INTRODUCTION TO
MANAGEMENT SCIENCE

INTRODUCTION TO
MANAGEMENT SCIENCE

Sang M. Lee
University of Nebraska

The Dryden Press

Chicago   New York   Philadelphia   San Francisco   Montreal   Toronto
London   Sydney   Tokyo   Mexico City   Rio de Janeiro   Madrid

Acquisitions Editor   Anne Elizabeth Smith
Developmental Editor   Paul D. Psilos
Project Editor   Kathleen Gleason
Design Director   Alan Wendt
Production Manager   Mary Jarvis
Managing Editor   Jane Perkins

Text and cover design by Alan Wendt
Copy editing by Mary Englehart
Indexing by Ann Heinrichs

Address orders to:
383 Madison Avenue
New York, New York 10017

Address editorial correspondence to:
One Salt Creek Lane
Hinsdale, Illinois 60521

Library of Congress Catalog Card Number: 82–72177
ISBN   0-03-059183-X
Printed in the United States of America
345-016-987654321

CBS College Publishing
The Dryden Press
Holt, Rinehart and Winston
Saunders College Publishing

To Tosca and Amy

PREFACE

Management science is concerned with the application of scientific approaches to improve management performance. In management science, special emphasis is placed on the systematic analysis of the nature of the problem, decision environment, objectives of the organization, judgment of the decision maker, and available decision alternatives. Thus, the field of management science encompasses a host of quantitative methodologies as well as behavioral aspects of decision making. The purpose of this text is to provide the student with a comprehensive coverage of how management science concepts and approaches can be applied to improve management decision making.

Management science is no longer a new field of study. Today, such terms as *cost/benefit analysis, simulation, system optimization, modeling,* and *data base management* are accepted as standard vocabulary. Management science concepts are widely known not only to businessmen and management scientists, but also to government planners, military analysts, space scientists, regional planners, health care administrators, and many other professionals. As the use of management science becomes broader, there is a greater need for a good introductory text. This book is such a text. It explains, in a simple manner with a minimum amount of mathematics, how to formulate management decision problems as models, how to solve them by using management science techniques, and then how to implement the solution results in the actual problem situation.

As managerial problems become more complex, management science tools are becoming more sophisticated. Consequently, great emphasis has been placed on the model solution, as if the modeling work is the end product in itself. An overwhelming emphasis on solution techniques often results in the neglect of other important issues such as the decision environment, the nature of the problem, the multiple organizational objectives, the decision maker's judgment, and the implementation of the model results. This book provides a comprehensive discussion of all of the major factors necessary for successful management science implementation. The emphasis throughout this book, is placed on the managerial perspective—improving the organizational performance through systematic analysis.

This book is directed toward the undergraduate student of business administration and the social sciences who has had no previous exposure to management science. A unique feature of the book is that it provides a highly readable yet comprehensive introduction to the standard topics of the first course in quantitative techniques, a course required in most schools of business.

The emphasis of the book is on the translation of mathematical modeling concepts into a presentation that is palatable to the undergraduate student of business with a minimum of mathematical background. Many topics are introduced by presenting realistic, practical examples in the form of casettes (small cases). Difficult techniques are presented within the framework of working examples, stressing an intuitive understanding of concepts rather than mathematical proofs.

In summary, *Introduction to Management Science* is all of the following:

1. A comprehensive yet easily readable presentation of various management science techniques.

2. An application orientation to realistic problems through the emphasis of the model formulation aspect of management science. Most chapters present interesting and realistic casettes as a means of demonstrating the model formulation, the solution process, and the interpretation of model results.

3. An up-to-date presentation of multiple objective decision making concepts.

4. A guide to the analysis of complex problems through the inclusion of casettes, computer-based solutions, numerous exercise problems, and a comprehensive *Study Guide*.

5. A managerial perspective of management science—problem formulation, analysis of the decision environment, multiple organizational objectives, and issues involved in implementation of model results.

A Note to the Student

Numerous books have been published in the area of management science, operations research, and quantitative methods. Most of these books, including several by this author, can be classified into two broad categories: (1) basic surveys that present a cookbook approach of management science techniques, and (2) comprehensive theoretical texts that represent the mathematical foundations of various quantitative tools. Few books have presented a comprehensive, introductory, application-oriented, fun-to-read, and up-to-date treatment of management science concepts. This book is intended to be such a book.

A major objective of this text is to avoid overwhelming you with mathematics. Rather, the purpose is to provide you with an opportunity to familiarize yourself with a wide variety of model building situations so that you come away from the introductory course with an ability to conceptualize the modeling approach in a managerial perspective. I attempt to achieve this purpose through a sound but interesting presentation of the underlying concepts through realistic casettes (small cases) and stories. I try to make the learning a fun experience for you.

Management science is not simply a collection of quantitative tools. It is a way of thinking and a philosophy of logical problem solving in any decision environment. By no means, after studying this book, should you come away with the idea that you now have a set of tools that can be simply plugged into the appropriate situations without carefully considering the assumptions of the models and the realities of the decision environments.

All of the techniques presented in this text are selected on the basis of their track record of real-world applications. Although most of the examples and casettes presented are relatively simple as compared to real-world problems, once you master these examples you will be much better prepared to tackle complex problems. Many real-world application examples are provided in the text to give you a general idea about the types of problems in which different techniques can be applied. The most important purpose of this book is to help you sharpen your conceptual skills in dealing with any decision problem. These skills will be invaluable throughout your career, whatever it may eventually be.

A Note to the Instructor

In writing this text, I had three basic objectives: (1) an emphasis on the managerial perspective—the basic role of management science is to improve organizational performance, (2) a comprehensive and interesting discussion of various management science topics through casettes, and (3) an application-oriented text presenting many real-world application examples and discussing the factors that are important for successful implementation of management science.

On the basis of two criteria, I selected those topics that are most appropriate for an introductory course in management science: (1) the current track record of the particular technique for solving real-world problems, and (2) the capacity of the technique for exposing the student to a variety of different modeling situations. The central theme of the book, which is carried through all of the chapters, stresses the concept of modeling in general. Thus, each chapter presents the identification of the model objective, the decision variables, the model parameters, the underlying assumptions of the model, the decision environment, the implementation of the solution, and real-world applications.

This book is organized so that the most frequently covered topics (most popular topics), such as linear programming and related topics, are presented first. Although most of the chapters present topics that are independent of other chapters, the topic of linear programming is presented in three chapters, ranging from introductory to more advanced material. Each chapter has the following aids to the student:

1. A brief introduction stating the purpose of the chapter.

2. A list of the learning objectives for the chapter.

3. Marginal terms to indicate key concepts and topics.

4. A brief summary of the topics covered in the chapter.

This text has over 50 casettes in the text and over 400 assignment problems at the ends of chapters. In addition, over 160 other problems and cases are presented in the *Study Guide* and the *Instructor's Manual*. Also, the text presents summaries of 17 real-world applications of management science. The *Study Guide* presents a list of suggestions for studying management science, a summary of the important concepts in each chapter, solutions to all of the odd-numbered assignment problems, additional problems and cases to prepare for tests, and a list of journals that are useful in studying the actual applications of management science. The *Instructor's Manual* presents solutions to all of the assignment problems, a suggested examination format with problems, discussion of some advanced topics that are not included in the text, suggested syllabi of the course at different levels, and the interactive linear programming and goal programming programs, as well as solutions of selected problems by the microcomputer. The Transparency Master for various figures and tables presented in the text will also be available from the publisher. The text and these accompanying materials present a comprehensive instructional support package for an introductory management science course.

Acknowledgments

In writing this book, I have relied heavily on the suggestions and criticisms of my colleagues and students. I have benefited greatly from discussion with my friends Fred Luthans, Lester Digman, and Gary Schwendiman at the University of Nebraska. I would like to thank my colleagues Eugene Kaczka (Clarkson), Patrick G. McKeown (University of Georgia), Spyros Economides (California State University—Hayward), James H. Patterson (University of Missouri), Bruce K. Blaylock (Virginia Polytechnique Institute), Charles J. Campbell (Memphis State University), A. Ravindran (University of Oklahoma), David L. Olson (Texas A&M), C. S. Kim (Kansas State University), and J. P. Shim (University of Wisconsin—La Crosse), who reviewed the entire manuscript several times. Special thanks go to my students S. H. Lee, Bruce Speck, A. Abdolhossein, Lucinda Galusha, and M. Abdel-Wahab at the University of Nebraska. They were indispensable in polishing the book through revisions and in preparing the *Instructor's Manual* and *Study Guide*. I am very grateful to my office staff: Joyce Anderson, Jane Chrastil, Cindy LeGrande, and Angela Sullivan for their expert word-processing skills. A tremendous thanks is expressed to the real professionals at The Dryden Press: Anne E. Smith, Senior Editor, Paul Psilos, Developmental Editor of this book and a good friend, Kathy Gleason, Project Editor, and Mary Englehart, Copy Editor, for their superb editorial work. Also, I express my thanks to Ada Chen at Boardworks for her beautiful art work. Finally, I could never have completed this book without the support of my family. I dedicate this book to my daughters Tosca and Amy, who made this book late by only several months.

Sang M. Lee

CONTENTS

1 THE ROLE OF MANAGEMENT SCIENCE

Management is basically a process of achieving a set of objectives in an effective way. To be effective managers, we must be rational in our problem solving and decision making. Management science is a discipline that includes a host of rational approaches to management decision making. In this chapter we will discuss what modern management is and how rational approaches of management science play important roles in today's complex organizations.

Learning Objectives *From the study of this chapter, you will learn the following:*

1. The basic process of management.
2. The importance of decision making in management.
3. How people ought to make decisions based on rationality.
4. How people actually make decisions in reality.
5. How management science can assist managers to make better decisions.
6. What types of techniques are most widely applied in practice.
7. A short historical background of management science.
8. How to build a proper perspective about the role of management science.
9. The meaning of the following terms:

Management	*Management science*
Decision making process	*Operations research*
Rational behavior	*Decision science*
Optimization	*Concept of economic person*
Bounded rationality	*Management information system*
Satisficing	*Scientific method*

WHAT'S IT ALL ABOUT?

Life consists of a continuous process of making decisions and solving problems. From the days of childhood to our teenage years and then our adult lives, we try to stay healthy, be happy, and do interesting things. In the process we make numerous types of decisions. The environment in which we live is complex, with various components such as laws, regulations, morality, socioeconomic realities, uncertainty about the future, many diseases, and the like. Thus, decision making is never simple.

Although we make decisions every day, we rarely spend time thinking about

Decision making

how we actually do make decisions. Perhaps we are too busy making decisions to think about decision making. Since we want to be successful in almost everything we do, we would like to do the right things at the right times. No one is a perfect decision maker, but each of us would like to be a successful one, at least for important decisions.

As individuals, we are experienced decision makers. Every day we make many routine decisions—how to dress, which road to take to school, where to have lunch, and so on. We also make many important decisions—whether to look for a part-time job at the library or at a local bank, whether to take computer science or anthropology as our minor, whether to join a karate club or a bridge club, whether to go to a graduate school or look for a job, and the like. Although the consequences of some of these decisions may be relatively minor, important decisions such as choosing a spouse or a career can change our lives.

Management science and decision making

Some people believe that good decision makers are born with special abilities. But we believe, and many empirical studies support our position, that decision making abilities can be acquired through learning and experience. Managerial decision making is not too much different from personal decision making. However, the magnitude, the nature, and the possible consequences are enormously greater for managerial problems. Thus, our purpose in studying management science is to learn the basics of rational decision making and how they can be applied to solving real-world management problems.

Mathematics as a language

A noted educator once stated that every American child should know at least two foreign languages: English and Mathematics. This educator had a rare perceptiveness in his definition of mathematics as a language. Mathematics is the language of rational thought. Thus, we will use mathematics in learning to be rational, consistent, and systematic in generating useful information for decision making. Mathematics allows us to be precise and succinct in expressing our thought. Furthermore, mathematics enables us to manipulate important characteristics of problems in answering ''what if'' questions. That makes mathematics a perfect tool for rational decision making.

Discussion of mathematics brings up an interesting and practical question: Can we really be perfectly rational in decision making? We know we cannot. Decision making in human organizations is never precise. We must analyze the inexact nature of human problems with imprecise tools and our limited analytical abilities. The manager knows this and therefore cannot be a total idealist. He or she must get desired results through practical means. Then, the rational decision making process based on mathematics must be practical. It can be and has been in many real-world applications.

MANAGEMENT AND DECISION MAKING

What is management?

The lifeblood of an organization is **management.** In spite of all else, if management falters, an organization cannot long survive. Although management is vital to our society, we have no universal definition of management; management has different meanings to different people. We know pretty much what a private does in the army, a secretary in an office, an assembly line worker in a General Motors plant, a salesperson in a shoe store, and a nurse in a municipal hospital. However, we have no standard view of a manager's job. What a manager is and what he does depend

Follet's definition of management

entirely upon the organization, the geographical location, the department, the expertise of the manager, the number of people working under him, and many other related factors.

Over a half century ago Mary Parker Follet defined management as "getting things done through people." This broad and vague definition is still a very good description of management. Management is a dynamic living system which integrates human, financial, and physical resources in such an effective way that the output becomes greater than the simple sum of its inputs. Thus, management emphasizes the following factors: (1) determination of definite directions for the organization—a set of objectives; (2) search for efficient ways to achieve the objectives through evaluating feasible alternatives; (3) analysis of the environmental constraints, both external and internal to the organization.

Management—art or science?

Traditionally, management has been regarded as the art of "getting things done." Thus, it emphasizes the "art" of performing the job. The individual manager's behavioral leadership qualities, with a strong connotation of a military commander's abilities, is an example of the "art" we are talking about. On the other hand, many recent studies have emphasized the "science" aspect of management—analytical approaches to problem solving and decision making.

In reality, we believe management is a combination of art and science in which both the behavioral and systematic approaches are required. In science, we can predict the phenomenon with a definite probability of occurrence when the ingredients of a process are accurately determined. For example, we can foretell with 99.99 percent accuracy the result of a chemical process when certain chemicals are added together in a given environment. However, such accuracy of scientific experimentation or prediction is impossible in a management process because the ingredients (people and other resources) are unpredictable and the environment is dynamic.

Importance of decision making

Simon's view

Management is a dynamic system which involves constantly changing environments, technologies, and philosophies. Thus the basic function of modern management has become management of disturbance, problem solving, or decision making. *Decision making is the most fundamental function of management.* As a matter of fact, Herbert A. Simon, an eminent scholar of management and a Nobel laureate in 1978, states that decision making is synonymous with management. Also, David W. Miller and Martin K. Starr, professors of management at Columbia University and well-known experts in management, point out that managers are evaluated on the basis of their performance in decision making.

What is management science?

In order to improve the quality of decision making, organizations and managers constantly seek ways to be more rational and systematic in making decisions. Thus, management science has become an integral part of modern management. Management science is a discipline which includes a host of rational approaches to management decision making. The central theme of management science is the application of scientific and rational methodologies to the process of management.

RATIONALITY IN DECISION MAKING

A relevant story

A well-known scientist decided that he had been a bachelor long enough, or at least that he should seriously consider whether to get married or not, and if so to whom. Being a rational man, he sat down and enumerated the advantages and disadvan-

tages of the marital state and the kind of qualities that he should look for in choosing a wife. As for the advantages—and I quote from his notes, "Children (if it please God), constant companion (and friend in old age), charms of music and female chit-chat." Among the disadvantages—"Terrible loss of time, if many children forced to gain one's bread; fighting about no society." But he continued, "What is the use of working without sympathy from near and dear friends? Who are near and dear friends to the old, except relatives?" And his conclusion was: "My God, it is intolerable to think of spending one's whole life like a neuter bee, working, working, and nothing after all. No, no won't do. Imagine living all one's day solitarily in smokey, dirty London house—only picture to yourself a nice soft wife on a sofa, with good fire and books and music perhaps—compare this vision with the dingy reality of Gt. Marlboro Street." His conclusion: "Marry, marry, marry." Having decided that he ought to get married and having listed the desirable qualities of a future spouse, he then proceeded to look for a suitable candidate. He had several female cousins, so that there was no need to search outside the family circle. He dispassionately compared their attributes with his list of objectives and constraints, made his choice and proposed to her. Needless to say, he lived happily ever after. The scientist in question—Charles Darwin; the year, 1837.[1]

Rationality in decision making

The above true story points out several important aspects of decision making. The first is that the rational decision making effort is really nothing new. As a matter of fact, the primary distinguishing characteristic of mankind has been the capacity to learn about his environment and to use such knowledge in an organized effort to accomplish desired goals. Some academicians trace the concept of decision making for objectives to the days of the Old Testament, the Koran, and the ancient Greek philosophers. There is no practical value in seeking a detailed genealogy of rational decision making. It should suffice to say that rational decision making effort has always been a major task of mankind.

Decision environment

The second aspect that we want to point out in the Darwin story is that decision making is constrained by environmental factors. Charles Darwin was a superb scientist. Thus, he was able to be rational in selecting his wife. The six wives of Henry VIII certainly must have wished that he was more rational in solving his marital problems. For some reason, Darwin limited his search for a bride to the family circle. Although he thought he made the best decision, it might not have been the best decision. This special constraint he imposed might have been due to his family training, his personality, or the accepted social norm during that period of time in England. In other words, the way we define the decision environment presents a host of constraints to the decision making process.

Multiple objectives

The third aspect of the Darwin story which deserves our attention is that complex real-world problems usually involve multiple, sometimes conflicting, objectives. Indeed, management by multiple objectives is a fact of life in the manager's job. This particular element of complexity presents a host of difficulties in decision making. Management by multiple objectives has been an important area of research in management science during the past ten years.

---

[1] S. Eilon, "Goals and Constraints in Decision Making," *Operational Research Quarterly*, 23: 1 (1973), 3. Quoted with the permission of the Society of Operational Research.

Whenever we discuss rationality in decision making, two basic approaches emerge: the scientific method and the concept of "economic person." We will now discuss them in detail.

The Scientific Method

The scientific method

The scientific method has evolved over a long period of time as a set of systematic steps for conducting research in the physical sciences—physics, chemistry, biology, astronomy, geology, and so on. It has been said that Sir Francis Bacon was the first person who formally suggested the method over four hundred years ago. Although the scientific method was established for the physical sciences, management scientists have borrowed the concept liberally for management decision making.

Table 1.1 presents the steps of the scientific method and their equivalent phases in management decision making.

Step 1: Define the Decision Problem This first step is the most crucial and difficult part. It has the preemptive role for the rest of the steps. For example, suppose that

Defining the problem

you defined your problem as "Should I work at the Pizza Parlor or the Radio Shack?" This statement excludes not only other workplaces but also many other types of decision you face, such as what to do about your fast-declining grades, how to handle the upcoming job interview, and where to spend the spring break—skiing in Colorado or hitchhiking to Florida. You may want to evaluate all of your pressing problems and come up with the most urgent one.

Suppose you decided to redefine your problem as follows: "I am broke. I need to make some money by taking a part-time job real quick." The nature of the problem has been changed drastically in that it has opened up all the possible work opportunities—the local library, the Pizza Parlor, a branch bank, K Mart, Mc-

Finding a good solution to a right problem

Donald's, Radio Shack, Pontillo's, The Underground Cousin, and so on. *Finding a good solution to a right problem is far superior to getting the best solution to a wrong problem.*

Step 2: Search for Data and Information In order to understand fully the nature of the problem at hand and its relationship to other problems, it is essential to have relevant data and information. For example, your financial problem discussed above may be due not to your lack of funds but to your undisciplined spending habits. Or it could be a result of your too frequent social activities. Thus, your financial problem, your declining grade-point average, and your extracurricular activities may be interrelated.

Table 1.1   Steps in the Scientific Method and Their Equivalents in Management Decision Making

The Scientific Method	Management Decision Making
1. Define the problem	1. Define the decision problem
2. Collect data	2. Search for data and information
3. Develop hypotheses	3. Generate alternative courses of action
4. Test hypotheses	4. Analyze feasible alternatives
5. Analyze results	5. Select the best course of action
6. Draw conclusion	6. Implement the decision and evaluate results

Collecting relevant data

It is important to collect relevant data and sort them out in such a way that they will provide information for decision making. For example, you may want to gather information about the different workplaces—wage rates, working conditions, type of work, potential value of the work experience, and perhaps, from some of your friends who have worked at these places, the personality of the boss you have to work for.

Generating additional alternatives

Step 3: Generate Alternative Courses of Action The next step is to generate alternative courses of action that could be taken for the decision problem. Most people limit their search for alternatives to those that are obvious and readily available. It is important to generate additional alternatives so that all feasible courses of action can be evaluated. For example, in searching for part-time work, you may want to check the local and state employment offices in addition to the classified ads.

Step 4: Analyze Feasible Alternatives Armed with information about the problem and the available courses of action, you must now turn to analyzing alternatives. The

Determining the objective criteria

primary standards to be used in the analysis are the objective criteria—the things that you would like to accomplish. For example, you may set several criteria about your part-time work such as wage rate, the number of hours you can work per week, work schedule (no graveyard shift, please), coordination with your class schedule and with important extracurricular activities, working conditions, and value of experience.

You should then evaluate each alternative against the objective criteria. You can easily eliminate several alternatives that are clearly inferior to others. Such alterna-

Nondominated solutions

tives are often referred to as *dominated solutions*. In order to evaluate the nondominated alternatives, you may wish to use your priorities for the objective criteria. For

Priorities of objectives

example, suppose that you have the following simple list of priorities written down on the back of an envelope:

Priority 1:   Total pay per week
Priority 2:   No conflict with class schedule
Priority 3:   Value of experience
Priority 4:   No midnight shift
Priority 5:   No conflict with extracurricular activities
Priority 6:   Working conditions
Priority 7:   Working hours per week

Now you should be able to further eliminate some alternatives on the list.

Step 5: Select the Best Course of Action Once the analysis of alternatives is com-

Selecting the best solution

pleted, you can make a decision by selecting the best course of action. The final decision will be based on a number of considerations, some quantitative and some judgmental. For example, how much money you can make in a week is a quantitative criterion. On the other hand, the value of experience, working conditions, undesirable working schedule, and conflict with other activities represent judgmental considerations. Evaluation of decision criteria in terms of their priorities to you is perhaps the most efficient way to select the best course of action.

Trade-off analysis

When we have a set of objective criteria we want to achieve, we often get into a tangle of trade-offs. In other words, sometimes we can achieve an important objective if we give up something else. You know exactly what we mean when you consider your flourishing social activities and your declining grade-point average. Analysis of trade-offs among the alternatives provides additional information which may be valuable in selecting the best course of action.

Implementing the decision

Step 6: Implement the Decision and Evaluate Results Decision making means taking a certain action. Implementation of action plans is the final phase of decision making. However, we do not stop there. We must always evaluate the results of the decision and ascertain whether or not the decision problem is resolved to our satisfaction. Suppose you took a part-time job in the library. Although the work is interesting and you have the opportunity to meet many people, your weekly earnings are simply not sufficient for you to survive financially through the school year. Perhaps your objective criteria and their priorities need to be modified. The feedback through an evaluation process is a very important element of the scientific method.

Feedback through an evaluation process

The Concept of Economic Person

Normative vs. descriptive decision making behavior

When we study human decision making behavior in organizations, we find two broad theoretical foundations—*normative* (prescriptive) and *descriptive* (behavioral). The normative theories are concerned with how rational decisions *ought* to be made, whereas the descriptive theories are concerned with how decisions *are* actually made.

The normative theory, which is also referred to as the classical theory, of rational decision making is conceptually neat. It assumes the decision maker as economic person who has perfect rationality. In other words, the decision maker is assumed to have complete information of all relevant aspects of the decision environment, to possess a stable system of preferences, and to have the ability to analyze the alternative courses of action. Thus, the decision maker is assumed to be a perfect individual to utilize the scientific method.

The concept of economic person presents a rational individual who always employs the scientific method to obtain the optimum solution for a single objective criterion for the organization. In other words, he always seeks global optimization. Global optimization in the context of economic person simply means that the decision maker seeks a solution that would result in the best overall organizational measure, such as finding the maximum profit or the least cost. Thus, several economic persons would reach the same solution to a given problem. Clearly, there is no decision maker in reality who behaves like economic person. Furthermore, decision makers have their own unique ways of approaching a problem, and it is not likely that a number of them would reach the same solution.

MANAGEMENT SCIENCE AND THE SYSTEMS APPROACH

Management science is concerned with the application of scientific approaches to generate concrete information that is relevant to the problem solving of the decision maker. Special emphasis is placed on the analysis of the nature of the problem, the decision environment, the objectives of the organization, the judgment of the decision maker, and the economic as well as noneconomic ramifications of the decision environment. As we have already discussed, management science is dedicated to finding the *best feasible* solution. When we say "feasible," it implies that the best solution we seek must be "workable," or "implementable."

The feasible solution

Since management science is a systematic and comprehensive approach to decision making, it inevitably involves what is called the **systems approach.** A system is a whole composed of a set of components, their attributes, and certain relationships among components that perform a function. Thus, a manufacturing firm is a man-

The systems approach

machine system. A stereo set, on the other hand, is a mechanical system; it is made up of components such as transistors, electronic converters, and speakers that transmit sound.

A precise analysis in human organizations, as contrasted to mechanical systems, is not possible because of uncertainties involved in human behavior such as motivation, performance, and cooperation among individuals. This fact further complicates the management decision making process. Nevertheless, management science attempts to seek the best solution for the organization as a whole. Any managerial problem should be put in proper perspective so that its impact on the whole organization and its environment can be analyzed. In other words, management science should be applied in a systems context.

Upon the solution of the original problem, management science applied in a systems context often uncovers new problems. This is a very important characteristic of management science. Therefore, the most effective way to apply management science is through continuous analysis rather than a one-shot solution approach.

Global optimization vs. suboptimization

The basic objective of management science is to find a feasible solution which is best for the organization, the global optimization. The process of finding a solution that is best for one or more parts of the organization is usually called *suboptimization*. Management science attempts to find a solution that is close to the global optimum by analyzing interrelationships among the system components that are involved in the problem.

Three basic management skills

Earlier in this chapter, we defined management as a process of achieving a set of objectives in an efficient manner. In performing such a function, a manager needs three basic skills: technical, conceptual, and human. The technical skills are those directly related to the performance of work that contributes to the production and distribution of goods and services. The conceptual skills represent the ability to synthesize, grasp the situation, plan for future actions, and make effective decisions. The human skills are related to the abilities to influence the attitudes and behaviors of others in achieving a common goal by encouraging, helping, and educating. As we move up the organizational ladder, we need more conceptual and human skills and fewer technical skills. The relationship between the organizational hierarchy and managerial skills is shown in Figure 1.1.

Management science and conceptual skills

Management science is useful in developing a manager's conceptual skills. Though management science can provide technical expertise for analyzing various decision problems, we believe that its primary purpose is to provide a manager with knowledge to conceptualize problems. It should be evident, then, that management science can provide valuable knowledge for middle- and higher-level managers.

The beginning of management science is unknown, as the birth of science itself is unknown. The roots of management science are as old as mankind's curiosity, civilization, and culture. There is evidence that some forms of scientific approaches to management existed during the era of the industrial revolution. Frederick W. Taylor, the father of **scientific management,** pioneered industrial engineering and systematic approaches to management through his time-and-motion studies in the late nineteenth century.

Taylor's scientific management

The origin of OR

However, the name **operations research** (OR), a term often used interchangeably with *management science,* began to be used only in the early 1940s. The origin of military operations research activities was in the United Kingdom during the early part of World War II. In order to devise the most effective military tactics and strategies, there was an urgent need for scientific approaches to analyze various logistics

Figure 1.1   *Organizational Hierarchy and Managerial Skills*

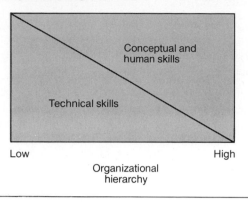

problems. The British, and later the American, military authorities formed groups of scientists to conduct research on military operations. It has been said that OR studies were instrumental in the victories in the air battle of Britain, the island campaign in the Pacific, the battle of the North Atlantic, and other phases of the war. The detailed history of management science will be presented in Chapter 15.

Synonyms for management science

Synonyms for the term *management science* are numerous. A frequent substitute is *operations research,* and other term such as *systems analysis, systems science, operations analysis, quantitative analysis, managerial analysis, decision analysis,* and *decision science* are also used. We have decided to use the term *management science* in this book because we are basically concerned with the systematic analysis of management decision problems. There is no organizational barrier for management science application. In other words, we can use management science for decision problems in government, military service, business and industry, academic institutions, health-care organizations, and many other areas.

HOW MANAGERS ACTUALLY MAKE DECISIONS

Now that we know something about rational decision making and management science, let us focus our attention on how managers actually make decisions in real-world situations. Management science permits the manager to utilize a scientific or analytical approach to problem solving. We believe management science has contributed more toward the acceptance of "purpose-oriented management" (often referred to as "management by objectives") than is usually appreciated by managers and scholars.

The role of management science today

The role of management science is especially important today because of the following factors:

The technology being used by organizations is getting more sophisticated every day (chemicals, electronics, lasers, industrial robots, etc.).

There is an increasing shortage of energy and critical materials (fossil fuels, certain vital metals, etc.).

Managerial problems involve complex processes (production and inventory control, assembly-line balancing, location allocation, working-capital management, customer-information processing, etc.

Managerial problems are not only complex but are becoming even more important (oil-importing decisions that involve international relations, development of computer-based information systems, design of the MX missile system, etc.).

The problems managers face are often new and there is no benefit to be drawn from past experience (the oil embargo of 1973, the Mt. St. Helens eruption, the continuous decline of productivity, and the like).

The emphasis on management planning and long-range objectives requires proactive decision making. Thus, managers attempt to forecast future problems and plan ahead before the problems actually emerge (public transit systems, synthetic fuel development, research on the electrical car, etc.).

Managers in reality

    Although we recognize the importance of management science in analyzing important decision problems, we also realize that management is a human process. There exists an enormous gap between the manager's aspirations for using the scientific method for problem solving and the actuality of trying to sort out a big mess from a disorganized chain of random events. In reality, the manager is not like economic person who is totally rational and effective in utilizing the scientific method for decision making.

    Recent developments and broad empirical investigations strongly indicate that the concept of economic person cannot be applied to today's managers. There is no evidence that the manager is capable of performing a completely rational analysis of complex decision problems. We also know that the manager's value system is not exactly identical to or congruent with the organization's objectives. Furthermore, the manager in reality is quite incapable of identifying the optimum choice, if there exists such a thing, either because of the lack of analytical ability or because of the complexity of the problem.

Descriptive theories of decision making

Bounded rationality

    As we discussed earlier, the descriptive theories of decision making are concerned with how decisions *are* actually made in reality. The descriptive theories are based on an abundance of empirical data that propose the now celebrated concept of "bounded rationality." Herbert A. Simon states that under bounded rationality individual decision makers strive to be as efficient as possible in achieving organizational objectives, given their limited information-processing abilities. Clearly, bounded rationality does not mean irrationality. The decision maker employs an "approximate" or "intentional" rationality in the process of attempting to do the best to achieve organizational goals within the given set of constraints.

    As we can imagine, management science models developed under the unrealistic conditions of complete rationality have very limited real-world implications. In order

Figure 1.2   Decision Making Process

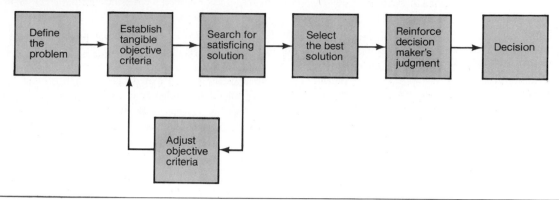

to implement decision models, then, either we must sufficiently simplify the model so that the optimum solution can be easily derived or we must design a realistic model and seek satisfactory solutions. The first is the traditional approach, whereas the second approach attempts to retain a richer set of properties of the real decision environment by giving up optimization. Although the two approaches are quite different, they are both "satisficing" approaches based on the concept of bounded rationality and have been widely applied by management scientists. The satisficing approach attempts to obtain a good solution that is sufficiently satisfactory for a complex decision problem.

Satisficing approaches

The global optimization model based on a single objective criterion (e.g., cost minimization or profit maximization) is often unrealistic. Perhaps the most practical way to develop a decision model would be to replace the abstract global optimization goal with tangible and measurable subgoals. These subgoals can be formulated on the basis of certain aspiration levels that are related to the organizational goals. Once a decision alternative satisfies a set of aspirations (or at least satisfies important ones), the search activity could be terminated. The satisficing model based on aspiration levels allows for a bounded rational decision by permitting reasonable amounts of analytical effort and incomplete information about the decision environment.

Answering "what if" questions

In reality, managers make decisions based not solely on solutions derived from management science models. As a matter of fact, management science models are often used to generate new information or to answer "what if" questions. Based on our discussion so far, we can present the decision making process as shown in Figure 1.2.

THE ROLE OF MANAGEMENT SCIENCE

If managers are not completely rational and systematic in decision making, what then is the role of management science? We can quickly come up with a number of important problems that we have not been able to solve with powerful computer-based management science models—the world population explosion, pollution, the energy shortage, international tension, hunger, decreasing natural resources, and so on. In the role of devil's advocate, let us ask ourselves what the world would be like today without systematic analysis of these complex problems. We are sure that the world would be in a worse situation than it is today. We believe management science will play an increasingly more important role in the future, precisely because of the manager's limited ability and rationality.

We are now quite comfortable with the notion that decision making must consider environmental factors, multiple objectives, satisficing, and bounded rationality. We should not view management science as a panacea for managerial decision problems. Decision making is and always will be based on human judgment, intuition, creativity, and perhaps courage, in addition to many systematic approaches. Much of the disillusionment and criticism of management science is the result of unrealistic expectations on the part of those who use it.

Important roles of management science

Management science plays the following important roles:

Purpose-oriented Decision Making Management science application requires an organization to be purpose-oriented. Work activities are planned and carried out according to organizational objectives rather than simply rationalizing habits by saying "we have always done it this way." The question "What does this activity contribute toward important organizational objectives?" is frequently asked before resources are committed.

The basic approach of management should be to pursue long-range achievement of the organizational purpose rather to seek only short-term monetary objectives. R. H. Hayes and W. J. Abernathy, management professors at Harvard University, contend that one of the primary reasons for the financial and productivity woes of many American corporations is their emphasis on short-term profit objectives, often at the expense of long-term organizational goals.[2] Management science can be a catalyst in coordinating management functions for purpose-oriented decision making in a long-term perspective.

A long-term perspective

Information and Analysis-based Decision Making Decision making based on management science requires an efficient information processing system. With the ever-increasing complexity of the environment and its vital impact on the organization's survival, information management becomes extremely important. Accurate and timely information must be processed in order to predict the future state of affairs with an acceptable degree of accuracy.

Management by information

Management science models can be used to generate additional information. The use of computers for everyday decision making is becoming more prevalent. With the availability of inexpensive but powerful micro- and minicomputers, even small organizations can effectively use management science.

Decision Making for Multiple Objectives Managers should be vitally concerned with the analysis of multiple objectives, not only with their formulation but with their priorities and trade-offs. We are keenly aware of the ever-increasing pressure for the simultaneous satisfaction of such factors as government regulations, economic optimization, industrial relations, and customer demands. Managers must analyze the direct

Multiple objective decision making

---

[2]Bibliographical data for all published material are given in the References at the ends of chapters.

conflict between the organization's economic survival and the other objectives that are related to social responsibilities.

Managers are being held increasingly more accountable for the legitimacy of their objectives, priorities, and resolutions of the conflicts among the objectives of the various interest groups. Thus, we expect to see more widespread application of systematic approaches in dealing with multiple goals and their trade-offs. Computer-based interactive approaches using management science models are finding wider applications in objective formulation and decision making.

Increasing productivity

Increased Emphasis on Productivity The essential purpose of management science is to increase the efficiency of the organization. In order to improve the effectiveness of the management process, three important areas should be evaluated: (1) productivity of human resources; (2) effective management of capital and materials; and (3) efficient decision making process. Management science can make important contributions to all three areas. We believe that the effective utilization of human resources is the key to the survival and prosperity of the organization.

Increased Attention to Group Behavior As we focus our attention on the effective utilization of human resources, group decision making behavior will become increasingly more important. Most management science projects are interdisciplinary in nature. In other words, people from several different departments such as production, finance, marketing, and personnel would work together to solve a common problem. It has been pointed out by many scholars that one of the important reasons for the poor showing of American workers in the world productivity race is management's failure to recognize the importance of workers' group behavior. Harvard sociologist Ezra F. Vogel, in his book *Japan as Number One: Lessons for America,* contends that perhaps the most important reason for the phenomenal productivity increase of Japanese workers is their group-conscious behavior patterns. It is extremely important for the Japanese people to belong to groups, and group loyalty and confidence in

Group decision making

group objectives are driving forces for Japanese workers. The study of group decision making behavior, especially the importance of the sense of shared purpose for organizational effectiveness, should receive greater attention from management in the United States.

Management of capital, energy, materials

Efficient Management of Capital, Energy, and Materials With the increasing scarcity and cost of acquiring capital, energy, and materials, the effective management of these resources is almost as important as the management of human resources. As economist Martin Feldstein points out, the American economy suffers from a lack of capital formation due to the low savings rate of the American people. He singles out inflation and government taxes that penalize savings as the main causes of declining savings. An efficient management of capital, energy, and materials requires systematic approaches based on computer-based information systems and management science. Cost savings from these resources represent a 100 percent contribution to profits while cost savings in other areas (e.g., marketing channels) may represent only a very small net contribution to profits.

More Systematic Contingency Management In the future, we will probably see more drastic changes in the environment than we have in the past. We will face a shortage of energy, materials, water, clean air, and many other resources. We will also see some important technological breakthroughs—cheaper and more powerful microcomputers, new methods for harnessing energy, new transportation methods, for example. We can also expect many political and economic crises in the international arena. All of these changes will have varying degrees of impact on the organizations.

Contingency management

However, an organization cannot be totally reactive to situations, functioning without plans. Nor can it be totally proactive, with every possible contingency planned for changing situations. But with the aid of management science, management can establish the basic targets and explore the means to get there. With the availability of information systems, management science models, and computational facilities, contingency management can be more systematic and orderly.

Management process as an open system

Closer Interaction with External Factors The management process is an open system. It breathes in external factors in the form of environmental constraints, needs, and information. The use of management science requires such information so that the entire system remains current and effective. Thus, management science necessitates that the organization have closer interactions with external forces: government agencies, international situations, socioeconomic factors of the environment, consumer concerns, changing market situations, and the like.

PRACTICAL APPLICATION OF MANAGEMENT SCIENCE

Management science is being applied to a wide range of managerial problems in all types of organizations. Applications of management science have been especially prevalent since the 1960s. However, there have been relatively few published studies about the actual success of management science application. It is therefore somewhat difficult to obtain the true picture of the role of management science in organizations.

Surveys of management science applications

A survey conducted by the American Management Association (AMA) in 1957 gave some early indication of the extent of management science application. The survey of 324 organizations that were using management science revealed that 40 percent of the firms reported "considerable improvement" in their operations due to management science. Less than 1 percent of the sample indicated the intent to reduce the application of management science.

In a 1966 survey by William Vatter, 360 respondents were questioned about the use of operations research in American companies. This survey asked about any use of operations research and the results obtained from its use. Overall, linear programming, PERT/CPM, inventory models, simulation, regression analysis, and statistical sampling appeared to be used frequently by the sample companies. Also, the majority of the ratings of tool performance were reported as fair or good.

G. Thomas and J. A. DaCosta surveyed 260 of *Fortune*'s top 500 corporations and 160 of the largest California-based firms in 1978. Table 1.2 presents the results of this survey concerning the corporate use of management science techniques. It is apparent that the most widely used management science techniques are simulation, linear programming, PERT/CPM, and inventory theory. These topics will be thoroughly treated in this text.

A survey was conducted by this author especially for this book in early 1981. A questionnaire was mailed to 950 nonacademic (practicing) members of the Operations Research Society of America. Table 1.3 presents the overall results. Based on 142 usable questionnaires returned, this study is similar to previous studies in that statis-

Table 1.2   Results of the Thomas and DaCosta Survey, 1978

Techniques	Firms Using the Technique
Statistical analysis	93%
Simulation	84
Linear programming	79
PERT/CPM	70
Inventory theory	57
Queuing theory	45
Nonlinear programming	36
Heuristic programming	34
Bayesian decision analysis	32
Dynamic programming	27
Risk analysis	3
Integer and mixed programming	2
Delphi	1
Financial methods	1

Table 1.3   Results of the Lee Survey, 1981

Technique	Use		
	Frequently	Sometimes	Not at All
Statistical analysis	60.6%	37.9%	1.5%
Simulation	45.1	45.1	9.8
Linear programming	29.8	50.4	19.8
Other mathematical programming	23.4	46.1	30.5
PERT/CPM	16.5	45.7	37.8
Inventory models	15.0	42.5	42.5
Multicriteria methods	9.5	34.1	56.4
Search techniques	7.2	35.2	57.6
Queuing models	5.6	45.2	49.2
Game theory	2.4	20.8	76.8

tical analysis, simulation, and linear programming are reported to be the most frequently used techniques. However, the study also reveals several interesting facts. First, PERT/CPM methods, although still popular, are not so widely applied as previously reported. Second, multicriteria methods are more frequently used now than search techniques, queuing models, or game theory. Third, the game theory is not being used much at all in real-world situations.

BUILDING A PROPER PERSPECTIVE

How exact a solution?

As you study this book, you will be learning many analytical techniques and will be trying to find exact solutions to various problems. No doubt you will wonder whether or not it is worth the time and trouble to find *exact* solutions to the problems. For example, you might ask, "Is it necessary to find $x_1 = 1.285714$ or is it sufficient to

Table 1.4   *Key Considerations in the Modeling Process*

Key Considerations	Modeling Approach	
	Complex Model Accurate Solutions	Simple Model Approximate Solutions
Resources Required		
Cost	High	Low
Time	High	Low
Manpower	High	Low
Organizational Acceptance		
Involving people	Low	High
Understanding the effort	Low	High
Implementation of the result	Low	High
Solution to the Real Problem	Good	Approximate

say that $x_1 = 1.286$?'' There is no clear-cut answer, but it all depends on the type of problem. For example, if the variable x_1 represents the number of cups of sugar to put into a cookie mix, either solution would be acceptable. On the other hand, if x_1 is the amount of a chemical required to test a chemical reaction, the second solution may not be acceptable.

The purpose of modeling

What we should remember is that a management science model is a simple representation of reality. The purpose of building a model in the first place is to simplify a complex real problem so that we can understand and analyze it. In other words, if a model is almost as complex as the real problem it represents, it has lost its value.

Law of critical few

As we shall see in Chapter 2, there is a law of *critical few* in natural phenomena. We can analyze a management problem by examining critical few variables. The modeling approach is based on this principle. Thus, management science models represent good approximations of the real problems. Solutions we derive by management science are solutions to the approximate models but not solutions to real problems. We must remember this important fact. The role of management science must be put in a proper perspective with this understanding in mind.

Proper perspective about modeling

When we attempt to build more accurate models and more exact solutions to the models, we must be prepared to expend greater amounts of time, energy, and resources. The critical issue is whether or not such efforts would be cost effective. In other words, additional resources required to obtain more accurate solutions should be justified by the benefits derived from the better solutions to the real problems. However, there are other important considerations concerning organizational acceptance of the modeling effort. Generally speaking, complex modeling efforts tend to turn off the interest of those persons who would be implementing the solution. Thus, we must build a proper perspective about modeling in view of the trade-off considerations presented in Table 1.4.

Some people think management science is a panacea for managerial problems. This is far from the truth. Managerial problems usually involve economic, human, physical, engineering, and environmental considerations. Thus, an accurate and completely objective analysis is not possible. Management science must be used as a

Generating new information

Creativity and desire for change

means to generate new information to improve and sharpen the manager's decision making abilities, rather than as a black box that spits out solutions to problems.

For a successful application of management science, a considerable amount of artistic creativity and the desire for change are required. Management problems are like a big mess of Jello that is hard to handle. In order to capture important features of a problem and analyze it for practical application, we must be imaginative, creative, and persistent. Also, we need to find ways to stimulate people who will be using the information generated by models. Management scientists must serve as catalysts in their rejection of the status quo and of any hang-ups about systematic analysis. Such dedication is much needed to implement management science.

SUMMARY

This chapter has provided a broad introduction to management science in terms of its meaning, role, history, and application to decision making. You are not expected to be an expert in management science after reading this chapter, but you should have a good feel for what the management science is about. You should also have learned to use several new jargonistic terms such as optimization, the concept of economic person, scientific method, bounded rationality, satisficing, and management information systems.

The ideas we have discussed in this chapter are useful in guiding our approaches to management problems and in deriving pertinent information that is essential for decision making. We will be using mathematics throughout this book as a language of rational thought. Mathematical models are effective tools in transforming disorganized and complex real problems into simple and manageable toy problems. Perhaps the most important single item we should remember is that we must keep a proper perspective about the value, role, and limitations of management science.

References

AMA Management Report, No. 10. *Operations Research Considered*. New York: AMA, 1958.

Churchman, C. S., Ackoff, R. L., and Arnoff, E. L. *Introduction to Operations Research*. New York: Wiley, 1957.

Eilon, S. "Goals and Constraints in Decision Making." *Operational Research Quarterly,* 23: 1 (1972), 3–16.

Gallagher, C. A., and Watson, J. H. *Quantitative Methods for Business Decisions*. New York: McGraw-Hill, 1980.

Hayes, R. H., and Abernathy, W. J. "Managing Our Way to Economic Decline," *Harvard Business Review,* 58: 4 (1980), 67–77.

Lee, S. M. *Management by Multiple Objectives*. Princeton, N.J.: Petrocelli Books, 1982.

Lee, S. M., and Moore, L. J. *Introduction to Decision Science*. New York: Petrocelli-Charter, 1975.

Lee, S. M., Moore, L. J., and Taylor, B. W. *Management Science*. Dubuque, Iowa: W. C. Brown, 1981.

Miller, D. W., and Starr, M. K. *Executive Decisions and Operations Research*. 2nd ed. Englewood Cliffs, N.J.: Prentice-Hall, 1969.

Simon, H. A. *Administrative Behavior*. 2nd ed. New York: Macmillan, 1957.

Simon, H. A. "Rational Decision Making in Business Organizations." *American Economic Review,* 69: 4 (1979), 493–513.

Taylor, F. W. *Principles of Scientific Management*. New York: Harper, 1911.

Thomas, G., and DaCosta, J. A. "A Sample Survey of Corporate Operations Research." *Interfaces,* 9: 4 (Aug., 1979), 102–111.

Vatter, W. "The Use of Operations Research in American Companies." *The Accounting Review,* 42: 4 (1967), 712–730.

Vogel, E. F. *Japan as Number One: Lessons for America*. Cambridge, Mass.: Harvard University Press, 1979.

Wagner, H. M. *Principles of Operations Research*. 2nd ed. Englewood Cliffs, N.J.: Prentice-Hall, 1975.

Assignments

1.1 What is the difference between management and management science?

1.2 What is the relationship between management science and the broad area of management?

1.3 Try to recall a decision you made today. Discuss how you made the decision. Now follow the steps of the scientific method to see whether you would reach the same decision again.

1.4 Is management an art or science? Discuss your own ideas.

1.5 What are the advantages and disadvantages of the scientific method?

1.6 What is the concept of economic person? How is economic person different from a decision maker in today's organizations?

1.7 Contrast the normative and descriptive theories of decision making.

1.8 Provide a one-sentence definition of each of the following terms: *global optimization, suboptimization, satisficing, bounded rationality, systems approach.*

1.9 What is the relationship between management science and the systems approach?

1.10 What are three basic skills of management?

1.11 What are the most widely used synonyms for management science?

1.12 In your opinion what are three of the most important reasons behind the expanding role of management science?

1.13 Consider a personal problem you have right now. Are there multiple objectives involved? Are they congruent, complimentary, or in conflict? Discuss in detail.

1.14 In your opinion what are the three most important roles of management science?

1.15 "Management science is not a panacea for management problems, but it is the best medicine we have." Discuss your ideas about this statement.

MODELING IN MANAGEMENT SCIENCE

In management science we approach various managerial problems in the context of models. We attempt to scale down complex real problems to approximate simple relationships so that we can understand and analyze them. It is because models play such an important role in management science that this chapter is devoted to modeling and its functions in the process of management science.

Learning Objectives *From the study of this chapter, you will learn the following:*

1. The meaning and classifications of models.
2. The advantages and limitations of management science models.
3. Classifications of decision making models.
4. The process of management science.
5. The meaning of the following terms:

Model	*Decision making under certainty*
Deterministic	*Decision making under risk*
Probabilistic	*Decision making under uncertainty*
Static	*Decision making under conflict*
Dynamic	*Independent variables*
Mental model	*Dependent variables*
Symbolic model	*Model parameter*
Iconic model	*Random variables*

INTRODUCTION TO MODELING

"Man is a thinking animal." We have heard this old saying many times. The primary characteristic distinguishing human beings from other animals is that they can think. The mental ability to think is the source of our ability to solve problems. Imagination and creativity enable human beings to recognize their existence in the environment. Imagination is basically the ability to build mental images of complex objects without actually observing them. In other words, human beings often solve problems by building models.

Using imagination and creativity

While taking your morning shower, you no doubt think about all the things you need to do during the day: stop at the bank for some cash, get a haircut, go to classes in the afternoon, finish the computer programming project, play a game of racquetball

A mental model

at Wallbanger's, and pick up your watch at the repair shop. As you think about all these activities, you are organizing the sequence of activities based on the geographic locations of where you need to be, the duration of expected activity times, and the scheduled times of the activities. After a short period of mental modeling time, you decide upon the following sequence of activities: stop at the bank on the way to school—finish the computer project—play a game of racquetball—have a quick lunch after a shower—go to classes—get a haircut at the student union—pick up the watch on the way back to the apartment.

The advantage of modeling

The mental model you constructed above is, of course, quite incomplete and fuzzy. You might ask the question, "Should I make the model more complete by analyzing all the details of the events?" We should say not. You have a simple abstraction of the actual situation, and the simplicity of the model allows you to solve the scheduling problem. If you were to spend five hours to develop a detailed model, you would not gain anything. The advantage of modeling is that the model we build captures pertinent details of the problem but is simpler than the complex reality. In essence, then, modeling is a process used to develop a simple representation of a problem; the model's solution is then applied to the situation in reality that it represents.

What Is a Model?

The model defined

There are all types of models around us. Perhaps the models we see and use most often are photographs, road maps, model airplanes, and Raggedy Anns. Mathematical equations, chemical molecule relations, conceptual theories, and our own mental images are also some examples of models. Every model has one basic purpose—to represent some aspects of reality by means of a simple object. So, let us state it one more time: the primary purpose of modeling is to understand a complex problem through a simpler, less expensive, and less cumbersome object.

Model Classification

Types of models

There are many different ways to classify models. However, the most widely accepted taxonomy for models is *abstract* and *exact*. Abstract models are extremely fuzzy and ill-structured representations of reality. As with your mental model discussed earlier, they have no physical or symbolic configuration. Exact models, on the other hand, have some physical characteristics that resemble the reality under study. Most physical models are such things as model airplanes, dolls, and an architect's scaled-down buildings. Between these two extremes there are symbolic models such as theories, written statements, and mathematical relationships. Figure 2.1 presents the classifications of models based on the degree of abstraction.

1. *Mental Models.*   Mental models are the most abstract representation of reality, such as imagination, as we discussed previously.

2. *Verbal Models.*   Verbal models represent written versions of mental models such as poetry, plays, novels, theories, and a policeman's report of a traffic accident.

Figure 2.1   Model Classification

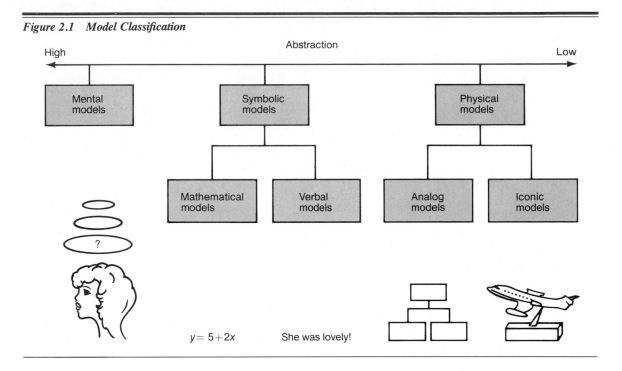

3. *Mathematical Models.*   Mathematical models are also symbolic models but they consist of mathematical relationships rather than words. Most management science models we will be studying in this book are mathematical models.

4. *Analog Models.*   Analog models are also physical models that may or may not look like the reality under study but they also perform some basic functions. Maps, blueprints, and organizational charts are good examples of analog models.

5. *Iconic Models.*   Iconic models are physical replicas of a reality, usually smaller or bigger in scale than the actual object. Many three-dimensional models such as model airplanes, buildings, and Raggedy Anns or two-dimensional paintings and photographs are good examples of iconic models.

MANAGEMENT SCIENCE MODELING

Among all the models discussed above, only mathematical models enable us to communicate precisely with the model builder without any misunderstanding. For example, we cannot always comprehend accurately what others have in mind when they verbalize their mental models, but if someone presents us his annual income as $I = 12x$, where x = monthly income of $2,000, there is no communication problem as to what his yearly income is.

Using the language of mathematics

Since mathematical models employ the language of mathematics in describing the system under study, we can also manipulate the models so that we can test the behavior of a system under varying conditons. For example, in the income model $I = 12x$, we can easily determine a new annual income when x is increased from $2,000 to $2,500. We can easily expand the model by adding other variables such as interest earned, dividends, and other income.

Mathematical models

Management science models are good examples of mathematical models. They are formulated and used to understand or predict certain management systems. One obvious disadvantage of a management science model is that it represents something less than the real system it represents. However, this aspect of a model is also an advantage. Since a model is simple, by analyzing it we can understand how the complex system functions. Thus, we can test the behavior of the system under different conditions. The real challenge of modeling is to build as simple a model as possible by including only pertinent attributes of the system.

Determining which model to build for a certain problem is an art in itself. Designing an appropriate model depends on the nature of the problem under study and the desired outcome of the study. For example, a production scheduling model can be formulated only after the production system is thoroughly analyzed and the purpose of the scheduling system is clearly established.

The basic law of critical few

In the natural phenomenon there exists the basic law of *critical few*. According to this law, there are a handful of critical attributes or variables that explain the major portion of the system's functions. For example, several key employees contribute 80 percent of the new ideas, two or three persons are responsible for the project delays, and 10 percent of the items contribute 85 percent of sales. Thus, we must identify these critical few attributes and include their performance in the model. The art of modeling can be mastered only through a good knowledge of management science, experience in model building, and creativity in fitting available tools to complex problems.

The Model Structure

Equations and inequalities

Management science models are usually in the form of mathematical relationships such as equations or inequalities. For example, your pocket money situation can be expressed as a relationship between your income (wage from a part-time job, a loan, and your parents' support) and expenses as follows:

$$PM = I - E$$

where
$$PM = \text{pocket money}$$
$$I = \text{income}$$
$$E = \text{expenses}$$

You may also want to find out how much you can spend for expenses. Since you cannot have a negative pocket money, the money you can spend must be equal to or less than your income. Thus you can express this relationship as:

$$E \leq I$$

The two types of models we have examined are perhaps the simplest examples of management science models. The complexity as well as the nature of the model will, of course, depend on the nature of the problem under study and the purpose of the analysis. We will discuss many other types of models in a later part of this chapter.

The Model Components

Model variables

When we attempt to construct a model, the first step is to abstract important components that explain the behavior of the system we are about to analyze. Such components are usually referred to as **variables.** In our pocket money model I and E are good examples of variables. In a broad sense, we classify variables into two categories: *dependent* and *independent*.

Dependent variables

The Dependent Variables The dependent variables are sometimes referred to as *criterion variables*. The value taken on by a dependent variable reflects the level of performance achievement of the system. For example, in our pocket money model, PM is the dependent variable. When your $PM = 0$, we know what kind of situation you are in—dead broke. On the other hand, if your $PM = \$500$, it shows either that you have been successful in bringing in more income or that lately your spending habit has been greatly disciplined. The value of the dependent variable is based on the values of the independent variables in the model.

In business organizations we can find a number of widely recognized dependent or criterion variables. As shown in Figure 2.2, some examples of dependent variables are: quantity of products processed, quality of products, customer satisfaction, total profit, market share, and return on investment.

Independent variables

The Independent Variables The independent variables are those that are not dependent on other variables in the model. In general, there are two types of independent variables: the *decision* (controllable) variables and the *exogenous* (uncontrollable) variables.

Decision variables

The Decision Variables The decision variables are often the most important components in management science models. It is the values of these variables for which a solution is sought. For example, let us formulate your total wage earnings model as follows:

$$W = 3.50H$$

where
$$W = \text{total wage income}$$
$$3.50 = \text{wage rate per hour}$$
$$H = \text{number of hours worked}$$

After evaluating the prospects of a loan and your parents' support, you decided that you need at least $700.00 from the part-time job during the next two months. Now you are trying to determine how many hours you have to work to earn $700.00. Thus, H is your decision variable in this model. You can easily determine the value of H as follows:

$$700.00 = 3.50H$$
$$H = 700.00/3.50$$
$$H = 200$$

Some of the typical decision variables in business organizations are also presented in Figure 2.2.

Exogenous variables

The Exogenous Variables The second type of independent variables, the exogenous variables, affects the outcome of the model and the system, but we have very little control over them. For a production problem, exogenous variables may include the cost of materials, availability of materials and human resources, and pollution-control regulations.

Figure 2.2   A Production Scheduling Model

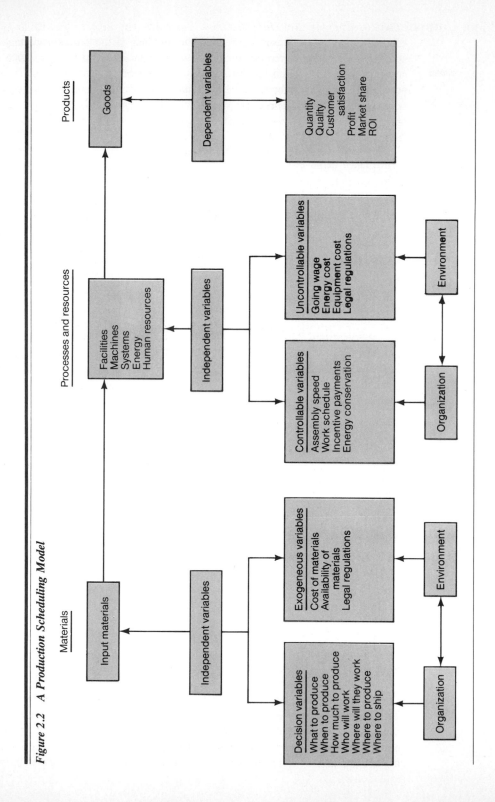

The Controllable and Uncontrollable Variables The independent variables may be defined as controllable and uncontrollable variables in the production processes of a production scheduling problem, as shown in Figure 2.2. The controllable variables may include such things as the speed of the assembly line, the work schedule for various assembly teams, employee incentive payment systems, and energy conservation targets. The uncontrollable variables may include the going wage rates for different types of work forces, current energy cost, equipment cost, and government regulations for worker safety and environmental protection.

Controllable and uncontrollable variables

The types of variables we have discussed thus far are not always so clearly discernible as described above. For example, in a production scheduling model it is not a simple task to classify neatly all the variables as independent and dependent. Our independent variable may become the dependent variable for someone else. Figure 2.2 illustrates some important variables and their classifications in a production situation.

Model Parameters The parameters are the remaining components of the model that are essential in developing the relationships among the variables. Parameters are generally classified into two categories: *constant* and *random*.

Two types of parameters

Constant Parameters The parameters are often assumed to be constant; that is, there exists a static state. Such an assumption may be valid for a short period of time before major environmental or organizational factors change. In the example of your pocket money model, the functional relationship of the total wage *(W)* and the hours worked *(H)* contains a parameter of $3.50, the hourly wage rate.

Constant parameters

Random Parameters In a more dynamic or complex situation, the model parameters may not have a constant relationship but rather the parameters themselves vary according to some probability distribution. For example, in your wage model let us assume that you accepted the option of getting 100 percent of your wages in tips rather than the $3.50/hour constant wage rate. In this case your total wage may be expressed as:

Random parameters

$$W = tH$$

where
t = amount of tip received per hour

Obviously, t is not a constant parameter but a random parameter.

Relationships within the Model

The essence of management science models is the representation of the relationships among the various components of the model. The relationship *can be illustrated graphically*. For example, your wage model $W = 3.50H$ can be presented graphically as shown in Figure 2.3.

Graphical illustration

Most of the management science models presented in this introductory text will be relatively complete so that we can derive a solution. When such a complete model cannot be constructed because of either lack of data or complexity of the system, computer programs may be employed as tools for analysis. The computer-based simulation to analyze waiting lines at a bank is a good example of such an approach.

Figure 2.3   Graphical Representation of the Wage Model

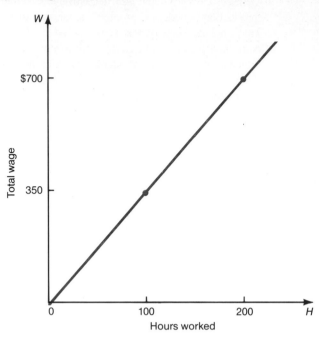

DECISION MAKING ENVIRONMENT

States of decision environment

Management science is primarily concerned with searching for information about feasible courses of action. The type of management science models used may be based both on the nature of the problem at hand and on the decision environment. Basically, there are four different states of decision environment: *certainty, risk, uncertainty,* and *conflict.* In Table 2.1 a summary is presented about the types of decision environments, the expected solutions, and some of the typical management science techniques applied. We shall discuss each type of decision environment in greater detail.

Decision Making under Certainty

Certainty condition

If we have all the information required to make a decision, we have a decision making situation under certainty. In other words, under certainty we can predict exactly the outcome of each alternative course of action. For example, in the linear programming problem presented in Chapters 3, 4, and 5, we know exactly how much of different resources are required to produce a product; thus, we can accurately predict its unit profit.

Many of the decision problems we face daily are under certainty. Where to purchase a racquet—K-Mart, Woolco, or Sports World? Where to have lunch—McDonald's, Burger King, the Crib, or the University Club? You know exactly how

Table 2.1 Decision Environment, Solutions, and Management Science Techniques

Decision Environment	Solutions	Typical Techniques
Certainty	Deterministic	Linear programming Goal programming Transportation and assignment models Dynamic programming Inventory models under certainty Some queuing and network models
Risk	Probabilistic	Probabilistic decision models Probabilistic inventory models Queuing models Simulation models
Uncertainty	Unknown	Decision analysis under uncertainty
Conflict	Contingent upon opponents' actions	Various custom-built models Game theory

much a racquet or a meal costs at each of the locations and you know the quality you will receive for your money.

Most of the management science techniques we will be studying in this book are for decision making under the condition of certainty. For example, linear programming; goal programming; transportation and assignment models; and analytical approaches of inventory, queuing, and PERT/CPM models are all deterministic models for decision making under certainty.

Decision Making under Risk

Risk condition

The risk condition refers to the situation in which the probabilities of certain decision outcomes occurring are known. For example, let us suppose that you are thinking about scalping some tickets at the forthcoming football game with your school's archrival. Your immediate concern is to decide how many tickets to get from your friends. You can buy student tickets at the regular cost of $5 from friends who are going home for the weekend. You are planning to sell the tickets at $25 each. If you have unsold tickets, they are of course worthless.

After a discussion with friends who have been scalping tickets for years, you arrive at the following estimates of ticket sales for the next game:

Tickets	Probability
2	0.10
3	0.25
4	0.30
5	0.25
6	0.10
	1.00

With the above data, you are able to determine the number of tickets you should purchase for resale on Saturday.

For decision problems under risk, the theory of probability is used extensively. Decision theory, decision trees, probabilistic linear programming, stochastic inventory, queuing models, and simulation are some of the examples of decision making models under risk.

Decision Making under Uncertainty

Uncertainty condition

The uncertainty state refers to the condition in which the probabilities of certain outcomes occurring are not known at all. Under uncertainty it is impossible even to estimate the probabilities of the various consequences. In your ticket scalping scheme, for example, the sales of tickets may be totally unpredictable because there are too many factors affecting the sales—ranking of the teams, the weather, what the opposing coaches say about the upcoming game, and so on.

Although it may sound like a helpless case, in reality, decision making under uncertainty is perhaps the most prevalent situation. Obviously, we cannot just give up decision making because there exists uncertainty. We must find ways to reduce uncertainty, and there have been several approaches suggested for decision making under uncertainty.

The first approach is to obtain additional information about the problem. This process may yield at least partial probabilities of consequences. Then the problem is not completely a "shot in the dark" but rather a "shot in a fog." Although additional information can make the problem clearer, the question of the cost of additional information becomes important. The benefit derived from additional information must exceed the cost of obtaining such information.

Another approach for handling decision making under uncertainty is to reduce it to a problem under risk by incorporating our own subjective feelings or estimates as probabilities. There are several strategies we can employ for this purpose. We will discuss this topic thoroughly in Chapter 9 when we study decision theory.

Decision Making under Conflict

Conflict condition

A condition of conflict exists when the interests of two or more decision makers are in a competitive situation. For example, if decision maker A benefits from a course of action he takes, it is possible only because decision maker B has also taken a certain course of action. Hence, in the decision analysis the decision makers are interested not only in what they do individually but also in what both of them do. There are many such situations when firms are involved in competitive market strategies, new product development, recruitment of experienced executives, or advertising campaigns.

Although decision making under conflict may sound simple, in reality it is extremely complex. We may have a decision making problem under uncertainty that is further compounded by fierce opponents or competitors. Thus, game theory has been suggested as a theoretical approach to decision making under conflict. However, in real-world applications game theory has been disappointingly ineffective, as clearly shown by the several surveys we reviewed in Chapter 1. In a conflict situation the problem is usually analyzed by designing custom-built models or by using other management science techniques rather than game theory. Therefore, game theory, which is theoretically neat but which has little practical value, will not be discussed in this book.

THE PROCESS OF MANAGEMENT SCIENCE MODELING

Several major steps

Management science is the application of scientific approaches to management decision making. There is no one correct way to apply management science. Every practitioner of management science may have his own way of doing things. However, there are several major steps that almost everyone agrees are important in management science application. These steps are:

1. Formulation of the Problem
    A. Orientation period
    B. Definition of problem components
        (1) The decision maker
        (2) The decision objectives
        (3) The decision environment
        (4) Alternative courses of action

2. Development of the Model

3. Model Validation

4. Solution of the Model

5. Implementation of the Solution

Let us discuss these major phases, as outlined above, in order to signify the role of modeling in management science.

Formulation of the Problem

What are we trying to do?

One aspect of the scientific approach that is absolutely necessary is determining what one is trying to do. As an old saying goes, a problem well put is half solved. As a matter of fact, understanding the problem seems to be the most difficult aspect of management decision making. Quite often when we are faced with a problem, we tend to deal with symptoms rather than a diagnosis. For example, let us suppose that you have been experiencing a foreboding that you are about to go broke. Just yesterday you had to make an excuse to Susan about why you could not go out Saturday night (the $3 you have in your wallet would not even get you to the main street, much less to your favorite hangout, the Starship). And today you received a notice from the Registrar's Office that your second tuition payment is overdue. These are important symptoms of your financial problem, but you cannot diagnose (understand and define) the nature of the problem without obtaining additional information, such as your undisciplined spending habits or your inability to generate adequate income.

Although management science application begins with the formulation of a problem, this step must be a continuous process until the completion of the project. Once an initial formulation of the problem is completed and subsequent steps proceed, the problem under study is subjected to continuous modification and refinement. Consequently, a continuous updating or modification of the problem is necessary in order to assure the validity of the model solution.

Each decision making problem may require a unique approach to formulate it. However, there are several generalized steps in the problem formulation phase.

Steps of problem formulation

Orientation Period The orientation period provides us with an opportunity to assess the overall picture of the problem. During this period we can obtain a broad understanding of the organizational climate, the objectives of the organization, and the purpose of the management science analysis. The orientation period can be used to specify the conditions that are required to carry out the analysis, such as time and resource requirements, administrative arrangements, the scope of the application, and the like.

Definition of Problem Components Before the problem can be formulated, its components must be clearly defined. The first component to be defined is the decision maker who is not satisfied with the current state of affairs. The second component to be analyzed is the objectives of the decision maker. What are the things that the decision maker is trying to achieve through the analysis? The third component is the decision environment or decision system that embraces the problem in question. Finally, a problem cannot be evaluated unless the decision maker has alternative courses of action. We shall now discuss these components in greater detail.

The Decision Maker For any decision analysis we must identify the decision maker who has the authority to initiate, modify, and terminate the activities that control the system or organization under study. In some instances the authority of decision making may rest upon more than one individual. In such an event it is essential to acquire a good understanding of how the decision group reaches certain decisions. Is the decision process based on majority vote or unanimous vote? Who has the authority to approve or veto their decision? These questions must be cleared up at this stage.

The role of decision maker

The Decision Objectives Perhaps the most crucial factor in decision analysis is the identification of decision objectives (or criteria). The decision maker may have a specific set of objectives that he wants to achieve through the analysis. In such a case analysis of the objectives is relatively simple. However, sometimes the decision maker cannot specify objectives for the problem. Then it may be necessary to list all the possible outcomes of the project and obtain the decision maker's ideas concerning the desirability of obtaining certain outcomes. Based on this analysis, and the approval of the decision maker, we can establish objectives.

Decision objectives

In analyzing the objectives of the decision maker, two distinct types of objectives must be evaluated. First, it is necessary to consider objectives that the decision maker has already obtained and that he wants to retain. For example, he may want to maintain a stable employment level or to preserve the good community image of the firm. These are *maintenance objectives*. The second type of objectives involves the

Maintenance objectives

Innovative objectives

achievement of a higher degree of performance or achievement from either existing or new activities. For example, the decision maker may want to increase the market share, increase profits, decrease personnel turnover, decrease production costs, or install a new computer system. These are *innovative objectives*.

In most managerial problems there are some objectives that are to be obtained and others that are to be maintained. In addition to the identification of objectives, it is also essential to obtain the decision maker's priority structure for the objectives. Since it is not always possible to achieve all the objectives to the degree desired by the decision maker, the priority consideration allows a concentration of efforts on the higher priority objectives. We will discuss this topic thoroughly in Chapter 6.

Key components of decision environment

The Decision Environment Any organized system involves several key components, such as managers (administrators), employees who carry out policies, financial and other resources necessary for policies to be carried out, outsiders who are affected by the organization, and the social and ecological environment in which the organization functions. It is essential, therefore, to analyze the effects and repercussions of the decision from the system's perspective. For example, the decision maker's objectives for the problem may be in conflict with the interests of outsiders and the social environment (e.g., profit maximization while neglecting pollution). Through the analysis of the system components and their objectives, the initial set of the decision maker's objectives may be further modified.

Choice of actions

Alternative Courses of Action A problem cannot exist unless the decision maker has a choice of actions. A number of possible courses of action is usually disclosed in the process of going through the steps of formulating the problem. However, the list of alternatives uncovered in this way might not be exhaustive. It may be necessary, therefore, to develop new alternatives through a thorough system analysis. It is extremely difficult to determine how extensive the alternative search should be, since the process may cost a great deal of money, time, and effort.

Development of the Model

Modeling—the crux of management science

Modeling is the crux of the management science approach. It is as important as laboratory experiments in physical science. We are getting into the fine details of the problem in this phase. Developing a model allows a comprehensive analysis by means of a logical expression of the complexities, unique characteristics, and possible uncertainties of the problem. The logical expression requires a mathematical formula to represent the interrelationships among the system's elements.

The model serves as a convenient vehicle that helps to analyze a complex reality in a concise and relatively simple manner. A model clarifies the feasible decision alternatives, the economic and noneconomic consequences of these alternatives, and the optimum alternative for the problem. A systematic analysis is possible only when the relationships among the components and their objective criteria are expressed in a comprehensive but manageable mathematical model.

Validation of the Model

Once the model is developed, it is important to test the model concerning the validity of its assumptions. The problem at hand may change over time, and thus a continuous updating and validating of the model components, their relationships, and the

Evaluating objective criterion
objective criteria may be necessary. It is imperative that the objective criteria be continuously evaluated, as management goals often change in time with the changes in the decision environment.

Frequently it is necessary to modify a model, even when the model is perfectly acceptable, because required data are not available or are too costly to obtain. Although the initial model development may be simple, its modification may be extremely difficult. Thus, it may be necessary to go through several cycles of model validation and search for more data. Each model leads to a search for data that may not always yield the required information. However, the search process often reveals how the model should be modified in order to use the available data.

Solution of the Model

The optimum solution
Once a mathematical model is formulated, the next phase is deriving an optimum solution from the model. The *optimum solution* presents the model result that optimizes the given decision criterion (objective). As pointed out earlier, a mathematical model is a simple abstract of reality. If the model represents almost every characteristic of the problem, it may be too complex to allow easy formulation, manipulation, and solution. On the other hand, if the model is too simple, it may not represent all the relevant aspects of the problem. Therefore, the model solution phase may point out whether or not the model is an appropriate one for the problem. This phase may give rise to a continuous review of the problem-formulation/model-development/ model-solution/model-validation cycle until a satisfactory solution is found.

Implementation of the Solution

Putting the solution to actual use
The true value of management science is realized when the model solution is put to actual use. This phase usually requires a translation of the solution into a set of management policies or operating procedures that can be easily implemented by the operating personnel. A problem that plagues most management science practitioners is that the system under investigation keeps changing. Consequently, a control process must be established over the solution so that the model can be updated continuously.

Organizational change
Implementation of an important management science model usually affects the entire organization. Such an organizational change requires modification of management practices, which in turn necessitates behavioral changes on the part of employees affected. It is only natural to expect that employees will resist change, whether it is good for the organization or not. It is imperative, therefore, that many key employees be directly involved in the management science project. Such an employee involvement, coupled with strong top management support for implementation, appears to be the key to the success of management science application. Chapter 15 is devoted entirely to the implementation process of management science.

The approximate optimum solution
We should always remember that the model does not yield the optimum solution to the real problem under analysis. Instead, the model provides only an optimum or approximately optimum solution to the model we formulated from the problem. Thus, we should never expect that the problem will be solved exactly as the model solution indicates.

The solution procedure we choose may also vary according to the type of model we formulate for a given problem. For instance, we can employ an analytical, nu-

Analytical procedures

merical, iterative, or a simulation-based procedure in order to solve a model. Analytical procedures involve the application of various mathematical tools to express the problem in an abstract manner. An analytical model usually allows the substitution of its solution values for various model variables. Sometimes, a model only allows

Numerical procedures

for numerical solutions. Numerical procedures are based on three basic steps: (1) assign certain values to the decision variables in the model; (2) compare the model solutions; and (3) select the set of values for the decision variables that yields the best solution. Numerical procedures may range from a very primitive trial-and-error

Iterative procedures

type analysis to a very systematic iterative analysis. An iterative analysis employs a successive solution that approaches the optimum solution on a step-by-step basis. It is often the case that the problem does not allow either analytical or numerical analysis. In such cases the only feasible approach may be a computer-based simulation. Simulation will be treated in greater detail in Chapter 14.

EXAMPLES OF MANAGEMENT SCIENCE MODELS

The most important aspect of management is decision making that seeks the best course of action given certain environmental and resource constraints. Allocating scarce resources to competing alternatives in order to achieve organizational objectives is the major interest of the decision maker. You are only too familiar with the resource allocation problems you face daily. Trying to live the whole week with $20 in your pocket, scheduling your week so that you could study for the midterm exam in the management science course and still date Susan at least three evenings, attempting to go home over the weekend and visit friends by covering 285 miles with a tankful of gas in your car—these may be some examples of your resource allocation problems.

Management science models are very useful in deriving new information that is essential for management planning and control. Management science models are especially valuable in deriving an optimum solution and "what if" type information for complex management problems that involve many interrelated decision variables.

Illustrative problems

In order to provide some initial understanding of how management science can be used for decision making, we present the following illustrative casettes ("little cases," so named to destinguish them from the more definitive case studies commonly found in the social sciences). In subsequent chapters we shall discuss the details of each technique that can be applied to these casettes.

CASETTE 2.1   *PRODUCTION SCHEDULING AT SANZO, LTD.*

Sanzo, Ltd., a Japanese electronics firm, recently constructed a new joint-venture electronics company. With the most advanced production technology, Sanzo has decided to produce two products: video cassette recorders (VCR) and stereo receivers (SR). The firm has set up two assembly lines within the plant. Most of the production work is done by industrial robots programmed by computer. Each video cassette recorder, with the label of Sanzuki, requires three hours in Assembly Line 1 and one hour in Assembly Line 2. Each stereo receiver, with the label of Frontier, requires one hour in Assembly Line 1 and two hours in Assembly Line 2. In addition, each product requires manpower in the Packaging Department. The packaging time required is 50 minutes for each unit of Sanzuki and 30 minutes for each unit of Frontier.

The firm has normal weekly operation time of 150 hours for Assembly Line 1 and 120 hours for Assembly Line 2 because of robot operation specifications. Also, the packaging department operates 80 hours per week. The Cost Accounting Department of Sanzo estimates that the unit profit for Sanzuki is $200 and for Frontier it is $140. The resource requirements and unit contributions can be summarized as follows:

Resource	Resource Requirements per Unit		Available Resources per Week
	Sanzuki VCR	Frontier SR	
Assembly Line 1	3 hr.	1 hr.	150 hr.
Assembly Line 2	1 hr.	2 hr.	120 hr.
Packaging	50 min.	30 min.	4,800 min.
Unit profit	$200	$140	

The problem facing the Sanzo management is to determine the quantity of Sanzuki VCR and Frontier SR to produce with the given amounts of resources in order to maximize profit. Since the firm is in the pioneering stage of its operation in the United States, it is primarily concerned with the profitability and marketability of its new products.

Now that the management has formulated the problem, the next step is to develop a management science model. In order to develop the model, the decision variables must first be defined. As the management attempts to determine the quantity of each product to produce, it must consider the following variables:

x_1 = the quantity of Sanzuki VCR to be produced per week

x_2 = the quantity of Frontier SR to be produced per week

The objective to be pursued in this problem is to maximize the total profit. The total profit equation to be maximized is referred to as the *objective function*. The total profit will be the sum of profits from Sanzuki VCR units and Frontier SR units. For example, if the firm produces 5 Sanzuki VCRs and 5 Frontier SRs, the total profit will be determined as follows:

$$\text{Profit from Sanzuki VCRs} = \$200 \times 5 = \$1,000$$
$$\text{Profit from Frontier SRs} = \$140 \times 5 = \$700$$
$$\text{Total profit} = \$1,000 + \$700 = \$1,700$$

Since values of the decision variables x_1 and x_2 are not known at present, the objective function is expressed as follows:

$$\text{Maximize total profit, } Z = \$200x_1 + \$140x_2$$

If the firm does not have resource constraints, the Sanzo management would try to produce as many units of Sanzuki VCR and Frontier SR as possible in order to maximize the total profit. However, the firm can try to maximize profit only within the limits imposed by the available resources. The relationships between the products' resource requirements and the available resources to be formulated are referred to as *constraints*. For example, the available weekly operation hours of Assembly Line 1 are 150. Each Sanzuki VCR unit requires 3 hours and each Frontier SR unit takes 1 hour in Assembly Line 1. Thus, the total weekly operation hours required to produce Sanzuki and Frontier units would be:

$$\text{Sanzuki VCR} = 3x_1$$
$$\text{Frontier SR} = 1x_2$$
$$\text{Total weekly operation hours} = 3x_1 + x_2$$

Since the total available weekly operation hours in Assembly Line 1 is 150, the total number of hours Sanzo can operate Assembly Line 1 must be equal to or less than the available 150 hours. The inequality sign "$\leq$" represents the "less than or equal to" relationship. Then, the first constraint of the model for Assembly Line 1 can be expressed by:

$$3x_1 + x_2 \leq 150 \qquad \textit{Assembly Line 1}$$

The remaining two constraints, Assembly Line 2 and the Packaging Department operations, can be formulated in a similar manner as follows:

$$x_1 + 2x_2 \leq 120 \qquad \textit{Assembly Line 2}$$
$$50x_1 + 30x_2 \leq 4800 \qquad \textit{Packaging Department}$$

Finally, we must recognize that negative units of production are not acceptable. Thus, we can formulate the following nonnegativity constraint:

$$x_1, x_2 \geq 0 \qquad \textit{Nonnegativity}$$

Now the complete model can be presented as:

$$\text{Maximize } Z = \$200x_1 + \$140x_2$$
$$\text{subject to} \quad 3x_1 + x_2 \leq 150$$
$$x_1 + 2x_2 \leq 120$$
$$50x_1 + 30x_2 \leq 4800$$
$$x_1, x_2 \geq 0$$

The above model is a typical maximization problem of *linear programming*. The model attempts to solve for decision variables x_1 and x_2 that will satisfy all the constraints and optimize the objective function. Chapters 3, 4, and 5 are devoted to linear programming and related topics.

CASETTE 2.2   *TRANSPORTATION PROBLEM OF J. R. DISTRIBUTORS, INC.*

J. R. Distributors, Inc. is a family-owned restaurant equipment manufacturer headquartered in Omaha, Nebraska. J. R. has been a specialist in constructing and distributing various restaurant refrigeration equipment ever since it was founded by James Richardson in 1946. The company has three plants, located in Kansas City, Missouri; Des Moines, Iowa; and Omaha.

The company is under contract to supply large refrigerators to three warehouses of a fast-food restaurant chain, Queen Burgers, Inc., located in Lincoln, Nebraska; Iowa City, Iowa; and Lawrence, Kansas. The decision problem facing the management of J. R. is to determine the quantity of refrigerators to be transported from three plants to the three Queen Burgers warehouses while minimizing the total transportation cost. The Cost Accounting Department at J. R. analyzed the unit transportation cost from each plant to each of the warehouses. The supply capacities at the three plants, the demand requirements of the warehouses, and the unit transportation costs from plants to warehouses are summarized as follows:

	Unit Transportation Cost			
Plant	**Lincoln**	**Iowa City**	**Lawrence**	**Supply**
Kansas City	$60	$70	$15	24
Omaha	20	40	60	16
Des Moines	80	30	50	16
Demand	30	14	12	56

The management of J. R. Distributors seeks to determine the optimum transportation scheme that will satisfy supply and demand requirements while minimizing the total transportation cost. This problem can be formulated and solved as a linear programming model. We can denote the quantity of refrigerators to be transported from each plant to each warehouse as follows:

	Warehouse		
Plant	**Lincoln**	**Iowa City**	**Lawrence**
Kansas City	x_1	x_2	x_3
Omaha	x_4	x_5	x_6
Des Moines	x_7	x_8	x_9

The objective function of the model is to minimize the total transportation cost, which is simply a sum of transportation costs from each plant to each warehouse. For example, the total transportation cost from Kansas City to Lincoln will be simply the unit transportation cost of refrigerators times the quantity transported, or $60x_1$. Thus, we can formulate the objective function as:

$$\text{Minimize } Z = 60x_1 + 70x_2 + 15x_3 + 20x_4 + 40x_5 + 60x_6 + 80x_7 + 30x_8 + 50x_9$$

The model constraints involved in this problem are the supply and demand requirements. This particular problem is a balanced transportation case where total supply equals total demand. Thus, each of the supply and demand constraints can be expressed as an equality. For example, the supply requirement for the Kansas City plant is that the total number of refrigerators supplied to the Lincoln, Iowa City, and Lawrence warehouses must equal 24 (the supply capacity). Thus, the supply constraint for the Kansas City plant can be expressed by:

$$x_1 + x_2 + x_3 = 24$$

Now, we can formulate the complete linear programming model as follows:

$$\text{Minimize } Z = 60x_1 + 70x_2 + 15x_3 + 20x_4 + 40x_5 + 60x_6 + 80x_7 + 30x_8 + 50x_9$$

$$\text{subject to} \quad \left.\begin{array}{l} x_1 + x_2 + x_3 = 24 \\ x_4 + x_5 + x_6 = 16 \\ x_7 + x_8 + x_9 = 16 \end{array}\right\} \text{supply constraints}$$

$$\left.\begin{array}{l} x_1 + x_4 + x_7 = 30 \\ x_2 + x_5 + x_8 = 14 \\ x_3 + x_6 + x_9 = 12 \end{array}\right\} \text{demand constraints}$$

$$x_j \geq 0 \quad \text{nonnegativity constraint}$$

When a transportation problem is formulated as a linear programming model, it becomes rather complex. The transportation method, a special case of linear programming, is a simple approach that takes advantage of the unique features of a transportation problem. Chapter 7 is devoted to the transportation method.

CASETTE 2.3   *INVENTORY PROBLEM OF THE MIDLAND UTILITIES*

The Midland Utilities provides electric service in three midwestern states. The company has constructed two new coal-fired units in view of the increasing cost of natural gas and oil as well as the uncertainty surrounding the future of nuclear power generation.

The manager of the Materials Management Division is attempting to determine the inventory policy in order to negotiate a long-term contract with a coal mining firm in Wyoming. Each of the coal-fired generating plants requires 200 tons of coal per day to operate, and the units are in operation 360 days per year. The manager has received information from the Cost Accounting Department that the average ordering cost (cost involved in processing an order) is $80 per order and the cost of storing coal is 25 percent of the purchase price of the average quantity held.

The coal mining company has presented a tentative contract which calls for $30 per ton for the coming year with an average lead time (the time required to receive the shipment from the time an order is processed) of 30 weeks. The manager of the Materials Management Division is trying to determine the optimum order quantity in order to minimize the total inventory cost.

The total inventory cost is the sum of the total ordering cost and the total holding cost. It is not a simple task to find the optimum order quantity as the total inventory cost is a nonlinear function. However, this problem can be easily solved by the inventory model. Chapter 11 is devoted to inventory models.

CASETTE 2.4   *QUEUING PROBLEM OF THE CHECKER TAXI COMPANY*

The Checker Taxi Company is the largest company in town that provides taxi service. Currently the company has 10 taxicabs with an average mileage of 60,000 miles (and an average age of only 8 months). One of the most frustrating and costly problems of Checker has been the mechanical breakdown of its taxis. The firm hired Jack Stolley, a recent business college graduate with a quantitative management background.

Jack has investigated the past year's data concerning taxi breakdowns, repair times in the shop, and the company policy about the repair priority when more than one taxi is out of service. The major findings are: (1) the average time between taxi breakdowns is three days, distributed according to a known distribution; (2) the average time to repair a taxi is two days, also distributed according to a known distribution; and (3) a single mechanic repairs the taxis in the order in which they break down.

The owner of the company has asked Jack to find answers to the following critical problems:

1. Probability that the mechanic would be idle.

2. Mean number of cabs waiting to be repaired.

3. Mean waiting time for break-down cabs to be repaired.

4. Probability that three or more cabs would be out of service at one time.

These problems can be analyzed by using a queuing model, which will be presented in Chapter 12.

KEEPING A PROPER PERSPECTIVE ABOUT MODELS

In this chapter we have discussed the modeling concept and many different types of models. You may be getting enough of modeling by now. Now let us try to put modeling in proper perspective.

Modeling in management science

Modeling is the crux of management science. Without models it is virtually impossible to analyze complex business systems. Determining which modeling approach to use and building a custom-made model for a particular problem involve much more than just management science knowledge. Artistic creativity and humanistic skills are also required to build and implement a useful model.

Requirements of a model

Perhaps the most important aspect of modeling is that a model represents something less than the true reality under study. In other words, a model must be simpler and less precise than the reality. We must always keep this in mind. Of primary importance is the decision of how simple we want to build a model and how much precision we want to sacrifice. The trade-off considerations we must contemplate lead us to a modeling approach somewhere between the so-called *quick and dirty* and the *slow and clean* modeling approaches.

The quick and dirty approach

In the quick and dirty modeling approach, a model is built by identifying only the key variables with relatively small amounts of effort, time, and cost. This ap-

*The slow and clean
approach*

proach is especially useful when an emergency situation requires a quick overall analysis, when there are insufficient time and personnel for the study, or when the study is not important enough to draw heavily on organizational resources.

The slow and clean approach to modeling attempts to build a model in the most deliberate and intricate manner. This approach is appropriate when analyzing a long-term policy issue, when there are sufficient organizational resources for a long-term study, or when the study is so important that it deserves the most elaborate and careful analysis. As mentioned above, in most real-world situations the modeling approach taken would be somewhere between the quick and dirty and the slow and clean extremes. The modeling effort may be based on a host of situational variables such as the importance of the problem, the work burden of the management science personnel, the time and cost required to finish the study, the availability of the necessary data, and the like.

*An optimum solution—
only for the model.*

Another important point we must remember about modeling is that the optimum solution to a model is the best solution only with respect to the model. In other words, the optimum model solution is not necessarily the best solution to the real problem. At best it could be an approximate optimum solution to the real problem. Therefore, the efforts required to build a very intricate model must be weighed against the costs and benefits associated with such efforts.

Management scientists are often denounced by practicing managers for their "hang-up" or passion for building complex and incomprehensible models. On the other hand, managers often want certain information on a moment's notice regardless of its source and method of obtainment. Now you can see why developing a proper perspective about modeling is so important. We must view a model as what it is—a convenient vehicle to help us understand a complex business system. But a modeling effort costs money and human resources. Thus, we must develop a model that is an effective and economical way to analyze important decision problems.

References

Beer, S. *Management Sciences: The Basic Use of Operations Research.* Garden City, N.Y.: Doubleday, 1968.

Churchman, C. W.; Ackoff, R. L.; and Arnoff, E. L. *Introduction to Operations Research.* New York: Wiley, 1957.

Lee, S. M. *Goal Programming for Decision Analysis.* Philadelphia: Auerbach, 1972.

Lee, S. M., and Moore, L. J. *Introduction to Decision Science.* New York: Petrocelli-Charter, 1975.

Turban, E., and Meredith, J. R. *Fundamentals of Management Science.* Dallas: Business Publications, 1977.

Assignments

2.1 Define the term *model* and give some examples of models you see around you every day.

2.2 Classify models based on the degree of their abstraction and provide some examples of such models.

2.3 What are the primary advantages of a mathematical model over other models? Why are these advantages important?

2.4 What are the components of a management science model? Define them and also discuss their relationships.

2.5 Let us assume that you are about to deposit $1000 in a passbook savings account that pays an annual interest of 8 percent. Develop a model that will determine the total amount of money you will have in the account at the end of the first year. Also, define all of the model components.

2.6 You were just notified by the Student Aid and Scholarships Office that you would receive a regents scholarship of $1000 for the coming academic year. Furthermore, your application for a work-study program was also accepted. You will be allowed to work up to 15 hours a week at an hourly wage rate of $3.40. The academic year has a total of 30 weeks of school. You estimate that the total deductions from the scholarship and work-study wages would be as follows: scholarship, 5 percent handling charges; work-study, 12 percent tax; and 5 percent health insurance. Develop a model that will determine your total cash situation during the next academic year, and define all of the model components.

2.7 Define four primary states of the decision making environment.

2.8 Provide examples of decision problems you face frequently under the four different states of the decision environment.

2.9 What are the primary differences between the deterministic and probabilistic models?

2.10 What is the role of modeling in the management science process?

2.11 Define the process of management science. Discuss a simple decision problem you face frequently in relation to the process of management science.

2.12 Most objectives can be classified into two types: maintenance and innovative. Classify the objectives you have for the coming year into the two types.

2.13 Many decision problems have multiple and often conflicting objectives. Discuss your objectives for this school year and set priorities by assigning A for the most important objective, B for the second most important objective, and so on.

2.14 The solution procedure for a model may vary according to the nature of the problem. Define the analytical, numerical, iterative, and simulation methods of solution.

2.15 What is the most important consideration in keeping a proper perspective about management science models?

3   INTRODUCTION TO LINEAR PROGRAMMING

The allocation of limited resources to competing demands is the most prevalent decision problem in organizations. Resource allocation problems may range from a simple daily work-scheduling problem to a complex capital-budgeting problem that encompasses several years. Mathematical programming *is the general term used for a host of management science techniques developed to solve management problems involving resource allocation. Linear programming is the most popular and most widely applied technique of mathematical programming. In this chapter we will walk through the basic concepts, the model formulations, and the graphical solution method of linear programming.*

Learning Objectives   From the study of this chapter, you will learn the following:

1. *The basic approach and history of linear programming.*
2. *The types of management problems that can be analyzed by linear programming.*
3. *The formulation of various types of problems as linear programming models.*
4. *The solution of simple linear programming models by the graphical method.*
5. *The performance of a simple sensitivity analysis of a model through graphical interpretation.*
6. *The meaning of the following terms:*

Mathematical programming	*Divisibility*
Linear programming	*Equality and inequality*
Objective function	*Graphical method*
Constraints	*Linearity*
Area of feasible solutions	*Additivity*

BASIC CONCEPTS OF LINEAR PROGRAMMING

The problem of resource allocation

A typical decision problem in organizations is one concerned with the allocation of scarce or limited resources to achieve certain objectives. Scarce resources may be money, manpower, materials, machine capacity, facilities, knowledge, skills, time, space, or technology. The objective of the decision maker is to achieve the best possible outcome or outcomes with the available resources. The desired outcome may be measured by such things as profits, costs, market shares, sales, return on investment, time, distance, or welfare of the public.

The desired outcome in the problem could be expressed as a mathematical relationship of decision variables, thus forming the objective function. The amounts of available resources, also expressed as mathematical relationships, become constraints that restrict the solution space for the problem. Linear programming is a powerful yet simple method to aid management decision making by identifying the best combination of scarce resources so as to optimize the desired objective.

A Brief History

History of linear programming

The origins of mathematical programming techniques may go far back in mathematical antiquity to the theories of mathematical equations. However, George B. Dantzig is widely recognized as the person who pioneered the technique of linear programming. Dantzig began his pioneering work when he was involved in military logistics problems of the U.S. Air Force during World War II. There were other scholars who complemented Dantzig's work, such as J. von Neumann, L. Kantorovich, T. C. Koopmans, and L. Hurwicz.

Dantzig named the technique *linear programming* after it was first introduced as "programming of interdependent activities in a linear structure." The basic solution technique of linear programming, the simplex method, was developed by Dantzig in 1947. Since then many scholars have joined Dantzig in developing the technique and exploring the applications of linear programming. Some of the best known of these scholars are Marshall Wood, Alex Orden, A. Charnes, W. W. Cooper, A. Henderson, and W. Orchard-Hays.

During its early stage of development, linear programming was applied primarily to military logistics problems such as transportation, assignment, and deployment decisions. However, after the war linear programming became a popular technique in business organizations. One of the earliest industrial applications of linear programming was conducted by A. Charnes and W. W. Cooper for the gasoline blending problem. Since then it has become one of the most widely applied management science techniques in business organizations, governmental agencies, and nonprofit institutions, as we learned in Chapter 1. Today numerous business firms apply linear programming to such managerial problems as petroleum blending, animal-feed blending, food processing, production scheduling and inventory control, personnel assignment and development, transportation of goods and services, and capital investments.

Wide applications

Basic Requirements

Requirements of linear programming

In order to apply linear programming to a particular problem, we must ascertain that the problem under analysis meets several requirements. These requirements restrict the applicability of linear programming. However, understanding the limitations of linear programming imposed by these requirements is very important for keeping a proper perspective about the true value of the technique.

The Objective Criterion A linear programming problem must have one explicit (quantitatively defined) objective criterion—to optimize. Examples of things one might want to optimize include profit, cost, market share, product exposure, productivity, and defective items. Thus, the objective function must be one of either maximization or minimization of the criterion, but never both. The single-objective optimization is an important requirement of linear programming.

Limited Resources Linear programming is a useful technique for analyzing decision problems that involve activities requiring the consumption of limited resources. The limited resources could be money, production capacity, personnel, time, or technology. The amounts of limited resources are expressed as constraints for the linear programming problem. The constraints impose restrictions on the activities (decision variables) in optimizing the objective function.

Linear Relationships Another requirement of linear programming is that all relationships among the variables in the model must be mathematically linear. The term *linear* simply implies that relationships among the decision variables (products, activities, etc.) must be directly proportional. **Proportionality** means that the relationship between outcome and resource usage is constant. In a production problem, for example, if we increase the required materials by 10 percent, we can expect a 10 percent increase in production.

Proportionality

Linear relationships also require that the total measure of the objective criterion and the total sum of resource usage must be additive. For example, suppose that we have a profit maximization problem for a furniture company that produces two products—desks and chairs. The **additivity** requires that the total profit must be the sum of the profits earned from desks and chairs. Also, the amount of resources used for production must exactly equal the sum of the resources required for producing desks and chairs.

Divisibility Another requirement of linear programming is that the solution values for the decision variables and the amount of resources used need not be integer (whole-number) valued but can be continuous. In other words, fractional values for the decision variables and resources must be permissible in obtaining an optimum solution. In the furniture production case, a production program requiring 100.79 oak boards and 25.27 hours of manpower to produce 29.13 desks and 15.25 chairs should be acceptable. In many decision problems it is perfectly acceptable to have fractional values for decision variables and resources. For example, we can use 2.75 cups of sugar and 1.33 pounds of flour to make 3.15 dozens of cookies. However, there are occasions when decision variables have physical significance or meaning only if they are in integer values. For example, we cannot assign 1.29 persons to a job, we cannot construct 0.67 percent of a power plant, and we cannot take 1.33 credit hours. Other extensions of linear programming will handle these problems, and they will be discussed in Chapter 5.

Divisibility

Deterministic Parameters In linear programming all of the model coefficients (e.g., the profit contribution of each product, the amount of resources required per unit of product, and the amount of available resources) are assumed to be known with certainty. In other words, linear programming implicitly assumes a decision problem in a static state. In real-world situations, however, model parameters are never completely deterministic but vary over time. Techniques have been developed to handle linear programming problems with uncertain parameters.

Deterministic parameters

Nonnegativity In most linear programming models there is an implicit requirement that all decision variables must take on nonnegative values. In other words, negative production of certain goods, negative investments, negative amount of foods served, and the like are not permissible. The nonnegative requirement certainly makes sense in most problems. If we need a decision variable which can be negative (e.g., the

Nonnegativity

rate of change in the unemployment level), we must make a slight adjustment to the decision variable so that the model satisfies the nonnegativity requirement.

Application Areas

Application areas

As we discussed earlier, linear programming has been a very popular technique that has been widely applied to all types of decision making problems. As a matter of fact, it is difficult to find a decision problem that has not been analyzed by linear programming. Thus, it would be a major undertaking to list all of the functional problem areas that have seen linear programming applications. Instead we will simply look at broad classifications of problem types that have been solved by linear programming.

Resource Allocation Problems Most business organizations are involved in the production of goods or services. General Motors Corporation, Texas Instruments, IBM, McDonald's, Kentucky Fried Chicken, Mutual of Omaha, The First National Bank, and St. Elizabeth's Hospital are all engaged in the production of goods or services. There may be many different types of limited resources these organizations use in producing a number of different possible outcomes. The typical decision problem would be to determine a combination of input resources that will result in the optimum outcome. Linear programming is perfectly suited for this type of resource allocation problem.

Allocating limited resources

Some of the most widely known resource allocation problems that have been analyzed by linear programming are as follows:

Manufacturing
  Production mix determination
  Blending (e.g., concrete mixing, cattle feed, sausage blending)
  Assembly line scheduling
  Inventory control

Marketing
  Sales effort allocation
  Sales territory determination
  Advertising budget allocation
  Sales quota allocation

Finance
  Capital budgeting
  Working capital management
  Investment portfolio determination
  Cash flow analysis

Personnel
  Manpower allocation and assignment
  Wage and salary administration
  Personnel mix determination

Hospital Administration
   Budget allocation
   Personnel allocation
   Space allocation (e.g., work space determination)

University Administration
   Faculty and staff allocation
   Office space and classroom allocation
   Allocation and reallocation of the operating budget
   Admissions procedure

Pursuing objectives

Planning and Scheduling Problems Most decision problems involve some degree of planning and/or scheduling. In order to achieve certain objectives in the future, a decision must be made concerning present and future actions that would contribute to the objectives. Stated in a different way, to accomplish the desired results, the optimum combination of inputs in certain time periods must be determined. Linear programming is effective for analyzing such problems as production scheduling, financial planning, manpower planning, construction scheduling, traveling salesperson scheduling, course offering scheduling, and student flow scheduling.

Diet Problems The diet problem is so labeled because one of the earliest applications of linear programming was in determining the most economical diet for human beings. Various food-related problems are concerned with the determination of the most economical (least total cost) mix of ingredients while meeting the desired nutrient values. We are familiar with this type of problem from our experience in college dining halls, hospitals, military chow halls, and summer camps.

Planning diet

For example, let us consider a diet problem in a local hospital. In planning a menu for the maternity ward patients, the hospital dietitian is considering 30 different types of food. Because she is concerned about the minimum nutritional requirements for new mothers, she analyzes the amount of nutrient in a unit of each of the foods being considered. The dietitian may formulate a linear programming problem that will specify a menu that meets all the nutritional requirements while minimizing the total cost.

Transportation Problems In a typical transportation problem we attempt to determine the quantities of a particular good to be transported from a number of origins (e.g., plants) to a number of destinations (e.g., retail outlets) in such a way that we can minimize the total transportation cost. The solution to the problem must satisfy the supply capacity of each origin and the demand requirement of each destination.

Transportation logistics

For example, let us consider the transportation problem of a concrete mixing firm. The company has three plants where concrete is mixed and four construction sites where concrete must be supplied. The firm has determined the unit transportation cost (cost involved in transporting a truckload of concrete from each plant to each construction site). Also, the firm has a concrete mixing capacity at each plant and a contracted agreement for supply to each site. The decision problem is to determine how many truckloads of concrete should be transported from each plant to each construction site so that the total transportation cost is minimized.

*Making the best
assignment*

Assignment Problems In assignment problems, we attempt to identify the most efficient way to assign certain objects (e.g., people, machines, or tools) to various destinations to optimize the objective criterion. For example, in a machine loading problem, linear programming can be applied to determine the optimum assignment of jobs to various machines so that the total production cost can be minimized. Assignment of police patrol cars to various areas of a city to minimize the total time required to reach trouble spots, and assignment of snowplows to various spots in an area to minimize the total time required to clear all major roads are also good examples of assignment problems.

MODEL FORMULATION

We know that linear programming has been widely applied to many different decision problems. It has been extensively used in business and industry, agriculture, engineering, the sciences, and the military sector. In addition, many applications can be found in architecture, economics, political science, and forestry management. The list of applications of linear programming is expected to grow, especially in new areas of study such as urban planning and development, ecology management, pollution control, population planning, and energy management. Several examples of real-world applications of linear programming are presented in a later section of this chapter.

Computer-based solution

During the past 15 years linear programming has become more readily available for practical use, primarily because of the continuous development of computer technology. Most of the major computer manufacturers have developed large-scale "canned" linear programming packages for their clients. Even mini- or microcomputers can be easily used for linear programming applications. The solution process, therefore, is not the difficult part of linear programming application. The most difficult aspect of linear programming application is model formulation—formulating a linear programming model for a complex real-world problem.

*Model formulation
examples*

In order to gain some experience and insight in formulating linear programming models, we will examine a variety of examples in this section. One key to successful application of the technique is the ability to recognize when a problem can be solved by linear programming and to formulate the corresponding model.

CASETTE 3.1   *PRODUCT MIX PROBLEM OF GALAXY ELECTRONICS*

Galaxy Electronics, Inc. is a specialist in the emerging field of microcomputers. The firm currently produces two products: a personal computer with the label GE-1000 and a small business-oriented computer with the label GE-2000. The company has set up two modern production assembly lines. The assembly time requirements, the production capacities of assembly lines, and the unit profit for the two products are as follows:

	Production Process (Hours/Unit)		Production Capacity (Hours/Week)
	GE-1000	GE-2000	
Assembly Line 1	4	2	80
Assembly Line 2	1	3	60
Unit profit	$150	$250	

The management of Galaxy Electronics is attempting to determine the best possible weekly production schedule for GE-1000 and GE-2000 in order to maximize total profit. To formulate a linear programming model for Galaxy, we must first define the decision variables.

Decision Variables

The variables whose values we are trying to determine in the model are the quantities of the two computers Galaxy should produce on a weekly schedule. Thus, there are two decision variables.

Decision variables

x_1 = the number of GE-1000 computers to be produced per week

x_2 = the number of GE-2000 computers to be produced per week

Model Constraints

Model constraints represent limited resources that impose restrictions on the decision variables. In this problem, constraints are the limited production hours available in each of the two assembly lines. Since each product requires assembly time in each line, the total production time required in Assembly Line 1 will be the sum of the production time required to produce GE-1000 and the production time for GE-2000. A unit of GE-1000 requires 4 hours in Assembly Line 1. Thus, the total production time required in Assembly Line 1 to produce GE-1000 will be $4x_1$. Similarly, we can easily determine the production time required in Assembly Line 1 for GE-2000 as $2x_2$.

Constraints

Since the number of available production hours per week in Assembly Line 1 is 80, the amount of production time we utilize for producing both GE-1000 and GE-2000 units must be limited to 80 hours. In order to express the limited resources, we can use a mathematical symbol $\leq$, which simply means that the left-hand side must be *less than or equal to* the value on the right-hand side. Then we can express the production time constraint for Assembly Line 1 as

$$4x_1 + 2x_2 \leq 80 \qquad \qquad \textit{Assembly 1}$$

The constraint for Assembly Line 2 can be formulated in a similar manner. A GE-1000 unit requires 1 hour and a GE-2000 unit takes 3 hours in Assembly Line 2. The available production capacity for Assembly Line 2 is 60 hours of operation time on a weekly basis. Thus, the second constraint is

$$1x_1 + 3x_2 \leq 60 \qquad \qquad \textit{Assembly 2}$$

As discussed in the section on the requirements of linear programming, a linear programming model also needs nonnegativity constraints. In other words, the quantities of GE-1000 and GE-2000 computers cannot be negative. These nonnegative constraints can be expressed as

$$x_1 \geq 0, \qquad x_2 \geq 0 \qquad \textbf{\textit{Nonnegativity constraints}}$$

The Objective Function

The objective function

The objective of Galaxy is to maximize total profit. The total profit Galaxy can expect is simply the sum of the profits from GE-1000 and GE-2000. The profit that can be gained by GE-1000 is the unit profit, $150, times the quantity of GE-1000 units produced for sale, or $150x_1$. Similarly, profit from GE-2000 will be $250x_2$. If we express total profit by the symbol Z, the objective function of this problem becomes

$$\text{Maximize } Z = 150x_1 + 250x_2 \qquad \textbf{\textit{Objective function}}$$

Now we can formulate the complete linear programming model for the Galaxy Electronics product mix problem as follows:

$$\begin{aligned}
\text{Maximize } Z = {} & 150x_1 + 250x_2 \\
\text{subject to} \quad & 4x_1 + 2x_2 \leq 80 \\
& x_1 + 3x_2 \leq 60 \\
& x_1, x_2 \geq 0
\end{aligned}$$

The solution of this model will determine the optimum values for the decision variables x_1 and x_2. From the optimum solution we can easily calculate the maximum possible profit Z based on the production schedule determined by the model.

Satisfying linear programming requirements

Now we can examine the above linear programming model and ascertain whether or not it satisfies the requirements of linear programming.

1. *The Objective Criterion.*   The Galaxy Electronics model has a single objective for maximizing total profits. The objective function is expressed by: Maximize $Z = 150x_1 + 250x_2$.

2. *Limited Resources.*   In the Galaxy Electronics problem, the limited resources are expressed by the available production hours in Assembly Lines 1 and 2.

3. *Linear Relationships.*   The objective function and the two constraints are all expressed as linear functions.

4. *Divisibility.*   The number of GE-1000 and GE-2000 computers to be determined by the model can take fractional values.

5. *Deterministic.*   In the Galaxy Electronics problem, unit contribution rates of the two computers and the amount of resources required to produce each computer are known with certainty.

6. *Nonnegativity.*   The quantity of GE-1000 and GE-2000 computers to be produced must be nonnegative.

| CASETTE 3.2 | *DIET PROBLEM OF THE FRESHMEN ORIENTATION PROGRAM* |

CASETTE 3.2   **DIET PROBLEM OF THE FRESHMEN ORIENTATION PROGRAM**

The university is planning the annual freshmen orientation program during the first week of June. All prospective freshmen and their parents have been invited to the campus for a three-day period. Since the summer school will not start until the third week of June, the university will make the dormitories available for most participants in the program.

In order to provide an ample amount of free time for the participants to roam around the campus and downtown areas on their own, the dormitories will serve only breakfast. For lunch and dinner, participants will be encouraged to explore a number of interesting restaurants on and around the campus. The dietitians at the dining halls are planning breakfast for the first day of the orientation period. Once the first day's breakfast menu is determined, the second and third days' breakfasts will be decided upon. The dietitians are attempting to provide the participants with a menu that not only is appetizing but also satisfies the nutrient requirements at the lowest possible cost.

The dietitians easily come up with the beverages to serve: orange juice, tomato juice, coffee, tea, and milk. However, based on their experience in recent years, there has been some disagreement among the dietitians concerning the types of food to serve. After a lengthy discussion, they decide to provide a very simple breakfast: scrambled eggs and "smokies" sausage.

The dietitians' responsibility is to provide an adequate amount of the following nutrients in the breakfast: vitamin A, vitamin B, and iron. Another important consideration is that the menu must be provided at the lowest possible cost. The nutritional contents (milligrams per scoop of scrambled eggs and per smokie), the minimum nutrient requirements, and the unit cost of the foods being considered are as follows:

Nutrient	Food Nutrient Content (mg.)		Nutrient Requirement (mg.)
	Scrambled Egg	Smokie	
Vitamin A	3	3	30
Vitamin B	4	2	24
Iron	1	2	12
Unit Cost	8¢	10¢	

Decision Variables

The dietitians attempt to determine how much of each type of food to serve in order to meet the nutrient requirements and also minimize the total cost. Since there are only two types of food to be served (not including beverages), there are two decision variables in the problem:

$$x_1 = \text{number of scoops of scrambled eggs served}$$
$$x_2 = \text{number of smokies served}$$

Model Constraints

In this diet problem, the model constraints represent the nutrient requirements that need to be satisfied for vitamin A, vitamin B, and iron. The dietitians have already determined the nutritional content for each unit of food being considered for breakfast. For example, a scoop of scrambled eggs contains 3 mg. of vitamin A, and one smokie sausage also contains 3 mg. of vitamin A. Since the minimum requirement for vitamin A is 30 mg., the total amount of vitamin A provided by the scrambled eggs and smokies must be *equal to or greater* than 30 mg. Thus, we can formulate the constraint for vitamin A as:

$$3x_1 + 3x_2 \geq 30 \qquad \textit{Vitamin A}$$

The constraint for vitamin B can be formulated in a similar manner. A scoop of scrambled eggs contains 4 mg. and a smokie 2 mg. of vitamin B. The minimum requirement for vitamin B is 24 mg. The constraint for vitamin B is:

$$4x_1 + 2x_2 \geq 24 \qquad \textit{Vitamin B}$$

The constraint for iron can be easily constructed in a similar way:

$$x_1 + 2x_2 \geq 12 \qquad \textit{Iron}$$

The Objective Function

The objective of the breakfast menu problem for the freshmen orientation program is to minimize the total cost of breakfast. The total cost of breakfast is simply the sum of the costs of the eggs and smokies to be served. Since we already know that a scoop of scrambled eggs costs 8 cents, we can determine the total cost of serving scrambled eggs by multiplying 8 cents by the number of scoops of scrambled eggs, or $8x_1$. Similarly, the total cost of serving smokies will be $10x_2$. If we express the total cost by the symbol Z, the objective function of this diet problem becomes

$$\text{Minimize } Z = 8x_1 + 10x_2 \qquad \textit{Objective function}$$

Now we can formulate the complete linear programming model for the breakfast menu problem of the freshmen orientation program as follows:

$$
\begin{aligned}
\text{Minimize } Z = {}& 8x_1 + 10x_2 \\
\text{subject to} \quad & 3x_1 + 3x_2 \geq 30 \\
& 4x_1 + 2x_2 \geq 24 \\
& x_1 + 2x_2 \geq 12 \\
& x_1, x_2 \geq 0
\end{aligned}
$$

The solution of this linear programming model will enable the dietitians to determine the optimum values for the decision variables x_1 and x_2. From the optimum solution determined by the model, they can easily calculate the minimum total cost possible based on the menu of scrambled eggs and smokie sausages.

CASETTE 3.3   **VEHICLE PURCHASING PROBLEM OF UR#1 LIMOUSINE SERVICE COMPANY**

UR#1 is a newly chartered transportation corporation in town. UR, as the company is known in financial circles, will be the primary limousine service between the municipal airport and the hotels in the downtown area. The company has done extensive research on the air traffic, passenger flows, hotel occupancy rates, vehicle costs, operation costs, vehicle maintenance costs, facility requirements, and personnel requirements. However, one aspect of the problem that needs an immediate decision is the exact number of different types of vehicles that should be placed on order.

Terry Anderson, the company treasurer and a CPA, has been charged with the decision problem. After examining the company's research material several times, he was able to come up with the following basic data:

1. There are three types of vehicles under consideration by UR: station wagons, vans, and buses. Each vehicle will serve a different purpose. A station wagon will be dispatched to the airport when small airplanes of regional airlines need transportation service or when individual requests are received. Vans will be used as regularly scheduled limousines at 45-minute intervals between the airport and the hotels. Buses will be used at specific times of the day when national airline flights are scheduled and a large number of passengers need the service.

2. If an order is placed immediately, the purchase price for each type of vehicle will be:

Station wagon	$9,500
Van	$12,500
Bus	$45,000

3. The Board of Directors has authorized $1 million for the purchase of vehicles.

4. The company has already hired 40 new drivers who will complete their 8-week training program before the new vehicles arrive from the manufacturer. The drivers will be fully qualified to operate all three types of vehicles. The company is planning a 16-hour-a-day operation schedule (6 AM–10 PM). It is expected that the maximum number of drivers on duty at any given time will be 30. Thus, the company does not wish to purchase more than 30 vehicles.

5. The maintenance shop will be fully functional when the company begins its limousine service. The department will have the capacity for performing maintenance service for 80 station wagons. In terms of using the maintenance resources, a van is estimated to be equivalent to 1.5 station wagons and a bus is equivalent to 3 station wagons.

6. The Cost Accounting Department has estimates of the expected net annual profit of the vehicles as follows:

Station wagon	$2,500 per vehicle
Van	$3,500 per vehicle
Bus	$10,000 per vehicle

7. Based on the experience of other airport transportation companies in other cities, the Board of Directors has adopted the following policies:
    a. In view of rising energy costs, the number of station wagons should be at least 30 percent of all the vehicles.

b. Since buses are often required to handle large tourist groups, the company should purchase at least 2 buses.

c. The regularly scheduled limousine service will be provided by vans. Thus, the company should have at least 10 vans in its fleet of vehicles.

The vehicle purchasing problem of UR is to determine the number of station wagons, vans, and buses to purchase, while meeting various constraints, in order to maximize the total profit. Since Terry Anderson could not solve the problem, he consulted with the systems specialist, Susan Kraft, who has just completed her master's degree in management science. After a lengthy discussion with Terry, Susan studied her old class notes and came up with a linear programming model.

Decision Variables

In this problem, the model should determine the number of each type of vehicle to be purchased. Thus, the decision variables are:

$$x_1 = \text{number of station wagons to be purchased}$$
$$x_2 = \text{number of vans to be purchased}$$
$$x_3 = \text{number of buses to be purchased}$$

Model Constraints

There are a number of constraints in this problem. Susan Kraft decided to formulate the constraints as follows:

1. *Budget for the Vehicles to Be Purchased.*   The Board of Directors allocated $1 million for the purchase of the vehicles. Since station wagons cost $9,500, vans $12,500, and buses $45,000, the budget constraint becomes

$$9,500x_1 + 12,500x_2 + 45,000x_3 \leq 1,000,000$$

2. *The Number of Drivers.*   Although the company will have a total of 40 drivers, the maximum number of drivers on duty at any given time will be 30. Thus, there is no reason to purchase more than 30 vehicles. The constraint is

$$x_1 + x_2 + x_3 \leq 30$$

3. *The Maintenance Department Capacity.*   One of the important considerations that requires attention is the maintenance capacity. Since the vehicles must be used virtually constantly to secure the expected return on investment, maintenance is a very important aspect of the total operation at UR. The capacity of the maintenance shop is equivalent to 80 station wagons. In terms of using the maintenance resource, a van accounts for 1.5 station wagons, and a bus is equivalent to 3 station wagons. Thus, Susan formulates the constraint as

$$x_1 + 1.5x_2 + 3x_3 \leq 80$$

4. *The Board of Directors' Policy Constraints.* Based on other firms' experience and its judgment about the composition of the vehicle fleet, the Board has further imposed these additional constraints:

a. *The number of station wagons.* The Board decided that the number of station wagons should be at least 30 percent of all the vehicles. Thus, Susan initially formulated this constraint as

$$x_1 \geq .30 \, (x_1 + x_2 + x_3)$$

Susan decided to further simplify the constraint as follows:

$$x_1 \geq .30x_1 + .30x_2 + .30x_3$$
$$x_1 - .30x_1 - .30x_2 - .30x_3 \geq 0$$
$$.70x_1 - .30x_2 - .30x_3 \geq 0$$

b. *The minimum number of buses.* The Board also decided to purchase at least 2 buses. This simple constraint is

$$x_3 \geq 2$$

c. *The minimum number of vans.* The Board would like to purchase at least 10 vans as the regularly scheduled limousines. This constraint is

$$x_2 \geq 10$$

The Objective Function

The objective of UR in this problem is to maximize the total annual profit from the limousine service operation. The Cost Accounting Department estimates the net annual profit per vehicle as follows:

Station wagon	$2,500
Van	$3,500
Bus	$10,000

Thus, the objective function can be formulated as

$$\text{Maximize } Z = 2,500x_1 + 3,500x_2 + 10,000x_3$$

Now the complete model can be presented:

$$\text{Maximize } Z = 2,500x_1 + 3,500x_2 + 10,000x_3$$
$$\text{subject to} \quad 9,500x_1 + 12,500x_2 + 45,000x_3 \leq 1,000,000$$
$$x_1 + x_2 + x_3 \leq 30$$
$$x_1 + 1.5x_2 + 3x_3 \leq 80$$
$$.70x_1 - .30x_2 - .30x_3 \geq 0$$
$$x_3 \geq 2$$
$$x_2 \geq 10$$
$$x_1, x_2, x_3 \geq 0$$

CASETTE 3.4   MANPOWER SCHEDULING PROBLEM OF LEON'S GROCERIES

Leon's Groceries is a well-known, privately owned food store. Since it was first opened in 1935 by the late Herschel Leon, Leon's has been best known for its fine meat department. Leon's store hours have increased steadily over the years. Rufus Leon, the new president fresh out of the university with an MBA degree, has decided to keep the store open 24 hours a day. He has been able to make the necessary arrangements with vendors, the trucking company, and the local banks for the expanded store operation.

One of the nagging problems of Rufus Leon has been the manpower planning for the workers. Rufus has tentatively set up the management teams and workers for 3 daily shifts as shown in Figure 3.1. Since 5 meat cutters need to work for the 8 AM–4 PM daily schedule, the most critical problem is scheduling cashiers and baggers/stockers on a daily basis. Based on the experience of Leon's and that of other stores operating on a 24-hour basis, Rufus has been able to determine the minimum necessary manpower for each 4-hour period as follows:

Time Period	Cashiers	Baggers/Stockers
8 AM–12 Noon	3	5
12 Noon–4 PM	4	4
4 PM–8 PM	6	6
8 PM–12 Midnight	3	3
12 Midnight–4 AM	1	2
4 AM–8 AM	2	7

One of the factors complicating the problem is that cashiers and baggers/stockers are not interchangeable. Cashiers need special training for dealing with money and operating the cash register. On the other hand, baggers/stockers need physical strength to handle the stocking carts and the weight of goods. Leon's has only full-time employees who report to work for a 8-hour shift. Overtime work and part-time work are available only in emergencies or during holiday seasons.

The employees usually report for work at 8 AM, 12 Noon, 4 PM, 8 PM, 12 Midnight, and 4 AM and work for an 8-hour shift. The wages for employees working at different time periods are as follows:

Time Period	Wage	
	Cashiers	Baggers/Stockers
8 AM–12 Noon	$4.00	$3.60
12 Noon–4 PM	4.00	3.60
4 PM–8 PM	4.20	4.00
8 PM–12 Midnight	4.60	4.40
12 Midnight–4 AM	5.00	4.80
4 AM–8 AM	4.80	4.60

Rufus believes that the total number of cashiers and baggers/stockers should not be more than 60 since the current manpower level for the 16-hour-a-day operation is 45.

The decision problem is to determine how many cashiers and baggers/stockers should be scheduled to work in order to meet the minimum manpower requirement of the store and also to minimize the total daily wages.

Decision Variables

In this problem, Rufus attempts to determine the number of cashiers and baggers/stockers who will report at the beginning of each of the 4-hour segments during the

Figure 3.1   Daily Operation System for Leon's Groceries

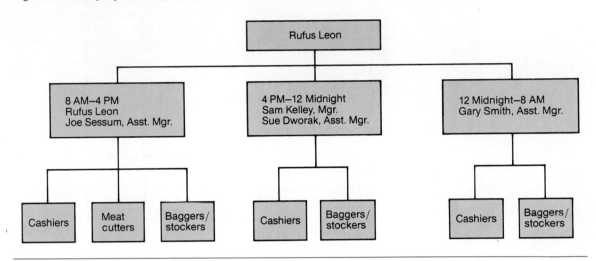

24-hour period. We can describe the decision variables schematically as shown in Figure 3.2. The variables can be defined as follows:

x_i = number of cashiers reporting to work during the day at the ith 4-hour intervals starting at 8 AM ($i = 1,2,\cdots,6$)

y_i = number of baggers/stockers reporting to work during the day at the ith 4-hour intervals starting at 8 AM ($i = 1,2,\cdots,6$)

Model Constraints

In this problem, there are basically two types of constraints: the required minimum number of employees during certain time periods of the day, and the total manpower limit of 60 per day. For the first type of constraint, let us consider the number of cashiers needed during the 8 AM–12 Noon period. The number of cashiers working during that period (see Figure 3.2) is the total number of cashiers who reported at 4 AM and those who reported at 8 AM. For example, we can easily show the cashiers working from 8 AM to 12 Noon and the minimum number of cashiers required as follows:

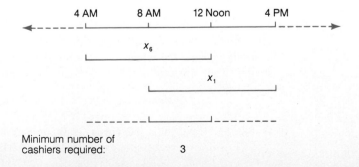

Figure 3.2   *Decision Variables of the Leon's Groceries Manpower Scheduling Problem*

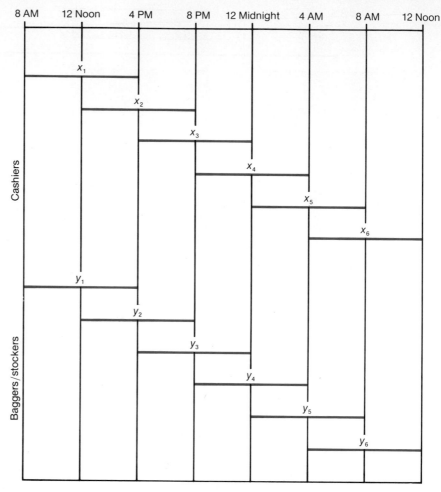

Since the minimum number of cashiers required for the 8 AM–12 noon period is 3, the constraint can be expressed as

$$x_1 + x_6 \geq 3$$

The same reasoning can be applied to all of the other constraints for the cashiers. In a similar manner, the required numbers of baggers/stockers can be expressed as constraints. Thus, we can formulate the following constraints:

$$
\begin{array}{lll}
\textit{Cashiers} & x_1 + x_2 \geq 4 & \text{12 Noon–4 PM} \\
& x_2 + x_3 \geq 6 & \text{4 PM–8 PM} \\
& x_3 + x_4 \geq 3 & \text{8 PM–12 Midnight} \\
& x_4 + x_5 \geq 1 & \text{12 Midnight–4 AM} \\
& x_5 + x_6 \geq 2 & \text{4 AM–8 AM}
\end{array}
$$

Figure 3.3 Average Wage Rate for the Cashiers at Leon's Groceries

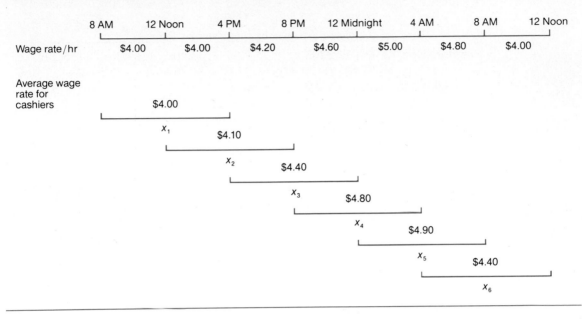

$$Baggers/ \quad y_1 + y_6 \geq 5 \qquad \text{8 AM–12 Noon}$$
$$Stockers \quad y_1 + y_2 \geq 4 \qquad \text{12 Noon–4 PM}$$
$$y_2 + y_3 \geq 6 \qquad \text{4 PM–8 PM}$$
$$y_3 + y_4 \geq 3 \qquad \text{8 PM–12 Midnight}$$
$$y_4 + y_5 \geq 2 \qquad \text{12 Midnight–4 AM}$$
$$y_5 + y_6 \geq 7 \qquad \text{4 AM–8 AM}$$

Another constraint we need to develop is the maximum number of 60 cashiers and baggers/stockers Rufus set as the ceiling for the manpower. This constraint can be formulated as

$$x_1 + x_2 + x_3 + x_4 + x_5 + x_6 + y_1 + y_2 + y_3 + y_4 + y_5 + y_6 \leq 60$$

The Objective Function

The objective of the Leon's Groceries manpower scheduling problem is to minimize the total daily payroll cost. Since the total daily payroll is the sum of hours worked times the wage rate for the employees, we must first analyze the wage rates for the employees during the different time periods. For example, Figure 3.3 indicates the hourly rates during the different 4-hour periods and the average wage rate for the cashiers during their respective 8-hour shifts. Thus, the total payroll Z will be:

$$Z = 32.00x_1 + 32.80x_2 + 35.20x_3 + 38.40x_4 + 39.20x_5 + 35.20x_6$$
$$+ 28.80y_1 + 30.40y_2 + 33.60y_3 + 36.80y_4 + 37.60y_5 + 32.80y_6$$

In the above expression, the first parameter, $32.00 for variable x_1, is simply the average hourly wage rate of $4.00 for cashiers working the 8 AM–4 PM shift multiplied by 8 hours for the shift. For example, if 3 cashiers work during the 8 AM–4 PM shift ($x_1 = 3$), the total wage for the 3 cashiers would be $32.00 × 3, or $96.00.

We can write the objective function as follows:

$$\text{Minimize } Z = 32.00x_1 + 32.80x_2 + 35.20x_3 + 38.40x_4 + 39.20x_5 + 35.20x_6$$
$$+ 28.80y_1 + 30.40y_2 + 33.60y_3 + 36.80y_4 + 37.60y_5 + 32.80y_6$$

Now the complete model can be formulated as follows:

$$\text{Minimize } Z = 32.00x_1 + 32.80x_2 + 35.20x_3 + 38.40x_4 + 39.20x_5 + 35.20x_6$$
$$+ 28.80y_1 + 30.40y_2 + 33.60y_3 + 36.80y_4 + 37.60y_5 + 32.80y_6$$

$$\begin{array}{ll}
\text{subject to} & x_1 + x_6 \geq 3 \qquad y_1 + y_6 \geq 5 \\
& x_1 + x_2 \geq 4 \qquad y_1 + y_2 \geq 4 \\
& x_2 + x_3 \geq 6 \qquad y_2 + y_3 \geq 6 \\
& x_3 + x_4 \geq 3 \qquad y_3 + y_4 \geq 3 \\
& x_4 + x_5 \geq 1 \qquad y_4 + y_5 \geq 2 \\
& x_5 + x_6 \geq 2 \qquad y_5 + y_6 \geq 7
\end{array}$$

$$x_1 + x_2 + x_3 + x_4 + x_5 + x_6 + y_1 + y_2 + y_3 + y_4 + y_5 + y_6 \leq 60$$

$$x_1, x_2, x_3, x_4, x_5, x_6, y_1, y_2, y_3, y_4, y_5, y_6 \geq 0$$

GRAPHICAL SOLUTION METHOD

The graphical method for simple problems

Two basic solution methods of linear programming will be presented in this text: the graphical method and the simplex method. The main purpose of presenting the graphical method is to provide you with a basic knowledge of the linear programming approach. The graphical method is never used in real-world applications of linear programming. It is a solution method used only for toy problems. The simplex method will be presented in Chapter 4 as the solution method of linear programming.

We can effectively depict on a graph those linear programming problems that involve only two dimensions (decision variables). We will therefore study the graphical method through simple problems that have only two decision variables. We can depict three-variable problems graphically, but the procedure becomes quite tedious when they have many constraints. Consequently, for complex real-world problems, we apply computer-based simplex programs. The graphical solution method, however, provides us with a conceptual framework for understanding the solution process of linear programming. Thus, we gain much insight into the linear programming approach and the type of information we can generate from the model.

Some Basics

Basics of linear algebra

Before we jump into the graphical method of linear programming, it is useful to review some of the properties of linear equalities and inequalities. The linear equality is simply a mathematical expression where two sides of the expression must be equal and all variables in the relationship must be of the first degree. For example, recall the wage earnings model we discussed in Chapter 2:

$$W = 3.50H$$

$$\begin{array}{ll}
\text{where} & W = \text{total wage income} \\
& 3.50 = \text{wage rate per hour} \\
& H = \text{number of hours worked}
\end{array}$$

This model is a linear equality. All linear equalities involving only one or two variables appear geometrically as straight lines in two-dimensional space. Linear equalities involving more than two variables will be represented by hyperplanes in multi-dimensional space.

The general form of a linear equality is $y = a + bx$, where a is the y intercept and b is the slope of the function. Now let us examine two simple linear equalities:

$$y = 40 - 2x$$
$$y = 20 - \frac{2}{3}x$$

In the first equality, we can easily identify the following: y intercept $= 40$, slope $= -2$. Similarly, in the second equality we can identify the y intercept as 20 and the slope as $-2/3$.

The y intercept

The slope

The y intercept indicates the point on the y axis that the straight line passes through when the value of x is zero. The slope of the linear function is simply the change in y associated with one unit change in x. Thus, we can define the slope as:

$$\text{Slope, } b = \frac{\text{change in } y}{\text{change in } x}$$

Graphical illustration

Now, let us plot the first equality on a graph. The usual placement of variables is y as the vertical axis and x as the horizontal axis. Since the linear equality is a straight line, if we can identify two points on the graph we can simply extend the line that goes through these points and plot the function on the graph. We already know one point that the function will go through: the y intercept is 40 when $x = 0$. We can find the x intercept as the second point. The x intercept is the point on the x axis that the line passes through when the value of y is zero. Thus, we can determine the x intercept as

$$y = 40 - 2x$$
$$0 = 40 - 2x$$
$$2x = 40$$
$$x = 20$$

Now, we can graph the first linear equality as a straight line by first plotting the two intercept points ($x = 0$, $y = 40$; $x = 20$, $y = 0$) as shown in Figure 3.4. Then we can connect the two points and extend the straight line as shown in Figure 3.5.

Similarly, we can determine the two intercept points for the second linear equality as follows:

Intercept points

y intercept point: ($x = 0$, $y = 20$)
x intercept point: ($x = 30$, $y = 0$)

The second equality function can be graphed as shown in Figure 3.6.

The intersecting point

The two equality lines plotted on the graph in Figure 3.6 intersect at point $x = 1$ and $y = 0$. When two linear functions intersect, we can easily find the intersecting point by solving the two equalities simultaneously. For example, since the values of x and y must be identical at the intersecting point for the two equalities, we can write

$$y = 40 - 2x \qquad\qquad \textit{Equality 1}$$
$$y = 20 - \frac{2}{3}x \qquad\qquad \textit{Equality 2}$$

Figure 3.4   Two Intercept Points of y = 40 − 2x

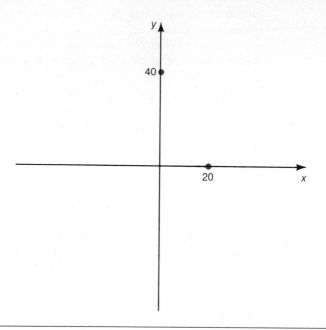

Figure 3.5   Plotting the Straight Line for y = 40 − 2x

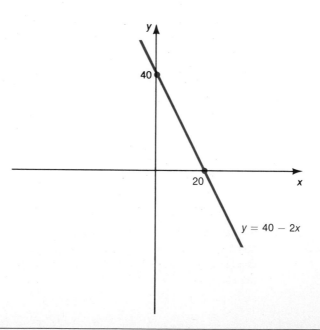

Figure 3.6   Graphical Presentation of the Two Equalities

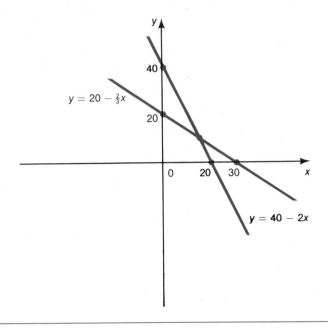

Therefore,

$$40 - 2x = 20 - \frac{2}{3}x$$

$$-2x + \frac{2}{3}x = 20 - 40$$

$$-\frac{4}{3}x = -20$$

$$x = 20 \times \frac{3}{4}$$

$$x = 15$$

By substituting $x = 15$ in Equality 1, we can find the value of y as

$$y = 40 - 2x$$
$$y = 40 - 2(15)$$
$$y = 10$$

Linear inequalities

Many real-world decision problems cannot be expressed by exact equalities. As we have seen in our casette problems, most linear programming problems have their constraints expressed by inequalities. Inequalities are also mathematical expressions that specify certain relationships and conditions. For example, let us make the following slight modifications in the two equalities we discussed:

$$x_2 \leq 40 - 2x_1 \qquad \qquad \textit{Inequality 1}$$

$$x_2 \leq 20 - \frac{2}{3}x_1 \qquad \qquad \textit{Inequality 2}$$

Figure 3.7   Graphical Presentation of Two Inequalities

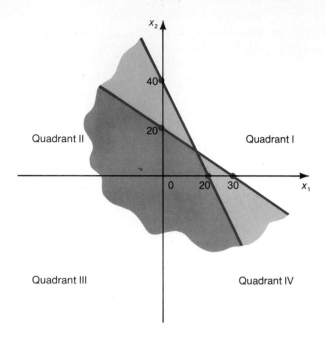

Figure 3.8   Two Inequality Constraints in Quadrant I

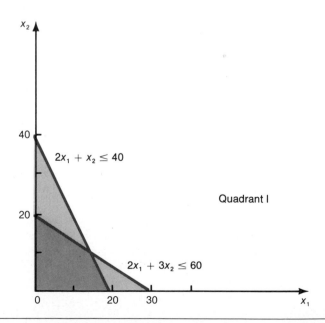

The two inequalities presented above are depicted in Figure 3.7. For the first inequality any point on the straight line $x_2 = 40 - 2x_1$ and below (to the left of the line) will satisfy the inequality condition. Similarly, for the second inequality any point on the straight line $x_2 = 20 - 2/3\ x_1$ and below (to the left of the line) will satisfy the inequality condition.

The inequality condition

There is another important aspect of linear inequalities that deserves our attention. As we recall from the linear programming models we formulated for various casettes, the nonnegativity constraint requires that all decision variables in the model be nonnegative. In other words, variables can take on only positive or zero values. This requirement makes good sense, as we cannot conceive of producing -200 units of record players, hiring -5 cashiers, or providing -2 scrambled eggs for breakfast. Because of the nonnegativity constraint for the decision variables, the graphical solution requires only the first quadrant of a rectangular coordinate system. For example, if we had the same two constraints $2x_1 + x_2 \leq 40$ and $2x_1 + 3x_2 \leq 60$, we can plot the two inequalities as shown in Figure 3.7. The graphical presentation of the same two inequalities with the nonnegativity constraint is shown in Figure 3.8.

Only the first quadrant needed

A Simple Maximization Problem

A maximization problem

To demonstrate the graphical solution method, we will use a simple maximization problem which we formulated in Casette 3.1. The management of Galaxy Electronics attempts to determine the number of GE-1000 (personal microcomputers) and GE-2000 (business-oriented microcomputers) to be produced in order to maximize total profit. In this problem, there are two constraints representing limited production hours available in Assembly Line 1 and Assembly Line 2. The linear programming model we developed for Galaxy was:

$$\text{Maximize } Z = 150x_1 + 250x_2$$
$$\text{subject to} \quad 4x_1 + 2x_2 \leq 80$$
$$x_1 + 3x_2 \leq 60$$
$$x_1, x_2 \geq 0$$

where
x_1 = number of GE-1000s to be produced
x_2 = number of GE-2000s to be produced

The process of the graphical method, regardless of whether it is used for a maximization or a minimization problem, consists of the following steps:

Step 1 Graphical representation of constraints

Step 2 Identification of the area of feasible solutions

Step 3 Identification of the optimum solution

We will follow these steps in solving the Galaxy Electronics problem by the graphical method.

Step 1: Graphical Representation of Constraints The problem has two linear inequalities as constraints. They are:

$$4x_1 + 2x_2 \leq 80 \qquad \textit{Constraint 1 (Assembly Line 1)}$$
$$x_1 + 3x_2 \leq 60 \qquad \textit{Constraint 2 (Assembly Line 2)}$$

Figure 3.9   Graphing of $4x_1 + 2x_2 = 80$

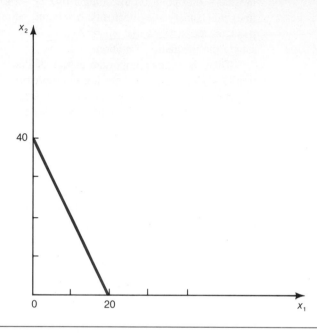

Plotting constraints

Let us analyze these constraints one at a time. For plotting constraints on the graph, we will treat variable x_1 as the horizontal axis and x_2 as the vertical axis.

Initially, the constraints will be plotted on the graph by treating them as linear equalities; then the appropriate inequality conditions will be indicated by the shaded areas. For example, let us consider the first constraint as an equality $4x_1 + 2x_2 = 80$. We can arrange the equality in the customary way, solving for the vertical axis x_2 as

$$4x_1 + 2x_2 = 80$$
$$2x_2 = 80 - 4x_1 \text{ (transposing } 4x_1)$$
$$x_2 = 40 - 2x_1 \text{ (dividing both sides by 2)}$$

The above equality indicates an x_2 intercept of 40 and a slope of -2. We can easily determine the x_1 intercept as 20 by assuming $x_2 = 0$ in the equality: $0 = 40 - 2x_1$; $2x_1 = 40$; $x_1 = 20$. Now the equality can be plotted on the graph as shown in Figure 3.9. Next, the inequality condition of the constraint must be satisfied. If we solve for x_2, as we did above, while maintaining the inequality sign, it becomes

$$4x_1 + 2x_2 \leq 80$$
$$2x_2 \leq 80 - 4x_1$$
$$x_2 \leq 40 - 2x_1$$

In the above inequality function, x_2 must be equal to or less than the straight line $x_2 = 40 - 2x_1$. Thus, the inequality condition can be satisfied by the shaded area

The inequality condition

Figure 3.10   Graphing of $4x_1 + 2x_2 \leq 80$ and Test Points

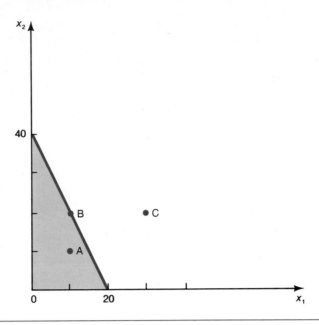

shown in Figure 3.10. Any point within the shaded area satisfies the constraint and any point outside of it does not meet the requirement. For example, let us examine the following three points, also shown in Figure 3.10:

Point A: $(x_1 = 10, x_2 = 10)$
$$4 \times 10 + 2 \times 10 \leq 80$$
$$60 < 80 \qquad \textit{Satisfies the constraint}$$

Point B: $(x_1 = 10, x_2 = 20)$
$$4 \times 10 + 2 \times 20 \leq 80$$
$$80 = 80 \qquad \textit{Satisfies the constraint}$$

Point C: $(x_1 = 30, x_2 = 20)$
$$4 \times 30 + 2 \times 20 \leq 80$$
$$160 > 80 \qquad \textit{Does not satisfy the constraint}$$

It should be apparent that any production combination of GE-1000 and GE-2000 computers within the shaded area can be processed in Assembly Line 1 with the available production time. Any production combination outside the shaded area cannot be handled with the given production capacity.

In a similar manner, we can plot the second constraint as follows:

$$x_1 + 3x_2 \leq 60$$
$$3x_2 \leq 60 - x_1 \qquad \text{(transposing } x_1\text{)}$$
$$x_2 \leq 20 - \frac{1}{3}x_1 \qquad \text{(dividing both sides by 3)}$$

Figure 3.11   *Graphing of* $x_1 + 3x_2 \leq 60$

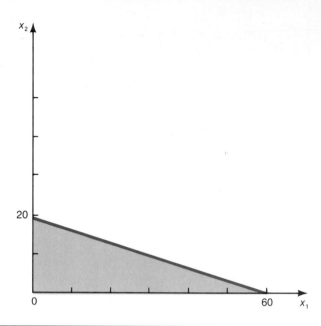

The second equality is plotted on the graph and the inequality condition of $x_2 \leq 20 - 1/3x_1$ is satisfied by the shaded area, as shown in Figure 3.11.

Step 2: Identification of the Area of Feasible Solutions Production of either type of microcomputer requires processing time in both assembly lines. Thus, the only feasible production area will be one in which both constraints are satisfied simultaneously. Such an area can be easily identified graphically as the crosshatched region where the two shaded areas of constraints overlap, as shown in Figure 3.12. This area is referred to as the *area of feasible solutions* or a *feasible region*.

The feasible region

The area of feasible solutions represents a region that satisfies conditions specified by all of the model constraints. Any point within the area is a feasible solution and any point external to it is an infeasible solution. For example, in Figure 3.12 the area of feasible solutions is 0ABC. The area ABD (but not on the line segment AB) satisfies the first constraint $4x_1 + 2x_2 \leq 60$. In other words, Assembly Line 1 has enough production capacity to handle the production combination in this area, but Assembly Line 2 does not have enough production capacity to accommodate such a production schedule.

In area BCE (but not on line segment BC) Galaxy Electronics has enough production capacity in Assembly Line 2 but not in Assembly Line 1. In the area above DBE (but not including point B), neither assembly line has enough production capacity to handle the production combinations. Thus, it is clear that area 0ABC is the feasibility area.

Figure 3.12   Graphing of the Two Constraints, $4x_1 + 2x_2 \leq 80$ and $x_1 + 3x_2 \leq 60$

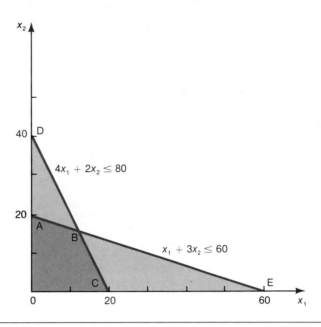

Step 3: Identification of the Optimum Solution

The Search Approach The simplest way to identify the optimum solution is to examine all the possible candidate solutions in the feasible region. For example, in the Galaxy Electronics problem the area of feasible solutions is formed by four corner points, 0, A, B, and C, as shown in Figure 3.13. Corner point 0, the origin, cannot be the optimum solution in a maximization problem because the total profit will be zero when $x_1 = 0$ and $x_2 = 0$.

Searching the optimal solution

Let us now examine a feasible solution, point D ($x_1 = 10$, $x_2 = 10$), inside the area of feasible solutions as shown in Figure 3.14. This solution yields 10 GE-1000 computers and 10 GE-2000 computers. Thus, the total profit at point D will be $Z = \$150(10) + \$250(10) = \$4,000$. However, point D is not optimum. We can increase production of x_2 to 16 2/3 units by moving up to point E. We can also increase production of x_1 to 15 units if we move over to point F. Or, we can increase production of both x_1 and x_2 by moving up diagonally toward point B.

The total profits at points D, E, and F are computed as follows:

Point D: $Z = \$150(10) + \$250(10) = \$4,000.00$
Point E: $Z = \$150(10) + \$250(16\ 2/3) = \$5,666.67$
Point F: $Z = \$150(15) + \$250(10) = \$4,750.00$

From this computation, it should be apparent that points E and F are superior to point D. In other words, solution points on the boundary of the feasible region are always superior to solution points inside the feasible region. Consequently, *the optimum point*

Figure 3.13   Examining the Corner Points of the Feasibility Area

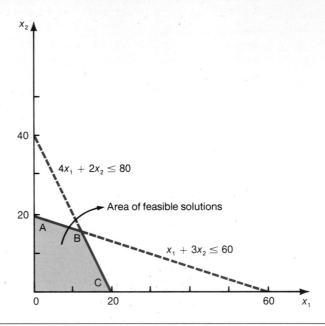

Figure 3.14   The Area of Feasible Solutions

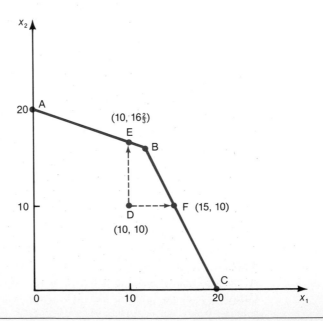

must be on the boundary, and it must also be at a *corner point* (also referred to as an *extreme point*) formed by the intersection of two constraints.

The concept of corner points (extreme points) is a very important property of linear programming. The boundary of the area of feasible solutions is made up of straight lines (or planes) that converge at intersecting corner points. Thus, the boundary has no indentions. This is why the feasible region is sometimes referred to as a

convex set. Because of this property (i.e., convexity) of the feasible region, the optimum solution must be at a corner point. Owing to this property, linear programming is sometimes referred to as an *extremal optimization method*.

Now we are ready to examine the remaining (excluding the origin) three corner points A, B, and C.

Total profits at points A and C can be easily calculated since the exact values of x_1 and x_2 are already known. We can calculate total profits at these points as follows:

$$\text{Point A:} \quad x_1 = 0, x_2 = 20$$
$$Z = 150 \times 0 + 250 \times 20$$
$$Z = 5,000$$
$$\text{Point C:} \quad x_1 = 20, x_2 = 0$$
$$Z = 150 \times 20 + 250 \times 0$$
$$Z = 3,000$$

At point A, Galaxy specializes in producing GE-2000 computers. On the other hand, at point B only GE-1000 computers are being produced. Since $2,000 more profit is

made at point A, if Galaxy desires to specialize in producing only one computer, it should be GE-2000.

Now we can proceed to calculate the total profit at point B. Before we can do this, we must first calculate the exact values of x_1 and x_2 at this point. Point B is the intersecting point of the two straight lines. Thus, we can solve the two equalities simultaneously as follows:

$$x_2 = 40 - 2x_1 \tag{1}$$

$$x_2 = 20 - \frac{1}{3}x_1 \tag{2}$$

Then,

$$40 - 2x_1 = 20 - \frac{1}{3}x_1$$

$$-\frac{5}{3}x_1 = -20$$

$$x_1 = 12$$

Substituting this value of x_1 into (1), we have

$$x_2 = 40 - 2 \times 12$$
$$x_2 = 16$$

Now, the total profit at point B can be derived as $Z = 150 \times 12 + 250 \times 16 = 5,800$. Since this total profit is $800 more than the $5,000 figure we found at point A, the optimum solution to the Galaxy Electronics problem is point B. At point B, Galaxy would produce 12 GE-1000 computers and 16 GE-2000 computers. This solution yields the maximum profit of $5,800.

The search approach we have discussed is obviously a very simple method for determining the optimum solution when the problem under study has a small number of constraints and thus very few corner points of the feasibility area. However, if a problem has a large number of constraints that form the area of feasible solutions, there would be a large number of corner points to search. Hence, the graphical search procedure is not a practical approach to identifying the optimum solution.

The iso-profit function

The Iso-profit Function Approach Perhaps the most practical approach to identifying the optimum solution through the graphical method is concerned with an analysis of the iso-profit function. As the prefix *iso-* implies, the *iso-profit function* is a straight line on which every point has the same total profit. We can derive the iso-profit function (or iso-cost function in a minimization problem) when the objective function is solved for the vertical axis variable (x_2 in our Galaxy Electronics problem). The objective function can be solved for x_2 as follows:

$$Z = 150x_1 + 250x_2 \qquad \textit{Objective function}$$
$$250x_2 = Z - 150x_1$$
$$x_2 = \frac{Z}{250} - \frac{150}{250}x_1$$
$$x_2 = \frac{Z}{250} - \frac{3}{5}x_1 \qquad \textit{Iso-profit function}$$

The iso-profit function derived above has an x_2 intercept of $Z/250$ and a slope of $-3/5$. The x_2 intercept $Z/250$ can be determined only when a total profit value Z is known. For example, if $Z = 1,500$, we can easily determine the x_2 intercept as $Z/250 = 1500/250 = 6$. Thus, the iso-profit function will be $x_2 = 6 - 3/5\ x_1$. If the total profit is doubled, then $Z = 3,000$, and the iso-profit function becomes $x_2 = 12 - 3/5x_1$. Although the x_2 intercept changes as the total profit Z is changed, the slope of the iso-profit function remains constant.

Moving upward from the origin

We can plot an infinite number of total profit lines on the graph. As we increase the total-profit value Z, the total-profit function moves gradually upward from the origin. In this maximization problem, then, we should attempt to move upward from the origin with the slope of the iso-profit function as far as we can within the feasibility area. Then, the optimum point is the last point we go through in the feasibility area. For example, let us plot a series of total-profit lines as shown in Figure 3.15. As we move upward from the origin the total profit increases; thus, $Z_1 < Z_2 < Z_3 < Z_4$. The maximum feasible profit is found to be $Z_3 = \$5,800$ at point B. The total profit $Z_4 = \$7,500$ is much greater than the $\$5,800$ we found at point B. However, this profit is infeasible because the profit line is outside of the feasibility area. The iso-profit function approach further reinforces the property of corner points we discussed earlier in the search method section.

The slope comparison approach

The Slope Comparison Approach Another approach that can be effective in solving simple linear programming problems is the slope comparison approach. In this approach, we compare the slope of the iso-profit function with the slopes of the constraints that form the area of feasible solutions. In the Galaxy Electronics problem, the slopes of two constraints are -2 and $-1/3$. As long as the slope of the iso-profit function ($-3/5$) falls between these two slopes, the optimum point is the intersecting

Figure 3.15 Total Profit Functions with Various Intercepts

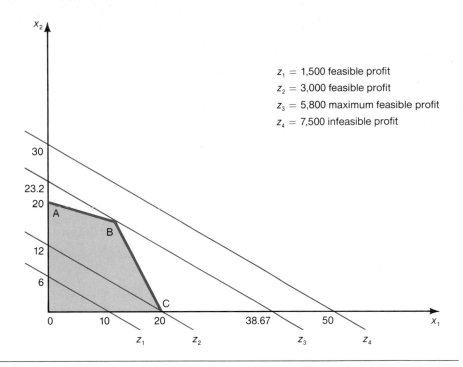

point of the two constraints, as shown in Figure 3.16. The slope $-3/5$ is not as steep as -2 but is steeper than $-1/3$; therefore, the iso-profit function will pass through the intersecting point of the two constraints at the tip of the area of feasible solutions.

If the iso-profit function had a slope of -3, which is steeper than either of the two slopes of the constraints, the optimum point would be the extreme point on the horizontal axis (Point C: $x_1 = 20$, $x_2 = 0$), as shown in Figure 3.17. By applying the same reasoning, if the iso-profit function had a slope of $-1/4$, which is flatter than either of the two constraint slopes, the optimum solution would be the extreme point on the vertical axis (Point A: $x_1 = 0$, $x_2 = 20$), also shown in Figure 3.17.

Comparing slopes of critical constraints

If the iso-profit function has a slope that is identical to one of the slopes of the *critical constraints* (constraints that form the feasibility area), the optimum solution would be a portion of that constraint. For example, if the slope of the iso-profit function were $-1/3$ in the Galaxy problem (e.g., $Z = 100x_1 + 300x_2$), any point on the line segment AB would be the optimum solution, as shown in Figure 3.18. In such a case, obviously, we have multiple optimum solutions. Usually, however, the decision maker is faced with a choice between points A and B. At point A the firm will be producing only one product (GE-2000), whereas at point B the firm will be producing both products. Since the total profit is identical at either solution point, the decision criteria would be some other, noneconomic considerations.

Figure 3.16   Graphical Representation of the Slope Comparison Approach

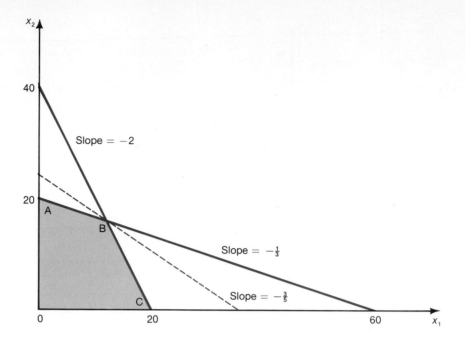

Figure 3.17   Slopes of the Iso-profit Function and the Optimum Solution

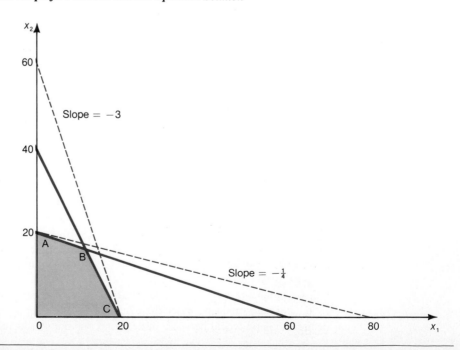

Figure 3.18 **The Multiple Optimum Solution Case**

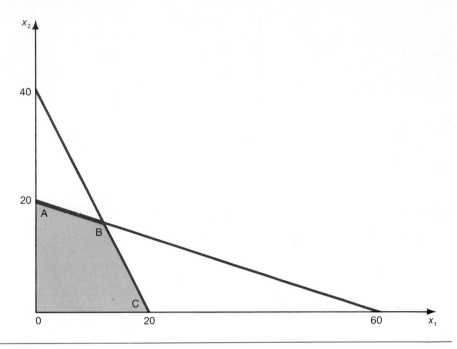

Now we can summarize the slope comparison approach for a maximization problem as follows:

Iso-profit Function Slope	Optimum Solution
Flatter than all constraint slopes	Extreme point on vertical axis
Steeper than all constraints	Extreme point on horizontal axis
Between two slopes of constraints	Intersecting point of the two constraint lines
Identical to the slope of a constraint	Multiple optimum solutions on the line segment of the constraint

Thus far in our discussion of the slope comparison approach, we have emphasized the fact that we should consider the slopes of only those constraints that form the boundary of the area of feasible solutions. In other words, we must graph all the constraints and identify the feasibility area before attempting to compare slopes. Oth-

The redundant constraint erwise, we may consider slopes of the *redundant constraints* (constraints that are not critical and do not form the feasibility area). Consequently, we may possibly identify a solution that is infeasible (a solution outside of the feasibility area) or one that violates the nonnegativity condition (one or more solution values of the decision variables are negative).

It should also be noted here that care must be taken in using the slope compari-

Figure 3.19   A Problem with Mixed Constraints

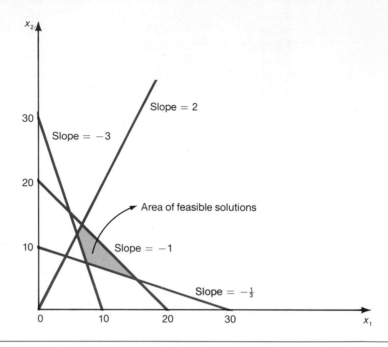

son approach if the problem involves mixed constraints. For example, suppose we have a linear programming model as follows:

$$\text{Maximize } Z = 12x_1 + 8x_2$$
$$\text{subject to} \quad x_1 + x_2 \leq 20$$
$$3x_1 + x_2 \geq 30$$
$$2x_1 + 6x_2 \geq 60$$
$$2x_1 - x_2 \geq 0$$
$$x_1, x_2 \geq 0$$

Mixed constraints

This maximization problem has mixed constraints—one is a "less than or equal to" and three are "greater than or equal to" type of constraint. Furthermore, one constraint has a zero right-hand-side value. It should be noted here that *a maximization problem does not need to have only "less than or equal to" constraints, and a minimization problems does not need to have only "greater than or equal to" constraints.* A linear programming problem, whether it is a maximization or a minimization prob-

Three types of constraints

lem, can have any combination of the three possible types of constraints: $\leq$, $=$, or $\geq$.

The maximization problem with mixed constraints presented above has the area of feasible solutions as shown in Figure 3.19. In this problem, you may have difficulty in finding the optimum solution by simply comparing slopes. For such problems it is more appropriate to use the iso-profit (or iso-cost) function approach.

A Simple Minimization Problem

A minimization problem

Thus far we have discussed the graphical method of linear programming for a maximization problem. The basic approaches used for a maximization problem can also be applied to a minimization problem. Let us consider the "Diet Problem of the Freshmen Orientation Program" that we formulated in Casette 3.2. The problem is concerned with the determination of the number of scoops of scrambled eggs and the number of smokie sausages to serve for breakfast in order to minimize the cost per serving. The constraints involved in the problem are to meet vitamin A, vitamin B, and iron requirements.

The diet problem we formulated was

$$\text{Minimize } Z = 8x_1 + 10x_2$$

$$\begin{array}{lll} \text{subject to} & 3x_1 + 3x_2 \geq 30 & \textit{Vitamin A} \\ & 4x_1 + 2x_2 \geq 24 & \textit{Vitamin B} \\ & x_1 + 2x_2 \geq 12 & \textit{Iron} \\ & x_1, x_2 \geq 0 & \end{array}$$

where x_1 = number of scoops of scrambled eggs served

x_2 = number of smokies served

Right-hand-side values minimum requirements

The objective function is expressed in terms of cents rather than dollars. The right-hand-side values of the constraints specify the *minimum* requirements for the three nutrients. Thus, the inequalities are shown as "greater than or equal to" constraints.

Based on the knowledge we have gained so far, we can easily plot the three constraints and identify the area of feasible solutions on a graph, as shown in Figure 3.20, by going through the following procedure:

$$3x_1 + 3x_2 \geq 30 \tag{1}$$
$$3x_2 \geq 30 - 3x_1$$
$$x_2 \geq 10 - x_1$$

$$4x_1 + 2x_2 \geq 24 \tag{2}$$
$$2x_2 \geq 24 - 4x_1$$
$$x_2 \geq 12 - 2x_1$$

$$x_1 + 2x_2 \geq 12 \tag{3}$$
$$2x_2 \geq 12 - x_1$$
$$x_2 \geq 6 - \frac{1}{2}x_1$$

The area of feasible solutions is represented by the shaded area on and above the lines outlined by ABCD. The problem can be solved by using any of the three approaches we have discussed. The optimum solution is the point where the total cost is minimum. If we did not have the model constraints, the optimum solution would be at the origin, point 0. Hence, the optimum solution within the area of feasible solutions must be one of those corner points that are close to the origin and that form the feasibility area.

Solution approaches

If we use the *search approach,* we can simply examine the total cost at each of the four corner points A, B, C, and D. If the *iso-cost function approach* is used ("cost" because this is a cost minimization problem), the optimum point will be the

Figure 3.20   The Graphical Presentation of the Diet Problem

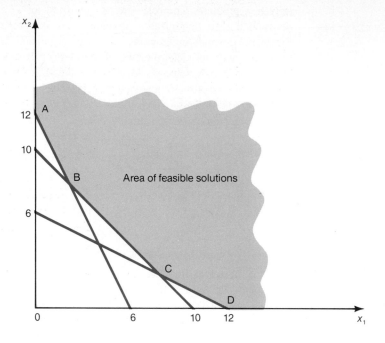

Figure 3.21   Graphical Solution of the Diet Problem by the Iso-cost Function Approach

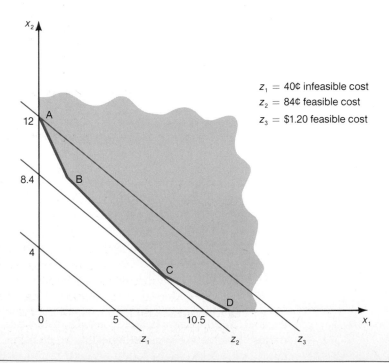

first point we touch within the feasibility area as we move out from the origin with the slope of the iso-cost function $-4/5$. For example, the iso-cost function can be developed as follows:

$$Z = 8x_1 + 10x_2$$
$$10x_2 = Z - 8x_1$$
$$x_2 = \frac{Z}{10} - \frac{4}{5}x_1$$

If the *slope comparison approach* is used, the slopes of the three constraints $(-2, -1, \text{ and } -1/2)$ should be compared with the slope of the iso-cost function, $-4/5$.

Let us use the iso-cost function approach to identify the optimum point. We can move out from the origin with a number of total-cost functions, as shown in Figure 3.21. The total cost of the three iso-cost functions have the relationship $Z_1 < Z_2 < Z_3$. We can easily identify point C as the optimum solution. Exact values of x_1 and x_2 at point C can be easily calculated when the two constraint equalities are solved simultaneously. The two constraints are the vitamin A and iron requirements.

We can solve for x_1 and x_2 as

$$x_2 = 10 - x_1 \qquad (1)$$

$$x_2 = 6 - \frac{1}{2}x_1 \qquad (3)$$

Thus,
$$10 - x_1 = 6 - \frac{1}{2}x_1$$

$$-\frac{1}{2}x_1 = -4$$

$$x_1 = 8$$

Substituting this value of x_1 into (1), we have
$$x_2 = 10 - 8$$
$$x_2 = 2$$

Now the total cost at point C can be derived as
$$Z = 8 \times 8 + 10 \times 2 = 84$$

A Problem with an Equality Constraint

In our discussion thus far we have dealt with linear programming problems having only inequality constraints. However, in certain problems we may actually have

An equality constraint

equality constraints. Let us consider the following simple maximization problem:

$$\text{Maximize } Z = \$18x_1 + \$12x_2$$
$$\text{subject to} \quad 2x_1 + x_2 \leq 40$$
$$x_2 \geq 10$$
$$x_1 + x_2 = 20$$
$$x_1, x_2 \geq 0$$

This problem, which is illustrated graphically in Figure 3.22, has all three types of constraints: $\leq$, $\geq$, and $=$. We already know how to define the feasibility area for an inequality constraint. For an equality constraint, the feasibility area is simply the straight line itself. Thus, the feasibility area for this problem is the line segment $\overline{AB}$.

Figure 3.22   A Problem with an Equality Constraint

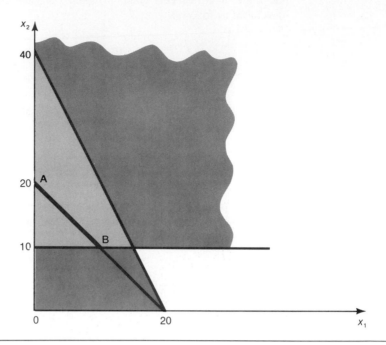

The iso-profit function of this problem is

$$Z = 18x_1 + 12x_2$$

$$x_2 = \frac{Z}{12} - \frac{3}{2}x_1$$

Since the slope of the iso-profit function is $-3/2$ and the slope of the line segment $\overline{AB}$ is -1, the optimum solution is point B. Now we can easily determine the optimum solution as $x_1 = 10$, $x_2 = 10$, $Z = \$400$.

SIMPLE SENSITIVITY ANALYSIS

Thus far we have discussed the model formulation and the graphical solution method of linear programming. Another very important aspect of linear programming that deserves our attention is sensitivity analysis. Sensitivity analysis attempts to evaluate the sensitivity of the optimum solution to changes in the model parameters. Because real-world problems always involve a degree of uncertainty, some model parameters are not known with certainty. Thus, decision makers are keenly interested in sensitivity analysis.

Answering "what-if" questions

If the optimum solution is very sensitive to changes in a certain parameter, special efforts should be directed to accurately forecasting the future values of the parameters. On the other hand, if the optimum solution is not very sensitive to changes in

Figure 3.23 *Graphical Solution of the Sensitivity Analysis Problem*

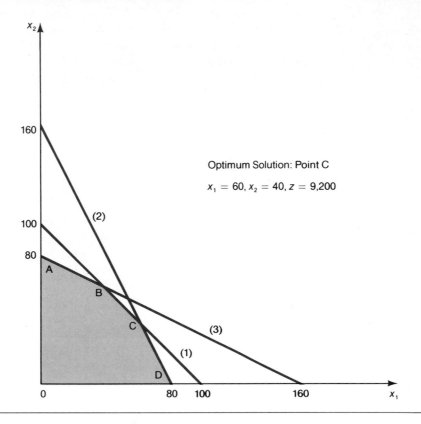

Optimum Solution: Point C

$x_1 = 60, x_2 = 40, z = 9,200$

a parameter, it will be a waste of time and effort to estimate the value of the parameter more accurately.

Three types of sensitivity analysis

In a simple sensitivity analysis, we examine the effects of changes in unit contribution rates of the objective function, technological coefficients (e.g., use of resources) in constraints, and the right-hand-side values (e.g., amount of resources available) of constraints. By way of introducing the sensitivity analysis, let us examine the following problem:

$$\text{Maximize } Z = 100x_1 + 80x_2$$
$$\text{subject to} \quad x_1 + x_2 \leq 100$$
$$2x_1 + x_2 \leq 160$$
$$x_1 + 2x_2 \leq 160$$
$$x_1, x_2 \geq 0$$

Figure 3.23 depicts this problem on a graph. A brief examination of the graph indicates that the optimum solution is at point C ($x_1 = 60$, $x_2 = 40$), with $Z = \$9,200$. Does the optimum solution remain the same when there are changes in unit profits, technological coefficients, or resource levels? We are trying to answer these questions by sensitivity analysis.

Change in Contribution Rates

Contribution rates

In many real-world problems, contribution rates (unit profits or unit costs of the decision variables in the objective function) change frequently. For example, on Wall Street the prices of most stock change daily, in grocery stores the cost of food seems to go up every month, and hospital care costs vary considerably depending on the location and reputation of the hospital.

In our example, suppose the unit profit of x_1 changes from \$100 to \$120 while the unit profit of x_2 remains at \$80. Notice that the only change is in the unit contribution rate of x_1 in the objective function. In other words, the area of feasible solutions remains exactly the same but the slope of the iso-profit function is changed from

A change in the iso-profit function

$-5/4$ to $-3/2$. If we denote the unit contribution rates of x_1 and x_2 as c_1 and c_2 respectively, the slope of the iso-profit function is simply $-(c_1/c_2)$. Thus, if we employ the slope comparison method, it is evident that point C ($x_1 = 60$, $x_2 = 40$) remains as the optimum solution. Of course, the total profit is increased from \$9,200 to \$10,400.

From our knowledge of the slope comparison approach, it is clear that point C would remain the optimum solution as long as the iso-profit function has a slope between -1 and -2. If the iso-profit function has a slope of -2, any point on the line segment $\overline{CD}$ will be an optimum solution (a case of multiple optimum solutions). On the other hand, if the slope of the iso-profit function is -1, any point on the line segment $\overline{BC}$ can be an optimum solution (note that this is also a case of multiple optimum solutions). Consequently, we can summarize the combination of optimum solutions and the slopes of the iso-profit function as follows:

Slope of the Iso-profit Function	Optimum Solution
$-\dfrac{c_1}{c_2} > -\dfrac{1}{2}$	Point A
$-\dfrac{c_1}{c_2} = -\dfrac{1}{2}$	Line segment $\overline{AB}$
$-1 < -\dfrac{c_1}{c_2} < -\dfrac{1}{2}$	Point B
$-\dfrac{c_1}{c_2} = -1$	Line segment $\overline{BC}$
$-2 < -\dfrac{c_1}{c_2} < -1$	Point C
$-\dfrac{c_1}{c_2} = -2$	Line segment $\overline{CD}$
$-\dfrac{c_1}{c_2} < -2$	Point D

The range of contribution rates

Now we can ask a simple question. If the unit profit of x_2 remains constant at \$80 but the unit profit of x_1 fluctuates, what kind of profit range should there be for x_1 in order for us to select point B as the optimum solution? We can easily analyze the problem as follows:

$$c_1 = ?, \quad c_2 = 80$$

The requirement for point B being the optimum solution,

$$-1 \leq -\frac{c_1}{c_2} \leq -\frac{1}{2}$$

$$-1 \leq -\frac{c_1}{80} \leq -\frac{1}{2}$$

The upper limit of the range can be found by

$$-1 \leq -\frac{c_1}{80}; \quad c_1 \leq 80$$

The lower limit of the range can be found by

$$-\frac{c_1}{80} \leq -\frac{1}{2}; \quad c_1 \geq 40$$

If the unit profit of x_2 remains constant at \$80, the required range of the unit profit of x_1 is $40 \leq c_1 \leq 80$ in order for point B ($x_1 = 40$, $x_2 = 60$) to be the optimum solution.

Change in Technological Coefficients

Changes in technological coefficients

Technological coefficients are those parameters that are associated with the decision variables in model constraints. For example, in our problem the second constraint is $2x_1 + x_2 \leq 160$. Thus, the technological coefficients for x_1 and x_2 in this constraint are 2 and 1 respectively. Changes in technological coefficients occur frequently as the result of technological innovations (e.g., new types of machines require shorter production time in Assembly 1), the learning curve or a higher employee morale (e.g., employees become more efficient on the job), or new product specifications or government regulations. Such changes may have profound effects on the problem solution.

Changing the slope of constraints

Changes in technological coefficients have no effect on the objective function of the problem. Thus, the iso-profit (or iso-cost) function will not be altered. Changes in technological coefficients affect the constraints and thereby usually bring changes in the area of feasible solutions. For example, suppose the second constraint is changed from $2x_1 + x_2 \leq 160$ to $2x_1 + 2/3\, x_2 \leq 160$. The coefficient of x_2 is changed from 1 to 2/3 in the constraint. This change will result in changes in the slope of the constraint and the x_2 intercept, as shown in Figure 3.24. The new area of feasible solutions is now 0ABED. Thus, the new optimum solution will be point E ($x_1 = 70$, $x_2 = 30$), where $Z = \$9,400$.

A change in a technological coefficient does not always result in a change in the optimum solution. For example, if point B were the previous optimum solution, the change in the technological coefficient of x_2 in the second constraint discussed above (i.e., $2x_1 + x_2 \leq 160$ is changed to $2x_1 + 2/3\, x_2 \leq 160$) would have no effect on the optimum solution. In this case, point B remains the optimum solution.

Change in the Right-hand-side Value

Changes in available resources or requirements

The right-hand-side value of a constraint usually represents the available resource. A change in the right-hand-side value of a constraint will result in changes in the intercepts of the constraint function. Consequently, it may result in changes in the area of

Figure 3.24   Effect of a Change in the Technological Coefficient on the Optimum Solution

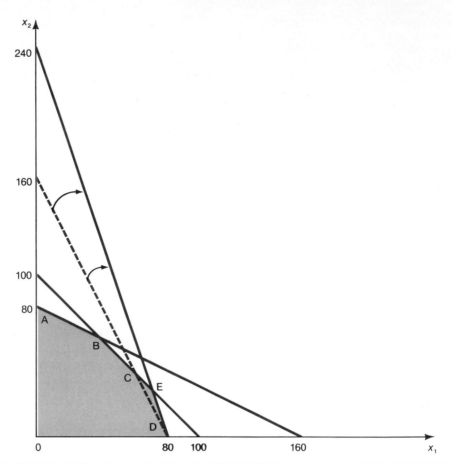

feasible solutions. For example, in our original problem let us suppose the third constraint is changed from $x_1 + 2x_2 \leq 160$ to $x_1 + 2x_2 \leq 120$.

The change in the intercepts and consequently in the area of feasible solutions is shown in Figure 3.25. Note that a change in the right-hand side does not affect the slope of the constraint. The new area of feasible solutions, as shown in Figure 3.25, is 0FGD. By applying the slope comparison method, it is clear that the optimum solution is point G ($x_1 = 66\ 2/3$, $x_2 = 26\ 2/3$), where $Z = \$8,800$. Once again, a change in the right-hand-side value does not always result in a change in the optimum solution.

In Figure 3.23 we identified the optimum solution as point C, where $x_1 = 60$, $x_2 = 40$, and $Z = \$9,200$. Point C is the intersecting point of Constraints 1 and 2. Thus, the critical (binding) constraints are 1 and 2. The noncritical (unbinding) constraint for the optimum solution is Constraint 3. Thus, if we can increase our resources in any of the three constraints, an increase in the right-hand-side value should be made in either Constraint 1 or Constraint 2 but not in Constraint 3.

Changing the intercepts of constraints

Figure 3.25 *Effect of a Change in Resource on the Optimum Solution*

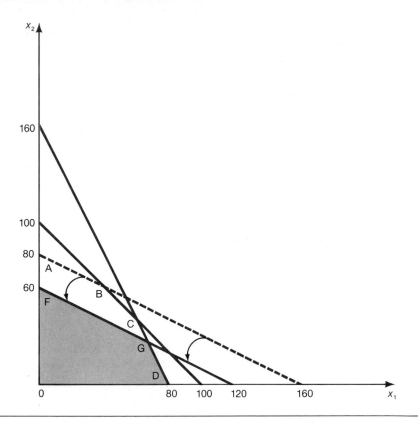

In order to decide whether we should increase the right-hand-side value in Constraint 1 or Constraint 2, we can simply check which choice yields a greater increase in profit. For example, if we increase the right-hand-side value of Constraint 1 by one unit of resource, a new optimum solution becomes:

$$x_1 + x_2 \leq 101 \qquad \qquad \textit{Constraint 1}$$
$$2x_1 + x_2 \leq 160 \qquad \qquad \textit{Constraint 2}$$

The optimum point is the intersecting point of Constraints 1 and 2. Intersecting point: $x_1 = 59$, $x_2 = 42$, where $Z = \$9,260$.

On the other hand, if we increase the right-hand-side value of Constraint 2 by one unit of resource, a new optimum solution will be:

$$x_1 + x_2 \leq 100 \qquad \qquad \textit{Constraint 1}$$
$$2x_1 + x_2 \leq 161 \qquad \qquad \textit{Constraint 2}$$

The optimum point is still the intersecting point of Constraints 1 and 2. Intersecting point: $x_1 = 61$, $x_2 = 39$, where $Z = \$9,220$.

Increasing and decreasing resources

From the above analysis, it is obvious that we should increase our resource in Constraint 1, rather than in Constraint 2, in order to maximize the total profit. Now we can see clearly that an across-the-board increase (an increase of the resources in all three constraints by the same proportions), which we see so often in many organizations, is not always the best way to allocate resources.

We can also analyze the problem in the same manner when resources must be reduced from constraints. Any reduction in resources (the right-hand-side value) must come first in the noncritical constraints. In this problem, the right-hand-side should be reduced in Constraint 3. Once again, we can see that an across-the-board decrease in resources, so often observed in organizations, really is inefficient. We will discuss these points in greater detail in Chapter 5.

From the above discussion, the net change in the total profit when we increase or decrease one unit of resource in each of the two binding constraints is as follows:

Constraint 1: $60 ($9260 − $9200 = $60)

Constraint 2: $20 ($9220 − $9200 = $20)

These two figures represent the marginal value of additional unit of exhausted resources and they are often referred to as the *shadow prices*. They will be discussed in greater detail in Chapters 4 and 5.

EXAMPLES OF REAL-WORLD APPLICATIONS OF LINEAR PROGRAMMING

Wide real-world applications

Since linear programmimg is a systematic method of selecting the best alternative among a large number of solution combinations, it is reasonable to expect extensive real-world applications of this technique. Indeed, there have been a large number of papers published about the application of linear programming to various management decision problems. However, it is extremely difficult to determine the number of real-world applications of linear programming in actual decision making settings. It is even harder to ascertain what percentage of these applications were actually implemented and resulted in positive consequences.

Examples of real-world applications

Since many business firms consider any innovative application of management science as a comparative advantage, they do not often reveal their management science applications. The profession of management science, however, has emphasized the publication of real-world applications. For example, the Institute of Management Science (TIMS) has an annual award ($6,000 cash prize) for the best paper describing a real-world application of management science. In this section we will introduce three real-world applications of linear programming.

Crude Oil Sales

The Naval Petroleum Reserves in California (NPRC), made up of NPR#1 (Elk Hills field) and NPR#2 (Buena Vista field), are important sources of crude oil in the United States. This case study[1] reports the bid and evaluation procedures as applied to crude oil sales at Elk Hills. The Elk Hills field is jointly owned by the federal government and Chevron, USA. A major problem associated with bringing Elk Hills into production was the structuring of sales contracts with private firms for marketing the oil.

[1]B. Jackson and J. Brown, "Using LP for Crude Oil Sales at Elk Hills: A Case Study," *Interfaces,* 10:3 (1980), 65–69.

Public Law 94-258 (the Naval Petroleum Production Act of 1976) required that the Secretary of Energy sell the government's share of the oil to the highest bidder, while limiting sales to any single bidder to 20 percent of total sales. The bid evaluation procedures at Elk Hills oil sales involved the determination of the average amount of oil available for sale at each of the six delivery points and a sequential evaluation of bids to determine award quantities. Bidders were allowed to bid on the entire quantity available at a given delivery point or on any portion desired. This problem involved a "mini-max" bid model of linear programming that attempted to maximize the total revenue from the bidding while satisfying various constraints.

The result of the study was reported to be very satisfactory. The model was used as a bid award procedure for the Elk Hills oil sales. Although the exact amount of additional revenue directly attributable to the model was not reported, this linear programming model represented an innovative application example.

A Facilities Location Model

The Coastal Construction Company of Portsmouth, Virginia, operates a precast-prestressed concrete products plant.[2] The plant was originally used to produce components for large bridges and tunnels. The company currently produces items such as bridge girders, pilings, and other marine construction components. The company decided to produce and market a new product, transmission poles for electrical utilities. The company attempted to determine two new production facilities for the new product.

The company's three existing facilities were a concrete batching plant, a steel manufacturing area, and a shipping-gate checking and weighing area. The company estimated an average sale of 40 poles per day. Forty poles would require approximately 10 cubic yards of concrete and 8,400 pounds of manufactured steel. The handling equipment required for producing 40 poles was: (1) concrete: 3-cubic-yard brickets on flatbed trucks; (2) steel: front end loader in drums; (3) poles: Drott travel lift crane and flatbed trailer.

The company was able to estimate the handling costs, which included the distance-costs associated with required trips to the existing facilities and equipment. The company designed a linear programming model that would minimize the total daily materials-handling costs involved in locating the two new facilities while meeting various production mix constraints. The solution of the model indicated two new facilities to be located in one location adjacent to the steel manufacturing area for maximum cost savings. The solution was successfully implemented by the company.

Assigning Students to Schools

A number of upstate New York consolidated school districts have several elementary schools serving a large geographical area.[3] The basic policy of the school districts is to use busing to transport the great majority of students. The major concerns of the school administrators have been rising fuel costs, decreasing enrollments, and the

---

[2]R. Lore and L. Yerex, "An Application of a Facilities Location Model in the Prestressed Concrete Industry," *Interfaces*, 6:4 (1976), 45–49.

[3]P. McKeown and B. Workman, "A Study in Using Linear Programming to Assign Students to Schools," *Interfaces*, 6:4 (1976), 96–101.

need either to use the available classrooms efficiently or to decide which schools to close.

A large-scale linear programming routine was set up to assign students to schools in a pattern that would minimize the total student-miles traveled in the district. Since the vast majority of students were bused to schools, the study used clustered bus stops in order to simplify the model. Data were collected (from the bus drivers) concerning the number of students in each grade at each bus stop.

The linear programming model minimized the total student-miles at 460.14. This figure indicated a reduction of approximately 447 student-miles from the current student-miles traveled, as measured by a survey. This study is an interesting application of linear programming to a public-sector problem. Although the result may not be exact, owing to the bus stop clustering procedure, it could be a useful piece of information for the school administrators as they attempt to solve their busing problem.

SUMMARY

Popularity of linear programming

Linear programming is a powerful mathematical technique for determining the optimum solutions to decision problems that involve linear objective functions and linear constraints. Linear programming has been widely applied by industry, government, and nonprofit organizations. Two reasons for this popularity appear to be its relatively simple concept and its applicability to many real-world problems. Another very important reason is the availability of the simplex technique as a solution algorithm. Today, there are numerous simplex-based computer programs available. These programs enable the decision maker to solve complex linear programming problems with relative ease. The most critical problem in applying linear programming is the model formulation. It requires a good understanding of the basic concept, requirements, and application areas of linear programming.

Model formulation—the key

In this chapter, we have seen how linear programming assists the decision maker in selecting the most effective course of action from various alternatives. We have studied the important aspects of linear programming through various casette examples and the graphical solution method. We have also learned how a decision maker can gain clearer insight into the nature of a problem by performing sensitivity analysis.

References

Charnes, A., and Cooper, W. W. *Management Models and Industrial Applications of Linear Programming*. New York: Wiley, 1961.

Dantzig, G. B. *Linear Programming and Extensions*. Princeton, N.J.: Princeton University Press, 1963.

Kwak, N. K. *Mathematical Programming with Business Applications*. New York: McGraw-Hill, 1973.

Lee, S. M., and Moore, L. J. *Introduction to Decision Science*. New York: Petrocelli-Charter, 1975.

Lee, S. M.; Moore, L. J.; and Taylor, B. *Management Science*. Dubuque, Iowa: W. C. Brown, 1981.

Loomba, N. P., and Turban, E. *Applied Programming for Management*. New York: Holt, Rinehart & Winston, 1974.

Assignments

3.1 What are the most important reasons why linear programming is one of the most widely applied techniques of management science?

3.2 List six major requirements of linear programming.

3.3 Define the following terms by using examples: *proportionality, additivity, divisibility, nonnegativity, deterministic.*

3.4 Discuss a problem you are familiar with that can be solved by linear programming.

3.5 Discuss the three different types of constraints that are used in linear programming.

3.6 What is the main difference between a linear equality and a linear inequality?

3.7 What is the iso-profit function? Why is it useful for the graphical method?

3.8 What is a redundant constraint?

3.9 When do we face a case of multiple optimum solutions?

3.10 When is the slope comparison approach not appropriate?

3.11 What is the purpose of sensitivity analysis? What are the model parameters that we examine in sensitivity analysis?

3.12 Graph the following equalities:
  a. $7x_1 + 7x_2 = 28$
  b. $12x_1 + 8x_2 = 72$
  c. $x_1 = 6$
  d. $x_1 + 2x_2 = 18$
  e. $x_2 = 9$

3.13 Graph the following inequalities:
  a. $2x_1 + 2x_2 \leq 16$
  b. $2x_1 \leq 24$
  c. $x_2 \geq 6$
  d. $6x_1 + 4x_2 \leq 48$
  e. $1/2x_1 + x_2 \leq 6$

3.14 Graph the following constraints and indicate the area of feasible solutions:

$$\text{subject to} \quad 3x_1 + 3x_2 \leq 300$$
$$6x_1 + 3x_2 \leq 480$$
$$3x_1 + 3x_2 \leq 480$$
$$x_1, x_2 \geq 0$$

3.15 Graph the following constraints and indicate the area of feasible solutions:

$$\text{subject to} \quad 7x_1 + 14x_2 \leq 56$$
$$42x_1 + 28x_2 \leq 168$$
$$x_1, x_2 \geq 0$$

3.16 Solve the following linear programming problem by the graphical method:

$$\text{Maximize } Z = \$18x_1 + \$14x_2$$
$$\text{subject to} \quad 4x_1 + 2x_2 \leq 80$$
$$2x_1 + 6x_2 \leq 60$$
$$x_1, x_2 \geq 0$$

3.17 Solve the following linear programming problem by the graphical method:

$$\text{Maximize } Z = \$9x_1 + \$15x_2$$
$$\text{subject to} \quad 3x_2 \leq 18$$
$$9x_1 + 6x_2 \leq 54$$
$$x_1, x_2 \geq 0$$

3.18 Solve the following linear programming problem by the graphical method:

$$\text{Maximize } Z = \$40x_1 + \$44x_2$$
$$\text{subject to} \quad 16x_1 + 12x_2 \leq 96$$
$$12x_1 + 16x_2 \leq 96$$
$$14x_1 + 14x_2 = 88$$
$$x_1, x_2 \geq 0$$

3.19 Solve the following linear programming problem by the graphical method:

$$\text{Maximize } Z = 80x_1 + 60x_2$$
$$\text{subject to} \quad x_1 + x_2 = 200$$
$$x_1 \leq 50$$
$$x_2 \geq 80$$
$$x_1, x_2 \geq 0$$

3.20 The Gloria Haig Company is a producer of two lines of designer jeans, Chic and Fancy. Ms. Haig supervises two production operation departments—Design and Cut, and Sewing. The company has a definite commitment to Bloomdust Department Store for 8,000 jeans. There is no inventory for the new season's designer jeans. Thus, the company must produce at least 8,000 new jeans for the coming season. Production of one lot of 100 jeans requires the following operations:

	Chic	Fancy
Design and Cut	20 hr.	40 hr.
Sewing	40 hr.	40 hr.

The company has secured the necessary manpower to operate the two departments for the following number of hours during the next month: Design and Cut Department, 400 hours; Sewing Department, 600 hours. Gloria is confident, as usual, that she can sell all the jeans to be produced next month. The expected unit profits are: Chic, $13; Fancy, $20.

    a. Formulate a linear programming model to determine the mix of Chic and Fancy designer jeans that will maximize profits.

    b. Solve the above problem using the graphical method.

3.21 The Neverfail Recorder Company produces two types of tape recorders—a reel-to-reel model and a cassette model—on two assembly lines. The company must process each tape recorder on each assembly line, and it has found that the following production times are required:

	Reel-to-Reel	Cassette
Assembly Line 1	6 hr.	2 hr.
Assembly Line 2	4 hr.	2 hr.

The production manager says that Assembly Line 1 will be available 40 hours per week while Assembly Line 2 will be available only 30 hours per week. After these hours of operation each line must be checked for repairs. The company realizes a profit of $30 on each reel-to-reel tape recorder and $12 on each cassette recorder.

    a. Formulate a linear programming model to determine how many recorders of each type should be produced each week to maximize profits.

    b. Solve the above problem using the graphical method.

3.22 The Airwaves Company has been a producer of picture tubes for television sets and certain printed circuits for radios. The company has just expanded into full-scale production and marketing of AM and AM-FM radios. It has built a new plant that can operate 48 hours per week. Production of an AM radio in the new plant will require 2 hours and production of an AM-FM radio will require 3 hours.

Each AM radio will contribute $4 to profits and each AM-FM radio will contribute $8 to profits. The Marketing Department, after extensive research, has determined that a maximum of 15 AM radios and 10 AM-FM radios can be sold each week.

    a. Formulate a linear programming model to determine the optimum production mix of AM and AM-FM radios that will maximize profits.

    b. Solve the above problem using the graphical method.

3.23 The Arts and Craft Shop is sponsoring a boomerang-throwing contest each week for the next four weeks. Each week's contest will be only for those people who have not participated in a previous week's contest. All boomerangs must be purchased from the Arts and Craft Shop. The shop sells two models of boomerang—the regular model and the "Super Bender."

Each model requires two processes—carving, and painting and varnishing. There is a maximum of 75 hours available per week for carving and 100 hours available per week for painting and varnishing. Production of a regular boomerang requires 1 hour of carving and 2 hours of painting and varnishing. Production of a "Super Bender" requires 3 hours of carving and 2 hours of painting and varnishing. Profit from the sale of a regular boomerang is $2 and a "Super Bender" provides a $5 profit.

    a. Formulate a linear programming model to determine the number of each type of boomerang that should be produced each week in order to maximize profits.

    b. Solve the above problem using the graphical method.

3.24 The Browning Clothing Store is making plans for its annual shirt and pants sale. The owner, Mr. Jarvis, is planning to use two different forms of advertising—radio and newspaper—to promote the sale. Based on past experience, Mr. Jarvis feels confident that each newspaper ad will reach 40 shirt customers and 80 pants customers. He estimates that each radio ad will reach 30 shirt customers and 20 pants customers.

    The cost of each newspaper ad is $100 and the cost of each radio spot is $150. An advertising agency will prepare the advertising, and it will require 5 man-hours of preparation for each newspaper ad and 15 man-hours of preparation for each radio spot.

    Mr. Jarvis's sales manager says that a minimum of 75 man-hours should be spent on the preparation of advertising in order to fully utilize the services of the advertising agency. Mr. Jarvis feels that, to have a successful sale, the advertising must reach at least 360 shirt customers and at least 400 pants customers.

    a. Formulate a linear programming model to determine how much advertising should be done using each of the two forms of media in order to minimize costs and still attain the objectives Mr. Jarvis has set.

    b. Solve the above problem using the graphical method.

3.25 The Cover Girl Company is expanding its operations and attempting to expand its sales territory. The sales manager has a staff of experienced salesladies who are each paid $200 per week. He is planning to hire some new sales trainees for $100 per week.

    Based on past experience, an experienced saleslady can generate $10,000 worth of sales per week. A sales trainee can generate an average of $6,000 worth of sales per week. The company has budgeted $800 for a training program for the new trainees. The estimated cost of training is $100 per trainee. The sales manager's payroll budget is $1,600 per week. Furthermore, the company has decided that the sales force should be limited to 10 or fewer salesladies. The decision problem of the sales manager is to determine the optimum number of experienced salesladies and new trainees in order to maximize total sales.

    a. Formulate a linear programming model for the problem.

    b. Identify the optimum solution and the total sales by using the graphical method.

    c. If the weekly sales of the experienced salesladies remain relatively constant at $10,000 per week but the weekly sales of the trainees fluctuate widely, how much should the average sales per trainee per week be before the company should limit its sales staff to two experienced salesladies and eight trainees?

d. In the original problem, if the training cost per trainee is $200 rather than $100, how would the optimum solution be changed?

e. In the original problem, if the company increases the number of salesladies from 10 to 12, how would the solution be changed?

3.26 The Global Chemical Company produces only one product, Compound X, which it can produce using either of two processes. Both processes produce not only Compound X but also a by-product known as Compound Y. Until recently, Compound Y was worthless, but a new, quite profitable market has been developed for it.

Using the first process, the company can produce 60 grams of Compound X per hour and 15 grams of Compound Y per hour. The second process produces 40 grams of Compound X and 30 grams of Compound Y per hour. To meet its contract commitments, Global must produce at least 3,600 grams of Compound X per month. The company would also like to produce at least 1,200 grams of Compound Y per month in order to gain a substantial share of the new market. The cost of using either process to produce Compound X and Compound Y is $30 per hour.

a. Formulate a linear programming model to determine how many hours per month each process should be operated in order to produce the desired quantities and still minimize costs.

b. Solve the above problem using the graphical method.

3.27 The Appalachian Mining Company operates two gold mines. The mines are located in different parts of the country, and they have different production capacities. After crushing, the ore is graded into three classes: premium, good, and regular. There is some demand for each grade of ore.

The company has a contract to provide a smelting plant with 18 tons of premium, 12 tons of good, and 36 tons of regular grade ore per week. The first mine costs $3,000 per day to operate, whereas the second mine costs only $2,400 per day. The average production per day for the first mine is 9 tons of premium, 3 tons of good, and 6 tons of regular grade ore. The second mine produces 3 tons of premium, 3 tons of good, and 18 tons of regular grade ore daily. The management's problem is to determine how many days a week the company should operate each mine in order to fulfill its contract obligations most economically.

a. Formulate a linear programming model for the problem.

b. Illustrate the model graphically by identifying the following: axis of graph, constraints, area of feasible solutions, point of optimum solution, and values of the decision variables at the optimum point.

c. Given the optimum solution, determine the operation cost per week, and for each mine determine the number of tons of each grade of ore produced each week.

d. Would there be any change in the optimum solution if the daily operation cost of the first mine is reduced to $2,250 while the daily operation cost of the second mine remains at $2,400?

e. In the original problem, what would be the effect if the firm has to ship only 9 tons of good grade instead of 12 tons?

3.28 The dietitian at a girls' camp is planning breakfast for the first day of camp. The dietitian has the responsibility of providing a menu that satisfies the minimum nutrient requirements at the lowest cost. Two types of foods are being considered for the breakfast: toast and sausage.

A piece of toast contains 2 mg. of vitamin A, 3 mg. of vitamin B, and 2 mg. of iron. On the other hand, a sausage contains 4 mg. of vitamin A, 1.5 mg. of vitamin B, and 2 mg. of iron. The minimum breakfast requirements of these nutrient elements are estimated to be:

Nutrient	Requirement (mg.)
Vitamin A	20
Vitamin B	15
Iron	16

The American Medical Association has published an article which reported that having more than four sausages for breakfast is not recommended for young people. The dietitian considers this one of the most important constraints. The unit costs of the food are: toast, 4¢; sausage, 8¢.

a. Formulate a linear programming model for the problem.

b. Solve this problem graphically.

3.29 Lee Fortune Cookies, Inc. produces two types of fortune cookies: love and happiness. The major decision problem to be solved is the product mix determination in order to maximize profits. The production of a dozen fortune cookies requires the following resources and capacity (the available resources and capacity are presented in the last column):

Requirement per Dozen	Love	Happiness	Available
Cookie mix	1.0 lb.	0.6 lb.	120 lb.
Icing mix	0.4 lb.	0 lb.	32 lb.
Labor	0.15 hr.	0.10 hr.	15 hr.
Oven capacity	1 doz.	1 doz.	120 doz.

The expected profit for love cookies is 40¢ per dozen and for happiness cookies it is 30¢ per dozen.

a. Formulate a linear programming model for the problem.

b. Solve the above problem graphically.

c. Provided that the profit per dozen for love cookies remains at 40¢, what kind of profit range should happiness cookies have in order for 80 love cookies and 30 happiness cookies to be the optimum solution?

3.30 Old Dominion Chemicals, Inc. produces two products: Formula Y and Formula Z. Production of both products requires the same two processes. A unit of Formula Y requires 3 hours in the first process and 4 hours in the second process. A unit of Formula Z requires 5 hours in the first process and 2 hours in the second process. The maximum available production time in each of the two processes is: first process, 60 hours; second process, 70 hours.

The production of Formula Z results in a by-product, Formula ZX. Some of Formula ZX can be marketed at a profit. However, production of Formula ZX in excess of 10 units is not desirable because of the limited market. The production process for Formula Z yields 4 units of Formula ZX for each unit of Formula Z. The unit profits of Formula Y and Formula Z are $5 and $10 respectively. The by-product, Formula ZX, yields a $3 unit profit. If Formula ZX cannot be sold, it should be destroyed, at a unit cost of $2. The marketing department reports that the demand for Formula Y and Formula Z is unlimited, but that only 10 units of Formula ZX can be sold at the present time.

Formulate a linear programming model that will determine the maximum number of units of Formula Y, Formula Z, and Formula ZX to be produced in order to maximize total profits.

3.31 Your grandfather has just left you $1 million. You plan to invest this money in four alternative investment plans: stocks, bonds, savings, and real estate. Investments in stocks and bonds are available at the beginning of each of the next six years. Each dollar invested in stocks at the beginning of each year returns an average of $1.20 (a profit of $.20) two years later, in time for immediate reinvestment. Each dollar invested in bonds at the beginning of one year returns $1.40 three years later for reinvestment.

In addition, money-making investments in savings (in a credit union) and in real estate will be available at the beginning of each year. Each dollar invested in the credit union at the beginning of each year returns $1.10 one year later. Each dollar invested in real estate at the beginning of a year hence returns $1.30 two years later.

You would also like to diversify your investments in order to minimize the risk. The total amount invested in stocks should not exceed 30 percent of the total investment in the other alternatives. Furthermore, you wish to invest at least 25 percent of the total investment in the credit union savings plan. In addition, you are planning to get married at the end of the third year, and you would like to make sure that the amount of cash you will have at that time (to show off to your bride but not to spend) would be at least $150,000.

If you are attempting to maximize the amount of money (cash) you will have at the end of the sixth year, how would you formulate a linear programming model?

4   SIMPLEX METHOD OF LINEAR PROGRAMMING

In this chapter, we get into the nitty-gritty part of linear programming—the simplex method. The simplex method is the general solution technique of linear programming. It is a systematic procedure that seeks the optimum solution to a problem through progressive operations. We will study the simplex solution procedure and its application to a wide range of linear programming problems.

Learning Objectives   *From the study of this chapter, you will learn the following:*

1. The simplex method as the general solution technique of linear programming
2. The simplex solution procedure
3. Interpretation of the simplex tableau
4. Solution of any type of linear programming problem by the simplex method
5. Ways to resolve several types of complications faced in linear programming
6. The meaning of the following terms:

Simplex method	*Testing the optimality*
Pivot element	*Testing the feasibility*
Entering variable	*Slack variable*
Leaving variable	*Artificial variable*
Surplus variable	*Big M method*
Degeneracy	

THE SIMPLEX METHOD

The graphical method of linear programming that we studied in Chapter 3 is a straightforward technique for solving simple linear programming problems. However, most real-world management problems are too complex to be solved by the graphical method. As a matter of fact, many resource allocation problems faced by management may involve several thousand variables and several hundred constraints. Clearly, these types of problems cannot be solved by the graphical method. Systematic procedures have been developed to solve complex linear programming problems. The best-known technique is the simplex method.

The simplex method developed by Dantzig

    The simplex method of linear programming was developed by George B. Dantzig in 1947 and has since been further refined by many other contributors. This method is simply a mathematical procedure that employs an iterative process so that

Figure 4.1   The Simplex Solution Process

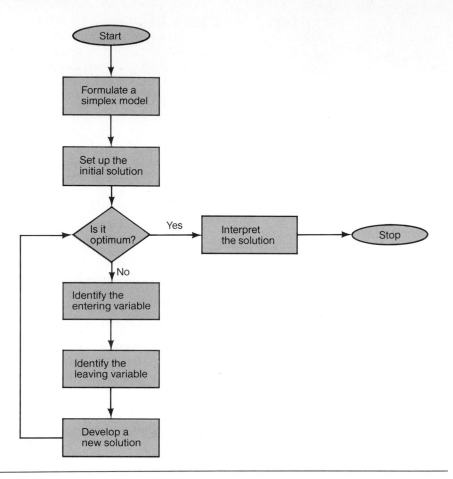

An iterative method

*A repeated solution
process*

the optimum solution is achieved through progressive operations. In other words, in a maximization problem, the last solution yields a total profit that is equal to or greater than the profit yielded by the previous solution. Although it may sound like a formidable task, the basic procedure is quite simple. In fact, if you follow the simplex procedure outlined in this chapter, a lack of knowledge of algebra will not be a problem.

The simplex method is nothing more than the repeated solution process of a set of linear equations. The simplex method is similar to the graphical method in that they both test optimality at extreme points within the area of feasible solutions. That is precisely why linear programming is often referred to as an extremal optimization method. The simplex method starts the search for the optimum solution from the origin and moves to another corner point whose objective value is equal to or better than that of the current solution. This process continues until there is no better solution to be found in the feasibility area.

The simplex procedure

The overall process of the simplex method is shown in Figure 4.1. Once the problem is properly arranged, an initial solution is set up in the simplex tableau and it is tested for optimality. If the solution is not optimum (the initial solution is, of course, usually not optimum), a new solution is derived in the second simplex tableau by identifying the incoming and outgoing variables as well as by completing the simplex operations. The new solution is also tested for optimality. If it is the optimum solution, its interpretation will terminate the process. If it is not optimum, the procedure is repeated until an optimum solution is found.

The simplex tableau at each step represents a new solution. Thus, the first (initial) solution is determined in the first tableau and the optimum solution in the final tableau. The value of the objective function in any tableau must always be *equal to or greater than* that of the previous solution in a maximization problem, and *equal to or less than* that of the previous solution in a minimization problem.

THE SIMPLEX SOLUTION PROCEDURE

Understanding the concept

We have already discussed the simplex method process through a flowchart. In this section we will go through the details of the solution procedure. In learning about the simplex method, the important thing is to *understand* the underlying concepts rather than *memorize* the solution mechanics. First we will walk slowly through the method until you get the general idea, and then we will breeze through other examples.

As a vehicle to explain the simplex procedure, let us discuss the following simple problem.

| *EXAMPLE 4.1* | *CANDEX CAMERA WORKS, LTD.* |

A maximization problem

Candex Camera Works, Ltd. specializes in precision photographic equipment. The company currently produces two well-known 35-mm. cameras: Candex A1 and Candex ZX. The modern production process involves two assembly lines. The production time requirements in the two assembly lines for each camera, the production capacities in the assembly lines, and the unit profit for each camera are as follows:

Production Resource	Time Requirements		Production Capacity
	Candex A1	Candex ZX	
Assembly Line 1	3 hr.	3 hr.	90 hr.
Assembly Line 2	2 hr.	4 hr.	80 hr.
Unit Profit	$40	$50	

The decision problem facing the Candex management is to determine the product mix for Candex A1 and Candex ZX that will maximize the total profit with the given weekly production capacities in the two assembly lines.

With the model formulation experience we have had, we can easily develop the following linear programming model for Candex:

$$\text{Maximize } Z = \$40x_1 + \$50x_2$$
$$\text{subject to} \quad 3x_1 + 3x_2 \leq 90$$
$$2x_1 + 4x_2 \leq 80$$
$$x_1, x_2 \geq 0$$

where
$$x_1 = \text{number of Candex A1 to be produced}$$
$$x_2 = \text{number of Candex ZX to be produced}$$

Step 1: Develop the Simplex Model

The simplex model

The first step of the simplex method procedure is to develop the simplex model. The regular linear programming model usually includes a number of linear inequalities, such as $\leq$ or $\geq$. It is necessary to transform such inequalities to equalities so that we can develop a standard simplex model.

For example, let us review the two assembly line constraints for Candex.

$$3x_1 + 3x_2 \leq 90 \qquad \textit{Assembly Line 1}$$
$$2x_1 + 4x_2 \leq 80 \qquad \textit{Assembly Line 2}$$

It is quite possible that the optimum product mix solution may not use up all the production time in the two assembly lines. For example, if an optimum solution happened to be at $x_1 = 30$, $x_2 = 0$, then the resource usage would be as follows:

$$3(30) + 3(0) = 90 \qquad \textit{Assembly Line 1}$$
$$2(30) + 4(0) \leq 80 \qquad \textit{Assembly Line 2}$$

In Assembly Line 1 we need all 90 hours of the available production time. But, in Assembly Line 2 we require only 60 hours, and thus 20 of the 80 available production hours will not be used.

In a *less than or equal to* constraint, the left-hand-side value of the inequality could be *less than* the right-hand-side value. Thus, in order to convert the constraint into an equality, we must add something to the left-hand side so that it can be brought up to the value on the right-hand side. This something we add to the left-hand side is called the *slack variable*. The slack variable represents the amount of unused resource in a given constraint. We need as many slack variables as there are *less than or equal to* constraints.

The slack variable

In the two assembly line constraints of the Candex problem, we need the following two slack variables:

$$s_1 = \text{slack variable for Assembly Line 1}$$
$$s_2 = \text{slack variable for Assembly Line 2}$$

Now we can transform the two inequality constraints to equalities as follows:

Time required to process x_1 units + Time required to process x_2 units

+ Unused resource = 90 hours available in Assembly Line 1

Time required to process x_1 units + Time required to process x_2 units

+ Unused resource = 80 hours available in Assembly Line 2

$$3x_1 + 3x_2 + s_1 = 90 \qquad \textit{Assembly Line 1}$$
$$2x_1 + 4x_2 + s_2 = 80 \qquad \textit{Assembly Line 2}$$

The use of slack variables allows the equalities to be general enough to hold under any situation. For example, we can examine closely the two constraints in Figure

Figure 4.2   The Two Constraints in the Candex Problem

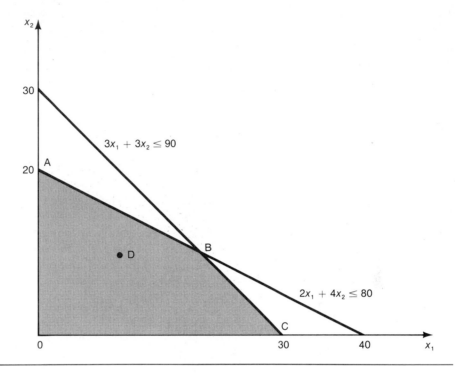

4.2. The area of feasible solutions is shown by the shaded area OABC. Any point in the feasibility area can be expressed by x_1, x_2, s_1, and s_2. For example, let us examine all of the extreme points of the feasibility area and point D, which is within the feasible region, as shown in Figure 4.2.

At point O (the origin), both of the decision variables are zero ($x_1 = 0$, $x_2 = 0$). Substituting these values in the two equalities, we can determine the values of slack variables as follows:

$$3x_1 + 3x_2 + s_1 = 90 \qquad \textit{Assembly Line 1}$$
$$3(0) + 3(0) + s_1 = 90$$
$$s_1 = 90$$

$$2x_1 + 4x_2 + s_2 = 80 \qquad \textit{Assembly Line 2}$$
$$2(0) + 4(0) + s_2 = 80$$
$$s_2 = 80$$

The same approach can be used at all of the other feasible points, as analyzed in Table 4.1. A very important point is revealed in Figure 4.2 and Table 4.1. The

Constraint lines represent maximum bounds

constraint lines represent the maximum possible production possibilities in the two assembly lines. Thus, on any point on line segment BC in Figure 4.2, production would require all of the 90 hours available in Assembly Line 1, and thus $s_1 = 0$. The same logic applies to any solution point on line segment AB. At any point on

Table 4.1   *Analysis of Some Feasible Points*

Feasible Point	Values of Decision Variables	Values of Slack Variables
O	$x_1 = 0, x_2 = 0$	$s_1 = 90, s_2 = 80$
A	$x_1 = 0, x_2 = 20$	$s_1 = 30, s_2 = 0$
B	$x_1 = 20, x_2 = 10$	$s_1 = 0, s_2 = 0$
C	$x_1 = 30, x_2 = 0$	$s_1 = 0, s_2 = 20$
D	$x_1 = 10, x_2 = 10$	$s_1 = 30, s_2 = 20$

$\overline{AB}$, production would require all of the 80 hours available in Assembly Line 2, and thus $s_2 = 0$. Therefore, at point B all available production hours in both assembly lines would be used, and thus $s_1 = 0$, and $s_2 = 0$.

We can also express the objective function in terms of the decision and appropriate slack variables. Since we have introduced two slack variables in the constraints, we must also add them in the objective function. Since slack variables represent unused resources, they contribute nothing to profit. Thus, the objective function becomes:

$$\text{Maximize } Z = 40x_1 + 50x_2 + 0s_1 + 0s_2$$

Now we can formulate the simplex model as follows:

$$\text{Maximize } Z = 40x_1 + 50x_2 + 0s_1 + 0s_2$$
$$\text{subject to} \quad 3x_1 + 3x_2 + s_1 + 0s_2 = 90$$
$$2x_1 + 4x_2 + 0s_1 + s_2 = 80$$
$$x_1, x_2, s_1, s_2 \geq 0$$

Notice in the above model that slack variables must also be nonnegative just like the decision variables because we cannot have negative unused resource amounts in the constraints.

Step 2: Determine the Initial Solution

The initial solution

The Initial Solution We are now ready to start the solution process by determining the first extreme solution point of the linear programming problem. In the simplex method, we initiate the solution procedure from the origin (where we do not produce any product). Since the values of the two decision variables are zero at the origin ($x_1 = 0, x_2 = 0$), the two constraint equalities will be

$$3x_1 + 3x_2 + s_1 + 0s_2 = 90$$
$$3(0) + 3(0) + s_1 + 0s_2 = 90$$
$$s_1 = 90$$

and

$$2x_1 + 4x_2 + 0s_1 + s_2 = 80$$
$$2(0) + 4(0) + 0s_1 + s_2 = 80$$
$$s_2 = 80$$

Table 4.2   The Simplex Tableau

c_b \ c_j	Basis	Solution	x_1	x_2	$\cdots$	s_1	s_2	$\cdots$
	z_j $c_j - z_j$							

c_j = the unit contribution rate associated with each of the variables in the objective function.
c_b = the unit contribution rate of each of the basis variables (variables in the solution basis).
Basis = the variables of the current solution. These variables usually have nonzero values.
Solution = the current solution values of the basic variables.

The basic variable

In the initial solution, the slack variables take on the values shown on the right-hand side. In other words, the only variables with nonzero values are s_1 ($s_1 = 90$) and s_2 ($s_2 = 80$). These nonzero-value variables are often referred to as *basic* or *basis* variables. We will explain this in greater detail later when we use the simplex tableau.

The objective function, then, becomes

$$\text{Total profit } Z = 40x_1 + 50x_2 + 0s_1 + 0s_2$$
$$= 40(0) + 50(0) + 0(90) + 0(80)$$
$$= 0$$

Obviously, the total profit is zero when the production plant is completely idle at Candex.

The simplex tableau

The Simplex Tableau As we discussed earlier, the simplex method is based on an iterative process. It is essential, therefore, to employ a simplified tableau for analysis and iteration. Although many different formats of the simplex tableau have been suggested, the functions of the tableau are basically the same. The simplex tableau we will use is shown in Table 4.2.

In Table 4.2 we can observe the following important points:

1. *The variable columns.*   There are as many variable columns as the number of variables (decision variables, slack variables, etc.). The variable columns are listed in the subscript sequence first for the decision variables and then for the slack variables.

The c_j row

2. *The c_j row.*   The c_j represents the unit contribution rate associated with each variable. We obtain c_j values from the objective function and list them above the variable labels in each of the variable columns.

3. *The* c_b *column*.   The c_b represents the unit contribution rate of each of the basic (basis) variables. The basic variables are those in the solution set. In the initial solution, s_1 and s_2 are the two basic variables.

4. *The basis column*.   The basis column is reserved for listing the basic variables. In our example, s_1 and s_2 are the two basic variables in the initial solution. In the simplex tableau, regardless of its iteration order, there are as many basic variables as the number of model constraints. In our example, we have two constraints. Thus, we have two basic variables in the simplex tableau at each iteration. The nonbasic variables are those that are not in the solution basis. In our example, x_1 and x_2 are not in the solution basis. Thus, x_1 and x_2 are the nonbasic variables. By definition, values

of the nonbasic variables are zero ($x_1 = 0$, $x_2 = 0$ at the initial solution). There are as many nonbasic variables in the simplex tableau as the number of variables less the number of basic variables. In our example problem, we have four variables and two basic variables (two constraints). Thus, the number of nonbasic variables will be $4 - 2 = 2$.

5. *The solution column*.   The solution column is reserved for the solution values of the basic variables. In the initial solution of our example problem, the solution values of the two basic variables are $s_1 = 90$ and $s_2 = 80$. Thus, we list 90 in the s_1 row and 80 in the s_2 row.

The First Simplex Tableau   The first simplex tableau contains the initial solution (solution at the origin) of the linear programming problem. As we found out earlier, in the initial solution $x_1 = 0$, $x_2 = 0$, $s_1 = 90$, and $s_2 = 80$. Since the nonzero-value variables are s_1 and s_2, they are the *basic* variables. Their solution values are 90 for s_1 and 80 for s_2.

The objective function in the simplex model is: Maximize $Z = 40x_1 + 50x_2 +$

$0s_1 + 0s_2$. Thus, we can list c_j values for all of the variables in the simplex tableau accordingly. We can also determine the c_b values, which represent the contribution rates of the basic variables. The two basic variables we determined are s_1 and s_2. Their contribution rates in the objective function are both zero. Now we can list all the information in the simplex tableau, as shown in Table 4.3.

The next step is to list the coefficients of the model variables in the main body of the tableau. The two constraints of the simplex model are

$$3x_1 + 3x_2 + s_1 + 0s_2 = 90$$
$$2x_1 + 4x_2 + 0s_1 + s_2 = 80$$

We list the coefficient of each variable in the appropriate columns and rows. For example, in the first constraint equality the coefficient of x_1 is 3. Thus, it should be listed in the x_1 column of the first row (the s_1 row). All the variable coefficients are listed in Table 4.4.

The coefficients listed in each of the variable columns represent the *marginal*

rates of substitution between the variables headed by the columns and rows. For example, in the x_1 column we have coefficients of 3 and 2 in the s_1 and s_2 rows respectively. In order to produce one unit of x_1 (one Candex A1 camera), we must

Table 4.3 Basic Variables, c_j, and c_b in the Simplex Tableau

c_b	c_j Basis	Solution	40 x_1	50 x_2	0 s_1	0 s_2
0	s_1	90				
0	s_2	80				
	z_j					
	$c_j - z_j$					

Table 4.4 Technical Coefficients in the Simplex Tableau

c_b	c_j Basis	Solution	40 x_1	50 x_2	0 s_1	0 s_2
0	s_1	90	3	3	1	0
0	s_2	80	2	4	0	1
	z_j					
	$c_j - z_j$					

use 3 units of s_1 (3 hours of idle production time in Assembly Line 1) and 2 units of s_2 (2 hours of idle production time in Assembly Line 2). The marginal rates of substitution between x_2 and s_1 and s_2 are 3 and 4 respectively. The marginal rate of substitution between s_1 and s_1 and between s_2 and s_2 will be, of course, 1. Since s_1 and s_2 are not related to each other, their substitution rates are zero.

The next step is to calculate z_j and $c_j - z_j$ values. The z_j and $c_j - z_j$ can be defined as follows:

z_j (solution column): The total profit (or total cost in a minimization problem) of the given solution.

z_j (variable column): The amount of profit lost for each unit of variable that is brought into the solution at the current iteration.

$c_j - z_j$: The *net* increase in profit (or cost in a minimization problem) associated with one unit of each product (variable) that is brought into the solution at the current iteration.

Now we can proceed to calculate values in the z_j row. First, we will calculate the z_j value in the solution column. The z_j value is the sum of c_b times the appropriate solution-column values. For example, we can calculate the z_j (solution) as follows:

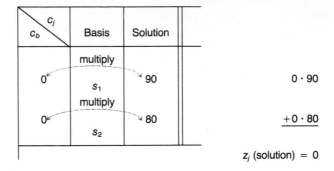

c_b \ c_j	Basis	Solution		
		multiply		
0	s_1	90		$0 \cdot 90$
		multiply		
0	s_2	80		$+0 \cdot 80$
				$z_j \text{ (solution)} = 0$

We can calculate the z_j values in various variable columns by following the same procedure except that we multiply c_b with the coefficients in each column rather than the solution-column values. For example, the z_j value in the x_1 column can be calculated as follows:

c_b \ c_j	Basis	Solution	x_1	
0	s_1	90	3	$0 \cdot 3$
0	s_2	80	2	$+0 \cdot 2$
				$z_j(x_1) = 0$

We can calculate z_j in the x_2 columns in a similar manner:

c_b \ c_j	Basis	Solution	x_1	x_2	
0	s_1	90		3	$0 \cdot 3$
0	s_2	80		4	$+0 \cdot 4$
					$z_j(x_2) = 0$

The same computational procedure is used for $z_j(s_1)$ and $z_j(s_2)$. Now we can list the z_j values in the tableau, as shown in Table 4.5.

Table 4.5 **z_j Values in the Simplex Tableau**

c_b	c_j Basis	Solution	40 x_1	50 x_2	0 s_1	0 s_2
0	s_1	90	3	3	1	0
0	s_2	80	2	4	0	1
	z_j $c_j - z_j$	0	0	0	0	0

We should note here once again that the coefficients listed in each of the variable columns represent the marginal rates of substitution. In order to bring one unit of x_1 into the solution, we need 3 units of s_1 and 2 units of s_2. Thus, the total profit we must give up for producing one unit of x_1 will be: $c_b(s_1) \cdot 3 + c_b(s_2) \cdot 2 = 0 \cdot 3 + 0 \cdot 2 = 0$. In this case, $z_j(x_1) = 0$ because slack variables have zero unit contribution rates. The total profit we must give up in order to bring one unit of a variable into the solution can be regarded as the implicit cost involved in the production process.

The $c_j - z_j$ *values*

$c_j - z_j$ represents the net increase in profit (or cost in a minimization problem) associated with one unit of each product. In the tableau we have the c_j value at the top and the z_j value at the bottom of each column. For example, in the x_1 column a Candex A1 camera brings in $40 profit ($c_1$). At the initial solution, where the firm has idle production time, no profit is lost in producing the Candex A1 camera ($z_1 = 0$). Therefore, the net per-unit profit contribution for Candex A1 is $40. In other words, $c_1 - z_1$ ($c_j - z_j$ in the first variable column) is $40 - 0 = $40, as shown below.

c_b	c_j Basis	Solution	40 x_1		
0	s_1	90	minus		
0	s_2	80			
	z_j $c_j - z_j$	0	0 40		

$$\begin{array}{r} 40 \\ -\ 0 \\ \hline \end{array}$$

$$c_1 - z_1 = 40$$

The same procedure can be applied to all other variable columns. Now we list the $c_j - z_j$ values in the tableau, and the complete initial simplex tableau is presented in Table 4.6.

Table 4.6   The Complete Initial Simplex Tableau

c_b \ c_j	Basis	Solution	40 x_1	50 x_2	0 s_1	0 s_2
0	s_1	90	3	3	1	0
0	s_2	80	2	4	0	1
	z_j	0	0	0	0	0
	$c_j - z_j$		40	50	0	0

Step 3: Test the Optimality

The optimality test

Now that we have completed the initial simplex tableau, we are ready to test the optimality. The optimality test is concerned with ascertaining whether or not the current solution is the optimum solution. This can be accomplished by analyzing the simplex criterion, the $c_j - z_j$ row.

As we discussed earlier, a $c_j - z_j$ value indicates the net per-unit contribution for each variable. If any one of the $c_j - z_j$ values is positive, it implies that we can further improve the total profit. Thus, the current solution is not optimum. On the other hand, if all $c_j - z_j$ values are either zero or negative, the current solution cannot be improved. Thus, we have reached the optimum solution.

The initial solution shown in Table 4.6 is obviously not an optimum solution. We have two positive $c_j - z_j$ numbers in Table 4.6. The x_1 column shows 40 and the x_2 column 50 as their $c_j - z_j$ values.

Step 4: Identify the Incoming Variable

The initial solution we derived for the Candex problem is simply a starting point where total profit is zero. In order to increase profit, Candex must produce some cameras and move out of the origin. The question, then, is not whether or not to move out of the origin, but rather where to move.

The incoming variable

Deciding which product we should introduce into the solution first is the process of identifying the entering variable. Since our objective is profit maximization, the first product we should introduce is the one that would increase total profit at the fastest rate.

The net increase of profit per unit of each product is represented by $c_j - z_j$. Then, the product to be introduced first will be the one with the largest positive value of $c_j - z_j$. Examining Table 4.6, we find that the largest positive $c_j - z_j$ value is $50 in the x_2 column. This indicates that x_2 (Candex ZX cameras) should be produced first in order to increase total profit at the fastest rate.

The pivot column

The column with the largest $c_j - z_j$ (x_2 in this problem) is usually called the *pivot column*. The variable in the pivot column is the incoming variable into the solution basis in the next simplex tableau. Since x_2 is the incoming variable, we will be moving vertically on the x_2 axis from the origin to point A, as shown in Figure 4.3. In other words, in the second solution, Candex will specialize in producing only Candex ZX cameras.

Figure 4.3   The Entering Variable

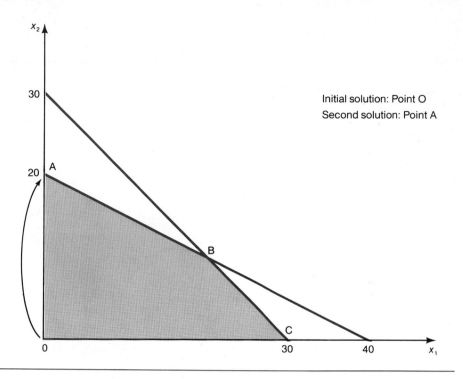

Initial solution: Point O
Second solution: Point A

There are two points we should note concerning the selection procedure of an entering variable. First, we must remember that the basic variables are those that are already in the basis with certain solution values assigned to them. For example, in the initial solution, s_1 and s_2 are the basic variables with solution values of 90 and 80 respectively. Since basic variables are already in the solution, one of them cannot be chosen as an entering variable. Therefore, the entering variable *must* be one of the nonbasic variables that have zero solution values.

The second point, as we can see in Table 4.6, is that all of the basic variable columns (s_1 and s_2 columns) have a $c_j - z_j$ of zero value. This is another reason why one of the nonbasic variables will always be selected as the entering variable.

Step 5: Determine the Outgoing Variable

The Candex problem has two constraints and thus there are only two basic variables. Since x_2 is the variable coming into the solution basis, one of the two basic variables must become zero in value and leave the solution basis.

The outgoing variable

Since we are trying to maximize profit at the fastest rate, we would like to produce as many Candex ZX cameras (x_2) as the constraints allow. Now, let us examine the maximum number of x_2's that can be processed in Assembly Line 1.

Table 4.7   The Pivot Column and the Pivot Row

c_b	c_j Basis	Solution	40 x_1	50 x_2	0 s_1	0 s_2
0	s_1	90	3	3	1	0
0	s_2	80	2	④	0	1
	z_j	0	0	0	0	0
	$c_j - z_j$		40	50	0	0

This maximum number can be determined if we use all of the available resource in Assembly Line 1 to produce only Candex ZX. Thus, we can analyze as follows:

$$3x_1 + 3x_2 + s_1 + 0s_2 = 90 \qquad \textit{Assembly Line 1}$$
$$3(0) + 3x_2 + 0 + 0s_2 = 90$$
$$3x_2 = 90$$
$$x_2 = 30$$

In Assembly Line 1, if we produce only x_2, the maximum number we can process is 30. We can also check the maximum quantity of Candex ZX we can process in Assembly Line 2 as follows:

$$2x_1 + 4x_2 + 0s_1 + s_2 = 80 \qquad \textit{Assembly Line 2}$$
$$2(0) + 4x_2 + 0s_1 + 0 = 80$$
$$4x_2 = 80$$
$$x_2 = 20$$

In Assembly Line 2, we can process up to 20 units of x_2. Since we must use both assembly lines to produce a camera, and Assembly Line 1 can process up to 30 units while Assembly Line 2 can produce only up to 20 units, the maximum number of units of x_2 we can produce is limited to 20.

In Table 4.7, we can see clearly that a unit of x_2 requires 3 hours of s_1 and 4 hours of s_2, as we already know from the marginal rates of substitution. The available idle production hours in the two assembly lines are 90 and 80 respectively, as shown in the solution column. Then, by dividing the solution values of s_1 and s_2 by the marginal substitution rates, we can also determine the maximum number of x_2 (Candex ZX) that each assembly line can produce. The computation is shown below.

Basis	Solution		x_2	
s_1	90	—Divide—	3	$90 \div 3 = 30$
s_2	80	—Divide—	4	$80 \div 4 = 20 \leftarrow$

In order to determine the maximum quantity of a variable that can be introduced to the solution, the only thing we have to do is identify the *minimum nonnegative value* when the solution values are divided by the coefficients (substitution rates) in the pivot column. Thus, the rows with either zero or negative coefficients in the pivot column must be excluded from consideration. This is a very important point to remember.

The pivot row

The row that indicates the minimum nonnegative value is the s_2 row. This is the *pivot row* and s_2 is the outgoing variable. In other words, in the second tableau, x_2 (Candex ZX) comes into the solution basis and it replaces s_2 (idle production time in Assembly Line 2). We can easily see this logic if we substitute $x_2 = 20$ into the two constraint equalities while holding the other variables to zero as follows:

$$3x_1 + 3x_2 + s_1 + 0s_2 = 90 \qquad \text{\textit{Assembly Line 1}}$$
$$3(0) + 3(20) + s_1 + 0s_2 = 90$$
$$60 + s_1 = 90$$
$$s_1 = 30$$

$$2x_1 + 4x_2 + 0s_1 + s_2 = 80 \qquad \text{\textit{Assembly Line 2}}$$
$$2(0) + 4(20) + 0s_1 + s_2 = 80$$
$$80 + s_2 = 80$$
$$s_2 = 0 \leftarrow \text{pivot row}$$

In the first constraint (Assembly Line 1), we will still have 30 hours of idle production time when we produce the maximum possible quantity of 20 units of x_2. In the second constraint (Assembly Line 2), however, we will be using all 80 of the available production hours, and thus $s_2 = 0$. When a variable has a zero value, it is relegated to a nonbasic variable. Now we know why x_2 comes into the solution basis and replaces s_2.

In Figure 4.4 we can reinforce our analysis. At the initial solution (the origin), we know that $x_1 = 0$ and $x_2 = 0$, and thus $s_1 = 90$ and $s_2 = 80$. When the incoming variable x_2 comes into the solution basis and replaces s_2, the new solution is at point A. At point A, we are on the maximum possible production line for the second constraint. Thus, we will be using all of the available resources in Assembly Line 2, and consequently $s_2 = 0$. However, point A is below the maximum possible production line for the first constraint. Hence, $s_1 > 0$. In fact, the exact value of $s_1 = 30$.

In Figure 4.4 we can easily see the change in the basic variables at solution points O and A. For the second solution (point A), the incoming variable is x_2 and the outgoing variable is s_2.

Step 6: Develop a New Solution

In order to develop the second solution, let us refer to Table 4.7, which indicates the *pivot column* and the *pivot row* by red numbers. The variable in the pivot column (x_2) is the incoming variable, and the variable in the pivot row (s_2) is the outgoing variable. The coefficient at the intersection of the pivot column and the pivot row is called the *pivot element*.

The pivot element

Then, in the second simplex tableau the first thing we should do is substitute x_2 for s_2. The unit contribution rate (c_j) of x_2 is \$50. This figure is entered as c_b for x_2 in Table 4.8.

Figure 4.4   The Incoming and Outgoing Variables for the Second Solution

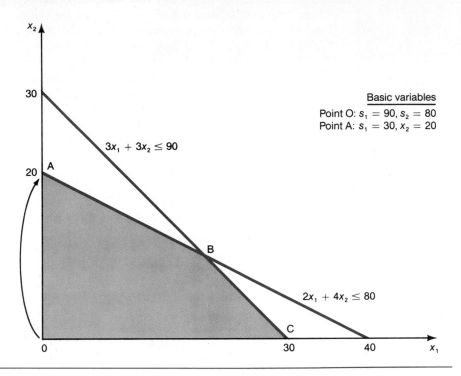

Basic variables
Point O: $s_1 = 90$, $s_2 = 80$
Point A: $s_1 = 30$, $x_2 = 20$

$3x_1 + 3x_2 \leq 90$

$2x_1 + 4x_2 \leq 80$

Table 4.8   The Partially Completed Second Simplex Tableau

c_b \ c_j	Basis	Solution	40 x_1	50 x_2	0 s_1	0 s_2
0	s_1					
50	x_2	20	1/2	1	0	1/4

Now we proceed to find new values in the pivot row (the x_2 row). The new solution value for x_2 is 20, as we explained in the pivot operation in Step 5. The procedure we used was to divide the old solution value (80) of s_2 by the *pivot element*. To find the new coefficients in the x_2 row (the pivot row in the initial simplex tableau), the same pivoting procedure should be used. For example, the initial tableau values and the second tableau values of the second row are shown following.

Basis	Solution	x_1	x_2	s_1	s_2

Tableau 1

Basis	Solution	x_1	x_2	s_1	s_2
s_2	80	2	④	0	1

Basis	Solution	x_1	x_2	s_1	s_2

Tableau 2

Basis	Solution	x_1	x_2	s_1	s_2
x_2	20	1/2	1	0	1/4

$$80 \div 4 = 20 \qquad 2 \div 4 = 1/2 \qquad 4 \div 4 = 1 \qquad 0 \div 4 = 0 \qquad 1 \div 4 = 1/4$$

Computing new values for the pivot row

Dividing all row values by the *pivot element* of 4, as shown above, yields new row values. The new values in the x_2 row are also listed in Table 4.8. Now we can write the computational procedure as:

New value (pivot row) = Old value ÷ Pivot element

The next step in completing the second simplex tableau is to calculate new values in the other constraint rows. First, let us calculate the new solution value for the s_1 row. In the initial solution there were 90 hours of idle production time in Assembly Line 1 (s_1). However, when we produce 20 Candex ZX cameras ($x_2 = 20$), the idle production capacity in Assembly Line 1 must be decreased. Since it requires 3 units of s_1 and 4 units of s_2 to produce a Candex ZX, production of 20 Candex ZX cameras will require 60 units of s_1 and 80 units of s_2 (refer to Table 4.7). Therefore, the leftover s_1 after the production of 20 Candex ZX cameras will be $90 - (3 \times 20) = 30$.

Computing new values for other rows

Now, let us have a slow-motion replay of the operation we have just performed. From the 90 units of s_1, which is the old solution value in the initial tableau, we substracted the product of the *row element* (3) and the new solution value in pivot row (20). We can summarize the calculations as follows:

The row element

New value (other rows)

$$= \text{Old value} - (\text{Row element} \times \text{New value in pivot row})$$

In order to maintain consistency, we must use the same procedure for calculating the new coefficients. After a period of practice, you will become so proficient in calculating the new row values that you may not even need a scrap of paper to write out the calculations. However, until that time comes you can use the following easy procedure:

Column	Old Row Value	−	(Row Element	×	New Value in Pivot Row)	=	New Row Value
Solution	90	−	(3	×	20)	=	30
x_1	3	−	(3	×	1/2)	=	3/2
x_2	3	−	(3	×	1)	=	0
s_1	1	−	(3	×	0)	=	1
s_2	0	−	(3	×	1/4)	=	−3/4

Table 4.9   The Complete Second Simplex Tableau

c_b $\diagdown$ c_j	Basis	Solution	40 x_1	50 x_2	0 s_1	0 s_2
0	s_1	30	3/2	0	1	−3/4
50	x_2	20	1/2	1	0	1/4
	z_j	1,000	25	50	0	12.50
	$c_j - z_j$		15	0	0	−12.50

In this procedure, the *row element* is the element at the intersection of the pivot column and the row under consideration (the s_1 row in this case). Thus, each row has its own element as the pivot row has the pivot element. Now we can list the new row values for the s_1 row, as shown in Table 4.9.

Computing the z_j value

Now that we have found all of the new values in the simplex tableau, we can proceed to complete the second simplex tableau, as shown in Table 4.9. The z_j value in the solution column ($1,000) indicates the total profit of the second solution, where we produce 20 Candex ZX cameras and have 30 hours of idle production time in Assembly Line 1.

In order to make sure that you still remember the procedure for calculating z_j values, the following computations are presented:

c_b $\diagdown$ c_j	Basis	Solution	40 x_1	50 x_2	0 s_1	0 s_2
0	s_1	30	3/2	0	1	−3/4
50	x_2	20	1/2	1	0	1/4

$$\begin{array}{c} 0 \cdot 30 \\ \underline{50 \cdot 20} \\ z_j \text{ (solution)} = \$1{,}000 \end{array}$$

$$\begin{array}{c} 0 \cdot 3/2 \\ \underline{50 \cdot 1/2} \\ z_j(x_1) = \$25 \end{array}$$

$$\begin{array}{c} 0 \cdot 0 \\ \underline{50 \cdot 1} \\ z_j(x_2) = \$50 \end{array}$$

$$\begin{array}{c} 0 \cdot 1 \\ \underline{50 \cdot 0} \\ z_j(s_1) = \$0 \end{array}$$

$$\begin{array}{c} 0 \cdot -3/4 \\ \underline{50 \cdot 1/4} \\ z_j(s_2) = \$12.50 \end{array}$$

The z_j and $c_j - z_j$ values are also shown in Table 4.9, which is the complete second simplex tableau. There are two points we should examine in Table 4.9. First, s_1 and x_2 are the basic variables and x_1 and s_2 are the nonbasic variables in the second

The basic-variable column coefficients

solution. In each of the basic-variable columns (x_2 and s_1), there is only one nonzero coefficient, a coefficient of 1 at the intersection of its row and column. For example, at the intersection of the s_1 row and the s_1 column there is a unit (1) coefficient. Also, at the intersection of the x_2 row and the x_2 column there is a coefficient of 1. That is precisely why c_j and z_j values are identical, and thus $c_j - z_j = 0$, in the basic-variable column. Secondly, in the nonbasic-variable column (x_1 and s_2), there usually are a number of nonzero coefficients and thus $c_j - z_j$ values usually are also nonzero.

Before we move on to the next step, let us examine more carefully the second simplex tableau presented in Table 4.9. In the original problem, production of a Candex A1 camera (x_1) required 3 hours in Assembly Line 1 and 2 hours in Assembly Line 2, as shown in Table 4.7. Then, why do we now have coefficients of 3/2 in the s_1 row and 1/2 in the x_2 row in Table 4.9? These coefficients represent the new marginal rates of substitution between x_1 and the basic variables s_1 and x_2.

Examining the simplex tableau

In the second simplex tableau we are producing 20 units of x_2 (Candex ZX cameras) by using 60 hours of s_1 and 80 hours of s_2. Thus, there is no production capacity left over in Assembly Line 2 to produce any x_1, although we still have 30 hours left over in Assembly Line 1. That is why s_2 has been removed from the solution basis while s_1 remains in the solution basis. Now it is obvious that the only way we can produce any x_1 is by sacrificing some units of x_2.

We have idle capacity of 30 hours in Assembly Line 1 ($s_1 = 30$). Therefore, the critical constraint is Assembly Line 2, where we have no slack time left over. A unit of x_1 requires 2 hours and a unit of x_2 requires 4 hours in Assembly Line 2. Therefore, to secure 2 hours that are required to produce one unit of x_1, we must sacrifice 1/2 unit of x_2. This rate of substitution is shown by the coefficient 1/2 in the x_1 column and x_2 row.

How about the coefficient 3/2 in the s_1 row? When we sacrifice 1/2 unit of x_2, we also get back 3/2 hours of production time in Assembly Line 1, as shown below.

Marginal rates of substitution

Production Resource	Time Requirement for One Unit of x_2	Time Recovered when 1/2 Unit of x_2 Is Sacrificed
Assembly Line 1	3 hr.	3/2 hr.
Assembly Line 2	4 hr.	2 hr.

A unit of x_1 requires 3 hours in Assembly Line 1. If we use the 3/2 hours that we get back from sacrificing 1/2 unit of x_2, then the actual use of s_1 required to produce one unit of x_1 will be 3/2 hours (3/2 + 3/2 = 3 hours). Now the whole thing makes sense. The total amount of profit lost when we sacrifice 1/2 unit of x_2 is $1/2 \cdot \$50 = \$25$. Since the unit contribution of x_1 is $40, the net contribution of one unit of x_1 at this solution point is \$15 ($40 - 25 = 15$). This is precisely the $c_j - z_j$ value of the x_1 column.

We can also examine the marginal rates of substitution for the x_2 column. In the x_2 column, we have coefficients of 0 in the s_1 row and 1 in the x_2 row. These coefficients indicate that production of one unit of x_2 requires, at this stage of the simplex solution, 0 unit of s_1 and 1 unit of x_2. In other words, the only way we can produce one additional unit of Candex ZX camera is by sacrificing a Candex ZX we have produced. This same relationship exists for every basic variable.

How about the coefficients in the s_2 row? s_2 is a nonbasic variable. Thus, $s_2 = 0$. s_2 became zero when we produced 20 units of x_2. In order to make $s_2 = 1$, we must sacrifice some units of x_2. A whole unit of x_2 requires 4 hours in Assembly Line 2. Thus, if we want to make $s_2 = 1$, we must sacrifice 1/4 unit of x_2. This coefficient, 1/4, is shown at the intersection of the s_2 column and the x_2 row.

When we sacrifice 1/4 unit of x_2 in order to create one hour of idle production time in Assembly Line 2 ($s_2 = 1$), we also get back 3/4 hour in Assembly Line 1 because a whole unit of x_2 requires 3 hours in Assembly Line 1. The coefficient, $-3/4$, at the intersection of the s_2 column and the s_1 row indicates this relationship. The negative substitution rate shows that the solution value of s_1 will be increased by 3/4 if we make $s_2 = 1$. In other words, if we decide to make $s_2 = 1$, then the solution values of the basic variables will be $s_1 = 30\ 3/4$, $x_2 = 19\ 3/4$.

The net effect of making $s_2 = 1$ will be the lost profit incurred from the sacrifice of 1/4 unit of x_2. Since a whole unit of x_2 contributes \$50, the 1/4 unit of x_2 we sacrifice results in a loss of \$12.50 profit. This lost profit (\$12.50) is shown as the $c_j - z_j$ value in the s_2 column.

Step 7: Test the Optimality and Repeat the Procedure

Now that we have gone through one simplex iteration, we must test the optimality of the solution and repeat the solution procedure, if the solution is not optimal. As we discussed earlier, the optimality test is simply examining whether or not the new solution still has any positive $c_j - z_j$ value. In Table 4.10, there is a positive $c_j - z_j$ value of \$15 in the x_1 column. Thus, the second solution is not optimum.

Repeating the solution procedure

Now we prepare the second iteration by identifying the incoming variable (the pivot column) and the outgoing variable (the pivot row). The pivot column has already been identified. Since the x_1 column is the only column with a positive $c_j - z_j$, it is the pivot column. The incoming variable is x_1. In order to determine the outgoing variable, we divide the solution values of the basic variables by their corresponding coefficients in the pivot column as follows:

Row	Solution Value		Coefficient		
s_1	30	$\div$	3/2	=	20 $\leftarrow$
x_2	20	$\div$	1/2	=	40

Table 4.10   The Pivot Column and Pivot Row in the Second Tableau

c_b	c_j Basis	Solution	40 x_1	50 x_2	0 s_1	0 s_2
0	s_1	30	(3/2)	0	1	$-3/4$
50	x_2	20	1/2	1	0	1/4
	z_j	1,000	25	50	0	12.50
	$c_j - z_j$		15	0	0	-12.50

The minimum nonnegative (i.e., minimum positive or zero) value we find is 20, in the s_1 row. Thus, the pivot row is the s_1 row and s_1 is the outgoing variable. The *pivot element* is 3/2, as identified in Table 4.10.

In order to find new values, we can easily perform the pivot operation as follows:

For the s_1 row (pivot row):

Column	Old Value	÷	Pivot Element	=	New Row Value
Solution	30	÷	3/2	=	20
x_1	3/2	÷	3/2	=	1
x_2	0	÷	3/2	=	0
s_1	1	÷	3/2	=	2/3
s_2	−3/4	÷	3/2	=	−1/2

For the x_2 row:

Column	Old Row Value	−	Row Element	×	New Value in Pivot Row	=	New Row Value
Solution	20	−	(1/2	×	20)	=	10
x_1	1/2	−	(1/2	×	1)	=	0
x_2	1	−	(1/2	×	0)	=	1
s_1	0	−	(1/2	×	2/3)	=	−1/3
s_2	1/4	−	(1/2	×	−1/2)	=	1/2

The new row values are listed in the third simplex tableau shown in Table 4.11. The z_j and $c_j - z_j$ values are determined in a manner similar to the previous two simplex tableaux.

Now that a new solution is found, the simplex procedure is to be repeated: Test the optimality, identify the entering variable, determine the outgoing variable, complete a new solution tableau. When we test the optimality in Table 4.11, it is immediately obvious that there is no positive $c_j - z_j$ value. In the x_1 and x_2 columns, the $c_j - z_j$ values are zero as they are the basic-variable columns. In the nonbasic-variable columns, s_1 and s_2, the $c_j - z_j$ values are negative. Thus, there is no non-basic viarable that can improve the total profit. In other words, we have found the optimum solution.

The optimum solution   The optimum solution is also shown graphically in Figure 4.5. The optimum solution is:

$$x_1 = 20$$
$$x_2 = 10$$
$$Z = \$1,300$$

Since the optimum point B is at the intersecting point of the two constraint lines, there will be no idle resources. Thus, at point B, $s_1 = 0$ and $s_2 = 0$.

Figure 4.5   *The Optimum Solution*

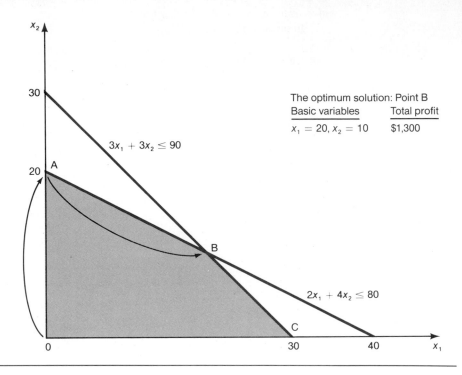

Table 4.11   *The Third Simplex Tableau*

c_b \ c_j	Basis	Solution	40 x_1	50 x_2	0 s_1	0 s_2
40	x_1	20	1	0	2/3	−1/2
50	x_2	10	0	1	−1/3	1/2
	z_j	1,300	40	50	10	5
	$c_j - z_j$		0	0	−10	−5

Step 8: Interpret the Optimum Solution

The linear program solution procedure does not end at simply getting the optimum solution. As we discussed in Chapter 3, we may want to ask a series of "what-if" questions about the stability of the optimum solution in the fickle decision environment.

A detailed discussion of the optimum-solution interpretation will be presented in Chapter 5 when we study duality and complex sensitivity analysis. Here we will limit our discussion to some simple, obvious, but important matters. From the final simplex tableau we can easily identify the following:

	Basic Variables	Nonbasic Variables	Total Profit
Interpreting the optimum solution	$x_1 = 20$	$s_1 = 0$	$Z = \$1,300$
	$x_2 = 10$	$s_2 = 0$	

"How about the two negative $c_j - z_j$ values we see in the s_1 and s_2 columns?" you will ask. That is a very constructive question. The $c_j - z_j$ values are -10 in the s_1 and -5 in the s_2 column respectively. Thus, if we attempt to enter s_1 into the solution basis (i.e., making some production time idle in Assembly Line 1), the total profit will decrease by \$10 per unit of s_1. Similarly, if we introduce s_2 into the solution basis, the total profit will decrease by \$5 per unit of s_2.

Analyzing $c_j - z_j$ in the nonbasic variable column

Now, you may wonder how we get such information. Let us examine the partial tableau of the final solution as shown below:

c_b \\ c_j	Basis	Solution	x_1	x_2	0 s_1	0 s_2
40	x_1	20			2/3	$-1/2$
50	x_2	10			$-1/3$	1/2
	z_j	1,300			10	5
	$c_j - z_j$				-10	-5

When we say that we want to introduce s_1 into the solution, that simply means that we want to pick s_1 as the pivot column. Although we would not pick s_1 as the pivot column because it has a negative $c_j - z_j$, let us assume that we would do this for a test. The rates of substitution between s_1 and the basic variables x_1 and x_2 are 2/3 and $-1/3$. Thus, when we introduce one unit of s_1 into the solution, we have to reduce the solution value of x_1 by 2/3 unit (from 20 to 19-1/3) and also increase the solution value of x_2 by 1/3 unit (from 10 to 10-1/3). A positive substitution rate will decrease the solution value, and a negative substitution rate will increase the solution value for the corresponding basic variables.

Then, in the optimum solution, if we let $s_1 = 1$ (i.e., taking away one production hour in Assembly Line 1 and making only 89 hours available instead of the previous 90 hours), the change in the solution values will be:

$$x_1 = 20 \quad \rightarrow x_1 = 19\ 1/3$$
$$x_2 = 10 \quad \rightarrow x_2 = 10\ 1/3$$
$$Z = 1,300 \quad Z = 1,290$$

The change in the total profit can be more easily calculated by:

Product	Unit Profit	Change in Profit
x_1: decrease of 2/3 unit	\$40	$-80/3$
x_2: increase of 1/3 unit	\$50	$+50/3$
	Net change in profit =	$-\$10$

Figure 4.6   A New Optimum Solution with a Changed Right-hand-side Value of Constraint 1

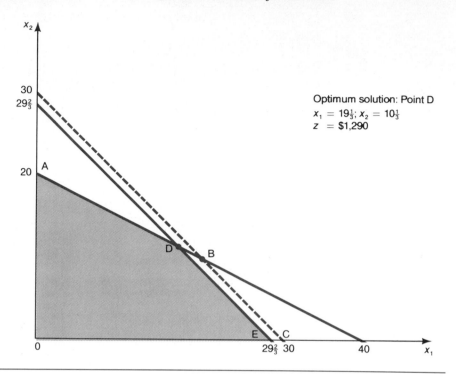

We can easily see the change in solution values in the graph shown in Figure 4.6. Since we are reducing the right-hand-side value of the constraint from 90 to 89 hours, the intercepts of the first constraint will be changed accordingly. Thus, the new feasible region is OADE and the optimum solution will be point D. When we move from point B to point D, the value of x_1 will be decreased by 2/3 and the value of x_2 will be increased by 1/3. We can see these changes clearly in the figure.

We can make a similar interpretation for s_2. If we let $s_2 = 1$, the solution value of x_1 will increase by 1/2 (from 20 to 20 1/2) and the solution value of x_2 will decrease by 1/2 (from 10 to 9 1/2). The net change in total profit will be $-\$5$. The $c_j - z_j$ values of the nonbasic-variable columns are often referred to as *shadow prices*. The reason is that the same $c_j - z_j$ value applies whether we increase or decrease the resource in a given constraint.

The shadow price

For example, if we reduce the available production time in Assembly Line 1 by one hour (from 90 to 89), the total profit will be *decreased* by $10. On the other hand, if we increase the available resource by one unit (from 90 hours to 91 hours), the total profit will be *increased* by the identical $10. Thus, the shadow price is like a mirror image.

Now, suppose Candex is thinking about expanding its production capacity by 2 percent by hiring additional manpower. The question may be raised as to how this manpower increase should be allocated to the two assembly lines. From the analysis of shadow prices in the s_1 and s_2 columns, we can logically conclude that additional manpower must be allocated to Assembly Line 1. If Candex is considering a reduction in production capacity, we also know that the reduction must be initiated in Assembly Line 2.

As we discussed earlier, many organizations (especially notorious are the governmental and nonprofit agencies) often increase or decrease the resources of various departments on an equal proportion basis. For example, if a state government wants to reduce its overall budget by 5 percent, each department is ordered to reduce its budget by 5 percent. Obviously it is assumed that all departments have exactly the same shadow price. This is, of course, a fallacy. Thus, a careful interpretation of the final simplex tableau is a very important part of the linear programming solution process.

Summary of the Simplex Solution Procedure

Now that we have completed our discussion of the simplex solution procedure through the Candex example, let us summarize all the steps we have taken.

Step 1: Develop the Simplex Model We convert all of the linear programming constraints into equalities by introducing appropriate slack variables. The objective function is also modified in such a way that it includes all slack variables.

Step 2: Determine the Initial Solution The initial solution is at the origin. Thus, all of the decision variables have zero values, and the slack variables become the basic variables. The initial simplex tableau is developed at this step and all elements are computed.

Step 3: Test the Optimality The current solution is tested as to whether or not it is optimum. This is accomplished by looking for positive $c_j - z_j$ values. If no positive $c_j - z_j$ is found, the solution is optimum. Go to Step 8. If there exists at least one positive $c_j - z_j$, the solution is not optimum. Continue with the procedure.

Step 4: Identify the Incoming Variable We identify a nonbasic-variable column with the largest positive $c_j - z_j$ value. This is the *pivot column*. The nonbasic variable in this column is the incoming variable.

Step 5: Determine the Outgoing Variable The solution values of the basic variables are divided by the corresponding coefficients in the pivot column. The row that yields the minimum nonnegative value is the *pivot row*. The variable in the pivot row is the outgoing variable.

Step 6: Develop a New Solution The incoming variable replaces the outgoing variable in the solution basis. New values are computed in the following manner:

$$\text{New value (pivot row)} = \text{Old value} \div \text{Pivot element}$$
$$\text{New value (other rows)} =$$
$$\text{Old value} - (\text{Row element} \times \text{New value in pivot row})$$

The z_j and $c_j - z_j$ values are also computed.

Step 7: Test the Optimality and Repeat the Procedure For the new solution that we have derived, we again test the optimality. Thus, this step is simply a return to Step 3.

Step 8: Interpret the Optimal Solution We examine the final simplex tableau and find the optimum solution in terms of the basic variables and their values as well as the total profit derived by the solution. We analyze shadow prices and also perform the appropriate sensitivity analysis.

SIMPLEX SOLUTION OF A PROBLEM WITH MIXED CONSTRAINTS

A problem with mixed constraints

Thus far, we have solved only one type of linear programming problem—a maximization problem with *less than or equal to* type constraints. However, in many real-world problems there are other types of constraints such as *exactly equal to* or *greater than or equal to*. In this section we will tackle one such problem.

EXAMPLE 4.2   *A MAXIMIZATION PROBLEM WITH MIXED CONSTRAINTS*

Let us examine the following simple problem that has all three types of constraints:

$$\text{Maximize } Z = 5x_1 + 7x_2$$
$$\text{subject to} \quad x_1 + 2x_2 = 50$$
$$x_1 \geq 20$$
$$x_2 \leq 20$$
$$x_1, x_2 \geq 0$$

In this problem, the first constraint may be a production constraint. It implies that the second product (x_2) requires twice as much productive resource as the first product (x_1). It also indicates that the firm has 50 units of productive resource, and it must use precisely what it has, no less and no more. Many production process constraints are often *exactly equal to* types, especially those of chemical processes.

The second and third constraints could be sales constraints. If we want to produce and market the first product, we must produce a minimum of 20 units. For the second product, however, the market is quite limited. Thus, the maximum quantity we can produce and sell is limited to 20 units.

The first step of the simplex procedure is to set up a simplex model for the problem. In order to convert all constraints to simplex equalities, let us examine the first constraint.

An equality constraint

We normally start by converting an inequality constraint to an equality function. But the first constraint is already an equality. How should we convert it to an equality? Our first reaction would be to leave it as it is. But we remember, of course, that the initial solution of the simplex method is at the origin, where $x_1 = 0$ and $x_2 = 0$. If we substitute these values into the constraint, we obtain

$$x_1 + 2x_2 = 50$$
$$0 + 2(0) = 50$$
$$0 = 50$$

This result is obviously an unacceptable outcome. First of all, $0 \neq 50$! Thus, the equality does not hold. Clearly, we need to add a variable on the left-hand side of the equality so that we can assign some value to this variable when $x_1 + 2x_2$ is less than 50. We may be tempted to add a slack variable. However, we remember that

Figure 4.7   The Equality Constraint

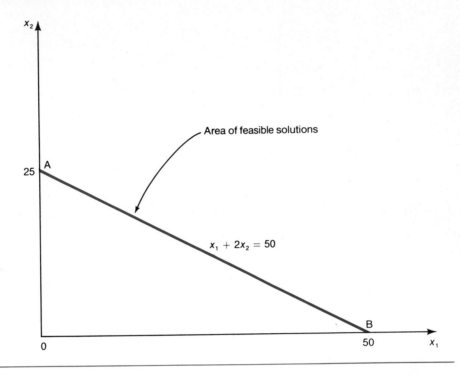

slack variables are used only to satisfy the "<" inequality sign. For example, in Example 4.1 we had a constraint $3x_1 + 3x_2 \leq 90$. In order to convert the inequality into an equality and eliminate the "<" sign, we added a slack variable to derive $3x_1 + 3x_2 + s_1 = 90$.

In the constraint under consideration, $x_1 + 2x_2 = 50$, we do not have an inequality sign to eliminate by adding a slack variable. For cases like this, we need to

The artificial variable

create a new variable, often referred to as an *artificial variable*. With the addition of an artificial variable, the equation becomes

$$x_1 + 2x_2 = 50 \rightarrow x_1 + 2x_2 + A_1 = 50$$

The function of A_1 can be seen in Figure 4.7. Since the constraint equality indicates that solutions must be on the straight line $\overline{AB}$ exactly, this line segment itself represents the area of feasible solutions. However, the initial solution is at the origin. In other words, the initial solution is outside of the area of feasible solutions. In order to facilitate preliminary solutions outside of the feasibility area, we must use

The function of an artificial variable

the artificial variable. For example, at the origin the constraint will be as follows:

$$x_1 + 2x_2 + A_1 = 50$$
$$0 + 2(0) + A_1 = 50$$
$$A_1 = 50$$

At the origin, $x_1 = 0$, $x_2 = 0$, and $A_1 = 50$. Thus, the constraint equality holds.

Figure 4.8   Graphical Presentation of $x_1 \geq 20$

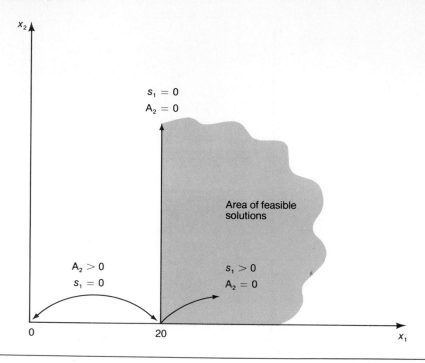

The second constraint of the problem, $x_1 \geq 20$, presents a new difficulty for us. This is the first time we are facing a *greater than or equal to* constraint in conjunction with the simplex method. Since x_1 can be greater than or equal to 20, x_1 can be as much as 100. Knowing that the slack variable is used to remove an inequality sign, we can convert this constraint into an equality by subtracting a slack variable, as $x_1 - s_1 = 20$. Whenever we subtract a slack variable, that variable is usually referred to as a *surplus variable*. The word *surplus* is appropriate in that the variable takes value only when $x_1 > 20$. For example, if $x_1 = 100$, then the equality becomes

The surplus variable

$$x_1 - s_1 = 20$$
$$100 - s_1 = 20$$
$$s_1 = 80$$

The use of s_1 has solved the problem nicely. Or so we thought. There is one more problem. At the initial solution (at the origin), $x_1 = 0$. Therefore, the equality will be

$$x_1 - s_1 = 20$$
$$0 - s_1 = 20$$
$$s_1 = -20$$

Since the nonnegativity constraint applies to all variables, including slack, surplus, and artificial variables, the above situation is unacceptable. Figure 4.8 depicts our predicament. At the origin, the solution is clearly outside of the feasibility area for the second constraint. Then, in order to facilitate preliminary solutions until we get into the area of feasible solutions, we must introduce an artificial variable. Thus, the equality becomes $x_1 - s_1 + A_2 = 20$. At the origin, the equality will be

$$x_1 - s_1 + A_2 = 20$$
$$0 - 0 + A_2 = 20$$
$$A_2 = 20$$

The function of a surplus variable

In this relationship, $s_1 = 0$ at the origin because s_1 can take a positive value only when $x_1 > 20$. This reasoning should be obvious from our previous explanation that a surplus variable is subtracted in order to remove the ">" sign from the relationship $x_1 \geq 20$. Now we can test several points where x_1 takes on different values and see whether or not our new simplex equality holds up.

If $x_1 = 10$,

$$x_1 - s_1 + A_2 = 20$$
$$10 - 0 + A_2 = 20$$
$$A_2 = 10$$

If $x_1 = 20$,

$$x_1 - s_1 + A_2 = 20$$
$$20 - 0 + 0 = 20$$
$$20 = 20$$

If $x_1 = 100$,

$$x_1 - s_1 + A_2 = 20$$
$$100 - s_1 + 0 = 20$$
$$s_1 = 80$$

In these tests, when $x_1 = 20$ the value of A_2 becomes zero, because the solution is now feasible for the $x_1 \geq 20$ constraint. But, since x_1 is not yet greater than 20, s_1 is also zero. When $x_1 = 100$, this solution is feasible and thus $A_2 = 0$. However, since $x_2 > 20$, s_1 takes a positive value. Figure 4.8 explains our reasoning quite clearly.

It is very easy to convert the third constraint of the problem, $x_2 \leq 20$, into a simplex equality. Simply by adding a slack variable, we can generate an equality $x_2 + s_2 = 20$.

Before we move along too far, we should restate the conditions needed for the use of a slack, surplus, or an artificial variable:

Type of Variable	Purpose
A slack or a surplus variable	To remove an inequality sign ($<$ or $>$) and create an equality relationship
An artificial variable	To facilitate preliminary solutions outside the feasibility area for the given constraint

We can further summarize the conversion process for linear programming constraints into simplex equalities as follows:

Type of Constraint	Adjustment Required
Less than or equal to ($\leq$)	Add a slack variable
Exactly equal to ($=$)	Add an artificial variable
Greater than or equal to ($\geq$)	Subtract a surplus variable and add an artificial variable

We are now about ready to formulate the complete simplex model. "It's about time," you will probably say. But we are not quite there as yet. In the objective function, we must also include all the variables in the constraint equalities. There is no problem in assigning a zero c_j value to the slack or surplus variable. But how about the artificial variable? If we assign a zero value to c_j, it is possible that the artificial variable may be in the solution basis of the optimum solution. What we do not want or need is to have an artificial variable in the final solution.

The artificial variable in the objective function

One way we can be assured of an optimum solution without an artificial variable is by assigning a very large negative c_j value to the artificial variable. In this way the artificial variable becomes so costly that we may never end up with it in the final solution. This approach is known as the *big M method* because the c_j value assigned to the artificial variable is a large negative-value M (negative million or billion dollars, let us say).

The big M method

Now we are finally ready to formulate a simplex model for the problem as follows:

$$\text{Maximize } Z = 5x_1 + 7x_2 + 0s_1 + 0s_2 - MA_1 - MA_2$$
$$\text{subject to} \quad x_1 + 2x_2 + A_1 = 50$$
$$x_1 - s_1 + A_2 = 20$$
$$x_2 + s_2 = 20$$
$$x_1, x_2, s_1, s_2, A_1, A_2 \geq 0$$

In the initial solution, we are once again at the origin ($x_1 = 0$, $x_2 = 0$). The three simplex equalities will be

$$x_1 + 2x_2 + A_1 = 50 \qquad \textit{Constraint 1}$$
$$0 + 2(0) + A_1 = 50$$
$$A_1 = 50$$

$$x_1 - s_1 + A_2 = 20 \qquad \textit{Constraint 2}$$
$$0 - 0 + A_2 = 20$$
$$A_2 = 20$$

$$x_2 + s_2 = 20 \qquad \textit{Constraint 3}$$
$$0 + s_2 = 20$$
$$s_2 = 20$$

The basic variables are A_1, A_2, and s_2. You should take notice here that whenever there is an artificial variable in a simplex equality, it becomes a basic variable and consequently appears in the solution basis in the initial solution. The solution values for A_1, A_2, and s_2 are 50, 20, and 20 respectively. They are listed in the appropriate column in Table 4.12.

In the initial tableau, z_j values are computed in the usual manner. For example, in the solution column, z_j is calculated as follows:

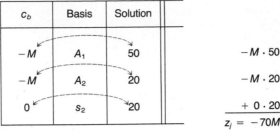

c_b	Basis	Solution	
$-M$	A_1	50	$-M \cdot 50$
$-M$	A_2	20	$-M \cdot 20$
0	s_2	20	$+ 0 \cdot 20$
			$z_j = -70M$

The z_j values in the variable columns are calculated in a similar fashion.

The $c_j - z_j$ values are also computed in the usual manner. For example, in the x_1 column, c_j is 5 and z_j is $-2M$. Therefore, $c_1 - z_1 = 5 - (-2M) = 5 + 2M$. Then, $c_j - z_j$ for the x_2 column will be $c_2 - z_2 = 7 - (-2M) = 7 + 2M$.

In Table 4.12 we can easily identify the pivot column and the pivot row. The pivot column is the x_2 column, since it has the largest $c_j - z_j$ value. Thus, the incoming variable is x_2. In order to determine the pivot row, we divide the solution values by each of the corresponding coefficients. As we discussed earlier, we can use only *positive* coefficients. The minimum nonnegative value of 20 is found in the s_2 row. Hence, this is the pivot row, and s_2 is the outgoing variable.

In Table 4.13 we find the second solution to the problem. In completing the second simplex tableau, you might use the following helpful tips:

Pivot Row: (1) s_2 is replaced by x_2.
   (2) c_b is now 7 instead of $-M$.
   (3) Since all row values are divided by the pivot element 1, the new values will be the same as the old ones.

A_1 Row: (1) Find new row values by
   Old value $-$ (Row element $\times$ New value in pivot row)
   (2) The old row values will remain the same in those columns where there is zero value in the pivot row.

A_2 Row: (1) Since the row element of the A_2 row is zero, the old row values will remain the same in the new tableau.

Eliminating the outgoing artificial variable

In Table 4.13 we can easily identify the x_1 column as the pivot column and the A_1 row as the pivot row. In Table 4.14, which presents the third solution, we notice that the A_1 column has been completely eliminated from the tableau. When an artificial variable is replaced by either a decision, slack, or surplus variable in the solution basis, that artificial variable is no longer needed in the simplex operation. This is completely logical because the artificial variable is used only to facilitate preliminary solutions outside of the feasible area for a given constraint. When an artificial variable is being kicked out of the solution, we know immediately that the new solution is now in the feasible solution area for the constraint.

For example, in the first constraint, A_1 is replaced by x_1 in Table 4.14. The quantity of x_1 being produced is 10, and x_2 has 20 units in the third solution. The

Table 4.12   *The Initial Solution for the Mixed Constraint Problem*

c_b	c_j Basis	Solution	5 x_1	7 x_2	0 s_1	0 s_2	$-M$ A_1	$-M$ A_2
$-M$	A_1	50	1	2	0	0	1	0
$-M$	A_2	20	1	0	-1	0	0	1
0	s_2	20	0	①	0	1	0	0
	z_j	$-70M$	$-2M$	$-2M$	M	0	$-M$	$-M$
	$c_j - z_j$		$5 + 2M$	$7 + 2M$	$-M$	0	0	0

Table 4.13   *The Second Solution for the Mixed Constraint Problem*

c_b	c_j Basis	Solution	5 x_1	7 x_2	0 s_1	0 s_2	$-M$ A_1	$-M$ A_2
$-M$	A_1	10	①	0	0	-2	1	0
$-M$	A_2	20	1	0	-1	0	0	1
7	x_2	20	0	1	0	1	0	0
	z_j	$140 - 30M$	$-2M$	7	M	$2M + 7$	$-M$	$-M$
	$c_j - z_j$		$5 + 2M$	0	$-M$	$-2M - 7$	0	0

Table 4.14   *The Third Solution for the Mixed Constraint Problem*

c_b	c_j Basis	Solution	5 x_1	7 x_2	0 s_1	0 s_2	$-M$ A_2
5	x_1	10	1	0	0	-2	0
$-M$	A_2	10	0	0	-1	②	1
7	x_2	20	0	0	1	0	1	0
	z_j	$190 - 10M$	5	7	M	$-3 - 2M$	$-M$
	$c_j - z_j$		0	0	$-M$	$3 + 2M$	0

Table 4.15   *The Fourth Solution for the Mixed Constraint Problem*

c_b	c_j Basis	Solution	5 x_1	7 x_2	0 s_1	0 s_2
5	x_1	20	1	0	-1	0
0	s_2	5	0	0	$-1/2$	1
7	x_2	15	0	1	①/2	0
	z_j	205	5	7	-1.5	0
	$c_j - z_j$		0	0	1.5	0

Table 4.16   The Optimum Solution for the Mixed Constraint Problem

c_b	c_j / Basis	Solution	5 x_1	7 x_2	0 s_1	0 s_2
5	x_1	50	1	2	0	0
0	s_2	20	0	1	0	1
0	s_1	30	0	2	1	0
	z_j	250	5	10	0	0
	$c_j - z_j$		0	-3	0	0

Figure 4.9   The Mixed Constraint Problem

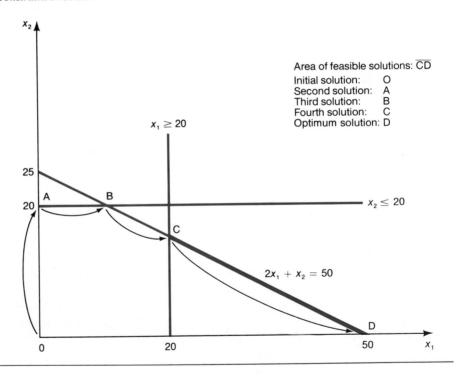

Area of feasible solutions: $\overline{CD}$

Initial solution: O
Second solution: A
Third solution: B
Fourth solution: C
Optimum solution: D

$x_1 \geq 20$

$x_2 \leq 20$

$2x_1 + x_2 = 50$

first constraint of the problem, $x_1 + 2x_2 = 50$, suggests that the left-hand side should be exactly equal to 50. Since we began the solution at the origin, we needed A_1 until we moved up to the equation line $x_1 + 2x_2 = 50$. Now, however, we no longer need A_1 as we are on this line (the feasibility area). In subsequent iterations, we will not and cannot go back into an infeasible area for the constraint. Thus, we can eliminate A_1 from the tableau.

Table 4.15 presents the fourth solution. Since A_2 is replaced by s_2, we eliminated the A_2 column in the tableau. The optimum solution, derived in Table 4.16, is: $x_1 = 50$, $x_2 = 0$, $s_1 = 30$, $s_2 = 20$, and $Z = \$250$. The simplex solution process of the problem can be seen clearly in Figure 4.9.

SIMPLEX SOLUTION OF A MINIMIZATION PROBLEM

Thus far, we have solved two maximization problems by the simplex method. The same solution procedure can be applied to minimization problems. Let us review the minimization problem we formulated and solved graphically in Chapter 3 as Casette 3.2.

EXAMPLE 4.3

A minimization problem

DIET PROBLEM OF THE FRESHMEN ORIENTATION PROGRAM

This problem is concerned with the determination of scoops of scrambled eggs and the number of smokie sausages to serve for breakfast in order to meet vitamin A, vitamin B, and iron requirements while minimizing the cost per serving. The problem was formulated as

$$\text{Minimize } Z = 8x_1 + 10x_2$$

$$
\begin{aligned}
\text{subject to} \quad 3x_1 + 3x_2 &\geq 30 & \textit{Vitamin A}\\
4x_1 + 2x_2 &\geq 24 & \textit{Vitamin B}\\
x_1 + 2x_2 &\geq 12 & \textit{Iron}\\
x_1, x_2 &\geq 0
\end{aligned}
$$

where, x_1 = number of scoops of scrambled eggs served

  x_2 = number of smokies served

The first step of the simplex solution procedure is, of course, to formulate a simplex model by introducing appropriate slack, surplus, and/or artificial variables. Since the problem has three *greater than or equal to* constraints, we need to subtract a surplus variable and add an artificial variable in each of the constraints as follows:

$$
\begin{aligned}
3x_1 + 3x_2 - s_1 + A_1 &= 30\\
4x_1 + 2x_2 - s_2 + A_2 &= 24\\
x_1 + 2x_2 - s_3 + A_3 &= 12
\end{aligned}
$$

A positive M *value to the artificial variable*

In a maximization problem, we assign a large negative c_j value, $-M$, to the artificial variable in the model. In a minimization problem, on the other hand, we must assign to the artificial variable a large positive M as a c_j value. Since we are trying to minimize total cost, the positive M value assigned to the artificial variable would make it very costly, and thus the procedure assures us a final solution without the artificial variable. Now, the simplex model is formulated as:

$$\text{Minimize } Z = 8x_1 + 10x_2 + 0s_1 + 0s_2 + 0s_3 + MA_1 + MA_2 + MA_3$$

$$
\begin{aligned}
\text{subject to} \quad 3x_1 + 3x_2 - s_1 + A_1 &= 30\\
4x_1 + 2x_2 - s_2 + A_2 &= 24\\
x_1 + 2x_2 - s_3 + A_3 &= 12\\
x_1, x_2, s_1, s_2, s_3, A_1, A_2, A_3 &\geq 0
\end{aligned}
$$

The first solution is at the origin, where we do not provide any eggs or sausage for breakfast. Thus, we can easily determine the basic variables in the first simplex tableau as:

$$
\begin{aligned}
3x_1 + 3x_2 - s_1 + A_1 &= 30 & \textit{Constraint 1}\\
3(0) + 3(0) - 0 + A_1 &= 30\\
A_1 &= 30
\end{aligned}
$$

Table 4.17 **The Initial Solution of the Diet Problem**

c_j / c_b	Basis	Solution	8 x_1	10 x_2	0 s_1	0 s_2	0 s_3	M A_1	M A_2	M A_3
M	A_1	30	3	3	−1	0	0	1	0	0
M	A_2	24	④	2	0	−1	0	0	1	0
M	A_3	12	1	2	0	0	−1	0	0	1
	z_j	66M	8M	7M	−M	−M	−M	M	M	M
	$z_j - c_j$		8M − 8	7M − 10	−M	−M	−M	0	0	0

$$4x_1 + 2x_2 - s_2 + A_2 = 24 \qquad \textit{Constraint 2}$$
$$4(0) + 2(0) - 0 + A_2 = 24$$
$$A_2 = 24$$

$$x_1 + 2x_2 - s_3 + A_3 = 12 \qquad \textit{Constraint 3}$$
$$0 + 2(0) - 0 + A_3 = 12$$
$$A_3 = 12$$

$z_j - c_j$ *replaces* $c_j - z_j$

With the simplex knowledge we have gained, it is now a simple task to complete the initial tableau presented in Table 4.17. You will notice one obvious change in the simplex tableau. We reversed the simplex criteria from $c_j - z_j$ to $z_j - c_j$. By reversing the computation procedure, we can still identify the pivot column by selecting a nonbasic-variable column with the *largest positive* $z_j - c_j$. Also, the $z_j - c_j$ value in each of the nonbasic-variable columns represents the net per-unit decrease of cost for each corresponding variable. The pivot column is the x_1 column and the pivot row is the A_2 row, as identified in Table 4.17.

The second simplex tableau is obtained in Table 4.18. Since A_2 was replaced by x_1 in the solution basis, we can eliminate the A_2 column. The second solution is an infeasible solution because we still have artificial variables in the basis. Also, it is not an optimum solution because we still have positive $z_j - c_j$ values in some of the

Table 4.18 **The Second Solution of the Diet Problem**

c_j / c_b	Basis	Solution	8 x_1	10 x_2	0 s_1	0 s_2	0 s_3	M A_1	M A_3
M	A_1	12	0	3/2	−1	3/4	0	1	0
8	x_1	6	1	1/2	0	−1/4	0	0	0
M	A_3	6	0	③/2	0	1/4	−1	0	1
	z_j	18M + 48	8	3M + 4	−M	M − 2	−M	M	M
	$z_j - c_j$		0	3M − 6	−M	M − 2	−M	0	0

Table 4.19   The Third Solution of the Diet Problem

c_b \\ c_j	Basis	Solution	8 x_1	10 x_2	0 s_1	0 s_2	0 s_3	M A_1
M	A_1	6	0	0	−1	1/2	①	1
8	x_1	4	1	0	0	−1/3	1/3	0
10	x_2	4	0	1	0	1/6	−2/3	0
	z_j	6M + 72	8	10	−M	1/2 M − 1	M − 4	M
	$z_j − c_j$		0	0	−M	1/2 M − 1	M − 4	0

Table 4.20   The Fourth Solution of the Diet Problem

c_b \\ c_j	Basis	Solution	8 x_1	10 x_2	0 s_1	0 s_2	0 s_3
0	s_3	6	0	0	−1	⑴/2	1
8	x_1	2	1	0	1/3	−1/2	0
10	x_2	8	0	1	−2/3	1/2	0
	z_j	96	8	10	−4	1	0
	$z_j − c_j$		0	0	−4	1	0

Table 4.21   The Final Solution of the Diet Problem

c_b \\ c_j	Basis	Solution	8 x_1	10 x_2	0 s_1	0 s_2	0 s_3
0	s_2	12	0	0	−2	1	2
8	x_1	8	1	0	−2/3	0	1
10	x_2	2	0	1	1/3	0	−1
	z_j	84	8	10	−2	0	−2
	$z_j − c_j$		0	0	−2	0	−2

nonbasic-variable columns. The incoming variable is x_2 and the outgoing variable is A_3.

The third solution is presented in Table 4.19. This solution is still infeasible because A_1 remains in the solution basis. The fourth solution, shown in Table 4.20, indicates that it is a feasible solution because all artificial variables have been eliminated from the solution basis. However, this solution is not an optimum solution because there exists a positive $z_j − c_j$ value in the s_2 column. One more iteration gives us the final solution, as shown in Table 4.21. The nonbasic-variable columns

Figure 4.10   The Diet Problem Solution Process

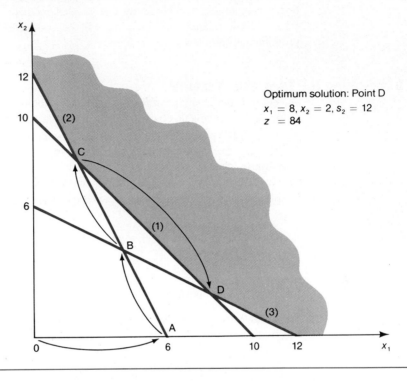

Optimum solution: Point D
$x_1 = 8, x_2 = 2, s_2 = 12$
$z = 84$

(s_1 and s_3) indicate negative $z_j - c_j$ values. Thus, we have reached the optimum solution. The simplex solution process is graphically presented in Figure 4.10.

The optimum solution   The optimum solution to the diet problem is $x_1 = 8$, $x_2 = 2$, $s_2 = 12$, and $Z = 84¢$. This solution corresponds with the solution we derived in Chapter 3 by the graphical method. The dietitians should provide 8 scoops of scrambled eggs and 2 smokies for breakfast with the per-serving cost of 84¢. Since s_1 and s_3 are nonbasic variables, we know that the breakfast does not provide any surplus vitamin A and iron requirements. In other words, the breakfast will provide precisely the minimum requirements of 30 mg. of vitamin A and 12 mg. of iron. However, since $s_2 = 12$ in the solution base, the breakfast provides 12 mg. beyond the minimum requirement of 24 mg. of vitamin B. Thus, the total vitamin B content of the breakfast would be 36 mg.

Shadow prices   Another interesting piece of information we can derive from the final simplex tableau is that the shadow prices of s_1 and s_3 are identical, -2. Thus, if we can decrease the minimum requirement of vitamin A from 30 mg. to 29 mg., the cost of the breakfast can be reduced by 2¢ (from 84¢ to 82¢). Similarly, if the minimum requirement of iron is reduced by 1 mg. (from 12 mg. to 11 mg.), the cost of the breakfast will decrease by 2¢. If, on the other hand, the minimum requirement for vitamin A or iron is increased by 1 mg., the per-serving cost of the breakfast will increase by 2¢.

SOME UNIQUE SITUATIONS

Unique situations
There are several unique situations that might give us some trouble when solving linear programming problems by the simplex method. Once we learn how to take care of these unique situations, we will be completely ready to tackle any linear programming problem.

Tie in Selecting the Incoming Variable

Selection of the incoming variable or the pivot column is based on the $c_j - z_j$ value of the nonbasic-variable columns. If two or more nonbasic-variable columns have the identical largest $c_j - z_j$ (or $z_j - c_j$ in a minimization problem) value, we have a tie in selecting the incoming variable. When we are faced with such a situation, the selection of the incoming variable can be made arbitrarily. Selection of one of the tied variable columns will carry us eventually to the optimum solution. To minimize the number of iterations required to reach the optimum solution, the following simple steps would be helpful:

Step 1 If there is a tie between two decision variable columns, selection can be made arbitrarily.

Step 2 If there is a tie between a decision variable and a slack (or surplus) variable, the decision variable should be selected as the incoming variable.

Step 3 If there is a tie between two slack (or surplus) variables, again, the choice can be made arbitrarily.

Tie in Selecting the Outgoing Variable (Degeneracy)

To determine the outgoing variable or the pivot row, the solution values of the basic variables are divided by the coefficients in the pivot column. Then, the row with the minimum nonnegative value is selected. The occurrence of two or more basic-variable rows with identical minimum nonnegative values presents the problem of *degeneracy*.

The degeneracy

The degeneracy case can be best explained by an example. Suppose we have the following linear programming problem:

$$\text{Maximize } Z = 80x_1 + 70x_2$$
$$\text{subject to} \quad 2x_1 + x_2 \leq 120$$
$$x_1 \quad\quad \leq 70$$
$$x_1 + x_2 \leq 60$$
$$x_1, x_2 \geq 0$$

We can easily determine the initial solution as shown in Table 4.22. The pivot column is the x_1 column because it has the largest positive $c_j - z_j$. When we divide the solution values by the coefficients in the pivot column, we find a tie between the s_1 and s_3 rows as candidates for the pivot row. If we select the s_1 row as the pivot row, the second solution can be obtained as shown in Table 4.23.

Zero solution values

In the second solution, the basic variable s_3 has a solution value of zero. As we discussed earlier, only nonbasic variables are to have zero solution values. In the case of degeneracy, however, a basic variable with zero value remains in the solution basis. This fact does not present any serious problem. The case of degeneracy in the

Table 4.22   The Initial Solution of the Degeneracy Case

c_b	c_j Basis	Solution	80 x_1	70 x_2	0 s_1	0 s_2	0 s_3
0	s_1	120	2	1	1	0	0
0	s_2	70	1	0	0	1	0
0	s_3	60	1	1	0	0	1
	z_j	0	0	0	0	0	0
	$c_j - z_j$		80	70	0	0	0

Table 4.23   The Second Solution of the Degeneracy Case

c_b	c_j Basis	Solution	80 x_1	70 x_2	0 s_1	0 s_2	0 s_3
80	x_1	60	1	1/2	1/2	0	0
0	s_2	10	0	−1/2	−1/2	1	0
0	s_3	0	0	(1/2)	−1/2	0	1
	z_j	480	80	40	40	0	0
	$c_j - z_j$		0	30	−40	0	0

two-variable case can occur any time a combination of three constraints and/or axes meet at an extreme point. For example, in Figure 4.11 we can see clearly that the first and third constraint lines and the x_1 axis intersect at an extreme point A ($x_1 =$ 60, $x_2 = 0$).

The problem of degeneracy

Theoretically, it is possible that a degeneracy problem can generate an indefinite number of iterations without improving the solution. Fortunately, in most real-world problems only rarely do we face any difficulty with degeneracy.

Multiple Optimum Solutions

A case of multiple optimum solutions involves a situation where the slope of the iso-profit function (or the iso-cost function in a minimization problem) is identical to the slope of a constraint that forms the area of feasible solutions. Let us examine the following problem with multiple optimum solutions:

$$\text{Maximize } Z = 60x_1 + 60x_2$$
$$\text{subject to} \quad 3x_1 + 3x_2 \leq 90$$
$$2x_1 + 4x_2 \leq 80$$
$$x_1, x_2 \geq 0$$

134

Figure 4.11   A Case of Degeneracy

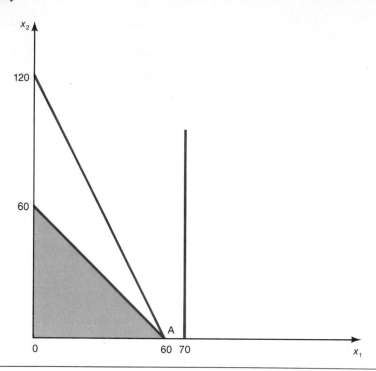

This problem is illustrated graphically in Figure 4.12. The slope of the iso-profit function is -1. Thus, the optimum solution is the line segment $\overline{BC}$. Consequently, we have a case with multiple optimum solutions.

When we solve a linear programming problem by the simplex method, we cannot examine the slopes as such. However, there is another way we can detect a case

Multiple optimum solutions

of multiple optimum solutions. Let us consider the final simplex solution to the above problem, as shown in Table 4.24. Since there is no positive $c_j - z_j$ value, the optimum solution has been found, and thus the simplex procedure is terminated. The

Zero $c_j - z_j$ in a nonbasic-variable column

usual final simplex solution yields zero $c_j - z_j$ values in all basic-variable columns and negative $c_j - z_j$ values in all nonbasic-variable columns. However, the x_2 column, which is a nonbasic-variable column, indicates a zero $c_j - z_j$ value.

We recall that a $c_j - z_j$ value represents the per-unit profit increase for a nonbasic variable. Since $c_j - z_j$ is zero for a nonbasic-variable s_2, entering s_2 in the solution will yield a different solution with the same total profit. For example, the new solution is shown in Table 4.25. The decision maker now has the option of deciding which optimum solution to implement on the basis of noneconomic factors.

Negative Right-hand-side Value

It is possible for a constraint to have a negative right-hand-side (rhs) value. Since the solution value for the basic variable must be nonnegative, the simplex method requires nonnegative rhs value. Let us consider the following constraint:

$$2x_1 - x_2 + 3x_3 \leq -10$$

Figure 4.12   A Problem with Multiple Optimum Solutions

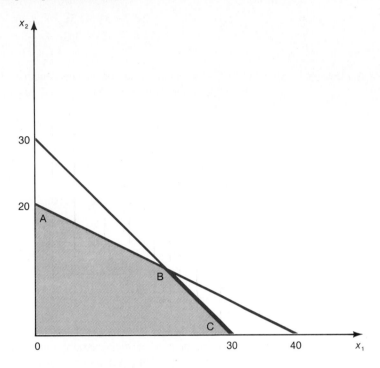

Table 4.24   A Problem with Multiple Optimum Solutions

c_b	c_j Basis	Solution	60 x_1	60 x_2	0 s_1	0 s_2
60	x_1	20	1	0	2/3	−1/2
60	x_2	10	0	1	−1/3	1/2
	z_j	1,800	60	60	20	0
	$c_j - z_j$		0	0	−20	0

Table 4.25   An Alternate Optimum Solution

c_b	c_j Basis	Solution	60 x_1	60 x_2	0 s_1	0 s_2
60	x_1	30	1	1	1/3	0
0	s_2	20	0	2	−2/3	1
	z_j	1,800	60	60	20	0
	$c_j - z_j$		0	0	−20	0

In the initial solution, $x_1 = 0$, $x_2 = 0$, and $x_3 = 0$. Thus, the simplex equality will be

$$2x_1 - x_2 + 3x_3 + s_1 = -10$$
$$2(0) - 0 + 3(0) + s_1 = -10$$
$$s_1 = -10$$

A negative right-hand-side value

Since $s_1 \geq 0$, the above condition is unacceptable. This problem can be easily re-solved by multiplying both sides by -1 and handling the constraint in the initial solution as follows:

$$2x_1 - x_2 + 3x_3 \leq -10$$
$$-2x_1 + x_2 - 3x_3 \geq 10 \text{ (multiplying both sides by } -1)$$
$$-2x_1 + x_2 - 3x_3 - s_1 + A_1 = 10$$
$$-2(0) + 0 - 3(0) - 0 + A_1 = 10$$
$$A_1 = 10$$

An Infeasible Problem

A problem is infeasible when it has conflicting or mutually exclusive constraints. Such a problem is simple to identify if it involves only two decision variables because we can plot the constraints graphically.

An infeasible problem

When we use the simplex method, an infeasible problem is not that easily detected, especially for large-scale problems. When a problem is completely solved by the simplex method, the final simplex tableau indicates zero or negative $c_j - z_j$ values. But if one or more artificial variables are in the solution basis, it is an infeasible problem. However, if the problem is degenerate (involving a tie in selecting the outgoing variable) and the artificial variable in the solution basis has a zero value, it is not an infeasible problem.

For example, let us consider the following problem:

$$\text{Minimize } Z = 10x_1 + 8x_2$$
$$\text{subject to} \quad 2x_1 + 2x_2 \leq 6$$
$$x_1 + 2x_2 \geq 10$$
$$x_1, x_2 \geq 0$$

The problem is illustrated graphically in Figure 4.13. Since the two constraints do not overlap, there is no feasible region. Thus, this problem is infeasible and cannot be solved by linear programming.

The final simplex solution tableau for the problem is shown in Table 4.26. Since the $c_j - z_j$ values of all the nonbasic-variable columns are negative, it is the final simplex tableau. However, an artificial variable A_1 is still in the basis with a solution value of 4. Thus, this is an infeasible problem.

An Unbounded Problem

An unbounded problem

If a maximization problem is unbounded, total profit can increase indefinitely without a bound. When we use the simplex method, the solution procedure continues for a while until the unbounded condition becomes obvious. Suppose we select a pivot column (the column with the largest positive $c_j - z_j$ value). The next step is to determine the pivot row (the row with the minimum nonnegative value when the solution values are divided by the positive coefficients in the pivot column). If the

Figure 4.13 An Infeasible Problem

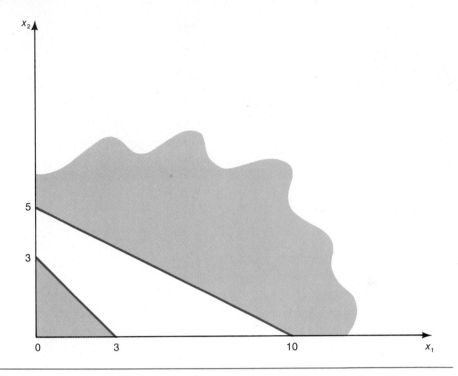

Table 4.26 Simplex Solution of an Infeasible Problem

c_b \ c_j	Basis	Solution	10 x_1	8 x_2	0 s_1	0 s_2	M A_1
8	x_2	3	1	1	1/2	0	0
M	A_1	4	-1	0	-1	-1	-1
	z_j	$24 + 4M$	$8 - M$	8	$4 - M$	$-M$	M
	$z_j - c_j$		$-2 - M$	0	$4 - M$	$-M$	0

pivot column has only zero or negative coefficients, there is no pivot row. Thus, the problem can be detected as unbounded.

For example, let us consider the following unbounded problem:

$$\text{Maximize } Z = 20x_1 + 30x_2$$
$$\text{subject to } \quad -4x_1 + 4x_2 \leq 32$$
$$x_2 \leq 12$$
$$x_1, x_2 \geq 0$$

Figure 4.14   An Unbounded Problem

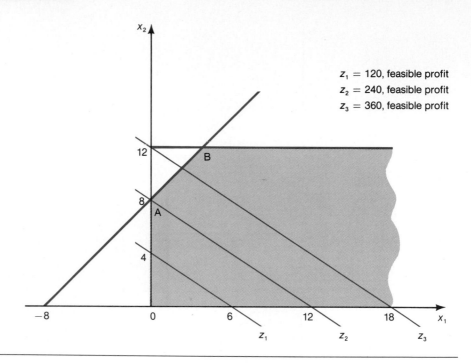

Table 4.27   Simplex Solution of an Unbounded Problem

c_b	c_j Basis	Solution	20 x_1	30 x_2	0 s_1	0 s_2
30	x_2	12	0	1	0	1
20	x_1	4	1	0	$-1/4$	1
	z_j	440	20	30	-5	50
	$c_j - z_j$		0	0	5	-50

This problem is graphically presented in Figure 4.14. The area of feasible solutions is defined by the shaded area outlined on the right of OAB. We can see clearly that there is no binding constraint on the right side of the feasible region. Thus, when we move out from the origin with the iso-profit functions Z_1, Z_2, and Z_3, the total profit increases without any bound. Unbounded cases can occur only when the model developer leaves out important constraints that restrict the feasible region.

The final simplex tableau for the above problem is presented in Table 4.27. The tableau indicates that we have not yet reached the optimum solution because the s_1 column indicates a positive $c_j - z_j$ value of 5. Thus, the s_1 column is the pivot column. However, there is no positive coefficient in the s_1 column. Therefore, we cannot select a pivot row. Hence, this problem is an unbounded problem.

COMPUTER-BASED SOLUTION OF LINEAR PROGRAMMING

Solving linear programming problems by computers

The graphical method presented in Chapter 3 and the simplex method we have explored in this chapter are effective in solving linear programming problems manually. We cannot and should not attempt to apply the manual simplex method to solve large-scale linear programming problems. Therefore, a computer-based solution is a prerequisite for any meaningful application of linear programming.

The popularity and wide application of linear programming are primarily due to the standardized solution procedure of electronic computers. Although the computer programs utilize the basic logic of the simplex method, the computer-based solution method has been greatly refined in recent years. The computer programs use the most advanced matrix-manipulation techniques that take advantage of the unique conditions of each problem under consideration.

Linear programming packages

The standardized computer solution programs are often referred to as *linear programming codes* or *canned linear programming packages*. Almost every major computer manufacturer has developed a linear programming package for its computer system. This certainly indicates that linear programming is a very popular management science technique. There are linear programming computer codes available from IBM, UNIVAC, RCA, NCR, Control Data, Honeywell, and other companies. Many mini- and microcomputer manufacturers are also busy introducing linear programming packages for their systems.

"What-if" questions

Many computer programs have augmented interactive systems that can easily file and modify data. This increased capacity allows the user to ask "what if" type questions through sensitivity analysis. Appendix 1 presents an interactive linear programming program with an example solution.

SUMMARY

In this chapter, we have learned about the simplex method of linear programming. We have studied the simplex solution procedure through a maximization problem, a problem with mixed constraints, and a case of minimization. We have also discussed several types of situations that often present us with problems, and we have seen how we can resolve these difficulties when solving linear programming problems by the simplex method.

The simplex solution procedure presented in this chapter is the key to understanding the topics to be discussed in subsequent chapters. Thus, if you have some difficulty in understanding the simplex method at this point, you should go back and study the chapter again.

References

Charnes, A., and Cooper, W. W. *Management Models and Industrial Applications of Linear Programming.* New York: Wiley, 1961.

Kwak, N. K. *Mathematical Programming with Business Applications.* New York: McGraw-Hill, 1973.

Lee, S. M.; and Moore, L. J.; *Introduction to Decision Science.* New York: Petrocelli-Charter, 1975.

Lee, S. M.; Moore, L. J.; and Taylor, B. W. *Management Science.* Dubuque, Iowa: W. C. Brown, 1981.

Assignments

4.1 Why do you think we have to study the simplex method, knowing that linear programming problems are usually solved by the computer?

4.2 What is the major difference between the graphical method and the simplex method of linear programming?

4.3 Convert the following constraints into simplex equalities:

$2x_1 + 3x_2 \leq 36$ $\qquad\qquad$ $x_1 + x_2 + 3x_3 = 45$

$4x_1 + x_2 - x_3 \geq 10$ $\qquad\qquad$ $-x_1 + x_2 + 2x_3 \geq -5$

$3x_1 - 2x_2 + x_3 \geq -2$

4.4 How is the pivot column determined in a maximization problem?

4.5 Define each of the following terms: c_j, c_b, z_j, $c_j - z_j$, *basic variable, nonbasic variable, pivot element, shadow price, slack variable, surplus variable, artificial variable, big M method.*

4.6 How is the pivot row determined?

4.7 In selecting the pivot column in a maximization problem, if there is a tie between two nonbasic variables both having the largest positive $c_j - z_j$ value, how would you break this tie?

4.8 When does a degeneracy occur and how would you handle the situation?

4.9 What is an infeasible problem? How is such a situation identified during the simplex solution process?

4.10 What is an unbounded problem? How can a problem be identified as unbounded?

4.11 Solve the following linear programming problem by the simplex method:

$$\text{Maximize } Z = \$40x_1 + \$30x_2$$
$$\text{subject to} \quad 2x_1 + 2x_2 \leq 240$$
$$2x_1 \leq 120$$
$$2x_2 \leq 80$$
$$x_1, x_2 \geq 0$$

4.12 Solve the following linear programming problem by the simplex method:

$$\text{Maximize } Z = \$48x_1 + \$64x_2$$
$$\text{subject to} \quad 16x_1 + 12x_2 \leq 96$$
$$8x_1 + 16x_2 \leq 80$$
$$4x_1 \leq 16$$
$$x_1, x_2 \geq 0$$

4.13 Solve the following linear programming problem by the simplex method:

$$\text{Minimize } Z = \$2x_1 + \$3x_2$$
$$\text{subject to } \quad 2x_1 + 5x_2 \geq 30$$
$$4x_1 + 2x_2 \geq 28$$
$$x_1, x_2 \geq 0$$

4.14 Solve the following linear programming problem by the simplex method:

$$\text{Maximize } Z = \$70x_1 + \$80x_2$$
$$\text{subject to } \quad -2x_1 + x_2 \geq -20$$
$$x_1 + x_2 \leq 14$$
$$x_1 + 2x_2 \leq 20$$
$$x_1, x_2 \geq 0$$

4.15 Lincoln Meatless Sausage, Inc. prepares its famous meatless sausage from two ingredients: soy concentrate and cornmeal. Each kilogram (kg.) of soy concentrate contains 90 milligrams (mg.) of protein, 6 mg. of iron, and 120 calories. Each kilogram of cornmeal contains 45 mg. of protein, 18 mg. of iron, and 120 calories. To satisfy the nutritional requirements of the USDA, each kilogram of sausage must contain at least 90 mg. of protein and 18 mg. of iron. Also, in order to appeal to the weight-watcher segment of the market, a kilogram of sausage should not exceed 360 calories. The soy concentrate costs 72¢/kg. and the cornmeal costs 18¢/kg.

    a. Formulate a linear programming model for this problem.

    b. Find the optimum solution (by the graphical method) that minimizes the total cost while satisfying all of the constraints.

    c. What are the basic variables and their values in the optimum solution? What are the nonbasic variables and their values?

    d. If the USDA changed the minimum requirement of iron from 18 mg. to 24 mg. for each kilogram of sausage, what would be the change in the optimum solution?

    e. In the original problem, if the cost of cornmeal is increased to 54¢/kg., how would the optimum solution be changed?

4.16 The Uptown Haberdashery is having its Annual After Holiday Dog Day Sale of unsold winter garments. Due to a very mild winter, Mr. Brown, the store manager, has the following inventory for sale: 5,000 men's overcoats, 7,500 women's wool sweaters, and 2,250 children's wool sweaters.

Mr. Brown is in the process of designing an advertising campaign for the sale. The types of advertising he plans to use and the estimated number of customers that each type is expected to reach are: newspaper—1,000 customers per ad, radio—750 customers per ad, and mail—1,500 customers per ad. The cost of each type of advertising is: newspaper—$120 per ad, radio—$90 per spot, and mail—$200 per ad.

The Hutter Advertising Agency has conducted an advertising survey and found the percentage of the market for men, women, and children reached by each type of advertising to be as follows:

	Type of Advertising		
Market	**Newspaper**	**Radio**	**Mail**
Men	45%	20%	50%
Women	40	55	40
Children	15	25	10

Mr. Brown has decided that to sell his inventory he must reach at least the following number of customers: 6,000 men, 8,500 women, and 3,500 children.

    a. Formulate a linear programming model to determine how much of each type of advertising Mr. Brown should use to minimize the total advertising cost and still sell his inventory.

    b. Use the simplex method and go through one iteration (two simplex tableaux including the initial tableau).

    c. Solve this problem by using the computer, if one is available.

4.17 Kay Manning, Manager of Sales, has two salesmen working for her. The ability of each salesman to secure new accounts had historically been as follows: Salesman 1—4 new accounts per 10 visits to prospects, and Salesman 2—3 new accounts per 10 visits to prospects. As of May 1, Salesman 1 has 20 established customers that he must call on each month if he is to retain their monthly orders. Salesman 2 has 15 established accounts that he is attempting to maintain.

    The average time each salesman spends with each type of customer per visit is as follows:

	Type of Customer	
Salesman	**New Account**	**Established Account**
1	10	5
2	8	6

Each new order yields the company an average profit of $150, whereas orders from established accounts are usually smaller and yield an average profit of $50 an order. Salesman 1 has a larger area to cover than Salesman 2, and as a result he has only 120 hours of time (net of traveling time) to spend with his customers each month. Salesman 2 has 135 hours available to spend with his customers, since his traveling time is less.

    a. Formulate a linear programming model to determine how many new and how many old customers each salesman should call on in May in order to maximize profits.

    b. Solve this problem by the simplex method.

4.18 Ms. Osborne, Marketing Manager of the Midwest Typewriter Co., is trying to decide how to allocate her salespersons to the company's three primary markets. Market Area 1 is an urban area and the salespersons can sell, on the average, 40 typewriters per week. The salespersons in the other two markets can sell, on the average, 36 and 25 typewriters per week respectively.

For the coming week, three of the salespersons will be on vacation, leaving only 12 people available for duty. Also, because of a limited number of company cars, a maximum of 5 salespersons can be allocated to Market Area 1. The selling expenses per week for each salesperson in each area are: $80/week for Market Area 1, $70/week for Market Area 2, and $50/week for Market Area 3. The budget for the next week is $750. The profit margin per typewriter is $15.

   a. Formulate a linear programming model to determine how many salespersons should be assigned to each area next week in order to maximize profits.
   b. Use the simplex method and go through one iteration.

4.19 The new cars for the upcoming year are about to be introduced and Mr. Weimer, Sales Manager of Roadside Motors, has a very large stock of last year's cars. Almost all of the current stock are large luxury cars that are not selling because of their poor gas mileage. To move these cars, Mr. Weimer is planning a large advertising campaign and sale. He plans to use the following types of advertising: (1) radio spots, which cost $40 per spot and reach an estimated 200 potential customers per ad; (2) newspaper ads, which cost $50 per ad and reach an estimated 300 potential customers per ad; and (3) mail ads, which cost $45 per ad and reach an estimated 325 potential customers per ad.

Mr. Weimer has estimated that he must reach at least 5,000 potential customers in order to reduce his inventory. At the present time the company has a contract for a minimum of 10 radio spots, 5 newspaper ads, and 5 mail ads each month.

   a. Formulate a linear programming model to determine how many ads of each type Mr. Weimer should purchase in order to minimize total costs.
   b. Solve this problem using the simplex method.

4.20 The Downing Plastics Company has just received a government contract to produce three different plastic valves: Exhaust, Intake, and Bypass. These valves will be used in the Explorer spacecraft. The valves must be highly heat and pressure resistant. The company has developed a three-stage production process that will provide the valves with the necessary properties.

The process involves work in three different chambers. Chamber 1 provides the necessary pressure resistance and can process valves for 1,200 minutes each week. Chamber 2 provides heat resistance and can process valves for 900 minutes a week. Chamber 3 tests the valve and can operate for 1,300 minutes a week. The three valve types and their time requirements in each chamber are:

Valve	Time Requirement		
	Chamber 1	Chamber 2	Chamber 3
Exhaust	5 min.	7 min.	4 min.
Intake	3 min.	2 min.	10 min.
Bypass	2 min.	4 min.	5 min.

The government will purchase all the valves that can be produced and the company will receive the following profit on each valve: Exhaust, $1.50; Intake, $1.35; and Bypass, $1.00.

a. Formulate a linear programming model to determine how many valves of each type the company should produce each week in order to maximize profits.

b. Go through one iteration by the simplex method.

4.21 The Willis Office Furniture Company is a small business operating in Rhode Island. It has two warehouses in the state from which it fills customers' orders. Due to a recent business slump, the company is attempting to institute a cost reduction campaign. A customer has just ordered 10 desks and 8 tables and Mr. North, the Distribution Manager, wishes to minimize shipping costs. The shipping costs of tables and desks from each warehouse are:

| | Shipping Cost | |
Furniture	Warehouse 1	Warehouse 2
Desk	$15	$12
Table	7	9

The company delivers all orders using their own trucks. Trucks coming from Warehouse 2 can haul no more than 7 tables and desks, but trucks coming from Warehouse 1 can transport up to 14 tables and desks. Mr. North has also instituted another policy that he hopes will reduce shipping costs. He has decided that the inventories at the two warehouses should be approximately equal. Therefore, he says that the difference in the number of tables and desks shipped from either warehouse cannot exceed 2.

a. Formulate a linear programming model to determine how many tables and desks should be shipped from each warehouse in order to minimize total shipping costs.

b. Solve this problem by the simplex method.

4.22 The Venus Candy Company makes three different candy bars: Saturn, Moon, and Venus. The ingredients for each candy bar are as follows:

| | Ingredients | | |
Candy Bar	Chocolate	Nuts	Caramel
Saturn	12 g.	4 g.	15 g.
Moon	6 g.	10 g.	8 g.
Venus	10 g.	2 g.	15 g.

The company's suppliers have limited the company to the following ingredients per week: chocolate, 25,000 grams; nuts, 15,000 grams; and caramel, 30,000 grams.

The Marketing Department estimates that the maximum demand for the Saturn will be 900 per week and for the Moon 700 per week. The Venus is a relatively new product and demand for this bar appears to be very large at the present time. Per-unit profit contributions for each candy bar are as follows: Saturn, 2¢; Moon 2.5¢; and Venus 1.5¢. The company would like to know how many candy bars of each type to produce next week in order to maximize total profits. Solve this problem by the simplex method.

4.23 Consider the following linear programming problem:

$$\text{Minimize } Z = \$15x_1 + \$25x_2$$

$$\begin{aligned}
\text{subject to} \quad 3x_1 + 4x_2 &\geq 12 \\
2x_1 + x_2 &\geq 6 \\
3x_1 + 2x_2 &\geq 9 \\
x_1, x_2 &\geq 0
\end{aligned}$$

a. Solve this problem by the simplex method.

b. Is the optimum solution valid? Why or why not?

4.24 The General Bulb Company produces three kinds of light bulb: a 60-watt soft-lite bulb, a 60-watt regular bulb, and a 100-watt bulb. The bulbs each take one hour per case in Production Line 1. In Production Line 2 a case of the soft-lites takes 2 hours and a case of each of the others takes 1 hour. Production Line 1 has 25 hours per week available and Production Line 2 has 40 hours per week available.

The company has determined that the two types of 60-watt bulb are considered substitute products by most people and that their combined demand will not be more than 25 cases per week. The demand for the 100-watt bulbs will never be greater than 60 cases per week. If the soft-lite bulbs earn a profit of $7 per case and the other two types of bulbs earn a profit of $5 per case, how many cases per week should the company produce of each type in order to maximize total profits?

4.25 The American Inland Oil Company is faced with a problem. It has only enough oil to keep its refineries operating for one more year. The company has determined that it has three possible alternatives for increasing its oil supply. The company has decided that it can spend no more than $5 million and that this investment must provide at least 2.5 million barrels of oil a year for at least the next 150 years.

Alternative 1 is to invest in more oil wells in this country. The company has determined that the total cost of a new well is $2 million with an expected yield of 500,000 barrles a year for 10 years. Alternative 2 is to invest in oil wells in South America. A well there costs $8 million initially and will yield 1 million barrels a year for 25 years. Alternative 3 is to invest in research for the recovery of shale oil. It is estimated that this research will cost $20 million but will yield 1.5 million barrels a year for 75 years. Unlike the other alternatives, only one research project is possible.

a. Formulate a linear programming model to determine the optimum choice of alternative that will maximize the company's oil supply.

b. Solve this problem by the simplex method.

4.26 The Ozark Brewing Company produces custom-blended whiskey to order. The components of the blend are rye whiskey and bourbon. The company has received an order for a minimum of 600 gallons of custom-blended whiskey. The customer has specified that the order must contain at least 40 percent rye and not more than 375 gallons of bourbon. The customer has also specified that the blend should be mixed in the ratio of two parts rye to one part bourbon.

The company can produce at the rate of 750 gallons a week, regardless of the blend, and it wishes to fill the order in one week of production. The company has agreed to furnish the blend for a price of $15 a gallon. Its cost per gallon of rye and bourbon used are $6 and $3 respectively. To meet the customer's requirements and maximize total profits, the management wishes to determine the blend the company should produce during one week's production. Formulate the problem as a linear programming problem and solve it by the simplex method. Now answer the following:

    a. How much total blend should be produced?
    b. How much of each component should be produced?
    c. What is the maximum profit yielded?
    d. Which restrictions are constrainting the solution?
    e. If the Ozark Brewing Company could sell only 600 gallons, how much of each component would they produce, and what would be the total profit?

4.27 The Roller Products Company produces roller skates and skateboards. It has three production lines. Production Line 1 makes skateboard platforms. Production Line 2 makes skate assemblies. Production Line 3 mounts wheels on both products. The Marketing Department has determined virtually unlimited demand for both products. Profit per pair of roller skates is $10, and per skateboard it is $6. Production Line 1 can produce 6 skateboard platforms per day and Production Line 2 can produce 5 pairs of shoes per day. Production Line 3 can mount 20 wheel sets per day. Each skateboard requires 2 wheel sets, and each pair of roller skates requires 4 wheel sets.

    a. How many skateboards and roller skates should be scheduled per day to maximize total profits?
    b. Solve this problem by the simplex method.

4.28 A gardener has 1,000 sq. yd. of land available to devote to cash crops. Profits for the planned crops are as follows: lima beans—$20 per 10 sq. yd., spinach—$10 per 10 sq. yd., zucchini—$15 per 10 sq. yd.

The gardener has $200 available to invest. Total preparation costs for 10 sq. yd. are: $4 for lima beans, $2 for spinach, and $1 for zucchini. The gardener has 200 hours of time available for gardening. Each 10 sq. yd. requires the following amount of time: lima beans—2 hours, spinach—1 hour, and zucchini—3 hours.

    a. Formulate a linear programming model to determine the optimum areas in square yards for each of the three crops.
    b. Using the simplex method, go through three iterations.

4.29 The Ladies Hanen, Inc. produces two types of ladies bathing suits—bikini and topless. These two products are manufactured in three sewing centers (SC). On the average, a bikini requires 6 minutes in SC I, 6 minutes in SC II, and 4 minutes in SC III. A topless bathing suit requires 4 minutes in SC I, 7.5 minutes in SC II, and 10 minutes in SC III. The maximum amount of time available for production per day is as follows: SC I—2 hours, SC II—2.25 hours, and SC III—2.5 hours. The expected profits are $12 from a bikini and $14 from a topless.

a. Using the graphical technique, find the optimum product mix that will maximize total profits.

b. What are the basic and nonbasic variables in the optimum solution?

c. If the firm has to cut manpower, where should it cut and by how many minutes without sacrificing the total profit?

4.30 Jack Phillips is the Social Chairman of the Sigma Delta Sigma Fraternity. He is planning a special drink for the upcoming open house. He has decided to serve Phillips screwdrivers. Although some friends swear that a Phillips screwdriver contains one part vodka and two parts Phillips Milk of Magnesia, it actually contains 5 oz. of vodka and frozen orange juice.

For the open house, Jack has obtained the following ingredients: premium vodka—400 oz.; cheap vodka—500 oz.; premium orange juice—800 oz.; and cheap orange juice—400 oz. Jack plans four different-quality Phillips screwdrivers. The recipes for the drinks and the prices that will be charged are as follows:

Drinks	Vodka	Orange Juice	Price
Phillips screwdriver—The Thing	4 oz. premium	1 oz. premium	$2.50
Phillips screwdriver—Deluxe	3 oz. premium	2 oz. cheap	2.20
Phillips screwdriver—Regular	3 oz. cheap	2 oz. premium	2.00
Phillips screwdriver—All The Way	2 oz. cheap	3 oz. cheap	1.70

From past experience, Jack knows that the maximum number of drinks he can sell are: 125 drinks that contain cheap vodka and 150 drinks that contain cheap orange juice. He also feels that he can sell at least 40 Phillips screwdrivers—The Thing.

Formulate a linear programming model to determine the optimum quantity of each type of drink to prepare in order to maximize total revenue.

5 ADDITIONAL TOPICS OF LINEAR PROGRAMMING

The purpose of linear programming is not just to derive an optimum solution. Since we live in an environment of uncertainty, we seek additional information from the simplex solution in order to answer "what if" type contingency questions. For example, a linear programming model may be formulated to answer such questions as the impacts of inflation, materials shortage, increase or decrease of the budget, technological improvements, change in market situations, and integer requirements for certain variables. In this chapter, we will study three major topics: duality, sensitivity analysis, and integer programming.

Learning Objectives   From the study of this chapter, you will learn the following:

1. The concept and purpose of duality.
2. The relationship between primal and dual models of linear programming.
3. How to formulate a dual model for any linear programming problem.
4. Dual simplex method of linear programming.
5. How to perform sensitivity analysis for complex problems.
6. How to solve integer programming problems.
7. The meaning of the following terms:

Duality theory   *Dual simplex*
Branch and bound   *Cost of indivisibility*
Stochastic programming   *Chance-constrained programming*
Multiple objective linear programming

DUALITY IN LINEAR PROGRAMMING

The primal vs. dual model

The term *duality* simply means that every linear programming problem can be formulated and analyzed in two different ways. The first form is the ordinary linear programming model, often referred to as the *primal*. The second model is the other side of the primal, often called the *dual*. Every primal linear programming model can be formulated as a dual model. For example, a profit maximization problem can be formulated as a problem of cost minimization. Or, a cost minimization can be viewed as a problem of maximizing the efficiency of using available resources.

Thus far, our discussion of linear programming has been limited to seeking the optimum solution to the primal. Each primal maximization problem has a corresponding minimization problem. Similarly, each primal minimization problem has a corresponding dual maximization problem. Therefore, the dual of a dual problem is the primal of the given problem.

The purpose of a dual model

You may ask, "Why should we worry about another way to solve the same problem?" Most management science texts offer two primary reasons. First, the dual solution provides valuable information concerning economic ramifications of the problem. Secondly, for certain problems the dual approach requires less computational effort than the primal because fewer iterations are required to reach the optimum solution.

If we are proficient in interpreting the primal solution, we can obtain all the information the dual model provides. This is especially true in view of the availability of many interactive linear programming programs. Thus, our discussion of duality will be relatively brief, and our emphasis will be on formulating the dual model and explaining the relationship between the primal and the dual.

The Primal-Dual Relationship

The primal solution provides us with the optimum values for the basic variables and the objective function. We can interpret the final simplex tableau to identify the shadow prices discussed in Chapter 4. To begin our discussion, let us go back to the familiar Candex Camera Works problem.

EXAMPLE 5.1   *CANDEX CAMERA WORKS, LTD.*

$$\text{Maximize } Z = 40x_1 + 50x_2$$
$$\text{subject to} \quad 3x_1 + 3x_2 \le 90$$
$$2x_1 + 4x_2 \le 80$$
$$x_1, x_2 \ge 0$$

where x_1 = number of Candex A1 cameras produced

x_2 = number of Candex ZX cameras produced

The primal-dual relationship

In order to formulate a dual model for this problem, the following chart of the primal-dual relationship can be used:

Model Feature	Primal	Dual
1. Objective function	Maximization Minimization	Minimization Maximization
2. Number of variables	Number of decision variables (x_j)	Number of model constraints
3. Number of constraints	Number of model constraints	Number of decision variables (u_i)
4. Objective function coefficients	Unit contribution rates in the objective function	Right-hand-side value
5. Resources	Right-hand-side value	Unit contribution rates in the objective function
6. Matrix coefficients	Technical coefficients	Transposed technical coefficients
7. Direction of constraints	$\le$ $\ge$	$\ge$ $\le$

Table 5.1   The Primal and Dual Candex Problem

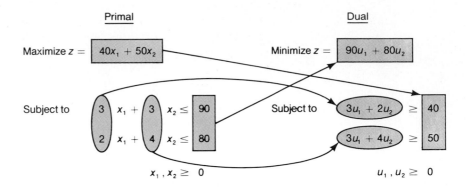

Now we can formulate the dual model for the Candex problem, as shown in Table 5.1. Let us follow the primal-dual relationship summarized above to make some sense out of the dual model formulation process.

1. Since the primal problem is for maximization, the dual problem becomes a minimization problem.

2. The primal problem has two decision variables. Thus, the dual model will have two model constraints.

The dual variables

3. The primal model has two constraints. Thus, the dual model will have two decision variables, u_1 and u_2. We can define these variables as follows:

u_1 = the marginal value of one hour of production time in Assembly Line 1
u_2 = the marginal value of one hour of production time in Assembly Line 2

4. The objective function coefficients in the primal model are \$40 and \$50 for x_1 and x_2 respectively. Thus, these two coefficients become the right-hand-side values (resources) of the dual constraints.

5. The amounts of resources available in the primal model are 90 hours in Assembly Line 1 and 80 hours in Assembly Line 2. These figures become the unit contribution rates in the objective function for u_1 and u_2.

6. The technological coefficients in the primal model are transposed for the dual model. In other words, the column-wise coefficients in the primal become the row-wise coefficients in the dual.

Interpretation of the Dual Model

Interpreting the dual model

In the dual model, decision variables u_1 and u_2 represent the marginal value of a resource unit (one production hour) in the two assembly lines. Since a Candex A1 (x_1) requires 3 hours in Assembly Line 1 and 2 hours in Assembly Line 2, the total cost of resources committed to produce one Candex A1 will be $3u_1 + 2u_2$. The unit profit for x_1 is \$40, as shown in the primal objective function. The

Figure 5.1   Optimum Solutions for the Primal and Dual Problems

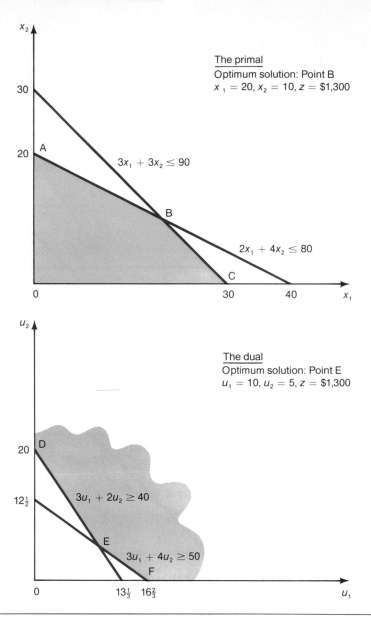

The primal
Optimum solution: Point B
$x_1 = 20, x_2 = 10, z = \$1,300$

$3x_1 + 3x_2 \le 90$

$2x_1 + 4x_2 \le 80$

The dual
Optimum solution: Point E
$u_1 = 10, u_2 = 5, z = \$1,300$

$3u_1 + 2u_2 \ge 40$

$3u_1 + 4u_2 \ge 50$

condition necessary to commit $3u_1 + 2u_2$ worth of resources to produce a Candex A1 is that it produce at least \$40 profit. If the resources committed in producing a Candex A1 do not return at least \$40 profit, then the management of Candex should use the resources for other purposes. Thus, the first constraint of the dual model is expressed as

$$3u_1 + 2u_2 \ge 40$$

Table 5.2   The Optimum Solution of the Primal Problem

c_b	c_j Basis	Solution	40 x_1	50 x_2	0 s_1	0 s_2
40	x_1	20	1	0	2/3	−1/2
50	x_2	10	0	1	−1/3	1/2
	z_j	1,300	40	50	10	5
	$c_j - z_j$		0	0	−10	−5

Table 5.3   The Optimum Solution of the Dual Problem

c_b	c_j Basis	Solution	90 u_1	80 u_2	0 s_1	0 s_2
90	u_1	10	1	0	−2/3	1/3
80	u_2	5	0	1	1/2	−1/2
	z_j	1,300	90	80	−20	−10
	$z_j - c_j$		0	0	−20	−10

The second constraint of the dual model can be formulated in a similar manner. Production of a Candex ZX camera (x_2) requires 3 hours in Assembly Line 1 and 4 hours in Assembly Line 2. Therefore, the total worth of resources committed to the production of one Candex ZX will be $3u_1 + 4u_2$. The unit contribution rate of Candex ZX is $50. Hence, the second constraint becomes

$$3u_1 + 4u_2 \geq 50$$

In the primal model, the available production resources are 90 hours in Assembly Line 1 and 80 hours in Assembly Line 2. The objective function is to minimize the total cost involved in producing Candex A1 and Candex ZX cameras by utilizing these available resources. Thus, the objective function is

$$\text{Minimize } Z = 90u_1 + 80u_2$$

The optimum solutions for the primal and dual problems are presented graphically in Figure 5.1. The simplex solutions are also presented for the primal and dual problems in Tables 5.2 and 5.3 respectively. The shadow prices are shown as the $c_j - z_j$ values of the nonbasic-variable columns in the primal optimum solution. These *The shadow prices* shadow prices (without minus signs) correspond to the basic-variable solution values in the dual optimum solution. We can contrast the two optimum solutions and analyze their relationship as follows:

Primal Solution	Dual Solution
Basic variables $x_1 = 20$ $x_2 = 10$	Nonbasic variable $z_j - c_j$ (shadow price) s_1 column: -20 s_2 column: -10
Nonbasic variable $c_j - z_j$ (shadow price) s_1 column: -10 s_2 column: -5	Basic variables $u_1 = 10$ $u_2 = 5$
Slack column coefficients	Slack column coefficients ($-$transposed)

$$
\begin{array}{cc}
s_1 & s_2 \\
\hline
2/3 & -1/2 \\
-1/3 & 1/2
\end{array}
\qquad
\begin{array}{cc}
s_1 & s_2 \\
\hline
-2/3 & 1/3 \\
1/2 & -1/2
\end{array}
$$

The Dual of a Problem with Mixed Constraints

A dual model for a problem with mixed constraints

As we discussed in Chapter 4, frequently the primal problem may have mixed constraints. While some constraints will be *less than or equal to* or *greater than or equal to* types, others will be *equality* type constraints. In such a case the formulation of a dual model becomes somewhat complicated. As we discussed previously, the direction of the dual constraints must be exactly opposite to the direction of the primal constraints. This procedure is not easy to follow when the primal model has mixed constraints.

Perhaps the easiest way to resolve this problem is to adjust the primal constraint in such a way that the directions of all the constraints are the same. Let us consider the following primal problem.

EXAMPLE 5.2

$$\text{Maximize } Z = 10x_1 + 8x_2 + 6x_3$$
$$\text{subject to} \quad 2x_1 + x_2 + 3x_3 \leq 90$$
$$x_2 + x_3 \geq 20$$
$$x_1 + x_2 + x_3 = 10$$
$$x_1, x_2, x_3 \geq 0$$

In order to formulate the dual model for the above problem, let us try to make all the primal constraints $\leq$ types. The first constraint is already a $\leq$ type. The second constraint is a $\geq$ type. The direction of this constraint can be changed as follows:

$$x_2 + x_3 \geq 20$$
$$-x_2 - x_3 \leq -20 \text{ (multiplying both sides by } -1)$$

An equality constraint

The *third* constraint is an equality ($=$) constraint. Thus, the *third* dual variable is unrestricted in sign. In order to avoid this complexity, we can easily replace an equality constraint with two inequality constraints. For example, $x_1 + x_2 + x_3 = 10$ can be expressed by the following two inequalities:

$$x_1 + x_2 + x_3 \leq 10$$
$$x_1 + x_2 + x_3 \geq 10$$

If the model satisfies the two inequality constraints, the original equality constraint will be completely satisfied. Now we change the direction of the second constraint as follows:

$$x_1 + x_2 + x_3 \geq 10$$
$$-x_1 - x_2 - x_3 \leq -10$$

Now we can formulate the dual model for the problem as follows:

$$\text{Minimize } Z = 90u_1 - 20u_2 + 10u_3 - 10u_4$$

$$
\begin{aligned}
\text{subject to} \quad 2u_1 \quad\quad\quad + \quad u_3 - u_4 &\geq 10 \\
u_1 - u_2 + \quad u_3 - u_4 &\geq 8 \\
3u_1 - u_2 + \quad u_3 - u_4 &\geq 6 \\
u_1, u_2, u_3, u_4 &\geq 0
\end{aligned}
$$

Computational aspect of the dual

In addition to facilitating the economic interpretation of the problem, the dual is often formulated for computational purposes. Let us consider a problem with 10 decision variables and 30 constraints. The number of constraints frequently (not always) determines the maximum number of iterations required to solve the problem. The primal solution, therefore, can take the maximum of about 30 iterations. However, if we formulate a dual model for the problem, it will involve 30 decision variables and 10 constraints. Thus, the computation time required to solve it can be reduced significantly.

The ellipsoid algorithm

Another reason we study duality is that the mathematical property of the primal-dual relationship can be useful in developing advanced models of management science. For example, the *ellipsoid algorithm* of linear programming, proposed by the Russian mathematician L. G. Khachian, utilizes the primal-dual relationship in developing the algorithm. However, the mathematical property of the primal-dual relationship is obviously beyond the scope and purpose of this book.

THE DUAL SIMPLEX METHOD

The dual simplex method

The dual simplex method is also a simplex-based solution method for linear programming problems. The underlying concept of this technique is that the optimum solution to a given linear programming problem is found when the primal and dual solutions to the problem are both feasible. Although the word *dual* may confuse you, the dual simplex method is based strictly on the primal simplex solution method.

Why dual simplex?

You may once again ask, "Why should we worry about an alternate simplex method when the ordinary simplex method works fine?" The dual simplex method is by no means more efficient than the ordinary simplex method. However, it is an extremely valuable tool for sensitivity analysis. Thus, we will have just a large enough dose of the dual simplex method to understand it and use it in the sensitivity analysis section.

The dual simplex procedure

The dual simplex method works almost the same way as the ordinary simplex method, once we get started. It starts with a *better than optimum but infeasible* solution rather than a solution that is not optimum but feasible. Thus, the $c_j - z_j$ values (or $z_j - c_j$ values in a minimization problem) of the nonbasic variables must be nonpositive so that the initial solution is better than optimum. When this happens, the initial solution is infeasible and the solution values are negative. As the dual simplex solution process continues, the value of the objective function deteriorates while maintaining nonpositive $c_j - z_j$ values (or $z_j - c_j$ values in a minimization problem) in the nonbasic-variable columns. The optimum solution is found when all of the basic variables have nonnegative solution values.

The dual simplex method solution steps are:

Step 1: Determine the initial solution such that the $c_j - z_j$ (or $z_j - c_j$) values are nonpositive in the nonbasic-variable columns.

Step 2: If the solution derived is feasible (all the solution values are nonnegative), this is the optimum solution. If the solution is infeasible, continue the solution process.

Step 3: Determine the pivot row first, rather than the pivot column. The pivot row is the one that has the smallest negative solution value (or the largest negative number).

Step 4: Select the pivot column. The pivot column is a nonbasic-variable column that has the minimum value when the $c_j - z_j$ (or $z_j - c_j$) value is divided by the corresponding *negative* coefficient in the pivot row. We ignore columns with zero or positive coefficients.

Step 5: Find a new solution by the ordinary pivoting and return to Step 2.

To illustrate the dual simplex method, let us examine the familiar diet problem.

EXAMPLE 5.3   **DIET PROBLEM OF THE FRESHMEN ORIENTATION PROGRAM**
The diet problem is formulated as follows:

$$\text{Minimize } Z = 8x_1 + 10x_2$$
$$\text{subject to} \quad 3x_1 + 3x_2 \geq 30$$
$$4x_1 + 2x_2 \geq 24$$
$$x_1 + 2x_2 \geq 12$$
$$x_1, x_2 \geq 0$$

To solve this problem by the ordinary simplex method, we convert the $\geq$ inequalities to simplex equalities by subtracting a surplus variable and adding an artificial variable in each of the constraints. In the dual simplex method, both sides of the constraints are multiplied by -1. This procedure results in $\leq$ type constraints and thus eliminates the necessity of using artificial variables. By simply adding slack variables to the constraints, we obtain the following simplex model:

Rearranging the constraints

$$\text{Minimize } Z = 8x_1 + 10x_2 + 0s_1 + 0s_2 + 0s_3$$
$$\text{subject to} \quad -3x_1 - 3x_2 + s_1 = -30$$
$$-4x_1 - 2x_2 + s_2 = -24$$
$$-x_1 - 2x_2 + s_3 = -12$$

The initial solution, derived in the usual manner, is shown in Table 5.4. Now we follow the dual simplex method steps as shown below.

Step 1: The initial solution has been determined. The solution values of the basic variables are negative, and also the $z_j - c_j$ values of the nonbasic-variable columns (x_1 and x_2) are nonpositive.

Table 5.4 The Initial Dual Simplex Solution

c_b	Basis	Solution	8 x_1	10 x_2	0 s_1	0 s_2	0 s_3
0	s_1	-30	-3	-3	1	0	0
0	s_2	-24	-4	-2	0	1	0
0	s_3	-12	-1	-2	0	0	1
	z_j	0	0	0	0	0	0
	$z_j - c_j$		-8	-10	0	0	0

Table 5.5 The Second Dual Simplex Solution

c_b	Basis	Solution	8 x_1	10 x_2	0 s_1	0 s_2	0 s_3
8	x_1	10	1	1	$-1/3$	0	0
0	s_2	16	0	2	$-4/3$	1	0
0	s_3	-2	0	-1	$-1/3$	0	1
	z_j	80	8	8	$-8/3$	0	0
	$z_j - c_j$		0	-2	$-8/3$	0	0

Step 2: This is not an optimum solution because it is infeasible. That is, the basic variables have negative solution values.

Step 3: The pivot row is the one that has the largest negative solution number. Thus, the s_1 row is the pivot row.

Step 4: The pivot column is determined as follows:

Nonbasic Variable	$z_j - c_j$	$\div$	Pivot Row Coefficient	Ratio
x_1 column	-8	$\div$	-3	8/3 ← pivot column
x_2 column	-10	$\div$	-3	10/3

The x_1 column is the pivot column. Thus, the incoming variable is x_1 and the outgoing variable is s_1.

Step 5: The second dual simplex solution is derived in Table 5.5. This solution is still infeasible because the basic variable s_3 has a solution value of -2. Thus, we repeat the process. The third solution shown in Table 5.6 is feasible. Thus, this is the optimum solution.

Table 5.6   The Optimum Dual Simplex Solution

c_b \\ c_j	Basis	Solution	8 x_1	10 x_2	0 s_1	0 s_2	0 s_3
8	x_1	8	1	0	$-2/3$	0	1
0	s_2	12	0	0	-2	1	2
10	x_2	2	0	1	$1/3$	0	-1
	z_j	84	8	10	-2	0	-2
	$z_j - c_j$		0	0	-2	0	-2

No need to deal with artificial variables

The optimum dual simplex solution corresponds to the optimum solution derived by the ordinary simplex method presented in Table 4.19. It is interesting to note that the dual simplex method required two iterations to find the optimum solution whereas the ordinary simplex method required four iterations. The main reason for this difference is that the dual simplex method does not have to deal with a number of artificial variables. When a model involves a large number of artificial variables, many iterations are required to eliminate these variables from the solution basis.

SENSITIVITY ANALYSIS

The optimum solution we obtain for a given linear programming model represents a solution under a set of restrictive assumptions, such as the certainty of the decision environment. In real-world situations, as we have discussed many times already, the decision environment is dynamic rather than static. Thus, the decision maker is vitally *Answering "what if"* interested in the "what if" questions concerning the effects of change in model pa- *questions* rameters on the optimum solution.

In Chapter 3 we considered simple sensitivity analysis using the graphical method. The same approach, of course, cannot be used for problems that involve more than two decision variables. In this section we will use the interpretation of the final simplex tableau to perform the sensitivity analysis.

Interactive linear programming systems

With the availability of many efficient interactive systems of linear programming, sensitivity analysis is often performed by solving the problem again by making simple changes in the model parameters. This process can be simplified by establishing a data file so that changes can be easily made in the file. However, if we need to *Interactive system vs.* perform sensitivity analysis of many small changes in the parameters, the interactive *sensitivity analysis* approach may be both costly and time consuming. Thus, the simplex-tableau-based sensitivity analysis can be a very useful tool.

We will limit our discussion of sensitivity analysis to the following: (1) change in the unit contribution rates (c_j); (2) change in available resources (b_i); (3) change in the technological coefficients (a_{ij}); (4) addition of a new constraint; and (5) addition of a new variable.

CASETTE 5.1

An example for sensitivity analysis

DRINK BLENDING PROBLEM OF ALPHA BETA SIGMA

Alpha Beta Sigma is a social fraternity at the university. The coming weekend is the annual Homecoming festivity. In addition to the traditional contests for the Homecoming Queen and the best Homecoming decorations among all of the dormitories, Greek houses, and other student organizations, many other activities are planned for the parents and returning alumni. Preparations for the brunch before the game and the dance Saturday night have already been completed.

The officers of Alpha Beta Sigma would like to have a special "Victory Celebration Happy Hour" right after the game. After a lengthy and sometimes heated discussion, the officers decided to serve the house special, the "Red Baron" frozen drink, which contains bourbon and tomato juice. Based on past experience and the increasing excitement about the upcoming big game against the perennial archrival, the officers have purchased the following ingredients: regular bourbon—360 oz., cheap bourbon—400 oz., regular tomato juice, 260 oz., and cheap tomato juice, 300 oz.

In the past, Alpha Beta Sigma asked the alumni to make small donations for the financial solvency of the house. This year, however, the house needs major repair work, and the officers have decided to use this occasion to raise some funds. The house plans to serve four types of Red Barons, each of a different quality. The type of drinks to be served, the secret house recipes, and the prices are as follows:

Type of Red Baron	Recipe	Price
Supreme	4 oz. reg. bourbon + 1 oz. reg. tomato juice	$3.00
Deluxe	3 oz. reg. bourbon + 2 oz. cheap tomato juice	2.40
Regular	3 oz. cheap bourbon + 2 oz. reg. tomato juice	2.00
Maybe	2 oz. cheap bourbon + 3 oz. cheap tomato juice	1.40

The Red Barons are jumbo drinks containing 5 ounces each. As such, the number of drinks that can be sold is often limited because most customers want to stay red barons rather than "sick barons." Past experience indicates that the demand for the drinks that contain regular bourbon has never exceeded 50. Also, the officers feel that they should not push more than 80 drinks that contain cheap tomato juice (a real heartburner). The officers decided to include the above two considerations as constraints.

The decision problem for the officers of Alpha Beta Sigma is to determine the number of each type of Red Baron drinks to prepare and freeze in order to maximize the total revenue. To have real "body" and color before freezing, it is essential that the ingredients be mixed at least 24 hours in advance. Therefore, mixing and freezing the drinks in advance requires a linear programming model.

Decision Variables

The officers are trying to determine the number of each type of Red Baron drink to prepare while meeting the ingredient supply requirements and other constraints in order to maximize the total revenue. Since there are four different Red Barons they intend to prepare, the decision variables can be defined as follows:

$$x_1 = \text{number of Red Baron Supremes to be prepared}$$
$$x_2 = \text{number of Red Baron Deluxes to be prepared}$$
$$x_3 = \text{number of Red Baron Regulars to be prepared}$$
$$x_4 = \text{number of Red Baron Maybes to be prepared}$$

Model Constraints

In this drink blending problem, the model constraints reflect both the amount of ingredients already purchased and sales forecast considerations. The blending of the ingredients has previously been determined by the house's secret recipes. First, let us consider the recipes and the available quantities of ingredients:

Ingredients	Red Baron Recipe				Quantity Available
	Supreme	Deluxe	Regular	Maybe	
Regular bourbon	4 oz.	3 oz.			360 oz.
Cheap bourbon			3 oz.	2 oz.	400 oz.
Regular tomato juice	1 oz.		2 oz.		260 oz.
Cheap tomato juice		2 oz.		3 oz.	300 oz.

The types of drinks that use regular bourbon are Supreme and Deluxe. Since each Red Baron Supreme requires 4 oz. and each Deluxe 3 oz. of regular bourbon, the total amount of regular bourbon to be used will be $4x_1 + 3x_2$. This total amount of regular bourbon must be *equal to or less than* the already purchased quantity of 360 oz. The constraint can be expressed as

$$4x_1 + 3x_2 \leq 360 \qquad \qquad \textbf{\textit{Regular bourbon}}$$

Following the same procedure, we can formulate the remaining three ingredient constraints as follows:

$$3x_3 + 2x_4 \leq 400 \qquad \qquad \textbf{\textit{Cheap bourbon}}$$
$$x_1 + 2x_3 \leq 260 \qquad \qquad \textbf{\textit{Regular tomato juice}}$$
$$2x_2 + 3x_4 \leq 300 \qquad \qquad \textbf{\textit{Cheap tomato juice}}$$

There are two additional constraints that are related to past sales experience. Not more than 50 drinks that contain regular bourbon should be made. Since the drinks that require regular bourbon are Supreme and Deluxe, we can write

$$x_1 + x_2 \leq 50 \qquad \qquad \textbf{\textit{Drinks with regular bourbon}}$$

Also, drinks that contain cheap tomato juice should be limited to 80. Only Deluxe and Maybe require cheap tomato juice. Thus,

$$x_2 + x_4 \leq 80 \qquad \qquad \textbf{\textit{Drinks with cheap tomato juice}}$$

The Objective Function

The drink blending problem of Alpha Beta Sigma has the primary objective of maximizing the total revenue. The total revenue will be a function of the price per drink and the number of each drink sold. In other words, the total revenue will be the sum of the revenues from sales of each type of drink. For example, the revenue from the Red Baron Supreme will be $3.00 multiplied by the quantity of drinks to be sold, or $3.00x_1$. The objective function, then, will be

$$\text{Maximize } Z = 3.00x_1 + 2.40x_2 + 2.00x_3 + 1.40x_4$$

Now the complete model can be formulated as follows:

$$\text{Maximize } Z = 3.00x_1 + 2.40x_2 + 2.00x_3 + 1.40x_4$$

$$
\begin{aligned}
\text{subject to} \quad 4x_1 + 3x_2 \qquad\qquad &\leq 360 \\
3x_3 + 2x_4 &\leq 400 \\
x_1 \qquad + 2x_3 \qquad &\leq 260 \\
2x_2 \qquad + 3x_4 &\leq 300 \\
x_1 + x_2 \qquad\qquad &\leq 50 \\
x_2 \qquad + x_4 &\leq 80 \\
x_1, x_2, x_3, x_4 &\geq 0
\end{aligned}
$$

The optimum simplex solution tableau is presented in Table 5.7. The optimum solution is $x_1 = 50$, $x_3 = 80$, $x_4 = 80$, $s_1 = 160$, $s_3 = 50$, $s_4 = 60$, and $Z = \$442.00$. For our discussion of sensitivity analysis, we will use the solution tableau presented in Table 5.7.

Change in the Unit Contribution Rates

Impact of a change in contribution rates

Checking the optimality

In real-world situations, unit contribution rates (objective function coefficients) change frequently. The decision maker is interested in knowing the effects of change in unit contribution rates as they relate to the optimum solution. One thing we should remember about a change in a unit contribution rate (c_j) is that it does not affect the area of feasible solutions. Thus, the only thing we have to check is the *optimality*—that is, whether or not all nonbasic variables have nonpositive $c_j - z_j$ values. We will discuss the change of a unit contribution rate first for a nonbasic variable and then for a basic variable.

For a nonbasic decision variable

Change in the Contribution Rate of a Nonbasic Variable The determination as to whether or not a decision variable appears in the optimum solution, and if so in what quantity, is based on two things: (1) the contribution rate of the decision variable in relation to the contribution rates of the other variables; and (2) the use of resources to produce the decision variable in relation to the resource uses of the other variables.

Among the decision variables in our drink blending example, x_2 (Red Baron Deluxe) is the only one not in the solution basis. In other words, x_2 is a nonbasic variable. The fact that x_2 is a nonbasic variable indicates that its unit contribution rate, $c_2 = \$2.40$, is not sufficient, in relation to its relative resource requirements, to warrant its preparation. Consequently, if c_2 decreases for some reason, x_2 would remain a nonbasic variable. On the other hand, if c_2 increases by a substantial amount, x_2 may become attractive enough to warrant its introduction into the solution base.

Only a positive change is relevant

The only thing we have to check, then, is whether or not the *positive* change in the contribution rate of x_2 will be sufficient to make the $c_j - z_j$ value positive in the column. Since the current $c_j - z_j$ value in the x_2 column is -0.67, the positive change in the contribution rate of x_2 should be at least 0.67 before x_2 can become a basic variable.

Table 5.7   The Final Simplex Tableau of the Alpha Beta Sigma Problem

c_b	Basis	Solution	3.00 x_1	2.40 x_2	2.00 x_3	1.40 x_4	0 s_1	0 s_2	0 s_3	0 s_4	0 s_5	0 s_6
0	s_1	160	0	-1	0	0	1	0	0	0	-4	0
1.40	x_4	80	0	1	0	1	0	0	0	0	0	1
2.00	x_3	80	0	$-2/3$	1	0	0	1/3	0	0	0	$-2/3$
0	s_4	60	1	-1	0	0	0	0	0	1	0	-3
3.00	x_1	50	1	1	0	0	0	0	0	0	1	0
0	s_3	50	0	1/3	0	0	0	$-2/3$	1	0	-1	4/3
	z_j	422.00	3.00	3.07	2.00	1.40	0	.67	0	0	3.00	.07
	$c_j - z_j$		0	$-.67$	0	0	0	$-.67$	0	0	-3.00	$-.07$

If we express the change in the contribution rate of x_2 as Δc_2, the following statement can be made:

$\Delta c_2 > -(c_2 - z_2)$	A new solution results in x_2 as a basic variable.
$\Delta c_2 = -(c_2 - z_2)$	The previous optimum solution is still optimum but an alternate optimum solution exists.
$\Delta c_2 < -(c_2 - z_2)$	The previous optimum solution is still optimum.

For a basic decision variable

Change in the Contribution Rate of a Basic Variable When the contribution rate of a basic variable is changed, there are three possible consequences: (1) the change in the contribution rate is not sufficient to change the optimum solution; (2) the change in the contribution rate is sufficient to warrant a new optimum solution; or (3) the change in the contribution rate does not affect the total profit (or cost), but there is an alternate optimum solution (a case of multiple optimum solutions).

Since the variable under consideration is a basic variable, a change in its contribution rate will affect the z_j (and thus the $c_j - z_j$) values in the nonbasic-variable columns. In the basic-variable row, there are only nonzero coefficients in its own column and in the nonbasic-variable column. For example, in Table 5.7 we can easily see that in the x_1 row there are coefficients of 1 only in the x_1 column itself and in the nonbasic-variable columns x_2 and s_5. Consequently, when the unit contribution rate of a basic variable changes, the results are as shown below:

A positive or negative change?

	The Nonbasic-Variable Column	
Change in c_j	**With Positive Coefficients**	**With Negative Coefficients**
Increase $(+\Delta)$	Becomes less attractive	Becomes more attractive
Decrease $(-\Delta)$	Becomes more attractive	Becomes less attractive

If a nonbasic variable becomes less attractive, it remains a nonbasic variable. In other words, the previous optimum solution remains optimum. Therefore, we are primarily concerned with the circled conditions in the above summary: if the contribution rate *increases,* we want to examine the nonbasic-variable columns where there are *negative* coefficients in the basic-variable row; if the contribution rate *decreases,* we want to analyze the nonbasic-variable columns where there are *positive* coefficients in the basic-variable row.

Checking the row coefficients

Now we are ready to examine a change in the unit contribution rate of a basic variable in our example. Let us suppose that the contribution rate of x_3 (c_3) is increased by a certain amount, Δ. We can substitute $2 + \Delta$ for the previous contribution rate c_3 ($\$2.00$), as shown in Table 5.8. Notice that this change will affect the z_j (and consequently the $c_j - z_j$) values of the three nonbasic-variable columns x_2, s_2, and s_6. Since c_3 is being increased, the s_2 column becomes less attractive because of its positive coefficient of 1/3 in the x_3 row. Thus, we can concentrate our attention on the x_2 and s_6 columns.

Finding a required change Δ for a new solution

As soon as the $c_j - z_j$ value of either the x_2 or the s_6 column becomes zero or positive as c_3 increases, we can have a new optimum solution. Then, we can analyze

Table 5.8   Change in the Contribution Rate of x_3

c_B	Basis	Solution	3.00 x_1	2.40 x_2	2+Δ x_3	1.40 x_4	0 s_1	0 s_2	0 s_3	0 s_4	0 s_5	0 s_6
0	s_1	160	0	−1	0	0	1	0	0	0	−4	0
1.40	x_4	80	0	1	0	1	0	0	0	0	0	1
2+Δ	x_3	80	0	−2/3	1	0	0	1/3	0	0	0	−2/3
0	s_4	60	0	−1	0	0	0	0	0	1	0	−3
3.00	x_1	50	1	1	0	0	0	0	0	0	1	0
0	s_3	50	0	1/3	0	0	0	−2/3	1	0	−1	4/3
z_j		422.00 +80Δ	3.00	3.07 − .67Δ	2+Δ	1.40	0	2/3 + Δ/3	0	0	3.00	1/15 − 2Δ/3
$c_j - z_j$			0	−.67 + .67Δ	0	0	0	−2/3 − Δ/3	0	0	−3.00	−1/15 + 2Δ/3

as follows the value of Δ that will make the $c_j - z_j$ values in the x_2 and x_6 columns positive:

x_2 column

$$c_j - z_j \geq 0$$
$$-.67 + .67\Delta \geq 0$$
$$.67\Delta \geq .67$$
$$\Delta \geq 1.00$$

s_6 column

$$c_j - z_j \geq 0$$
$$-1/15 + 2\Delta/3 \geq 0$$
$$2\Delta/3 \geq 1/15$$
$$\Delta \geq 1/10$$
$$\Delta \geq .10$$

It is clear that if c_3 increases by \$.10, the $c_j - z_j$ value in the s_6 column becomes zero and thus results in a case of multiple optimum solutions. If the increase of c_3 is over \$.10, s_6 becomes a basic variable and we will have a new solution. Since the required change of c_3 for the s_6 column is smaller than that for the x_2 column (\$.10 vs. \$1.00), the upper limit of change in c_3 becomes

Finding the upper and lower limits

$$\text{Upper limit} = \text{Current contribution rate} + \text{Required change} = \$2.00 + \$.10$$
$$\text{Upper limit } (c_3) = \$2.10$$

If c_3 decreases, we can substitute $2 - \Delta$ for 2.00 and evaluate the nonbasic-variable columns that have positive coefficients. Since we have only one positive coefficient in the s_2 row (other than 1 in its own column x_3), we can perform our analysis as follows:

s_2 column:

$$c_j - z_j \geq 0$$
$$-2/3 - \Delta/3 \geq 0$$
$$-\Delta/3 \geq 2/3$$
$$\Delta \leq -2.00$$

If c_3 is decreased by \$2.00, the $c_j - z_j$ value of the s_2 column will become zero and therefore an alternate optimum solution exists. Thus, the lower limit of change in c_3 is

$$\text{Lower limit} = \text{Current contribution rate} + \text{Required change} = \$2.00 - \$2.00$$
$$\text{Lower limit } (c_3) = 0$$

The range of c_3 is \$0 (lower limit) to \$2.10 (upper limit). If the contribution rate of x_3 is within this range, the current optimum solution remains optimum. If c_3 increases above \$2.10, a new optimum solution will result since the $c_j - z_j$ value of s_6 becomes positive. On the other hand, if the contribution rate of x_3 is exactly equal to either \$0 or \$2.10, there will be an alternate optimum solution.

A similar analysis can be made for the contribution rates of x_1 and x_4. A brief examination of the x_1 and x_4 rows in Table 5.8 indicates that there is no negative coefficient in either of these two rows. Thus, there will be only lower limits but no upper limits.

To simplify the process, you are provided with the following simple procedure for deriving the upper or lower limits of contribution rates:

Simple formulas

$$\text{Lower limit: } \quad c_{kl} = \max\left(c_k + \frac{c_j - z_j}{a_{kj}}\right) \text{ for } a_{kj} > 0$$

$$\text{Upper limit:} \quad c_{ku} = \min\left(c_k + \frac{c_j - z_j}{a_{kj}}\right) \text{ for } a_{kj} < 0$$

where

c_k = contribution rate of the kth basic variable in the solution basis

$c_j - z_j$ = the $c_j - z_j$ value of the jth variable that is nonbasic

a_{kj} = the coefficient in the kth basic-variable row and jth variable column that is nonbasic

In our example, we can again find the range of the contribution rate of x_3 as follows:

$$c_{3l} = \max\left(c_3 + \frac{c_{s2} - z_{s2}}{a_{3,s2}}\right)$$

[the only positive coefficient is in the x_3 row and the s_2 column]

$$= \left(2.00 + \frac{-2/3}{1/3}\right)$$
$$= (2.00 - 2.00)$$
$$= 0$$

$$c_{3u} = \min\left(c_3 + \frac{c_2 - z_2}{a_{3,2}}; c_3 + \frac{c_{s6} - z_{s6}}{a_{3,s6}}\right)$$

[there are two negative coefficients in the x_3 row: one in the x_2 column and the other in the s_6 column]

$$= \min\left(2.00 + \frac{-2/3}{-2/3}; 2.00 + \frac{-2/30}{-2/3}\right)$$
$$= \min(3.00; 2.10)$$
$$= 2.10$$

We can summarize our sensitivity analysis of changes in the unit contribution rates of basic variables as follows:

Basic Variable	Contribution Rate Ranging		
	Lower Limit	Current Rate	Upper Limit
x_1	$2.33	$3.00	No limit
x_3	$0.00	$2.00	$2.10
x_4	$1.33	$1.40	No limit

Changes in the Available Resources

Changes in the available resources are, indeed, quite frequent in actual decision problems. You are undoubtedly familiar with a situation such as: "How can my $9.50 check at the Pizza Parlor bounce? I had $75 in my checking account just last Monday!" *C'est la vie!*

Change in the right-hand-side value

In this section we will discuss the effect of a change in the right-hand-side value (b_i) of a constraint on the optimum solution. A change in b_i does not affect $c_j - z_j$. You will remember from our discussion of sensitivity analysis in Chapter 3 that a change in b_i affects only the intercepts of the constraint. Thus, the only thing we have to check is whether or not the new solution values of the basic variables are still nonnegative after a change in b_i. If they are nonnegative, the previous optimum solution is still optimum. If there is a negative solution value for a basic variable, the previous optimum solution is infeasible. Thus, we are not interested in checking the optimality but rather the *feasibility*.

Checking the feasibility

We can develop a simple approach for determining a b_i range within which the previous optimum solution mix of basic variables would remain in the solution basis. For example, let us assume that the fifth constraint of the model has been changed from $x_1 + x_2 + s_5 = 50$ to $x_1 + x_2 + s_5 = 50 + \Delta$. In other words, b_5 has been increased by Δ units. If we substitute $b_5 = 50 + \Delta$ for the original b_5 and solve the problem, the simplex solution results in the final simplex tableau shown in Table 5.9.

Notice that in Table 5.9 there is no change in any coefficients in the mode, except for the changes in the solution values for the s_1, x_1, and s_3 rows. The coefficients of Δ in the solution column correspond to the coefficients in the s_5 column, as shown below:

Basis	Δ Coefficient in Solution Column	Coefficient in s_5 Column
s_1	-4Δ	-4
x_4	0	0
x_3	0	0
s_4	0	0
x_1	$+\Delta$	1
s_3	$-\Delta$	-1

The above result is no accident. The slack variable s_5 appears only in the fifth constraint, where b_5 has been changed. Therefore, the coefficients in the s_5 column indicate what multiples of b_5 have been added to the solution values of the other rows.

Determining the range of a change

Now let us refer to Table 5.9 once more. As long as a change in b_5 expressed by Δ does not result in a negative solution value in the basis, the previous solution mix remains the optimum mix. Thus, we can easily determine the range of Δ as follows:

$$
\begin{aligned}
s_1 \text{ row:} \quad 160 - 4\Delta &\geq 0 \\
-4\Delta &\geq -160 \\
4\Delta &\leq 160 \\
\Delta &\leq 40 \\
x_1 \text{ row:} \quad 50 + \Delta &\geq 0 \\
\Delta &\geq -50 \\
s_3 \text{ row:} \quad 50 - \Delta &\geq 0 \\
-\Delta &\geq -50 \\
\Delta &\leq 50
\end{aligned}
$$

We can arrange the value of Δ as follows:

$$-50 \leq \Delta \leq 40 \leq 50$$

It should be clear in the above relationship that we can discard 50 because it is preempted by 40. In other words, the solution value of the s_1 row becomes negative

Table 5.9 *The Final Simplex Tableau with* $b_5 = 50 + \Delta$

c_j			3.00	2.40	2.00	1.40	0	0	0	0	0	0
c_b	Basis	Solution	x_1	x_2	x_3	x_4	s_1	s_2	s_3	s_4	s_5	s_6
0	s_1	$160 - 4\Delta$	0	−1	0	0	1	0	0	0	−4	0
1.40	x_4	80	0	1	0	1	0	0	0	0	0	1
2.00	x_3	80	0	−2/3	1	0	0	1/3	0	0	0	−2/3
0	s_4	60	0	−1	0	0	0	0	0	1	0	−3
3.00	x_1	$50 + \Delta$	1	1	0	0	0	0	0	0	1	0
0	s_3	$50 - \Delta$	0	1/3	0	0	0	−2/3	1	0	−1	4/3
z_j		$422.00 + 3\Delta$	3.00	3.07	2.00	1.40	0	.67	0	0	3.00	.07
$c_j - z_j$			0	−.67	0	0	0	−.67	0	0	−3.00	−.07

when Δ exceeds 40. Thus, the range of change Δ is $-50 \leq \Delta \leq 40$. Since the current value of $b_5 = 50$, the range of b_5 is as follows:

$$50 - 50 \leq b_5 \leq 50 + 40$$
$$0 \leq b_5 \leq 90$$

Within the above range of b_5 the solution mix of basic variables remains in the optimum solution. However, the solution values of the basic variables do not remain the same. For example, suppose that b_5 is changed from 50 to 60. Then the optimum solution will be as follows:

Previous Optimum Solution		New Optimum Solution	
Basis	**Solution**	**Basis**	**Solution**
s_1	160	s_1	$160 - 4\,(10) = 120$
x_4	80	x_4	80
x_3	80	x_3	80
s_4	60	s_4	60
x_1	50	x_1	$50 + 1\,(10) = 60$
s_3	50	s_3	$50 - 1\,(10) = 40$
	$Z = \$422$		$Z = \$452$

The impact of coefficient signs

From our discussion thus far it is easy to ascertain that when a b_i increases, the solution value of the basic-variable row that has a negative coefficient in the corresponding slack-variable column decreases. For example, when b_5 was increased from 50 to 60, as illustrated above, the solution values for the s_1 and s_3 rows decreased because of their negative coefficients in the s_5 column. Thus, we should be primarily concerned with the circled conditions in the following summary box:

	Basic-variable Solution Values	
Change in b_i	**With Positive Slack Coefficients**	**With Negative Slack Coefficients**
Increase $(+\Delta)$	Increase	(Decrease)
Decrease $(-\Delta)$	(Decrease)	Increase

To simplify the process of determining the right-hand-side value ranging, you are provided with the following simple procedure. Do not try to memorize the formulas, but simply learn to use them.

Simple formulas

$$\text{\textit{Lower limit:}} \quad b_{il} = \max \left(b_i - \frac{B_k}{a_{ki}^*} \right) \text{ for } a_{ki}^* > 0$$

$$\text{\textit{Upper limit:}} \quad b_{iu} = \min \left(b_i - \frac{B_k}{a_{ki}^*} \right) \text{ for } a_{ki}^* < 0$$

where
b_i = the original right-hand-side value of the ith constraint
B_k = the solution value of the kth basic-variable
a_{ki}^* = the coefficient in the kth row and ith slack-variable
column where b_i has been changed

Now let us go back to our drink blending example. The optimum solution was presented in Table 5.7. The interpretation of the shadow price (the $c_j - z_j$ value of the nonbasic slack variable) is that the objective function will be changed by the amount shown by the shadow price within the right-hand-side range for that particular constraint. For example, the interpretation of the shadow price in the s_5 column is that one additional unit in b_5 would be worth \$3.00. Thus, if we relax this constraint by one unit, our revenue would be increased by \$3.00. On the other hand, if we tighten the constraint by reducing b_5 by one unit, our revenue would be decreased by \$3.00. This shadow price is valid within the lower and upper limits of b_5. The range can be calculated as

Shadow prices and the range of a change

$$b_{5l} = \max\left(b_5 - \frac{B_{x1}}{a_{x1,\ s5}}\right)$$

[there is only one positive coefficient in the s_5 column]

$$= \left(50 - \frac{50}{1}\right)$$
$$= 0$$

$$b_{5u} = \min\left(b_5 - \frac{B_{s1}}{a_{s1,\ s5}};\ b_5 - \frac{B_{s3}}{a_{s3,\ s5}}\right)$$

[there are two negative coefficients in the s_5 column, in the s_1 row, and in the s_3 row]

$$= \min\left(50 - \frac{160}{-4};\ 50 - \frac{50}{-1}\right)$$
$$= \min\ (50 + 40;\ 50 + 50)$$
$$= 90$$

The range of b_5 is zero (lower limit) to 90 (upper limit) drinks. If b_5 is within this range, the current optimum solution mix remains the same. Within this range, therefore, the shadow price of \$3.00 for the s_5 column remains valid. By using the same procedure, we can determine the right-hand-side value ranging for all constraints as follows:

	Right-hand-side Ranging		
Constraint Number	Lower Limit	Current Value	Upper Limit
1	200	360	No limit
2	160	400	475
3	210	260	No limit
4	240	300	No limit
5	0	50	90
6	42 1/2	80	100

Changes in the Technological Coefficients

In real-world situations, the technological coefficients (a_{ij}) change frequently as a result of the varying efficiency of manpower or because of technological improvements. Surely you are familiar with this situation: frequently you can study almost a whole chapter in one hour while listening to music, but sometimes you cannot study even a single page during an entire evening.

The decision maker is interested in the impact of changes in technological coef-

Change in technological coefficients

ficients on the optimum solution. The effect of a change in an a_{ij} depends on whether the coefficient is for a basic decision variable or a nonbasic decision variable.

Change in an a_{ij} of a Nonbasic Decision Variable When the a_{ij} coefficient of a nonbasic decision variable is changed, it does not affect the feasibility of the previous optimum solution. In other words, if we repeat the simplex solution with the changed a_{ij} coefficient of a nonbasic decision variable, the only possible changes would be in the coefficients of that nonbasic-variable column. Thus, the same solution must be obtained and it must be feasible. Since the variable is nonbasic ($x_j = 0$ in the final solution), the only thing we have to check is whether or not the new coefficients in this variable column have made the $c_j - z_j$ value positive.

For a nonbasic decision variable

Checking the optimality

In our drink blending example, let us suppose that coefficient a_{52} is changed from 1 to $1 + \Delta$. Then, the constraint becomes $x_1 + (1 + \Delta)x_2 + s_5 = 50$. Table 5.10 on pages 172 presents the final simplex tableau with $a_{52} = 1 + \Delta$ substituted in the model. You will notice immediately that several coefficients are changed in the x_2 column.

For example, we can contrast the old and new coefficients as follows:

Row	Old Coefficients in x_2 Column	New Coefficients in x_2 Column	Coefficients in s_5 Column
s_1	-1	$-1 - 4\Delta$	-4
x_4	1	1	0
x_3	$-2/3$	$-2/3$	0
s_4	-1	-1	0
x_1	1	$1 + \Delta$	1
s_3	$1/3$	$1/3 - \Delta$	-1

Checking the slack column coefficients

It should be apparent that the Δ coefficients in the x_2 column correspond exactly to the coefficients in the s_5 column. As long as the $c_j - z_j$ value of the x_2 column remains nonpositive, the previous optimum solution remains optimum. The range of a_{52}, over which the previous optimum solution remains optimum, can be determined by analyzing the optimality condition as follows:

$$c_j - z_j \leq 0$$
$$-2/3 - 3\Delta \leq 0$$
$$-3\Delta \leq 2/3$$
$$\Delta \geq -2/9$$

Since $a_{52} = 1 + \Delta$,

$$\Delta = a_{52} - 1$$

Thus,

$$a_{52} - 1 \geq -2/9$$
$$a_{52} \geq 7/9$$

If a_{52} is less than 7/9, the $z_j - c_j$ value becomes positive in the x_2 column, and thus x_2 is the incoming variable. One more iteration would yield a new optimum solution. As long as $a_{52} \geq 7/9$, the previous solution is still optimum.

For a basic decision variable

Change in an a_{ij} of a Basic Decision Variable Analyzing the impact of a change in an a_{ij} is more complex when the variable involved is a basic variable. Since $x_j > 0$ in the final solution because it is a basic variable, a change in an a_{ij} will have some effect on the solution values of other basic variables. Therefore, a new solution must be checked for its feasibility as well as its optimality.

Table 5.10   The Final Simplex Tableau with $a_{52} = 1 + \Delta$

c_j $\diagdown$ c_b	Basis	Solution	3.00 x_1	2.40 x_2	2.00 x_3	1.40 x_4	0 s_1	0 s_2	0 s_3	0 s_4	0 s_5	0 s_6
0	s_1	160	0	$-1 - 4\Delta$	0	0	1	0	0	0	-4	0
1.40	x_4	80	0	1	0	1	0	0	0	0	0	1
2.00	x_3	80	0	$-2/3$	1	0	0	1/3	0	0	0	$-2/3$
0	s_4	60	0	-1	0	0	0	0	0	1	0	-3
3.00	x_1	50	1	$1 + \Delta$	0	0	0	0	0	0	1	0
0	s_3	50	0	$1/3 - \Delta$	0	0	0	$-2/3$	1	0	-1	4/3
	z_j	422.00	3.00	$3.07 + 3\Delta$	2.00	1.40	0	.67	0	0	3.00	.07
	$c_j - z_j$		0	$-2/3 - 3\Delta$	0	0	0	$-.67$	0	0	-3.00	$-.07$

First, we must calculate the new coefficients of x_j in the simplex tableau by the same procedure we have already described when a change in an a_{ij} occurs for a nonbasic variable. Since x_j is a basic variable, all coefficients in the x_j column should be zero except for a coefficient of 1 in its own basic-variable row. This condition must be restored algebraically in order to test the feasibility and optimality of the revised solution.

To illustrate the procedure, let us go back to our problem. Suppose the second constraint is changed from the original $3x_3 + 2x_4 + s_2 = 400$ to $3x_3 + x_4 + s_2 = 400$ (coefficient a_{24} is changed from 2 to 1). We can easily determine the required change as follows:

Row	Coefficients in x_4 Column	Coefficients in s_2 Column	New Coefficient in x_4 Column
s_1	0	0	0
x_4	1	0	1
x_3	0	1/3	−1/3
s_4	0	0	0
x_1	0	0	0
s_3	0	−2/3	2/3

Restoring the simplex tableau condition

Since the change in a_{24} is -1, $\Delta = -1$. Thus, the coefficients in the s_2 column are multiplied by -1. That is how, in Table 5.11, we determined $-1/3$ and $2/3$ in the x_3 and s_3 rows respectively. To restore the condition of the basic-variable column coefficients, we must pick the x_4 column as the pivot column and the x_4 row as the pivot row in Table 5.11.

A new solution is derived in Table 5.12. This solution restored the condition of the basic-variable column coefficients in the x_4 column. However, this process resulted in an infeasible solution because s_3 has a solution value of $-10/3$. To find a feasible solution, we apply the dual simplex method. The pivot row is the s_3 row and the pivot column is the s_2 column.

One more iteration yields the new optimum solution shown in Table 5.13.

Checking both feasibility and optimality

A similar analysis can be made for the remaining basic decision variables x_1 and x_3. Since we have to check both the feasibility and the optimality of the solution when the a_{ij} of a basic variable changes, we cannot simply determine the coefficient ranging. However, we can determine the coefficient ranging for the solution feasibility. Such a solution may not be optimum, however, and it may require additional iterations to determine the optimum solution.

Addition of a New Constraint

Adding a new constraint

After the optimum solution has been obtained for a linear programming problem, it may become necessary to add a new constraint. Such a situation may occur as a result of a development such as a new government regulation, a new company policy, a new organizational structure, a change in the economic situation, or an error in overlooking a resource constraint in the model formulation process. If the decision maker decides to add a new constraint after the final solution has been reached, the solution mix may be changed.

Table 5.11   The Simplex Tableau with $a_{24} = 1$

c_j			3.00	2.40	2.00	1.40	0	0	0	0	0	0
c_b	Basis	Solution	x_1	x_2	x_3	x_4	s_1	s_2	s_3	s_4	s_5	s_6
0	s_1	160	0	-1	0	0	1	0	0	0	-4	0
1.40	x_4	80	0	1	0	1	0	0	0	0	0	1
2.00	x_3	80	0	-2/3	1	-1/3	0	1/3	0	0	0	-2/3
0	s_4	60	0	-1	0	0	0	0	0	1	0	-3
3.00	x_1	50	1	1	0	0	0	0	0	0	1	0
0	s_3	50	0	1/3	0	2/3	0	-2/3	1	0	-1	4/3
	z_j	422.00	3.00	3.07	2.00	.73	0	.67	0	0	3.00	.07
	$c_j - z_j$		0	-.67	0	.67	0	-.67	0	0	-3.00	-.07

Table 5.12 *New Optimum Solution with $a_{24} = 1$*

c_j / c_b	Basis	Solution	3.00 x_1	2.40 x_2	2.00 x_3	1.40 x_4	0 s_1	0 s_2	0 s_3	0 s_4	0 s_5	0 s_6
0	s_1	160	0	−1	0	0	1	0	0	0	−4	0
1.40	x_4	80	0	1	0	1	0	0	0	0	0	1
2.00	x_3	320/3	0	−1/3	1	0	0	1/3	0	0	0	−1/3
0	s_4	60	0	−1	0	0	0	0	0	1	0	−3
3.00	x_1	50	1	1	0	0	0	0	0	0	1	0
0	s_3	−10/3	0	−1/3	0	0	0	−2/3	1	0	−1	2/3
	z_j	475.33	3.00	3.73	2.00	1.40	0	2/3	0	0	3.00	.73
	$c_j - z_j$		0	−1.33	0	0	0	−2/3	0	0	−3.00	−.73

Table 5.13 *The New Optimum Solution by the Dual Simplex Method*

c_j / c_b	Basis	Solution	3.00 x_1	2.40 x_2	2.00 x_3	1.40 x_4	0 s_1	0 s_2	0 s_3	0 s_4	0 s_5	0 s_6
0	s_1	160	0	−1	0	0	1	0	0	0	−4	0
1.40	x_4	80	0	1	0	1	0	0	0	0	0	1
2.00	x_3	105	0	−2/3	1	0	0	0	1/2	0	−1/2	0
0	s_4	60	0	−1	0	0	0	0	0	1	0	−3
3.00	x_1	50	1	1	0	0	0	0	0	0	1	0
0	s_2	5	0	1/2	0	0	0	1	−3/2	0	3/2	−1
	z_j	472.00	3.00	3.07	2.00	1.40	0	0	1.00	0	2.00	1.40
	$c_j - z_j$		0	−.67	0	0	0	0	−1.00	0	−2.00	−1.40

A new constraint can
never expand the feasible
region

The addition of a new constraint does not affect the objective function. If the new constraint is binding, it will further reduce the area of feasible solutions, and thus the total profit, z_j, will decrease. On the other hand, if the new constraint is not binding (i.e., if it is redundant), the previous optimum solution is still feasible and optimum. We should always remember that a new constraint can only further reduce the solution space, but it can never expand the feasibility area.

Checking the feasibility

The only thing we have to check, when we add a new constraint, is whether or not the previous optimum solution is still feasible. This can easily be done by examining whether or not the solution values of the basic variables satisfy the new constraint. If the new constraint is not satisfied, the previous optimum solution is now an infeasible solution.

If the previous optimum solution is infeasible, the solution value of the new slack variable in the basis will be negative. In this case we can utilize the dual simplex method to find a new optimum solution. To illustrate the procedure, let us consider two possible cases.

A New Constraint, $x_1 \leq 70$ Suppose that we decide to add a new sales constraint, $x_1 \leq 70$, to the Alpha Beta Sigma model. This constraint simply says that we should restrict the number of Red Baron Supremes to 70 drinks. The previous optimum solution indicates that currently we are scheduled to make 50 Red Baron Supremes (i.e., $x_1 = 50$). We can easily check the previous optimum solution and see that it satisfies the new constraint. Thus, the previous solution is still optimum.

A nonbinding new
constraint

A binding new constraint

A New Constraint, $x_4 \leq 60$ Let us suppose that we decide to add a new constraint, $x_4 \leq 60$, which says that the number of Red Baron Maybes should be limited to 60. The current optimum solution shows $x_4 = 80$. Consequently, the new constraint is not satisfied and the current solution is infeasible.

First, we develop a new simplex equality, $x_4 + s_7 = 60$. Then, we introduce s_7 into the solution basis and list the appropriate coefficients in the simplex tableau, as shown in Table 5.14. In the x_4 column, since x_4 is a basic variable, the only nonzero coefficient must be the 1 in the x_4 row. To restore this condition, we select the x_4 column as the pivot column and the x_4 row as the pivot row.

The new solution, after the iteration, is shown in Table 5.15. This solution is clearly infeasible because the solution value of s_7 is negative (-20). Now, we employ the dual simplex method to derive a new solution. The pivot row is the s_7 row, and the s_6 column is the pivot column. The new optimum solution is obtained in Table 5.16.

Addition of a New Variable

Adding a new decision
variable

After we solve a linear programming problem, we may discover, for example, that we omitted an important decision variable in the model, or that the firm decided to introduce a new product that uses the same basic production resources. Including an additional variable in the model requires an appropriate c_j coefficient in the objective function and appropriate a_{ij} coefficients in the constraints.

Is the new variable
profitable?

The important question is whether or not the new variable is attractive enough to be brought into the solution basis. This question can be answered simply by analyzing the new product's resource requirements and its contribution rate. For exam-

Table 5.14   Addition of a New Constraint, $x_4 \leq 60$

c_j			3.00	2.40	2.00	1.40	0	0	0	0	0	0	0
c_b	Basis	Solution	x_1	x_2	x_3	x_4	s_1	s_2	s_3	s_4	s_5	s_6	s_7
0	s_1	160	0	−1	0	0	1	0	0	0	−4	0	0
1.40	x_4	80	0	1	0	⨀1	0	0	0	0	0	1	0
2.00	x_3	80	0	−2/3	1	0	0	1/3	0	0	0	−2/3	0
0	s_4	60	0	−1	0	0	0	0	0	1	0	−3	0
3.00	x_1	50	1	1	0	0	0	0	0	0	1	0	0
0	s_3	50	0	1/3	0	0	0	−2/3	1	0	−1	4/3	0
0	s_7	60	0	0	0	1	0	0	0	0	0	0	1
	z_j	422.00	3.00	3.07	2.00	1.40	0	.67	0	0	3.00	.07	0
	$c_j - z_j$		0	−.67	0	0	0	−.67	0	0	−3.00	−.07	0

Table 5.15   An Infeasible New Solution

c_j			3.00	2.40	2.00	1.40	0	0	0	0	0	0	0
c_b	Basis	Solution	x_1	x_2	x_3	x_4	s_1	s_2	s_3	s_4	s_5	s_6	s_7
0	s_1	160	0	−1	0	0	1	0	0	0	−4	0	0
1.40	x_4	80	0	1	0	1	0	0	0	0	0	1	0
2.00	x_3	80	0	−2/3	1	0	0	1/3	0	0	0	−2/3	0
0	s_4	60	0	−1	0	0	0	0	0	1	0	−3	0
3.00	x_1	50	1	1	0	0	0	0	0	0	1	0	0
0	s_3	50	0	1/3	0	0	0	−2/3	1	0	−1	4/3	0
0	s_7	−20	0	−1	0	0	0	0	0	0	0	⨀−1	1
	z_j	422.0	3.00	3.07	2.00	1.40	0	.67	0	0	3.00	.07	0
	$c_j - z_j$		0	−.67	0	0	0	−.67	0	0	−3.00	−.07	0

Table 5.16   The New Optimum Solution

c_j → c_b ↓	Basis	Solution	3.00 x_1	2.40 x_2	2.00 x_3	1.40 x_4	0 s_1	0 s_2	0 s_3	0 s_4	0 s_5	0 s_6	0 s_7
0	s_1	160	0	−1	0	0	1	0	0	0	−4	0	0
1.40	x_4	60	0	0	0	1	0	0	0	0	0	0	1
2.00	x_3	93 1/3	0	0	1	0	0	1/3	0	0	0	0	2/3
0	s_4	120	0	2	0	0	0	0	0	1	0	0	3
3.00	x_1	50	1	1	0	0	0	0	1	0	1	0	0
0	s_3	23 1/3	0	−1	0	0	0	−2/3	1	0	−1	0	−4/3
0	s_6	20	0	1	0	0	0	0	0	0	0	1	−1
	z_j	420.67	3.00	3.00	2.00	1.40	0	.67	0	0	3.00	0	2.73
	$c_j - z_j$		0	−.60	0	0	0	−.67	0	0	−3.00	0	−2.73

ple, let us suppose that a new variable, x_5 (Red Baron Super), is to be added. Let us assume that the new variable x_5 requires 3 units of Resource 1 (regular bourbon), 2 units of Resource 3 (regular tomato juice), 1 unit of Resource 5 (limited sales of drinks that contain regular bourbon), and has a price (unit contribution rate) of \$2.75.

From Table 5.7 the shadow prices for the three resources can be found as follows:

$$\text{Resource 1:} \quad \text{shadow price in the } s_1 \text{ column} = \$0.00$$
$$\text{Resource 3:} \quad \text{shadow price in the } s_3 \text{ column} = \ \ 0.00$$
$$\text{Resource 5:} \quad \text{shadow price in the } s_5 \text{ column} = \ \ 3.00$$

Thus, the cost of producing one unit of x_5 is found by multiplying each resource requirement by its respective shadow price and adding:

$$Z(x_5) = (3 \times 0) + (2 \times 0) + (1 \times 3.00) = 3.00$$

With a c_j of \$2.75 for x_5, the net contribution becomes

$$c_j - z_j = 2.75 - 3.00 = -0.25$$

Thus, x_5 will not be brought into the solution basis, and the previous solution is still optimum.

If the $c_j - z_j$ value for the new variable is positive, we can either solve the problem again with the new model or use a dual model to check the optimality. Remembering the formulation procedure of the dual model, we find that the addition of a new decision variable in the primal model is the same as adding a new constraint in the dual model. Therefore, the dual optimum solution remains feasible if the solution satisfies the new constraint. In such a case, the primal solution is still optimum. Otherwise, more simplex iterations may be required. We can proceed to find the new optimum solution via the dual model by following the same procedure we used above for the addition of a new constraint.

INTEGER PROGRAMMING

Linear programming assumes that all variables can take any nonnegative continuous values in the solution. The divisibility requirement presents no special difficulty for

Unacceptable fractional solution values

most decision problems. For example, it is perfectly acceptable to spend \$129.79 to pour 1.25 cubic feet of concrete, or to use 1.679 ounces of a chemical in an experiment.

In certain problems, however, decision variables cannot take continuous values. For example, we cannot take 1.337 courses at the university, it is impossible to construct 0.29 nuclear power plant, and we cannot assign 2.79 people to complete a task. For these types of problems, linear programming is not directly applicable.

One approach we can take to derive an integer solution is simply to round off the linear programming solution. However, it is not a simple task to round off the fractional solution values of the basic variables while satisfying all of the constraints

The rounded solution

of the model. As a matter of fact, a rounded solution may actually be infeasible with the given set of constraints. Or, a rounded solution may be inferior to the optimum integer solution.

Integer programming is a special extension of linear programming, one which has been developed to derive the optimum integer solution to linear programming

Characteristics of integer programming

problems. The integer programming model must have the following characteristics: (1) a linear objective function; (2) a set of linear constraints; (3) a nonnegativity constraint for model variables; and (4) integer-value constraints for certain variables. When the model requires all integer values for the basic variables, it is generally referred to as an *all-integer* problem. If the model requires only certain variables to be integers, it is a *mixed-integer* problem. A special case of an integer programming problem requires each of its decision variables to have only a value of zero or 1. Such a problem is often referred to as a *zero-one* integer programming problem.

Different types of integer programs

There are many different types of integer programming techniques available. The best known, and perhaps the simplest and most efficient, technique is the *branch and bound* method. Thus, our discussion will be centered around the branch and bound method for all-integer problems. We will begin our discussion of integer programming with the rounding approach and the graphical method.

The Rounding Approach

The rounding approach

The easiest and often the most practical approach to solving integer programming problems is the rounding approach. This approach is simple and certainly economical in terms of the effort and cost required to derive an integer solution. In this approach, we first use the ordinary linear programming method to derive the optimum continuous (or fractional) solution. Then, the solution values of the basic variables are rounded off to their nearest integer values.

The major disadvantage

The major disadvantage of this approach is that the rounded solution may not correspond to the true integer optimum solution. Because the rounded solution may be significantly inferior to the optimum integer solution, the cost and effort required to find the best integer solution may be fully warranted. Or, the rounded solution may be an infeasible solution with the given set of constraints.

Let us examine the following two problems:

$$\text{Problem A:} \quad \text{Maximize } Z = 9x_1 + 10x_2$$
$$\text{subject to} \quad 3x_1 + 4x_2 \leq 30$$
$$2x_1 + x_2 \leq 12$$
$$x_1, x_2 \geq 0$$

$$\text{Problem B:} \quad \text{Maximize } Z = 10x_1 + 22x_2$$
$$\text{subject to} \quad 2x_1 + 5x_2 \leq 20$$
$$6x_1 + 4x_2 \leq 24$$
$$x_1, x_2 \geq 0$$

Table 5.17 presents a comparison of the standard simplex solution with no integer requirements, rounded solutions, and optimum integer solutions for these two problems. For Problem A, the rounded solution yields a total profit of $86, which is $4.60 more than the profit in the continuous solution. Obviously, this is an infeasible solution. We must always remember that an integer solution is never better than a continuous solution, and in most cases the integer solution is inferior to the continuous solution. The reason is, of course, that the additional integer requirement was imposed upon the model. Additional constraints can only shrink the solution space, never expand it. The difference between the continuous and integer solutions is often referred to as the *cost of indivisibility*.

The cost of indivisibility

For Problem B, the rounded solution is feasible but it is inferior to the optimum integer solution. The rounded solution indicates a total profit that is only $2 less than

Table 5.17　Comparison of Continuous, Rounded, and Integer Solutions

Problem	Continuous Solution	Rounded Integer Solution	Optimum Integer Solution
A	$x_1 = 3\ 3/5$ $x_2 = 4\ 4/5$ $Z = \$81.40$	$x_1 = 4$ $x_2 = 5$ $Z = \$86$ (infeasible)	$x_1 = 2$ $x_2 = 6$ $Z = \$78$
B	$x_1 = 1\ 9/11$ $x_2 = 3\ 3/11$ $Z = \$90.18$	$x_1 = 2$ $x_2 = 3$ $Z = \$86$ (feasible)	$x_1 = 0$ $x_2 = 4$ $Z = \$88$

the total profit derived by the optimum integer solution. However, if the unit contribution rates happen to be expressed in millions of dollars, it certainly is cost effective to invest the necessary effort and time to derive the optimum integer solution rather than use the rounded solution.

The Graphical Approach

The graphical approach

If an integer programming problem involves only two decision variables, we can easily solve it by the graphical method. This approach is no different from the graphical method of linear programming we discussed in Chapter 3, except that we must satisfy the integer requirements. The best way to apply the graphical approach of integer programming is to use graph paper and plot all of the integer points within the area of feasible solutions. Then, identify the optimum integer solution through either the iso-profit (or iso-cost) function or the search approaches.

EXAMPLE 5.4　　**CREATIVE DESIGNER JEANS, INC.**

An example

Julia Klein, a junior majoring in Textiles and Design at the university, has decided to create designer jeans and sell them at several boutiques in town. Julia has developed two distinct and simple designs called "Coed" and "Julia." The designs are changed slightly every week so that each boutique will have different jeans to market. Currently, Creative Designer Jeans has orders for the next six months' production.

Julia has set up two production processes: Process 1—cutting and patching, and Process 2—final sewing. With the help of a friend, Julia has set up the following operations:

Process	Time Requirement per Pair		Production Capacity
	Coed	Julia	
Cutting and Patching	2 hr.	3 hr.	12 hr.
Sewing	5 hr.	3 hr.	15 hr.
Unit Profit	$20	$16	

Figure 5.2   Graphical Solution of the Creative Designer Jeans Problem

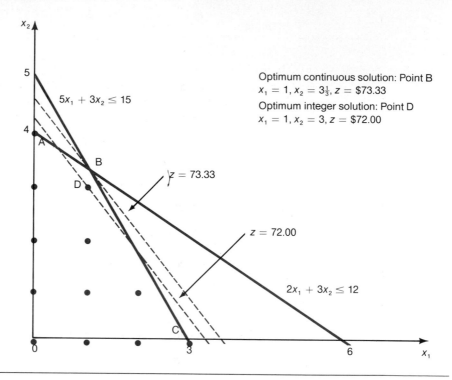

Since the designs are changed every week, the weekly production requires an integer solution. Julia is attempting to determine the optimum number of Coed and Julia jeans to produce every week in order to maximize total profit. A noninteger solution is not acceptable for this problem.

We can formulate the problem as an integer programming model as follows:

$$\text{Maximize } Z = 20x_1 + 16x_2$$
$$\text{subject to} \quad 2x_1 + 3x_2 \leq 12$$
$$5x_1 + 3x_2 \leq 15$$
$$x_1, x_2 = 0 \text{ or nonnegative integer}$$

where x_1 = number of Coed jeans produced per week

x_2 = number of Julia jeans produced per week

This model is the same as any linear programming model except for the last constraint, which specifies the integer requirement for the decision variables. The graphical solution to this problem is presented in Figure 5.2.

The area of feasible solutions is OABC. The optimum continuous solution is identified as point B, where $x_1 = 1$, $x_2 = 3\ 1/3$, and $Z = \$73.33$. To determine the integer optimum solution, we must depart from the continuous optimum point (point B) and retreat toward the origin with the slope of the iso-profit function ($-5/4$). The optimum integer solution is the first integer point intersecting the iso-profit function. This point is point D, where $x_1 = 1$, $x_2 = 3$, and $Z = \$72.00$.

The Branch and Bound Method

The branch and bound method

The general solution method most widely used for integer programming is the branch and bound method. Since a problem has a certain finite number of integer solutions, we can use an enumeration procedure to pick the best solution. The branch and bound method is basically a systematic search routine of enumeration that greatly reduces the solution combinations to be examined.

The basic steps of the branch and bound method of integer programming for a maximization problem can be outlined as follows:

The basic steps

Step 1 Solve the problem by the standard simplex method without the integer requirements.

Step 2 Examine the optimum solution. If the basic variables with integer requirements are all integer valued, the optimum integer solution is found. Stop. If any of the basic variables does not satisfy the integer requirements, continue the process.

Step 3 The set of feasible noninteger solution values is branched into two subproblems. This *branching* is accomplished by introducing two mutually exclusive constraints that are necessary to satisfy the integer requirement of a chosen variable.

Step 4 The *bounding* procedure is as follows: For each subproblem, the objective function value of the optimum noninteger solution is determined as the *upper bound*. The best integer solution derived in any subproblem becomes the *lower bound*. Those subsets having upper bounds that are less than (inferior to) the current lower bound are excluded from further analysis. If there is a feasible integer solution, one that is as good as or better than the upper bound for any subset, it is the optimum integer solution. If no such solution exists, a subproblem with the best upper bound is selected to continue branching. Repeat the process by returning to Step 3.

To illustrate the branch and bound method, let us consider the Creative Designer jeans problem:

$$\text{Maximize } Z = 20x_1 + 16x_2$$
$$\text{subject to} \quad 2x_1 + 3x_2 \leq 12$$
$$5x_1 + 3x_2 \leq 15$$
$$x_1, x_2 = \quad 0 \text{ or nonnegative integer}$$

Step 1 The optimum solution to the problem without the integer requirements was derived in Figure 5.2. The optimum solution is $x_1 = 1$, $x_2 = 3\ 1/3$, $Z = \$73.33$.

Step 2 The optimum solution that is derived is not an integer solution. Thus the branch and bound process must continue.

Step 3 To branch the problem into two subproblems, the variable with the noninteger solution value that has the greatest fractional part is selected. In our solution, only x_2 has a fractional value. Thus, x_2 is selected to develop two mutually exclusive constraints for the two subproblems.

To eliminate the fractional part of x_2, two new constraints are developed. The two integer values closest to 3 1/3 are 3 and 4. Thus, we develop two subproblems by introducing one additional constraint to the original problem, $x_2 \leq 3$ or $x_2 \geq 4$ in each of the subproblems. These two mutually exclusive constraints eliminate all possible fractional values for x_2 between 3 and 4. The two subproblems are as follows:

$$\text{Subproblem A:} \quad \text{Maximize } Z = 20x_1 + 16x_2$$
$$\text{subject to} \quad 2x_1 + 3x_2 \leq 12$$
$$5x_1 + 3x_2 \leq 15$$
$$x_2 \leq 3$$
$$x_1, x_2 \geq 0$$

$$\text{Subproblem B:} \quad \text{Maximize } Z = 20x_1 + 16x_2$$
$$\text{subject to} \quad 2x_1 + 3x_2 \leq 12$$
$$5x_1 + 3x_2 \leq 15$$
$$x_2 \geq 4$$
$$x_1, x_2 \geq 0$$

Step 4 The two subproblems are solved by the graphical method of linear programming, as shown in Figure 5.3. Subproblem A yields a noninteger solution with a total profit of $72.00. This is the upper bound. Subproblem B, on the other hand, has an integer solution. Thus, this integer solution ($x_1 = 0$, $x_2 = 4$, $Z = \$64.00$) is the lower bound. The noninteger solution of Subproblem A has a total profit ($72.00) that is greater than the lower bound ($64.00). Therefore, it is possible that a further branching of Subproblem A may yield an integer solution that is better than the lower bound.

The bounding is achieved by setting the lower bound ($64.00) of the integer solution derived in Subproblem B. Any subproblem that yields solutions with less

than $64.00 total profit will be eliminated from further consideration. We now branch Subproblem A into two subparts, Subproblem A1 and Subproblem A2. Subproblem A1 has an additional constraint, $x_1 \leq 1$, and Subproblem A2 has an additional constraint, $x_1 \geq 2$.

$$\text{Subproblem A1:} \quad \text{Maximize } Z = 20x_1 + 16x_2$$
$$\text{subject to} \quad 2x_1 + 3x_2 \leq 12$$
$$5x_1 + 3x_2 \leq 15$$
$$x_2 \leq 3$$
$$x_1 \leq 1$$
$$x_1, x_2 \geq 0$$

$$\text{Subproblem A2:} \quad \text{Maximize } Z = 20x_1 + 16x_2$$
$$\text{subject to} \quad 2x_1 + 3x_2 \leq 12$$
$$5x_1 + 3x_2 \leq 15$$
$$x_2 \leq 3$$
$$x_1 \geq 2$$
$$x_1, x_2 \geq 0$$

The graphical solutions for the two subproblems are shown in Figure 5.4. Subproblem A1 yields an integer solution ($x_1 = 1$, $x_2 = 3$, $Z = \$68.00$). Since this solution is better than the current lower bound, it becomes the new lower bound. Subproblem A2 yields a noninteger solution ($x_1 = 2$, $x_2 = 1$ 2/3, $Z = \$66.67$).

Figure 5.3   Graphical Solution of Subproblems A and B

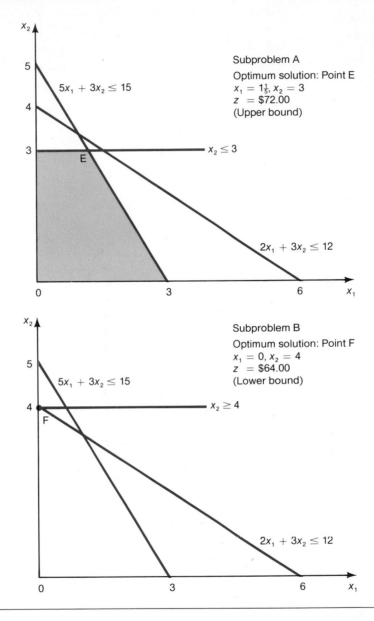

This solution, however, is inferior to the current lower bound ($68.00 derived in Subproblem A1). Thus, no further branching will be necessary from Subproblem A2. There is no upper-bound solution that is better than the lower bound. The optimum integer solution has been obtained. The optimum integer solution is the current lower bound $x_1 = 1$, $x_2 = 3$, $Z = \$68.00$.

Figure 5.4   Graphical Solution of Subproblems A1 and A2

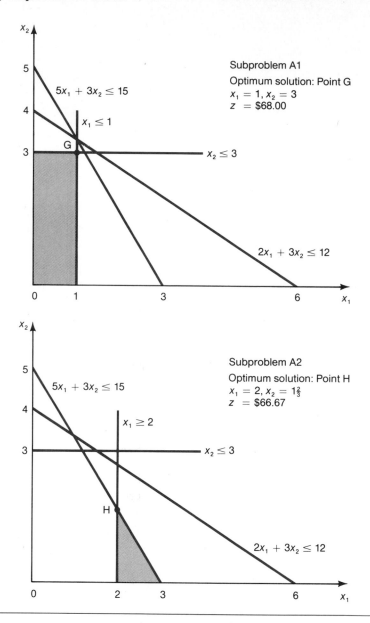

*When to terminate the
procedure*

In the branch and bound procedure, further analysis is terminated when (1) a subproblem results in a solution that is inferior to the current lower bound solution, and (2) further branching yields infeasible solutions.

When the search process is completed, the best integer solution is selected as the optimum solution. The branch and bound procedure for the Creative Designer Jeans problem is presented in Figure 5.5.

Figure 5.5   Complete Branch and Bound Solution

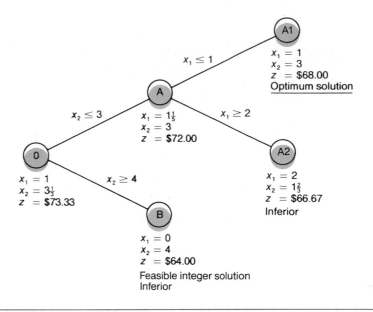

Real-world Applications of Integer Programming

*Real-world application
examples*

In many real-world problems, the solution values must be in integers. It seems logical, then, to expect a wide use of various integer programming techniques. However, integer programming has seen only limited real-world application. We suspect that there is a great deal of "rounding" going on in many organizations. Also, some of the successful applications of integer programming are probably not reported in the literature.

Recently, an increasing number of studies have been reported about the real-world applications of integer programming approaches. One study reported that a mixed-integer programming method was applied in the planning of a steel mill operation in Sweden.[1] This application was successful in determining the optimum mix of ingredients for different types of steel while reducing the materials cost by about 6 percent ($200,000 a year). Another study also reported an application of mixed-integer programming for a warehouse location problem of a large manufacturing firm.[2] The purpose of the study was to reduce the warehouse and distribution costs by identifying alternate warehouse locations. The study reported a potential savings of about 22 percent ($550,600). Yet another study reported an application of mixed-integer programming for the optimum operation of a thermal power station in an

[1]Carl-Henrick Westerberg, Bengt Bjorklund, and Eskil Hultman, "Application of Mixed Integer Programming in a Swedish Steel Mill," *Interfaces,* 7:2 (1977), 39–43.

[2]I. Brosh, M. Hersh, and E. Shlifer, "A Mixed Integer Programming and Heuristic Algorithm for a Warehouse Location Problem," *Omega,* 2:6 (1974), 805–808.

industrial company.[3] The study suggested a significant reduction in the operating cost of the power station.

OTHER TOPICS IN ADVANCED LINEAR PROGRAMMING

In this section we will briefly review several topics of advanced linear programming for those of you who would like to conduct independent studies. Some of these topics are related to the development and extension of the theory of linear programming. Other topics relate to the new applications of linear programming.

Linear Programming under Uncertainty

As we have discussed earlier, the general linear programming approach is deterministic. This assumption makes linear programming an extremely simple technique to use. However, this assumption is also a source of limitation in the practical application of linear programming. The true value of model parameters is usually not known until after the decision based on a linear programming solution is actually implemented. The primary reason for this is that frequently all or some of the parameters are random variables—variables that are influenced by random events in the decision environment.

Several different approaches have been suggested for the solution of the linear programming problem under uncertainty. However, we can express their common characteristic as the "extreme difficulty of solution." There is no general solution method of linear programming under uncertainty, such as the simplex method for the deterministic linear programming problem.

Probabilistic linear programming

There are basically two distinct approaches to linear programming under uncertainty. The first approach, which is generally referred to as *stochastic programming*, attempts to solve the problem through making two or more decisions by selecting model parameters at different points in time. This approach sounds very logical. Its practical application, however, is enormously complex, especially when the model is large.

Stochastic programming

Chance-constrained programming

The second approach, called *chance-constrained programming*, a deterministic model equivalent to the problem-under-uncertainty model, is developed by analyzing the probability distribution of the parameter values. If you are interested in studying this topic further, you should consult the works of Charnes and Cooper, Hillier and Lieberman, Madansky, and Simonnard (see References at the end of this chapter).

Linear Programming and Game Theory

Game theory in a linear programming framework

The relationship between linear programming and game theory was first explored by von Neumann and Dantzig in 1947. The formal relationships between the two fields were further analyzed by A. W. Tucker and his associates. These studies received tremendous attention from management scientists because of their great potential for practical application and because of their theoretical breakthrough in game theory.

---

[3]F. Cavalieri, A. Roversi, and R. Ruzzeri, "Use of Mixed Integer Programming to Investigate Optimum Running Conditions for a Thermal Power Station and Possible Extension to Capacity," *Operational Research Quarterly,* 22:3 (1971), 221–236.

Although the linear programming formulation of a game problem is very interesting mathematically, it has yet to expand the existing knowledge of game theory in any significant way. Those interested in studying this area should consult the many advanced books on mathematical programming, such as the works of Dantzig, Hillier and Lieberman, and Loomba and Turban (see References).

Multiple Objective Linear Programming

Multiple objective linear programming

In linear programming, we can handle only one basic objective—maximize or minimize an objective criterion subject to a set of constraints. In most real-world problems, it is only rarely that we find a decision problem that has a single objective. As a matter of fact, in most of the decision problems we face in life, we have multiple, and sometimes conflicting, objectives.

For example, you are going to a university or a college to gain valuable knowledge in many different areas. Academic programs for a degree, extracurricular activities for your personal interests, dating or meeting many different people in order to socialize and grow, having a part-time job at a local bank to gain some work experience, and living with others to develop friendships—these could be some examples of your objectives. It is extremely difficult or almost impossible to analyze a problem involving multiple objectives by linear programming.

Examples of multiple objectives

We have seen some advances in the area of multiple objective linear programming during the past five years. The basic procedure is to optimize one objective at a time. For example, let us suppose that we have three different objectives, arranged according to priority, as follows:

1. Minimize payroll cost.

2. Achieve a profit level of $150,000.

3. Provide a 10 percent bonus to employees.

The linear programming model can initially be solved to achieve the first objective subject to a set of constraints. When the first objective is achieved as desired or to the extent possible with the given set of constraints, it can be used as an additional constraint. Then, the second objective is pursued. This procedure is repeated until all of the objectives are pursued, and then the final result is analyzed in terms of the attainment of the objectives. Those interested in this topic should consult the work of Steuer (see References).

Although many interesting approaches of multiple objective linear programming have been proposed, they are still at the developmental stage. In this book we devote Chapter 6 to goal programming, an effective technique for multiple objective decision making. Goal programming is an extension and further modification of linear programming. It is a powerful tool in dealing with multiple and conflicting objectives.

Parametric Programming

In many decision problems, model parameters change simultaneously and continuously, rather than discretely as in sensitivity analysis. Parametric programming is also a postoptimum analysis, like sensitivity analysis, but it is concerned with the analysis

Analyzing continuous changes in parameters of continuous changes in the model parameters. A detailed discussion of parametric programming is certainly beyond the scope of this book. However, readers interested in parametric programming are encouraged to read the works of Hillier and Lieberman, and Kim (see References).

SUMMARY

Every linear programming problem, whether it is a maximization or a minimization problem, has a dual model corresponding to its primal. The optimum solution to the dual model provides useful information for the decision maker. The values of the objective functions (z_j in the solution column) in the primal and dual models are always the same when the optimum solutions are reached. The dual decision variables in the optimum solution are usually referred to as the *shadow prices*.

The dual simplex method applies directly to infeasible but better-than-optimum solutions and works toward feasibility. This method is especially useful for problems with many mixed constraints that require a number of artificial variables.

The simplex algorithm is a technique used to derive the optimum solution to a linear programming problem with constant model parameters. However, in real-world situations, model parameters change frequently. Sensitivity analysis is perhaps as important a part of linear programming as the derivation of the optimum primal solution. The decision maker is extremely concerned with the sensitivity of the optimum solution to changes in the model parameters. In this chapter, we have reviewed five possible changes in model parameters, decision variables, and model constraints.

Integer programming is a special type of linear programming in which all or some of the model variables are required to have integer values in the optimum solution. The branch and bound method is a useful tool for general integer programming problems, especially when the variables are constrained by upper and lower bounds.

There are several advanced topics that deserve brief discussion. Therefore, in this chapter we reviewed linear programming under uncertainty, linear programming and game theory, multiple objective linear programming, and parametric programming.

References

Ackoff, R. L., and Sasiani, M. F. *Fundamentals of Operations Research*. New York: Wiley, 1968.

Baumol, W. J. *Economic Theory and Operational Analysis*, 2nd ed. Englewood Cliffs, N.J.: Prentice-Hall, 1965.

Charnes, A., and Cooper, W. W. *Management Models and Industrial Applications of Linear Programming*. New York: Wiley, 1961.

Dantzig, G. B. *Linear Programming and Extensions*. Princeton, N.J.: Princeton University Press, 1963.

Dantzig, G. B., and Wolfe, P. "Decomposition Principles for Linear Programs." *Operations Research,* 8:1 (1960), 101–111.

Hillier, F. S., and Lieberman, G. J. *Introduction to Operations Research,* 3rd ed. San Francisco: Holden-Day, 1980.

Khachian, L. G. "A Polynomial Algorithm in Linear Programming." *Doklady,* 244:6 (1979), 1093–1096.

Kim, C. *Introduction to Linear Programming*. New York: Holt, Rinehart & Winston, 1971.

Kornai, J., and Liptak, T. "Two Level Planning." *Econometrica,* 33:1 (1965), 141–169.

Kwak, N. K. *Mathematical Programming with Business Applications*. New York: McGraw-Hill, 1973.

Lee, S. M. *Linear Optimization for Management*. New York: Petrocelli-Charter, 1976.

Loomba, N. P., and Turban, E. *Applied Programming for Management*. New York: Holt, Rinehart & Winston, 1974.

Madansky, A. "Methods of Solution of Linear Programs under Uncertainty." *Operations Research*, 10:4 (1962), 463–471.

Simonnard, M. *Linear Programming*. Englewood Cliffs, N.J.: Prentice-Hall, 1966.

Steuer, R. E. "An Interactive Multiple Objective Linear Programming Procedure." *TIMS Studies in Management Science*, 6 (1977), 225–239.

Wagner, H. M. *Principles of Operations Research*, 2nd ed. Englewood Cliffs, N.J.: Prentice-Hall, 1975.

Assignments

5.1 What are the important benefits of formulating and solving a dual model?

5.2 Is the dual simplex method a special solution method for a dual model of linear programming? Explain.

5.3 If a primal model has 10 constraints and 15 decision variables, how many constraints and decision variables would its corresponding dual model have?

5.4 Why is sensitivity analysis useful in analyzing linear programming problems?

5.5 What are some of the possible reasons for changes in the technological coefficients in real-world situations?

5.6 What is the cost of indivisibility?

5.7 What are some examples of problems in which we need integer solution values?

5.8 Discuss a problem that would require a mixed-integer or zero-one integer programming model.

5.9 The rounding approach is a simple and practical approach to solving some integer programming problems. What are the possible dangers involved in using the rounding approach?

5.10 What is the difference between sensitivity analysis and parametric programming?

5.11 Can we apply the branch and bound method to a mixed-integer programming problem?

5.12 Discuss a case where we may need to add a new constraint to the problem.

5.13 Discuss a case where we may want to add a new decision variable to the problem.

5.14 Is chance-constrained programming a way to reduce the chance of making errors in linear programming? Explain.

5.15 Discuss a problem that involves multiple and conflicting objectives.

5.16 Is game theory a useful method of winning games when all other predictive models fail? Explain.

5.17 Formulate the dual of the following linear programming problem:

$$\text{Maximize } Z = 240x_1 + 225x_2$$
$$\text{subject to} \quad 3x_1 + 9x_2 \leq 12$$
$$6x_1 + 15x_2 \leq 24$$
$$x_1, x_2 \geq 0$$

5.18 Formulate the dual of the following linear programming problem:

$$\text{Maximize } Z = 80x_1 + 120x_2$$
$$\text{subject to} \quad 4x_1 + 8x_2 \leq 240$$
$$8x_1 - 4x_2 \geq 36$$
$$x_1, x_2 \geq 0$$

5.19 Formulate the dual of the following linear programming problem:

$$\text{Maximize } Z = 40x_1 + 36x_2$$
$$\text{subject to} \quad 16x_1 + 8x_2 = 80$$
$$2x_2 \leq 8$$
$$x_1, x_2 \geq 0$$

5.20 Formulate the dual of the following linear programming problem:

$$\text{Minimize } Z = -20x_1 + 40x_2$$
$$\text{subject to} \quad -2x_1 + 2x_2 \leq 2$$
$$6x_1 + 4x_2 \leq 24$$
$$x_1, x_2 \geq 0$$

5.21 Paul, the butcher at the local meat market, has a meat loaf mixing problem that requires linear programming. He is attempting to determine the optimum mix of two types of meat loaf: regular and hot.

A tray of regular meat loaf requires 1 hour of mixing time, and a tray of hot meat loaf takes 2 hours. A tray of regular meat loaf takes 3 feet of shelf space, and a tray of hot meat loaf requires only 2 feet. From past experience, Paul has determined that the profit per tray is $8 for regular and $12 for hot meat loaf. He estimates that the maximum mixing time available per day is 9 hours, and the shelf space available is 16 feet. The maximum daily sale of meat loaf is estimated to be 6 trays.

    a. Formulate the primal linear programming model and solve it by the graphical method.

    b. Formulate the dual model for this problem.

    c. Solve the primal problem by the simplex method.

    d. If we assume that the profit per tray of hot meat loaf is steady at $12, but that the profit per tray of regular meat loaf fluctuates considerably, what profit range should there be for a tray of regular meat loaf in order for Paul to mix and sell 4 trays of regular and 2 trays of hot meat loaf? Refer to the final simplex tableau obtained in part (c).

    e. In the original problem, formulated and solved in part (c), if Paul hires an assistant and the mixing time is increased to 12 hours, what will be the change in the optimum solution?

    f. Again in the original problem, if Paul purchases a new mixer that can mix a tray of hot meat loaf in 1 hour (everything else remaining the same), what will be the effect on the optimum solution?

5.22 The Student Center is preparing a special breakfast for the visiting high school seniors. The center's dietitians have decided to serve only two types of food: eggs and toast (plus all the water one wishes to drink). The minimum vitamin requirements for the breakfast and the vitamin content in a unit of each food are shown on the following page.

Vitamin	Vitamin Content per Unit		Minimum Requirement
	Egg	Toast	
A	4 mg.	5 mg.	20 mg.
B	12 mg.	3 mg.	30 mg.
C	3 mg.	2 mg.	12 mg.

a. If the unit cost for an egg is 3¢ and it is 2¢ for toast, find the optimum solution by the simplex method.

b. Formulate the dual model for this problem.

c. If the minimum requirement for vitamin A is increased from 12 to 18 mg., what will be the change in the final solution?

d. In the original problem solved in part (a), if the unit cost for toast is increased to 4¢, what will be the impact of this change on the optimum solution?

e. Solve the dual problem by the simplex method.

5.23 The Craft Shop is sponsoring its annual yo-yo contest. All yo-yos must be purchased from the shop. The shop sells two models of yo-yos—Super Climber and Hugging Yo. Each model requires three production processes: molding, painting, and finishing. The shop has secured the maximum of 100 hours for molding, 40 hours for painting, and 20 hours for finishing.

Production of a batch of 100 Super Climbers requires 2 hours of molding, 30 minutes of painting, and 30 minutes of finishing. Production of a batch of 100 Hugging Yos requires 2 hours of molding, 1 hour of painting, and 15 minutes of finishing. The Sales Manager reports that the maximum expected sales for Super Climber is 3,500 (35 batches of 100 each), since to use this yo-yo requires a special skill. The manager also reports that they can sell all the Hugging Yos that the shop produces. The management of the firm has decided to use this number of expected sales as a model constraint.

The expected profit from the sale of one batch (100) of Super Climbers is $30, and for a batch (100) of Hugging Yos it is $20.

a. Solve this problem by using the graphical method, and determine the exact number of batches of each type of yo-yo to be produced.

b. What are the basic variables and their values at the optimum point?

c. Because of the unexpected popularity of the Hugging Yo, its unit profit per batch has increased from $20 to $35. What will be the impact of this change on the optimum solution?

d. Solve the original problem in part (a) by the simplex method, and identify the shadow prices. Within what ranges are these shadow prices valid?

5.24 The local credit union has $500,000 to invest in various investment alternatives. The credit union does not wish to invest in mutual funds or common stocks, as it views these as risky alternatives in view of the current economic instability. Instead, it prefers to diversify its investments by allocating the funds among the following alternatives: personal loans to the members of the credit union, government bonds, deposits in a savings and loan association, and preferred stock.

The credit union is simply trying to determine the optimum allocation of funds to be invested in the four alternatives so that the maximum return can be realized.

The actual investment in a specific choice (e.g., preferred stock of General Motors Corp.) within the given investment area will be determined at a later date.

The current yield rates for each of the four alternatives are: personal loans, 7.0 percent; government bonds, 8.0 percent; savings and loan association, 6.5 percent; and preferred stocks, 7.5 percent. The credit union wishes to invest the entire $500,000 so that there will be no idle funds.

Because of the risk elements and the lengths of investment periods required, the management of the credit union has set the following guidelines:

1. Investment in preferred stock should not exceed the amount invested in government bonds or the amount invested in the savings and loan association.

2. The amount of loans to the members should not exceed the total investment in the other three alternatives.

3. At least 30 percent of the total investment funds should be allocated for personal loans to the members.

a. Formulate the primal model for this problem.
b. Solve the model by a computer program, if one is available.
c. Suppose the management has decided to introduce this additional constraint: that the total investment in government bonds should be at least $50,000. What would be the effect of this new constraint on the optimum solution?

5.25 Consider the final simplex tableau on page 195 for a linear programming problem:

a. Identify the optimum solution.
b. What is the marginal value of an additional unit of resource in the first constraint? What is the range of b_1 within which the marginal value is valid ($b_1 = 120$)?
c. Is there an alternative optimum solution? If so, identify the new solution.
d. Suppose that the firm can obtain 10 additional units of resource for the fourth constraint at $10 each ($b_4 = 20$). Should it obtain these additional units? Why or why not?
e. Suppose that the firm can obtain additional resources for the second constraint at $1 per unit ($b_2 = 160$). Should it purchase the additional resources? If so, how many units?
f. Suppose the firm signed a trade agreement with its competitor, and the agreement resulted in a new constraint, $x_1 \leq 8$. Derive the new solution with this additional constraint.

5.26 Solve the following problem by the branch and bound technique:

$$\text{Maximize } Z = 12x_1 + 15x_2$$
$$\text{subject to} \quad 8x_1 + 16x_2 \leq 100$$
$$4x_1 \leq 32$$
$$8x_2 \leq 40$$
$$x_1, x_2 = 0 \text{ or nonnegative integer}$$

5.27 Solve the following problem by the branch and bound technique:

| c_j → | | | 40 | 24 | 52 | 23 | 0 | 0 | 0 | 0 | 0 | 0 |
c_b	Basis	Solution	x_1	x_2	x_3	x_4	s_1	s_2	s_3	s_4	s_5	s_6
24	x_2	50	0	1	1/2	0	-1/5	2/5	0	0	0	-1
0	s_4	10	0	0	-1	0	-3/5	1/5	0	1	0	-3
0	s_3	530	0	0	2 1/2	0	-5	0	1	0	0	-13
40	x_1	10	1	0	1	0	3/5	-1/5	0	0	0	3
0	s_5	16	0	0	1	0	0	0	0	0	1	0
23	x_4	10	0	0	0	1	0	0	0	0	0	-1
	z_j	1830	40	24	52	23	19.20	1.60	0	0	0	73
	$c_j - z_j$		0	0	0	0	-19.20	-1.60	0	0	0	-73

$$\text{Maximize } Z = 51x_1 + 68x_2$$
$$\text{subject to} \quad 17x_1 + 17x_2 \leq 8500$$
$$17x_1 + 17x_2 \geq 6800$$
$$102x_1 - 68x_2 \geq 0$$
$$17x_1 - 34x_2 = 0$$
$$x_1, x_2 = 0 \text{ or nonnegative integer}$$

5.28 Solve the following problem by the branch and bound technique:

$$\text{Maximize } Z = \$4x_1 + \$20x_2$$
$$\text{subject to} \quad x_1 + 10x_2 \leq 20$$
$$x_1 \leq 2$$
$$x_1, x_2 = 0 \text{ or nonnegative integer}$$

5.29 Solve the following problem by the branch and bound technique:

$$\text{Maximize } Z = 3x_1 + 4x_2$$
$$\text{subject to} \quad x_1 + x_2 \leq 500$$
$$x_1 + x_2 \geq 400$$
$$x_1 - 2x_2 = 0$$
$$6x_1 - 4x_2 \geq 0$$
$$x_1, x_2 = 0 \text{ or nonnegative integer}$$

5.30 The dietitian at the local hospital is preparing the breakfast menu for the maternity ward patients. She is planning a special nonfattening diet and has chosen cottage cheese and scrambled eggs for breakfast. She is primarily concerned with the vitamin E and iron requirements for the breakfast.

According to the American Medical Association (AMA), new mothers must get at least 12 mg. of vitamin E and 24 mg. of iron from breakfast. The AMA handbook reports that a scoop of cottage cheese contains 3 mg. of vitamin E and 3 mg. of iron. An average scoop of scrambled eggs contains 2 mg. of vitamin E and 8 mg. of iron. The AMA handbook also recommends that new mothers eat at least two scoops of cottage cheese for breakfast. The dietitian considers this to be one of the model constraints.

The hospital Accounting Department estimates that a scoop of cottage cheese costs 5¢ and a scoop of scrambled eggs also costs 5¢. The dietitian is attempting to determine the optimum breakfast menu that satisfies all the requirements and minimizes the total cost. The cook insists that he can serve foods only by the full scoop, thus necessitating an integer solution.

Solve this problem by the branch and bound technique to determine the optimum integer solution.

6 GOAL PROGRAMMING

In Chapters 3, 4, and 5 we studied linear programming as a decision making technique for problems that involve a single objective. In most linear programming problems we discussed, the objective was to maximize total profit or minimize total cost subject to a set of constraints imposed by the decision environment. In most real-world situations, however, organizations have multiple and sometimes conflicting objectives. Decision making with multiple objectives has been a new challenge of management science during the past decade. Goal programming is a powerful and most promising technique for decision problems that involve multiple objectives. In this chapter, we will study the concept, model formulation, and solution methods of goal programming.

Learning Objectives   From the study of this chapter, you will learn the following:

1. The basic concept and approach of goal programming.
2. The types of management problems that can be analyzed by goal programming.
3. Formulating various decision problems as goal programming models.
4. Solving simple goal programming problems by the graphical method.
5. Solving complex goal programming problems by the modified simplex method.
6. The meaning of the following terms:

Goal programming	*Deviational variables*
Multiple objectives	*Aspiration levels*
Incompatible objectives	*Overachievement*
Priority structure	*Underachievement*
Preemptive weights	*System constraints*
Cardinal weights	*Goal constraints*

THE CONCEPT OF GOAL PROGRAMMING

The value of experience

As we learned in Chapters 1 and 2, decision making is the primary task of management. In the past, management practice has been based primarily on experience and intuition. There is no denying that experience is often the foundation of knowledge. We always try to learn from others' experiences in order to avoid making the same mistakes ourselves. For example, we have learned a great deal from our grandpas' story telling, from nonfiction books, from "how to" handbooks, and from management case studies.

Confucius, some 2,400 years ago, told us the value of experience when he said, "I hear and I forget, I see and I remember, I do and I understand." However, the value of experience is decreasing because of the rapidly changing decision environment. We cannot use the decision making approach we used last year to solve a similar problem we will face five years from now.

The traditional modeling approach

In Chapter 1, we discussed the concept of economic person. In the traditional normative approach to decision making, the student of management science has been taught that the systematic way to solve a decision problem is to follow faithfully a set of rules such as:

1. Determine the decision variables.

2. Formulate an objective function, which is either to maximize or to minimize a single objective criterion.

3. Develop a set of constraints representing resource limitations and environmental restrictions.

4. Seek the global optimum solution for the single objective.

This general approach has become so ingrained that we tend to follow the procedure without even pausing to consider the real-world problem, the cognitive limitations of the decision maker, the complexity of the environment, and the assumptions of the model formulation process. Today, we have a large mass of data that supports the descriptive approach to decision making. Thus, we try to develop new ways to solve management problems rather than use the traditional approach.

Bounded rationality and satisficing

The descriptive approach to decision making is based on the *bounded rationality* that we discussed in Chapter 1. The idea of "intentionally" rational decision behavior is the foundation of bounded rationality. Under bounded rationality, the *satisficing* approach replaces the *optimizing* approach. In the satisficing approach, an abstract single objective for the organization is replaced by tangible and measurable goals. These measurable goals may be formulated on the basis of certain aspiration levels that are related to organizational goals.

Multiple objective decision making

Today, *management by multiple objectives* (also referred to as multicriteria decision making or multiobjective decision making) is one of the most important areas of management science. There have been various techniques introduced for multiple objective decision making, such as multiattribute utility theory, multicriteria linear programming, heuristic search methods, goal programming, and learning models. Of these, *goal programming* is one of the most powerful and popular techniques for multiple objective decision making.

The concept of goal programming

Initially, goal programming was developed as an extension of the optimization technique of linear programming. Goal programming is much more than a mere extension of linear programming. It has the additional capabilities to analyze the decision maker's multiple aspiration levels, to relax some of the model constraints, and to incorporate the decision maker's preference system for multiple conflicting goals. Thus, goal programming can transform a decision model into a satisficing model. This special feature of goal programming allows the decision maker to incorporate environmental, organizational, and judgmental considerations into the model through the determination of aspiration levels and their priorities.

The history of goal programming

The concept of goal programming was originally introduced by A. Charnes and W. W. Cooper (see References). The concept was further developed as a distinct management science technique for multiple objective decision problems through the efforts of many other scholars, especially the contributions of Y. Ijiri and S. M. Lee. Goal programming can be applied to various decision problems having a single goal and multiple subgoals, as well as to problems with multiple conflicting goals and subgoals.

The idea of satisficing

If there are multiple conflicting goals in a model, it may not be possible to achieve every goal to the desired extent. In such a case, the goal programming model attempts to obtain satisfactory levels of goal attainment that would be the best feasible solution in view of the importance of these goals to the organization. Thus, there is a need for a weighting system for the goals such that the less important goals are considered only after the very important goals have achieved the levels beyond which no further improvements are desired. These weights can be established on the basis of absolute ordinal priorities or on numerical (cardinal) weights such as utility.

Ordinal or numerical weights

Preemptive priority

The ordinal weighting scheme is based on the *preemptive* priority weights for the goals. Thus, the most important objective is sought before the other goals are considered. Once the most important goal has been attained as desired or has reached the maximum possible level of attainment within the constraints of the problem, the second most important objective will be sought. This sequential approach continues until the most satisfactory solution is identified.

The numerical weighting scheme, on the other hand, is based on a system that converts all of the goals into a universal criterion such as number of points, utilities, or effectiveness values. For example, the military services have established many job or performance evaluation systems based on points. This scheme allows a conversion of multiple objectives to a single criterion by considering the *perceived degree of magnitude or importance* of the various goals. However, this approach has many inherent difficulties and has not been widely accepted by practicing managers.

Assumptions of goal programming

Goal programming is similar to linear programming in many aspects. It has the same basic limitations, assumptions, and requirements as linear programming. As in linear programming, we can apply the graphical method or the simplex method but in a modified form. Although goal programming is a powerful and flexible technique for multiple objective decision problems, it is by no means a panacea for problems of this type. It is still a relatively new technique and there are many areas open to further development. Nevertheless, it has been an increasingly popular technique among the practitioners of management science.

APPLICATION AREAS OF GOAL PROGRAMMING

Application areas of goal programming

We are sure that you can readily identify with multiple objective decision problems in your daily life. Let us suppose that you have only $50 in your checking account to cover your expenses for the coming month. You would like to allocate this very scarce resource in such a way that you could accomplish the following:

1. Drive home next weekend to see your parents and then down to Broken Bow to spend some time with Peggy, your high school sweetheart (expected cost, $12).

2. Buy enough groceries to survive the month (your average weekly grocery bill is about $10).

3. Invite Susan (a classmate in your Quantitative Analysis course) over for a nice candlelight dinner (steak, salad, soup, pie, and wine—expected cost, $20).

4. Go out with Susan to the Starship for an evening of dancing and then a movie (expected cost $25).

This list clearly shows that you have a resource allocation problem with multiple conflicting objectives. Sooner or later, preferably very soon indeed, you must be realistic about your goals in view of your distressing financial situation. An analysis of the problem, in which you set your goal priorities, may provide you with information that indicates which goals must be satisfied at the expense of other goals. It may also provide answers as to how much resource will be required to attain all of the goals. You can then explore ways to secure the resources.

Types of goal programming analysis

In general, a goal programming model performs three types of analysis: (1) it determines the required resources to achieve a set of desired objective; (2) it determines the degree of attainment for the established goals with given resources; and (3) it provides the best satisficing solution under the varying amounts of resources and the priority structures for the goals. If the goal programming approach is to be taken for a decision problem, it must be carefully examined by the decision maker to fully utilize its advantage.

Some application examples

Goal programming has been applied to a wide range of decision problems in business firms, government agencies, and nonprofit organizations. The most popular application areas of goal programming have been resource allocation, planning and scheduling, and policy analysis problems. Applications of goal programming include the following examples:

Advertising media planning	Marketing strategy planning
Manpower planning	Environmental protection
Production planning and inventory control	Health care delivery planning
	Blood bank logistics
Academic planning	Insurance planning
Financial analysis	Location-allocation decisions
Economic policy analysis	Police force deployment
Transportation logistics	Zero base budgeting, and many others

It is impossible to provide even a brief summary of all of these goal programming examples here. However, later in this chapter we will examine three real-world applications of goal programming. It should suffice to state that goal programming is one of the most popular techniques for multiple objective decision making among scholars and practitioners of management science.

MODEL FORMULATION

Examples of model formulation

To gain some experience in formulating multiple objective decision problems as goal programming models, we will examine many different situations by means of several casettes. It is important to recognize quickly which of the problems under consideration can be solved by goal programming, and then be able to formulate a corresponding model for those that can be solved.

A Single Objective Problem

A single objective model

We will start our discussion of goal programming model formulation with the simplest possible case, one in which we have a single objective. You may quickly recognize that such a problem can be formulated as a linear programming model. Goal programming can solve any single objective or multiple objective problem as long as it satisfies the basic requirements. Therefore, goal programming is capable of solving any linear programming problem as well as many different types of problems that involve multiple objectives.

CASETTE 6.1   **CENTURY ELECTRONICS, INC.**

Century Electronics, Inc. is a small manufacturer of tape deck players. The company produces only two types of deck players: cassette and 8-track. Century has a production plant where all of its deck players are processed. Past experience has shown that production of either a cassette player or an 8-track player requires an average of 1 hour in the plant. The plant has a normal production capacity of 40 hours per week.

The Marketing Department of Century reports that a *maximum* number of 24 cassette and 30 8-track players can be sold each week. The expected profit from the sale of a cassette player is $60, whereas it is $40 for an 8-track player. Currently, the company has only one goal—maximizing the total profit from its weekly operation under normal production and market conditions.

Linear Programming Model

This problem can be easily formulated as a linear programming problem as follows:

$$\text{Maximize } Z = 60x_1 + 40x_2$$

subject to		
$x_1 + x_2 \le 40$	*Production constraint*	
$x_1 \le 24$	*Sales constraint*	
$x_2 \le 30$	*Sales constraint*	
$x_1, x_2 \ge 0$		

where x_1 = number of cassette players produced per week

x_2 = number of 8-track players produced per week

This problem can be solved by the graphical method, as shown in Figure 6.1. The solution indicates that the company should produce 24 cassette players and 16 8-track players, and the total weekly profit will be $2,080. It is obvious that Century has some slack market for 8-track players, as it produces only 16 units whereas the market can accommodate 30 units.

Goal Programming Model

The above single objective problem can also be formulated and solved by goal programming. Let us discuss each component of the model.

The system constraint

System Constraints. A goal programming model has two types of constraints: system and goal. System constraints represent absolute restrictions imposed by the decision environment on the model. For example, there arc only seven days in a week (time

Figure 6.1   The Century Electronics Problem

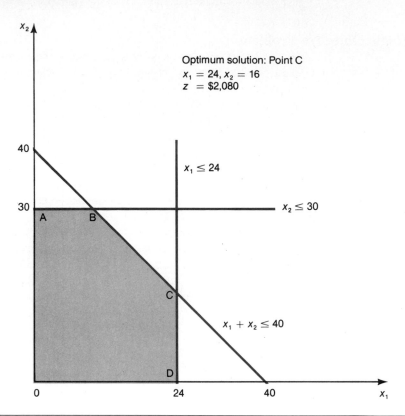

constraint), the production or sales capacity in the short run is limited to certain existing conditions (capacity constraint), and the production should be limited to demand and storage capacity (physical constraint). System constraints must be satisfied before any of the goal constraints can be considered.

In this problem, there are three system constraints:

$$x_1 + x_2 \leq 40 \qquad \textit{Production constraint}$$
$$x_1 \leq 24 \qquad \textit{Sales constraint for cassette players}$$
$$x_2 \leq 30 \qquad \textit{Sales constraint for 8-track players}$$

Goal Constraints. Goal constraints represent aspiration levels for certain goals or objectives. Desired level of profit, desired level of pollution control, desired market share, desired diversification of investments among various available alternatives are several illustrations of goal constraints.

The goal constraint

In the Century Electronics problem, there is only one goal constraint because there is a single goal. The only goal is to maximize the total weekly profit. The company has no specific desired level of profit, but it seeks to maximize the total profit. Therefore, the right-hand-side value is not set. To maximize the total profit, we can set the right-hand-side value unrealistically high (say $100,000) and then try to achieve this level. Now we can formulate the goal constraint for profit maximization as follows:

$$60x_1 + 40x_2 + d_1^- - d_1^+ = \$100,000$$

where
$$d_1^- = \text{underachievement of the } \$100,000 \text{ profit goal}$$
$$d_1^+ = \text{overachievement of the } \$100,000 \text{ profit goal}$$

The deviational variable

We need to explain the d_1^- and d_1^+ variables in greater detail. These variables, referred to as *deviational variables,* can be thought of as slack and surplus variables. For example, if the total profit attained is less than $100,000, then the negative deviational variable d_1^- will have a certain value while the positive deviational variable d_1^+ will be zero. On the other hand, if the total profit achieved happens to exceed $100,000, then d_1^+ will have a certain value while d_1^- will be zero.

Since we are attempting to maximize the total profit, we must minimize d_1^- as much as possible. If we could minimize it all the way to zero, then our total profit will be $100,000. On the other hand, if we were interested in limiting our profit level to $100,000, then we must minimize d_1^+. If we could minimize it all the way to $d_1^+ = 0$, then our total profit will be $100,000 or less. If both of the deviational variables, d_1^- and d_1^+, are minimized to zero, then the total profit level will be exactly $100,000.

Relationship between negative and positive deviations

From the above discussion, it should be obvious that at least one deviational variable is always zero. Also, since d_1^- and d_1^+ are complementary to each other if $d_1^- > 0$, then $d_1^+ = 0$, and if $d_1^- = 0$, then $d_1^+ > 0$. Thus, it is always true that $d_1^- \times d_1^+ = 0$.

Now, we can summarize as follows the three options open for the goal constraints and their corresponding consequences:

Minimize	Goal	If the Goal Is Achieved
d_1^-	$60x_1 + 40x_2 \geq 100,000$	$d_1^- = 0, d_1^+ \geq 0$
d_1^+	$60x_1 + 40x_2 \leq 100,000$	$d_1^- \geq 0, d_1^+ = 0$
$d_1^- + d_1^+$	$60x_1 + 40x_2 = 100,000$	$d_1^- = 0, d_1^+ = 0$

Objective Function. The Century Electronics problem has a single goal of profit maximization. This goal can be achieved if d_1^- is minimized. Thus, the objective function becomes

$$\text{Minimize } Z = d_1^-$$

Now, the complete model can be developed as follows:

$$\text{Minimize } Z = d_1^-$$
$$\text{subject to} \quad x_1 + x_2 \leq 40$$
$$x_1 \leq 24$$
$$x_2 \leq 30$$
$$60x_1 + 40x_2 + d_1^- - d_1^+ = 100,000$$
$$x_1, x_2, d_1^-, d_1^+ \geq 0$$

Figure 6.2   The Goal Programming Model

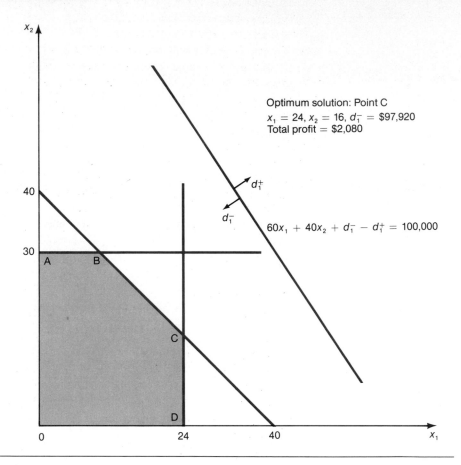

In this model, we have used an arbitrarily large profit figure of $100,000, which is totally unattainable. Thus, we can easily eliminate d_1^+ in the goal constraint, because d_1^+ will always be zero.

The same goal programming model formulation approach can be applied to any problem which has a single objective, whether it be a maximization or a minimization problem. For example, if the problem is a minimization problem, we can formulate it in the following manner:

$$\text{Minimize } Z = d_1^+$$
$$\text{subject to} \quad x_1 + x_2 \leq 40$$
$$x_1 \leq 24$$
$$x_2 \leq 30$$
$$60x_1 + 40x_2 + d_1^- - d_1^+ = 0$$
$$x_1, x_2, d_1^-, d_1^+ \geq 0$$

In the goal constraint described above, the right-hand-side value of zero is an unrealistic total cost. As we attempt to minimize d_1^+, the positive deviation from zero cost, the process becomes a cost minimization approach.

Solution of the Goal Programming Model. The goal programming model we formulated for Century Electronics to maximize profit can be easily solved by the graphical method. As the goal constraint has such a large right-hand-side value, this constraint line will be far above the other system constraints. However, the slope of the goal constraint is $-3/2$, exactly the same as the slope of the iso-profit function of the linear programming model.

A graphical solution

The first step of the solution process is to identify the area of feasible solutions defined by the system constraints. Figure 6.2 shows the feasibility area OABCD. The next step is to minimize d_1^- from the goal constraint line. We plotted the goal constraint line unrealistically close to the feasibility area for the purpose of illustration. To minimize the value of d_1^-, we must move in toward the origin with the slope of the goal constraint ($-3/2$) from the outer space. Actually, this is the same procedure as the iso-profit function approach except that it moves from the opposite direction (toward the origin rather than away from the origin).

The optimum solution can be found by identifying the first point within the feasibility area as we move in toward the origin with the slope of the goal constraint. The optimum solution point is identified as point C in Figure 6.2. The optimum solution is $x_1 = 24$, $x_2 = 16$, $d_1^- = \$97,920$, and total profit $= \$2,080$.

A Multiple Objective Problem

The next case of goal programming we will study is a multiple objective problem. Such a problem may have both system and goal constraints or it may have only a set of goal constraints. When there are multiple and often conflicting objectives, a preference weighting system must be introduced. If there are definite reasons and sufficient information to allow conversion of all of the objectives into a common criterion such as utility or profit, the multiple objective problem can be reduced to a single objective problem.

A multiple objective problem

In many real-world problems, however, some of the objectives may not only be incompatible but they may also be incommensurable. For example, a problem may have an employment goal (measured in number of full-time employees), a profit goal (measured in dollars), and a pollution control goal (measured in terms of tons of chemical wastes). Thus, it is often impossible to convert these goals into a common criterion such as utility or profit. A powerful alternative approach is to weight the multiple objectives. This system of preference employs *ordinal weights* or *preemptive priorities*.

The meaning of preemptive priorities

The preemptive priority system can be simply explained as a process in which the objectives are pursued in an ordinal sequence based on their importance. Let us suppose that a problem has five different goals. The most important objective is pursued first until it is attained as fully as desired or until it reaches a point beyond which further improvement is impossible because of the system constraints. Then, the second goal is sought within the solution space defined by the system constraints and the first priority goal. This process continues until all five goals have been considered.

CASETTE 6.2   MODERN FASHIONS, INC.

Modern Fashions, Inc. is a producer of ladies' bathing suits. The company specializes in producing two basic styles: regular and bikini. The production of all bathing suits is done in a modern sewing center. A regular bathing suit requires an average of 5 minutes in the sewing center and a bikini requires an average of 8 minutes. The normal operation time available in the sewing center is, for two shifts, 80 hours per week. The unit profit for each type of bathing suit is: regular—$2.50, bikini—$3.00.

Carol Schrader, the aggressive president of the company, has set the following goals, listed in the order of their importance:

1. Achieve the profit goal of $2,000 per week.

2. Limit the overtime operation of the sewing center to a maximum of 8 hours per week.

3. Meet the sales goal of 400 bikini bathing suits per week.

4. Meet the sales goal of 500 regular bathing suits per week.

Goal Constraints

In this problem we have only goal constraints. To formulate a goal programming model, we must first develop the following goal constraints:

Formulating goal constraints

Profit Goal. Achievement of the $2,000 profit goal is a function of the number of each type of bathing suit produced and its unit profit:

$$2.50x_1 + 3.00x_2 + d_1^- - d_1^+ = 2,000$$

where

$$x_1 = \text{number of regular bathing suits produced per week}$$
$$x_2 = \text{number of bikini bathing suits produced per week}$$
$$2.50 = \text{unit profit for regular bathing suits}$$
$$3.00 = \text{unit profit for bikini bathing suits}$$
$$d_1^- = \text{underachievement of the profit goal}$$
$$d_1^+ = \text{overachievement of the profit goal}$$
$$2,000 = \text{profit goal per week}$$

Overtime Operation. Modern Fashions attempts to limit the overtime operation of the sewing center to 8 hours per week. Since the normal operation time available per week is 80, the maximum acceptable number of operation hours will be 88 per week. If we express the operation hours in terms of minutes, then we can express this goal constraint as follows:

$$5x_1 + 8x_2 + d_2^- - d_2^+ = 5,280$$

where

$$d_2^- = \text{negative deviation from 5,280 minutes of operation}$$
$$d_2^+ = \text{overtime operation in excess of 5,280 minutes}$$
$$5 = \text{unit production time for regular bathing suits}$$
$$8 = \text{unit production time for bikini bathing suits}$$
$$5,280 = \text{desired maximum operation time, 88 hours}$$

Sales Goal for Bikini Bathing Suits. The company is attempting to achieve the sales goal of 400 bikini bathing suits, which can be expressed as:

$$x_2 + d_3^- - d_3^+ = 400$$

where

d_3^- = underachievement of the sales goal for bikini bathing suits
d_3^+ = overachievement of the sales goal for bikini bathing suits
400 = desired sales goal for bikini bathing suits

Sales Goal for Regular Bathing Suits. The desired sales goal for regular bathing suits can be expressed as:

$$x_1 + d_4^- - d_4^+ = 500$$

where

d_4^- = underachievement of the sales goal for regular bathing suits
d_4^+ = overachievement of the sales goal for regular bathing suits
500 = desired sales goal for regular bathing suits

The Objective Function

Now we are ready to formulate the objective function. We have four priority goals. The preemptive priority weights can be defined as follows:

P_1: The highest priority is assigned to achieving the profit goal. This can be accomplished by minimizing the underachievement of the profit goal, or d_1^-.

Priorities defined

P_2: The second priority is assigned to limiting the overtime operation of the sewing center to 8 hours. This goal can be achieved by minimizing the overtime operation of the sewing center in excess of 5,280 minutes, or d_2^+.

P_3: The third priority is assigned to the achievement of the sales goal for 400 bikini bathing suits. This goal can be achieved by minimizing the underachievement of the sales goal for bikini bathing suits, or d_3^-.

P_4: The last priority is assigned to the achievement of the sales goal for 500 regular bathing suits. This goal can be achieved by minimizing the underachievement of the sales goal for regular bathing suits, or d_4^-.

Now we can formulate the objective function of the Modern Fashions problem as follows:

$$\text{Minimize } Z = P_1 d_1^- + P_2 d_2^+ + P_3 d_3^- + P_4 d_4^-$$

In this objective function, it should be noted that Z is not a single-dimensional criterion such as profit or cost. Instead, Z is like a fruit basket that contains different types of fruit—an apple, a banana, two pears, a melon, several oranges, and so on. In other words, Z is a multidimensional function composed of various priority factors representing incommensurable objective criteria.

Multidimensional objective function

Another point we should remember in the objective function is that the priority factors represent ordinal weights. In other words, priority factor P_1 takes priority over P_2. Thus, we can express our four priority weights as $P_1 >>> P_2 >>> P_3 >>> P_4$.

This relationship simply means that P_1 is more important than P_2, P_2 is more important than P_3, and so on.

Now we can formulate the complete goal programming model for the Modern Fashions problem as follows:

$$\text{Minimize } Z = P_1d_1^- + P_2d_2^+ + P_3d_3^- + P_4d_4^-$$

$$\begin{aligned}
\text{subject to } \quad 2.50x_1 + 3.00x_2 + d_1^- - d_1^+ &= 2,000 \\
5x_1 + 8x_2 + d_2^- - d_2^+ &= 5,280 \\
x_2 + d_3^- - d_3^+ &= 400 \\
x_1 + d_4^- - d_4^+ &= 500 \\
x_1, x_2, d_1^-, d_2^-, d_3^-, d_4^-, d_1^+, d_2^+, d_3^+, d_4^+ &\geq 0
\end{aligned}$$

A Multiple Objective–Multiple Subgoal Problem

In certain goal programming problems, it is possible that there may be several subgoals at a certain priority level. For example, let us suppose the second goal of a problem is to maintain the firm's current market share for its products. If the firm currently has five different products, the second priority goal will involve five subgoals—market share goals for the five products.

A problem with multiple goals and subgoals

If we are totally indifferent about market share goals for the five products, we can assign the same numerical weight to each of the five subgoals. On the other hand, if there is a good reason to assign different numerical weights (e.g., there are different unit profits for the five products), differential weights can be assigned. Thus, it is necessary for multiple subgoals at a given priority level to be commensurable.

CASETTE 6.3   *BIG SOUND RECORDS, INC.*

Big Sound Records, Inc. is a popular record store located next to the university campus. It is by far the largest record shop in town, in terms of both total sales and record selections. The owner of the shop, Robert Ryman, was an MBA student who conducted a feasibility study for a record shop next to the campus as a term project in the Small Business Management course. After receiving his degree, Bob Ryman was convinced that he could actually implement his feasibility study. He opened Big Sound Records two years ago with a $10,000 loan from the U.S. Small Business Administration. He has been a very successful small businessman ever since.

The record shop employs 10 full-time and 8 part-time salespeople. Every salesperson is trained on the job to handle both sales and cash registers. The normal numbers of working hours per month are 160 for a full-time salesperson and an average of 80 hours per month for a part-time salesperson.

According to the past sales records, average sales have been 10 records per hour for the full-time salespeople and 6 records per hour for the part-time salespeople. The average hourly wage rates are $6 for full-time employees and $4 for part-time employees. The average gross profit from the sale of a record is $1.50.

In view of past sales records, aggressive promotional efforts, and an increased enrollment at the university, Bob feels that the sales goal for the next month should be 22,000 records. Since the store is open six days a week, overtime work is often required of the salespeople (not necessarily overtime, but extra hours for the part-time salespeople).

Bob is convinced that good employer-employee relations have been an essential factor in his business success. Therefore, he feels that a stable employment level with an occasional overtime requirement is a better practice than an unstable employment level with no overtime. However, he also believes that overtime of more than 200 hours per month among the full-time employees should be avoided because fatigue is related to declining sales effectiveness.

Multiple goals
Bob has established the following goals for the next month's operation in the order of their priority:

1. The first goal is to achieve sales of 22,000 records in the next month.

2. The second goal is to limit the overtime of full-time salespersons to 200 hours.

3. The third goal is to provide job security for the salespeople. Bob feels that full utilization of full-time employees is twice as important as full utilization of part-time salespeople.

4. The fourth goal is to achieve a gross profit of $31,000 for the next month.

5. The last goal is to minimize the overtime work of the full-time and part-time employees. Bob wants to assign differential weights to the minimization of overtime given to full-time and part-time salespeople according to their marginal profit ratios per hour.

The Big Sound Records problem involves no system constraints, only goal constraints.

Sales Goal

Achievement of the sales goal, which is set at 22,000 records, is a function of the total working hours of the full-time and part-time salespeople and their productivity (sales per hour) rates:

$$10x_1 + 6x_2 + d_1^- - d_1^+ = 22,000$$

where

x_1 = total full-time salespeople hours per month.
x_2 = total part-time salespeople hours per month
d_1^- = underachievement of the sales goal
d_1^+ = overachievement of the sales goal
10 = sales of records per hour for full-time salespeople
6 = sales of records per hour for part-time salespeople
22,000 = sales goal for month

The sales goal will be achieved if we minimize d_1^-, the underachievement of the sales goal of 22,000 records.

Overtime Work for Full-time Salespeople

In the goal programming approach, to achieve a certain goal we must have a deviational variable to minimize. If we do not have such a deviational goal, we must create one by formulating a new goal constraint. In the Big Sound Records problem,

Bob's second goal is to limit the overtime of the full-time employees to 200 hours during the next month.

We do not have a deviational variable to limit the overtime work of the full-time employees. Thus, we must first determine the regular working hours for the full-time employees. We have defined x_1 as the total full-time salespersons' hours per month. With 10 full-time employees, the total regular working hours per month will be $10 \times 160 = 1,600$ hours:

$$x_1 + d_2^- - d_2^+ = 1,600$$

where

d_2^- = underutilization of regular full-time salespeople hours per month

d_2^+ = overtime given to full-time salespeople hours per month

To limit the overtime work of the full-time salespeople to 200 hours, we should introduce the following constraint:

$$d_2^+ + d_3^- - d_3^+ = 200$$

where

d_3^- = underutilization of the allowed overtime of 200 hours for full-time salespeople

d_3^+ = overtime in excess of 200 hours for full-time salespeople

A decomposed goal

We have introduced both the negative and positive deviations from the allowed overtime of 200 hours because the actual overtime work for the full-time salespeople may, in fact, be less than, equal to, or even greater than 200 hours. Now we have a deviational variable (d_3^+) to minimize in order to achieve the second goal. It should be noted that this constraint can also be expressed in a different way. For example, we can add the allowed overtime of 200 hours to the right-hand-side value of the regular working-hour constraint of the full-time salespeople and obtain the following:

$$x_1 + d_3^- - d_3^+ = 1,800$$

In this problem, either of the above constraints can be used to formulate a goal programming model. The second goal can be achieved by minimizing d_3^+ (overtime in excess of 200 hours for full-time employees).

Job Security Goal

Bob would like to provide job security for his full-time and part-time salespeople. This goal can be achieved if the salespeople are provided with at least their regular working hours and if no one is laid off. We have already formulated the regular working hours for the full-time salespeople $(x_1 + d_2^- - d_2^+ = 1,600)$. The total regular working hours for the 8 part-time salespeople will be $8 \times 80 = 640$ hours/ month. Thus, we can formulate the following constraint:

$$x_2 + d_4^- - d_4^+ = 640$$

where

d_4^- = underutilization of the total regular part-time salespeople hours per month

d_4^+ = extra working hours given to part-time salespeople per month

The third goal can be achieved by minimizing d_2^- *and* d_4^- (underutilization of the regular working hours for full-time and part-time salespeople respectively).

Profit Goal

Multiple subgoals

Bob's fourth goal is to achieve a gross profit of $31,000 for the next month. Big Sound Records' average gross profit margin per record is $1.50. Thus, the total gross profit will be a function of the total expected sales of records and the average profit per record. The expected sales of records per hour for the full-time and part-time salespeople are 10 and 6 respectively. Thus, the goal constraint becomes:

$$15x_1 + 9x_2 + d_5^- - d_5^+ = 31,000$$

where

d_5^- = underachievement of the profit goal
d_5^+ = overachievement of the profit goal
15 = gross profit per hour generated by full-time salespeople
(10 records $\times$ $1.50 = $15)
9 = gross profit per hour generated by part-time salespeople
(6 records $\times$ $1.50 = $9)

The profit goal can be achieved by minimizing d_5^- (the underachievement of the profit goal of $31,000).

Overtime Minimization Goal

The last goal of the owner of Big Sound Records is to minimize the overtime work of the full-time and part-time employees. We have already formulated the regular working-hour constraints for the full-time and part-time salespeople. Thus, there is no need to reformulate these constraints in order to identify the deviational variables being minimized to achieve this goal. The two constraints that contain the overtime work as deviational variables are as follows:

$$x_1 + d_2^- - d_2^+ = 1,600$$
$$x_2 + d_4^- - d_4^+ = 640$$

The overtime minimization goal can be achieved by minimizing d_2^+ and d_4^+ (overtime work assigned to full-time and part-time employees respectively).

The Objective Function

Now we are ready to formulate the objective function for the problem. Let us formulate the function by adding the priority goals in the sequence of their ordinal ranking.

Sales Goal. In order to achieve the sales goal, we must minimize the underachievement of the sales goal to zero in the following goal constraint:

$$10x_1 + 6x_2 + d_1^- - d_1^+ = 22,000$$

Thus, the highest priority factor P_1 should be assigned to the minimization of d_1^-. The objective function becomes

$$\text{Minimize } Z = P_1 d_1^-$$

Overtime Work for Full-Time Sales Persons. Bob wants to limit the overtime work of the full-time salespeople to 200 hours. This goal can be achieved if we minimize the deviational variable that represents overtime in excess of 200 hours in either of the following constraints:

$$d_2^+ + d_3^- - d_3^+ = 200$$

or

$$x_1 + d_3^- - d_3^+ = 1,800$$

The second priority factor, P_2, should be assigned to the minimization of d_3^+. The objective function now becomes

$$\text{Minimize } Z = P_1 d_1^- + \mathbf{P_2 d_3^+}$$

Job Security. Bob's third goal is to provide job security to the full-time and part-time employees. Since we must consider two separate goal constraints, we have multiple subgoals at the third priority level. If Bob were completely indifferent to a preferential handling of the job security of full-time and part-time employees, we could assign the same weight to these subgoals. However, he has already indicated that he would like to assign twice the weight to providing job security for full-time employees as for part-time employees.

Assigning differential weights

The two goal constraints involved in the third priority level are:

$$x_1 + d_2^- - d_2^+ = 1,600$$
$$x_2 + d_4^- - d_4^+ = 640$$

To achieve the job security goal, we must minimize d_2^- and d_4^- but with differential weights assigned as follows:

$$\text{Minimize } Z = P_1 d_1^- + P_2 d_3^+ + \mathbf{2P_3 d_2^-} + \mathbf{P_3 d_4^-}$$

Profit Goal. The fourth goal is to achieve a gross profit of $31,000. This goal can be achieved by minimizing d_5^- in the following goal constraint:

$$15x_1 + 9x_2 + d_5^- - d_5^+ = 31,000$$

The fourth priority goal is assigned to the minimization of d_5^- as follows:

$$\text{Minimize } Z = P_1 d_1^- + P_2 d_3^+ + 2P_3 d_2^- + P_3 d_4^- + \mathbf{P_4 d_5^-}$$

Overtime Minimization Goal. The last goal is concerned with minimization of overtime work for full-time and part-time salespeople. Once again, we have a case of multiple subgoals at a given priority level. We could achieve this goal if we could minimize d_2^+ and d_4^+ to zero in the following goal constraints:

$$x_1 + d_2^- - d_2^+ = 1,600$$
$$x_2 + d_4^- - d_4^+ = 640$$

Computing differential weights

We are interested in determining the differential weights to be assigned to d_2^+ and d_4^+. Full-time salespeople receive an average hourly wage of $6. Thus, an overtime hourly wage rate will be $9, time-and-a-half pay. With this payroll cost, Big Sound Records can expect sales of 10 records, which would result in $15 gross profit. Thus, the expected profit/payroll ratio is

$$\frac{\$15}{\$9} = \frac{5}{3}$$

Part-time salespeople do not receive overtime pay but rather the regular hourly wage rate of $4 for any work beyond their normal monthly working schedule of 80 hours. With an extra overtime hour, a part-time salesperson is expected to sell 6 records, resulting in $9 gross profit. Thus, the expected profit/payroll ratio is

$$\frac{\$9}{\$4} = \frac{9}{4}$$

It should be clear now that if we have to provide overtime in order to achieve the higher priority goals, we should provide overtime to the part-time employees rather than to the full-time employees. The profit/payroll ratios for full-time and part-time salespeople are as follows:

	Salespeople	
Ratio	Full-time	Part-time
Actual	$\dfrac{5}{3}$	$\dfrac{9}{4}$
Integer (multiply by 4 or 3)	20	27

Since the profit/payroll ratio is lower for the full-time employee group, the relative cost of overtime is higher for the full-time salespeople. Thus, we can reverse the differential weight assignment so that minimization of overtime for the full-time salespeople will be given a greater weight than that for the part-time salespeople. The objective function becomes

$$\text{Minimize } Z = P_1 d_1^- + P_2 d_3^+ + 2P_3 d_2^- + P_3 d_4^- + P_4 d_5^- + \mathbf{27P_5 d_2^+} + \mathbf{20P_5 d_4^+}$$

Now the complete goal programming model for the Big Sound Records problem can be formulated as follows:

$$\text{Minimize } Z = P_1 d_1^- + P_2 d_3^+ + 2P_3 d_2^- + P_3 d_4^- + P_4 d_5^- + 27P_5 d_2^+ + 20P_5 d_4^+$$

$$
\begin{aligned}
\text{subject to} \quad & 10x_1 + 6x_2 + d_1^- - d_1^+ = 22{,}000 \\
& x_1 + d_2^- - d_2^+ = 1{,}600 \\
& d_2^+ + d_3^- - d_3^+ = 200 \\
& x_2 + d_4^- - d_4^+ = 640 \\
& 15x_1 + 9x_2 + d_5^- - d_5^+ = 31{,}000 \\
& x_1,\, x_2,\, d_i^-,\, d_i^+ \geq 0 \qquad (i = 1, 2, \ldots, 5)
\end{aligned}
$$

A Problem with System Constraints and Multiple Objectives

A problem with system constraints

In this section, we will examine a more complex case in which there are a number of system constraints and multiple objectives. With the model formulation experience we have accumulated thus far, it should be relatively simple to formulate a goal programming model for an additional problem.

CASETTE 6.4   *BLEEKER COLLEGE FOUNDATION*

Bleeker College is a private fine arts college with a long tradition. With decreasing student enrollment and rising educational cost, Bleeker has been very aggressively engaged in alumni fund-raising activities. Recently, Dr. Joseph Anthony's estate informed the college that the late physician had left his entire Western art collection to Bleeker.

The Bleeker College Foundation has been successful in negotiating with the Guggenheim Museum for the sale of the entire collection of 42 fine paintings by early Western artists. The basic agreement is that Bleeker will receive a total of $2,000,000 during the next four years. The payment schedule will be as follows: Year 1, $1,200,000; Year 2, $500,000; Year 3, $200,000; Year 4, $100,000.

The conditions of this gift are complex. The most restrictive condition is that funds from the sale of the paintings must be safely invested. The bequest specifically indicated that the funds could be invested only in real estate, government bonds, money market funds, and local bank stocks. The current annual yield rates of the investment alternatives are as follows: real estate, 15 percent; government bonds, 12 percent; money market funds, 16 percent; and bank stocks, 10 percent. The Anthony family also specified the following required expenditures from the gift during the first five years:

1. Establish a distinguished professorship with the name of Joseph Anthony Professor of Free Enterprise in the School of Business with a salary of at least $40,000 per academic year. Also, provide an operating budget of $10,000 for the clerical and office expenses of the professorship. Both the professorship and the operating budget must be increased by 10 percent per year during the next five years.

2. Establish at least two $2,000 scholarships in each of the following departments: Basic Science, Premed, Fine Arts, Romance Languages, and Business Management.

3. Create a dean's discretionary account in the School of Business during the third year at an annual allocation of $100,000.

The Board of Directors of the Bleeker College Foundation decided to set the following goals for the Anthony Gift in the order of their importance:

1. Invest at least 50 percent of all funds available in the most liquid investment vehicles—government bonds and money market funds.

2. Invest at least $200,000 in The First National Bank stocks, which have shown the most stable growth of the available alternatives during the past several years.

3. Establish the chaired professorship, Joseph Anthony Professor of Free Enterprise, and the operating budget for this professorship; secure enough funds for all of the required scholarships; and create the School of Business discretionary fund.

4. Maximize the cash value of this gift by the end of the fifth year.

The Bleeker College Foundation would like to determine how the cash proceeds of the Anthony gift should be invested during the next five years in order to achieve the established objectives.

System Constraints

In this problem, the cash inflow and outflow during the five-year period can be visualized as shown in Figure 6.3. Cash outflow in a given year must be limited to available cash. It is assumed that the Foundation will normally invest all of the funds available after cash expenses for the professorship, scholarships, and dean's fund

Figure 6.3   Cash Flows for the Bleeker College Foundation Problem

Cash Inflows	Year					
	1	2	3	4	5	6
Cash	$1,200,000	$500,000	$200,000	$100,000		
Real estate		$1.15RE_1$	$1.15RE_2$	$1.15RE_3$	$1.15RE_4$	$1.15RE_5$
Government bonds		$1.12B_1$	$1.12B_2$	$1.12B_3$	$1.12B_4$	$1.12B_5$
Money market fund		$1.16M_1$	$1.16M_2$	$1.16M_3$	$1.16M_4$	$1.16M_5$
Bank stock		$1.1BS_1$	$1.1BS_2$	$1.1BS_3$	$1.1BS_4$	$1.1BS_5$

Cash Outflows	Year				
	1	2	3	4	5
Real estate	RE_1	RE_2	RE_3	RE_4	RE_5
Government bonds	B_1	B_2	B_3	B_4	B_5
Money market fund	M_1	M_2	M_3	M_4	M_5
Bank stock	BS_1	BS_2	BS_3	BS_4	BS_5
Professorship & operating budget	$50,000	$55,000	$60,500	$66,550	$73,205
Scholarships	$20,000	$20,000	$30,000	$30,000	$30,000
Dean's fund, School of Business			$100,000	$100,000	$100,000

have been deducted from the available money. Thus, we can formulate the following system constraints:

Year 1:

$$RE_1 + B_1 + M_1 + BS_1 \leq 1,200,000$$

Year 2:

$$RE_2 + B_2 + M_2 + BS_2 \leq 500,000 + 1.15RE_1 + 1.12B_1 + 1.16M_1 + 1.1BS_1$$

Year 3:

$$RE_3 + B_3 + M_3 + BS_3 \leq 200,000 + 1.15RE_2 + 1.12B_2 + 1.16M_2 + 1.1BS_2$$

Year 4:

$$RE_4 + B_4 + M_4 + BS_4 \leq 100,000 + 1.15RE_3 + 1.12B_3 + 1.16M_3 + 1.1BS_3$$

Year 5:

$$RE_5 + B_5 + M_5 + BS_5 \leq 1.15RE_4 + 1.12B_4 + 1.16M_4 + 1.1BS_4$$

Goal Constraints

In addition to the system constraints listed above, the Bleeker College Foundation has the following goal constraints:

1. At least 50 percent of all funds invested should be in government bonds and money market funds. Thus, the constraint is

$$\sum_{i=1}^{5} B_i + \sum_{i=1}^{5} M_i \geq .5 \left(\sum_{i=1}^{5} RE_i + \sum_{i=1}^{5} B_i + \sum_{i=1}^{5} M_i + \sum_{i=1}^{5} BS_i \right)$$

By introducing deviational variables and rearranging the variables, we obtain the following constraint, in which we minimize d_1^-.

$$- .5 \sum_{i=1}^{5} RE_i + .5 \sum_{i=1}^{5} B_i + .5 \sum_{i=1}^{5} M_i - .5 \sum_{i=1}^{5} BS_i + d_1^- - d_1^+ = 0$$

2. At least \$200,000 should be invested in The First National Bank stocks. This investment is assumed to satisfy the gift condition that some money should be invested in local bank stocks. Thus, we have the following constraint:

$$\sum_{i=1}^{5} BS_i + d_2^- - d_2^+ = 200,000$$

In this constraint, we should minimize d_2^-.

3. Sufficient funds should be secured for the \$40,000 chaired professorship. This constraint can be satisfied if cash inflow exceeds cash outflow by at least \$70,000. The constraint for the first year is

$$1,200,000 - RE_1 - B_1 - M_1 - BS_1 \geq 70,000$$

Thus, we can develop the following goal constraint and minimize d_3^+:

$$RE_1 + B_1 + M_1 + BS_1 + d_3^- - d_3^+ = 1,130,000$$

Goal constraints for the remaining four years can be formulated in a similar manner as follows:

$$RE_2 + B_2 + M_2 + BS_2 - 1.15RE_1 - 1.12B_1 - 1.16M_1 - 1.1BS_1$$
$$+ d_4^- - d_4^+ = 425,000$$

$$RE_3 + B_3 + M_3 + BS_3 - 1.15RE_2 - 1.12B_2 - 1.16M_2 - 1.1BS_2$$
$$+ d_5^- - d_5^+ = 9,500$$

$$1.15RE_3 + 1.12B_3 + 1.16M_3 + 1.1BS_3 - RE_4 - B_4 - M_4 - BS_4$$
$$+ d_6^- - d_6^+ = 96,550$$

$$1.15RE_4 + 1.12B_4 + 1.16M_4 + 1.1BS_4 - RE_5 - B_5 - M_5 - BS_5$$
$$+ d_7^- - d_7^+ = 203,205$$

In the above constraints d_4^+, d_5^+, d_6^-, and d_7^- should be minimized. We transformed the sixth and seventh goal constraints because their right-hand-side values were negative. We simply multiply both sides by -1 and then minimize the negative deviational variable rather than the positive deviational variable.

4. The cash value of the Anthony gift should be maximized by the end of the fifth year. In Figure 6.3 it is obvious that the cash inflow by the end of the fifth year will be determined by the sum of $1.15RE_5 + 1.12B_5 + 1.16M_5 + 1.1BS_5$. We can set an arbitrarily large right-hand-side value of \$100,000,000 and then attempt to minimize the underachievement, or d_3^-:

$$1.15RE_5 + 1.12B_5 + 1.16M_5 + 1.1BS_5 + d_8^- - d_8^+ = 100,000,000$$

Now we formulate the complete goal programming model for the Bleeker College Foundation problem as follows:

Minimize $Z = P_1 d_1^- + P_2 d_2^- + P_3(d_3^+ + d_4^+ + d_5^+ + d_6^- + d_7^-) + P_4 d_8^-$

subject to

$$RE_1 + B_1 + M_1 + BS_1 \leq 1,200,000$$

$$-1.15RE_1 + RE_2 - 1.12B_1 + B_2 - 1.16M_1 + M_2 - 1.1BS_1 + BS_2 \leq 500,000$$

$$-1.15RE_2 + RE_3 - 1.12B_2 + B_3 - 1.16M_2 + M_3 - 1.1BS_2 + BS_3 \leq 200,000$$

$$-1.15RE_3 + RE_4 - 1.12B_3 + B_4 - 1.16M_3 - M_4 - 1.1BS_3 + BS_4 \leq 0$$

$$-1.15RE_4 + RE_5 - 1.12B_4 + B_5 - 1.16M_4 - M_5 - 1.1BS_4 + BS_5 \leq 0$$

$$-.5\sum_{i=1}^{5} RE_i + .5\sum_{i=1}^{5} B_i + .5\sum_{i=1}^{5} M_i - .5\sum_{i=1}^{5} BS_i + d_1^- - d_1^+ = 0$$

$$\sum_{i=1}^{5} BS_i + d_2^- - d_2^+ = 200,000$$

$$RE_1 + B_1 + M_1 + BS_1 + d_3^- - d_3^+ = 1,130,000$$

$$RE_2 + B_2 + M_2 + BS_2 - 1.15RE_1 - 1.12B_1 - 1.16M_1 - 1.1BS_1 + d_4^- - d_4^+ = 425,000$$

$$RE_3 + B_3 + M_3 + BS_3 - 1.15RE_2 - 1.12B_2 - 1.16M_2 - 1.1BS_2 + d_5^- - d_5^+ = 9,500$$

$$1.15RE_3 + 1.12B_3 + 1.16M_3 + 1.1BS_3 - RE_4 - B_4 - M_4 - BS_4 + d_6^- - d_6^+ = 96,550$$

$$1.15RE_4 + 1.12B_4 + 1.16M_4 + 1.1BS_4 - RE_5 - B_5 - M_5 - BS_5 + d_7^- - d_7^+ = 203,205$$

$$1.15RE_5 + 1.12B_5 + 1.16M_5 + 1.1BS_5 + d_8^- - d_8^+ = 100,000,000$$

$$RE_i, B_i, M_i, BS_i, d_i^-, d_i^+ \geq 0$$

THE GRAPHICAL METHOD OF GOAL PROGRAMMING

Let us remember that the objective of goal programming is not the maximization or minimization of a single objective criterion. Instead, the objective is to achieve a set of multiple goals as close to the desired levels as possible. The basic approach we will take is to minimize the deviations between the goals and what we can achieve within the given set of system constraints. The deviation from the goal with the highest priority factor will be minimized to the fullest possible extent, and the deviation from the second goal will be minimized after considering the first goal, and so

The graphical method of goal programming

on. Thus, in goal programming, *the optimum solution is optimum only in the sense that it is the most attractive satisficing solution for multiple objectives.*

The goal programming model is, therefore, always a minimization problem. To explain the graphical solution of goal programming, let us consider the following problem.

EXAMPLE 6.1   AN ELECTRONICS MANUFACTURING FIRM

A small electronics manufacturing firm produces AM-FM and AM radios. A radio, regardless of its type, requires an average of one hour in the production plant. Currently, the company has a normal production capacity of 40 hours per week. The expected weekly sales for each type of radio are: AM-FM—20, AM—30. The unit profit for each type of radio is: AM-FM—$40, AM—$30.

The Plant Manager has the following goals for next week's plant operation, listed in the order of their importance:

Figure 6.4   Achievement of the First Goal

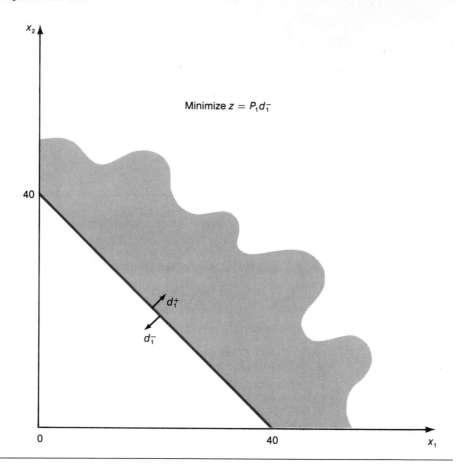

1. Minimize underutilization of normal production capacity.

2. Achieve the sales goal for AM-FM radios by producing at least 20 radios.

3. Avoid overtime operation of the plant in excess of 10 hours.

4. Achieve a weekly profit goal of $1,800.

5. Achieve the sales goal for AM radios by producing at least 30 radios.

With the model formulation experience we have acquired in this chapter, we can easily formulate the following goal programming model for the problem:

$$\text{Minimize } Z = P_1 d_1^- + P_2 d_2^- + P_3 d_3^+ + P_4 d_4^- + P_5 d_5^-$$

$$\begin{aligned}
\text{subject to} \quad x_1 + \quad x_2 + d_1^- - d_1^+ &= 40 \\
x_1 \quad\quad\quad + d_2^- - d_2^+ &= 20
\end{aligned}$$

Figure 6.5 Achievement of the First and Second Goals

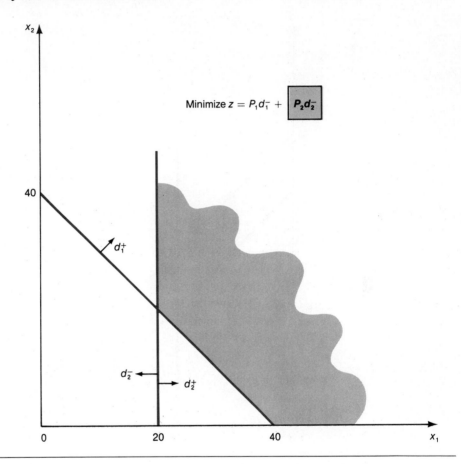

$$x_1 + x_2 + d_3^- - d_3^+ = 50$$
$$40x_1 + 30x_2 + d_4^- - d_4^+ = 1{,}800$$
$$x_2 + d_5^- - d_5^+ = 30$$
$$x_1, x_2, d_i^-, d_i^+ \geq 0$$

where

x_1 = number of AM-FM radios to be produced

x_2 = number of AM radios to be produced

A sequential solution procedure

To solve this problem, we will plot one constraint at a time according to the objective function. For example, the most important goal is to minimize the capacity (the negative deviation) in the first constraint. Thus, we can plot the normal production capacity constraint and minimize d_1^-, as shown in Figure 6.4. When we minimize d_1^-, the feasible area becomes the shaded area. Any point in the shaded area will satisfy the first goal because the total production hours will be 40 or more.

The second goal is to minimize the underachievement of the sales goal for AM-

Figure 6.6   Achievement of the First, Second, and Third Goals

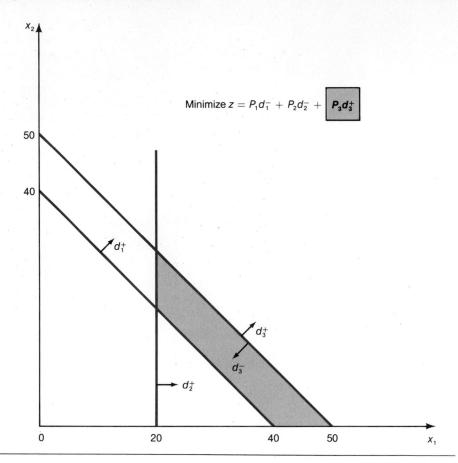

FM radios. This can be accomplished by minimizing d_2^- in the second constraint. However, this goal must be sought within the feasible area already defined by satisfying the first goal. Thus, the feasible area becomes further reduced, as shown in Figure 6.5.

The third goal is to limit overtime operation of the plant to 10 hours. This goal would be achieved if we could minimize d_3^+ to zero within the feasible area. As can be seen in Figure 6.6, the third goal is achieved and the feasible area is now a narrow strip. Within this shaded area, any solution would satisfy the first three most important goals.

The fourth goal, to achieve the weekly profit goal of $1,800, can be satisfied by minimizing d_4^- in the fourth constraint. The process further reduces the feasible area. The narrow space of feasible area that remains is shown in Figure 6.7.

The last goal of the problem is to achieve the sales goal for AM radios. We must minimize d_5^- as much as possible. In the feasible area already defined by ABC

Figure 6.7   Achievement of the First, Second, Third, and Fourth Goals

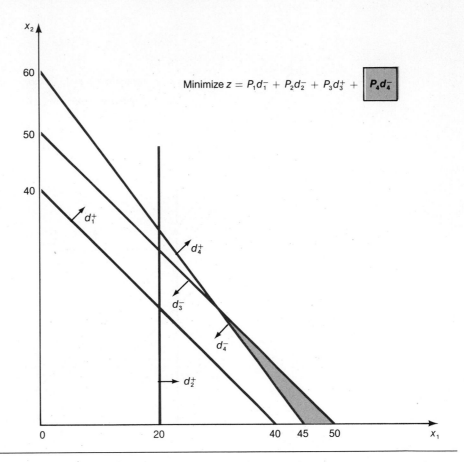

in Figure 6.8, it is impossible to minimize d_5^- all the way to zero. Thus, we must search for the point, within the feasible area, that is closest to the $x_2 = 30$ line. It is obvious that point A is the optimum solution.

At point A, we can easily derive the values of x_1 and x_2 by solving the two intersecting equalities simultaneously. We obtain $x_1 = 30$ and $x_2 = 20$. By substituting these values in all of the goal constraints, we find the following basic variables:

The solution

$$x_1 = 30, \quad x_2 = 20, \quad d_1^+ = 10, \quad d_2^+ = 10, \quad d_5^- = 10,$$
$$\text{other variables} = 0$$

Based on the solution values, we can interpret the degree of goal attainment as follows:

Goal achievement

P_1: Attained (plant is in operation for 50 hours)

P_2: Attained (30 AM-FM radios sold)

P_3: Attained (overtime operation of the plant is limited
to 10 hours)

Figure 6.8   The Optimum Solution for the Electronics Firm Problem

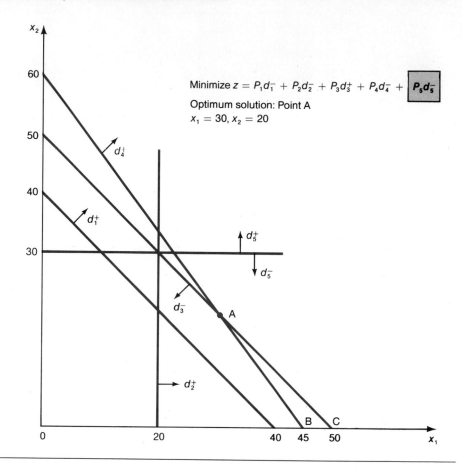

Minimize $z = P_1 d_1^- + P_2 d_2^- + P_3 d_3^+ + P_4 d_4^- + \boxed{P_5 d_5^-}$

Optimum solution: Point A

$x_1 = 30, x_2 = 20$

P_4:   Attained (profit of \$1,800 is attained)

P_5:   Not attained (produced only 20 AM radios—
        underachievement of 10 AM radios)

EXAMPLE 6.2   JEANS GALORE, INC.

Jeans Galore, Inc. is a small local company that produces women's jeans with various flare and pocket designs. It produces two basic types of jeans: ladies and juniors. Joyce, the owner, has set up a sewing center where both types of jeans are cut, sewn, and washed before they are shipped to retailers.

The sewing center currently has normal operation hours of 80 per week. The average production time for a pair of jeans, regardless of type or size, is one hour in the sewing center. The company has weekly orders from several local specialty shops. The estimated weekly demand for each type of jeans is: ladies—70, junior—45. Joyce has established for the next week the following operational goals in the order of their importance:

1. Operate the sewing center for at least 80 hours.

2. Avoid weekly overtime operation of the plant in excess of 10 hours.

3. Achieve the following sales goals: ladies—70 jeans, junior—45 jeans. Assign differential weights to these two goals based on their net profit figures. The estimated unit profit for each type of jeans is: ladies—$15, junior—$9.

4. Minimize overtime operation of the sewing center as much as possible.

With the model formulation experience we have accumulated, we can easily formulate the problem as follows:

$$\text{Minimize } Z = P_1 d_1^- + P_2 d_4^+ + 5P_3 d_2^- + 3P_3 d_3^- + P_4 d_1^+$$
$$\text{subject to} \quad x_1 + x_2 + d_1^- - d_1^+ = 80$$
$$x_1 + d_2^- - d_2^+ = 70$$
$$x_2 + d_3^- - d_3^+ = 45$$
$$x_1 + x_2 + d_4^- - d_4^+ = 90$$
$$x_1, x_2, d_i^-, d_i^+ \geq 0$$

where

$$x_1 = \text{number of ladies jeans produced}$$
$$x_2 = \text{number of junior jeans produced}$$

The first goal of the model is to minimize the underutilization of the normal operation hours in the sewing center. When we minimize d_1^-, the feasible area will become the shaded area shown in Figure 6.9. The second goal is to minimize weekly overtime operation in excess of 10 hours in the sewing center. When we minimize d_4^+, the feasible area becomes further restricted to the narrow strip of shaded area shown in Figure 6.10.

Any solution point in the feasible area will satisfy Joyce's first two most important goals. The third goal is to minimize d_2^- in the second constraint and also d_3^- in the third constraint. Obviously, we have two subgoals at the third priority level. We have differential weights assigned to these two subgoals based on their unit profit ratios: $15 to $9, or 5 to 3. Since d_2^- has a weight of 5, as compared to 3 assigned to d_3^-, d_2^- should be minimized first (the actual solution procedure is more clearly demonstrated in the modified simplex method section).

In Figure 6.11, notice that when we minimize d_2^- the feasible area is restricted to ABCD. Now let us attempt to minimize d_3^-. Clearly, it is impossible to minimize d_3^- all the way to zero. Thus, we must identify the point, within the feasible area, that is closest to the line $x_2 = 45$. This point is obviously A.

The fourth and last goal is to minimize overtime operation of the sewing center as much as possible. To minimize d_1^+, we must move from point A to point B. However, if we move to point B, we will be further removed from the line $x_2 = 45$, and thus d_3^- will be increased. Since we assigned P_3 to the achievement of the sales

Figure 6.9   Achievement of the First Goal

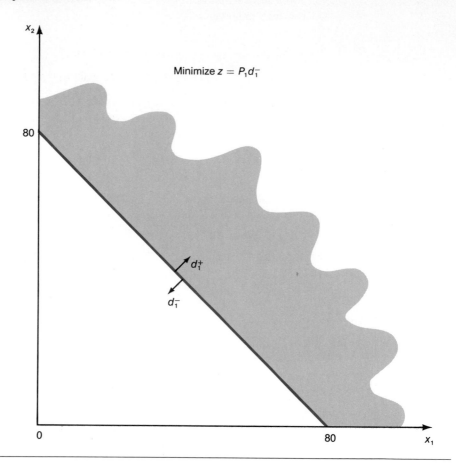

goal for junior jeans, and P_4 to the minimization of the overtime operation in the sewing center, we are not willing to sacrifice the third goal in order to achieve the fourth goal. Thus, the optimum solution is identified as point A. We can interpret the optimum solution as follows:

$$x_1 = 70, \quad x_2 = 20, \quad d_1^+ = 10, \quad d_3^- = 25, \quad \text{all other variables} = 0$$

Based on the solution values, we can interpret the degree of goal attainment as follows:

P_1:   Attained

P_2:   Attained

P_3:   Not completely attained ($d_3^- = 25$)

P_4:   Not completely attained ($d_1^+ = 10$)

There is one point we must clear up before terminating our discussion of the graphical method of goal programming. To apply the graphical method, all system

Figure 6.10   Achievement of the First and Second Goals

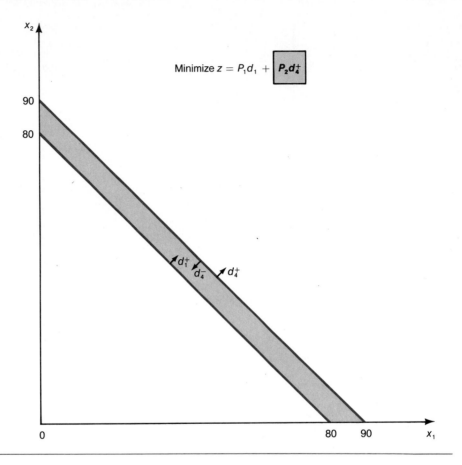

and goal constraints in the model must be expressed in terms of x_1 and/or x_2. Otherwise, we would not know how to plot a constraint on the graph. Occasionally, we have constraints composed entirely of deviational variables. This situation arises when we decompose a goal into two or more goals. In such cases, we must convert these constraints into functions that are expressed in terms of decision variables.

Handling a decomposed goal

For example, in Casette 6.3, we expressed the overtime restriction goal for full-time salespersons as follows:

$$d_2^+ + d_3^- - d_3^+ = 200$$

To transform this constraint into one that contains decision variables, we can take the following steps:

$$d_2^+ = 200 - d_3^- + d_3^+$$

Now we substitute this value of d_2^+ into the second constraint:

Figure 6.11   Analysis of the First, Second, Third, and Fourth Goals

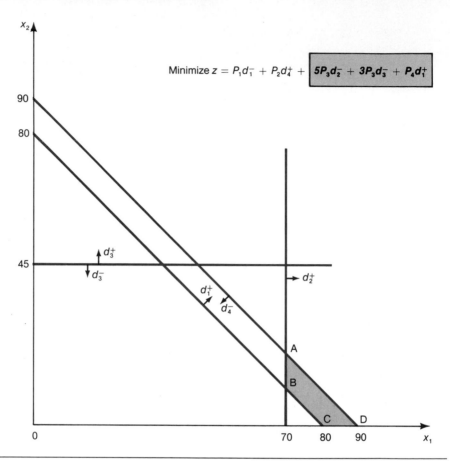

$$x_1 + d_2^- - d_2^+ = 1{,}600$$
$$x_1 + d_2^- - (200 - d_3^- + d_3^+) = 1{,}600$$
$$x_1 + d_2^- + d_3^- - d_3^+ = 1{,}800$$

In this constraint, the right-hand-side value of 1,800 hours represents overtime of 200 hours. In other words, we are trying to determine how much overtime should be allowed for the full-time employees. The deviational variable d_2^- (underutilization of the 1,600 regular working hours), therefore, must be zero. Thus, we can eliminate d_2^- in this constraint. The goal constraint is now expressed as

$$x_1 + d_3^- - d_3^+ = 1{,}800$$

The above constraint can be easily plotted on the graph.

THE MODIFIED SIMPLEX METHOD OF GOAL PROGRAMMING

The modified simplex method

There have been several solution methods introduced for goal programming. Some methods are more efficient than others in terms of computation time on the computer. However, almost every solution technique is based on the basic solution approach known as the *modified simplex method*. This method, developed by S. M. Lee, takes advantage of the unique features of the goal programming model in applying the simplex technique.

Some of the best-known solution techniques of goal programming, such as the goal partitioning algorithm and the revised simplex method of goal programming, are based on the modified simplex method framework augmented by efficient matrix manipulation methods. We will summarize the steps involved in the modified simplex method of goal programming in a later section of this chapter. However, the basic steps we will be following are presented in the simple flow diagram shown in Figure 6.12.

In this section, we will study the modified simplex method of goal programming. Let us use the problem presented as Example 6.2, which we examined earlier as a vehicle for the study of the modified simplex method:

An example

$$\text{Minimize } Z = P_1 d_1^- + P_2 d_4^+ + 5P_3 d_2^- + 3P_3 d_3^- + P_4 d_1^+$$
$$\text{subject to } x_1 + x_2 + d_1^- - d_1^+ = 80$$
$$x_1 + d_2^- - d_2^+ = 70$$
$$x_2 + d_3^- - d_3^+ = 45$$
$$x_1 + x_2 + d_4^- - d_4^+ = 90$$
$$x_1, x_2, d_i^-, d_i^+ \geq 0$$

Before we jump into the modified simplex method of goal programming, we must remember several key features of the goal programming model:

Key features of a goal programming model

1. In a goal programming model, our objective is not to optimize one criterion but to achieve multiple objectives. The basic approach we take is to minimize the deviational variables through the use of priority factors and differential weights.

2. Since the objective function is expressed by priorities and associated differential weights, c_j or c_b values are represented by these weights rather than by unit contribution rates.

3. The preemptive priority weights are not one-dimensional values but multidimensional values. Therefore, z_j or $z_j - c_j$ requires a matrix because it cannot be represented by a single row.

4. Since the simplex criterion $z_j - c_j$ is a matrix, the selection of the pivot column must be determined by the priority factors. In other words, we must select the pivot column that would improve the highest unachieved priority goal by the greatest amount.

5. The modified simplex method of goal programming attempts to satisfy the system constraints, if there are any, by assigning the superpriority P_0 to the appropriate

Figure 6.12   Goal Programming Solution Process by the Modified Simplex Method

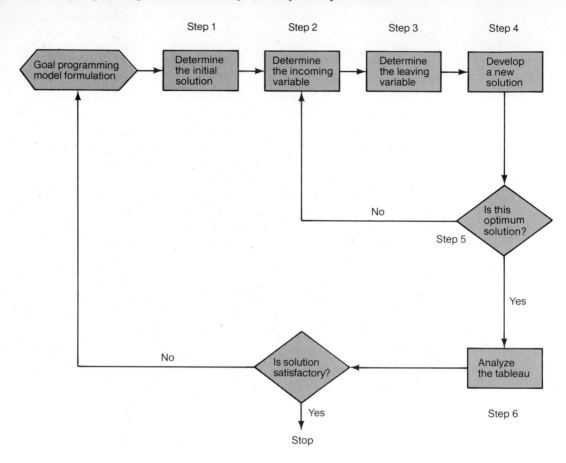

deviational variables. Then, it proceeds to achieve the most important goal to the fullest possible extent, then the second goal, and so on in sequence.

6. A goal programming model is a minimization problem. Thus, we must calculate $z_j - c_j$ rather than $c_j - z_j$.

Developing the Initial Simplex Tableau

This step is similar to that of the simplex method of linear programming. We assume that the initial solution is at the origin, where we do not produce anything. Thus, $x_1 = 0$ and $x_2 = 0$. Substituting these values of the decision variables in the constraints, we can determine the basic variables.

The initial simplex tableau In the first constraint, because $x_1 = 0$ and $x_2 = 0$, then d_1^+ (e.g., overtime operation to produce the two products) must be zero. Thus, d_1^- will take the right-hand-side value as shown following.

Table 6.1   The Initial Simplex Tableau

c_b	c_j Basis	Solution	0 x_1	0 x_2	P_1 d_1^-	$5P_3$ d_2^-	$3P_3$ d_3^-	0 d_4^-	P_4 d_1^+	0 d_2^+	0 d_3^+	P_2 d_4^+
P_1	d_1^-	80	1	1	1	0	0	0	-1	0	0	0
$5P_3$	d_2^-	70	①	0	0	1	0	0	0	-1	0	0
$3P_3$	d_3^-	45	0	1	0	0	1	0	0	0	-1	0
0	d_4^-	90	1	1	0	0	0	1	0	0	0	-1
	P_4	0	0	0	0	0	0	0	-1	0	0	0
$z_j - c_j$	P_3	485	5	3	0	0	0	0	0	-5	-3	0
	P_2	0	0	0	0	0	0	0	0	0	0	-1
	P_1	80	1	1	0	0	0	0	-1	0	0	0

$$x_1 + x_2 + d_1^- - d_1^+ = 80$$
$$0 + 0 + d_1^- - 0 = 80$$
$$d_1^- = 80$$

The basic variable for the first constraint is d_1^-, and the solution value is 80.

In a similar manner, we can determine that d_2^-, d_3^-, and d_4^- are also basic variables. As a matter of fact, it is a rule that the negative deviational variables (d_i^-) in each of the constraints become the basic variables in the initial tableau.

The basic variables in the initial tableau

The initial simplex tableau is presented in Table 6.1. The c_j and c_b values are obtained from the objective function of the model. For example, P_1 was assigned to d_1^- in the objective function. Thus, P_1 is listed as c_j in the d_1^- column and in the d_1^- row.

The simplex criterion $z_j - c_j$ is computed first, rather than the z_j values first and then the $z_j - c_j$. By omitting the z_j matrix, we can greatly simplify the simplex tableau. In the basis column, we list the priorities in the ascending order, from the lowest at the top to the highest at the bottom. In this way we can determine the pivot column from the bottom of the tableau.

Computing z_j values

In the solution column, we simply calculate the z_j value. The z_j value in the solution column is calculated by the same procedure we used in linear programming:

$$z_j \text{ (solution)} = \Sigma \, (c_b \times \text{solution values})$$
$$= (P_1 \times 80) + (5P_3 \times 70) + (3P_3 \times 45) + (0 \times 90)$$
$$= 80P_1 + 485P_3$$

The z_j value in the solution column

The z_j value in the solution column represents the unattained portion of each goal. For example, in the initial tableau, z_j values in the solution column are $P_1 = 80$, $P_2 = 0$, $P_3 = 485$, and $P_4 = 0$. In other words, the first and third goals are not completely attained, but the second and fourth goals are completely attained. How can this be possible when our solution is at the origin, where we are not even operating the sewing center? When we examine the objective function, it is clear that the second goal is to limit the overtime operation of the sewing center to 10 hours and the fourth goal is to minimize the total overtime operation of the sewing center as much as possible. Since we are not even operating the sewing center, there is no overtime operation.

The underachievement of the first goal is 80 because our goal is to operate the sewing center for at least 80 hours, and presently it is idle. The unattained portion of the third goal is 485. This value is a bit difficult to explain. The third goal is concerned with achieving the sales goals for the ladies' jeans and junior jeans. We assigned differential weights of 5 and 3 to the achievement of the sales goals for the ladies' jeans and the junior jeans respectively. These two subgoals are commensurable (i.e., they are measured in number of jeans). Since we have not achieved the sales goal of 70 ladies' jeans and 45 junior jeans, the total unattained portion of this goal will be $(70 \times 5) + (45 \times 3) = 485$.

For the variable columns, we must calculate the $z_j - c_j$ value in one operation. First, we must compute the z_j value in each of the variable columns. We must remember that the $z_j - c_j$ value is zero in the basic-variable columns. Therefore, we can eliminate the d_1^-, d_2^-, d_3^-, and d_4^- columns from the $z_j - c_j$ calculation. Calculation of z_j in a variable column can be accomplished by the following procedure:

Computing $z_j - c_j$ values

$$z_j \text{ (variable column)} = \Sigma \, (c_b \times \text{coefficients})$$

Thus, the z_j value in the x_1 column is

$$z_j \, (x_1) = (P_1 \times 1) + (5P_3 \times 1) + (3P_3 \times 0) + (0 \times 1)$$
$$= P_1 + 5P_3$$

The c_j value in the x_1 column is zero, as shown at the top of the column. Thus, $z_j - c_j$ for the x_1 column is $(P_1 + 5P_3) - 0 = P_1 + 5P_3$.

Since P_1 and P_3 are not commensurable, we must list them separately in the P_1 and P_3 rows of the simplex criterion. Thus, we list 1 at the P_1 level and 5 at the P_3 level. In a similar manner, we can derive the $z_j - c_j$ value in the x_2 column:

$$z_j \, (x_2) = (P_1 \times 1) + (5P_3 \times 0) + (3P_3 \times 1) + (0 \times 1)$$
$$= P_1 + 3P_3$$

The c_j value is also zero in the x_2 column. Therefore, $z_j - c_j = P_1 + 3P_3$. We also list 1 at the P_1 level and 3 at the P_3 level.

The $z_j - c_j$ values in the basic-variable columns d_1^-, d_2^-, d_3^-, and d_4^- will all be zero. For the d_1^+ column, the z_j value is $-P_1$. Since the c_j value of the column is P_4, the $z_j - c_j$ value wil be $-P_1 - P_4$. Therefore, -1 is listed in the P_1 row and also in the P_4 row. It should be a simple task to calculate $z_j - c_j$ in the d_2^+ and d_3^+ columns. They are $-5P_3$ and $-3P_3$ respectively. In the last column, d_4^+, the z_j value is zero. But its c_j value is P_2. Thus, the $z_j - c_j$ value will be $-P_2$. Accordingly, we list -1 in the P_2 row.

As we discussed earlier, we combined into one the calculational procedures for determining z_j and $z_j - c_j$ in the simplex tableau. The single procedure obviously requires more mental calculations, but it certainly makes the tableau simpler to handle. If a problem containing 5 preemptive priorities and 20 variables is being analyzed, we can avoid a 5×20 matrix by calculating $z_j - c_j$ in one operation.

Selecting the pivot column

Now, let us move on to the selection of the pivot column and the pivot row. The criterion we use in determining the pivot column is the rate of contribution of each nonbasic variable in achieving the highest unattained objective in terms of the priorities. In Table 6.1, the highest unattained priority goal is P_1, where we have 80 hours of unattained goal. Thus, we are searching for a nonbasic-variable column that has the largest positive $z_j - c_j$ value at the P_1 level.

In Table 6.1, there are two identical positive values in the x_1 and x_2 columns. To break this tie, we check the next lower priority level. Since there is a greater value (5) in the x_1 column at the P_3 level as compared to the x_2 column (3), we select x_1 as the pivot column.

Determining the pivot row

The pivot row selection procedure is exactly the same as that employed in linear programming. The pivot row is the row that has the minimum nonnegative value when we divide the solution values by the positive coefficients in the pivot column. For example, we have three positive coefficients in the x_1 column in the d_1^-, d_2^-, and d_4^- rows. Thus, we can divide the solution values by the positive coefficients as follows:

Row	Solution	÷	Coefficient	=	Quotient
d_1^-	80	÷	1	=	80
d_2^-	70	÷	1	=	70 ← pivot row
d_4^-	90	÷	1	=	90

The pivot row is selected as the d_2^- row. In Table 6.1, the boldface numbers identify x_1 as the pivot column and d_2^- as the pivot row.

The First Iteration

The first iteration

Now we are ready to develop the second simplex tableau. We can apply the regular simplex procedure to complete the first iteration.

In the initial tableau shown in Table 6.1, we identified x_1 as the incoming variable and d_2^- as the outgoing variable. The pivot element is also identified by the circle. To find the new values in the pivot row and in the other rows, we use the following procedures:

Pivot Row
    New value = Old value ÷ Pivot element

Computing new values

Other Rows
    New value = Old value − (Row value × New value in pivot row)

Table 6.2 presents the simplex tableau after the first iteration. The solution indicates that the sewing center is in operation for 70 hours to produce 70 ladies' jeans ($x_1 = 70$). Therefore, the underutilization of the normal operating hours in the sewing center is 10 hours ($d_1^- = 10$). We have now completely achieved the sales goal for ladies' jeans, and, therefore, d_2^- has been removed from the solution basis.

Interpreting the simplex tableau

Since we are yet to produce any junior jeans, underachievement of the sales goal for junior jeans is 45 ($d_3^- = 45$). Currently, the sewing center is in operation for 70 hours. Since the acceptable overtime operation of the sewing center is 10 hours, we are underutilizing 20 hours from the total allowed operation hours of 90 ($d_4^- = 20$).

The z_j values in the solution column in Table 6.2 indicate that the unattained portion of the first goal has been decreased considerably, from 80 to 10. This is a good sign because the goal programming model is a minimization problem, and the value of z_j should decrease at each step toward the optimum solution. As our immediate concern is the achievement of the most important goal, we can simply examine whether z_j has decreased at the P_1 level at each iteration. When z_j is at the P_1 level and is completely minimized to zero, we can then focus our attention on the z_j value at the P_2 level, and so on. In Table 6.2, z_j at the P_3 level has also decreased by 350, as the production of 70 ladies' jeans enables the achievement of the sales goal for ladies' jeans.

The Second Iteration

The second iteration

In the second simplex tableau shown in Table 6.2, we can identify x_2 as the pivot column. The best way to achieve the most important goal is by producing 10 junior jeans, thereby operating the sewing center for a total of 80 hours. Thus, the pivot row is the d_1^- row.

Table 6.3 presents the third simplex tableau. The solution indicates that production of 70 ladies' jeans and 10 junior jeans is sufficient to achieve the first, second, and fourth goals. However, the third goal is not completely attained since the sales goal of junior jeans is still 35 short of attainment ($d_3^- = 35$ shown in the solution basis).

Interpreting goal attainment

A very interesting point we discover in Table 6.3 is that when a goal is attained there should be only zero or negative $z_j - c_j$ values at the given priority level. For example, we can ascertain that the P_1 goal is attained when z_j at the P_1 level is zero. Therefore, all $z_j - c_j$ values at the P_1 level are either zero or negative. The same result is found at the P_2 and P_4 levels. However, since the P_3 goal is not attained (i.e., the z_j value is 105), there should be at least one positive $z_j - c_j$ value at the P_3 level. We can find a positive $z_j - c_j$ value of 3 in the d_1^+ column.

The Optimum Solution

The optimum solution

The selection of the pivot column should be determined at the P_3 level. The d_1^+ column is the pivot column and d_4^- is the pivot row. The fourth simplex tableau is presented in Table 6.4. This solution is the optimum solution. Notice that the z_j value at the P_3 level was decreased from 105 to 75. To decrease the underachievement of the third goal, we sacrificed the attainment of the fourth goal by 10 units, as shown by the z_j value at the P_4 level.

The optimum solution is $x_1 = 70$, $x_2 = 20$, $d_3^- = 25$, and $d_1^+ = 10$. In other words, the company should produce 70 ladies' jeans and 20 junior jeans with 10 hours of overtime operation of the sewing center, resulting in the underachievement of the sales goal for junior jeans by 25. With this solution the company's goal attainment will be as follows:

Goal attainment

P_1:   Attained

P_2:   Attained

P_3:   Not attained (underachievement of sales goal for junior jeans by 25)

P_4:   Not attained (10 hours of overtime operation in the sewing center)

In Table 6.4, since the third goal is not attained, there is a positive $z_j - c_j$ value at the P_3 level. This value is 3 in the d_4^+ column. Obviously, we can attain the third goal if we introduce d_4^+ into the solution. We find, however, a negative $z_j - c_j$ value

Table 6.2 The Second Simplex Tableau

c_b	Basis	Solution	0 x_1	0 x_2	P_1 d_1^-	$5P_3$ d_2^-	$3P_3$ d_3^-	0 d_4^-	P_4 d_1^+	0 d_2^+	0 d_3^+	P_2 d_4^+
P_1	d_1^-	10	0	①	1	-1	0	0	-1	1	0	0
0	x_1	70	1	0	0	1	0	0	0	-1	0	0
$3P_3$	d_3^-	45	0	1	0	0	1	0	0	0	-1	0
0	d_4^-	20	0	1	0	-1	0	1	0	1	0	-1
$z_j - c_j$	P_4	0	0	0	0	0	0	0	-1	0	0	0
	P_3	135	0	3	0	-5	0	0	0	0	-3	0
	P_2	0	0	0	0	0	0	0	0	0	0	-1
	P_1	10	0	1	0	-1	0	0	-1	1	0	0

Table 6.3 The Third Simplex Tableau

c_b	Basis	Solution	0 x_1	0 x_2	P_1 d_1^-	$5P_3$ d_2^-	$3P_3$ d_3^-	0 d_4^-	P_4 d_1^+	0 d_2^+	0 d_3^+	P_2 d_4^+
0	x_2	10	0	1	1	-1	0	0	-1	1	0	0
0	x_1	70	1	0	0	1	0	0	0	-1	0	0
$3P_3$	d_3^-	35	0	0	-1	1	1	0	1	-1	-1	0
0	d_4^-	10	0	0	-1	0	0	1	①	0	0	-1
$z_j - c_j$	P_4	0	0	0	0	0	0	0	-1	0	0	0
	P_3	105	0	0	-3	-2	0	0	3	-3	-3	0
	P_2	0	0	0	0	0	0	0	0	0	0	-1
	P_1	0	0	0	-1	0	0	0	0	0	0	0

Table 6.4   The Optimum Solution Tableau

c_b	Basis	Solution	0 x_1	0 x_2	P_1 d_1^-	$5P_3$ d_2^-	$3P_3$ d_3^-	0 d_4^-	P_4 d_1^+	0 d_2^+	0 d_3^+	P_2 d_4^+
0	x_2	20	0	1	0	-1	0	1	0	1	0	-1
0	x_1	70	1	0	0	1	0	0	0	-1	0	0
$3P_3$	d_3^-	25	0	0	0	1	1	-1	0	-1	-1	1
P_4	d_1^+	10	0	0	-1	0	0	1	1	0	0	-1
	P_4	10	0	0	-1	0	0	1	0	0	0	-1
$z_j - c_j$	P_3	75	0	0	0	-2	0	-3	0	-3	-3	3
	P_2	0	0	0	0	0	0	0	0	0	0	-1
	P_1	0	0	0	-1	0	0	0	0	0	0	0

Interpreting the final simplex tableau

(-1) at a higher priority level (i.e., at the P_2 level). This implies that if we introduce d_4^+ into the solution, we would improve the achievement of the third goal (P_3) at the expense of achieving the second goal (P_2). Of course, we are not willing to accept this trade-off. Thus, we cannot introduce d_4^+ into the solution.

The same logic applies to the d_4^- column. We find a positive $z_j - c_j$ value of 1 at the P_4 level in the d_4^- column. However, there is a negative $z_j - c_j$ value of -3 at a higher priority level (i.e., P_3). Therefore, d_4^- cannot be selected as the pivot

Optimality conditions

column. The optimum solution must satisfy one of the following two conditions:

1. The z_j values in the solution column are zero at all priority levels. This is a case in which all priority goals are attained. This case can occur only when there is no conflict among the goals.

2. There is no pivot column to be selected because all of the positive $z_j - c_j$ values at the various priority levels have accompanying negative $z_j - c_j$ values below them (i.e., at higher priority levels). This is a case in which some of the goals are in conflict. Thus, all goals cannot be achieved as desired.

The complete modified simplex solution procedure for the Jeans Galore problem is shown in Figure 6.13.

Analysis of Goal Conflicts

We can derive some valuable information from the final simplex tableau. From an analysis of the $z_j - c_j$ values, we can point out where conflict exists among the goals. For example, in Table 6.4 we can easily identify the conflict between the second and third goals in the d_4^+ column. Also, there is a conflict between the third

Analyzing goal conflicts

and fourth goals in the d_4^- column. Now we can determine precisely how we must rearrange the priority structure if the underachieved goals at the lower levels are to be attained. This process of analyzing goal conflicts provides an opportunity for us to evaluate the soundness of our priority structure for the goals.

Figure 6.13 **The Modified Simplex Solution Procedure for the Jeans Galore Problem**

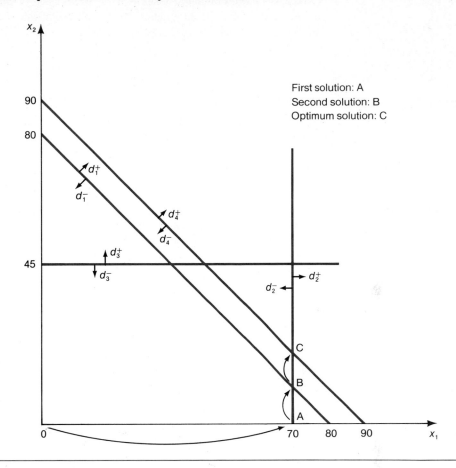

We can also analyze the coefficients in the main body of the final simplex tableau in order to identify the exact trade-offs between the goals that are in conflict. For example, in Table 6.4 we can see that if we introduce 25 units of d_4^+ into the solution, the third goal will be completely attained. However, this procedure will "undo" the second goal by the same quantity, and the degree of attainment of the fourth goal will also be deteriorated by the same quantity. The marginal substitution rate in this case is 1:1, as can be seen by the coefficients shown below:

c_j / c_b	Basis	Solution	. . .	P_2 d_4^+
	⋮	⋮	⋮	
$3P_3$	d_3^+	25		1
P_4	d_1^+	10		-1

The same type of analysis can be made in the d_4^- column. The trade-off rate between the third and fourth goals is 1:1. An analysis of the final simplex tableau provides a great deal of information about and insight into the decision environment and the decision maker's goal priority structure.

SOME UNIQUE SITUATIONS IN GOAL PROGRAMMING

Unique situations in goal programming

As in linear programming, there are several unique situations in goal programming. Some of these situations are common to all linear optimization techniques. However, certain unique features of goal programming provide us with ways to resolve some of these complications.

Negative Right-hand-side Value

A negative right-hand-side value

It is possible that the right-hand-side value of a certain goal constraint may be negative. In such a case, we must first multiply both sides by -1 and then introduce the appropriate deviational variables. For example, let us consider the following goal constraint:

$$-2x_2 + x_3 - x_4 \geq -10$$

The goal is to make the left-hand side of the inequality greater than or equal to -10. Now we multiply both sides by -1 and obtain

$$2x_2 - x_3 + x_4 \leq 10$$

Then, we introduce the deviational variables and attempt to minimize the positive deviation in the goal constraint:

$$2x_2 - x_3 + x_4 + d_1^- - d_1^+ = 10$$

A Tie in Selecting the Pivot Column

Breaking a tie in selecting the pivot column

This situation has already been explained thoroughly. If there is a tie in selecting the pivot column, the $z_j - c_j$ values at the lower priority levels of the two tied columns should be compared. If the tie cannot be broken, select the column that has a lower priority factor as its c_j value. If the tie is still not broken, selection between the contending variable columns can be made arbitrarily.

A Tie in Selecting the Pivot Row

Breaking a tie in selecting the pivot row

This situation has also been explained previously. To determine the pivot row, the solution values are divided by the positive coefficients in the pivot column. The row that has the minimum nonnegative value is the pivot row. If we have a tie among two or more rows each with the identical minimum nonnegative quotient, the tie is broken by selecting the variable row with the highest priority factor.

Multiple Optimum Solutions

Multiple optimum solutions

For certain problems, it is possible that two or more extreme points yield solutions that achieve exactly the same goal levels. Such a situation never occurs if: (1) there is a single goal at each of the priority levels; (2) differential weights are assigned among the subgoals when there is more than one goal at a given priority level; and (3) conflicts exist among some of the goals.

An Unbounded Problem

An unbounded problem

For some problems, it is possible in theory that lack of system constraints or realistic goal levels may allow one or more variables to increase without bound. However, in most real-world situations such a situation never occurs because of restrictive system constraints or goal conflicts.

An Infeasible Problem

An infeasible problem

When there is a conflict among the system constraints, the problem is infeasible. We can assign the superpriority P_0 to the deviational variables in the system constraints. Then, in the final simplex tableau, the z_j value in the solution column should be zero if the problem is to be feasible. If the z_j value at the P_0 level is positive, the problem is infeasible. In such a case, the system constraints must be carefully analyzed to determine whether or not the conflict among system constraints can be resolved.

REAL-WORLD APPLICATIONS OF GOAL PROGRAMMING

Applying goal programming to real-world problems

There have been a number of interesting real-world applications of goal programming reported in management literature. Some of these applications have been for decision problems in business firms, and others have been for decision problems in governmental agencies and nonprofit organizations. Most of these applications are primarily concerned with resource allocations, planning or scheduling, and policy analysis. We will examine three applications in this section.

An Application of Goal Programming at Lord Corporation

An application of goal programming reported by A. Salvia[1] is concerned with resource allocation among competing research and development projects at Lord Corporation. The company was attempting to allocate resources to 25 potential research and development projects in order to achieve 10 different goals. The goals listed by the Lord management were:

1. No one project should require more than 10 percent of the allocated resources.

2. Sales growth of 15 percent per year should be achieved through the projects.

3. The discounted cash flow amount should exceed a 30 percent rate of return.

4. Projects selected should have 5-year capital limits.

5. Projects should promote constructive change in the industry.

6. Projects should help the company to play a leadership role in the industry.

---

[1]A. Salvia, "An Application of Goal Programming at Lord Corporation," *Interfaces*, 9:4 (1979), 129–133.

7. Projects must develop new technology for the company.

8. Projects should develop advanced technology that is interrelated to other exciting technology.

9. Projects should provide diversification for future projects and market strategies.

10. The current balance of resource allocations among the various units should be maintained.

After a goal programming model was developed, four different computer runs were tried with different priority structures and goal levels. These computer runs were used to generate "what if" type sensitivity analysis. The study reported that results of the model were very useful in determining the final resource allocation among the 25 research and development projects at Lord Corporation.

Ballistic Missile Defense Technology Management with Goal Programming

Another interesting application of goal programming was reported by J. M. Mellichamp, W. L. Dixon, and S. L. Mitchell[2] concerning the selection of a mission-efficient set of ballistic missile defense (BMD) research projects and the determination of the appropriate level of support for the selected programs. There is currently a strategic arms limitation agreement between the United States and the Soviet Union. This agreement prohibits the deployment of antiballistic missile (ABM) systems for nationwide defense and also limits the number of ABM sites that each nation can deploy for defending a particular geographic location. However, there is no restraint placed on ABM research.

The defense organization responsible for administering the ABM research effort is the Ballistic Missile Defense Advanced Technology Center (BMDATC). To select the most efficient set of BMD research projects, three basic goals were considered: (1) the desired enhancement of defense effectiveness required from the research projects; (2) allocation of a certain proportion of available funds to low-risk projects that are expected to result in improved defense effectiveness; and (3) limiting project expenditures to the allocated budget.

The study evaluated six available projects. The model determined the level of funding for each of the six projects in order to achieve the three goals as closely as possible. The study reported that the model results generated some valuable information for the management of BMD research projects.

Formulating Blood Rotation Policies with Goal Programming

Another unusual and innovative application of goal programming was reported by K. E. Kendall and S. M. Lee[3] concerning the formulation of human blood rotation policies. Human blood is a very valuable resource that is highly perishable. Thus, it is desirable to redistribute blood systematically to hospital blood banks where it will have a high probability of transfusion.

[2]J. M. Mellichamp, W. L. Dixon, and S. L. Mitchell, "Ballistic Missile Defense Technology Management with Goal Programming," *Interfaces,* 10:5 (1980), 68–74.

[3]K. E. Kendall and S. M. Lee, "Formulating Blood Rotation Policies with Multiple Objectives," *Management Science,* 26:11 (Nov., 1980), 1145–1157.

This study is based on data collected from the American Red Cross—Midwest Region, based in Omaha, Nebraska. This regional blood center serves urban and rural areas in parts of Nebraska, Iowa, Kansas, and South Dakota. A total of 105 hospital blood banks participate in this region. The large and sparsely populated geographical area further reinforces the need for effective management of blood inventory. This goal programming model involved the following six goals:

1. Limit to a certain acceptable level the frequency of blood shortage experienced by hospitals.

2. Prevent the overstocking of blood in order to minimize cost.

3. Secure the supply of a sufficient amount of fresh blood to accommodate special types of surgery such as open heart surgery.

4. Limit the average number of units of outdated blood, and thereby prevent waste of human blood.

5. Limit the average age of blood in each hospital so that relatively fresh blood would be available.

6. Keep to an acceptable level the total cost of the entire regional operation, including blood collection, inventory control, distribution, and rotation.

This study reported that the model results were very useful to the regional administrator in determining how blood should be rotated among the member hospitals so that the goals and priorities unique to the region could be achieved. The goal programming approach is especially well suited for analyzing blood rotation policies because it allows the administrators to take part in the design of a policy that is tailored to the region's specific needs.

COMPUTER-BASED ANALYSIS OF GOAL PROGRAMMING

Using the computer for goal programming solutions

Many real-world problems are too complex to solve by the modified simplex method of goal programming. To apply goal programming to practical problems, therefore, we often need a computer-based analysis. Currently, there are available only a few computer programs for goal programming. Appendix 2 presents a computer solution using the modified simplex method of goal programming as a demonstration tool for analyzing exercise problems. There are more advanced programs available to analyze large-scale real-world problems.

SUMMARY

In recent years an increasing amount of attention has been given to goal programming as a decision making tool for problems that involve multiple and conflicting objectives. Goal programming is a powerful technique that allows the decision maker to incorporate into the model his or her judgment about the unique decision environment, the bureaucratic decision process, and the organizational goals and their priorities. The goal programming solution process yields valuable information about goal conflicts, soundness of the priority structure for goals, and trade-offs among the conflicting objectives.

During the past several years there have been a number of important advances made in the area of goal programming, including sensitivity analysis, integer goal programming, interactive goal programming, decomposition goal programming, separable goal programming, chance-constrained goal programming, and several advanced solution methods. If you are interested in doing some research in these topics, consult the following list of references.

References

Charnes, A., and Cooper, W. W. *Management Models and Industrial Applications of Linear Programming*. New York: Wiley, 1961.

Ignizio, J. P. *Goal Programming and Extensions*. Lexington, Mass.: Lexington Books, 1976.

Ijiri, Y. *Management Goals and Accounting for Control*. Chicago: Rand-McNally, 1965.

Lee, S. M. *Goal Programming for Decision Analysis*. Philadelphia: Auerbach, 1972.

Lee, S. M. *Linear Optimization for Management*. New York: Petrocelli-Charter, 1976.

Lee, S. M. *Goal Programming Methods for Multiple Integer Programs*. Atlanta: American Institute of Industrial Engineers, 1979.

Assignments

6.1 What is the set of steps that has been advocated for decision making in the traditional normative approach of decision making?

6.2 What is the foundation of the descriptive approach of decision making? How is this approach different from the normative approach?

6.3 Contrast satisficing and optimizing.

6.4 What are the major differences between linear programming and goal programming?

6.5 Explain in one paragraph the basic concept of goal programming.

6.6 Outline a problem you face frequently that involves multiple conflicting objectives.

6.7 What are the major differences between system and goal constraints?

6.8 In a goal programming model, what are the three options to achieve certain objectives through minimizing the deviational variables?

6.9 Explain the difference between cardinal weights and preemptive priority weights.

6.10 Why must all goals in a given priority level be commensurable in goal programming?

6.11 What are the major differences between the ordinary simplex method of linear programming and the modified simplex method of goal programming?

6.12 What is a trade-off? Is there a trade-off between two goals only when they are in conflict?

6.13 Solve the following goal programming problem by the graphical method:

$$\text{Minimize } Z = P_1 d_2^- + P_2 d_1^- + P_3 d_1^+ + P_4 d_3^-$$
$$\text{subject to } \quad x_1 + x_2 + d_1^- - d_1^+ = 80$$
$$x_1 + d_2^- - d_2^+ = 100$$
$$x_2 + d_3^- = 45$$
$$x_j, d_i^-, d_i^+ \geq 0$$

6.14 Solve the following goal programming problem by the graphical method:

$$\text{Minimize } Z = P_1 d_1^- + P_2 d_4^+ + 3P_3 d_2^- + P_3 d_3^- + P_4 d_2^+ + 3P_4 d_3^+$$
$$\text{subject to } \quad 5x_1 + 2x_2 + d_1^- - d_1^+ = 550$$
$$x_1 + d_2^- - d_2^+ = 80$$
$$x_2 + d_3^- - d_3^+ = 32$$
$$x_1 + d_4^- - d_4^+ = 90$$
$$x_j, d_i^-, d_i^+ \geq 0$$

6.15 Solve the Modern Fashions, Inc. problem, presented in this chapter as Casette 6.2, by the graphical method.

6.16 Solve the Big Sound Records, Inc. problem, Casette 6.3 in this chapter, by the graphical method.

6.17 The manufacturing plant of an electronics firm produces two types of television sets: color and black-and-white. Past experience indicates that production of either a color or a black-and-white set requires an average of 3 hours in the plant. The plant has a normal production capacity of 120 hours a week. The Marketing Department reports that the estimated number of color and black-and-white sets that can be sold each week are 25 and 30 respectively. The gross profit from the sale of a color set is $80, whereas it is $40 from the sale of a black-and-white set. The president of the company has set the following goals, arranged in the order of their importance to the organization:

1. Avoid any underutilization of normal production capacity (no layoffs of production workers).
2. Sell as many television sets as estimated by the Marketing Department. Since the gross profit from the sale of a color television set is twice the amount from a black-and-white set, the president has twice as much desire to achieve the sales goal for color sets as for black-and-white sets.
3. Minimize the overtime operation of the plant as much as possible.

Solve this problem by the graphical method of goal programming.

6.18 Oriental Rugs, Inc. produces the world's finest factory-made oriental rugs. The company's production facility consists of two production lines. Line 1 is staffed with skilled workers who can produce an average of 2 rugs per hour. Line 2 is capable of producing an average of 1-1/2 rugs per hour, as it is staffed with relatively new employees. The regular production capacity for the next week is 40 hours for each line. The profit from an average rug is $200. It is estimated that the operating costs of the two lines are virtually the same. The president of the firm has listed, in ordinal ranking of importance, the following multiple goals to achieve in the coming week:

1. Meet the production goal of 170 rugs for the week.
2. Limit the overtime operation of Line 1 to 5 hours.
3. Avoid the underutilization of the regular working hours of Line 1 as specified by the union contract.
4. Limit the overtime operation for each of the production lines. (Apply differential weights according to the relative cost of overtime.)

Formulate a goal programming model for the problem and solve it by the graphical method.

6.19 A production manager faces the problem of job allocation between his two teams. The processing rate of the first team is 5 units per hour and the processing rate of the second team is 6 units per hour. The normal production capacity for each team is 8 hours per day. The production manager has the following goals for the next day, arranged in order of importance:

1. Avoid any underachievement of the production level, which is set at 120 units of product.
2. Avoid any overtime operation of Team 2 beyond 3 hours.
3. The total overtime should be minimized. (Assign differential weights according to the relative cost of overtime hours. Assume that the operating cost for the two teams is identical.)
4. Any underutilization of regular working hours should be avoided. (Again assign weights according to the relative productivity of the two teams.)

a. Formulate a goal programming model for this problem.
b. Solve this problem by the graphical method.

6.20 Sunny Electronics, Inc. produces the most sophisticated color television sets on the market. The company has two production lines. The production rate of Line 1 is 4 sets per hour, whereas it is 3 sets per hour in Line 2. The regular production capacity is 40 hours a week for each line. The expected profit from an average color television set is $100. The top management of the firm has set the following goals for the week (in ordinal ranking):

1. Meet the production goal of 360 sets for the week.
2. Limit the overtime of Line 1 to 10 hours.
3. Avoid the underutilization of the regular working hours for both lines. (Assign differential weights according to the production rate of each line.)
4. Limit the overtime operation for each line. (Assign differential weights according to the relative cost of an overtime hour. Assume that the cost of operation is identical for the two production lines.)

a. Formulate a goal programming model for this problem.

b. If top management desires to put the profit goal of $38,000 for the week as the first-priority goal over the stated four goals, how would the model be changed?

c. If top management has only the one goal of profit maximization, subject to the regular production capacity of both lines, how would the goal programming model be formulated?

6.21 Valley Products, Inc. plans to schedule its annual advertising campaign. The total advertising budget is set at $1,000,000. The firm can purchase local radio spots at $50 per spot, local television spots at $300 per spot, or local newspaper advertising at $100 per insertion. The payoff from each advertising medium is a function of its audience size and audience characteristics. The generally accepted objective criterion for advertising is audience points. Audience points for the three advertising vehicles are:

Radio: 50 points per spot
Television: 250 points per spot
Newspaper: 200 points per insertion

The president of the firm has established the following goals for the advertising campaign, listed in the order of their importance:

1. The total budget should not exceed $1,000,000.
2. The contract with the local radio and television station requires that the firm spend at least $300,000 for television and radio ads.
3. The company does not wish to spend more than $200,000 for newspaper ads.
4. Audience points from the advertising campaign should be maximized.

Formulate a goal programming model for this problem.

6.22 Otani Electronics produces two types of radios: AM and FM. According to past experience, production of either type of radio requires an average of 30 minutes in the plant. The plant has a normal production capacity of 80 hours a week. The marketing department reports that the *maximum* number of AM and FM radios that can be sold each week are 80 and 100 respectively. The unit profits are: AM—$30, FM—$20. The president of the company has set the following multiple goals, listed in the order of their importance:

1. Avoid any underutilization of the normal production capacity.
2. Achieve the sales goals of 80 AM and 100 FM radios. (Assign differential weights according to the unit profits.)
3. Minimize the overtime operation of the plant as much as possible.

a. In this problem, if the president of the firm had only the single goal of profit maximization within the normal production capacity and sales constraints, how would you set up a goal programming model?

b. Formulate a goal programming model for this problem and solve it by the simplex method.

6.23 Omaha Computer Hardwares, Inc. produces three different types of computers: Epic, Galaxie, and Utopia. The production of all computers is conducted in a complex and modern assembly line. The production of an Epic requires 5 hours in the assembly line, a Galaxie requires 8 hours, and a Utopia requires 12 hours. The normal number of operating hours of the assembly line is 200 per month. The Marketing Department and the Accounting Department have estimated that profits per unit for the three types of computers are \$100,000 for the Epic, \$120,000 for the Galaxie, and \$150,000 for the Utopia. The Marketing Department further reports that demand is such that the firm can expect to sell all the computers it produces in the next month. The president of the firm has established the following goals, listed according to their importance:

1. Avoid underutilization of the production capacity of the assembly line.
2. Meet the demand of the northeastern sales district for 5 Epics, 5 Galaxies, and 8 Utopias (no differential weights).
3. Limit the overtime operation of the assembly line to 20 hours.
4. Meet the sales goal for each type of computer: Epic—15, Galaxie—12, and Utopia—12 (no differential weights).
5. Minimize the total overtime operation of the assembly line.

a. Formulate a goal programming model for this problem.
b. Work through two iterations (three tableaus) by the simplex method of goal programming.

6.24 Your grandmother has just won \$40,000 in the "Lifebuoy Sweepstakes." Because of her advanced age, you plan to "have fun" helping her to invest in these five alternatives: stock options, real estate, bonds, savings accounts, and diamonds. Real estate and bonds yield an estimated 17 percent and 12 percent per year respectively, and the savings account yields 6 percent. Since options and diamonds are risky, you cannot assume they will have any yield. You have established the following goals, in order of their importance:

1. Minimize the risk by diversifying the investment. No more than 40 percent of the total investment should be in any one alternative.
2. Since diamonds are rumored to be profitable, try to invest at least \$10,000 in this alternative.
3. The amount invested in speculative ventures (options and diamonds) should not exceed the amount invested in safer plans.
4. Guarantee that Granny will earn at least \$5,000 annually from your investments.

Formulate a goal programming model that will determine the amount of money to be invested in each of the various alternatives.

6.25 Old Dominion Electronics, Inc. produces two types of tape deck players: cassette players and 8-track players. The production of both products is done in two assembly centers. Each cassette player requires 4 hours in Assembly Center 1 and 2 hours in Assembly Center 2. Each 8-track player requires 2 hours in Assembly Center 1 and 6 hours in Assembly Center 2. Additionally, each product requires some in-process inventory. Each cassette player requires \$100 worth of in-process inventory; an 8-track player requires \$60 worth of in-process inventory. The normal monthly operation capacity for the assembly centers are: Assembly Center 1—240 hours; Assembly Center 2—300 hours. The average monthly in-process inventory is \$8,000. According to the Marketing Department, the estimated sales for the cassette player and 8-track player are 55 and 65 respectively for the coming month.

a. If the president of the firm is simply trying to maximize profit, how would you set up a linear programming model within the limits of the normal monthly production capacity, average inventory level, and forecasted sales?

b. Solve this problem by the graphical method of linear programming.

c. The president of the firm has established the following multiple goals according to their importance:

1. Achieve the sales goal of 55 cassette players for the month.

2. Not more than $8,500 may be tied up in in-process inventory.

3. Avoid any underutilization of the regular operation hours of both assembly centers (no differential weights).

4. Limit the overtime operation of Assembly Center 1 to 40 hours.

5. Achieve the sales goal of 65 8-track players.

6. Limit the overtime operation of each assembly center (no differential weights).

Set up a goal programming model and work through three tableaus by the simplex method.

6.26 Consider the following goal programming problem:

$$\text{Minimize } Z = P_1 d_1^- + 3P_2 d_2^- + 2P_2 d_3^- + P_3 d_1^+$$
$$\text{subject to} \quad x_1 + x_2 + d_1^- - d_1^+ = 40$$
$$x_1 + d_2^- = 24$$
$$x_2 + d_3^- = 28$$
$$x_j, d_i^-, d_i^+ \geq 0$$

a. Solve this problem by the graphical method.

b. Solve this problem by the modified simplex method.

c. In the final simplex tableau, analyze the goal conflicts and trade-offs.

6.27 Solve the following goal programming problem using the modified simplex method:

$$\text{Minimize } Z = P_1 d_1^+ + P_2 d_3^- + P_3 d_4^- + P_4 d_2^-$$
$$\text{subject to} \quad x_1 + d_1^- - d_1^+ = 8$$
$$x_2 + d_2^- = 8$$
$$x_1 + x_2 + d_3^- - d_3^+ = 10$$
$$x_1 + d_4^- - d_4^+ = 1$$
$$x_j, d_i^-, d_i^+ \geq 0$$

6.28 Solve the following goal programming problem using the modified simplex method:

$$\text{Minimize } Z = P_1 d_2^- + P_2 d_3^- + P_3 d_1^- + P_4 d_{31}^+ + P_5 d_1^+$$
$$\text{subject to} \quad 10x_1 + 12x_2 + d_1^- - d_1^+ = 1{,}000$$
$$x_1 + d_2^- - d_2^+ = 40$$
$$x_2 + d_3^- - d_3^+ = 40$$
$$d_{31}^- + d_3^+ - d_3^+ = 5$$
$$x_j, d_i^-, d_i^+ \geq 0$$

6.29 The Midtown City Council is reviewing housing proposals for a new development area. There is some dispute among various interest groups as to what goals should be sought. The Zoning Committee has recommended three types of housing: one-family houses, deluxe condominiums, and apartments.

The Zoning Committee has also compiled the following data for each type of housing:

	Housing Type		
	One-family	**Deluxe Condo**	**Apartment**
Land usage, acres per unit	.25	.30	.125
Families housed per unit	1	4	6
Tax base generated per unit	$50,000	$100,000	$25,000
Taxes requires for city services	$4,000	$8,000	$6,000

There are 20 acres available for zoning. The League for Better Housing has conducted a campaign to gain housing for at least 500 families. The Taxpayers' Union has strongly lobbied for an added tax base of $4,000,000. The Gray Panthers have disrupted the City Council meetings and demanded that taxes for city services be no more than $250,000.

The City Council hired a public-opinion survey company to assess the priorities of the citizens. The poll results are as follows:

	Priority		
Goal	**1**	**2**	**3**
Housing for 500 families	55%	35%	10%
Tax base of $4,000,000	40	30	30
Taxes for services, $250,000	15	20	65

Based on this survey, the City Council has established the following priorities:

P_1: Provide housing for at least 500 families.

P_2: Establish at least $4,000,000 worth of new tax base.

P_3: Taxes for city services should be limited to $250,000.

a. Formulate this problem as a goal programming model.

b. Solve this problem by using the computer program if it is available.

6.30 Donald White was recently named by Governor Wilson as the campaign director for his upcoming reelection campaign. Governor Wilson thinks that if he can get his message to 2 million people in the state, he has a good chance to win a large chunk of votes at the Republican Convention.

Donald White has obtained the following information about advertising media availability and their costs:

Medium	Voter Exposure per $1,000 Spent	Cost per Insertion	Maximum Units Available
Television (prime-time)	20,000	$500	60
Television (nonprime-time)	8,000	400	60
Radio	7,000	300	100
Newspaper	5,000	200	120
Billboards	750	100	150

Governor Wilson has a campaign fund of $160,000 available, which, according to the state election law, cannot be exceeded. Furthermore, no more than $60,000 can be spent on television ads (a legal limit of 60 units).

Governor Wilson's priorities are as follows:

P_1: Obtain exposure to 2 million voters.

P_2: Avoid spending over $160,000.

P_3: Spend at least $15,000 on newspaper ads.

P_4: Maximize voter exposure.

Donald White is attempting to formulate the advertising strategies for Governor Wilson. As a special consultant, you have been asked to help Mr. White. Formulate this problem as a goal programming model.

THE TRANSPORTATION PROBLEM

A prevalent managerial decision problem for many organizations is the transportation of goods and services from sources to a number of destinations while minimizing the total transportation cost. In this chapter, we will study various techniques that are useful in analyzing the transportation problem. The graphical and simplex methods presented in Chapters 3 and 4 are for the general linear programming problems. Some special types of linear programming problems can be analyzed more efficiently by using special techniques. The transportation method is such a special technique. In this chapter, we will study the transportation solution method as a tool to determine the optimum transportation of goods from a number of sources to a number of destinations at a minimum total cost.

Learning Objectives   *From the study of this chapter, you will learn the following:*

1. The basic nature of the transportation problem.
2. The formulation of a linear programming model for the transportation problem.
3. The development of an initial solution to the transportation problem.
4. The solution of the transportation problem by different techniques.
5. The analysis of an unbalanced transportation problem.
6. The application of the transportation method to real-world problems.
7. The meaning of the following terms:

Balanced transportation problem   *Modified distribution method*
Unbalanced transportation problem   *Cost improvement index*
Northwest corner method   *Degenerate transportation solution*
Minimum cell-cost method   *Multiple optimum solutions*
Vogel's approximation method   *Prohibited transportation route*
Opportunity cost   *Transshipment problem*
Stepping-stone method   *Multiple objective transportation*
Stepping-stone path   *problem*

THE NATURE OF THE TRANSPORTATION PROBLEM

The transportation problem

The transportation problem is concerned with the transportation of a product (or service) from a number of sources that have specific quantities of supply to a number of destinations with certain quantities of demand. For example, a petroleum company has six refineries (sources) and twenty fuel depots (destinations) at various locations. For a given period of time, each refinery has a specific capacity of supply of gasoline and each depot has a specific demand for gasoline. If we know the unit transportation cost from each refinery to each depot, we may be able to determine the quantity of gasoline to be transported from specific refineries to specific depots in order to minimize the total transportation cost.

Types of transportation problems

The transportation method has a wide spectrum of real-world applications. One such application would be the military logistics problem of transporting troops and supplies from various camps and supply depots to several hot spots (such as the Persian Gulf, the Middle East, and the Far East) while minimizing the total transportation time. You can easily identify with the problem of locating dormitories on campus to accommodate student residence requirements while minimizing the average distance that students must walk around the campus.

A brief history

Mathematical analysis of the transportation problem was not undertaken until 1941, when F. L. Hitchcock published his study, "The Distribution of a Product from Several Sources to Numerous Localities." Since then, the transportation problem has been further studied by such scholars as T. C. Koopmans, George B. Dantzig, A. Charnes, W. W. Cooper, and many others (see References). As a matter of fact, many variations of the transportation method have been developed. Examples include the assignment method, location-allocation problems, and distribution problems. In this chapter, we will study the more widely used techniques for transportation problems.

To illustrate the transportation method, we will examine a simple problem in Casette 7.1.

CASETTE 7.1   *GULF COAST OIL COMPANY, INC.*

Gulf Coast Oil Company, Inc. is a petroleum refinery company headquartered in Dallas, Texas. The company does not operate its own oil wells. Instead, it purchases crude oil from a number of small offshore drilling companies on a long-term contract basis. The company has three refineries, located in Houston, Corpus Christi, and Fort Worth and it has three distribution depots, located in San Antonio, Texarkana, and El Paso. The company's most important product is gasoline for automobiles.

An example

The transportation problem faced by Gulf Coast Oil is to supply the required quantity of gasoline to each of the distribution depots from the three refineries, each with specific production capacity, to minimize total transportation costs. The transportation problem can be visualized on the map in Figure 7.1. We must remember here that only refineries can produce and supply gasoline to depots. A depot cannot supply gasoline to another depot.

The decision variables

The problem is further illustrated by the network in Figure 7.2. The network also presents the supply capacity at each of the refineries, the demand requirements at each of the distribution depots, and the unit transportation costs. The decision variables can be defined as follows:

x_{ij} = quantity of gasoline to be transported from refinery i to distribution depot j

Figure 7.1   *Gulf Coast Oil Transportation Problem*

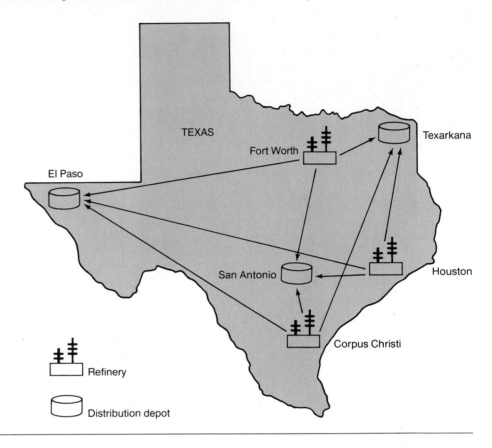

A linear programming model

where $i = 1$ Houston $j = 1$ San Antonio
            $i = 2$ Corpus Christi $j = 2$ Texarkana
            $i = 3$ Fort Worth $j = 3$ El Paso

As can be seen in Figure 7.2, this is a balanced transportation problem in which total supply exactly equals total demand. We can formulate a linear programming model that will minimize the total transportation costs subject to the supply and de-. mand constraints as follows:

$$\text{Minimize } Z = 20x_{11} + 9x_{12} + 5x_{13} + 6x_{21} + 10x_{22} + 18x_{23} + 2x_{31}$$
$$+ 15x_{32} + 12x_{33}$$

$$\text{subject to} \quad
\left.\begin{array}{l}
x_{11} + x_{12} + x_{13} = 150 \\
x_{21} + x_{22} + x_{23} = 100 \\
x_{31} + x_{32} + x_{33} = 250
\end{array}\right\} \text{ Supply}$$

$$\left.\begin{array}{l}
x_{11} + x_{21} + x_{31} = 200 \\
x_{12} + x_{22} + x_{32} = 120 \\
x_{13} + x_{23} + x_{33} = 180
\end{array}\right\} \text{ Demand}$$

$$x_{ij} \geq 0$$

Figure 7.2   Gulf Coast Oil Transportation Network

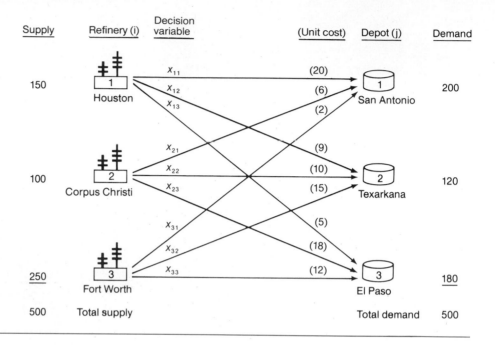

The Gulf Coast Oil transportation problem can be succinctly summarized in tableau form, as shown in Table 7.1. The tableau indicates the sources, destinations, supply capacity (in 1,000 gallons) at each of the sources, demand requirements (in 1,000 gallons) at each of the distribution depots, and unit transportation costs from each source to each destination.

THE BALANCED TRANSPORTATION PROBLEM

A balanced problem

In a balanced transportation problem, the total supply at sources and the total demand at destinations are exactly equal. Although not many real-world transportation problems are balanced cases, once we learn to solve a balanced case, any unbalanced case can be easily solved by making simple modifications.

Sources and destinations

To illustrate the balanced transportation problem, let us once again consider the Gulf Coast Oil transportation problem. This balanced transportation problem can be summarized in tableau form, as shown in Table 7.2. The numbers in the "From" column indicate the refineries that are the sources of the gasoline, and the numbers in the "To" row refer to the distribution depots that are the final destinations of the gasoline.

The transportation quantity and cost

Each cell at the intersection of a source and a destination is where we are attempting to allocate some quantity to be transported. For example, if cell (1,1) has the number 40 recorded in it, this quantity means that 40,000 gallons of gasoline will

Table 7.1 Tableau Form of the Gulf Coast Oil Problem

Destinations / Sources	1 San Antonio	2 Texarkana	3 El Paso	Supply (1,000 Gallons)
1 Houston	$20	$9	$5	150
2 Corpus Christi	6	10	18	100
3 Fort Worth	2	15	12	250
Demand (1,000 Gallons)	200	120	180	500

Table 7.2 Transportation Tableau for the Gulf Coast Oil Problem

From / To	1	2	3	Supply
1	20 x_{11}	9 x_{12}	5 x_{13}	150
2	6 x_{21}	10 x_{22}	18 x_{23}	100
3	2 x_{31}	15 x_{32}	12 x_{33}	250
Demand	200	120	180	500

be transported from Source 1 (Houston) to Destination 1 (San Antonio). Each cell also has a boxed-in number in the upper left corner. This number indicates the unit transportation cost from a source to a destination. For example, cell (1,1) has a cost figure of 20. This figure tells us that the transportation cost of 1,000 gallons from Source 1 (Houston) to Destination 1 (San Antonio) is $20.

The solution procedure   The solution procedure for the general transportation problem is as follows:

Step 1: Define the Problem and Set Up the Transportation Tableau The first step

The transportation tableau   of the transportation method is to analyze the problem and set up the transportation tableau with all of the following information: supply capacity at each source, demand requirement at each destination, and unit transportation cost from each source to each destination.

Step 2: Develop an Initial Solution Just as in linear programming, we need an initial solution to start the solution process. In linear programming, the initial solution is always at the origin. However, in a transportation problem we need an initial solution other than the origin because we are using a tableau format that requires satisfaction of the supply and demand constraints. There are several different approaches that can

The initial solution   be used to generate an initial solution.

Step 3: Determine the Optimum Solution Once an initial solution is derived, we are ready to use the transportation method to generate improved solutions until we

An iterative method   determine the optimum solution. This step may require a number of iterations as we move toward the optimum solution.

Step 4: Evaluate the Optimum Solution The final step of the transportation method

Interpreting the optimum solution   is to analyze the optimum solution in terms of the transportation schedule, the total transportation cost, and alternative optimum solutions.

Since we have already discussed the transportation problem of Gulf Coast Oil and set up the transportation tableau, we will focus our attention on Step 2.

Developing an Initial Solution

As we discussed earlier, in a transportation problem the initial solution cannot be at the origin because of the tableau form of analysis we use. In developing an initial

The initial solution   solution, a number of different methods can be used. We will discuss the three most widely used methods: the northwest corner method, the minimum cell-cost method, and Vogel's approximation method.

Northwest Corner Method The northwest corner method is the simplest way to develop an initial solution. Although other methods may provide better initial solu-

The northwest corner method   tions, none is as simple and straightforward as the northwest corner method. As a matter of fact, the northwest corner method, although a very systematic method, is not based on logic or even on common sense. Thus, an initial solution derived by the northwest corner method usually yields the largest total transportation cost among the three methods we will be studying here.

A simplistic approach   The steps of the northwest corner method can be summarized as follows:

1. Starting from the northwest corner (upper left corner) of the transportation tableau, allocate as much quantity as possible to cell (1,1), from Source 1 to Destination 1, within the supply constraint of Source 1 and the demand constraint of Destination 1.

2. The first allocation will satisfy either the supply capacity of Source 1 or the de-

The steps of the method   mand requirement of Destination 1. (a) If the demand requirement for Destination 1

is satisfied but the supply capacity for Source 1 is not exhausted, move on to cell (1,2) for the second allocation. (b) If the demand requirement for Destination 1 is not satisfied but the supply capacity for Source 1 is exhausted, move on to cell (2,1) for the second allocation. (c) If the demand requirement for Destination 1 is satisfied and the supply capacity for Source 1 is also exhausted, move on to cell (2,2) for the second allocation.

3. Continue the allocation process in the same manner toward the southeast corner (lower right corner) of the transportation tableau until the supply capacities of all sources are exhausted and the demand requirements of all destinations are satisfied.

For the Gulf Coast Oil problem, the initial solution by the northwest corner method is presented in Table 7.3. The initial solution via the northwest corner method is obtained by following these steps:

Step 1: Cell (1,1) Cell (1,1) is the northwest corner cell in the tableau. Thus, we must transport as much quantity as possible from Source 1 to Destination 1. The supply capacity of Source 1 is 150 and the demand requirement of Destination 1 is 200. Therefore, the maximum quantity we can transport to cell (1,1) will be 150. By transporting 150 to cell (1,1), we will exhaust the supply capacity of Source 1. However, the demand of Destination 1 has not been satisfied as yet, since we are short by 50.

Step 2: Cell (2,1) As we follow the northwest corner method procedure, the unsatisfied demand of 50 for Destination 1 should be supplied by Source 2. Now the total quantity being transported to Destination 1 from Source 1 (quantity of 150) and Source 2 (quantity of 50) satisfies the total demand requirement.

Step 3: Cell (2,2) Since we have satisfied the demand of Destination 1, we move on to the next column, Destination 2. The total demand of Destination 2 is 120. After transporting 50 to Destination 1, Source 2 can transport only the remaining supply capacity of 50 to Destination 2.

Step 4: Cell (3,2) Destination 2 still requires an additional quantity of 70 to meet the total demand of 120. Since Sources 1 and 2 have already exhausted their supply capacities, this quantity has to be transported from Source 3.

Step 5: Cell (3,3) Since this is a balanced problem in which total demand is equal to total supply, the demand of Destination 3 must be equal to the remaining supply capacity of Source 3.

Meeting the demand and supply requirements

The stair-step effect

Now we can check each column and row to see whether or not the demand and supply requirements are satisfied. The initial solution obtained by the northwest corner method shown in Table 7.3 indicates that we have satisfied all the demand and supply requirements. In this problem, we have 9 cells altogether because we have 3 sources and 3 destinations ($3 \times 3 = 9$). We transported to 5 cells (5 occupied cells) and did not transport to 4 cells (4 empty cells). One distinctive feature of the northwest corner solution is that the occupied cells usually form a stair-step effect from the upper left corner, as shown in Table 7.3 by the shaded cells. Now we are ready

Table 7.3   The Initial Solution by the Northwest Corner Method

To From	1	2	3	Supply
1	20 150	9	5	150
2	6 50	10 50	18	100
3	2	15 70	12 180	250
Demand	200	120	180	500

to calculate the total transportation cost of the initial solution we obtained in Table 7.3 as follows:

Cell	Σ (Quantity Transported	×	Unit Cost)	=	Total Cost
(1,1)	150	×	$20	=	$3,000
(2,1)	50	×	6	=	300
(2,2)	50	×	10	=	500
(3,2)	70	×	15	=	1,050
(3,3)	180	×	12	=	2,160
			Total Transportation Cost =		$7,010

The total transportation cost of this initial solution is $7,010. Of course, we remember that this is just an initial solution, a solution from which we initiate our search for the optimum solution. The northwest corner method is the simplest way to obtain an initial solution. However, this method usually yields the least attractive solution because it does not consider the unit transportation costs in making allocations. Consequently, when we initiate the solution process with the northwest corner method, the number of iterations required to reach the optimum solution will be greater than the number required by other methods.

Minimum Cell-Cost Method As we have observed, the northwest corner method is a simple way to develop an initial solution, but it is far from being scientific, to say the least. Another simple way to develop an *initial solution* is to use good common sense. For example, since the objective of the problem is to minimize total cost, we must try to allocate as much as possible to those cells in the tableau that have mini-

The minimum cell-cost method

Table 7.4 Initial Allocation by the Minimum Cell-Cost Method

From \ To	1	2	3	Supply
1	20	9	5	150
2	6	10	18	100
3	2 200	15	12	50 ~~250~~
Demand	200	120	180	500

mum unit transportation costs. This approach is referred to as the minimum cell-cost method.

A sensible approach

The steps of the minimum cell-cost method can be summarized as follows:

Steps of the method

1. Select the cell with the minimum cell-cost in the tableau and allocate as much to this cell as possible within the supply and demand constraints.

2. Select the cell with the next minimum cell-cost and allocate as much to this cell as possible within the demand and supply constraints.

3. Continue this procedure until all of the supply and demand requirements are satisfied. In a case of tied minimum cell-costs between two or more cells, the tie can be broken by selecting the cell that can accommodate the greater quantity.

Checking the demand and supply requirements

Let us consider the Gulf Coast Oil problem once again. In the entire transportation tableau, we can easily identify the minimum cell-cost as $2 in cell (3,1). We can make the initial allocation of 200 in cell (3,1) because the supply capacity of source 3 is 250 and the demand requirement of Destination 1 is 200. We always select the lesser of the supply and demand quantities as the amount of allocation. When we make this initial allocation, the demand requirement of Destination 1 is completely satisfied and the supply capacity of Source 3 is reduced to 50, as shown in Table 7.4. The shaded column in Table 7.4 indicates that we can eliminate this column from further consideration because the demand requirement is satisfied for Destination 1.

Table 7.5   First and Second Allocations by the Minimum Cell-Cost Method

To From	1	2	3	Supply
1	20	9	5 ____ 150	150
2	6	10	18	100
3	2 ____ 200	15	12	50 ~~250~~
Demand	200	120	30 ~~180~~	500

The cell with the next minimum cell-cost in the unshaded cells is $5 in cell (1,3). The maximum quantity we can allocate to cell (1,3) is 150, since Source 3 has a supply capacity of 150 even though Destination 3 has a demand requirement of 180. The second allocation is made in Table 7.5.

The next cell we allocate to is cell (2,2), which has the minimum cell-cost among the remaining four cells. The maximum quantity we can allocate is 100, as shown in Table 7.6. By allocating 100 to cell (2,2), we will exhaust the supply capacity of Source 2. Because we have exhausted the supply capacities of Sources 1 and 2, it is clear in Table 7.6 that the only source that still has some supply capacity left is Source 3. It has 50 available. On the other hand, Destinations 2 and 3 still have demand requirements of 20 and 30 respectively. Thus, we have no further choice but to allocate 20 to cell (3,2) and 30 to cell (3,3). Table 7.7 presents the complete initial solution by the minimum cell-cost method.

The total transportation cost of the initial solution shown in Table 7.7 is $2,810, calculated as follows:

Cell	Σ (Quantity Transported	×	Unit Cost)	=	Total Cost
(1,3)	150	×	$5	=	$750
(2,2)	100	×	10	=	1,000
(3,1)	200	×	2	=	400
(3,2)	20	×	15	=	300
(3,3)	30	×	12	=	360
			Total Transportation Cost	=	$2,810

As we compare the total transportation costs derived by the northwest corner method ($7,010) and the minimum cell-cost ($2,810) method, it is clear that the

Table 7.6 First, Second, and Third Allocations by the Minimum Cell-Cost Method

From \ To	1	2	3	Supply
1	20	9	5 ⟶ 150	150
2	6	10 ⟶ 100	18	100
3	2 ⟶ 200	15	12	50 ~~250~~
Demand	200	20 ~~120~~	30 ~~180~~	500

Table 7.7 The Initial Solution by the Minimum Cell-Cost Method

From \ To	1	2	3	Supply
1	20	9	5 ⟶ 150	150
2	6	10 ⟶ 100	18	100
3	2 ⟶ 200	15 ⟶ 20	12 ⟶ 30	250
Demand	200	120	180	500

common sense approach of the minimum cell-cost method has resulted in a savings of $4,200. Thus, we can conclude that the optimum solution could be reached a great deal faster by using the minimum cell-cost method rather than the northwest corner method.

Vogel's Approximation Method Another technique to develop an initial solution is Vogel's approximation method (VAM). This method makes allocations based on a rational approach—minimization of the penalty (or opportunity) cost. The penalty

Vogel's approximation method

cost can be defined as the amount we lose because of our failure to select the best alternative. For example, suppose you are considering two job offers. One offer is from a large electronics firm with an annual salary of $28,000. The second offer is from a family-owned wholesale restaurant equipment company with an annual salary of $16,000. Because of your desire to work in a small organization, you decide to accept the second offer. The penalty (opportunity) cost of this career decision is $12,000 in terms of the first year's salary.

A rational approach
The steps of VAM, which is also referred to as the *penalty* or *regret method,* can be summarized as follows:

1. Calculate the penalty cost for each row and each column. The penalty cost is simply the difference between the minimum cell-cost and next minimum cell-cost in a given row or column. Thus, the penalty cost represents the per-unit opportunity cost associated with the failure to allocate to the cell with the minimum cell-cost in

Steps of VAM

a given row or column.

2. Select the row or column that has the largest penalty cost. Allocate as much quantity as possible to the cell with the minimum cell-cost in the selected row or column. This procedure assures that we avoid paying the largest penalty cost. If there is a tie in selecting the largest penalty cost, select the row or column whose minimum cost-cell can accommodate the greatest quantity.

3. Adjust the demand and supply requirements after the allocation. Eliminate any rows and columns that have satisfied the demand or supply requirements and thus eliminate them from further consideration.

4. If there are additional allocation choices, recalculate the penalty costs and continue the allocation process. If all demand and supply requirements are fully satisfied, the initial solution has been determined.

Computing penalty costs

Now, let us apply VAM to set up the initial solution for the Gulf Coast Oil problem. In Table 7.8, we have calculated the penalty costs for the rows and columns. In the first row (Source 1), the minimum cell-cost is $5 in cell (1,3). The next minimum cell-cost is $9 in cell (1,2). Therefore, the penalty cost for the first row will be $9 − $5 = $4. This penalty cost of $4 is the extra amount we have to pay per unit if we fail to allocate to cell (1,3) and subsequently allocate to cell (1,2). The same procedure is used for calculating the penalty costs for all the rows and columns.

The largest penalty cost in Table 7.8 is $10 in Row 3. This penalty cost indicates that if we fail to allocate to the cell with the minimum cost, (3,1), we have to allocate to the next best cell, (3,3), and pay a $10 penalty per unit. To avoid paying this penalty, we must allocate as much as possible to cell (3,1). The maximum quantity we can allocate to cell (3,1) is 200, since the demand requirement of Destination 1 is only 200 whereas the supply capacity of Source 3 is 250. After making the initial allocation, we can eliminate Column 1 from further consideration as we have met its demand requirement, as shown in Table 7.8. Next, we adjust the supply capacity of Source 3 from 250 to 50 (250 − 200 = 50), as also shown in Table 7.8.

Table 7.8 Penalty Costs and the Initial Allocation by VAM

To From	1	2	3	Supply	Row penalty cost
1	20	9	5	150	4
2	6	10	18	100	4
3	2 200	15	12	50 ~~250~~	10*
Demand	200	120	180	500	
Column penalty cost	4	1	7		

Now that we have eliminated Column 1 from further consideration, the row penalty costs must be recalculated. In Table 7.9, it is obvious that Row 2 has the largest penalty cost. To avoid paying this penalty, we must allocate as much as possible to cell (2,2). The maximum quantity we can allocate to this cell is 100. This allocation will completely exhaust the supply capacity of Source 2. Thus, we can eliminate Row 2 from further consideration. The demand requirement of Column 2 is adjusted to 20. All of the adjustments are shown in Table 7.9.

In Table 7.10, we recalculate the column penalty costs because we have eliminated Row 2. The maximum penalty cost now appears in Column 3. Therefore, we must allocate as much as possible to cell (1,3). The maximum quantity we can allocate to cell (1,3) is 150. Table 7.10 presents the adjustments after this third alloca-

Adjusting demand and supply requirements

tion. Now, there are only two empty cells left. We need to allocate 20 to cell (3,2) and 30 to cell (3,3). We do not have a further allocation choice. Thus, we can make these allocations and identify the initial solution derived by VAM, as shown in Table 7.11.

The total transportation cost of this initial solution derived by VAM is $2,810, calculated as follows:

Cell	Σ (Quantity Transported	$\times$	Unit Cost)	$=$	Total Cost
(1,3)	150	$\times$	$5	$=$	$750
(2,2)	100	$\times$	10	$=$	1,000
(3,1)	200	$\times$	2	$=$	400
(3,2)	20	$\times$	15	$=$	300
(3,3)	30	$\times$	12	$=$	360
			Total Transportation Cost	$=$	$2,810

Table 7.9   The Second Allocation by VAM

To / From	1	2	3	Supply	Row penalty cost
1	20	9	5	150	4
2	6	10 / 100	18	100	8*
3	2 / 200	15	12	50 / ~~250~~	3
Demand	200	20 / ~~120~~	180	500	
Column penalty cost		1	7		

Table 7.10   The Third Allocation by VAM

To / From	1	2	3	Supply	Row penalty cost
1	20	9	5 / 150	150	4
2	6	10 / 100	18	100	
3	2 / 200	15	12	50 / ~~250~~	3
Demand	200	20 / ~~120~~	30 / ~~180~~	500	
Column penalty cost		6	7*		

Table 7.11   The Initial Solution by VAM

To From	1	2	3	Supply
1	20	9	5 150	150
2	6	10 100	18	100
3	2 200	15 20	12 30	250
Demand	200	120	180	500

This total transportation cost happens to be the same as the cost of the initial solution derived by the minimum cell-cost method; the solutions are identical.

VAM uses the concept of opportunity cost in developing the initial solution. This method is more logical than the minimum cell-cost method because it takes into account the relative cost of current and subsequent allocations. In general, VAM greatly reduces the number of iterations required to reach the optimum solution. Although, for the Gulf Coast Oil problem, the transportation cost derived by the minimum cell-cost method is the same as that derived by VAM, VAM generally yields a better initial solution than other methods. As a matter of fact, for simple transportation problems, VAM frequently yields the optimum solution or a solution that is a good approximate optimum solution. This is why this method is named Vogel's *approximation* method. As we will see later, the initial solution derived by VAM is in fact the optimum solution to our example.

The meaning of approximation

Determining the Optimum Solution

Once we develop an initial solution for the transportation problem, the next step is to improve the solution and eventually determine the optimum solution. To check whether or not we can improve the solution by further reducing the total transportation cost, we must analyze the possibility of reallocation to some of the empty cells (i.e., cells in which no allocations are made). We will study two different ways to determine the optimum solution: the *stepping-stone method* and the *modified distribution method*. These two methods are essentially the same variation of the simplex method with different procedures for computing the improvement index of an empty cell.

Solution methods

The Stepping-Stone Method When we walk into a beautiful Japanese garden, we may see a picturesque pond in the center. There are water lilies, golden carp, frogs, and dragonflies. Around the mirrorlike water, we find dwarf mugho pines and azaleas in lavish colors. Then, no doubt, a series of stepping-stones stretching across the pond will catch our eye. We can cross the pond only if we step carefully on these stones.

The stepping-stone method

The *stepping-stone method,* first suggested by A. Charnes and W. W. Cooper, is based on this pretty image of a Japanese garden. We evaluate all of the empty cells (those in which no allocation is made) by carefully stepping on the occupied cells (in which allocations have been made). We must remember that if we ever step on an empty cell, we will be in the water screaming "Help!"

To evaluate all of the empty cells in the tableau, we must meet one requirement. The number of occupied cells must be exactly equal to the sum of the number of rows (sources) and the number of columns (destinations) minus 1:

One important requirement

Number of occupied cells = (number of rows + number of columns) − 1

The occupied cells are none other than the basic variables in the simplex approach. Accordingly, the empty cells are simply the nonbasic variables. In the simplex tableau, the number of basic variables is exactly equal to the number of constraints. In a transportation problem, the total number of constraints is equal to the number of rows plus the number of columns. Now you may wonder why the number of occupied cells (i.e., the basic variables) is one less than the sum of the rows and columns. This is a valid question.

In a balanced transportation problem, total supply is equal to total demand. Now let us consider a three-row and three-column transportation problem. When two supply constraints and two demand constraints have been satisfied and an allocation is made to satisfy the third supply constraint, that allocation will simultaneously satisfy the third demand constraint. In other words, one of the six constraints becomes a redundant constraint. This is why we need only five occupied cells for a 3×3 problem.

The requirement explained

Let us evaluate the initial solution we derived by the northwest corner method for the Gulf Coast Oil problem, shown in Table 7.12. Let us evaluate all of the empty cells and check whether or not we can reduce the total transportation cost by reallocating some quantity to one of the empty cells. If an empty cell receives some reallocation, it will become a basic variable. Of course, we know that a nonbasic variable (i.e., an empty cell) can enter the solution basis and become a basic variable only if it is the variable that will reduce the total transportation cost by the maximum amount.

To determine the cost reduction possibility, we must step on the occupied cells and evaluate all the empty cells. The set of occupied cells we step on to evaluate an empty cell is called the *stepping-stone path*. Once we determine the stepping-stone loop, we can easily determine the net change in the transportation cost through a reallocation by the stepping-stone path. The net change in cost is often referred to as the *cost improvement index* (CII). The CII is actually nothing but a $c_j - z_j$ value in the simplex tableau.

Tracing the stepping-stone path

CII

Let us select cell (1,2) as the first empty cell to evaluate. Suppose that we transfer one unit from cell (1,1) to cell (1,2) (i.e., we transfer only 149 units from

Table 7.12   The Initial Solution by the Northwest Corner Method

To\From	1	2	3	Supply
1	20 / 150	9	5	150
2	6 / 50	10 / 50	18	100
3	2	15 / 70	12 / 180	250
Demand	200	120	180	500

Source 1 to Destination 1 and transfer one unit from Source 1 to Destination 2). To allow this transfer of one unit from cell (1,1) to cell (1,2) while satisfying the supply and demand requirements, we must also transfer one unit from Column 2 to Column 1. This reasoning can be seen in the following tableau:

From\To	1	2	3	Supply
1	149	1	0	150
2	50	50	0	100
3	0	70	180	250
Demand	199	121	180	500

Because cell (3,1) is an empty cell, we cannot transfer quantities from cell (3,2) to cell (3,1). Thus, the transfer must be made from cell (2,2) to cell (2,1). When we make this transfer, we can still satisfy the demand and supply requirements as follows:

From \ To	1	2	3	Supply
1	**149**	1	0	150
2	**51**	**49**	0	100
3	0	70	180	250
Demand	200	120	180	500

Horizontal transfers only

In Table 7.13, we indicate the flow of the transfer or reallocation by arrow lines. The change of quantity in each cell is indicated by a plus (increased quantity) or minus (decreased quantity) sign. The solid arrow lines represent the stepping-stone path. The stepping-stone path involves only *horizontal movements* because only sources can transport to destinations. The broken vertical arrow lines are used only as convenient connecting lines for the stepping-stone path. The stepping-stone path is simply a set of positive or negative coefficients in a nonbasic-variable column of a simplex tableau. The stepping-stone path for cell (1,2) is

$$\text{Cell } (1,2) = +12 - 11 + 21 - 22$$

Computing CII

The reason we trace the stepping-stone path is to determine whether the transfer of one unit will decrease or increase the total transportation cost. From the stepping-stone path we identified above, we can determine the CII. By reallocating one unit from cell (1,1) to cell (1,2), we have to incur $9 cost [i.e., the unit transportation cost in cell (1,2)]. But by shipping one unit less (only 149 units) from Source 1 to Destination 1, we can save $20 [i.e., the unit transportation cost in cell (1,1)]. Similarly, by transferring one unit from cell (2,2) to cell (2,1), we increase the cost by $6 in cell (2,1) and decrease it by $10 in cell (2,2). By following the stepping-stone path and analyzing the unit transportation cost in each cell, as shown in Table 7.13, we can derive the CII as:

$$\text{Cell } (1,2) = +(1,2) - (1,1) + (2,1) - (2,2)$$
$$\text{CII } (1,2) = +\$9 - \$20 + \$6 - \$10 = -\$15$$

Transfer to an empty cell with the largest negative CII

The amount $-\$15$ indicates that if we make a transfer of one unit from cell (1,1) to cell (1,2) and make the necessary adjustments, the total transportation cost will be decreased by $15 per each unit that we transfer to cell (1,2). This is certainly an attractive transfer. But before we go ahead and make this transfer, we must evaluate all of the empty cells and select the one that has the *largest negative CII*.

We now continue our evaluation of the other empty cells. Let us select cell (3,1); it is an easy cell to evaluate because it is surrounded by three occupied cells. The stepping-stone path of cell (3,1) is shown in Table 7.14. The CII for cell (3,1) can be found by tracing the stepping-stone path as follows:

Table 7.13.   *Stepping-Stone Path for Cell (1,2)*

To From	1	2	3	Supply
1	20 $-$ 150 $\longrightarrow$ $+$	9	5	150
2	6 $+$ 50	10 $-$ 50	18	100
3	2	15 70	12 180	250
Demand	200	120	180	500

$$\text{Cell } (1,2) = +(1,2) - (1,1) + (2,1) - (2,2)$$
$$\text{CII } (1,2) = +9 - 20 + 6 - 10 = -15$$

$$\text{Cell } (3,1) = + (3,1) - (3,2) + (2,2) - (2,1)$$
$$\text{CII } (3,1) = + \$2 - \$15 + \$10 - \$6 = -\$9$$

The CII for cell (3,1) indicates that if we transfer some units from cell (3,2) to cell (3,1), we can reduce the total transportation cost by \$9 per unit.

We can evaluate cell (2,3) in a similar manner, as it is also surrounded by three occupied cells, as shown in Table 7.15.

$$\text{Cell } (2,3) = + (2,3) - (2,2) + (3,2) - (3,3)$$
$$\text{CII } (2,3) = + \$18 - \$10 + \$15 - \$12 = +\$11$$

The analysis of cell (1,3), which we have put off long enough, is a rather involved process because its stepping-stone path is relatively hard to trace. Observing Row 1 in Table 7.16, we see that cell (1,1) is the only occupied cell from which we can make a transfer of one unit to cell (1,3). Now, we must increase one unit in Column 1. The only occupied cell, other than cell (1,1), that can accept a transfer of one unit is cell (2,1). When we transfer a unit from cell (2,2) to cell (2,1), we need one additional unit in Column 2. Cell (3,2) is the only cell in Column 2, other than cell (2,2), that can accept a transfer of one unit. Investigating Row 3, we find that this unit must come from cell (3,3). The stepping-stone path and the CII for cell (1,3) can be determined as follows:

$$\text{Cell } (1,3) = + (1,3) - (1,1) + (2,1) - (2,2) + (3,2) - (3,3)$$
$$\text{CII } (1,3) = + \$5 - \$20 + \$6 - \$10 + \$15 - \$12 = -\$16$$

Table 7.14   Stepping-Stone Path for Cell (3,1)

From \ To	1	2	3	Supply
1	20 150	9	5	150
2	6 − 50	10 + 50	18	100
3	2 +	15 − 70	12 180	250
Demand	200	120	180	500

$$\text{Cell } (3,1) = +(3,1) - (3,2) + (2,2) - (2,1)$$
$$\text{CII } (3,1) = +2 - 15 + 10 - 6 = -9$$

Table 7.15   Stepping-Stone Path for Cell (2,3)

From \ To	1	2	3	Supply
1	20 150	9	5	150
2	6 50	10 − 50	18 +	100
3	2	15 + 70	12 − 180	250
Demand	200	120	180	500

$$\text{Cell } (2,3) = +(2,3) - (2,2) + (3,2) - (3,3)$$
$$\text{CII } (2,3) = +18 - 10 + 15 - 12 = +11$$

Table 7.16   Stepping-Stone Path for Cell (1,3)

From \ To	1	2	3	Supply
1	20 150 − ↑	9	5 + →	150
2	6 50 + ←	10 50 − ↑	18	100
3	2	15 70 + ←	12 180 − ↓	250
Demand	200	120	180	500

Cell $(1,3)$ = $+(1,3)$ − $(1,1)$ + $(2,1)$ − $(2,2)$ + $(3,2)$ − $(3,3)$
CII $(1,3)$ = $+5$ − 20 + 6 − 10 + 15 − 12 = -16

Now we have evaluated all of the empty cells. We can summarize our evaluation of the empty cells as shown in Table 7.17. Clearly, the best empty cell to which we would make a transfer is cell $(1,3)$. If we make a transfer from cell $(1,1)$ to cell $(1,3)$, the total transportation cost could be reduced by $16 per unit.

Table 7.17   Evaluation of All Empty Cells

Empty Cell	Stepping-Stone Path	CII
$(1,2)$	$+(1,2) - (1,1) + (2,1) - (2,2)$	$+9 - 20 + 6 - 10 = -\$15$
$(3,1)$	$+(3,1) - (3,2) + (2,2) - (2,1)$	$+2 - 15 + 10 - 6 = -\$9$
$(2,3)$	$+(2,3) - (2,2) + (3,2) - (3,3)$	$+18 - 10 + 15 - 12 = +\$11$
$(1,3)$	$+(1,3) - (1,1) + (2,1) - (2,2) + (3,2) - (3,3)$	$+5 - 20 + 6 - 10 + 15 - 12 = -\$16$

The maximum transfer quantity

The next question we have to answer is: "How much can we transfer to cell $(1,3)$?" The stepping-stone path for cell $(1,3)$ has positive stones (cells with plus signs) at cells $(1,3)$, $(2,1)$, and $(3,2)$ and negative stones (cells with minus signs) at cells $(1,1)$, $(2,2)$ and $(3,3)$, as shown in Table 7.16. The maximum quantity we can transfer to cell $(1,3)$ is exactly the minimum quantity we find in the negative stones

Table 7.18   Determining the Maximum Quantity Transferable to Cell (1,3)

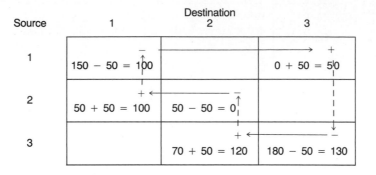

Source	Destination 1	2	3
1	150 − 50 = 100		0 + 50 = 50
2	50 + 50 = 100	50 − 50 = 0	
3		70 + 50 = 120	180 − 50 = 130

Table 7.19   The Second Solution by the Stepping-Stone Method

To From	1	2	3	Supply
1	20 100	9	5 50	150
2	6 100	10	18	100
3	2	15 120	12 130	250
Demand	200	120	180	500

Total Transportation Cost

$$
\begin{aligned}
100 \times \$20 &= \$2{,}000 \\
50 \times \ \ 5 &= \ \ \ \ 250 \\
100 \times \ \ 6 &= \ \ \ \ 600 \\
120 \times \ 15 &= \ 1{,}800 \\
130 \times \ 12 &= \ \underline{1{,}560} \\
&\ \ \ \ \$6{,}210
\end{aligned}
$$

of the stepping-stone path. Cell (1,1) has 150, cell (2,2) has 50, and cell (3,3) has 180. Therefore, the minimum quantity we find is 50 units in cell (2,2), and 50 is the maximum quantity we can transfer to cell (1,3). It should be obvious that if we transfer more than 50 units to cell (1,3), we have to assign some negative value to cell (2,2) in order to meet the demand and supply requirements, as shown in Table 7.18. Of course, we cannot transport negative quantity. Determination of the maximum quantity to be transferred among the negative stones is actually nothing more than the process of determining the pivot row in the simplex procedure. In other words, cell (1,3) is the incoming variable and cell (2,2) is the outgoing variable.

The new solution is shown in Table 7.19. Now we have completed the first iteration. The total transportation cost of the second solution is $6,210, as shown in Table 7.19. This cost is $800 less than the initial solution cost of $7,010 derived by the northwest corner method. Since the CII of cell (1,3) was −$16 and the quantity we transferred to cell (1,3) was 50, the total cost reduction would be $800 ($16 × 50 = $800). Now we must reevaluate the new empty cells to see if we can further improve the solution. Before we proceed to generate a new solution, there are several points we must remember about the stepping-stone method.

1. To evaluate all empty cells, there should be $m + n - 1$ number of occupied cells, where m is the number of sources and n is the number of desinations.

2. Only sources can transport goods to destinations. Thus, any reallocation or transfer can be made only rowwise but never columnwise.

Key features of the stepping-stone method

3. For any empty cell, there is only one unique stepping-stone path. The stepping-stone path is simply a set of nonzero coefficients in the pivot column in a simplex tableau.

4. The stepping-stone path is composed only of occupied cells.

5. The stepping-stone path can skip over empty cells or even over occupied cells.

The second iteration

Now we will start the second iteration by evaluating all of the empty cells. Before evaluating them, we can easily determine the CII of cell (2,2), the cell that we just emptied in the first iteration. We emptied cell (2,2) because the empty cell (1,3) had a CII of −$16. Therefore, if we evaluate cell (2,2) by using the same stepping-stone path, its CII will be +$16. We can easily determine the CII of all of the remaining empty cells, as shown in Table 7.20.

The cell with the best CII is cell (3,1) with −$25. We can reduce the total transportation cost by $25 per unit if we transfer some quantity from cell (3,3) to cell (3,1). The maximum quantity we can transfer is 100 because this is the minimum quantity in the negative stones of the stepping-stone path. Thus, the total transporta-

The third iteration

tion cost will be reduced by $2,500 ($25 × 100 = $2,500); hence, the total cost becomes $3,710. The result of the second iteration is shown in Table 7.21.

We will now begin the third iteration. Without calculating, we already know that the CII of cell (1,1) is +$25, since we just emptied this cell. We can evaluate the remaining empty cells in the usual manner, as shown in Table 7.22. Clearly, cell (2,2) has the best CII with −$9. The maximum quantity that can be transferred to cell (2,2) is 100 [100 units in cell (2,1)]. The solution we derive after the third iteration is shown in Table 7.23. The total transportation cost will be reduced by $900 ($9 × 100 = $900). Hence, the new total transportation cost is $2,810.

We repeat the procedure of evaluating the empty cells. Of course, we need not evaluate cell (2,1) because we already know that this cell has a +$9 CII. The three

The optimum solution

remaining empty cells are analyzed in Table 7.24. It is now apparent that no empty cell has a negative CII. In other words, we cannot improve the solution further by making a reallocation. Therefore, we have reached the optimum solution. It should be noted here that in a balanced transportation problem where all supply and demand quantities are integers, the solution will also be integer valued. The optimum solution of the Gulf Coast Oil problem has the transportation network shown in Figure 7.3.

Table 7.20   *The Stepping-Stone Paths and CIIs for Empty Cells*

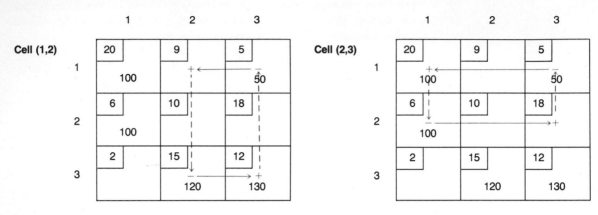

Cell (1,2) = +(1,2) − (1,3) + (3,3) − (3,2)
CII (1,2) = +9 − 5 + 12 − 15 = +1

Cell (2,3) = +(2,3) − (2,1) + (1,1) − (1,3)
CII (2,3) = +18 − 6 + 20 − 5 = +27

Cell (1,3) = +(3,1) − (3,3) + (1,3) − (1,1)
CII (1,3) = +2 − 12 + 5 − 20 = −25

The stepping-stone method we have applied can be summarized as follows:

1. Be sure that the number of occupied cells is exactly equal to $m + n − 1$, where m is the number of rows and n is the number of columns.

2. Evaluate each empty cell by tracing its stepping-stone path and determining its CII. If all CIIs have zero or positive values, an optimum solution is found. If there are negative indexes, find the cell with the largest negative CII. This is the cell in which a reallocation should be made.

Table 7.21   The Third Solution by the Stepping-Stone Method

From \ To	1	2	3	Supply
1	20	9	5 150	150
2	6 100	10	18	100
3	2 100	15 120	12 30	250
Demand	200	120	180	500

Total Transportation Cost
$$150 \times \$5 = \$750$$
$$100 \times 6 = 600$$
$$100 \times 2 = 200$$
$$120 \times 15 = 1,800$$
$$30 \times 12 = 360$$
$$\$3,710$$

Table 7.22   Evaluation of All Empty Cells

Empty Cells	Stepping-Stone Path	CII
(1,1)	+(1,1) − (1,3) + (3,3) − (3,1)	+20 − 5 + 12 − 2 = +$25
(1,2)	+(1,2) − (1,3) + (3,3) − (3,2)	+9 − 5 + 12 − 15 = +$1
(2,2)	+(2,2) − (2,1) + (3,1) − (3,2)	+10 − 6 + 2 − 15 = −$9
(2,3)	+(2,3) − (2,1) + (3,1) − (3,3)	+18 − 6 + 2 − 12 = +$2

Table 7.23   The Optimum Solution after Three Iterations

From \ To	1	2	3	Supply
1	20	9	5 150	150
2	6	10 100	18	100
3	2 200	15 20	12 30	250
Demand	200	120	180	500

Total Transportation Cost
$$150 \times \$5 = \$750$$
$$100 \times 10 = 1,000$$
$$200 \times 2 = 400$$
$$20 \times 15 = 300$$
$$30 \times 12 = 360$$
$$\$2,810$$

Table 7.24   Evaluation of the Empty Cells

Empty Cell	Stepping-Stone Path	CII
(1,1)	+(1,1) − (1,3) + (3,3) − (3,1)	+20 − 5 + 12 − 2 = +$25
(1,2)	+(1,2) − (1,3) + (3,3) − (3,2)	+9 − 5 + 12 − 15 = +$1
(2,3)	+(2,3) − (2,2) + (3,2) − (3,3)	+18 − 10 + 15 − 12 = +$11

Figure 7.3   Optimum Transportation Network for Gulf Coast Oil

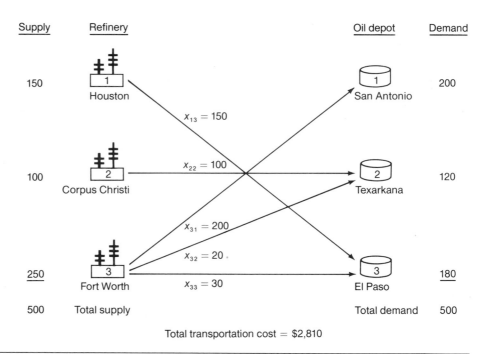

3. Determine the maximum quantity that can be reallocated or transferred to the selected empty cell. Trace the stepping-stone path for the cell and identify the minimum positive quantity in the negative stones. Transfer this quantity and find the new solution after the iteration. Repeat the solution procedure by going back to Step 1.

The MODI method

The Modified Distribution Method   Although the stepping-stone method is a systematic way to determine a transportation solution, it involves the cumbersome procedure of tracing the stepping-stone paths for all of the empty cells. The modified distribution method (MODI) is a more efficient procedure in evaluating the empty cells. Instead of evaluating the empty cells one at a time by tracing the stepping-stone path as in the stepping-stone method, in the MODI method we evaluate all of

Table 7.25   Initial Transportation Tableau by the MODI Method

		To From	1	2	3	Supply
k_j		$k_1 = 20$	$k_2 = 24$	$k_3 = 21$		
r_i						
$r_1 = 0$	1	20	9	5		150
		150		+		
$r_2 = -14$	2	6	10	18		100
		50	50			
$r_3 = -9$	3	2	15	12		250
			70	180		
	Demand	200	120	180	500

Total Transportation Cost = $7,010

the empty cells simultaneously. Consequently, in MODI we do not have to trace all of the stepping-stone paths of the empty cells. Instead, we trace the stepping-stone path of only the one empty cell that has the best CII. In using this method, therefore, we can eliminate the major portion of the cumbersome task of tracing the stepping-stone path!

The MODI method, originated by George B. Dantzig, is a variation of the stepping-stone method. It is based on the dual formulation of the primal transportation problem. To demonstrate this method, let us go back to the initial solution obtained by the northwest corner method for the Gulf Coast Oil problem, shown in Table 7.25. For the MODI operation, however, we must make a slight modification in the simplex tableau. We add the r_i row for row values and the k_j column for column values, as shown in Table 7.25.

Modifications in the tableau

For the *occupied cells* [cells where some quantities have been allocated, e.g., cells (1,1), (2,1), (2,2), (3,2), and (3,3)], the following relationships exist:

$$c_{ij} = r_i + k_j$$

where

Cost relationships for the occupied cells

c_{ij} = unit transportation cost at the occupied cell ij

r_i = ith row value

k_j = jth column value

For example, the unit transportation cost for the five occupied cells can be described as follows:

$$c_{11} = r_1 + k_1 = 20 \qquad \text{cell } (1,1)$$
$$c_{21} = r_2 + k_1 = 6 \qquad \text{cell } (2,1)$$
$$c_{22} = r_2 + k_2 = 10 \qquad \text{cell } (2,2)$$
$$c_{32} = r_3 + k_2 = 15 \qquad \text{cell } (3,2)$$
$$c_{33} = r_3 + k_3 = 12 \qquad \text{cell } (3,3)$$

In these equations, we have six unknown variables (row and column values) and five equations. To solve for the six unknown variables, one of the variables must be selected and assigned an arbitrary value. The usual procedure is to select r_1 and assign a zero value to it. With $r_1 = 0$, it is a simple task to identify the values of the remaining variables as follows:

Computing r_i and k_j

Occupied Cell	$c_{ij} = r_i + k_j$	Row or Column Value
$r_1 + k_1 = 20$	$0 + k_1 = 20,$	$k_1 = 20$
$r_2 + k_1 = 6$	$r_2 + 20 = 6,$	$r_2 = -14$
$r_2 + k_2 = 10$	$-14 + k_2 = 10,$	$k_2 = 24$
$r_3 + k_2 = 15$	$r_3 + 24 = 15,$	$r_3 = -9$
$r_3 + k_3 = 12$	$-9 + k_3 = 12,$	$k_3 = 21$

All of the row and column values are determined. As we can see in the above calculations, the row and column values are not always positive. We list these values in the transportation tableau, as shown in Table 7.25. We are now ready to evaluate all of the empty cells.

For the *empty cells,* the cost improvement index (CII) can be determined as follows:

$$\text{CII} = c_{ij} - r_i - k_j$$

As in the stepping-stone method, if a cell has a negative CII, it indicates that an improved solution is possible. When all of the CII values are zero or positive, an optimum solution is obtained. We can calculate the CII for each of the empty cells as follows:

CII for the empty cells

Computing CII

Empty Cell	$c_{ij} - r_i - k_j$	CII
(1,2)	$9 - 0 - 24$	-15
(1,3)	$5 - 0 - 21$	-16
(2,3)	$18 - (-14) - 21$	$+11$
(3,1)	$2 - (-9) - 20$	-9

The stepping-stone path

The CII values found above correspond with those we calculated in the stepping-stone method. The empty cell with the largest negative CII is cell $(1,3)$ with $-\$16$. The maximum quantity we can transfer to cell $(1,3)$ is the minimum quantity in the negative stones of the stepping-stone path. Therefore, we must determine the stepping-stone path for only one empty cell, the one with the best CII. From the stepping-stone method we know that the stepping-stone path for cell $(1,3)$ is $+(1,3) - (1,1)$

+ (2,1) − (2,2) + (3,2) − (3,3), as shown in Table 7.25. The maximum quantity we can transfer to cell (1,3) is 50 [the quantity in cell (2,2)].

After we implement this transfer, we derive the second solution. The second solution is evaluated by recalculating the row and column values and the CII as shown below:

Occupied Cell	$c_{ij} = r_i + k_j$	Row or Column Value
(1,1)	$20 = 0 + k_1$	$k_1 = 20$
(1,3)	$5 = 0 + k_3$	$k_3 = 5$
(2,1)	$6 = r_2 + 20$	$r_2 = -14$
(3,2)	$15 = 7 + k_2$	$k_2 = 8$
(3,3)	$12 = r_3 + 5$	$r_3 = 7$

Empty Cell	$c_{ij} - r_i - k_j$	CII
(1,2)	$9 - 0 - 8$	$+1$
(2,2)	$10 - (-14) - 8$	$+16$
(2,3)	$18 - (-14) - 5$	$+27$
(3,1)	$2 - 7 - 20$	-25

The second solution

Table 7.26 presents the second solution with the row and column values. The cell with the best CII is cell (3,1) with −$25. By tracing its stepping-stone path, as shown in Table 7.26, we can easily determine that the maximum quantity we can transfer is 100 [in cell (1,1)].

We repeat the process and derive the third solution, as shown in Table 7.27. The new row and column values and the CIIs are determined as follows:

Occupied Cell	$c_{ij} = r_i + k_j$	Row or Column Value
(1,3)	$5 = 0 + k_3$	$k_3 = 5$
(3,3)	$12 = r_3 + 5$	$r_3 = 7$
(3,2)	$15 = 7 + k_2$	$k_2 = 8$
(3,1)	$2 = 7 + k_1$	$k_1 = -5$
(2,1)	$6 = r_2 + (-5)$	$r_2 = 11$

Empty Cell	$c_{ij} - r_i - k_j$	CII
(1,1)	$20 - 0 - (-5)$	$+25$
(1,2)	$9 - 0 - 8$	$+1$
(2,2)	$10 - 11 - 8$	-9
(2,3)	$18 - 11 - 5$	$+2$

The third solution

Table 7.27 presents the third solution with row and column values. The cell with the best CII is cell (2,2) with −$9. We trace the stepping-stone path for cell (2,2), as shown in Table 7.27. The maximum quantity we can transfer to cell (2,2) is 100 [in cell (2,1)]. When we transfer 100 units to cell (2,1), we obtain the fourth solution, as shown in Table 7.28.

Table 7.26   The Second Solution by the MODI Method

| k_j | | $k_1 = 20$ | $k_2 = 8$ | $k_3 = 5$ | |

r_i	From \ To	1	2	3	Supply
$r_1 = 0$	1	20 — 100	9	5 → + 50	150
$r_2 = -14$	2	6 100	10	18	100
$r_3 = 7$	3	2 +	15 120	12 ↓ 130	250
	Demand	200	120	180	500

Total Transportation Cost = $6,210

Table 7.27   The Third Solution by the MODI Method

| k_j | | $k_1 = -5$ | $k_2 = 8$ | $k_3 = 5$ | |

r_i	From \ To	1	2	3	Supply
$r_1 = 0$	1	20	9	5 150	150
$r_2 = 11$	2	6 100	10 → +	18	100
$r_3 = 7$	3	2 + 100	15 120	12 30	250
	Demand	200	120	180	500

Total Transportation Cost = $3,710

Table 7.28 The Optimum Solution Obtained by the MODI Method

k_j		$k_1 = -5$	$k_2 = 8$	$k_3 = 5$	
r_i	To / From	1	2	3	Supply
$r_1 = 0$	1	20	9	5 150	150
$r_2 = 2$	2	6	10 100	18	100
$r_3 = 7$	3	2 200	15 20	12 30	250
	Demand	200	120	180	500

Total Transportation Cost = $2,810

Now we repeat the evaluation process by the MODI method and determine the row and column values and the CIIs for the empty cells as follows:

Occupied Cell	$c_{ij} = r_i + k_j$	Row or Column Value
(1,3)	$5 = 0 + k_3$	$k_3 = 5$
(3,3)	$12 = r_3 + 5$	$r_3 = 7$
(3,2)	$15 = 7 + k_2$	$k_2 = 8$
(3,1)	$2 = 7 + k_1$	$k_1 = -5$
(2,2)	$10 = r_2 + 8$	$r_2 = 2$

Empty Cell	$c_{ij} - r_i - k_j$	CII
(1,1)	$20 - 0 - (-5)$	$+25$
(1,2)	$9 - 0 - 8$	$+1$
(2,1)	$6 - 2 - (-5)$	$+9$
(2,3)	$18 - 2 - 5$	$+11$

The optimum solution

The CII values calculated for the empty cells indicate that they are all positive. Therefore, we have reached the optimum solution. This solution is exactly identical to the one we derived through the stepping-stone method.

We can summarize the MODI method as follows:

1. Starting with a solution, compute the row (r_i) and column (k_j) values by using the relationship $c_{ij} = r_i + k_j$ for all of the occupied cells. Assign $r_1 = 0$ and determine all of the r_i and k_j values.

2. Compute the CIIs for all of the empty cells by using the formula $\text{CII} = c_{ij} - r_i - k_j$.

3. Trace the stepping-stone path for the empty cell that has the largest negative CII. If there is no negative CII, the optimum solution is found.

4. Transfer to the empty cell selected the minimum quantity in the negative stones of the stepping-stone path.

5. Develop a new solution and repeat the procedure by going back to Step 1.

THE UNBALANCED TRANSPORTATION PROBLEM

The unbalanced problem

Our discussion thus far has focused on the balanced transportation problem, in which total supply equals total demand. In real-world situations, however, a balanced case is the exception rather than the rule. As a matter of fact, most transportation problems are unbalanced cases in which either supply exceeds demand or demand exceeds supply. To analyze an unbalanced transportation problem, we must make a minor modification in the transportation tableau so that the case becomes a balanced case. First we will discuss the case in which demand exceeds supply, and then the case in which supply exceeds demand.

Demand Exceeds Supply

Demand > supply

Let us consider the original transportation problem of Gulf Coast Oil Company. Suppose the demand for gasoline at the third destination (El Paso) has increased to 240 from the original demand of 180. The total demand from the three destinations is now 560, while the total supply remains at 500. This problem can be formulated as a linear programming model as follows:

$$\text{Minimize } Z = 20x_{11} + 9x_{12} + 5x_{13} + 6x_{21} + 10x_{22} + 18x_{23} + 2x_{31} + 15x_{32} + 12x_{33}$$

$$\text{subject to} \quad \left. \begin{array}{l} x_{11} + x_{12} + x_{13} = 150 \\ x_{21} + x_{22} + x_{23} = 100 \\ x_{31} + x_{32} + x_{33} = 250 \end{array} \right\} \text{ Supply}$$

$$\left. \begin{array}{l} x_{11} + x_{21} + x_{31} \leq 200 \\ x_{12} + x_{22} + x_{32} \leq 120 \\ x_{13} + x_{23} + x_{33} \leq 240 \end{array} \right\} \text{ Demand}$$

$$x_{ij} \geq 0$$

Since the demand is greater than ($>$) the supply, we will use every unit supplied by the sources. However, all of the quantity demanded by a destination may not be satisfied. In any unbalanced problem, whichever is the lesser quantity between the demand and supply requirements will always have exactly an *equal to* ($=$) type

Table 7.29   Initial Solution by the Minimum Cell-Cost Method for the Unbalanced Problem

From \ To	1	2	3	Supply
1	20	9	5 150	150
2	6	10 100	18	100
3	2 200	15 20	12 30	250
4 Dummy	0	0	0 60	60
Demand	200	120	240	560

A dummy source

Determining initial solutions

constraint, whereas the greater of the two will always have a *less than or equal to* ($\leq$) type constraint.

To make the unbalanced case a balanced problem, we can create an imaginary refinery (source) that can accommodate the excess demand. We introduce a *dummy* source to supply the increased demand of 60 at Destination 3. Now we can balance supply and demand. Since the dummy source is only an imaginary refinery, the unit transportation costs of all of the cells in the dummy row are zero.

The initial solution for the problem can be determined by the northwest corner, minimum cell-cost, or Vogel's approximation method. In using the northwest corner method or VAM, we treat the dummy row (or dummy column in a case of supply > demand) as if it were one of the regular rows. However, if we use the minimum cell-cost method, we cannot make the first unique assignment among the three zero-cost cells in the dummy row. For example, the supply quantity of 60 in the dummy row can be assigned to cell (4,1), (4,2), or (4,3) at the minimum cost of zero. Therefore, for the minimum cell-cost method it is better that we leave out the dummy row (or dummy column) from consideration until the end.

Let us consider the modified transportation tableau shown in Table 7.29. Notice that the unbalanced case has been modified to become a balanced case. We exclude the dummy row and start with the minimum cell-cost method. The cell with the minimum transportation cost is cell (3,1). We make the maximum possible assignment of 200 in this cell and continue as we did earlier in the minimum cell-cost method procedure (p. 256). After all assignments are made in the regular rows, as shown in Table 7.29, we consider the unique assignment in the dummy row. Obviously, the last assignment has to be made in cell (4,3).

Transporting from the
dummy source
Now we can proceed to solve the problem by using either the stepping-stone or the MODI method. If the optimum solution calls for the dummy row to transport some quantity to one or more destinations, this implies that the destination(s) will receive less than the quantity required. For example, if the optimum solution shows the dummy row supplying 60 units to Destination 3, in reality Destination 3 would receive only 180 units rather than the 240 it demanded.

Supply Exceeds Demand

Supply > demand
Now we can analyze the opposite case in which supply exceeds demand. Suppose, again in the Gulf Coast Oil problem, that the demand requirement at Destination 1 has decreased to 160 from the original 200. The total demand from the three destinations now amounts to only 460, whereas the total supply remains at 500. Clearly, this is a case in which supply exceeds demand. We can formulate a linear programming model for the unbalanced case as follows:

$$\text{Minimize } Z = 20x_{11} + 9x_{12} + 5x_{13} + 6x_{21} + 10x_{22} + 18x_{23} + 2x_{31} + 15x_{32} + 12x_{33}$$

$$\text{subject to} \quad \left. \begin{array}{c} x_{11} + x_{12} + x_{13} \leq 150 \\ x_{21} + x_{22} + x_{23} \leq 100 \\ x_{31} + x_{32} + x_{33} \leq 250 \end{array} \right\} \text{Supply}$$

$$\left. \begin{array}{c} x_{11} + x_{21} + x_{31} = 160 \\ x_{12} + x_{22} + x_{32} = 120 \\ x_{13} + x_{23} + x_{33} = 180 \end{array} \right\} \text{Demand}$$

$$x_{ij} \geq 0$$

A dummy destination
To balance the supply and demand requirements for the problem, we must create a dummy destination to absorb the excess supply of 40 units. The dummy column is added in the tableau and unit transportation costs of zero are assigned to the cells in the dummy destination column, as shown in Table 7.30. The initial solution by the northwest corner method is also presented in Table 7.30. As usual, we can proceed to improve the solution by using either the stepping-stone or the MODI method.

If Destination 4 (dummy column) receives some quantity from a source (or sources) in the final solution, this implies that the source (or sources) is not supplying up to its productive capacity. For example, if the dummy destination receives 40 units from Source 3, as shown in Table 7.30, Source 3 in reality is supplying only 210 units, or 40 below its supply capacity of 250. Thus, Source 3 (refinery at Fort Worth) may either produce gasoline up to its productive capacity and store the unsold quantity of 40 units, or produce 40 units less than its productive capacity and simply meet the demand.

SOME UNIQUE SITUATIONS

Unique situations
In many transportation problems, we face several unique situations that may cause some difficulty. In this section, we will discuss some of these situations.

Degeneracy

To improve a solution, we must evaluate all of the empty cells and determine their CII values. For the stepping-stone or MODI method, the number of occupied cells should be exactly $m + n - 1$ (m = number of rows, n = number of columns). If

Table 7.30   Initial Solution by the Northwest Corner Method for the Second Unbalanced Problem

From \ To	1	2	3	4 Dummy	Supply
1	20 / 150	9	5	0	150
2	6 / 10	10 / 90	18	0	100
3	2	15 / 30	12 / 180	0 / 40	250
Demand	160	120	180	40	500

Degeneracy

Not enough occupied cells

a transportation tableau has less than $m + n - 1$ occupied cells, the solution is referred to as *degenerate*. In a degenerate problem, we cannot evaluate all of the empty cells because, if we apply the stepping-stone method, the lack of occupied cells would make it impossible to develop the necessary stepping-stone paths. If we apply the MODI method, degeneracy would prohibit us from developing a sufficient number of $c_{ij} = r_i + k_j$ relationships to determine the row and column values.

Degeneracy can occur at any time during the transportation solution process, either in the initial solution or during the iterations. The cause of degeneracy is a unique allocation that satisfies the demand and supply requirements simultaneously. Let us discuss degenerate cases in the initial solution and also during the iterations.

Degeneracy in the Initial Solution   Suppose the Gulf Coast Oil problem has been slightly modified as shown in Table 7.31. The initial solution is derived by the northwest corner method. Since the demand at Destination 3 and supply at Source 3 are an identical 160 units, the unique allocation in cell $(3,3)$ satisfies the demand and supply requirements simultaneously. We have only four occupied cells, which results in a degenerate solution. We know from our previous discussion that the northwest corner method usually yields an initial solution with a chain of occupied cells that form a step effect. This chain is broken in Table 7.31.

To remedy the problem of degeneracy, we must restore the condition of $m + n - 1$ number of occupied cells for the solution. By assigning a very small quantity, ϵ (epsilon), to an empty cell, we will connect the broken chain of occupied cells. In our solution, shown in Table 7.31, there are two candidates, cell $(2,3)$ and cell $(3,2)$. By assigning ϵ to either cell $(2,3)$ or cell $(3,2)$, we can proceed with the solution process in the usual manner.

There are two characteristics of ϵ that we must know about. First, ϵ is such a small value that if we add some quantity to ϵ the sum will be exactly equal to the

Degeneracy in the initial tableau

Use of ϵ

Table 7.31 Degeneracy in the Initial Solution

From \ To	1	2	3	Supply
1	20 150	9	5	150
2	6 50	10 140	18	190
3	2	15	12 160	160
Demand	200	140	160	500

Table 7.32 A Positive ε Cell in the Stepping-Stone Path

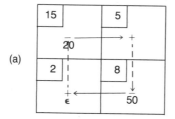

(a)

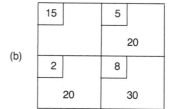

(b)

The role of ε

quantity just added. For example, let us consider the stepping-stone path for an empty cell as shown in Part (a) of Table 7.32. The ε cell is a positive stone. Thus, when we add the transfer quantity of 20 to ε, the new quantity in the ε cell becomes 20, as shown in Part (b) of Table 7.32. This transfer actually eliminated ε, as the problem is no longer degenerate.

The second characteristic of ε is that if ε is in a negative stone of the stepping-stone path, the quantity we can transfer to the empty cell will be ε. For example, let us consider the stepping-stone path shown in Part (a) of Table 7.33. Since the minimum quantity in the negative stones of the path is ε, this is the quantity that must be transferred, as shown in part (b) of Table 7.33. When ε is subtracted from the quantities of the occupied cells in the path, the old quantities remain the same because ε is such a minimal value. Thus, this transfer serves *no purpose*. Therefore, whenever ε is in a negative stone, we should ignore this path evaluation and move on to the next path that shows the greatest CII.

Table 7.33   A Negative ε Cell in the Stepping-Stone Path Serves No Purpose

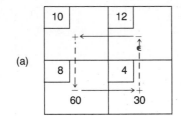
(a)

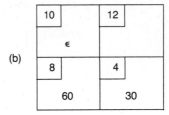
(b)

Table 7.34   The Initial Solution by the Northwest Corner Method

From \ To	1	2	3	Supply
1	20 120	9 (−15)	5 (−16)	120
2	6 30	10 120	18 (+11)	150
3	2 (−9)	15 20	12 210	230
Demand	150	140	210	500

Degeneracy in Subsequent Iterations Let us suppose that the Gulf Coast Oil problem has been modified as shown in Table 7.34. The initial solution is derived by the northwest corner method. This solution is not degenerate. From a brief analysis of the CII values, indicated by the circled numbers in each empty cell, it is obvious that cell (1,3) is where we must make a transfer. The stepping-stone path is also indicated in Table 7.34.

The maximum quantity we can transfer to cell (1,3) is 120. However, when this transfer is made, both cell (1,1) and cell (2,2) become empty, since these two negative stones have the identical minimum quantity of 120 in the negative cells of the stepping-stone path. The iteration yields a degenerate solution, as shown in Table 7.35. We can assign ε to one of the two negative cells that have become empty,

Degeneracy during iterations

Table 7.35   The Second Solution Tableau

To From	1	2	3	Supply
1	20	9	5 120	120
2	6 150	10 ε	18	150
3	2	15 140	12 90	230
Demand	150	140	210	500

namely cell (1,1) and cell (2,2). Now we can proceed with the solution process in the usual manner.

If a solution is degenerate, we cannot determine all of the row (r_i) and column (k_j) values when we apply the MODI method. From an analysis of the relationship $c_{ij} = r_i + k_j$, we can easily determine to which empty cell we must assign ε in order to calculate the r_i and k_j values. Once ε is assigned to an appropriate empty cell, we can proceed in the usual manner.

Prohibited or Impossible Transportation Routes

In certain transportation problems, shipment from a certain source to a certain destination is either prohibited by local traffic ordinances or physically impossible because of a union strike, road construction, seasonal hazards of the road (snow, flooding, etc.), weight limits on bridges, and the like. A transportation problem with prohibited

Impossible routes

or impossible routes can be handled in the usual manner by assigning a large unit transportation cost, M (similar to the large M method we used in linear programming), to each of the prohibited cells. The same result can be obtained if we block out those cells altogether. In such a case, the blocked-out cells are skipped over in the evaluation of the empty cells.

Multiple Optimum Solutions

In a transportation tableau, the optimum solution is obtained when all of the CII values for the empty cells are zero or positive. If there are one or more empty cells with zero CII values, the problem has alternate optimum solutions. Since the empty

Multiple optimum solutions

cells represent the nonbasic variables and their CII values are $c_j - z_j$ in the simplex concept, we can easily identify with the multiple optimum solution case. We can

Table 7.36 An Optimum Solution Tableau

To From	1	2	3	Supply
1	20 (+24)	9 (0)	6 150	150
2	6 (+9)	10 100	18 (+16)	100
3	2 200	15 20	12 30	250
Demand	200	120	180	500

Zero CII in an empty cell

make a transfer to an empty cell with a zero CII value and obtain an entirely different solution but with exactly the same total transportation cost.

For example, let us suppose that the optimum solution to a modified version of the Gulf Coast Oil problem is obtained as shown in Table 7.36. The circled CII values for the empty cells are also presented in the table. Cell (1,2) has a zero CII value. Thus, there is an alternate optimum solution.

From a brief analysis of the stepping-stone path for cell (1,2), shown in Table 7.36, we can easily determine that the maximum quantity we can transfer to cell (1,2) is 20. After this transfer, a new optimum solution is derived, as shown in Table 7.37. The total transportation cost remains the same, but an alternate optimum solution is identified. If management has a preference for a given solution, in consideration of such noneconomic factors as road conditions, traffic accident figures for certain routes, and union contracts, an analysis of multiple optimum solutions may be valuable.

The Transshipment Problem

The transshipment problem

In a typical transportation problem, only sources can transport goods to destinations. However, in many real-world problems, destinations can be intermediate points of transportation. For example, gasoline can be transported from a refinery in Houston to an oil depot in San Antonio, and then the San Antonio depot can transport it to another depot in El Paso. The *transshipment method* has an enormous potential for practical application. A special procedure is available to solve the transshipment problem by the regular transportation method, with some minor adjustments. If you are

Table 7.37   An Alternate Optimum Solution

From \ To	1	2	3	Supply
1	20	9 _20_	6 _130_	150
2	6	10 _100_	18	100
3	2 _200_	15	12 _50_	250
Demand	200	120	180	500

interested in this topic, possibly for the purpose of working on a term project, you should consult the publications of Hillier and Lieberman and of Lee, Moore, and Taylor (see References).

THE TRANSPORTATION PROBLEM WITH MULTIPLE OBJECTIVES

Multiple objective transportation problem

Many practical transportation problems often involve multiple conflicting objectives rather than the single objective of transportation cost minimization. In such cases, since the transportation method can handle only one objective criterion (i.e., the transportation cost), we must abandon this approach and instead apply the goal programming methodology. Many transportation-related problems with multiple objectives have been analyzed by goal programming in recent years. Some of these applications are location-allocation, manpower scheduling and allocation, school busing logistics, and transportation or transshipment problems. If you are interested in this topic, you should consult the References at the end of this chapter.

REAL-WORLD APPLICATIONS

Applications to real-world problems

There have been numerous real-world applications of the transportation method. Many transportation and transportation-related problems, such as location-allocation problems, are often formulated in the general transportation model framework and solved by linear programming. In this section, we will examine one example of a real-world application.

Determination of Electric Transmission Fees

Samkjoringen av Kraftverkene i Norge is the national electrical cooperative which organizes and coordinates the electrical power companies that have approximately 95 percent of the generating capacity in Norway.[1] Samkjoringen's primary responsibility is to manage the central electrical network. The central network represents the transmission grid system that is utilized for rational coordination and utilization of the member power stations for each time period. The central network includes approximately 2,540 kilometers of 275 kV lines, 3,640 kilometers of 132 kV lines, and various transformers that connect the different system voltages.

The central network has 75 subscribing companies that use the grid system. The central network is owned by a number of member companies of Sankjoringen. The ownership companies of the central network receive an annual compensation based on their fixed percentage of the capital invested in the grid system. The total compensation paid to the ownership companies equals the total sum paid by the subscribers to the central network.

The subscribers' annual fees are made up of three primary components: transmission fees, exchange fees, and connection fees. The transmission fees represent approximately 90 percent of the total subscription fees. This study was focused on the determination of the transmission fee for each subscriber. To formulate the transportation model upon which the study was based, the following definitions were specified:

Sources: points that feed electricity into the system

Sinks: points that use electricity

x_{ij}: amount of electricity (megawatts) transmitted from source i ($i = 1, \ldots, m$) to sink j ($j = 1, \ldots, n$)

a_i: amount of electricity (megawatts) supplied by source i to the network

b_j: amount of electricity (megawatts) used by sink j

c_{ij}: distance in kilometers from source i to sink j

The transportation model formulated was:

$$\text{Minimize } Z = \sum_{i=1}^{m} \sum_{j=1}^{n} c_{ij} x_{ij}$$

$$\text{subject to } \sum_{j=1}^{n} x_{ij} = a_i, \qquad (i = 1, \ldots, m)$$

$$\sum_{i=1}^{m} x_{ij} = b_j, \qquad (j = 1, \ldots, n)$$

$$x_{ij} \geq 0$$

This transportation problem was solved by the Norwegian Computer Center by means of a fast transportation computer code. The largest transportation problem solved had 75 sources and 92 sinks—161 constraints and 6,900 decision variables. The authors claim that the problem was solved in 16 seconds. Once the transportation

[1]O. Aarvik and Paul Randolph, "The Application of Linear Programming to the Determination of Transmission Fees in an Electrical Power Network," *Interfaces*, 61 (Nov., 1975), 47–49.

model was solved, the exact transmission fee could be determined for each subscriber.

In the past, Samkjoringen had used hand methods to solve simplified transportation models, a task often requiring several weeks. In addition to the enormous computation time consumed by using hand calculation, frequently the allocation that was used might not have been the optimum one. Thus, the use of a transportation model greatly improved the efficiency in determining the equitable transmission fees for the subscribers of the central electrical network in Norway.

SUMMARY

The transportation problem is a special type of linear programming problem, and its analysis has constituted one of the major areas of fruitful application of linear programming. The initial work done by F. L. Hitchcock and T. C. Koopmans in the 1940s paved the way for future research. Many scholars have since refined and extended the basic transportation model to include not only the determination of optimum transportation patterns but also the analysis of production scheduling problems, transshipment problems, and assignment problems (to be presented in Chapter 8).

In the general transportation problem, the objective is to minimize total transportation costs. The basic assumption underlying this method is that management is concerned primarily with cost minimization. However, this assumption is not always valid. In the transportation problem, there may be multiple objectives, such as the fulfillment of transportation schedule contracts, fulfillment of union contracts, provision for a stable employment level in various plants and transportation fleets, balancing of work among a number of plants, minimization of transportation hazards, and, of course, minimization of cost. The application of goal programming has broadened considerably our ability to solve complex transportation problems.

References

Ackoff, R. L., and Sasieni, M. W. *Fundamentals of Operations Research*. New York: Wiley, 1968.

Charnes, A., and Cooper, W. W. *Management Models and Industrial Applications of Linear Programming*. New York: Wiley, 1961.

Churchman, C. W.; Ackoff, R. L.; and Arnoff, E. L. *Introduction to Operations Research*. New York: Wiley, 1958.

Dantzig, G. B. *Linear Programming and Extensions*. Princeton, N.J.: Princeton University Press, 1963.

Hillier, F. S., and Lieberman, G. J. *Introduction to Operations Research*, 3rd ed. San Francisco: Holden-Day, 1980.

Hitchcock, F. L. "The Distribution of a Product from Several Sources to Numerous Localities." *Journal of Mathematics and Physics*, 20 (1941), 224–230.

Koopmans, T. C. (ed.). *Activity Analysis of Production and Allocation, Cowles Commission Monograph No. 13*. New York: Wiley, 1951.

Kwak, N. K. *Mathematical Programming with Business Applications*. New York: McGraw-Hill, 1973.

Lee, S. M., and Moore, L. J. "Optimizing Transportation Problems with Multiple Objectives." *AIIE Transactions*, 5:4 (1973), 333–338.

Lee, S. M., and Moore, L. J. "Multiple-Criteria School Busing Models." *Management Science*, 23:7 (1977), 703–715.

Lee, S. M.; Moore, L. J.; and Taylor, B. W. *Management Science*. Dubuque, Iowa: W. C. Brown, 1981.

Orden, A. "The Transshipment Problem." *Management Science*, 2 (1956), 276–285.

Reinfeld, V., and Vogel, R. *Mathematical Programming*. Englewood Cliffs, N.J.: Prentice-Hall, 1958.

Assignments

7.1 Why is the transportation method a special technique of linear programming?

7.2 Describe a problem familiar to you that can be solved by the transportation method.

7.3 What is the primary difference between a balanced and an unbalanced transportation problem?

7.4 In terms of logic or scientific reasoning, distinguish among the following three methods for developing an initial transportation solution: northwest corner method, minimum cell-cost method, and VAM.

7.5 Describe the opportunity cost concept by giving an example familiar to you.

7.6 What are the major differences between the stepping-stone method and the MODI method?

7.7 Is there more than one stepping-stone path for each empty cell? Why or why not?

7.8 How do you determine the maximum quantity that can be transferred or reallocated to an empty cell?

7.9 What is the cost improvement index (CII)?

7.10 What is the difficulty involved in dealing with a degenerate transportation solution? Discuss it for occasions when we solve the problem by the stepping-stone method and the MODI method.

7.11 Is there only one unique empty cell in which we must assign ϵ when a condition of degeneracy exists?

7.12 Discuss the implications of multiple optimum solutions to a transportation problem.

7.13 Describe a transportation problem that may have multiple conflicting objectives.

7.14 What are two approaches that can be used to handle prohibited transportation routes?

7.15 What are the equivalent simplex terms or conditions for the following transportation terms: *CII, stepping-stone path, degeneracy, the maximum quantity to be transferred to an empty cell.*

7.16 Consider the following transportation problem:

To From	A	B	C	D	Supply
1	$5	$12	$7	$10	50
2	4	6	7	6	50
3	2	8	5	3	60
Demand	40	20	30	70	

a. Determine initial solutions using the northwest corner method, the minimum cell-cost method, and VAM. Compute the total cost for each method.
b. Solve this problem by the MODI method.

7.17 Consider the transportation problem with the following parameters:

To From	1	2	3	4	Supply
A	$5	$5	$7	$6	40
B	4	2	3	5	70
C	7	8	4	4	40
Demand	30	20	30	40	

Derive initial solutions by the northwest corner method, minimum cell-cost method, and VAM. Indicate total transportation costs.

7.18 Consider the following transportation problem:

To Demand	A	B	C	Supply
1	$80	$90	$100	42
2	90	110	110	30
3	100	120	90	28
Demand	35	40	25	

a. Determine an initial solution using the northwest corner method.
b. Determine an initial solution using the minimum cell-cost method.
c. Formulate this problem as a general linear programming model.

7.19 Consider the following transportation problem:

To From	A	B	C	D	Supply
1	$50	$75	$30	$45	120
2	65	80	40	60	170
3	40	70	50	55	110
Demand	100	100	100	100	

a. Determine an initial solution by VAM.
b. Using an initial solution by VAM, find the optimum solution using the MODI method.

7.20 Given the following transportation problem:

To From	A	B	C	D	Supply
1	$120	$100	$90	$150	360
2	100	80	20	100	250
3	90	50	130	80	300
Demand	260	400	250	300	

a. Find an initial solution by the northwest corner method.
b. Solve the problem by the stepping-stone method.

7.21 Consider the following transportation problem:

To From	A	B	C	Supply
1	$40	$10	$20	800
2	15	20	10	500
3	20	25	30	600
Demand	1050	500	650	

a. Formulate a linear programming model for this problem.

b. Set up initial solutions by the northwest corner method, minimum cell-cost method, and VAM.

c. Starting with the initial solution derived by the northwest corner method, solve this problem by the MODI method.

7.22 Consider the following transportation problem:

To From	A	B	C	D	E	Supply
1	$21	$12	$28	$17	$9	50
2	15	13	20	50	12	60
3	18	17	22	10	8	40
4	*M*	2	10	5	1	70
5	33	29	35	27	23	50
Demand	40	30	50	60	50	

a. Determine an initial solution using VAM.

b. Solve this problem by the MODI method.

7.23 Oranges are transported and then stored in warehouses in Tampa, Miami, and Fresno. These warehouses supply oranges to markets in New York, Philadelphia, Chicago, and Boston. The following tableau gives the shipping costs per ton and the supply and demand requirements:

To From	New York	Philadelphia	Chicago	Boston	Supply
Tampa	$9	$14	$12	$17	200
Miami	11	10	6	10	200
Fresno	12	8	15	7	200
Demand	130	170	100	150	

Because of a distributor's agreement, shipments are prohibited from Miami to Chicago.

a. Set up the transportation tableau for this problem and determine an initial solution using the minimum cell-cost method.

b. Solve this problem by the MODI method.

c. Are there multiple optimum solutions to this problem? If there is an alternate optimum solution, identify it.

7.24 The Yankee Hill Stone Company has a contract to supply gravel for all road repairs in a certain county. The company maintains three stockpiles, each containing the following amount of gravel: 100 tons in Stockpile 1, 60 tons in Stockpile 2, and 80 tons in Stockpile 3. Because of recent flooding, numerous roads need repair. The company has received instructions to deliver the following amounts to the designated locations: Fremont—40 tons, Johnstown—90, and Marion—110. The company has had this contract for many years, and it is known that the transportation cost per ton from each stockpile to each location is as follows:

	Fremont	**Johnstown**	**Marion**
Stockpile 1	$4	$6	$2
Stockpile 2	8	7	10
Stockpile 3	6	1	4

a. Formulate a linear programming model for this problem.
b. Develop initial solutions by the minimum cell-cost method and VAM.
c. Starting with the initial solution derived by the northwest corner method, identify the cell with the best cost improvement index and the quantity that can be transferred to that cell.
d. Find the optimum solution by the stepping-stone method.
e. Is there an alternate optimum solution? If so, identify it.

7.25 Owen's Tree Farm is the primary supplier of Christmas trees for a tricity region in Colorado. Christmas trees are grown at three different farm locations and shipped to the three cities as orders are placed. Shipping costs per tree from each farm to each city have been estimated as follows:

	Boulder	**Colorado Springs**	**Denver**
Farm 1	25¢	9¢	18¢
Farm 2	13	15	12
Farm 3	20	17	22

This year's supply of trees is very good, and each farm has the following number of trees available: 1,500 in Farm 1; 800 in Farm 2; and 1,000 in Farm 3. Mr. Owen has received orders from tree distributors in the tricity area, and they have requested the following number of trees: Boulder—700, Colorado Springs—1,200, and Denver—1,600.

a. Formulate an initial solution by the minimum cell-cost method.
b. Find the optimum solution by the MODI method.

7.26 REBAL is an organization of students and staff at various local high schools who are interested in rebalancing the environment. REBAL groups in three high schools have conducted an extensive paper recycling drive during the holidays. They have collected the following amounts of waste paper: East High—175 tons; Northwest High—150 tons; and Central High—125 tons.

Currently, there are three paper recycling companies in the area. They are, however, relatively small firms and can process a very limited quantity per month. The three firms report that they can buy only up to the following quantities of waste paper: Colonial Recycling—200 tons; Systems Environment—100 tons; and Valley Ecology—100 tons. The companies have their own trucks for transportation. Their shipping costs per ton of waste paper from the three high school locations are as follows:

	Colonial	Systems	Valley
East High	$20	$19	$17
Northwest High	23	21	20
Central High	18	24	22

a. Formulate a linear programming model for the transportation problem.
b. Set up an initial solution by VAM.
c. Is the initial solution derived in part (b) degenerate? If so, what are some of the cells in which ϵ should be assigned?
d. Find the optimum solution by the MODI method.

7.27 The Grover Brewing Company brews an extremely popular brand of beer. However, to preserve quality, it produces beer in only three plants where spring water is available. The company ships to three wholesalers. The current inventory of beer at the three plants is: Colorado plant—18,000 cases; Minnesota plant—12,500 cases; and Washington plant—9,500 cases. The three wholesalers have just placed orders for the following quantities of beer: 15,000 cases for Wholesaler 1; 8,500 cases for Wholesaler 2; and 16,500 cases for Wholesaler 3. Since they are the only customers, the company has the following accurate shipping costs per 100 cases from each plant to each wholesaler:

	Wholesaler 1	Wholesaler 2	Wholesaler 3
Colorado plant	$8	$6	$4
Minnesota plant	4	7	3
Washington plant	5	8	6

The Colorado plant reports that, as a result of a recent snowstorm in the area, it is impossible to ship beer to Wholesaler 3.

a. Set up an initial solution by the minimum cell-cost method.
b. Find the optimum solution by the MODI method.

7.28 The Charmelle Dress Company has been producing summer dresses for the past several months in anticipation of orders from its customers. Charmelle stores its dresses in three warehouses, which at the present time have the following inventories: 2,600 dresses in Warehouse 1; 3,500 dresses in Warehouse 2; and 1,850 dresses in

Warehouse 3. Orders have begun to come in, and three large customers have placed the following orders to be shipped to the following cities: Chicago—2,400 dresses; New York—1,750 dresses; and Tampa—3,350 dresses. The Distribution Manager has computed the following shipping costs per 100 dresses from each warehouse to each city:

	Chicago	New York	Tampa
Warehouse 1	$15	$10	$13
Warehouse 2	15	14	12
Warehouse 3	11	12	15

    a. Starting with an initial solution derived by the minimum cell-cost method, solve the problem by the MODI method.

    b. Are there are alternate optimum m solutions? If so, identify them.

7.29 Through local radio stations, the management of Economy Discount Stores plans to advertise summer sales to be held in its four locations. The cost of advertising per minute varies because of differences in the sizes of the audiences reached. Management has information of the available advertising time for each of four radio stations, required advertising time by the stores, and costs, as shown in the following tableau:

Radio Stations \ Discount Stores	1	2	3	4	Available Time
WAAA	$50	$70	$65	$50	30
WBBB	45	60	75	60	40
WCCC	60	50	55	70	50
WDDD	65	50	60	75	50
Required Time	30	30	40	50	

Using the MODI method, determine the amount of advertising time to be used on each radio station in order to minimize total cost.

7.30 North Carolina Tobacco Company purchases tobacco and stores certain quantities in warehouses located in the following four cities:

Warehouse Location	Capacity (Tons)
A. Charlotte	90
B. Raleigh	50
C. Lexington	80
D. Danville	60

These warehouses supply tobacco to cigarette companies in three cities that have the following demands:

Cigarette Company	Demand (Tons)
1. Richmond	120
2. Winston-Salem	100
3. Durham	110

The following railroad shipping costs per ton have been determined:

From \ To	1	2	3
A	$7	$10	$5
B	12	9	4
C	7	3	11
D	9	5	7

Because of railroad construction, shipments are temporarily prohibited from Charlotte to Richmond.

   a. Set up the transportation tableau for this problem, determine the initial solution by VAM, and compute the total cost.

   b. Solve this problem by the MODI method.

   c. Are there multiple optimum solutions? If there are alternative optimum solutions, identify them.

8   THE ASSIGNMENT PROBLEM

In the assignment problem, we attempt to find the best way to match each of the given number of objects (people, tasks, etc.) to each of the given number of stations (machines, work areas, etc.). There are many real-world situations in which, for example, we try to assign employees to tasks, crews to projects, and ambulances to first-aid stations. The basic goal of the assignment problem is either to minimize the total cost of completing all of the required tasks or to maximize the total payoff (or benefit) from the assignments.

In Chapter 7, we studied the transportation problem as a variation of the general linear programming problem. Another variation of the linear programming problem is the assignment problem. The assignment problem is very closely related to the transportation problem. As a matter of fact, the assignment problem is simply a special type of transportation problem in which there are equal numbers of sources and destinations. Furthermore, the supply of each source and the demand of each destination must be exactly 1. Consequently, the quantity we assign to a given cell must be either 0 or 1.

Because of its simple structure, the assignment problem can be solved more efficiently by its unique solution method than by linear programming or transportation solution techniques. In this chapter, we will study the concept, solution approaches, and special features of the assignment problem.

Learning Objectives   *From the study of this chapter, you will learn the following:*

1. The basic nature of the assignment problem.
2. How to formulate a linear programming model for the assignment problem.
3. How to apply the transportation approach to the assignment problem.
4. How to solve an assignment problem by the Hungarian method.
5. How to solve an assignment problem by the branch and bound approach.
6. The meaning of the following terms:

Hungarian method	*Multiple optimum assignments*
Opportunity cost table	*Branch and bound approach*
Revised opportunity cost table	*Lower and upper limits*
Impossible assignment	*Branching operation*
Zero-one integer programming	

THE NATURE OF THE ASSIGNMENT PROBLEM

A variation of the transportation problem

The assignment problem is simply a variation of the transportation problem in which the numbers of sources and destinations are exactly equal and in which the supply capacity of each source and the demand requirement of each destination equals exactly 1. Pioneers in the development of solution methods for the assignment problem are P. S. Dwyer, M. M. Flood, and H. W. Kuhn (see References). Several variations have since been developed for the solution method, the best known of which is the *Hungarian method,* so named because the underlying theorem was first proved by

König's theorem

the Hungarian mathematician, D. König. More recently, the *branch and bound* and *zero-one* integer programming methods have been applied to solve assignment-related problems.

Typical assignment examples

In real-world situations, there are many managerial problems that involve the assignment of people, machines, or objectives. Several typical examples of assignment problems are:

Employees to machines

Snowplows to areas in a city

Service crews to different districts

Police teams to various precincts

Instructors to undergraduate and graduate courses

Scientists to various research projects

Ambulances to first-aid stations

Cashiers to checkout counters

Salespersons to various sales districts

In the general assignment problem, there are only a finite number of objects (people, crews, etc.) to be assigned to a finite number of stations (machines, projects, etc.). Also, the objects must be assigned to stations on a one-to-one basis. The typical objective criterion of the assignment problem is either to minimize the total cost of the assignment or to maximize the total payoff from the assignment.

CASETTE 8.1   *MARTHA WEINSTEIN COSMETICS, INC.*

Martha Weinstein Cosmetics, Inc. was founded in 1958 by the late Martha Weinstein, a pioneer in cosmetology and beauty care for women. The company has since developed a national chain of personal sales forces, known as Martha's Crusade. The company has regional sales offices where salespersons are recruited, trained, and assigned to specific territories. The company management believes that the most important factor behind the success of a salesperson, and consequently the success of the company, is effective assignment of each trained salesperson to a territory based on performance evaluation during on-the-job training.

Recently, the Midland Sales District sales office recruited and trained four new salespersons. The new salespersons were assigned to the four sales territories on a monthly rotation system. Each salesperson spent one month in each sales territory for the four-month on-the-job training program. Because of differences in the salespersons' familiarity with each territory as well as differences in their ability to deal with various types of customers, the time required to call on potential clients in each territory varies for each salesperson.

For each salesperson in each of the sales territories during the on-the-job training, the average time required (in minutes) to contact a potential new client is as follows:

| Salesperson | Sales Territory | | | |
	A	B	C	D
1	8 min.	10 min.	12 min.	16 min.
2	11	11	15	8
3	9	6	5	14
4	15	14	9	7

The task faced by the district sales manager is the assignment of the four salespersons to each of the four sales territories. As an incentive to develop the area, only one person is to be assigned to a specific territory. The basic decision problem, therefore, is to determine how each of the salespersons should be assigned in order to minimize the total time required to contact potential clients.

THE COMPLETE ENUMERATION METHOD

The assignment problem of Martha Weinstein Cosmetics can be presented in tableau form, as shown in Table 8.1. We note that there are identical numbers of rows and columns. Also, the quantity of supply in each row and the demand requirement in each column is exactly 1. These are unique characteristics of the assignment problem.

In the assignment problem described in Table 8.1, since there are 4 salespersons and 4 territories, the total number of possible assignments would be $4! = 4 \times 3 \times 2 \times 1 = 24$. Thus, one way we can identify the optimum assignment is to perform a *complete enumeration* of all of the possible solutions. Table 8.2 presents the complete enumeration of alternative assignments. Comparing the 24 possible assignments, alternatives 1 and 4 yield the minimum total customer-contact time of 31 minutes. In this problem, we have multiple optimum solutions.

An enumeration method

If we have a large number of objects and stations, it is impractical to use the complete enumeration method. For example, if we have 6 salespersons and 6 sales territories, the number of alternatives that must be evaluated will be $6! = 6 \times 5 \times 4 \times 3 \times 2 \times 1 = 720$. Obviously, this is not a useful technique for real-world assignment problems.

n! alternatives

Table 8.1   Tableau Form of the Martha Weinstein Assignment Problem

Salesperson ╲ Territory	A	B	C	D	Supply
1	8	10	12	16	1
2	11	11	15	8	1
3	9	6	5	14	1
4	15	14	9	7	1
Demand	1	1	1	1	4

A LINEAR PROGRAMMING MODEL FOR THE ASSIGNMENT PROBLEM

We can formulate an assignment problem as a linear (integer) programming problem. If we denote x_{ij} as the decision variable representing the assignment of the ith salesperson to the jth sales territory, it should be clear that x_{ij} must be either 1 or 0. If the ith salesperson is assigned to the jth territory, x_{ij} becomes 1. On the other hand, if the ith salesperson is not assigned to the jth territory, x_{ij} will be 0. If we denote c_{ij} as the time required for the ith salesperson to contact a potential new client in the jth territory, the assignment problem can be formulated as a linear programming problem as follows:

A linear programming model

$$\text{Minimize } Z = 8x_{11} + 10x_{12} + 12x_{13} + 16x_{14} + 11x_{21} + 11x_{22}$$
$$+ 15x_{23} + 8x_{24} + 9x_{31} + 6x_{32} + 5x_{33} + 14x_{34}$$
$$+ 15x_{41} + 14x_{42} + 9x_{43} + 7x_{44}$$

$$\text{subject to} \quad \left.\begin{array}{l} x_{11} + x_{12} + x_{13} + x_{14} = 1 \\ x_{21} + x_{22} + x_{23} + x_{24} = 1 \\ x_{31} + x_{32} + x_{33} + x_{34} = 1 \\ x_{41} + x_{42} + x_{43} + x_{44} = 1 \end{array}\right\} \text{Supply requirement}$$

$$\left.\begin{array}{l} x_{11} + x_{21} + x_{31} + x_{41} = 1 \\ x_{12} + x_{22} + x_{32} + x_{42} = 1 \\ x_{13} + x_{23} + x_{33} + x_{43} = 1 \\ x_{14} + x_{24} + x_{34} + x_{44} = 1 \end{array}\right\} \text{Demand requirement}$$

$$x_{ij} = 0 \text{ or } 1$$

Table 8.2   Complete Enumeration of Assignment Alternatives

Alternative	Assignment	Total Time
1	1A, 2B, 3C, 4D	8 + 11 + 5 + 7 = 31 ← minimum
2	1A, 2B, 4C, 3D	8 + 11 + 9 + 14 = 42
3	1A, 3B, 2C, 4D	8 + 6 + 15 + 7 = 36
4	1A, 3B, 4C, 2D	8 + 6 + 9 + 8 = 31 ← minimum
5	1A, 4B, 2C, 3D	8 + 14 + 15 + 14 = 51
6	1A, 4B, 3C, 2D	8 + 14 + 5 + 8 = 35
7	2A, 1B, 3C, 4D	11 + 10 + 5 + 7 = 33
8	2A, 1B, 4C, 3D	11 + 10 + 9 + 14 = 44
9	2A, 3B, 1C, 4D	11 + 6 + 12 + 7 = 36
10	2A, 3B, 4C, 1D	11 + 6 + 9 + 16 = 42
11	2A, 4B, 1C, 3D	11 + 14 + 12 + 14 = 51
12	2A, 4B, 3C, 1D	11 + 14 + 5 + 16 = 46
13	3A, 1B, 2C, 4D	9 + 10 + 15 + 7 = 41
14	3A, 1B, 4C, 2D	9 + 10 + 9 + 8 = 36
15	3A, 2B, 1C, 4D	9 + 11 + 12 + 7 = 39
16	3A, 2B, 4C, 1D	9 + 11 + 9 + 16 = 45
17	3A, 4B, 1C, 2D	9 + 14 + 12 + 8 = 43
18	3A, 4B, 2C, 1D	9 + 14 + 15 + 16 = 54
19	4A, 1B, 2C, 3D	15 + 10 + 15 + 14 = 54
20	4A, 1B, 3C, 2D	15 + 10 + 5 + 8 = 38
21	4A, 2B, 1C, 3D	15 + 11 + 12 + 14 = 52
22	4A, 2B, 3C, 1D	15 + 11 + 5 + 16 = 47
23	4A, 3B, 1C, 2D	15 + 6 + 12 + 8 = 41
24	4A, 3B, 2C, 1D	15 + 6 + 15 + 16 = 52

Characteristics of the assignment problem

From this assignment model, we can identify several interesting characteristics of the assignment problem. First, the assignment problem tableau is a square matrix because the problem has n sources and n destinations. Second, since a person (source) can be assigned to only one territory (destination), we have the following relationship:

$$\sum_{i=1}^{n} x_{ij} = \sum_{j=1}^{n} x_{ij} = 1$$

Consequently, the number of positive solution variables for an $n \times n$ problem must be exactly n. In the strict sense of the transportation model, then, the assignment problem is always a degenerate case because we need $2n - 1$ number of occupied cells in the $n \times n$ problem to avoid degeneracy. Third, the total number of possible assignment combinations for an $n \times n$ assignment problem is $n!$.

THE TRANSPORTATION APPROACH TO THE ASSIGNMENT PROBLEM

The transportation approach

Because the assignment problem is a special variation of the transportation problem, we can use the transportation approach to solve the Martha Weinstein Cosmetics problem described in Table 8.1. However, since the assignment problem has only a

Table 8.3   An Initial Solution by the Northwest Corner Method

Salesperson \ Territory	A	B	C	D	Supply
1	8	10	12	16	1
	1 - - - - - - → ϵ				
2	11	11	15	8	1
		1 - - - - - → ϵ			
3	9	6	5	14	1
			1 - - - - → ϵ		
4	15	14	9	7	1
				1	
Demand	1	1	1	1	4

limited number of occupied cells (*n* occupied cells in an *n* × *n* problem) a severe case of degeneracy will occur.

For example, in Table 8.3 an initial solution to the problem is derived by the northwest corner method. Since we have identical supply and demand requirements, a degenerate solution results. By assigning ϵ to cells (1,B), (2,C), and (3,D), we can achieve the stair-step effect of the initial solution and thus resolve the degeneracy. We can now proceed to solve the problem by either the stepping-stone or the MODI method. Obviously, this solution procedure is a very complex and time-consuming process. Thus, the transportation approach is not an efficient solution approach for the assignment problem.

THE HUNGARIAN METHOD OF ASSIGNMENT

The Hungarian method

The Hungarian method is based on the concept of opportunity cost, or penalty cost, which we discussed in Vogel's approximation method of transportation in Chapter 7. The opportunity cost is the cost associated with failing to take the best course of action. Thus, the Hungarian method attempts to minimize the opportunity cost of not using (assigning to) the cheapest cells.

The Hungarian method consists of the following steps:

Step 1: Develop the Opportunity Cost Table First derive the opportunity cost table for the rows. Then, develop the opportunity cost table for the columns from the row opportunity cost table. This is the complete opportunity cost table.

Table 8.4   The Martha Weinstein Problem

Salesperson ╲ Territory	A	B	C	D
1	8	10	12	16
2	11	11	15	8
3	9	6	5	14
4	15	14	9	7

Steps of the Hungarian method

Step 2: Analyze the Feasibility of an Optimum Assignment To test the feasibility of an optimum assignment, draw a minimum number of horizontal and/or vertical lines to cross out all of the zero values in the opportunity cost table. If the number of straight lines required is equal to the number of rows or columns, an optimum assignment can be made. Otherwise, proceed to Step 3.

Step 3: Develop a Revised Opportunity Cost Table In the opportunity cost table derived in Step 2, identify the minimum value that is not crossed out, and subtract this value from all of the other values not crossed out. This same minimum value is added to all of the values at the intersections of two straight lines.

Step 4: Repeat Steps 2 and 3 until an Optimum Solution Is Found

The Opportunity Cost Table

Developing the opportunity cost table

The first step of the Hungarian method of assignment is to develop the opportunity cost table. The initial opportunity table is obtained through rowwise reductions. In the Martha Weinstein problem, if a salesperson is assigned to a sales territory with the minimum customer contact time, obviously we chose the best alternative. For example, in Table 8.4, if Salesperson 1 is assigned to Territory A, an average of 8 minutes would be required to contact a potential new client. On the other hand, if we assign the same salesperson to Territory B, the required time would be 10 minutes. The best possible assignment for Salesperson 1, disregarding other employees for the time being, is clearly to Territory A.

The failure to assign Salesperson 1 to territory A and assigning him or her to Territory B will cost the firm 2 minutes (10 − 8 = 2), and thus result in a less than optimum level of sales performance. Since we are attempting to minimize the total

Table 8.5   The Initial Row-wise Opportunity Cost Table

Salesperson \ Territory	A	B	C	D
1	0	2	4	8
2	3	3	7	0
3	4	1	0	9
4	8	7	2	0

Computing the opportunity costs

time required to contact potential clients, our strategy should be to minimize the opportunity cost. First, let us find the initial opportunity cost table by analyzing each row. The procedure we follow in determining the row opportunity costs is to subtract the minimum value in each row from each of the other values in that row. For example, we can compute the opportunity cost for the first row as follows:

Cell	Cell Value	−	Minimum Row Value	=	Opportunity Cost
(1,A)	8	−	8	=	0
(1,B)	10	−	8	=	2
(1,C)	12	−	8	=	4
(1,D)	16	−	8	=	6

Table 8.5 presents the opportunity cost for each of the rows.

From our discussion thus far, it should be clear that the opportunity cost also exists for columns. Any of the 4 salespersons can be assigned to Territory A. Salesperson 1 has the minimum customer contact time of 8 minutes in Territory A. If Salesperson 2 is assigned to Territory A, we must absorb the opportunity cost of 3 minutes ($11 - 8 = 3$) because we failed to assign Salesperson 1 to that territory. The column opportunity cost must be computed from the row opportunity cost table we derived in Table 8.5. For example, the final opportunity costs for Column A can be calculated as follows:

Table 8.6   The Complete Opportunity Cost Table

Salesperson \ Territory	A	B	C	D
1	0	1	4	8
2	3	2	7	0
3	4	0	0	9
4	8	6	2	0

Cell	Cell Value	−	Minimum Column Value	=	Opportunity Cost
(1,A)	0	−	0	=	0
(2,A)	3	−	0	=	3
(3,A)	4	−	0	=	4
(4,A)	8	−	0	=	8

The complete opportunity cost table after the column reduction is shown in Table 8.6.

Analysis of Optimum Assignment Feasibility

Once we develop a complete opportunity cost table, the next step is to determine whether or not an optimum assignment can be made. An optimum assignment is possible if the final opportunity cost table has four *independent zeros* that allow four unique assignments. The "independent" zero indicates that assigning a salesperson to a cell with zero opportunity cost will not exclude assignments to other cells having zero costs.

Independent zero elements

When we make an assignment to a cell with zero opportunity cost, we are assured of the best possible assignment for a given row and a given column. That is why we are looking for as many independent zeros as the number of rows or columns. A convenient way to test optimality is to draw a *minimum* number of straight lines, horizontally or vertically but never diagonally, to cross out all of the zero values in the opportunity cost table.

Determining the minimum number of straight lines

Note that the word *minimum* is significant in this procedure. By minimizing the number of straight lines required to cover all of the zero values, we will be identify-

Table 8.7   The First Test of Optimum Assignment Feasibility

Sales-person \ Territory	A	B	C	D
1	0	1	4	8
2	3	(2)	7	0
3	4	0	0	9
4	8	6	(2)	0

Table 8.8   The Second Test of Optimum Assignment Feasibility

Sales-person \ Territory	A	B	C	D
1	0	(1)	4	8
2	3	2	7	0
3	4	0	0	9
4	8	6	2	0

ing the number of independent zeros in the opportunity cost table. Therefore, *the minimum number of straight lines must equal the number of rows or columns for an optimum assignment*. If the number of straight lines is less than the number of rows or columns, we do not have a sufficient number of independent zeros to make an optimum assignment.

Tables 8.7 and 8.8 present two different ways to cover all of the zeros in the table. It is evident that we need only three lines to cross out all of the zeros. Thus, an optimum assignment is not possible at this point.

The Revised Opportunity Cost Table

Revising the opportunity cost table

Since we need only three lines to cover all of the zeros in the opportunity cost table, we have only three independent-zero cells in which assignments can be made. In other words, one salesperson must be assigned to a cell in which we have a positive opportunity cost. To identify the cheapest cell to which the fourth salesperson can be assigned, we must revise the opportunity cost table. The procedure we use can be summarized as follows:

1. In the table identify the minimum opportunity cost that is not crossed out by a straight line.

2. Subtract this value from all of the other opportunity costs that are not crossed out by straight lines.

3. Add the same minimum value to those opportunity costs that are at the intersections of two straight lines.

4. Fill the remaining cells with the unchanged opportunity costs from the previous table.

This procedure is repeated, if necessary, until we can make an optimum assignment. This procedure is used to generate additional independent zeros while retaining the previously identified independent zero values. Each new independent zero is determined on the basis of the opportunity costs among the cells not crossed out. In other words, we are creating an opportunity cost table within an opportunity cost table. The cell with the minimum opportunity cost that is not crossed out becomes the cell with the zero opportunity cost.

Let us use the first test table shown in Table 8.7 to develop the revised opportunity cost table. Among the six opportunity costs not crossed out in the table, the minimum cost is 2 in cells (2,B) and (4,C). We subtract this value 2 from all of the costs not crossed out, and we also add this value to the two intersection values in cells (1,D) and (3,D). Note that the costs that are crossed out by only one line are unchanged in the revised opportunity cost table. The revised opportunity cost table is presented in Table 8.9.

Table 8.10 presents the two different ways to cross out all of the zeros in the revised opportunity cost table. We need four straight lines to cover all of the zeros. Consequently, it is possible to make an optimum assignment for the problem. In the revised opportunity cost table shown in Table 8.9, there are two zeros in each row and each column except the first row and first column. The first assignment must be made in a row or column where there is *only one* zero because it represents a unique assignment. Since there is only one zero in the first row, we will assign Salesperson 1 to Territory A.

Assigning to a row or column with only one zero

Table 8.9   The Revised Opportunity Cost Table

Salesperson \ Territory	A	B	C	D
1	0	1	4	10
2	1	0	5	0
3	4	0	0	11
4	6	4	0	0

Table 8.10   Two Tests of Optimum Assignment Feasibility

(a)

Salesperson \ Territory	A	B	C	D
1	0	1	4	10
2	1	0	5	0
3	4	0	0	11
4	6	4	0	0

Table 8.10   Continued

(b)

Sales-person \ Territory	A	B	C	D
1	0	1	4	10
2	1	0	5	0
3	4	0	0	11
4	6	4	0	0

After this assignment, three rows (2, 3, and 4) and three columns (B, C, and D) remain, as shown in Table 8.11.

Table 8.11   The Opportunity Cost Table after the Assignment of 1A

Sales-person \ Territory	A	B	C	D
1	0	1	4	10
2	1	0	5	0
3	4	0	0	11
4	6	4	0	0

*Multiple optimum
solutions*

Since each of the remaining rows and columns has two zeros, we cannot make a unique assignment. However, there are two optional assignments we can make. First, we can assign Salesperson 2 to Territory B. Then, the remaining assignments in the one-to-one pairing will be Salesperson 3 to Territory C and Salesperson 4 to Territory D. Second, we can assign Salesperson 2 to Territory D. Then, we have no other choice but to assign Salesperson 3 to Territory B and Salesperson 4 to Territory C. Thus, we have two optimum solutions. These solutions correspond to those we identified earlier by the complete enumeration method. The two possible optimum assignments and their total time are as follows:

Assignment 1		
Salesperson	**Territory**	**Time**
1	A	8 min.
2	B	11
3	C	5
4	D	7
	Total time =	31 min.

Assignment		
Salesperson	**Territory**	**Time**
1	A	8 min.
2	D	8
3	B	6
4	C	9
	Total time =	31 min.

A MAXIMIZATION ASSIGNMENT PROBLEM

A maximization problem

The Hungarian method of assignment can also be applied to a problem in which the basic objective is to maximize a criterion. In a maximization problem, the objective criterion is usually profit, system effectiveness, sales, market share, utility, and the like. When a person is assigned to different tasks, the person's work effectiveness may vary according to his or her experience, expertise, and interest. The work effectiveness of an employee in different tasks (or locations, work groups, projects, etc.) can be expressed by an assignment table. This table can be transformed into an opportunity cost table.

The opportunity cost is the difference between the actual effectiveness realized and the best possible effectiveness measure if the best assignment were to be made. Thus, the objective of the problem is to determine an optimum assignment schedule that will minimize the total opportunity cost.

CASETTE 8.2   *THE NEIGHBORHOOD TEAM-POLICING ASSIGNMENT*

Harristown is a medium-size city with a population of approximately 120,000. The Harristown Police Department (HPD) recently decided to institute a neighborhood-based team-policing system. The team-policing system is based on the general con-

Figure 8.1 Organizational Setup of the Team

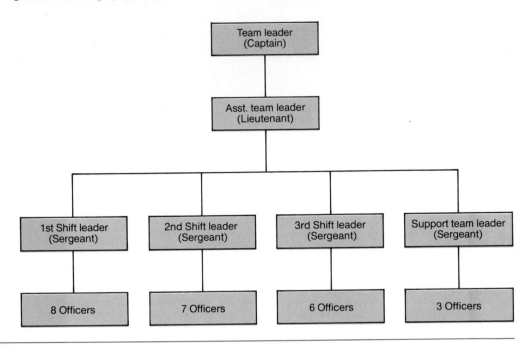

cept of decentralized management. Under this system, the city is divided into four team areas: northeast, southeast, northwest, and southwest. Each team will be assigned to a given area, and it is totally responsible for all police work on a 24-hours-a-day, 365 days-a-year basis.

The primary incentive behind the neighborhood-based team-policing system is that each team can exercise its own initiative in solving police problems in a given neighborhood. Furthermore, citizen participation in assisting the police department through a grassroots neighborhood-policing network is expected to be a major benefit of this system. Currently, four field teams have been organized and deployed throughout the city. The HPD headquarters team provides general support to the teams, such as record-keeping, central dispatcher system, public service assistance, computer-based information systems, planning and analysis, as well as the detective team and SWAT team.

Each team has the same organizational setup as shown in Figure 8.1. Although all of the team personnel assignments have been completed, the Police Chief has not been able to assign four captains to lead each team. The problem stems from the fact that each of the four captains would like to be the leader of the Southwest Area, where there tends to be more "action" because of its location. This area has the municipal airport, state penitentiary, and state mental correction institute, in addition to a number of newly opened restaurants and bars.

To be equitable and systematic in assigning the four captains to the four areas, the Chief decided to rotate their jobs so that each captain will work for a period of

Table 8.12   *Effectiveness Score Summary for the Four Captains in the Four Team Areas*

Captains \ Team Areas	1	2	3	4
1	20	28	24	26
2	18	15	16	20
3	30	28	25	23
4	17	22	21	22

one month in each of the four areas. After the four-month period of job rotation, their work performance in each area will be evaluated on the basis of a complicated scoring system. The scoring system is determined by each team's effectiveness under a given team leader in the following areas: (1) meeting service calls, (2) investigating major crimes, (3) performing preventive patrol duties in the team area, (4) doing community relations work, and (5) cooperating with the headquarters' support team. At the conclusion of the rotation period, the evaluation committee submitted the summary sheet presented in Table 8.12. The Police Chief now wants to make an optimum assignment of the four captains in order to maximize their total effectiveness score.

From a brief examination of Table 8.12, it is clear that Captain 1 performed best in Team Area 2. Thus, the opportunity cost of assigning Captain 1 to Team area 1 would be 8 points $(28 - 20 = 8)$. Now we can derive a row opportunity cost table by calculating the differences between the *highest* row score and each of the row scores, as shown in Table 8.13.

The complete opportunity cost table can be obtained from Table 8.13 by subtracting the *smallest* value in each column from each element in that same column. For example, in the third column, the smallest value is 1 in cell (4,3). Thus, subtracting this value of 1 from each element in Column 3, we obtain column opportunity costs of 3, 3, 4, and 0. The complete opportunity cost table is presented in Table 8.14.

We now use straight lines to cover all of the zero elements in Table 8.13. It is obvious that we need four lines, as shown in Table 8.14. Thus, an optimum assign-

Table 8.13   The Initial Row-wise Opportunity Cost Table

Captains \ Team Areas	1	2	3	4
1	8	0	4	2
2	2	5	4	0
3	0	2	5	7
4	5	0	1	0

Table 8.14   The Complete Opportunity Cost Table

Captains \ Team Areas	1	2	3	4
1	8	0	3	2
2	2	5	3	0
3	0	2	4	7
4	5	0	0	0

ment can be made. Since there is only one zero in row 1, we can assign Captain 1 to Team Area 2. Then, Captain 2 is assigned to Team Area 4. Now we have no further choice but to assign Captain 3 to Team Area 1 and Captain 4 to Team Area 3. The optimum assignment schedule and the total effectiveness score are as follows:

Captain	Team Area	Effectiveness Score
1	2	28
2	4	20
3	1	30
4	3	21
		Total score = 99

SOME UNIQUE SITUATIONS

Unique situations

As in the transportation problem, we may face a number of unique situations in real-world assignments. We will discuss several such situations here.

Unequal Rows and Columns

Unequal rows and columns

One very important requirement of the Hungarian method of assignment is that the number of rows (supply sources) must be exactly equal to the number of columns (demand destinations). In many practical problems, however, such an assignment problem is a very rare case indeed. For example, the number of employees to be assigned may be greater than the number of tasks to which they can be assigned. Or, there may be more jobs that need to be performed than the number of employees to do the work. In such cases we introduce either a dummy employee (row) or a dummy job (column) and balance the row-column requirements. The unit assignment costs for the dummy row or column will all be zero. This procedure is exactly the same as the one we used for the unbalanced transportation problem in Chapter 7.

CASETTE 8.3   *MISSISSIPPI BARGE TRANSPORTATION, INC.*

Mississippi Barge Transportation, Inc. (MBT) is a company located in St. Louis that specializes in loading and unloading cargo being transported by barges on the Mississippi River. The company has four docks on the riverfront with various loading and unloading equipment, crews with different areas of expertise, and different storage capacities. Thus, the efficiency of unloading certain cargo from barges varies among the docks.

MBT has just been notified that three barges are expected to arrive for unloading the next morning. Barge 1 contains coal destined for a public utility company. Barge 2 has a grain cargo to be shipped to a local gasohol plant. Barge 3 contains heavy equipment from Texas. The company wants to determine an optimum assignment of the three barges to three of the four available docks in order to minimize the total time required to unload the cargos from all of the barges. In analyzing the past performance records of the four docks in unloading these types of cargos, the dock

Table 8.15   The Cargo Unloading Problem

Barge \ Dock	A	B	C	D	Supply
1	5	8	3	6	1
2	4	5	7	4	1
3	6	2	4	5	1
Demand	1	1	1	1	4 / 3

Table 8.16   The Cargo Unloading Problem with a Dummy Row

Barge \ Dock	A	B	C	D
1	5	8	3	6
2	4	5	7	4
3	6	2	4	5
4 Dummy	0	0	0	0

manager estimated the number of hours required to unload each type of cargo by each of the four docks. His calculations are presented in Table 8.15.

To apply the Hungarian method, a dummy row (barge) is added with zero unloading hours. This problem is summarized in Table 8.16. Now we are ready to determine the initial row-wise opportunity cost table. The opportunity cost can be calculated by subtracting the minimum number of hours in a given row from each row element. The row-wise opportunity cost table is presented in Table 8.17.

Since the dummy row has all zero elements, the column opportunity cost will be exactly the same as the one shown in Table 8.17. Therefore, the complete opportunity cost table has been derived. Four straight lines are used to cross out all of the

Table 8.17   The Row-wise Opportunity Cost Table

Barge \ Dock	A	B	C	D
1	2	5	0	3
2	0	1	3	0
3	4	0	2	3
4 Dummy	0	0	0	0

Table 8.18   The Complete Opportunity Cost Table

Barge \ Dock	A	B	C	D
1	2	5	0	3
2	0	1	3	0
3	4	0	2	3
4 Dummy	0	0	0	0

zero elements in Table 8.18; thus, an optimum assignment can be made. There are two optimum assignments; as shown below.

Barge	Dock	Unloading Time
1	C	3 hrs.
2	A or D	4
3	B	2
	Total hours	= 9 hrs.

Impossible (or Prohibited) Assignments

There are many instances in which certain employees cannot be assigned to certain jobs, certain ships cannot be unloaded at certain docks, and the like. The reasons for such impossible assignments may be the physical requirements of the task, special

Prohibited assignments

equipment or facility required at a certain work station, or the personal preference of an individual. As in the transportation problem with prohibited routes, we can assign large costs *(M)* to the impossible assignments and solve the problem by the usual assignment method. Or we can block out those impossible assignments in the table and proceed in the usual manner.

Multiple Optimum Solutions

Multiple optimum solutions

As we have observed previously, for a given problem there may be two or more ways to cross out all of the zero elements in the final opportunity cost table. This implies that there are more than the required number of independent zero elements. In such a case, there will be multiple optimum solutions with the same total cost (profit) of assignment. The decision maker has the option to exercise his or her judgment or preference and select one particular optimum solution for the problem.

Multiple Objectives

A problem with multiple objectives

It is possible that an assignment problem may involve a set of multiple conflicting objectives. For example, the team leader assignment problem for the Harristown Police Department may involve such multiple objectives as matching each captain's police work experience with each of the team area's major policing problems, accommodating each of the captain's or team members' preference for a particular assignment, and the like. There are many real-world location-allocation problems that are variations of the assignment problem with multiple objectives. Some examples of such problems may be a fire station location, a new school-site decision, a warehouse location decision, and a manpower allocation.

Zero-one goal programming approach

The zero-one goal programming approach has been applied to many assignment-related problems involving multiple objectives. If an employee is assigned to a certain task, the solution value for the variable is 1; otherwise, it would be zero. Those of you who are interested in this topic should consult Lee and Franz (see References).

THE BRANCH AND BOUND APPROACH

Branch and bound approach

The assignment problem can also be solved by the branch and bound approach of integer programming discussed in Chapter 5. The assignment problem has a finite number of solution possibilities. Thus, we can utilize the branch and bound procedure to partition the set of all feasible assignments into smaller, mutually exclusive subsets for analysis. The basic solution procedure of the branch and bound method for a minimization assignment problem can be summarized as follows:

Step 1 The set of all feasible solutions is branched into several subsets, starting with the first station (column). Thus, each subset is determined by assigning each object (row) to the first station.

Step 2 For each subset, the *lower bound* is determined. The lower bound is computed by summing the cost of the initial assignment in Step 1 and the minimum costs in each of the remaining unassigned columns. If there are *feasible* assignments, the minimum value among their lower bounds is determined as the *upper bound*.

Table 8.19   The Martha Weinstein Cosmetics Assignment Problem

Salesperson \ Territory	A	B	C	D
1	(8)	10	12	16
2	11	11	15	8
3	9	(6)	(5)	14
4	15	14	9	(7)

Step 3 Those subsets having lower bounds that exceed the current upper bound must be excluded from further analysis. A subset with the best lower bound among the remaining subsets is selected and branched further.

Step 4 A feasible solution where the objective function value is not greater than the lower bound for any subset is to be found. This is the optimum solution. If such a solution does not exist, return to Step 3.

To illustrate the branch and bound approach to the assignment problem, let us consider the Martha Weinstein Cosmetics problem discussed earlier. The problem is presented in Table 8.19. The objective of the problem is to assign each of the four salespersons to each of the four sales territories so that the total time required to contact potential new clients is minimized. The problem can be represented with a 4 × 4 matrix. Therefore, the total number of feasible solutions would be 4! = 24.

In applying the branch and bound procedure, we should determine a tight lower bound for all 24 feasible solutions. The best way to determine such a tight lower bound is by summing the minimum costs in each of the columns, regardless of the feasibility of each assignment. In Table 8.19, the minimum column costs are circled. Thus, the lower bound is 8 + 6 + 5 + 7 = 26.

A tight lower bound

We can assign any one of the four salespersons to Territory A. Hence, all feasible solutions are initially branched into four subsets. If we assign Salesperson 1 to Territory A, the total number of feasible solutions becomes 3! = 6. The lower bound for this subset can be determined by summing the circled values in Table 8.20. The lower bound for branch 1A (assigning Salesperson 1 to Territory A) is 26. This lower bound is not the total time of a feasible solution because Salesperson 3 is assigned twice, to Territory B and Territory C.

Table 8.20   The Lower Bound of Branch 1A

Territory Salesperson	A	B	C	D
1	(8)			
2		11	15	8
3		(6)	(5)	14
4		14	9	(7)

Lower bound = 8 + 6 + 5 + 7 = 26

In a similar manner, the lower bounds for the subsets 2A, 3A, and 4A can be determined. For example, if Salesperson 2 is assigned to Territory A, the lower bound would be 11 + 6 + 5 + 7 = 29, as shown in Table 8.21. The lower bounds of branches 3A and 4A can be determined similarly.

Table 8.21   The Lower Bound of Branch 2A

Territory Salesperson	A	B	C	D
1		10	12	16
2	(11)			
3		(6)	(5)	14
4		14	9	(7)

Lower bound = 11 + 6 + 5 + 7 = 29

Figure 8.2   The First-Stage Branching Operation

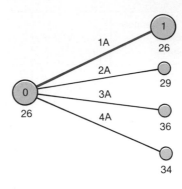

The lower bounds of the four subsets of solutions are presented below.

Subset	Lower Bound
1A	8 + 6 + 5 + 7 = 26 ← lower bound
2A	11 + 6 + 5 + 7 = 29
3A	9 + 10 + 9 + 7 = 36
4A	15 + 6 + 5 + 8 = 34

Determining the lower and upper bounds

The minimum value among the lower bounds of the four subsets is 26, the lower bound of subset 1A. This value, therefore, is the *lower bound* in the first-stage branching operation. The *upper bound* is represented by the minimum value among the lower bounds of the feasible solutions, if there are any at this stage. None of the solutions we have derived in the four subsets is feasible. Thus, there is no upper bound as yet.

The first-stage branching operation is presented in Figure 8.2. Subset 1A is selected for the second-stage branching operation because it has the current lower bound. Thus, we identify subset 1A by the circled node ①, as shown in Figure 8.2. Salesperson 1 has been assigned to Territory A. The next assignment we have to make is to appoint one of the three remaining salespersons to Territory B. Let us suppose that we are going to assign Salesperson 2 to Territory B. Then, the lower bound for this subset would be the sum of the assignment times of cells (1,A), (2,B), and the minimum elements in the remaining two columns, C and D, after deleting Rows 1 and 2. Therefore, the lower bound for subset 1A-2B is 8 + 11 + 5 + 7 = 31, as shown in Table 8.22. In a similar manner, we can calculate the lower bounds for the remaining two subsets.

Table 8.22   The Lower Bound of Branch 1A-2B

Territory Sales- person	A	B	C	D
1	⑧			
2		⑪		
3			⑤	14
4			9	⑦

Lower bound $= 8 + 11 + 5 + 7 = 31$

The lower bounds of the three branches from node 1 (1A) are presented below.

Subsets	Lower Bound
1A-2B	$8 + 11 + 5 + 7 = 31 \leftarrow$ upper bound
1A-3B	$8 + 6 + 9 + 7 = 30$
1A-4B	$8 + 14 + 5 + 8 = 35$

The minimum value among the lower bounds of the feasible assignments is identified as the upper bound. Subset 1A-2B is a feasible solution. Therefore, its lower bound, 31, computed above, is the upper bound. Subset 1A-4B should be eliminated from further consideration because it is not a feasible solution and its lower bound (35) is greater than the current upper bound (31). The second-stage branching operation is presented in Figure 8.3.

From Figure 8.3, it is obvious that subsets 3A, 4A, and 1A-4B can all be eliminated from further consideration because their lower bounds are greater than the current upper bound. Now, the lower bound is identified as 29, which is the lower bound of subset 2A. The next branching operation must take place at this node. Since we must come back to node 0 to examine subset 2A, this procedure is often referred to as *backtracking*.

In the 2A branch, we can calculate the lower bounds of the three subsets 2A-

The backtracking procedure

Figure 8.3   The Second-Stage Branching Operation

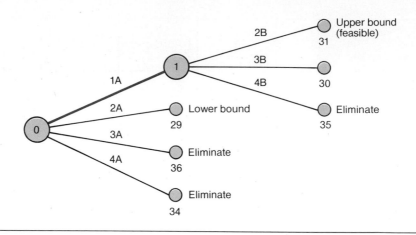

1B, 2A-3B, and 2A-4B. For example, the lower bound of subset 2A-1B can be calculated as shown in Table 8.23.

Table 8.23   The Lower Bound of Branch 2A-1B

Salesperson \ Territory	A	B	C	D
1		(10)		
2	(11)			
3			(5)	14
4			9	(7)

Lower bound = 11 + 10 + 5 + 7 = 33

The lower bounds of the three subsets are as follows:

Figure 8.4   The Third-Stage Branching Operation

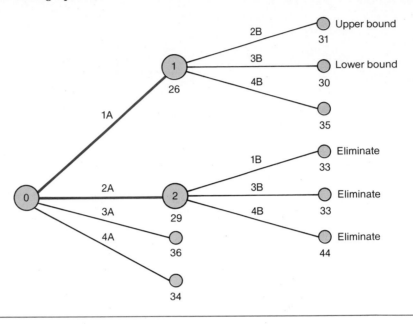

Subset	Lower Bound
2A-1B	11 + 10 + 5 + 7 = 33
2A-3B	11 + 6 + 9 + 7 = 33
2A-4B	11 + 14 + 5 + 14 = 44

None of the above three lower bounds is acceptable because they are all greater than the current upper bound. Thus, we must backtrack to subset 1A-3B, which has the new lower bound as shown in Figure 8.4.

In the 1A-3B branch, we can easily calculate the lower bounds of the two subsets as follows:

Subset	Lower Bound
1A-3B-2C	8 + 6 + 15 + 7 = 36
1A-3B-4C	8 + 6 + 9 + 8 = 31

The above two solutions are both feasible. The lower bound of subset 1A-3B-4C yields the total time, which is identical to the current upper bound. Thus, there are two optimum assignment schedules for this problem, which can be identified as follows:

Figure 8.5   The Complete Branch and Bound Solution Procedure

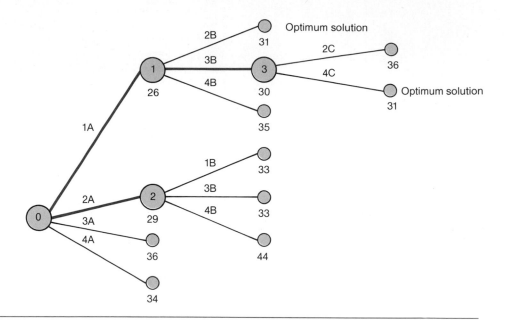

	Assignment 1			Assignment 2	
Sales-person	Territory	Time	Sales-person	Territory	Time
1	A	8 min.	1	A	8 min.
2	B	11	2	D	8
3	C	5	3	B	6
4	D	7	4	C	9
	Total time = 31 min.			Total time = 31 min.	

The above two solutions correspond to the optimum solutions we derived by the Hungarian method of assignment. The complete branch and bound analysis for the problem is shown in Figure 8.5. If the total time of the final two subsets (1A-3B-2C-4D and 1A-3B-4C-2D) both exceeded the upper bound (31), these solutions would have been eliminated from further consideration. In that case, a node with the new lower bound, if it is less than the current upper bound, would be selected for further branching. If no node meets this requirement, then the subset that yields the upper bound is the optimum solution.

The branch and bound procedure we have discussed thus far can also be applied to a maximization assignment problem. The approach is exactly the same as the one we applied to a minimization problem. The only differences are the calculation process for the lower and upper bounds and the branching procedure.

In a maximization, the lower bound is computed by summing the payoff of the

For a maximization problem

actual assignment and the maximum payoffs in each of the remaining unassigned columns. If there are feasible assignments, the maximum value among their lower bounds is determined as the upper bound. Then, only those subsets having lower bounds that exceed the current upper bound are selected for further analysis. A subset with the highest lower bound among the remaining subsets is selected and branched further. In continuing the branch and bound process, the optimum solution is found when the objective function value of a subset is not less than the lower bound for any subset.

SUMMARY

The assignment problem is a variation of the linear programming problem. As a matter of fact, the assignment problem is a special type of transportation problem in which there are equal numbers of sources and destinations and in which the supply of each source and the demand of each destination must equal exactly 1. The objective of the assignment problem is to determine the optimum allocation of resources to various tasks. In this chapter, we have discussed the two widely applied techniques of assignment: the Hungarian method and the branch and bound procedure.

References

Dwyer, P. S. "Solution to the Personnel Classification Problem with the Method of Optimal Regions." *Psychometrika*, 19 (1954), 11–26.

Flood, M. M. "On the Hitchcock Distribution Problem." *Pacific Journal of Mathematics*, 2 (1953), 369–386.

Kuhn, H. W. "The Hungarian Method for the Assignment Problem." *Naval Research Logistics Quarterly*, 2 (1955), 83–97.

Kwak, N. K. *Mathematical Programming with Business Applications*. New York: McGraw-Hill, 1973.

Lee, S. M. *Linear Optimization for Management*. New York: Petrocelli-Charter, 1976.

Lee, S. M. *Goal Programming Methods for Multiple Objective Integer Programs*. Atlanta: American Institute of Industrial Engineers, 1979.

Lee, S. M., and Franz, L. S. "Optimizing the Location-Allocation Problem with Multiple Objectives." *International Journal of Physical Distribution and Materials Management*, 9:6 (1979), 245–255.

Assignments

8.1 Why is the assignment problem a special variation of the transportation problem?

8.2 If we can formulate an assignment problem as a linear programming model, why do we need the assignment method?

8.3 Describe a problem with which you are familiar that can be solved by the assignment method.

8.4 How is a zero-one programming model different from a regular linear programming model?

8.5 Why do we refer to the general assignment method as the Hungarian method?

8.6 What is the logic behind the use of straight vertical and horizontal lines in the Hungarian method?

8.7 State the primary difference(s) between the Hungarian and the branch and bound methods?

8.8 In the branch and bound approach, how do we determine the lower and upper limits of a minimization assignment problem?

8.9 What is backtracking in the branch and bound procedure?

8.10 How can we handle an impossible or prohibited assignment when the Hungarian method is used?

8.11 Three secretaries are available to type three reports. Given below is the typing time (in hours) required for each secretary to type each report. Determine the optimum assignment by the Hungarian method.

		Report	
Secretary	A	B	C
Joyce	12	12	20
Jane	10	12	24
Cindy	15	15	24

8.12 Conformity Systems, Inc. has three employees: a typist, a clerk, and a stenographer. Each person will be assigned one of the following tasks: bookkeeping, filing, and report preparation. The manager wishes to assign workers to jobs so that the total cost is minimized. The costs for each possible job assignment are as follows:

		Job	
Employee	Bookkeeping	Filing	Report Preparation
Typist	$40	$50	$70
Clerk	50	40	60
Stenographer	60	50	50

Find the optimum assignment solution by the Hungarian method.

8.13 Given the following table for an assignment problem and using the Hungarian method, find the assignment requiring the least total time.

Job	Machine			
	A	B	C	D
1	10 min.	14 min.	15 min.	13 min.
2	12	13	15	12
3	8	12	12	11
4	13	16	18	16

8.14 An insurance firm has five salespersons that the firm wants to assign to five sales regions. Because of previously acquired contacts, the salespersons' efficiency in covering each region varies in terms of expected sales. The estimated sales per month (in thousands of dollars) by each salesperson for each of the regions are as follows:

Salesperson	Region				
	A	B	C	D	E
1	$15	$12	$14	$16	$18
2	14	10	15	10	14
3	16	13	10	19	16
4	18	17	12	17	14
5	12	16	10	14	13

Find the optimum assignment by the Hungarian method.

8.15 Given the following cost table for an assignment problem and using the branch and bound procedure, find the minimum-total-cost assignment of men to machines.

Man	Machine			
	A	B	C	D
1	$20	$30	$32	$36
2	28	26	32	20
3	22	18	16	36
4	26	26	22	18

8.16 The Checker Cab Company has a taxi waiting at each of four posts. Four customers have called and requested service. The distances, in miles, from the waiting taxis to the four customers are given below:

Cab Post	Customer			
	1	2	3	4
A	16	8	6	14
B	10	12	8	10
C	12	18	14	12
D	8	14	12	16

Using the branch and bound method and the Hungarian method, find the optimum assignment of taxis to customers that will minimize the total driving distance.

8.17 In a job shop operation, five jobs may be performed on any of four machines. The hours required for each job on each machine are presented in the following table:

Job	Machine 1	2	3	4
A	13	14	16	10
B	12	13	15	12
C	11	12	12	9
D	16	16	18	14
E	10	12	13	12

D–dummy

The plant foreman would like to assign the jobs so that the total time is minimized. Find the optimum solution by the Hungarian method.

8.18 Bay Laboratories, Inc. has five machines that need to be staffed by five operators. The time required to complete the given tasks by each operator with a given machine is shown below:

Operator	Machine A	B	C	D	E
1	8	10	10	15	2
2	14	21	17	10	2
3	14	18	22	25	3
4	16	19	20	24	2
5	8	11	11	10	2

a. Identify the optimum solution by the branch and bound method.
b. Find the optimum assignment solution by the Hungarian method.

8.19 The personnel director of a company facing severe financial difficulty must relocate four operations researchers from recently closed locations. Unfortunately, there are only three positions available. Salaries are the same throughout the company. Moving expenses will be used as the means of determining who goes where and who gets the opportunity to begin a new career. The estimated moving expenses are:

Operations Researcher	New Location Gary	Salt Lake	San Francisco
Allen	$5,000	$8,000	$4,000
Benson	7,000	3,000	5,000
Charles	2,000	1,000	6,000
David	4,000	3,000	1,000

Find the optimum assignment solution by the Hungarian method.

8.20 Given the following payoff table for an assignment problem and using the Hungarian method, find the maximum payoff assignment of employees to machines.

	Machine				
Employee	A	B	C	D	E
1	$12	$9	$8	$7	$12
2	17	15	11	12	6
3	14	10	14	16	8
4	5	4	6	5	5

8.21 A job shop has four machinists to be assigned to four machines. The hourly cost required to operate each machine by each machinist is:

	Machine			
Machinist	A	B	C	D
1	$12	$11	$8	$14
2	10	9	10	8
3	14	8	7	11
4	6	8	10	9

However, due to a lack of experience, Machinist 3 cannot operate Machine B.

    a. Formulate this problem as a general linear programming model.
    b. Find the optimum assignment of machinist to machine by the Hungarian method.
    c. Formulate an initial solution of the assignment problem by Vogel's approximation method.
    d. Go through one iteration by the MODI method based on the initial solution derived in part (c).

8.22 A sergeant must assign four soldiers to duties. Because these four soldiers have been especially recalcitrant, the First Sergeant decides to assign each soldier to the worst job possible. Each soldier rates the five duties by preference, with 5 being the most favorable rating. Since only one soldier can be assigned to each job, everyone's worst choice cannot be selected. But the assignment method can be used to obtain the worst set of assignments possible. Based on the ratings given below, find the worst assignment (from the viewpoint of the soldiers) by the Hungarian method.

	KP	Guard Duty	CQ	Driver	Club Guard
Fennegan	1	2	3	4	5
Hennigan	1	2	4	3	5
Lannigan	1	3	2	4	5
O'Toole	2	1	3	4	5

8.23 Brockwinkle's Transport of Poughkeepsie has five transport crews. Today they have four jobs scheduled. The estimated numbers of hours for each of the crews to accomplish the jobs are as follows:

Job No.	Crew				
	#12	#28	#37	#42	#58
#1292	9	6	5	4	2
#2862	7	6	3	2	won't
#3774	6	7	4	5	3
#4921	2	6	4	9	6

Crew #58 refuses to perform Job #2862, citing Clause 621.32A of its union contract.

    a. Find the assignment requiring the least total time by the Hungarian method.

    b. Are there multiple optimum solutions? If so, identify them.

    c. Solve this problem by the branch and bound method.

8.24 The Memphis Police Department has five hard-drug squads available for assignment to five drug cases. The Chief of Detectives wishes to assign the squads so that the total dollar value of the drugs confiscated from the cases is maximized. The estimated dollar value, in thousands of dollars, of the hard-drugs that can be confiscated by each squad in each case is as follows:

Squad	Case				
	1	2	3	4	5
A	14	7	3	7	27
B	20	7	12	6	30
C	10	3	4	5	21
D	8	12	7	12	21
E	13	25	24	26	8

Each squad has a different composition of personnel, expertise, equipment, and so on. Solve this maximization assignment by using the Hungarian method.

8.25 Matthews Insurance Company has been given four additional districts in recognition of its outstanding performance. Mr. Matthews has five agents with varying degrees of training and experience whom he can assign to handle this new business. He would like to assign only one agent to each district. Mr. Matthews has estimated the costs involved in contacting ten potential customers by each agent as follows:

Agent	District			
	1	2	3	4
A	$38	$32	$60	$36
B	34	44	48	50
C	40	38	52	60
D	38	58	42	46
E	35	39	45	48

Which agent should be assigned to which district in order to minimize total costs?

8.26 Trans-American Air Cargo Co. has five types of airplanes that it must assign to five different routes. Because of variations among the routes (distances, cargo characteristics, weather, airport facilities, etc.), the airplanes are not all equally adaptable to each route. The cost (in thousands of dollars) for each airplane over each route is as follows:

Airplane	Omaha-Chicago	Los Angeles-Denver	Detroit-Kansas City	New York-Reno	St. Louis-Phoenix
DC3	$10	$15	$17	$40	$45
DC7	8	12	20	38	43
B707	7	14	18	34	37
B727	6	13	12	30	32
B747	9	12	21	42	41

How should the airplanes be assigned in order to minimize the total costs?

8.27 A manufacturing firm has five employees and six machines. The firm is attempting to assign the employees to the machines in a manner that will minimize the total cost. A cost table showing the cost incurred by each employee on each machine is presented below:

Employee	Machine					
	A	B	C	D	E	F
1	$12	$7	$10	$14	$8	$10
2	10	14	13	20	9	11
3	5	3	6	9	7	10
4	9	11	7	16	9	10
5	10	6	14	8	10	12

However, due to union rules regarding departmental transfers, Employee 3 cannot be assigned to Machine E and Employee 4 cannot be assigned to Machine B.
 a. Solve this problem by indicating the optimum assignment and computing the total minimum cost.
 b. Formulate this problem as a general linear programming model.

8.28 Mr. John Sano is trying to decide where to locate three new machines that he has ordered for his shop. Some locations are more desirable than others for particular machines because of their proximity to work centers that would have heavy work flows to and from these machines. Mr. Sano has come up with the following table of estimated handling costs:

Machine	Location		
	A	B	C
1	$33	$15	$39
2	24	30	33
3	27	36	21

a. Which machines should be placed at which locations to minimize the handling costs? Solve this problem by the Hungarian method.

b. Solve this problem by the branch and bound method.

8.29 The Public Works Department of Saratoga Springs has seven snowplows. The Director wants to assign these plows to seven districts in the city to clean up the new snow in the shortest possible time. The amount of time (in minutes) required to clean up all major streets in each district by different snowplows is given in the following table. Solve the assignment problem.

Plow	Districts						
	A	B	C	D	E	F	G
1	44	52	27	41	60	22	35
2	58	47	65	33	42	39	51
3	43	36	50	41	53	32	25
4	49	55	34	46	40	28	32
5	42	49	57	63	45	36	43
6	34	42	35	46	31	18	27
7	58	64	43	59	72	50	48

8.30 The Overland Bus Company is trying to improve its municipal transit service in large cities. It is particularly interested in assigning one additional bus to each of four cities. The company has four buses of varying ages and conditions that have been removed from cross-country service because of the gas shortage problem. The company's Transportation Division has estimated that the operating profit per day for each bus in each city will be as follows:

Bus	Cities			
	Roanoke	Washington	Richmond	Norfolk
1	$150	$110	$130	$125
2	140	135	150	110
3	125	120	115	135
4	130	115	120	145

a. Which bus should be assigned to which city in order to maximize the total profits?

b. Are there alternate optimum solutions? If so, identify them.

DECISION THEORY

A famous philosopher once said, "Don't sacrifice today for an uncertain tomorrow." But we must and do sacrifice some of today precisely because tomorrows are uncertain. In this chapter we will study how probabilities can be used for decision making under the conditions of risk and uncertainty. We will study the concepts of expected value, payoff matrix, decision making criteria under uncertainty, and decision trees. Collectively, these concepts are often referred to as statistical decision theory.

Learning Objectives *From the study of this chapter, you will learn the following:*

1. *The four basic states of decision environment.*
2. *The use of probabilities for decision making under risk.*
3. *The value of perfect information.*
4. *Application of the expected value and expected loss criterion.*
5. *Simple inventory problem analysis by incremental analysis.*
6. *Decision making criteria under uncertainty.*
7. *Application of subjective probabilities for decision making.*
8. *Utility analysis as a decision making tool.*
9. *Decision tree analysis for decision making under risk.*
10. *The meaning of the following terms:*

Conditional payoffs	*Loss due to overstocking*
Expected payoffs	*Loss due to understocking*
Decision tables	*Incremental analysis*
Indifference probabilities	*Salvage value*
Expected loss	*Goodwill cost*
Perfect information	*Maximin*
Maximax	*Minimax*
Dominance test	*Coefficient of optimism*
Utility analysis	*Decision tree*
Bayes' theorem	

DECISION MAKING UNDER RISK

An amateur Confucian contends that Confucius once said, "Prediction is very difficult, especially when it is for the future." Life is interesting and challenging because we live in a very uncertain world. We can seldom predict or forecast future outcomes with certainty. For example, it is difficult to say what will be the inflation rate next year. Also, we don't know whether the All Star Baseball Game will be postponed next year because of a player strike.

The decision theory

People develop certain intuitive skills or a knack of making good decisions in probabilistic situations. For instance, a good investor seems to know just when to sell stocks and put the money in Treasury bills as the interest rate increases. When we are faced with a simple problem, even we can be pretty adept at making good decisions. However, if a complex or a very important decision problem is confronting us, we simply cannot rely on our intuitive judgment. Thus, decision theory is useful for making decisions under the conditions of risk and uncertainty.

States of decision environment

The type of scientific technique we use for decision making is not entirely based on the nature of the problem at hand. The decision environment also plays a major role. For example, an inventory problem for a country seed and fertilizer store and an inventory problem for Con-Agra would require different types of analyses. As we discussed briefly in Chapter 1, there are four basic states of decision environment: certainty, risk, uncertainty, and conflict. Probabilities are especially useful for decision making under the conditions of risk and uncertainty. Decision theory based on probabilities assists the decision maker in analyzing complex problems with numerous alternatives and consequences. The basic objective of decision theory is to provide the decision maker with concrete information concerning the relative likelihood of certain consequences. Such information is useful for identifying the best course of action.

The risk condition

The risk condition refers to the situation in which the probabilities of certain outcomes are known. For decision making under risk, we must identify the following components:

1. Alternative courses of action that are available and feasible.

2. Possible events that can occur and their probabilities.

3. Conditional payoff for a given course of action under a given possible event.

Alternative courses of action

Alternative Courses of Action Any decision problem must have alternative options. If a problem has only one course of action available, it is not a decision problem— we have no choice but to accept the option. In most real-world problems, however, we have a number of alternatives open to us. For example, in selecting a set of courses to take in a given semester, you have many (perhaps too many) options. You may not want to take Math 345 (Advanced Calculus) simultaneously with Computer Science 215 (Advanced FORTRAN) and Chemistry 306 (Inorganic Chemistry). So you choose not to take one of these three courses and to take either Drama 110, PE 101 (Tennis), or Fine Arts 120 (Music Appreciation). You have many alternative courses of action open to you.

In real-world situations, we simply cannot consider all possible courses of action. We must use our judgment in limiting the alternatives to those that are available and feasible, in terms of predetermined criteria. For example, in designing a new automobile engine, we may limit the possible fuel alternatives to gasoline, gasohol, liquefied gas, and diesel fuel. We exclude coal, solar energy, hydrogen, and other fuels because they are not economically feasible at present, though they may be technologically feasible. Selecting all of the available and feasible alternatives is an art in itself.

Possible Events and Probabilities The possible events are also referred to as the *states of nature*. An event may be a state of international situation, economy, weather condition, or a particular instructor in a given section of a course. An event is usually an uncontrollable condition that is the product of a complex interaction of external forces or it may simply be an act of God. The number of possible events for most decision problems under risk is usually finite and identifiable.

Events and probabilities

The possibilities or likelihood of each event occurring in the future represents the probability of that event. For example, one may ask, ''What is the probability that we will once again have a double-digit inflation rate next year?'' If the Chase Economic Forecasting model predicts it to be .25, then we may want to accept this figure as the probability. Regardless of the probability distribution among the possible events, the sum of all of the probabilities must be 1. In other words, only one event can occur in the future. Thus, we can write

$$p_1 + p_2 + \cdots + p_n = 1$$

where

$$p_j = \text{probability of event } j \text{ to occur}$$

Conditional Payoff The conditional payoff refers to the outcome associated with each of the alternative/event combinations. For example, if you take Chemistry 306 under Professor Leopold Lipscovitch, your expected grade might be D because that has been the average grade in his class. Typically, the conditional payoff is associated with a specific time period (e.g., a grade of D after a semester or 6 percent return after one year). The time period associated with the conditional payoff is often referred to as the *planning horizon* or *decision horizon*.

Conditional outcomes

Components of the decision problem under risk

The Typical Decision Problem Structure The above three basic components of the decision making problem under risk can be structured as a decision table. We can label the components as follows:

a_i = **alternative course *i* (independent controllable variables)**

e_j = **event *j* (independent uncontrollable variables)**

c_{ij} = **payoff for the alternative *i* and event *j* combination (dependent variables)**

It is not a simple task to determine the exact monetary payoff for each of the alternative/event combinations. Nevertheless, we believe that past records and work experience can be utilized to derive sufficiently accurate conditional payoffs for many decision problems under risk. The typical decision table is presented in Table 9.1. The events (column-wise) and course of action (row-wise) arrangements can be interchangeable depending on the structure of the problem under analysis.

The expected value

The dominant decision making criterion under the condition of risk is the *expected value*. The expected value for a decision alternative is the weighted average outcome (e.g., payoff or loss). Thus, the expected value is determined by the sum of the products of the conditional outcome of an alternative multiplied by the probability of each possible event. In applying the expected value criterion, we can use either the expected payoff or the expected loss criterion.

Table 9.1   The Decision Table Structure

Course of Action	Events and Probabilities					
	e_1 p_1	e_2 p_2	.	.	.	e_n p_n
a_1	c_{11}	c_{12}	.	.	.	c_{1n}
a_2	c_{21}	c_{22}	.	.	.	c_{2n}
.	.	.	.	.	.	.
.	.	.	.	.	.	.
.	.	.	.	.	.	.
a_m	c_{m1}	c_{m2}	.	.	.	c_{mn}

The Expected Payoff Criterion

The expected payoff

The *expected payoff (EP)* is a decision criterion that has the basic principle of maximizing the long-term economic payoff from the selection of a particular course of action. Let us consider the following casette.

CASETTE 9.1   ***FRIENDLY INVESTMENT CLUB***

The Friendly Investment Club (FIC) is an informal investment club composed of 50 junior managers from various local banks and stock brokerage firms. Each club member contributes $100 a month and the total monthly funds of $5,000 are invested in either stocks or bonds, but never in both. The actual selection of particular stocks or bonds (e.g., 100 shares of Baker International common stock) will be determined later.

The Club is attempting to determine whether the investment for September should be in stocks or in bonds. The payoff is primarily dependent on the economic condition in a given month. If the economic condition indicates an upswing (falling or stable interest rates, increasing productivity, etc.), investment in stocks tends to result in a greater payoff. On the other hand, if the economic condition is in the downswing, investment in bonds brings in a greater payoff. The investment alternatives, possible events (economic conditions), and conditional payoffs are presented in Table 9.2.

One difficult aspect of the investment problem is obtaining the probabilities of the events to occur in September. The Investment Research Committee evaluated the trends of a number of important economic indicators. The Committee's estimated probability of an economic upswing condition for September is 30 percent. Consequently, the probability of an economic downswing condition would be 70 percent.

The club decided to use the expected payoff (or expected monetary value) as the decision criterion. The expected payoff for an alternative course of action is the weighted average payoff, which is simply the sum of the products of the payoff of each event multiplied by the associated probability. Thus, the expected payoff of the two investment alternatives can be computed as follows:

$$EP(a_1) = (0.3 \times 1,000) + (0.7 \times 250) = \$475$$
$$EP(a_2) = (0.3 \times 600) + (0.7 \times 400) = \$460$$

Table 9.2 *Friendly Investment Club Problem*

	Events	
Investment Alternative	Economic Upswing	Economic Downswing
Stocks	$1,000	$250
Bonds	600	400

Indifference probabilities

In this computation, a_1 refers to Alternative 1—investment in stocks, and a_2 represents Alternative 2—investment in bonds. From the expected payoffs derived above, it is obvious that the investment plan in stocks is the better alternative because its expected payoff is $15 more than that for bonds.

Before making the final recommendation, the Investment Research Committee wanted to generate more information about the investment situation. The members of the committee were interested in finding the probabilities of the two alternatives that would result in exactly equal expected payoffs. Such probabilities are referred to as *indifference probabilities*. If the outcomes are identical, we will be indifferent toward the two investment alternatives.

If we denote p_1 as the probability of Event 1 (i.e., economic upswing) and p_2 as the probability of Event 2 (i.e., economic downswing), then $p_1 + p_2 = 1$. Thus, $p_2 = 1 - p_1$. Then, we can compute the expected payoffs of the two alternatives as follows:

$$EP(a_1) = 1,000 \, p_1 + 250 \, (1 - p_1) = 750p_1 + 250$$
$$EP(a_2) = 600 \, p_1 + 400 \, (1 - p_1) = 200p_1 + 400$$

The indifference condition requires $EP(a_1) = EP(a_2)$. Therefore, we can write

$$EP(a_1) = EP(a_2)$$
$$750p_1 + 250 = 200p_1 + 400$$
$$550p_1 = 150$$
$$p_1 = 0.2727$$

Since $p_1 = 0.2727$, we can easily compute $p_2 = 0.7273$. In other words, if the probability of an economic upswing is 0.2727, and consequently the probability of an economic downswing is 0.7273, we will be completely indifferent to whether the investments are to be in stocks or in bonds. The basic question we must ask is whether or not the probability of an economic upswing condition would be less than or greater than 0.2727. If $p_1 > 0.2727$, our choice will be stocks. On the other hand, if $p_1 < 0.2727$, investment in bonds will be our choice.

The meaning of the expected payoff

The expected payoff is an important decision criterion for decision making under risk. It should be pointed out, however, that the expected payoff is not exactly the eventual outcome of a decision. For example, $EP(a_1) = \$475$ does not mean that the payoff of investment in stocks would actually be $475. If we invest in stocks (a_1) and an economic upswing condition (e_1) occurs, the payoff will be $1,000. But if an economic downswing condition (e_2) occurs, a_1 will result in a payoff of $250. If the FIC makes the same monthly investment decisions over a long period of time, the average payoff for a_1 with the given probabilities (i.e., $p_1 = 0.3$ and $p_2 = 0.7$) for the events will be about the same as the expected value of $475.

If a decision problem is a repetitive type, the same problem will occur a great number of times. Since we attempt to maximize the long-term payoff, the expected payoff is a valid criterion for decision making under risk. The investment problem of FIC is precisely such a problem. Thus, the club decided to invest in stocks.

If a decision problem under risk is not repetitive but rather a "once in a lifetime" type problem, the expected payoff would be a less appropriate criterion to use. Also, *Only for repetitive* in certain problems under risk, we may not select a decision alternative if it has a *decisions* very large conditional loss, even if its expected payoff is much greater than that of the other alternatives.

The Expected Loss Criterion

The expected payoff criterion is appropriate for maximizing the long-term expected payoff. If we are interested in minimizing the long-term opportunity loss from the *The expected loss* selection of a particular course of action, the *expected loss* (or expected opportunity *criterion* loss or expected regret) criterion would be appropriate. The fundamental requirement for the two criteria remains the same—the decision problem must be a repetitive type over time. As a matter of fact, the solution is exactly the same whether we use the expected payoff or the expected loss criterion.

The concept of opportunity loss or opportunity cost was introduced in Chapter 7 (Vogel's approximation method of transportation) and in Chapter 8 (assignment method). The opportunity loss is simply the difference between the outcome of the best alternative and the outcome of a given alternative.

CASETTE 9.2   **THE STATE FAIR CONCESSION PROBLEM**

The State Fair will be once again in the fairgrounds during the last two weeks of August. The State A&M University is assigned the same exhibition hall to demonstrate the new advances in research, instruction, and public service at the university. Each college can have three booths and a concession stand. This year Sigma Alpha Epsilon is assigned the concession stand. One stipulation imposed by the university is that each concession stand can choose to sell only one product from among the following four choices: Coke, lemonade, coffee, and popcorn.

The officers of Sigma Alpha Epsilon are determined to do well this time around. Three years ago when the fraternity chose Coke, hoping to make a real "killing," it rained for 10 days and the total sales were only $149.30. The primary factor that affects the payoff is the weather condition. This year, the officers decided to minimize the expected loss rather than maximize the expected payoff. The past records indicate the relevant information shown in Table 9.3.

Table 9.3 Sigma Alpha Epsilon Concession Problem

	Events	
	Good Weather	Bad Weather
Alternatives	$p_1 = 0.6$	$p_2 = 0.4$
Coke (a_1)	$1,200	$150
Lemonade (a_2)	800	400
Coffee (a_3)	400	800
Popcorn (a_4)	500	500

The opportunity losses must be computed for each possible event, in this case the weather condition. If good weather prevails during the fair, the best course of action is selling Coke because it has the highest conditional payoff ($1,200). Thus, the opportunity loss for selling Coke under a good weather condition will be zero because it has the highest conditional payoff. The opportunity loss for the lemonade alternative will be $1,200 - 800 = 400$. Likewise, the opportunity loss for coffee is $1,200 - 400 = 800$ and for popcorn, $1,200 - 500 = 700$. If bad weather prevails, the best course of action will be to sell coffee. We can develop a conditional loss table, as shown in Table 9.4.

Table 9.4 Conditional Loss Table for the Sigma Alpha Epsilon Problem

	Events	
	Good Weather	Bad Weather
Alternatives	$p_1 = 0.6$	$p_1 = 0.4$
Coke (a_1)	$ 0	650
Lemonade (a_2)	400	400
Coffee (a_3)	800	0
Popcorn (a_4)	700	300

Now we can compute the expected loss *(EL)* for each alternative as follows:

$$EL(a_1) = 0(0.6) + 650(0.4) = 260$$
$$EL(a_2) = 400(0.6) + 400(0.4) = 400$$
$$EL(a_3) = 800(0.6) + 0(0.4) = 480$$
$$EL(a_4) = 700(0.6) + 300(0.4) = 540$$

From this computation, it is obvious that Coke is the best alternative because it has the minimum expected loss. Thus, Sigma Alpha Epsilon once again decided to sell Coke at the concession stand during the State Fair.

SIMPLE INVENTORY PROBLEMS UNDER RISK

A simple inventory problem

The expected value criterion we discussed in the previous section can be applied to a number of other types of decision problems under risk. In this section, we will expand the concept further and apply it to a relatively simple inventory problem under risk.

CASETTE 9.3   *NEW ENGLAND FISH MARKET*

Mr. Dan Brown owns and operates the New England Fish Market. This is the only fish market in town that sells fresh Maine lobsters. Lobsters are flown in from Boston once a week and they are kept in a salt-water tank for a period of one week. If the lobsters are not sold within a week, they are sold to a local restaurant at a loss. Determining the optimum number of lobsters to stock is a difficult task, especially because of a wide fluctuation in the demand for lobsters.

Mr. Brown purchases lobsters (an average of 1.5 pounds each) from a dealer in Boston at $5 each. The profit per lobster is $5, as the price charged is $10. At the end of each week the leftover lobsters are sold to a restaurant for $3 per lobster, a loss of $2 each. Mr. Brown has the sales records for the past 100 weeks, as shown in Table 9.5. Demand ranges from 1 to 7 lobsters per week. Based on the number of weeks in which the identical number of lobsters were sold, we can derive a probability distribution. For example, in 5 weeks out of the 100 weeks the demand for lobster was 1 lobster. Thus, the probability of demand for 1 lobster will be 5 ÷ 100 = 0.05.

Table 9.6 presents the possible weekly demand for lobsters and the probability distribution based on the past demand. This table represents the possible demand for lobsters if the past market situation remains constant. However, the future market situation may not be the same as the past records indicate. Thus, if drastic changes occur in the market situation (e.g., airline strikes, shortage of lobsters, etc.), we should not rely on the past records.

Conditional payoff and probabilities

The decision problem of Mr. Brown is to determine the optimum number of

---

Table 9.5   Past Demand for Lobsters

Weekly Sales	Number of Weeks
1	5
2	10
3	25
4	30
5	20
6	5
7	5
	100

Table 9.6 *Weekly Demand for Lobsters and Probability Distribution*

Weekly Demand	Probability
1	0.05
2	0.10
3	0.25
4	0.30
5	0.20
6	0.05
7	0.05
	1.00

lobsters to order weekly in order to maximize his profit. Clearly, if Mr. Brown orders more than what will be demanded, his profit will be reduced or he may actually have a loss because the unsold lobsters will be sold to a restaurant at a loss. On the other hand, if he orders an insufficient quantity of lobsters to meet the demand, his profit will be smaller because of lost sales due to shortage and associated goodwill costs.

Conditional Profits

Before we can calculate the *expected profit,* we must construct a table of conditional profits. In the New England Fish Market problem, the conditional profit of stocking a certain number of lobsters will be based on two conditions: (1) demand *(D)* is equal to or greater than the quantity stocked *(Q),* and (2) demand *(D)* is less than the quantity stocked *(Q).*

Sell all we have

Condition 1: $D \geq Q$ When the demand is equal to or greater than the quantity stocked, the market can sell all of the lobsters it has in stock. Since the cost of a lobster is $5 and it is sold for $10, the profit will be $5 per lobster. Therefore, the total profit is $5Q. For example, if Mr. Brown stocks 3 lobsters and the demand is for 3 or more lobsters, the total profit will be $5Q = $5 \times 3 = $15. The conditional profit *(CP)* when $D \geq Q$ will be

$$CP = \$5Q$$

Don't sell all we have

Condition 2: $D < Q$ When the demand for lobsters is less than the quantity stocked, Mr. Brown will have some unsold lobsters. The total cost will be $5Q, as Mr. Brown's purchasing cost is $5 per lobster. The total revenue from the lobsters sold will be $10D, since the selling price is $10 per lobster. The number of unsold lobsters is simply $Q - D$. Mr. Brown sells the leftover lobsters to a restaurant for $3 each. Thus, the revenue generated from the unsold lobsters will be $3(Q - D)$.

The conditional profit when $D < Q$ can be computed as follows:

Table 9.7   Conditional Profit Table for Lobsters Stocked and Demanded

Demand (D)	Quantity Stocked (Q)						
	1	2	3	4	5	6	7
1	$5	$3	$1	$−1	$−3	$−5	$−7
2	5	10	8	6	4	2	0
3	5	10	15	13	11	9	7
4	5	10	15	20	18	16	14
5	5	10	15	20	25	23	21
6	5	10	15	20	25	30	28
7	5	10	15	20	25	30	35

$$\text{Conditional profit} = \text{Total revenue} - \text{Total cost}$$
$$= \$10D + \$3\,(Q - D) - \$5Q$$
$$= \$10D + \$3Q - \$3D - \$5Q$$
$$CP = \$7D - \$2Q$$

For example, if Mr. Brown stocks 3 lobsters but has a demand for only 2 lobsters, the conditional profit will be ($7 × 2) − ($2 × 3) = $14 − $6 = $8. We can check this answer as follows:

Revenue from sale of 2 lobsters = $10 × 2 = $20
Revenue from 1 leftover lobster
   sold to a restaurant   = $ 3
                      Total revenue = $23

Total cost of purchasing 3 lobsters = $15
                Conditional profit = $ 8

Now we can prepare a conditional profit table, as shown in Table 9.7, by using the two conditional profit functions developed above. It should be noted here that the conditional profits presented in Table 9.7 represent the actual (explicit) monetary outcomes for specific quantities stocked under various demand conditions. In other words, conditional profits include losses due to overstocking, but they do not include the opportunity (implicit) costs due to understocking. In Table 9.7 we also placed the alternatives (quantity stocked) column-wise and the events (demand) row-wise for convenience.

Expected Profits

Computing expected profits

In order to compute the expected profit for stocking a certain number of lobsters, we must use the expected value *(EV)* concept we discussed earlier. First, we must obtain information about the possible demands and their probabilities, as shown in Table 9.6. Then, after we combine these probabilities and the conditional profits, as shown in Table 9.7, we can compute the expected profits.

For example, for the alternative of stocking 1 lobster, the expected profit can be computed as follows:

Stocking 1 Lobster ($Q = 1$):

Demand	Probability	Conditional Profit	Expected Profit
1	0.05	$5	$0.25
2	0.10	5	0.50
3	0.25	5	1.25
4	0.30	5	1.50
5	0.20	5	1.00
6	0.05	5	0.25
7	0.05	5	0.25
	1.00		Total = $5.00

Since the conditional profit is $5 for each possible demand, we can also compute the expected profit of stocking 1 lobster as $5 $\times$ 1.0 = $5. The same approach can be used to compute the expected profit of stocking 2 lobsters.

Stocking 2 Lobsters ($Q = 2$):

Demand	Probability	Conditional Profit	Expected Profit
1	0.05	$3	$0.15
2	0.10	10	1.00
3	0.25	10	2.50
4	0.30	10	3.00
5	0.20	10	2.00
6	0.05	10	0.50
7	0.05	10	0.50
	1.00		Total = $9.65

The conditional profit is $10 for 95 percent of the time and it is $3 for only 5 percent of the time. Thus, we can easily compute the expected profit by determining ($10 $\times$ 0.95) + ($3 $\times$ 0.05) = $9.65. Table 9.8 presents the expected profits of the various stock decisions.

Table 9.8 Expected Profit for Various Quantities Stocked

Demand	Probability	Quantity Stocked (Q)						
		1	2	3	4	5	6	7
1	0.05	$5	$3	$1	$-1	$-3	$-5	$-7
2	0.10	5	10	8	6	4	2	0
3	0.25	5	10	15	13	11	9	7
4	0.30	5	10	15	20	18	16	14
5	0.20	5	10	15	20	25	23	21
6	0.05	5	10	15	20	25	30	28
7	0.05	5	10	15	20	25	30	35
Expected profit		$5.00	$9.65	$13.60	$15.80	$15.90	$14.60	$12.95

The maximum expected profit is $15.90 when Mr. Brown stocks 5 lobsters. Thus, the optimum quantity to stock is 5 lobsters. If the New England Fish Market faces the lobster inventory problem every week over a long period of time, stocking 5 lobsters per week will provide the highest average weekly profit under the given demand and its probability distribution, unit cost, and unit profit conditions.

Expected Profit under Certainty

If the New England Fish Market could obtain perfect information about the exact demand for lobsters for the next week, Mr. Brown could eliminate the condition of risk. In fact, the decision problem then becomes one under the condition of certainty. Demand may still fluctuate from 1 to 7 lobsters per week with the given probability distribution. However, if we can obtain perfect information concerning demand in advance, Mr. Brown can easily determine the optimum quantity to stock.

Referring to Table 9.8, it is obvious that the conditional profit will be maximum for each Q (i.e., column) if the quantity stocked is exactly equal to the quantity demanded. In other words, when perfect information concerning demand is available, the only thing Mr. Brown has to do is order exactly the same quantity as demanded, or $Q = D$. Then, the conditional profits for the various demand-stock combinations will be as shown in Table 9.9.

Table 9.9   Conditional Profit Table with Perfect Information

Demand	Quantity Stocked 1	2	3	4	5	6	7
1	$5						
2		$10					
3			$15				
4				$20			
5					$25		
6						$30	
7							$35

Since $Q = D$ when certainty prevails, there will be no losses resulting from under- or overstocking. The expected profit under certainty can be derived in the same manner, as follows:

Demand	Probability	Conditional Profit	Expected Profit
1	0.05	$5	$0.25
2	0.10	10	1.00
3	0.25	15	3.75
4	0.30	20	6.00
5	0.20	25	5.00
6	0.05	30	1.50
7	0.05	35	1.75
	1.00		Total = $19.25

The expected profit under certainty (with perfect information) is $19.25. This value is the maximum profit possible under the condition of certainty. Without perfect information concerning demand, the best thing Mr. Brown could do was identify the inventory level that maximized the expected profit. The optimum quantity to stock was found to be 5 lobsters with the expected profit of $15.90. How much better off is he with perfect information than he was without it? We can easily determine that the value of perfect information is the difference between the expected profit of the optimum decision without perfect information ($15.90) and that with the perfect information ($19.25). Therefore, the value of perfect information will be $3.35, as this is the amount by which the profit can be increased with the additional information.

The value of perfect information

Conditional Loss

Conditional loss

The inventory problem of the New England Fish Market can also be solved by analyzing the expected loss. First, we shall determine the conditional loss associated with the combination of quantity stocked and quantity demanded. The conditional losses are based on two types of losses: actual (accounting) loss and opportunity (implicit) loss. The actual loss results from overstocking, and the opportunity loss from understocking.

Loss Due to Overstocking ($Q > D$) In our example, any lobster left over after one week must be sold to a restaurant at a loss of $2 (cost of $5 and selling price of $3). For example, if we stock 6 lobsters and sell only 5, the sixth lobster must be sold to a restaurant at a loss of $2. Consequently, the amount of loss due to overstocking would be $2 ($Q - D$).

Loss because of overstocking

Loss Due to Understocking ($Q < D$) If we stock less than the quantity demanded, the loss would be the lost profit. For example, if Mr. Brown stocked 4 lobsters and the demand was for 5, the demand for the fifth lobster could not be satisfied. If he had stocked the fifth lobster, he could have made a $5 profit from it. Therefore, the opportunity loss due to understocking would be $5 ($D - Q$).

Loss because of understocking

From our discussion of these two types of losses, it should be apparent that there will be no loss whatsoever if we stock exactly the quantity demanded. In other words, $Q = D$ would be the optimum stock quantity. We already know this, of course, because we discussed it when we considered the value of perfect information. Now we can construct the conditional loss table, as shown in Table 9.10.

Table 9.10   Conditional Loss Table

Demand	\multicolumn{7}{c}{Quantity Stocked}
	1	2	3	4	5	6	7
1	$0	$2	$4	$6	$8	$10	$12
2	5	0	2	4	6	8	10
3	10	5	0	2	4	6	8
4	15	10	5	0	2	4	6
5	20	15	10	5	0	2	4
6	25	20	15	10	5	0	2
7	30	35	20	15	10	5	0

Expected Loss

The expected loss

Once we have developed the conditional loss table, the next step is to compute the expected loss for stocking a certain quantity. The possible weekly demand and the probability distribution were shown in Table 9.6.

The expected loss can be found for a given quantity stocked by computing the weighted average loss, that is, the conditional loss multiplied by its probability. For example, the expected loss of stocking 1 lobster will be:

Demand	Probability	Conditional Loss	Expected Loss
1	0.05	$0	$0.00
2	0.10	5	0.50
3	0.25	10	2.50
4	0.30	15	4.50
5	0.20	20	4.00
6	0.05	25	1.25
7	0.05	30	1.50
	1.00		$14.25

Table 9.11 presents the expected loss resulting from various stocking decisions. The expected loss is the minimum ($3.35) if we stock 5 lobsters. This optimum stock level corresponds to the one we derived in our discussion of the expected profit. It does not matter whether we utilize the expected profit or the expected loss criterion; the same optimum stock level can be determined by either means.

The optimum stock quantity

The optimum quantity is found when the expected profit is the maximum, or when the change in the expected profit becomes negative as the stock level is gradually increased. When we look at the expected loss criterion, the optimum quantity is found when the expected loss is the minimum, or when the change in the expected loss becomes positive. Although the signs are opposite, because profit is the opposite of loss, the absolute incremental changes for both of the expected values are identical. For example, if we increase the stock level from 1 lobster to 2 lobsters, the expected profit increases by $4.65. This increase is possible if there is a corresponding de-

Table 9.11   Expected Loss Table for Various Stocking Decisions

Demand	Probability	Quantity Stocked						
		1	2	3	4	5	6	7
1	0.05	$0	$2	$4	$6	$8	$10	$12
2	0.10	5	0	2	4	6	8	10
3	0.25	10	5	0	2	4	6	8
4	0.30	15	10	5	0	2	4	6
5	0.20	20	15	10	5	0	2	4
6	0.05	25	20	15	10	5	0	2
7	0.05	30	25	20	15	10	5	0
Expected loss		$14.25	$9.60	$5.65	$3.45	$3.35	$4.65	$6.30

Table 9.12   Summary Table of Expected Profits and Expected Losses

Quantity Stocked (Q)	Expected Profit	Change in Expected Profit	Expected Loss	Change in Expected Loss
1	$5.00		$14.25	
		$+4.65		$-4.65
2	9.65		9.60	
		+3.95		-3.95
3	13.60		5.65	
		+2.20		-2.20
4	15.80		3.45	
		+0.10		-0.10
5	**15.90**		**3.35**	
		-1.30		+1.30
6	14.60		4.65	
		-1.65		-1.65
7	12.95		6.30	

crease of $4.65 in the expected loss. Table 9.12 presents the summary of the expected profits and the expected losses of various stock levels and their changes. The optimum stock quantity is 5 lobsters, as shown by the red-number row in Table 9.12.

Value of Perfect Information

We discussed briefly the value of perfect information in the section on expected profit under certainty. The real value of perfect information is simply the difference between the expected profit ($15.90) of the optimum quantity to stock under risk and the expected profit ($19.25) under certainty, that is, $3.35. If we use the expected loss criterion, we find the minimum expected loss to be the same as the value of perfect information.

If the demand for the next week is known in advance, no matter how many lobsters it may be, we can reduce the expected loss to zero by simply stocking exactly the quantity that will be demanded. For example, if perfect information suggests that the demand will be 5 lobsters, we will stock 5 and have no conditional loss. Therefore, the expected loss will be zero when perfect information is available, and the value of perfect information will be exactly equal to the expected loss of the optimum stock level under risk. The expected loss of the optimum stock level (5 lobsters in Table 9.12) is $3.35. Hence, this is the value of perfect information.

Although it is highly desirable to obtain perfect information about demand, in reality it is extremely difficult to obtain such information. The main purpose of determining the value of perfect information is to place an upper bound on the value of additional information.

INCREMENTAL ANALYSIS

A more convenient short cut for the inventory problem under risk is incremental analysis. Incremental analysis, first suggested by Robert Schlaifer, evaluates the inventory decision one unit at a time. For example, we analyze the difference between the expected loss of stocking the first unit and the expected loss of not stocking the first unit. If stocking the first unit has less expected loss than not stocking it, then we

Table 9.13   *Incremental Analysis for the First Lobster*

Event	Probability	Course of Action			
		Stock 1st Lobster		Don't Stock 1st Lobster	
		Cond. Loss	Exp. Loss	Cond. Loss	Exp. Loss
Demand for 1st lobster	1.0	$0	$0	$5	$5
No demand for 1st lobster	0.0	2	0	0	0
	1.0		$0		$5

Incremental analysis

proceed with the same incremental analysis for the second unit, and so on. If stocking the *i*th unit has a greater expected loss than not stocking the unit, the optimum stock quantity is found and the analysis terminated.

Stocking Decision for the First Unit

Let us go back to the familiar New England Fish Market problem. Table 9.13 presents the computation of the expected losses for the two possible courses of action concerning the first lobster: stock the first lobster or do not stock it. Regardless of which course of action Mr. Brown takes, there will be only two possible events that can occur: there may be demand for the first lobster or there may not be demand for it.

Analyzing one unit at a time

Referring to Table 9.11 for the probability distribution of demand, we can easily determine that there always will be demand for the first lobster. Since the demand ranges from 1 to 7 lobsters per week, we can always sell the first lobster if we stock it. The probability of demand for the first lobster is, therefore, 1.0. Conversely, the probability of no demand for the first lobster is zero.

If we stock the first lobster and there is demand for it, the conditional loss will be zero. However, if we stock the first lobster and there is no demand for it, the conditional loss will be $2, as we discussed earlier. The expected loss for stocking the first lobster will be

$$EL(Q=1) = (1.0 \times \$0) + (0 \times \$2) = \$0$$

On the other hand, if we do not stock the first lobster but there is demand, the conditional loss will be $5, the lost profit due to understocking. If we do not stock the first lobster and there is no demand, the conditional loss will, of course, be zero. The expected loss of not stocking the first lobster, therefore, will be

$$EL(Q=0) = (1.0 \times \$5) + (0 \times \$0) = \$5$$

Stocking Decision for the Second Unit

Since the expected loss of not stocking the first lobster ($5) is greater than that of stocking it ($0), we should stock the first lobster in order to avoid the loss. We can proceed to analyze the inventory decision concerning the second lobster in the same

Table 9.14 Incremental Analysis for the Second Lobster

Event	Probability	Course of Action			
		Stock 2nd Lobster		Don't Stock 2nd Lobster	
		Cond. Loss	Exp. Loss	Cond. Loss	Exp. Loss
Demand for 2nd lobster	0.95	$0	$0.00	$5	$4.74
No demand for 2nd lobster	0.05	2	0.10	0	0.00
	1.00		$0.10		$4.75

manner, as shown in Table 9.14. When we compare Tables 9.13 and 9.14, it should be apparent that the conditional losses remain the same for each incremental analysis. For example, if we stock the second lobster and there is demand for it, the conditional loss will be zero. But if we stock the second lobster and there is no demand, the loss will be $2 due to overstocking. Now, if we do not stock the second lobster but there is demand for it, the conditional loss will be $5 due to understocking. However, if we do not stock the second lobster and there is no demand for it, there will be no loss.

The only differences we find between Tables 9.13 and 9.14 are the probabilities of demand and of no demand for the second lobster. As long as there is demand for two or more lobsters, the second lobster will be sold. Therefore, the probability of demand for the second lobster will be 0.95. The only case in which there will be no demand for the second lobster is when only one lobster is demanded. Consequently, the probability of no demand for the second lobster will be 0.05. The expected loss of stocking the second lobster ($0.10) is still less than that of not stocking the second lobster ($4.75). Thus, we will stock the second lobster.

Stocking Decision for the *i*th Unit

Stocking decision for a certain unit

As we progress with the incremental analysis, the expected loss of stocking a certain lobster will gradually increase as the probability of demand for a greater number of lobsters decreases. Consequently, the expected loss of not stocking a certain lobster will gradually decrease as the probability of no demand for the lobster increases. Then, the optimum stock level will be found at the point where the expected loss of stocking that lobster is still less than the expected loss of not stocking that unit but where stocking one more unit will result in a greater loss. If the expected loss of stocking a certain lobster is exactly equal to that of not stocking it, we should be indifferent. In other words, we can either stock or not stock that particular lobster.

We can analyze the problem by formulating a stock decision for the generalized case (i.e., stocking the *i*th lobster), as shown in Table 9.15. The probability (p) that there will be demand for the *i*th lobster is the same as the probability that demand will be equal to or greater than *i* lobsters. Accordingly, there will be no demand for the *i*th lobster if demand is less than *i* lobsters. Of course, the sum of the two probabilities is 1.

Table 9.15   Incremental Analysis for Stocking the ith Lobster

		Course of Action			
		Stock *i*th Lobster		Don't Stock *i*th Lobster	
Event	Probability	Cond. Loss	Exp. Loss	Cond. Loss	Exp. Loss
Demand for *i*th lobster	$p(D \geq i)$	\$0	\$0	$\$L_u$	$L_u \cdot p(D \geq i)$
No Demand for *i*th lobster	$p(D < i)$	L_o	$L_o \cdot p(D < i)$	0	0
	1.0		$L_u \cdot p(D < i)$		$L_u \cdot p(D \geq i)$

L_o: Loss due to overstocking.
L_u: Loss due to understocking.
$p(D \geq i)$: Probability that demand will be at least *i*.
$p(D < i)$: Probability that demand will be less than *i*.

If we stock the *i*th lobster and there is demand for it, the conditional loss will be zero. But if we stock the *i*th lobster and there is no demand, the loss will be due to overstocking (L_o). The expected loss of stocking the *i*th lobster will be

$$EL(Q > i) = L_o \cdot p(D < i)$$

If we do not stock the *i*th lobster but there is demand for it, the conditional loss will be due to understocking (L_u). On the other hand, if we do not stock the *i*th lobster and there is no demand for it, there will be no loss. The expected loss of not stocking the *i*th lobster can be computed as

$$EL(Q < i) = L_u \cdot p(D \geq i)$$

The condition required for us to stock the *i*th lobster is that the expected loss of stocking it should be less than or equal to that of not stocking it. In other words, we can express the relationship as

$$L_o \cdot (D < i) \leq L_u \cdot (D \geq i)$$

We can rearrange the above relationship. The sum of the probabilities of the two possible events is equal to 1: $p(D < i) + p(D \geq i) = 1.0$.
Since $p(D \geq i) = 1 - p(D < i)$, we can write

$$L_o \cdot p(D < i) \leq L_u \cdot p(D \geq i)$$
$$L_o \cdot p(D < i) \leq L_u \cdot [1 - p(D < i)]$$
$$L_o \cdot p(D < i) \leq L_u - L_u \cdot p(D < i)$$

Adding $L_u \cdot p(D < i)$ to both sides, we have

$$L_o \cdot p(D < i) + L_u \cdot p(D < i) \leq L_u - L_u \cdot p(D < i) + L_u \cdot p(D < i)$$
$$L_o \cdot p(D < i) + L_u \cdot p(D < i) \leq L_u$$

Factoring out $p(D < i)$, we obtain

$$p(D < i) (L_o + L_u) \leq L_u$$

Table 9.16 Cumulative Probability p(D < i)

Demand (i)	Probability	Cumulative Probability $p(D < i)$
1	0.05	0.00
2	0.10	0.05
3	0.25	0.15
4	0.30	0.40
5	**0.20**	**0.70**
6	0.05	0.90
7	0.05	0.95

Dividing both sides by $(L_o + L_u)$, we derive

$$\frac{p(D < i)\,(L_o + L_u)}{(L_o + L_u)} \leq \frac{L_u}{(L_o + L_u)}$$

$$p(D < i) \leq \frac{L_u}{L_o + L_u}$$

Using the cumulative probabilities

The above relationship simply indicates that in order to stock the ith lobster, the cumulative probability of demand being less than i lobsters should be less than or equal to the ratio of loss due to understocking (L_u) over the sum of losses due to overstocking and understocking $(L_o + L_u)$. The probability $P(D < i)$ is simply a cumulative probability function, as shown in Table 9.16. For example, the probability that demand is less than 1 lobster will be zero because demand is always at least 1 lobster. The probability that demand is less than 2 lobsters is the same as the probability that demand is for only 1 lobster, that is, 0.05. The probability that demand is less then 3 lobsters is the same as the probability that demand is 1 or 2 lobsters. There is 0.05 probability that demand will be 1 lobster and 0.10 probability that demand will be 2 lobsters. Therefore, the sum of these two probabilities gives the cumulative probability 0.15 that demand is less than 3 lobsters.

In our New England Fish Market example, the loss due to overstocking, L_o, is $2, and the loss due to understocking, L_u, is $5. Therefore, we can compute:

$$p(D < i) \leq \frac{L_u}{L_o + L_u}$$

$$p(D < i) \leq \frac{5}{2 + 5}$$

$$p(D < i) \leq 0.7143$$

In other words, Mr. Brown should continue to stock lobsters as long as the cumulative probability $p(D < i)$ is less than or equal to 0.7143. Referring to Table 9.16, we find that the optimum stock level should be 5 lobsters, as shown by the red-number row. This answer corresponds to the one we derived when we used the expected profit and expected loss as decision criteria.

Now then, to solve the simple inventory problem under risk, the only things we

Key parameters

must know in order to determine the optimum stock level are: loss due to understocking (L_u), loss due to overstocking (L_o), and the cumulative probability function $p(D < i)$. By using the incremental analysis, we can avoid the cumbersome calculative work required by the expected profit and expected loss approaches.

Analysis of Salvage Value

Considering the salvage value

In the New England Fish Market problem, we assumed that any lobsters left over at the end of a week are sold to a restaurant for $3 per lobster. The $3 we receive from a restaurant is nothing but a salvage value. If leftover lobsters are thrown out at a total loss of $5 (cost) per lobster, then there would be no salvage value. Thus, we can reformulate the net loss due to overstocking as follows:

$$\text{Loss due to overstocking} = \text{preliminary loss due to overstocking} - \text{salvage value}$$

$$L_o = PL_o - S$$

If the salvage value of the leftover lobster is only $1, rather than $3 as assumed previously, the optimum stock quantity will be

$$p(D < i) \le \frac{L_u}{L_o + L_u}$$

$$p(D < i) \le \frac{L_u}{(PL_o - S) + L_u}$$

Since $L_u = \$5$, $PL_o = \$5$, and $S = \$1$,

$$p(D < i) \le \frac{5}{(5 - 1) + 5}$$

$$p(D < i) \le 0.5556$$

Referring to the cumulative probability distribution as shown below, we can easily determine the optimum stock level of 4 lobsters.

*i*th Lobster	$p(D < i)$
1	0.00
2	0.05
3	0.15
4	**0.40**
5	0.70
6	0.90
7	0.95

Since loss due to overstocking is $2 greater than the previous figure $4 vs. $2), the optimum stock level has been decreased by one lobster.

Computing the range of salvage value

Now we can determine what kind of salvage value is required to justify stocking a certain number of lobsters. For example, we can determine the range of salvage value required to stock 5 lobsters. From the incremental analysis we know that in order to stock 5 lobsters, $L_u \div (L_o + L_u)$ should be between 0.7 and 0.9, as shown above in the cumulative probability, $p(D < i)$.

The minimum salvage value required for stocking 5 lobsters can be determined by equating the $L_u \div (L_o + L_u)$ ratio to 0.7:

$$\frac{L_u}{L_o + L_u} = 0.7$$

$$\frac{L_u}{(PL_o - S) + L_u} = 0.7$$

$$\frac{5}{(5 - S) + 5} = 0.7$$

$$\frac{5}{10 - S} = 0.7$$

Multiplying both sides by $(10 - S)$, we obtain

$$5 = 0.7(10 - S)$$
$$5 = 7 - 0.7S$$
$$0.7S = 2$$
$$S = \$2.86$$

Similarly, the maximum salvage value required to justify stocking 5 lobsters can be computed as follows:

$$\frac{L_u}{(PL_o - S) + L_u} = 0.9$$

$$\frac{5}{(5 - S) + 5} = 0.9$$

$$\frac{5}{10 - S} = 0.9$$

$$5 = 0.9(10 - S)$$
$$0.9S = 4$$
$$S = \$4.44$$

To justify stocking 5 lobsters, then, the salvage value must be between \$2.86 and \$4.44. In order to stock a large number of lobsters in relation to the demand distribution, the salvage value must be relatively high. If the salvage value is higher than \$4.44, which is almost as much as the cost of purchasing a lobster, we can stock 6 lobsters.

Analysis of Goodwill Cost

Considering the goodwill cost

In the analysis thus far, we have assumed that the loss due to understocking is simply the amount of lost profit. In reality, however, such an assumption is rarely justified. Often, the unsatisfied or unserved customer may cause considerable amount of goodwill cost to the firm by simply not returning to the store or by broadcasting his or her bad experience to other current or potential customers. For example, suppose that there is a customer who purchases an average of \$50 worth of seafood per month from the New England Fish Market. Let us assume that her demand for lobsters was not satisfied because of understocking. Hence, she decided not to come back to the market for a whole month. The lost sales amount to \$50, and possibly the lost profit to the market may be as much as \$10.

It is extremely difficult to measure the actual goodwill cost. Nevertheless, in reality goodwill cost exists. Goodwill cost affects only the loss due to understocking because it occurs only when there is unsatisfied demand. Then, the total loss due to understocking, L_u, should include the preliminary loss due to understocking without the consideration of goodwill cost and goodwill cost per lobster:

Loss due to understocking = preliminary loss due to understocking
+ goodwill cost

$$L_u = PL_u + G$$

Now, let us suppose that the demand for lobsters and the probability distribution remain the same as presented earlier. Also, the following parameters are given:

$$PL_u = \$5$$
$$G = \$2$$
$$PL_o = \$5$$
$$S = \$3$$

Then, by employing the incremental analysis, we obtain

$$p(D < i) \leq \frac{L_u}{L_o + L_u}$$

$$p(D < i) \leq \frac{(PL_u + G)}{(PL_o - S) + (PL_u + G)}$$

$$p(D < i) \leq \frac{5 + 2}{(5 - 3) + (5 + 2)}$$

$$p(D < i) \leq \frac{7}{2 + 7}$$

$$p(D < i) \leq 0.7778$$

Referring to the cumulative probability distribution $p(D < i)$ in Table 9.16, we can easily determine that the optimum stock level is 5 lobsters.

By utilizing the approach shown in the salvage value section, we can also determine the range of goodwill cost that will justify stocking a certain number of lobsters. For example, by using the above information, let us determine the goodwill cost range required for stocking 6 lobsters. In order to stock 6 lobsters, the ratio of $(PL_u + G) \div [(PL_o - S) + (PL_u + G)]$ should be between 0.9 and 0.95, as we can observe in the $p(D < i)$ table.

Computing the range of goodwill cost

First, we can equate the ratio to 0.9 to determine the lower limit of the goodwill cost:

$$\frac{PL_u + G}{(PL_o - S) + (PL_u + G)} = 0.9$$

Since $PL_u = \$5$, $PL_o = \$5$, and $S = \$3$,

$$\frac{5 + G}{7 + G} = 0.9$$

$$5 + G = 0.9(7 + G)$$

$$5 + G = 6.30 + 0.9G$$

$$0.1G = 1.30$$

$$G = \$13.00$$

In order to find the upper limit of the range, we can equate the ratio to 0.95:

$$\frac{5 + G}{(5 - 3) + (5 + G)} = 0.95$$

$$\frac{5 + G}{7 + G} = 0.95$$

$$5 + G = 0.95(7 + G)$$

$$0.05G = 1.65$$

$$G = \$33.00$$

The above calculations indicate that the goodwill cost per understocked lobster should have a range between \$13.00 to \$33.00 in order for Mr. Brown to stock 6 lobsters. The above analysis clearly points out that in order to stock a relatively large number of lobsters, the per-unit goodwill cost should be quite high. Even when the exact amount of goodwill cost is not known, the analysis of goodwill cost provides management with a cost range that often contributes to a better inventory decision.

DECISION MAKING UNDER UNCERTAINTY

Decision making in an environment where the probabilities of certain events occurring are not known constitutes decision making under uncertainty. Decision making under uncertainty involves the following elements:

1. Alternative courses of action.

2. Possible events (states of nature).

3. Conditional payoffs for the action/event combinations.

4. Unknown probabilities of the events.

The uncertainty condition

Decision making under uncertainty is not a desirable or even a pleasant situation. Yet, this is the most prevalent decision environment we face in reality. We can recall many dramatic real-world experiences—the 1973 oil embargo, the Mount St. Helens eruption, and the Iranian crisis of 1980, for example. We often face uncertainties when completely new situations occur, such as a group of new employees, a new production process, a new inventory control system, a new market, or a new product line. For decision making under uncertainty, we can use one of several decision making criteria to generate more information for making the optimum decision. Let us consider the following casette as a means of studying several decision criteria under uncertainty.

CASETTE 9.4   *SAKURA MOTORS CORPORATION (SMC), USA*

Sakura Motors Corporation is a Japanese automotive manufacturing company. The company recently signed a contract to build a new production plant in the state of Kentucky. The plant will be a completely modern production facility with industrial robots, an interchangeable production setup, repetitive manufacturing systems, and a total quality-control system.

The company estimates that the new plant will cost approximately $100 million and that it will provide 800 new jobs in the community. Although the management of SMC is excited about this new venture, it could not decide on the best product line for the plant. The company plans to manufacture only one product in the Kentucky plant.

SMC can produce one of three products: the Sakura 1200X motorcycle, the Sakura jet ski, or the Sakura all-terrain three-wheeler. The company management believes that the conditional payoff of each alternative product line will be based on the American people's perception of the political relationship between the United States and Japan. There are three possible events: a favorable, normal, or strained relationship between the two countries. The conditional-payoff matrix for the problem is presented in Table 9.17.

Table 9.17   Conditional-Payoff Matrix for the Sakura Motors Problem

Product Line	U.S.-Japan Political Relationship		
	Favorable	Normal	Strained
	(Payoffs in Millions of Dollars)		
Motorcycle	$25	$18	$−12
Jet ski	20	16	2
Three-wheeler	10	10	10

If SMC produces the motorcycle, the conditional payoff will be $25 million if the political relationship is favorable, $18 million under a normal relationship, and −$12 million under a strained relationship. If SMC produces the jet ski, the conditional payoff will be $20 million, $16 million, and $2 million under each of the three respective relationships. On the other hand, if SMC produces the all-terrain three-wheeler, the conditional payoff is estimated to be $10 million regardless of the political situation between the two countries.

Decision Making with Partial Probabilities

If there is available a certain partial probability about the future political relationship between the United States and Japan, we may be able to exercise our educated judgment in decision making. For example, let us suppose that the Brookings Institute predicts that the probability of a normal relationship during the next year is 0.4.

Using the partial probabilities

With the available partial probability, we can at least compute the indifference probabilities for the three alternative products. The payoff of $10 million for the three-wheeler is a certainty. Therefore, we can compute the probabilities required of the favorable relationship and the strained relationship for SMC to be indifferent between the motorcycle and the jet ski alternatives. If we denote p as the probability of the favorable relationship, then $(0.6 - p)$ will be the probability of the strained relationship. The sum of all three probabilities of events will be 1.

$$0.4 + p + (0.6 - p) = 1.0$$

In order for us to be indifferent between the motorcycle and the three-wheeler alternatives, the two expected values must be exactly equal. Thus,

$$
\begin{aligned}
\textit{Motorcycle:} \quad EV &= 25p + 18(0.4) - 12(0.6 - p) \\
&= 25p + 7.2 - 7.2 + 12p \\
&= 37p
\end{aligned}
$$

$$
\begin{aligned}
\textit{Three-wheeler:} \quad EV &= 10 \\
EV \text{ (motorcycle)} &= EV \text{ (three-wheeler)} \\
37p &= 10 \\
p &= 0.2703
\end{aligned}
$$

If the probability of the favorable relationship is 0.2703, and thus the probability of the strained relationship is 0.3297 (i.e., $0.6 - 0.2703 = 0.3297$), we will be completely indifferent between the motorcycle and the three-wheeler alternatives. If the probability of the favorable condition is greater than 0.2703, we will, of course, prefer the motorcycle alternative.

Now we can proceed to compute the indifference probabilities between the jet ski and the three-wheeler alternatives in a similar manner:

$$
\begin{aligned}
\textit{Jet ski: } EV &= 20p + 16(0.4) + 2(0.6 - p) \\
&= 20p + 6.4 + 1.2 - 2p \\
&= 18p + 7.6
\end{aligned}
$$

$$
\begin{aligned}
\textit{Three-wheeler: } EV &= 10 \\
EV \text{ (jet ski)} &= EV \text{ (three-wheeler)} \\
18p + 7.6 &= 10 \\
p &= 0.1333
\end{aligned}
$$

We should be indifferent between the jet ski and the three-wheeler alternatives if the probability of the favorable relationship is 0.1333. Consequently, the required probability of the strained relationship is 0.4667.

We can also compute the indifference probabilities between the motorcycle and the jet ski alternatives as follows:

$$
\begin{aligned}
EV \text{ (motorcycle)} &= 25p + 18(0.4) - 12(0.6 - p) \\
EV \text{ (jet ski)} &= 20p + 16(0.4) + 2(0.6 - p) \\
EV \text{ (motorcycle)} &= EV \text{ (jet ski)} \\
25p + 7.2 - 7.2 + 12p &= 20p + 6.4 + 1.2 - 2p \\
37p &= 18p + 7.6 \\
p &= 0.4
\end{aligned}
$$

The required probabilities of the favorable relationship and the strained relationship are 0.4 and 0.2 respectively, in order for SMC to be indifferent between the motorcycle and the jet ski alternatives.

Figure 9.1   Expected Payoffs and the Probability of the Favorable Relationship

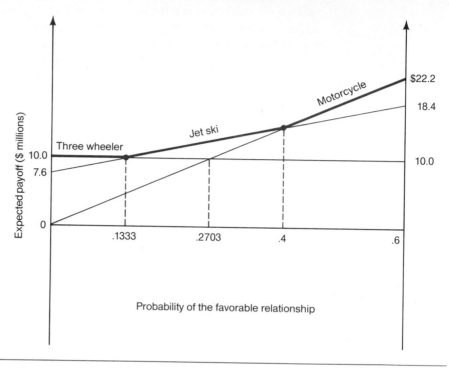

There is at least one certain payoff in this problem. It is the $10 million from the three-wheeler alternative. By analyzing the indifference probabilities, we can at least pinpoint the critical probabilities for the product line decision. In order to get the expected return of $10 million from the motorcycle, the favorable relationship must have a probability of 0.2703. On the other hand, we can derive the same $10 million expected payoff from the jet ski if the probability of the favorable relationship is only 0.1333. This implies that if the probability of the favorable relationship is relatively small, the choice will be between the jet ski and the three-wheeler. The indifference probability of the favorable relationship between the motorcycle and the jet ski is 0.4. Now we can construct the expected payoffs with the various probabilities of the favorable relationship, as shown in Figure 9.1.

This illustration presents two critical probabilities. First, if the probability of the favorable relationship is 0.1333 or less, the most attractive product line is the three-wheeler. If the probability is greater than 0.1333 but less than 0.4, the best alternative is the jet ski. If the probability of the favorable relationship is greater than 0.4, the motorcycle will be the best product line.

The Equal Probabilities (Laplace) Criterion

The Laplace criterion

The case of partial probabilities for the events is a rare situation. In most decision problems under uncertainty, even partial probabilities do not exist. In such situations, we may apply one of several decision making criteria under uncertainty.

Since the probabilities of future states of nature are not known, one approach we can take is to assign equal probabilities to all possible events. This approach is often referred to as the *Laplace* criterion. In our SMC problem, we should assign the identical 1/3 probability to the favorable, normal, and strained relationships. Then, the expected payoff becomes an appropriate criterion to use for decision making. For our SMC problem (see Table 9.17), the expected payoffs for the three product line alternatives can be computed as follows:

$$EP \text{ (motorcycle)} = \tfrac{1}{3}(25) + \tfrac{1}{3}(18) + \tfrac{1}{3}(-12) = \$10,333,333$$
$$EP \text{ (jet ski)} = \tfrac{1}{3}(20) + \tfrac{1}{3}(16) + \tfrac{1}{3}(2) = \$12,666,667 \leftarrow \text{optimum}$$
$$EP \text{ (three-wheeler)} = \tfrac{1}{3}(10) + \tfrac{1}{3}(10) + \tfrac{1}{3}(10) = \$10,000,000$$

Based on the Laplace criterion, the jet ski alternative has the highest expected payoff amount of \$12,666,667.

The Maximin (Wald) Criterion

The maximin criterion

The *maximin* criterion, also referred to as the *Wald* criterion (after Abraham Wald, who first suggested this criterion), is based on a completely pessimistic outlook (i.e., risk-avoiding behavior) for the future outcomes. Accordingly, we should expect the worst outcome (similar to *Murphy's Law*—whatever can possibly go wrong will) for each of the alternatives. Therefore, the minimum conditional payoffs for the alternatives are compared and the alternative that yields the maximum among the minimum payoffs should be selected. In the SMC problem, the minimum payoffs are as follows:

Alternative	Minimum Payoff
Motorcycle	\$ −12
Jet ski	2
Three-wheeler	10 ← optimum

Based on the above comparison, it is obvious that the optimum choice under the maximin criterion will be the three-wheeler. This alternative has the maximum-minimum payoff of \$10 million. One major weakness of this criterion is that it utilizes only partial information (i.e., analysis of the minimum payoffs). Thus, this approach can be a totally unrealistic way to analyze a decision making problem under uncertainty.

The Maximax Criterion

The maximax criterion

Since we have a very pessimistic outlook in the maximin criterion, we also ought to have a very optimistic outlook (i.e., risk-taking behavior). The *maximax* criterion is precisely such a criterion. It is based on a very aggressive, optimistic, perhaps even a desperate outlook about the future outcomes. The maximax criterion suggests that we should select the alternative that has the maximum among the maximum payoffs. The maximum payoffs for the three alternatives are as follows:

Alternative	Maximum Payoff
Motorcycle	\$25 ← optimum
Jet ski	20
Three-wheeler	10

The best alternative for SMC, according to the maximax criterion, is the motorcycle. This alternative has the highest maximum conditional payoff of $25 million. As is the case in the maximin criterion, this criterion does not utilize all of the available information. This weakness makes the maximax criterion an unrealistic way to analyze a real-world problem.

The Dominance Criterion

The dominance criterion

A somewhat similar approach to the maximax criterion is the *dominance* criterion. This approach is useful for decision making under uncertainty to the extent that it can reduce the number of viable alternatives. However, it does not always yield a unique optimum alternative course of action as the other criteria do.

An alternative is said to be dominated when there is another alternative that yields a higher payoff (or a more favorable outcome) regardless of the state of nature that may occur. We then gradually eliminate all of those alternatives that have been dominated by other alternatives. If there is only one alternative remaining after the elimination process, there will be an optimum course of action. But if the dominance test procedure yields a number of superior alternatives that cannot be eliminated any further, we must rely on another criterion in making the final choice.

For example, let us examine the following conditional payoff table:

	Conditional Payoffs under Events		
Alternatives	e_1	e_2	e_3
A*	$4,000	$3,000	$2,000
B	−6,000	2,000	1,500
C*	2,000	2,500	3,500
D	1,500	2,500	3,000
E*	2,000	4,000	2,500

When we compare Alternatives A and B, it is clear that A is superior to B under every feasible event in terms of conditional payoffs. Thus, Alternative B is dominated by A. When we compare Alternatives C and D, we find that C dominates D. However, when we compare Alternatives A, C, and E, none of these can be dominated. The undominated alternatives, indicated by the asterisks (*), must be analyzed by using another approach. In practice, the decision maker uses the dominance principle quite frequently, either consciously or unconsciously. Nevertheless, as we indicated earlier, this approach does not always yield the optimum course of action.

The Hurwicz Criterion

The Hurwicz criterion

The *Hurwicz* criterion, suggested by Leonid Hurwicz, is somewhat of a compromise between the maximin and maximax criteria. The decision maker in reality is not completely pessimistic as the maximin criterion suggests. On the other hand, the decision maker is not completely optimistic as suggested by the maximax criterion. Rather, the decision maker usually has some degree of pessimism and some degree of optimism simultaneously.

Hurwicz suggested the *coefficient of optimism* (α) as a measure of the decision maker's degree of optimism. The coefficient of optimism ranges from 0 to 1, just like a probability distribution. If $\alpha = 0$, the decision maker's coefficient of optimism is completely zero; that is, he or she is totally pessimistic. On the other hand, if $\alpha = 1$, the decision maker is completely optimistic. Thus, the coefficient of pessimism is $1 - \alpha = 0$.

Using the coefficient of optimism

According to the Hurwicz criterion, the weighted payoff for each alternative is obtained in the following manner:

Weighted payoff = α (maximum payoff) + $(1 - \alpha)$ (minimum payoff)

The best alternative is the one that has the maximum weighted payoff.

In the SMC problem, we can identify the following maximum and minimum payoffs for each alternative:

Alternative	Maximum Payoff	Minimum Payoff
Motorcycle	$25	$-12
Jet ski	20	2
Three-wheeler	10	10

Let us suppose that the decision maker's coefficient of optimism is $\alpha = 0.5$. Therefore, the coefficient of pessimism is $(1 - \alpha) = 0.5$. Now, we can compute the weighted payoffs *(WP)* as follows:

WP (motorcycle)   = 0.5(25) + 0.5(-12) = $ 6.5 million
WP (jet ski)   = 0.5(20) + 0.5(2)   = $11.0 million   ← optimum
WP (three-wheeler) = 0.5(10) + 0.5(10)   = $10.0 million

The jet ski alternative is the best choice as it has the highest weighted payoff of $11.0 million.

Let us suppose that the decision maker is completely optimistic ($\alpha = 1$). Then, he or she will select the motorcycle alternative because when $\alpha = 1$ the Hurwicz criterion is exactly the same as the maximax criterion:

WP (motorcycle)   = 1(25) + 0(-12) = $25 million   ← optimum
WP (jet ski)   = 1(20) + 0(2)   = $20 million
WP (three-wheeler) = 1(10) + 0(10)   = $10 million

Conversely, if $\alpha = 0$, the approach becomes the maximin criterion. Thus, the weighted payoffs will be:

WP (motorcycle)   = 0(25) + 1(-12) = $-12 million
WP (jet ski)   = 0(20) + 1(2)   = $ 2 million
WP (three-wheeler) = 0(10) + 1(10)   = $ 10 million   ← optimum

Thus, the optimum alternative will be the three-wheeler.

It is quite possible in reality that the decision maker cannot specify the exact α. In such a case, we can determine several critical α's and ask the decision maker whether his or her α is greater than these α's. Asking a series of questions, we can identify the best course of action.

Figure 9.2 presents the Hurwicz criterion analysis for the SMC problem. On the left side of the graph, where $\alpha = 0$, we plot the minimum payoffs, and on the right side of the graph, where $\alpha = 1$, we plot the maximum payoffs for the alternatives.

Figure 9.2   The Hurwicz Criterion Analysis

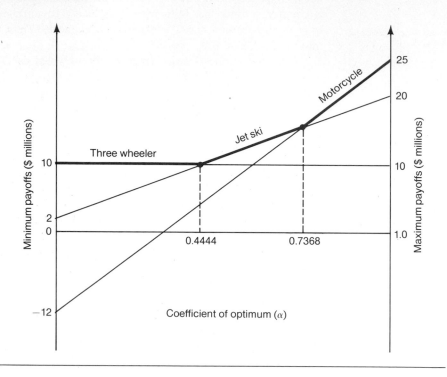

Now, the minimum and maximum payoffs of each alternative are connected by a straight line.

Determining critical α's

Since there are only three straight lines, we can easily determine their intersecting points and solve for the coefficient of optimism α. For example, at the intersecting point of the three-wheeler and the jet ski lines, we will be perfectly indifferent between the two alternatives because their weighted payoffs are identical. If we express the payoff as y and the coefficient of optimism α as x, then we can derive the function of the three lines as follows:

$$\text{Motorcycle:} \quad y = -12 + 37x$$
$$\text{Jet ski:} \quad y = 2 + 18x$$
$$\text{Three-wheeler:} \quad y = 10$$

In order to find α at the intersecting point of the three-wheeler and the jet ski lines, we can equate the two expressions as follows:

$$2 + 18x = 10$$
$$18x = 8$$
$$x = 0.4444$$

We can do the same for the jet ski and the motorcycle alternatives:

$$2 + 18x = -12 + 37x$$
$$-19x = -14$$
$$x = 0.7368$$

In Figure 9.2 we can clearly see that our decision choice varies as follows:

Optimum Decision	Coefficient of Optimism
Three-wheeler	$\alpha \leq 0.4444$
Jet ski	$0.4444 \leq \alpha \leq 0.7368$
Motorcycle	$\alpha \geq 0.7368$

Not universally applicable

The Hurwicz criterion is a good compromise between the maximin and maximax criteria. This criterion also incorporates the decision maker's personal judgment about the future outcome in the form of the coefficient of optimism. However, although this criterion is conceptually attractive, it is not universally applicable to all decision problems under uncertainty. For example, if two decision alternatives have the identical mimimun and maximum conditional payoffs, regardless of what kind of intermediate payoffs they have, under the Hurwicz criterion we would be indifferent between the two.

The Minimax (Regret) Criterion

The minimax criterion

The *minimax* criterion, which is also referred to as the *regret* criterion, is based on the concept of opportunity loss. The basic idea of this criterion, as proposed by L. J. Savage, is that the decision maker will experience an opportunity loss (or regret) when a state of nature occurs and the chosen alternative results in a payoff that is less than the maximum possible payoff for that state of nature.

The amount of opportunity loss or regret is the difference between the maximum conditional payoff and other payoffs under a given state of nature. Once the opportunity loss table is developed, we attempt to be conservative by utilizing the minimax principle—minimize the maximum opportunity loss.

In the SMC problem (see Table 9.17), we can construct the opportunity loss table as shown in Table 9.18. If we select the three-wheeler and the favorable relationship occurs, the payoff will be $10 million. However, had we selected the motorcycle alternative, the payoff would have been the maximum payoff of $25 million. Thus, the difference of $15 million represents the decision maker's opportunity loss for selecting the three-wheeler. If the jet ski alternative is chosen, the amount of opportunity loss will be $5 million. Since the motorcycle alternative has the maximum conditional payoff (i.e., $25 million), the opportunity loss for this alternative will be zero.

Table 9.18   The Opportunity Loss Table for the SMC Problem

Product Line	U.S.-Japan Political Relationship		
	Favorable	Normal	Strained
	(Opportunity Loss in Millions of Dollars)		
Motorcycle	$0	$0	$22
Jet ski	5	2	8
Three-wheeler	15	8	0

In Table 9.18 the maximum opportunity loss for each alternative is identified. Since we attempt to minimize the maximum opportunity loss, the jet ski alternative will be our choice, as shown below.

Alternative	Maximum Regret	
Motorcycle	$22	
Jet ski	8	← optimum
Three-wheeler	15	

Summary of Decision Making Criteria

In this section we have discussed several of the best-known decision making criteria under the condition of uncertainty. Since the uncertainty condition represents the most prevalent decision environment, an understanding of the various decision making criteria is important. As we have seen, each criterion emphasizes a certain principle or assumption. Thus, the decision maker has to determine which criterion is most appropriate for the problem under consideration. We can summarize the principle or assumption for each criterion as follows:

Decision Criterion	Principal Assumption
Laplace	Equal probabilities among the states of nature—maximize the expected value.
Maximin	Pessimistic view—maximize the minimum conditional payoff.
Maximax	Optimistic view—maximize the maximum conditional payoff.
Hurwicz	The coefficients of optimism and pessimism—maximize the weighted payoff.
Minimax	Conservative view—minimize the maximum opportunity loss.

For the casette problem of Sakura Motors Corporation, the optimum decision alternatives selected on the basis of different decision criteria can be summarized as follows:

Decision Criterion	Optimum Alternative
Laplace	Jet ski
Maximin	Three-wheeler
Maximax	Motorcycle
Hurwicz ($\alpha = 0.5$)	Jet ski
Minimax	Jet ski

Subjective Probabilities

Subjective probabilities

Another important concept about decision making under uncertainty is *subjective probability*. The traditional probability theory is based on the mathematical foundation of the *law of large numbers*. This traditional concept is often referred to as *mathematical* or *objective probability*. Subjective probability, in contrast, is based on one's degree of belief concerning the possible outcomes of a decision. Thus, it is possible that one's subjective probability may be quite different from the objective probability, if it is known. This certainly makes sense to us, as different decision makers usually do not have the same expectations concerning future outcomes. We have discussed several casettes in which we used subjective probabilities.

Many experiments and much empirical research clearly suggest that decision making under uncertainty is influenced by the decision maker's personal belief about the likelihood of future outcomes occurring. These studies support and reinforce the concept of subjective probability. The individual decision maker appears to be capable of assessing the value and probability of certain outcomes in the unique decision environment. Accepting this proposition, we believe the study of subjective probability will provide new insights about decision making in real-world situations.

Bayes' Decision Rule

Bayes' theorem

Another important area of study related to subjective probability is the *Bayes' decision rule* or *Bayes' theorem*. This decision rule was pioneered by Reverend Thomas Bayes, an eighteenth-century English Presbyterian minister and mathematician.

Prior or posterior probabilities

The Bayes decision rule is an orderly and consistent procedure of revising the probabilities of events (states of nature) based on additional information, experiments, or personal judgment. The basic principle of this rule is that the accuracy of event probabilities often can be improved by the utilization of additional information. The existing current probabilities are referred to as *prior probabilities,* whereas the revised or altered probabilities are referred to as *posterior probabilities*.

Let us discuss the Bayes decision rule by considering the following example.

EXAMPLE 9.1   *CENTENNIAL PRECISION WORKS, INC.*

Centennial Precision Works, Inc. is a manufacturer of precision chemical instruments. The company is very concerned about defective parts produced by its new plant in Kansas City. The quality control department has determined that the defective parts produced by the Kansas City plant were due to either human or mechanical error. The breakdown of the causes of the defective parts is as follows: human error, 60 percent; mechanical error, 40 percent.

The quality control chart indicates that 80 percent of the defective parts caused by mechanical problems have been detected at the inspection station. On the other hand, only 50 percent of the defective parts caused by human errors have been detected. In order to reduce the chance that any defective part would pass the inspection station without being detected, the quality control manager decided to take one sample part and inspect it. Thus, the manager asked a machine operator to produce a sample part, and it was found to be defective upon inspection. The manager would like to know the probability that this particular defective part was caused by a machine error.

The probabilities described in this problem can be defined as follows:

$p\ (DH)$ = probability of a defective part produced because of human error
$p\ (DM)$ = probability of a defective part produced because of machine error
$p\ (D|DH)$ = conditional probability that a defective part is detected by an inspector, given that the part was defective because of human error

Table 9.19   Posterior Probabilities of Defective Parts

Cause	Prior Probability	Conditional Probability	Posterior Probability
Human error	$P(DH) = 0.6$	$P(D\mid DH) = 0.5$	$P(DH\mid D) = 0.48$
Mechanical error	$P(DM) = \underline{0.4}$	$P(D\mid DM) = 0.8$	$P(DM\mid D) = \underline{0.52}$
	1.0		1.00

$p\ (D\mid DM)$ = conditional probability that a defective part is detected by an inspector, given that the part was defective because of mechanical error

From the information given, we can determine the following:

$$p(DH) = 0.6 \qquad p(D\mid DH) = 0.5$$
$$p(DM) = 0.4 \qquad p(D\mid DM) = 0.8$$

The conditional probability

The posterior probability we are interested in obtaining is the conditional probability that the defective part has been caused by a mechanical error, given that the sample part is detected as defective by an inspector. This conditional probability can be described as $p(DM\mid D)$. According to the Bayes decision rule, we can compute the posterior probability as follows:

$$p(DM\mid D) = \frac{p(D\mid DM)p(DM)}{p(D\mid DM)p(DM) + p(D\mid DH)p(DH)}$$

$$= \frac{(0.8)(0.4)}{(0.8)(0.4) + (0.5)(0.6)}$$

$$= 0.52$$

The only information the quality control manager had previously was that 40 percent of the defective parts were due to mechanical error. After a sample part was produced and found to be defective by an inspector, the manager now knows that there is a 0.52 probability that the part is defective because of mechanical error. Thus, the sampling provides additional information that allows the manager to revise the probability estimate as to whether or not the defective part is due to mechanical error. The improved, more accurate estimate will certainly enhance the manager's decision making capability concerning ways to improve the quality control effort.

A defective part detected at the inspection station is caused either by mechanical error or by human error. Therefore, the probability of selecting a defective part that was caused by mechanical error and detected by an inspector, $p(DM\mid D)$, and the probability of selecting a defective part that was caused by human error, $p(DH\mid D)$, are mutually exclusive. Furthermore, the sum of the two probabilities will be 1. Thus, we can write

$$p(DM\mid D) + p(DH\mid D) = 1.0$$

Therefore,

$$p(DH\mid D) = 1.0 - p(DM\mid D) = 1.0 - 0.52 = 0.48$$

Now we can determine the posterior probabilities concerning defective parts detected at the inspection station, as shown in Table 9.19. Such a table will be very useful to the decision maker.

Utility Analysis

Utility theory

We discussed briefly the use of utilities for multiple criteria decision making in Chapter 6. Although utility theory has been studied extensively in economics and theoretical management science/operations research, it has been severely criticized by practicing managers and pragmatic management scientists for its lack of real-world relevance and applicability. However, theoretical properties of utility theory are very neat indeed.

The meaning of utility

The word *utility* means the power to satisfy one's desires. In general, the concept of utility refers to a measure of satisfaction from the consumption of a good. Thus, it is natural that an individual's utility of a certain good differs from that of others.

Utility analysis has been suggested for decision making under uncertainty. One important problem we face in applying the minimax criterion is that the amount of opportunity loss is expressed in absolute monetary units (i.e., dollars). Since the relative value of money decreases as the amount of money increases (the diminishing

Diminishing marginal utility

marginal utility of money), utility analysis can be applied to measure and express the opportunity loss in relative values through utility. In this way the opportunity loss can represent the real loss perceived by the decision maker.

Let us examine the decision problem described in Table 9.20. The opportunity cost table for this problem is developed in Table 9.21. According to the minimax criterion, we should be completely indifferent between alternatives a_1 and a_2, since their maximum opportunity losses are identical. Are we really indifferent between the two alternatives? We should say not! Is the difference of $500,000 between the conditional payoffs of a_1 and a_2 under e_1 worth exactly the same as the difference of $500,000 we see under e_3 between a_1 and a_2? Under e_1, Alternative a_2 returns $1,000,000 and a_1 returns $1,500,000. Receiving $500,000 more on $1,000,000 would be very nice, of course. Under e_3, a_2 returns $250,000 and a_1 has a conditional

Using utility values

Table 9.20 An Alternative Decision Problem with Uncertainty

Alternative	State of Nature		
	e_1	e_2	e_3
a_1	$1,500,000	$500,000	$-250,000
a_2	1,000,000	500,000	250,000

Table 9.21 The Opportunity Cost for the Problem in Table 9.20

Alternative	State of Nature		
	e_1	e_2	e_3
a_1	$0	$0	$500,000
a_2	500,000	0	0

Figure 9.3   Utility Function for Monetary Payoffs

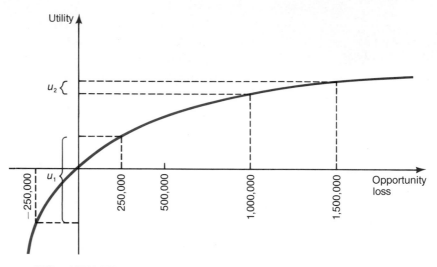

u_1 = Utility of $500,000 between −$250,000 and $250,000

u_2 = Utility of $500,000 between $1,000,000 and $1,500,000

payoff of −$250,000. The difference is still $500,000. However, this difference may mean a survival or a bankruptcy of the firm. Certainly, under e_3 we will prefer a_2 over a_1.

Let us suppose that a decision maker has the utility function of money shown in Figure 9.3. The utility of $500,000 between −$250,000 and $250,000 is expressed by U_1. The utility of $500,000 between $1,000,000 and $1,500,000 is expressed by U_2. It is obvious that U_1 is about 6 times greater than U_2. Based on the analysis of marginal opportunity cost, it is clear that a_2 is a superior alternative to a_1.

Although the marginal opportunity cost approach based on utility appears to be an ideal theoretical procedure for decision making under uncertainty, there is no satisfactory general methodology to develop the utility function for individuals in various situations. Furthermore, either people do not believe in a universal measure such as utility or they tend to be inconsistent in expressing their perceived value of certain criteria. Currently, the utility-based analysis is not widely applied to decision maker under uncertainty. However, when all other approaches or criteria are inappropriate for a certain problem, the utility analysis can be another way to analyze the problem.

Multiple Objectives

Multiple objective decision making

Decision problems under risk or uncertainty rarely involve only a single objective, such as maximizing profits or utilities, or minimizing total costs. As we discussed in Chapter 6, most decision problems involve multiple objectives. A firm may want to increase its market share, achieve a desired level of profit, develop its human resources, increase its service to the community, and develop new products or innovative management systems. Decision alternatives may yield varying measures of outcome for multiple objectives under different states of nature.

If we can somehow conveniently sum up the outcomes of a decision alternative for various multiple objectives in a cardinal measure $(1, 2, 3, \cdots)$ such as utilities, then the problem involves a single-objective decision making. However, as we have discussed previously, it is not always possible to convert heterogeneous objective measures into a common denominator.

For example, we are aware that providing job security to members of the organization is a superordinate goal in most Japanese firms. The Japanese never equate this supreme purpose of the organization with other functional objectives such as profit, market share, or operational efficiency. Furthermore, the process of converting everything into a convenient denominator like utilities often results in a fabrication or in a distortion of actualities in order to simplify the problem. In such problems, we believe that it would be a better idea to use probabilistic goal programming methods. If you are interested in pursuing this advanced topic of goal programming, please check the References for Chapter 6.

DECISION TREES

Decision trees

The decision making under risk and uncertainty that we have discussed thus far has been limited to cases involving a single time period as the planning horizon. Consequently, our approach has been to make a good decision at the begining of the planning horizon based on the estimated consequences at the end of a specific period of time. All of the information required for decision making has been neatly presented in payoff tables for various alternative-event combinations. However, many decision problems in the real world require a series of decisions ranging over several future time periods or several decision stages.

Since a decision made at a given time period may have an impact on future decisions, an analysis of the entire series of decisions is required in order to determine the optimum decision. A *decision tree* is a schematic presentation of a sequential or multiperiod decision making process under risk, and as such is a useful tool for evaluating sequential decision problems.

Decision trees provide a quick schematic presentation of the following sequential decision processes:

Decision points: **Specific points of time when a decision must be made are shown as decision points. Alternative decisions become decision branches from a square (☐) decision point.**

Event points: **A number of states of nature that may occur are shown as event points. The possible events become event branches from a circle (○) event point.**

Probabilities: **The known probabilities of events are presented above each of the event branches.**

Figure 9.4   *The Structure of a Decision Tree*

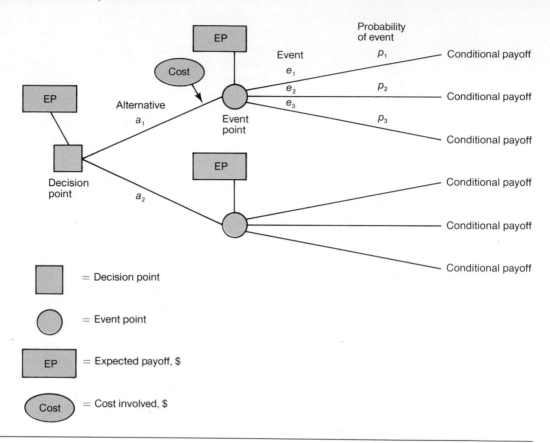

Conditional payoffs: **The conditional payoff of each eventual branch is known and recorded at the end of each branch.**

A typical decision tree is presented in Figure 9.4. A decision tree starts from the left side with one or more decision points. From the first decision point, all possible and feasible decision alternatives are branched out toward the right. At the end of each alternative branch, either an event point or another decision point is added as the problem requires. For each event branch stemming from an event point, the

Sequential decision process

corresponding probability is recorded. The tree branching continues until all the sequential processes are completed and the conditional payoffs are recorded. Then, each decision branch is evaluated by computing its expected payoff (or expected value) criterion.

CASETTE 9.5   *MOSTLY NUTS OF GEORGIA, INC.*

William Joseph (Billy Joe) Bodenhammer operates the family-owned peanut farm and the nut factory, Mostly Nuts of Georgia, Inc. Mostly Nuts, as the company is known nationwide, is a major producer of cocktail nuts, beer nuts for airlines, and peanut butter. The company is seriously considering a new product, a chocolate-covered candy bar with the label of Mostly Chocolate Nuts.

The developmental cost involved in introducing this new product is estimated to be $1.0 million. This cost includes marketing research, new equipment, new personnel, and training programs for the employees. The profit from Mostly Chocolate Nuts depends primarily on three things: (1) whether Galaxie Candy Company, the chief competitor of Mostly Nuts, would introduce a similar product or not; (2) the type of advertising campaign that Mostly Nuts launches; and (3) the type of advertising campaign that Galaxie uses to counter the promotional effort of Mostly Nuts.

If the company introduces Mostly Chocolate Nuts and Galaxie does not introduce a similar product, Mostly Nuts can launch a major advertising campaign and maximize profit. However, if Galaxie introduces a similar candy bar, the profit will depend on the advertising efforts of the firm and that of Galaxie. Mostly Nuts is considering three types of advertising campaigns based on the costs involved: a major campaign (with a cost of $0.5 million), a regular campaign (cost = $0.2 million), or a minor campaign (cost = $0.1 million).

Billy Joe has asked Barry Lorenzo, Vice-President of Marketing, to determine whether or not the new product should be introduced, and if so which advertising campaign the company should adopt. Barry Lorenzo, after spending a considerable amount of time reviewing his old management science texts, constructed the decision tree shown in Figure 9.5. The figure presents the sequence of decision points, event points, probabilities of events, and conditional profits involved in the problem.

At the first decision point, Mostly Nuts has two alternatives: the firm may introduce the product or it may not introduce the product. If Mostly Chocolate Nuts is not introduced, the conditional profit will of course be zero. If the company introduces Mostly Chocolate Nuts, Galaxie Candy Company has two alternatives as its reactions: (1) it may introduce a similar candy bar, or (2) it may not introduce a similar product. The probability of Galaxie introducing a similar candy bar is estimated to be 0.6 and thus the probability is 0.4 for not introducing the product.

At the second decision point, Mostly Nuts has three advertising strategies: a major campaign, a regular campaign, or a minor campaign. If Galaxie does not introduce a similar candy bar, the advertising effort of Mostly Nuts will not bring any reaction from Galaxie. However, if Galaxie introduces a similar candy bar, the advertising campaign selected by Mostly Nuts is expected to be challenged by one of the identical three types of advertising campaign of Galaxie's own.

For example, if Mostly Nuts launches a major advertising campaign, the probabilities of Galaxie's responses are: 0.5 for a major advertising campaign, 0.3 for a regular campaign, and 0.2 for a minor campaign. If Mostly Nuts' major campaign is answered by a major campaign from Galaxie, the conditional profit is estimated to be $1.0 million. The major-regular campaign combination results in $1.4 million, and the major-minor combination has a conditional profit of $2.5 million. These profit figures do not include the total development cost of $1.0 million. Other com-

Figure 9.5   Initial Decision Tree of the Mostly Nuts Problem

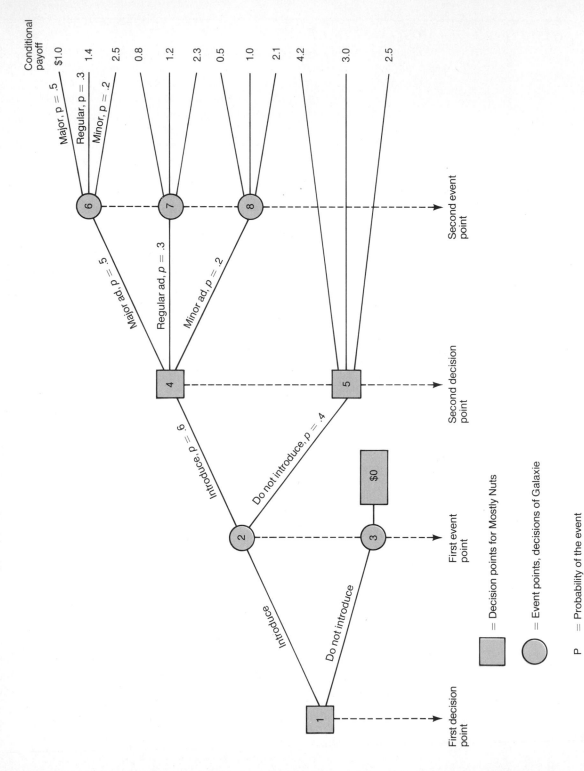

Conditional
payoff

Major, p = .5 $1.0
Regular, p = .3   1.4
Minor, p = .2   2.5

                     0.8
                     1.2
                     2.3

                     0.5
                     1.0
                     2.1

                     4.2

                     3.0

                     2.5

Major ad, p = .5
Regular ad, p = .3
Minor ad, p = .2

Introduce, p = .6

Do not introduce, p = .4

Introduce

Do not introduce

$0

First decision
point

First event
point

Second decision
point

Second event
point

= Decision points for Mostly Nuts

= Event points, decisions of Galaxie

P   = Probability of the event

binations of advertising campaigns, probabilities, and conditional profits are shown in Figure 9.6.

The best way to analyze the sequential decision problem of Mostly Nuts is to work from the end of each branch. Let us compare profit for each sequence of decisions. For example, the expected profit for the combination of Mostly Nuts to introduce the new product, Galaxie's introduction of a similar product, and the company's decision to launch a major ad campaign will be:

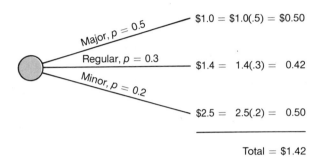

$1.0 = $1.0(.5) = $0.50

$1.4 = 1.4(.3) = 0.42

$2.5 = 2.5(.2) = 0.50

Total = $1.42

We can also compute the expected profits of Events 7 and 8 as follows:

$$EP(7) = 0.8(0.5) + 1.2(0.3) + 2.3(0.2) = \$1.22 \text{ million}$$
$$EP(8) = 0.5(0.5) + 1.0(0.3) = 2.1(0.2) = \$0.60 \text{ million}$$

When Mostly Nuts initiates an advertising campaign, it incurs costs for preparing the ad and running the ad in the various media selected. Launching a major ad is estimated to cost $0.5 million, a regular ad $0.2 million, and a minor ad $0.1 million. After subtracting these costs from the above computed expected profits, we obtain the following net expected profits:

Major ad: 1.42 − 0.50 = $0.92 million
Regular ad: 1.22 − 0.20 = $1.02 million*
Minor ad: 0.60 − 0.10 = $0.50 million

Based on the above computation, it is obvious that if Galaxie introduces a similar product the best decision at the second decision point for Mostly Nuts is to launch a regular advertising campaign. This alternative yields a net expected payoff of $1.02 million. This expected profit is recorded for Decision Point 4 in Figure 9.6. The other two inferior strategies are eliminated, as indicated by the // signs.

If Galaxie does not introduce a similar product, the maximum conditional profit is $4.2 million when Mostly Nuts adopts a major advertising strategy. Since a major ad campaign costs $0.5 million, the net conditional profit for this strategy is $3.7 million. We can compute the net conditional profits of the three advertising alternatives as follows:

Major ad: 4.2 − 0.5 = $3.70 million   ← optimum
Regular ad: 3.0 − 0.2 = $2.80 million
Minor ad: 2.5 − 0.1 = $2.40 million

The optimum strategy is, of course, the major advertising campaign. Therefore, we can eliminate the other two strategies as shown by the double-slash signs.

Figure 9.6 The Decision Tree and the Expected Profits

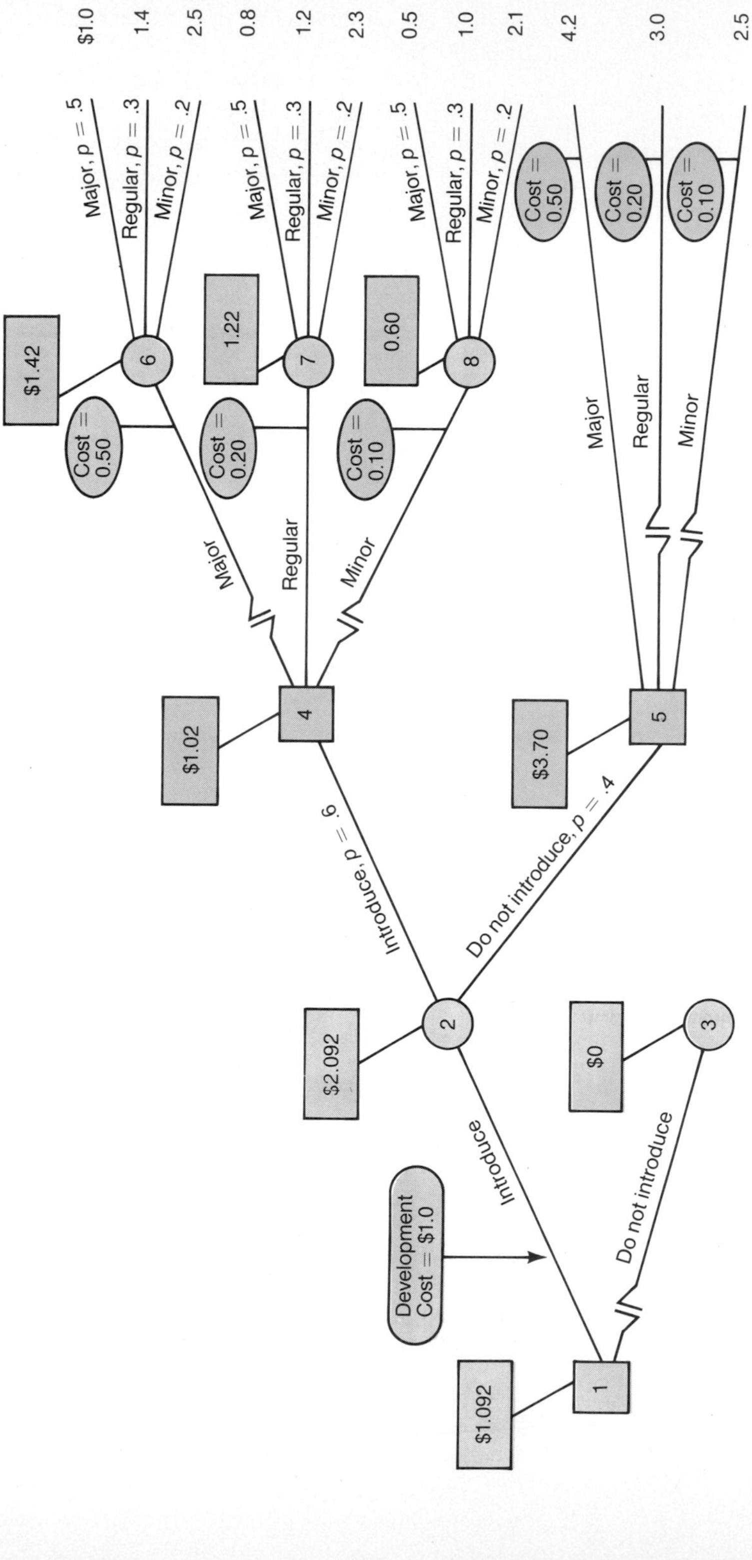

Now the expected profit of the Mostly Nuts new product can be computed. It is the sum of the expected profit in the event that Galaxie introduces a similar product ($1.02 million) multiplied by its probability (0.6) and the expected profit in the event that Galaxie does not introduce a similar product ($3.70 million) multiplied by its probability (0.4). Thus, the expected profit for Event 2 will be

Expected profit (2): $1.02(0.6) + $3.70(0.4) = $2.092 million

Developmental costs for the new product are estimated to be $1.0 million. Thus, the net expected profit of the new product is $1.092 million. Thus, Mostly Nuts of Georgia decided to introduce the new candy bar—Mostly Chocolate Nuts.

REAL-WORLD APPLICATIONS

Real-world applications

Decision analysis based on statistical methods, and especially on probability theories, is perhaps most popular in real-world situations. Many questionnaire surveys concerning the actual use of management science techniques, as we reviewed in Chapter 1, clearly indicate that statistical techniques are often the most widely applied tools for decision making. When we consider the use of simulation in conjunction with statistical analysis, decision theory approaches are indeed very important decision tools.

There are numerous real-world applications of decision theory techniques, from a simple newspaperboy problem (deciding how many copies to order) to a complex investment portfolio problem. In this section we will examine two interesting real-world applications of decision theory.

Determining Hotel Reservation Policy

Many service organizations use reservation systems.[1] Airlines, doctors' offices, hotels and motels, and automobile repair shops are good examples of such organizations. Setting an effective reservation policy is a vital factor in the success of these organizations. The problem is especially important during peak demand periods (e.g., the ski season for Colorado condominiums, summer hunting-fishing season in Alaska, and Christmas-New Year's holiday season for airlines).

The difficulty in formulating an effective reservation policy for a hotel stems from unpredictable human behavior. Some people make reservations and cancel them at the last minute. Worse yet, some people never show up—"no-shows." People often want to stay for longer or shorter periods than their reservations stipulate, and others simply walk in and expect to get a room right then—"walk-ins."

The types of costs involved in the hotel reservation problem are as follows:

1. *Underbooking cost:* Lost profit of $40 to $75 per day.

[1]Fred E. Williams, "Decision Theory and the Innkeeper: An Approach for Setting Hotel Reservation Policy," *Interfaces,* 7:4 (Aug., 1977), 18–30.

2. *Overbooking cost:* Each turnaway inflicts cost for goodwill and for securing accommodations for that person, perhaps twice as much as the underbooking cost.

An effective hotel reservation policy attempts to achieve a balance between the two costs described above. Currently, most hotel managers use several widely practiced intuitive rules of thumb such as, for example, "booking up to 110 percent of capacity."

In order to develop an effective reservation policy for a given day, three basic sources of demand must be accurately analyzed. They are:

1. *Stay-overs:* People who decide to stay beyond their original scheduled reservations.

2. *Reservations:* People who check in as scheduled with proper reservations.

3. *Walk-ins:* People who walk in without reservations and attempt to secure rooms.

There are many different ways to develop probability-based forecasting models for the above three sources of demand for rooms on a given day. Once a model is developed, the basic question becomes how many reservations should be accepted, given the number of occupants on the previous day and associated underbooking and overbooking costs.

The author of this study developed a methodology, based on decision theory, that determines the optimum number of reservations to accept on a certain day by analyzing the number of scheduled checkouts and stay-overs on the previous day. This application of decision theory is not only interesting but it also has great potential for real-world applications.

Selecting Business Targets

There are a number of large corporations that are heavily involved in bidding for government contracts in a very competitive environment.[2] In order to be successful in pursuing a select group of promising contract targets, a probability-based decision theory method can be applied.

The authors of this study developed such a method for the TRW Defense and Space Systems Group. In order to develop an optimum group of government contract targets to pursue, this method analyzed the following factors:

1. Probability of a target (project) to be funded by the government.

2. Probability of the organization being the successful bidder of the target contract.

---

[2]R. Bruce Gerding and David D. Morrison, "Selecting Business Targets in a Competitive Environment," *Interfaces,* 10:4 (Aug., 1980), 34–41.

3. Expected value of the target contract to the organization.

4. Amount of resources required to pursue the contract target.

Once the above information was compiled, the effectiveness-cost ratio (ECR) for each target was developed based on the following formulation:

$$ECR = \frac{\text{Return on investment for Target } j}{\text{Max}\left(\dfrac{\text{(Pursuit funds for Target } j \text{ in year } i)}{\text{(Pursuit funds constraint for year } i)}\right)}$$

Then the final selection methodology became a modified version of a decision tree in a sequence of planning time. This variation of the decision theory method has been said to be very effective in the planning process at TRW's Defense and Space Systems Group. Although the actual dollar amount saved or earned was impossible to compute, this method was credited with providing the TRW management with a common denominator for evaluating various business opportunities.

SUMMARY

Most real-world decision problems occur in an environment of risk or uncertainty. In this chapter we have studied many different approaches to decision making under risk and uncertainty. Utilizing these approaches improves the decision making capability of the manager when faced with difficult problems under risk or uncertainty. The expected payoff or expected opportunity cost criterion based on probabilities is the dominant approach for decision making under risk. The same basic approach can be applied to simple inventory problems where the costs of overstocking and understocking are to be balanced.

When the probabilities of the states of nature are not known, decision making under the condition of uncertainty exists. Several interesting approaches and criteria have been suggested for decision making under uncertainty. Although utility theory has been developed and published extensively in the literature of management science, it is rarely used in real-world situations. In reality, decision making under uncertainty is often converted to decision making under risk by using expert opinions or subjective probabilities.

Decision trees are useful tools for analyzing sequential decision problems under the condition of risk. A decision tree contains decision points, event points, probabilities associated with the events, and conditional payoffs of alternatives. By employing the expected payoff criterion, we can gradually eliminate inferior branches and identify the optimum sequence of decisions.

References

Holloway, C. A. *Decision Making under Uncertainty*. Englewood Cliffs, N.J.: Prentice-Hall, 1979.

Lee, S. M.; Moore, L. J.; and Tayler, B. W. *Management Science*. Dubuque, Iowa: W. C. Brown, 1981.

Luce, R. D., and Raiffa, H. *Games and Decisions*. New York: Wiley, 1957.

Raiffa, H. *Decision Analysis*. Reading, Mass.: Addison-Wesley, 1968.

Schlaiffer, R. *Probability and Statistics for Business Decisions*. New York: McGraw-Hill, 1959.

Schlaiffer, R. *Analysis of Decisions under Uncertainty*. New York: McGraw-Hill, 1969.

White, D. J. *Decision Methodology*. London: Wiley, 1975.

Assignments

9.1 What are the four states of decision environment? Discuss which management science techniques could be useful for decision problems under each of these states.

9.2 What are the important decision components that are needed for decision making under the condition of risk?

9.3 The expected payoff and the expected loss criterion result in the same optimum solution. What is the reason for this?

9.4 In reality, no one really has perfect information. Then why should we even bother computing the value of perfect information?

9.5 Contrast the loss due to overstocking and the loss due to understocking. In addition to simple inventory problems, to what type of decision problems can we apply these cost concepts?

9.6 The salvage value and goodwill cost can be important components of an inventory problem. How do they fit into the process of determining the optimum stock quantity?

9.7 What are some of the sources where we can obtain partial probabilities of events for a certain investment problem under the condition of uncertainty?

9.8 What is the major difference between the dominance criterion and other decision making criteria under uncertainty?

9.9 What is the major weakness of the Hurwicz criterion?

9.10 Utility analysis is a sophisticated theoretical approach to decision making. List a few of your personal decision problems that could be solved by utility analysis.

9.11 What is the difference between subjective probability and objective probability?

9.12 What are the important components of a decision tree? Explain each briefly.

9.13 Discuss a decision problem familiar to you that can be analyzed by using a decision tree.

9.14 When a decision problem under risk or uncertainty involves multiple objectives, what may be the possible solution approaches?

9.15 What is the major shortcoming of both the maximin and maximax criteria?

9.16 Given the following decision table, answer the questions below.

Alternative	State of Nature		
	e_1 ($p = 0.2$)	e_2 ($p = 0.3$)	e_3 ($p = 0.5$)
a_1	$3,000	$3,000	$3,000
a_2	2,800	3,600	3,600
a_3	2,600	3,400	4,200

a. Determine the expected payoff for each of the alternatives and select the optimum alternative.
b. Now construct the conditional loss table and determine the optimum alternative by the expected loss criterion.
c. What is the value of perfect information?

9.17 Given the following information, choose the best alternative by the expected value criterion.

Alternative	State of Nature	
	e_1 ($p = 0.5$)	e_2 ($p = 0.5$)
a_1	$200,000	− $40,000
a_2	0	0
a_3	400,000	360,000

9.18 Sugar Mountain Winter Sports, Inc. has just opened up a new ski slope. There is great potential for a successful ski business in the area, since it can draw customers from all over the South. However, the key factor for success is snow. If the winter brings an average of 60 or more inches of snow, the season could be a financial success. If the snowfall is between 40 and 60 inches, the firm can operate artificial snowmakers and still manage a moderate financial gain. However, if the snowfall is less than 40 inches, as was the case during the past 3 years, the firm will be operating in the red. Recently, a large firm in Vermont has offered $500,000 to lease the ski slope from Sugar Mountain Sports. The president of Sugar Mountain is contemplating whether the firm should operate the ski slope or lease it for the coming winter. The conditional payoffs for operating the ski slope under the three snow conditions are as follows:

	Snow: 60″ or More	Snow: 40″–60″	Snow: Less than 40″
Operate ski slope	$1,500,000	$600,000	− $400,000

a. If the National Weather Bureau forecasts that there is an equal probability of 0.4 for snowfall of more than 60 inches and for snowfall of less than 40 inches, should the firm operate or lease the ski slope?

b. If the National Weather Bureau can predict only the probability of snowfall of less than 40 inches as 0.4, what kind of probability for snowfall of more than 60 inches should there be before the firm should decide to operate the ski slope?

9.19 Ernie's Fish Market sells fresh trout. Trout are bought in Denver at $1.00 per fish (including transportation costs) and sold for $1.50. Any trout left over at the end of the week is sold to a cat food plant for $.20 per fish. According to past experience, the weekly demand for trout has been as follows:

Demand	Probability of Demand
15	0.10
16	0.20
17	0.40
18	0.20
19	0.10

a. Assuming that there is no goodwill cost involved for unmet demand, construct a payoff table for the various demand and stocking quantities.

b. Using the expected payoff criterion, determine the optimum quantity to stock per week.

c. Using the expected loss criterion, construct the conditional loss table and determine the optimum stock quantity.

d. Determine the value of perfect information.

9.20 The Cornhusker Market buys T-bone steak from the university's Animal Science Department. The purchase price is $2.50 per pound and the market sells the steak for $4.00 per pound. Any steak left over at the end of the week is sold to a local cannery for $0.50 per pound. According to the sales records for the past 100 weeks, demand has been as follows:

Weekly Demand (Lb.)	Number of Weeks
10	10
11	20
12	20
13	30
14	10
15	10
	100

a. Construct a payoff table for the various demand and stocking quantities.

b. If the market can obtain perfect information concerning the following week's demand for T-bone steak, what will be the expected profit?

c. Determine the optimum stock quantity.

9.21 The Airport Newsstand buys *House Decoration* magazine for $2.00 a copy and sells it for $3.00. Any copies remaining unsold are put on sale for $.40 a copy in the following month. According to the requests for *House Decoration* over the past 100 months, the demand distribution has been as follows:

Number Requested	Relative Frequency
10	0.05
11	0.15
12	0.20
13	0.30
14	0.15
15	0.10
16	0.05

a. What is the loss due to overstocking?

b. What is the loss due to understocking?

c. Construct a conditional loss table and identify the optimum quantity to stock.

d. What is the value of perfect information about demand for the magazine?

9.22 Given the following payoff table, determine the best alternative based on the criteria listed below.

	State of Nature		
Alternative	e_1	e_2	e_3
a_1	$3,250	$5,000	$-2,000
a_2	3,000	4,000	500
a_3	2,500	2,500	2,500

a. Laplace

b. Maximin

c. Maximax

d. Hurwicz ($\alpha = 0.4$)

e. Minimax

9.23 The Trust Department of the First Wild West Bank is contemplating 3 investment alternatives for a $10 million trust fund recently acquired. The investment alternatives are stocks, bonds, and real estate. The estimated returns of each of the alternatives under 3 possible economic conditions are as follows:

Investment Alternative	State of Nature		
	e_1	e_2	e_3
Stocks	$1,200,000	$600,000	$-400,000
Bonds	900,000	500,000	200,000
Real estate	1,800,000	800,000	800,000

a. If the Federal Reserve Bank predicts the probability of e_1 as 0.3, in which alternative should the bank invest the money? Explain your reasoning.
b. Construct a payoff graph based on the Hurwicz criterion. Determine all critical α's and identify the optimum alternative for the various α's.
c. Determine the best alternative under each of the following criteria:
  1. Laplace
  2. Maximin
  3. Maximax
  4. Minimax

9.24 A newsstand operator buys the Sunday Edition of the *Washington Post* for $1.00 per copy and sells it for $1.50. The distribution of demand for the Sunday edition over the last 100 weeks has been as follows:

Number Demanded	Relative Frequency
less than 40	0.00
40	0.02
41	0.04
42	0.07
43	0.10
44	0.12
45	0.13
46	0.14
47	0.12
48	0.10
49	0.08
50	0.05
51	0.02
52	0.01
over 52	0.00

a. Assuming that any newspaper left over has no value and that running short has no effect on any customer's tendency to return, determine the losses due to understocking and overstocking.
b. Based on the information from part (a), determine how many copies should be stocked. Use incremental analysis.
c. If any newspaper left over can be sold to a fish market for $0.10 per copy, how many copies should be stocked?
d. What is the smallest salvage value of each of the leftover newspapers that will justify the operator's actual stocking of 50 copies?
e. Given the salvage value of $0.10 per copy, what is the range of goodwill cost that will justify stocking 50 copies?

9.25 The General Hospital is widely recognized for its pioneering surgical procedures for heart patients. The chief surgeon, Dr. Marc Crosby, is extremely concerned about the availability of rare type blood, AB negative, for open-heart surgery. In order to analyze the problem, Dr. Crosby compiled the use of the AB negative blood during the past 100 days, as shown below:

Use of AB Negative Blood (Pints)	Number of Days
30	5
31	10
32	10
33	15
34	20
35	15
36	10
37	5
38	5
39	5
40+	0

The hospital purchases AB negative blood from the regional Red Cross for $100 per pint and charges the patient $300. Since only very fresh blood is used for open-heart surgery, the hospital purchases only the freshest blood (one day old from the donation). The hospital keeps it for a maximum of one week and any leftover blood is sold to other hospitals for $25 per pint.

In view of General Hospital's usage of the AB negative blood, Dr. Crosby is attempting to determine the weekly stocking policy of the blood.

a. If General Hospital is attempting to maximize the expected profit, how many pints should it stock?

b. If General Hospital runs out of blood, it can call the nearby metropolitan area Red Cross and have it delivered by helicopter in 25 minutes. However, the average cost of blood by this emergency means is $400 per pint.

How many pints of blood should General Hospital order per week?

9.26 A merchant at the farmers' market sells avocados. He purchases avocados from a dealer in California at $4 per case of 20 and sells them at $8 per case in the first week they are stocked (he sells only by the case). If there are any cases left over after the first week, he reduces the selling price to $2 per case in the following week. Any avocados that have not been sold by the end of the second week are scrapped at a total loss. The merchant, according to his previous experience, assigns the following probability distributions for the demand for fresh avocados and for week-old avocados:

Fresh Avocados		Week-old Avocados	
Demand	Probability	Demand	Probability
0	0	0	0.15
1	0.3	1	0.25
2	0.4	2	0.30
3	0.3	3	0.20
4+	0	4	0.10
	1.0		1.00

According to the merchant's experience, the demand for fresh avocados is not related to the demand for week-old avocados.

a. Construct a conditional payoff table for various stock levels.

b. How many cases of avocados should the merchant stock per week? (*Hint:* The events in the payoff table for this problem are of the type "demand for one case of avocados in the first week and demand for two cases in the second week.")

9.27 Mario's Pizza Company has four restaurants in the city. Currently, the company has a total of 200 employees. The Personnel Department files indicate the following breakdown of employees by sex and work status (full-time or part-time):

Sex	Work Status	
	Full-Time	**Part-Time**
Female	30	50
Male	80	40

a. If we select an employee at random, what is the probability that the employee will be a part-time employee?

b. What is the conditional probability that an employee is a female, given that she works full-time?

c. Suppose that an employee selected at random turns out to be a male. What is the chance that he is a part-time employee?

Use the Bayes' decision rule in answering this question.

9.28 The United States is seriously considering a substantial amount of military aid to Country A. Country A held a commanding military hardware superiority over the surrounding hostile countries before the recent outbreak. Today, however, the country maintains a relatively small superiority (55 percent on a 100 percent rating, where 50-50 is an exact balance). The U.S. government asserts that Country A must maintain a considerable amount of superiority in military arms in order to sustain a long-term peace in the area. However, any arms aid to Country A may result in immediate Russian aid to the hostile countries in the area. State Department experts estimate that the probability of Russian aid to the hostile countries subsequent to U.S. aid to Country A is 0.8. The Central Intelligence Agency has informed the State Department that Russia would most likely wait and see whether the amount of U.S. aid to Country A would be large, moderate, or small before it makes its move to neutralize the U.S. aid. If the U.S. aid to Country A is large, the most likely Russian reactions and their consequences in terms of Country A's relative military superiority are estimated as follows:

Event: Amount of Aid to Hostile States	Probability	Country A's Position
Large	0.7	50%
Moderate	0.2	60
Small	0.1	70

On the other hand, if the United States provides Country A with a moderate amount of arms aid, the expected Russian reactions and their consequences are estimated as follows:

Event: Amount of Aid to Hostile States	Probability	Country A's Position
Large	0.1	45%
Moderate	0.6	55
Small	0.3	60

If the amount of U.S. arms aid to Country A is small, the Russian reactions are expected to be as follows:

Event: Amount of Aid to Hostile States	Probability	Country A's Position
Large	0.1	45%
Moderate	0.3	50
Small	0.6	55

There exists, as mentioned above, a 20 percent probability that Russia may not make any equalizing arms aid to the hostile states even when the United States provides aid to Country A. In such a case, the expected outcomes are as follows:

Event: Amount of U.S. Aid to Country A	Country A's Position
Large	90%
Moderate	75
Small	60

If the U.S. government is determined to improve the military superiority of Country A in order to maintain the fragile peace in the area, what kind of decisions should it make? Analyze the problem by using decision trees.

9.29 Gulf Exploration International, Inc. is considering making a bid for the oil drilling rights off the Mexican shore. Through careful and thorough analysis, management of the firm has decided to set the bidding price at $520 million. The experts estimate that the firm has about a 60 percent chance of winning the contract for $520 million. Once the firm wins the contract, it has three alternatives for the extraction of oil: (1) the company can drill for oil on its own, (2) it can arrange a joint venture with Texas Oil Exploration, or (3) it can sell the drilling rights to foreign oil companies.

If the company wishes to drill on its own, the actual oil drilling operation is estimated to cost $80 million. The joint venture with Texas Oil Exploration is expected to cost $45 million. On the other hand, sales of the rights to foreign interests is expected to cost $2 million because of the long negotiating process.

The firm's scientists and consultants conclude that if Gulf Exploration drills on its own, the following possible outcomes and their probabilities are expected:

Event	Probability	Financial Outcome ($ Million)
Big find	0.6	$900
Medium find	0.2	600
Failure	0.2	250

If the firm makes a joint drilling arrangement with Texas Oil Exploration, the expected outcomes and associated probabilities are as follows:

Event	Probability	Financial Outcome ($ Millions)
Big find	0.6	$750
Medium find	0.3	500
Failure	0.1	200

The sale of the rights to foreign companies is expected to return a flat $600 million.

Construct a decision tree for the problem and determine the optimum decision strategy.

9.30 Smith Laboratories, Inc. has just developed a new drug called "Stress Ez." This drug has been tested thoroughly in laboratories as well as through voluntary drug testing programs with human beings. The company is attempting to decide the best way to market the product.

Currently the company has the following marketing options: (1) get approval from the Federal Drug Administration (FDA) and market the drug domestically; (2) if the FDA does not approve the drug, then market it overseas only; (3) market it overseas only.

The Marketing Manager has constructed the following decision tree with the associated conditional payoffs and probabilities. The conditional payoffs include various marketing and other related costs.

Determine the optimum marketing strategy for Smith Laboratories.

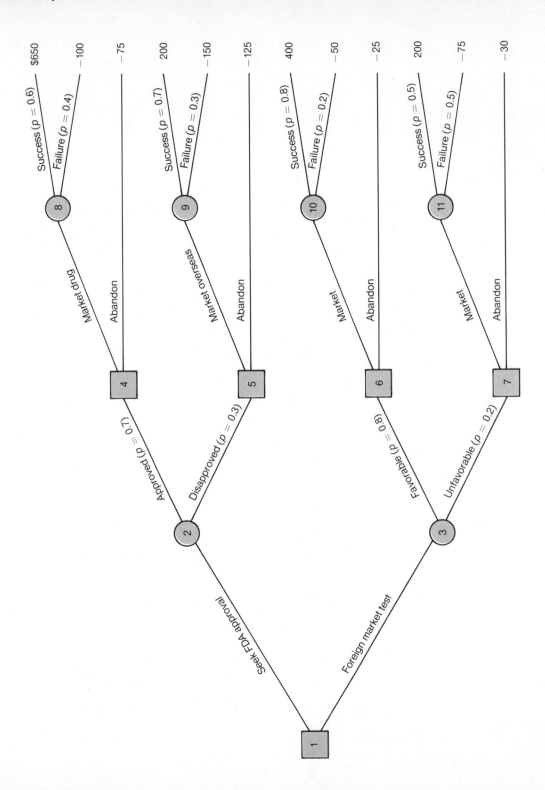

PROJECT PLANNING WITH PERT AND CPM

In many organizations, network analysis plays an important role in the area of project management. By analyzing a network, which is a graphical representation of a series of activities and events, we can formulate, plan, and control projects more efficiently. Among the several network analysis techniques available, PERT (Program Evaluation and Review Technique) and CPM (Critical Path Method) are the best known and most widely used techniques. In this chapter, we will study the concepts and solution procedures of PERT/CPM networks for managerial decision problems.

Learning Objectives *From the study of this chapter, you will learn the following:*

1. Several important characteristics of the project planning problem.
2. Development and use of the Gantt chart.
3. Development of networks with activities and events.
4. Development of a network from a Gantt chart.
5. Identification of the critical path through calculation of the earliest expected time and the latest allowable time.
6. Scheduling of activities of a project based on a network analysis.
7. Project crashing based on a time-cost trade-off analysis.
8. Estimation of the project completion time and associated probabilities for a PERT network.
9. The meaning of the following terms:

Gantt chart	*Earliest expected time*
Activities	*Latest allowable time*
Events	*Noncritical events*
Critical path	*Total slack time*
Network	*Shared (floating) slack*
Dummy activity	*Free slack time*
Project crashing	*Optimistic time*
Most likely time	*Pessimistic time*

CHARACTERISTICS OF THE PROJECT PLANNING PROBLEM

We may not be experts in project planning as yet, but we can certainly qualify as frequent project planners. Basically, a project is an undertaking that has a clear beginning point and a definite ending point. We have completed many projects—class

Some examples of projects

Figure 10.1   Three Phases of PERT/CPM Application

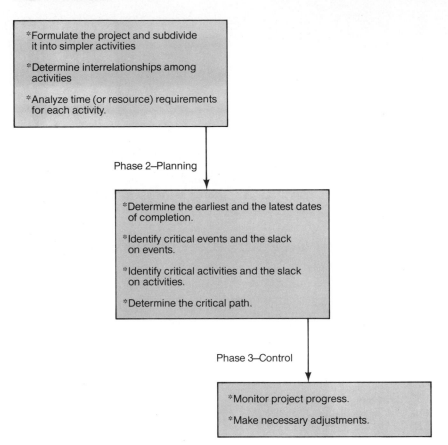

Phase 1–Formulation

*Formulate the project and subdivide
 it into simpler activities

*Determine interrelationships among
 activities

*Analyze time (or resource) requirements
 for each activity.

Phase 2–Planning

*Determine the earliest and the latest dates
 of completion.

*Identify critical events and the slack
 on events.

*Identify critical activities and the slack
 on activities.

*Determine the critical path.

Phase 3–Control

*Monitor project progress.

*Make necessary adjustments.

term projects, a house painting job, a spring cleaning chore, a vegetable garden planting, and the like. In business organizations, projects tend to cost great sums of money, take a long time, require a great deal of manpower, and may cause frequent ulcer attacks. Examples of such large projects might be the construction of a new shopping center, the development of a new medicine to combat hypertension, the Voyager 2 project, the Alaskan pipeline project, the design of a new neighborhood-based team-policing system, and the like.

The project planning techniques we will study in this chapter are widely applied to a variety of real-world projects. The federal government usually requests contractors to utilize project planning techniques for most of its projects. Construction and engineering firms frequently use project planning techniques for work planning and cost control. The project planning techniques are extremely valuable in determining the project duration time, critical tasks, and the probability of completing the project within the given amount of resources and time.

Projects usually involve a host of interrelated activities that are to be completed within specified limits of time and resources. Thus, we need to coordinate and schedule activities in order to complete a project efficiently. Project planning is often a complex and important management function. All project planning problems, whether involving physical operations or intellectual endeavors, complex or simple, large or small, have the following common characteristics:

A series of events and activities.

Interrelationships among the activities.

Importance of managing time (for the beginning, process, and completion).

Importance of managing resources.

Project planning based on PERT/CPM may include a number of steps and procedures. However, it generally involves three basic phases: formulation, planning, and control, as shown in Figure 10.1.

The Gantt chart

The simplest project scheduling tool available is the *Gantt chart,* developed by Henry L. Gantt in 1918. The value of the Gantt chart rests on its flexibility that provides ease in describing a project in terms of activities, time schedule of each activity, and the precedence relationships among some of the activities. Because of its simplicity and flexibility, the Gantt chart is a powerful project scheduling tool. Many sophisticated network-based projects are often initiated on the basis of a good Gantt chart. The Gantt chart is undoubtedly the tool most widely used by practicing managers today.

Suppose you decided to undertake your monthly car cleaning and polishing project with a friend. The project involves the following activities: washing the car, drying the car, applying the wax, cleaning the interior while the wax is drying, and then polishing the car. Table 10.1 presents the activity label, activity description, predecessor, and duration estimates (in minutes).

Table 10.1   Car Cleaning and Polishing Project

Activity	Description	Predecessor	Estimated Duration (minutes)
A	Wash the car	None	10
B	Dry the car	A	10
C	Wax the car	B	15
D	Clean the interior	B	30
E	Polish the car	C	25

Figure 10.2   A Gantt Chart for Cleaning and Polishing a Car

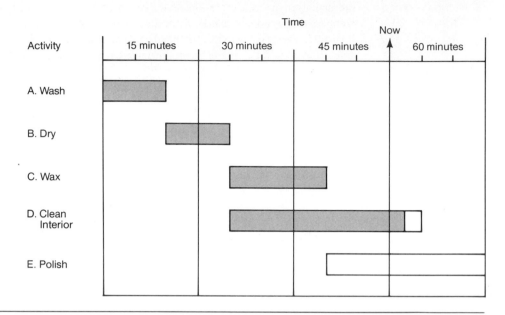

The Gantt chart
Figure 10.2 presents a Gantt chart for the car cleaning and polishing project. Activities are listed vertically on the left side of the bar chart. The horizontal axis represents time. The estimated duration of each project is represented by the length of the bar, from the beginning to the ending point. Since the length of the activity bar represents the total completion time, we can easily ascertain the progress of each activity. For example, in Figure 10.2 the shaded area represents the completed portions of the activities. Thus, it is clear that we are on or ahead of schedule on all activities except the polishing activity.

Precedence relationships
A Gantt chart can accommodate simple precedence relationships among the activities. For example, Activity B (drying the car) cannot take place until Activity A (washing the car) is completed. However, if we have a complex network under consideration, it is extremely difficult to express interrelationships among activities on the chart. This is the major weakness of the Gantt chart.

History of PERT and CPM

History of PERT and CPM
PERT and CPM were developed in the late 1950s as aids in the planning, scheduling, and controlling of complex, large-scale projects. PERT was developed by the U.S. Navy for planning and scheduling the Polaris missile project. CPM, on the other hand, was developed by the DuPont Company and the Univac Division of Remington Rand Corporation as a device to control the maintenance of chemical plants.

Differences between PERT and CPM
In many respects, PERT and CPM are similar in their basic concepts and methodology. But there is also a basic difference between the two techniques. CPM is most appropriate for a project in which the activity durations are known with cer-

tainty. Thus, it focuses on the trade-off between the project time and cost. On the other hand, PERT is useful for analyzing a project scheduling problem in which the completion time is uncertain (probabilistic). It emphasizes the uncertainties of activity completion times and attempts to reach a particular event (milestone) in a project.

Important factors of a network

While we keep the basic difference between PERT and CPM in mind, there are several factors that must always be considered whenever we deal with a project scheduling problem. These factors are:

The project completion time.

The most critical activities that must be completed on time.

The critical path (i.e., the longest path to completion) of the network.

Permissible delays of noncritical activities that would not cause a delay for the entire project.

The above described factors are essential in understanding the critical relationships among activities and also in identifying missing elements in the network.

DEVELOPING PROJECT NETWORKS

Activities and events

PERT/CPM networks consist of two basic elements: *activities* and *events*. An activity represents an operation of the project that requires resources and consumes time. An event, on the other hand, represents a certain point in time, such as the beginning or ending of an activity.

Representing activities and events

In the network model, activities are represented by arrows ($\rightarrow$) and events are shown as circles ($\bigcirc$). The activity arrows are called *arcs,* and the event circles are referred to as *nodes*. Thus, every activity is bounded by nodes. Let us consider a simple example, the finishing process of a house construction project. There are two activities involved: the exterior finishing and the interior finishing. Table 10.2 presents a network for the finishing work process. Figure 10.3 provides the graphical representation of the two activities and the three associated events.

Each activity is identified by its starting and ending events. Event 1 represents the start of Activity A (exterior finishing), and Event 2 indicates the end of Activity

Table 10.2 A House Finishing Network

Activity	Activity Description	Start and End Nodes	Duration Estimates (Weeks)
A	Exterior finishing	(1,2)	3
B	Interior finishing	(2,3)	5

Figure 10.3   A House Finishing Network

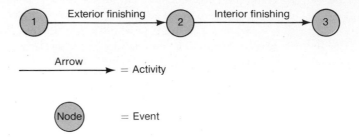

Figure 10.4   A Gantt Chart and a Corresponding Network

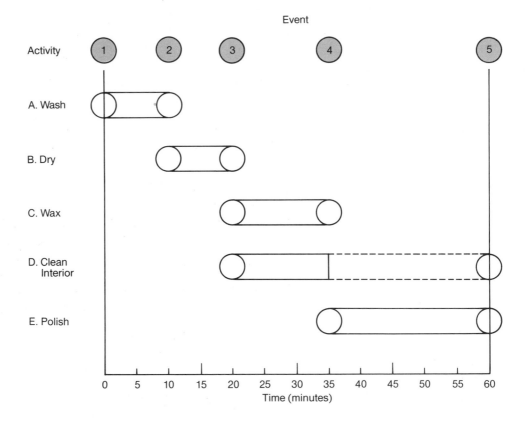

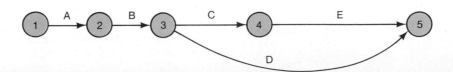

A. In other words, Activity A starts from Node 1 and ends at Node 2. Event 2 also represents the start of activity B (interior finishing). Then, Event 3 is the terminating point of Activity B.

Transforming a Gantt Chart into a Network

Developing a network from a Gantt chart

In order to start a project, we can begin by developing a simple Gantt chart. Then, we can easily transform this chart into a network to handle complex interrelationships among activities. The Gantt chart for our car washing and polishing project is presented in Figure 10.4. As a means of transforming the chart into a network, we added circles (nodes) at the beginning and ending points of each bar.

In order to develop a network diagram, the five nodes are placed in a row, and activities are drawn as arrows connecting them. The length of an arrow has no bearing on the duration of an activity that connects two nodes. The only determining factor for the network diagram is precedence.

We have already emphasized the importance of the precedence relationship. An event or a node is not realized until all contributing or incoming activities are completed. For example, in Figure 10.4, Event 5 will not be realized until both Activities D and E are completed. Also, an activity cannot commence until all incoming activities to the starting event are completed. Therefore, Activities C and D cannot begin until Activity B is completed.

Dummy Activities

In a network, the easiest way we can identify an activity is by referring to the event numbers at the beginning and ending points. In other words, we would like to provide unique event coordinates for each activity in the network diagram. In the network diagram shown in Figure 10.5(a), we have two activities, C and D, that start at a

---

Figure 10.5 Using a Dummy Activity

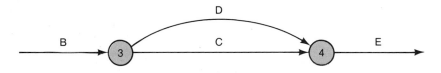

(a) A network without dummy

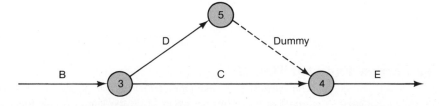

(b) A network with a dummy activity

same event (3) and also end at a same event (4). We would like to modify the diagram so that there will be only one activity between two events.

Dummy activities

In some PERT/CPM networks, it is necessary to include dummy activities to designate proper precedence relationships. Where there exists a doublet, we simply create a new event node to remove one of the activities. Then, in order to preserve the precedence relationship, we also create a dummy activity that connects the new event node and the old event node. Since dummy activities are only artificial (e.g., a dummy destination or a dummy source in a transportation problem), they require absolutely no time or resources to complete. As shown in Figure 10.5(b), dummy activities are indicated by a dotted arrow line rather than a solid arrow line.

IDENTIFYING THE CRITICAL PATH

The critical path

The *critical path* is the path that has the longest time through a network from start to finish. Identifying the critical path is of great importance as it represents the duration of the entire project. Thus, if any activity on the critical path is delayed for any reason, the entire project will be delayed accordingly. Every project network has a critical path. It is possible to have multiple critical paths if there are exact duplications among the longest paths.

EXAMPLE 10.1   *A SIMPLE NETWORK*

Let us consider the simple network shown in Figure 10.6. There are three possible paths for the network. They are (listed by event nodes):

Path	Length of Time	
①-②-④-⑥:	4 + 2 + 4 = 10 days	
①-②-⑤-⑥:	4 + 7 + 2 = 13 days	← critical path
①-③-⑤-⑥:	3 + 6 + 2 = 11 days	

Enumeration of possible paths

For this simple network, the critical path is found by enumerating all of the possible paths to the completion point. The second path is the critical path because it requires the longest period of time to completion. Thus, if any activity on this path (① - ② - ⑤ - ⑥) is not completed within the planned time, the whole project will be delayed. For most real-world problems, enumeration of all of the possible paths can be cumbersome and time-consuming. There are two analytical approaches we can use to identify the critical path: the earliest expected time and the latest allowable time.

The Earliest Expected Time *(ET)*

Earliest expected time

The *earliest expected time (ET)* is based on the activity time estimate. The earliest time that an event can occur is on the latest completion of an activity terminating at that event node. This is also referred to as the *time of event realization*. ET values for each event are computed in a *forward*, or a *left-to-right*, tracing of the network.

Figure 10.6   A Simple Network

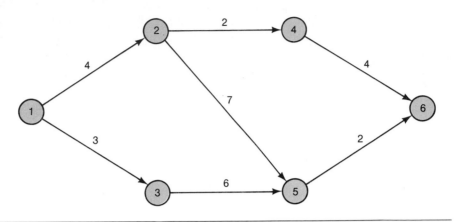

In the CPM network, the activity time is given as a single estimate of the time required to complete each activity. In the PERT network, on the other hand, the activity time is expressed by the *mean* of each activity completion time. We will discuss how to determine the mean time of each activity in a later section of this chapter. Here, let us focus our attention on the CPM network.

A single activity time

In the network shown in Figure 10.6, we can see that two paths go through Event 5. Event 5 cannot be realized until Activities 2–5 and 3–5 are both completed. Activity 2–5 has the starting event at 2 and the ending event at 5. Now we can compute the event realization time by tracing the activity time estimates.

Computing ET

The first event (the project starting event) is assigned an *ET* value of zero (*ET* = 0). To compute the *ET* for Event 2, we add the completion time of Activity 1–2 to the preceding *ET*, in this case the *ET* of Event 1:

$$ET = ET \text{ (preceding event)} + \text{activity time}$$
$$ET\ (1\text{--}2) = 0 + 3 = 3$$

In general, the computation procedure for determining the earliest expected time for each network event is as follows:

$$ET_j = \text{Max}\ (ET_i + t_{ij})$$

where

ET_j = the earliest expected time of Event j

ET_i = the earliest expected time that an activity leading to Event j can be started

t_{ij} = the estimated duration of an activity from Event i to Event j.

Event 5 cannot be realized until Activities 2–5 and 3–5 are completed. Thus, we must determine ET_5 as follows:

$$ET_5 = \text{Max}\ (ET_2 + t_{25};\ ET_3 + t_{35})$$
$$= \text{Max}\ (4 + 7;\ 3 + 6)$$
$$= \text{Max}\ (11;\ 9)$$
$$= 11$$

Table 10.3   Computation of ET's for Event 5 and Event 6

EVENT 5

Starting Event	ET_i	Activity	t_{ij}	ET_j
②	4	2–5	7	11*
③	3	3–5	6	9

EVENT 6

Starting Event	ET_i	Activity	t_{ij}	ET_j
④	6	4–6	4	10
④	11	5–6	2	13*

The *ET* value for Event 4 is computed by simply adding the completion time of Activity 2–4 to ET_2. Thus, $ET_4 = ET_2 + t_{24} = 4 + 2 = 6$. The *ET* value for Event 6, the final event, is determined by selecting the latest completion time of Activities 4–6 or 5–6. Thus, the *ET* for Event 6 would be

$$ET_6 = \text{Max } (ET_4 + t_{46}; ET_5 + t_{56})$$
$$= \text{Max } (6 + 4; 11 + 2)$$
$$= \text{Max } (10; 13)$$
$$= 13$$

Table 10.3 presents the computation of *ET* values for Event 5 and Event 6. Figure 10.7 presents the network with *ET* values for all events. The *ET* values are listed on the left of the T-bar above each event.

Figure 10.7   The Network with ET Values

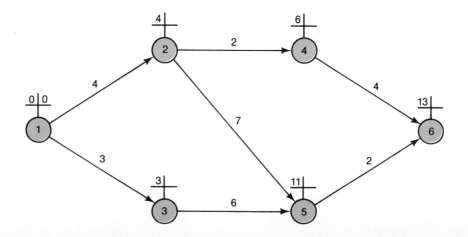

The Latest Allowable Time (*LT*)

The latest allowable time

Once the earliest expected time (*ET*) of the entire network is determined, the *latest allowable time* (*LT*) for an event can be computed. The *LT* for an event is the latest time that the event can be delayed without delaying the completion of the entire project.

The procedure we use in computing the *LT* value is to start from the final event of the network and work *backward* to the starting event in a *right-to-left* fashion. Let us examine our example network presented in Figure 10.6. First, the *LT* for the final event (Node 6) should be set equal to the *ET* value for Event 6, ET_6. In this case, $LT_6 = ET_6 = 13$. This *LT* value of 13 days is the latest time allowed to complete the entire project.

Computing LT

The *LT* value for an event can be computed by subtracting duration times of the activities that terminate at the last event from the preceding *LT* value. For example, the *LT* for Event 4 is $13(LT_6) - 4(t_{46}) = 9$. Similarly, the *LT* for Event 5 is $13(LT_6) - 4(t_{46}) = 9$. Similarly, the *LT* for Event 5 is $13(LT_6) - 2(t_{56}) = 11$. In the case in which two or more activities start from an event, such as Event 1 and Event 2 in our example, we must select the *LT* value that is the smaller. Let us examine the case for Event 2. Since both Activities 2-4 and 2-5 start from Event 2, there will be two *LT* values for Event 2. One is $7[9(LT_4) - 2(t_{24}) = 7]$ and the other is $4[11(LT_5) - 7(t_{25}) = 4]$. We select the smaller of the two. Thus, LT_2 is 4.

In general, the computation for the *LT* value for an event in a network is

$$LT_i = \text{Min } (LT_j - t_{ij})$$

where

LT_i = the latest allowable time of Event *i*

LT_j = the latest allowable time of Event *j* toward which Activity *i-j* is headed

t_{ij} = the estimated duration for an activity from Event *i* to Event *j*

The *LT* value for Event 3 is simply $LT_3 = 11(LT_5) - 6(t_{35}) = 5$. Activities 1-2 and 1-3 both start from Event 1. Thus, we can compute the *LT* value for Event 1 as follows:

$$
\begin{aligned}
LT_1 &= \text{Min } (LT_2 - t_{12}; LT_3 - t_{13}) \\
&= \text{Min } (4 - 4; 5 - 3) \\
&= \text{Min } (0; 2) \\
&= 0
\end{aligned}
$$

Computations of the latest allowable times for all of the events of the network are summarized in Table 10.4. It should be noted here that, by definition, at the beginning point of the network (Event 1) $ET_1 = LT_1 = 0$, and at the ending point (Event *n*) $ET_n = LT_n$.

The Critical Path

Critical and noncritical events

Once the values of *ET* and *LT* for all of the events are determined, we can easily identify the critical path of the network. If the values of *ET* and *LT* for an event are equal, then the event is referred to as the *critical event*. All other events for which the *LT* values are not equal to the respective *ET* values are *noncritical events*. Each noncritical event has a positive *slack*.

Table 10.4   Summary of LT Values for the Network Events

Starting Event (*I*)	Ending Event (*J*)	LT_J	Activity	t_{IJ}	LT_I
6	—	13	—	—	13
5	6	13	5-6	2	11*
4	6	13	4-6	4	9
3	5	11	3-5	6	5
2	4	9	2-4	2	7
2	5	11	2-5	7	4*
1	2	4	1-2	4	0*
1	3	5	1-3	3	2

Figure 10.8   The Network with ET, LT, and Slack Values

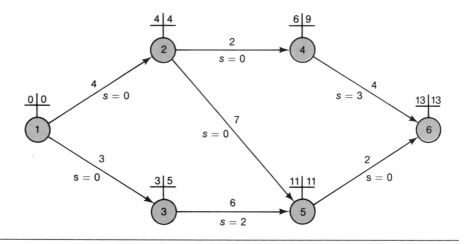

The slack time

The slack at a noncritical event is the difference between its *LT* and *ET* values $(S = LT - ET)$. The slack *(S)* represents an excess amount of time available for the activity. In other words, we can delay this *particular* event up to the amount of slack time without risking the delay of the entire project. Figure 10.8 presents the network of our example problem with respective *ET,* and *LT,* and slack values at each event. The *ET* values are listed on the left side of the T-bar, the *LT* values on the right side of the T-bar, and the slacks beneath each activity arrow.

The critical path

Now we can determine the critical path by tracing the critical events which have no slack values (i.e., *S* = 0). Thus, the critical path of our network is ① → ② → ⑤ → ⑥, as shown in Figure 10.9. It should be noted that the events on the critical

Figure 10.9   Critical Path of the Example Network

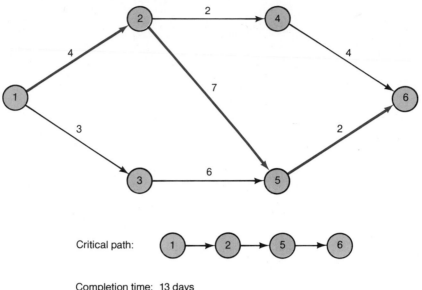

Critical path:

Completion time: 13 days

path have zero slacks, and consequently there is no time to spare or to delay without delaying the entire project. However, at noncritical events, activities can be delayed up to their respective slack times without delaying the entire project. For example, Event 3 has a slack of 2 days. Thus, we can delay Activity 1-3 for up to 2 days. Since t_{13} is 3, Activity 1-3 can take up to 5 days without delaying the entire project.

Activity Scheduling and Slack

When we computed slack times at noncritical events, we might have given the impression that we could delay activities up to the computed slack times. This is not usually the case because cumulative delays at noncritical events may actually delay the entire project. In this section we will consider activity scheduling in relation to the associated slack times at various events.

Activity scheduling

The time at which an activity must be scheduled can be computed from the *ET* and *LT* values we determined earlier. For instance, in our example network presented in Figure 10.8, Activity 2-4 must be scheduled to start no earlier than after 4 days ($ET_2 = 4$) and to end no later than after 9 days ($LT_4 = 9$). In other words, Activity 2-4 can be scheduled as shown in Figure 10.10. We can start Activity 2-4 at the beginning of the fifth day and complete it in two days (at the end of the sixth day). We can also start it at the beginning of the eighth day and complete it by the end of the ninth day. Or we can make any other arrangement from the fifth day to the end of the ninth day.

Total slack

There are two types of slack for each activity in a network. *Total slack* represents

Figure 10.10   Scheduling Activity 2-4

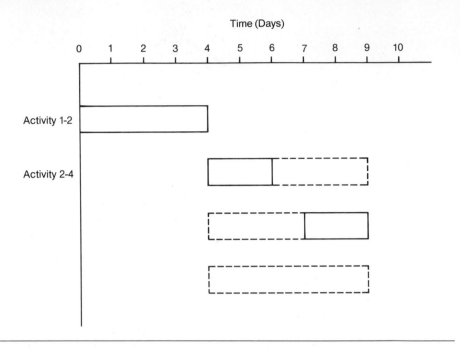

the maximum amount of time available to schedule an activity, as we discussed earlier. Total slack values can be determined as follows:

$$TS_{ij} = LT_j - ET_i - t_{ij}$$

where

TS_{ij} = total slack for Activity i-j

LT_j = the latest allowable time for Event j

ET_i = the earliest expected time for Event i

t_{ij} = the time duration for Activity i-j

For example, we can compute total slack for Activities 1-3 and 2-5 as follows:

$$TS_{13} = LT_3 - ET_1 - t_{13}$$
$$= 5 - 0 - 3$$
$$= 2$$
$$TS_{25} = LT_5 - ET_2 - t_{25}$$
$$= 11 - 4 - 7$$
$$= 0$$

The total slack for a given activity is based on the assumption that other activities on the same path will be completed during a certain time period. Whenever we have two or more noncritical activities in the same path, there may be *shared* or *floating* slack. For example, let us consider the network shown in Figure 10.11. The critical

Shared or floating slack

Figure 10.11   Shared or Floating Slack

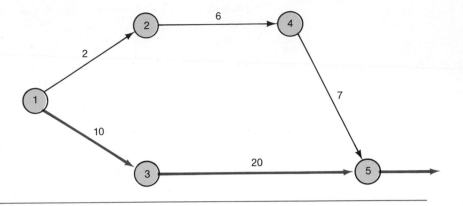

path 1-3-5 requires a total of 30 days. Activities 1-2, 2-4, and 4-5 are noncritical and they require a total of 15 days (2 + 6 + 7 = 15). Suppose the three activities have a total of only 10 free slack days. Then, there exists a five-day shared slack (15 − 10 = 5). This floating slack can be used anyway we want among the three activities.

Free slack   Now we need to compute free slack for each noncritical activity. *Free slack* is the length of time an activity can be delayed without causing any delay in the completion of the entire network. We can compute free slack for a given activity by the following formula:

$$FS_{ij} = ET_j - ET_i - t_{ij}$$

where

$$FS_{ij} = \text{free slack for Activity } i\text{-}j$$
$$ET_j = \text{the earliest expected time for Event } j$$
$$ET_i = \text{the earliest expected time for Event } i$$
$$t_{ij} = \text{the time duration for Activity } i\text{-}j$$

For example, we can compute free slack for Activities 3-5 and 4-6 in Figure 10.9 as follows:

$$FS_{35} = ET_5 - ET_3 - t_{35}$$
$$= 11 - 3 - 6$$
$$= 2$$
$$FS_{46} = ET_6 - ET_4 - t_{46}$$
$$= 13 - 6 - 4$$
$$= 3$$

It should be pointed out here that a free slack can occur only at merge events. Now we can summarize the results of all of our computations as shown in Table 10.5. This table is valuable in the sense that we can use the information to schedule our activities, determine the critical path, determine the length of the project, and calculate the total free slack.

Table 10.5   Summary Information for the Network

Activity	Activity Duration	Earliest Expected Time (ET_i)	Latest Allowable Time (LT_j)	Total Slack (TS_{ij})	Free Slack (FS_{ij})
1-2	4 days	0	4	0	0
1-3	3	0	5	2	0
2-4	2	4	9	3	0
2-5	7	4	11	0	0
3-5	6	3	11	2	2
4-6	4	6	13	3	3
5-6	2	11	13	0	0

▢ Critical path activities

CASETTE 10.1   SCHMIDT CONSTRUCTION, INC.

Hans Schmidt has been an independent contractor for over 20 years. He is a meticulous designer and worker who rejects any fast and sloppy job. This is the primary reason for his outstanding reputation as a quality builder in the city. Just recently he signed a contract to build a town house for a retiring banker. The contract indicates that Hans has to complete the house much faster than his normal pace will allow. He has never used any systematic approaches to conduct his building business.

His daughter Megan is home helping Hans do the bookkeeping work during the summer vacation. Megan is a management major at the university, and she has been lecturing Hans about how he should use modern management techniques in his operation. Hans decided that this is a perfect chance to test Megan and convince her that theory and practice do not always mix.

Network Construction

Megan accepted her father's challenge, although her confidence seemed to wane somewhat as she sat down and pondered where to begin. She quickly rejected linear programming, goal programming, and dynamic programming approaches when she realized that the problem did not fit their model requirements. Finally she decided to use a network approach based on PERT/CPM.

Identifying major activities

On the basis of conversations with Hans and past contract records, Megan identified several major activities and their estimated durations. She also asked Hans about special relationships among the activities. As a result of these inquiries, she was able to compile the relevant information shown in Table 10.6. Hans reviewed the table and was pleasantly surprised to find that Megan's expensive education was not a complete waste.

Examining the information in Table 10.6, Megan realized that she must connect Events 3 and 4 because the plumbing work (Activity F) can be started only when both Activities B and C have been completed. Fortunately, she recalled how to add a dummy activity to accommodate such a situation. Megan constructed a network for the town house project as shown in Figure 10.12.

Table 10.6   The Town House Project

Activity	(Nodes)	Description	Predecessor	Duration (Days)
A	(1-2)	Foundation and basement work	none	5
B	(2-3)	Erecting walls and roofing	A	10
C	(2-4)	Flooring work	A	6
D	(3-5)	Landscaping work	B	10
E	(3-6)	Electrical work	B	3
F	(4-6)	Plumbing work	B, C	4
G	(6-7)	Finishing work	D, E, F	15

Figure 10.12   The Town House Project Network Diagram

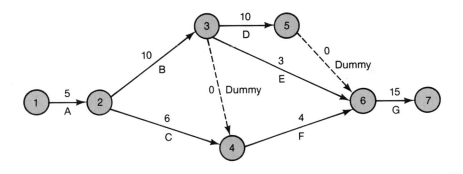

Network Analysis

In Figure 10.12, it is obvious that Activities B and C can be started at the end of 5 days from the beginning of the project. On completion of Activity B at the end of 15 days ($5 + 10 = 15$), Activity D can be started. Similarly, on completion of Activity C at the end of 11 days ($5 + 6 = 11$) and the dummy activity at the end of 15 days ($5 + 10 + 0 = 15$), we can begin Activity F. Thus, Activity F can be started at the end of 15 days.

In order to proceed with the network analysis, Megan decided to use the concepts of the earliest expected time and the latest allowable time by means of the following formulas:

Computing ET *and* LT

$$ET_j = \text{Max } (ET_i + t_{ij})$$
$$LT_i = \text{Min } (LT_j - t_{ij})$$

Also, based on the *ET* and *LT* values at each event in the network derived above, Megan was able to compute total slack and free slack with the following formulas:

$$TS_{ij} = LT_j - ET_i - t_{ij}$$
$$FS_{ij} = ET_j - ET_i - t_{ij}$$

Figure 10.13   The Town House Network with ET, LT, TS, *and* FS *Values*

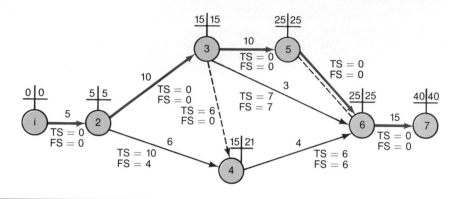

Figure 10.13 presents the town house project network with associated *ET, LT, TS,* and *FS* values. Megan identified 4 possible paths to complete the project. They are (expressed in event nodes):

Path	Length of Time	
①-②-③-⑤-⑥-⑦	5 + 10 + 10 + 0 + 15 = 40 days	← critical path
①-②-③-⑥-⑦	5 + 10 + 3 + 15 = 33	
①-②-③-④-⑥-⑦	5 + 10 + 0 + 4 + 15 = 34	
①-②-④-⑥-⑦	5 + 6 + 4 + 15 = 30	

The critical path is determined as ① - ② - ③ - ⑤ - ⑥ - ⑦ with a total duration time of 40 days. On the basis of this analysis, Megan prepared for her father the summary report shown in Table 10.7. She also prepared a construction schedule

Table 10.7   Summary Report of the Town House Project

1. Critical Activities and Time Duration

Foundation and basement work	5 days
Erecting walls and roofing	10
Landscaping work	10
Finishing work	15
	Total = 40 days

2. Noncritical Activities, Duration, and Slack Time

	Duration	Total Slack	Feedback
Flooring work	6	10	4
Electrical work	3	7	7
Plumbing work	4	6	6

3. Total Project Duration = 40 days

Figure 10.14   The Town House Construction Schedule

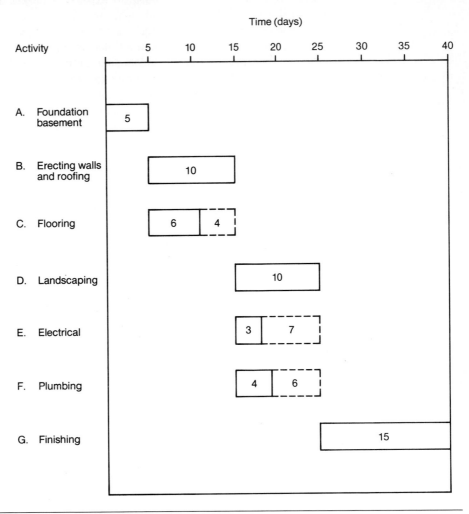

for the various activities, as shown in Figure 10.14. Hans was greatly impressed by the thoroughness of the study and very proud of his favorite network person.

CPM TIME AND COST TRADE-OFFS

Expediting a project

The critical path method is an effective tool in deriving valuable information about critical activities, noncritical activities, free slack times for noncritical activities, and total completion time for a project. One of the most important aspects of CPM network analysis is its capacity for evaluating alternative ways to expedite some or all of the network activities and then analyze their cost implications. In many real-world problems, it is often desirable to expedite a project even at a considerable additional cost. On the other hand, sometimes it is desirable not to expedite at all, depending on the nature of the project and the environment.

The time-cost trade-off

There was an interesting case in a Colorado ski resort town where three builders were each undertaking a large condominium project. One builder expedited his project at 50 percent cost overrun in order to open the condominium before the ski season. The second builder maintained his regular construction schedule, and the third contractor deliberately slowed down his schedule by 30 percent at a cost under-run of 15 percent. This particular ski season turned out to be a total disaster—the ski slopes were open for only 25 days out of the 140-day season because of a lack of snow. The first builder went bankrupt, the second builder sustained a substantial loss, and the third builder was not very happy either, but at least he was not complaining.

Project crashing

An important extension of project time analysis is project *time-cost trade-off* analysis. Expediting or rushing activities in order to shorten the project duration from the normal completion time is often referred to as project *crashing*. Cost analysis associated with project crashing is an important part of CPM analysis. However, time-cost trade-off can be applied to any project scheduling network, regardless of whether it is a CPM or PERT type network. The basic purpose of time-cost analysis is to determine certain activities of the network that can be expedited (by how much time and at what cost).

The time-cost analysis

In time-cost analysis, two time estimates and two cost estimates are used to develop the time-cost relationship. The two estimates used are: normal time vs. crash time, and normal cost vs. crash cost. The relationship between normal time/normal cost and crash time/crash cost for an activity is assumed to be linear. Let us suppose that an activity can be performed at a normal work pace requiring $200 and 4 days. Under an emergency situation, the same activity can be performed on a ''crash'' basis requiring $500 and only 2 days. The time-cost relationship can be developed as illustrated in Figure 10.15.

The slope of the straight line in Figure 10.15 represents the change in cost associated with one unit change in time. In other words, it represents the *crash cost per unit of time* (e.g., day, week, year). We can develop the slope as follows:

$$\text{Crash cost per unit of time} = \frac{\text{Crash cost} - \text{Normal cost}}{\text{Normal time} - \text{Crash time}}$$

$$\text{Slope} = \frac{CC - NC}{NT - CT}$$

For the problem illustrated in Figure 10.15, we can determine the crash cost per day as follows:

$$\text{Crash cost per day} = \frac{\$500 - \$200}{4 - 2}$$

$$= \frac{\$300}{2}$$

$$= \$150$$

Thus, if we are interested in reducing the total project completion time by expediting this particular activity, we can do so up to 2 days at a cost of $150 per day. One

Figure 10.15   Activity Time/Cost Relationship

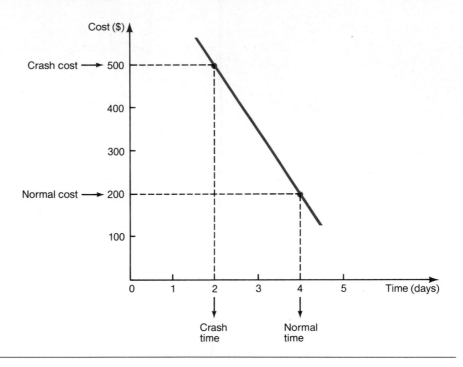

Changes of the critical path

thing we must realize when crashing a project is that the critical path may change while crashing. Therefore, we should take care to crash an activity without affecting the project completion time.

EXAMPLE 10.2   *PROJECT CRASHING*

Let us consider the project network presented in Figure 10.16. The normal and crash times (in parentheses) as well as the crash cost per day are also shown in the network. The time-cost information, including the computed crash cost per day, is provided in Table 10.8.

We can easily determine the critical path of the example network by computing *ET* and *LT* values for each activity. The critical path is ① - ② - ④ - ⑤ and the normal project completion time is 58 days.

In analyzing this project crashing, the type of questions that we need to answer are: Can we complete the project faster than the critical path indicates? If so, at what additional cost? What is the minimum cost required to complete the project in 10 weeks? What would be the best way to schedule the project, given that we have a $2 million budget?

Project crashing procedure

Now we are ready to examine the project crashing. As we go through the analysis procedure, we must pay close attention to any change in the critical path through-

Figure 10.16   A Network for Cost Analysis

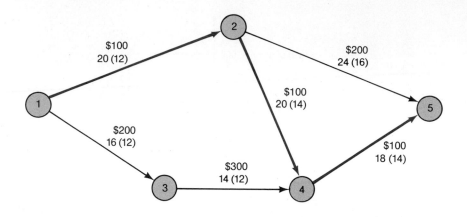

Project completion time = 58 days

Table 10.8   The Network Crashing Information

Activity	Time (Days)		Cost (Dollars)		Crash Cost/Day
	Normal	Crash	Normal	Crash	
1-2*	20	12	$1,800	$2,600	$100
1-3	16	12	800	1,600	200
2-5	24	16	3,200	4,800	200
2-4*	20	14	1,600	2,200	100
3-4	14	12	2,400	3,000	300
4-5*	18	14	800	1,200	100
			10,600	15,400	

*Critical path.
The normal project completion time = 58 days.
The completely crashed completion time = 40 days.

out the crashing process. The time-cost trade-off analysis involves the following steps:

Step 1. Identify and crash the critical activity that has the minimum crash cost per unit of time. In a case in which there are multiple critical paths, select the joint critical activity that has the minimum crash cost per unit of time. If no such joint critical activity exists, select the activity from each critical path that has the minimum crash cost per unit of time.

Step 2. Completely revise the network by adjusting the time and cost of the crashed activity. Identify the critical path. If the normal project completion time

Joint critical activity

Updating the network

Figure 10.17 Cost Network with Activity 1-2 Crashed

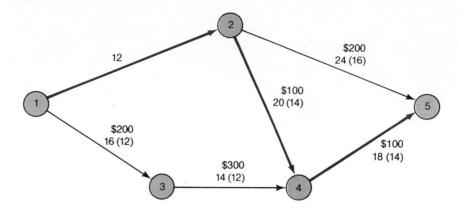

Project completion time = 50 days

equals the crashed completion time, terminate the procedure. Otherwise, repeat the procedure by going back to Step 1.

The First Crashing

In our example, the crash costs of three critical activities, 1-2, 2-4, and 4-5, are identical, $100. Thus, we may choose any one of them. Let us arbitrarily choose Activity 1-2 to crash. Activity 1-2 can be crashed by 8 days: 20 (normal time) − 12 (crash time) = 8. Thus, the associated crashing cost is $800: $100 (crash cost per day) × 8 (days) = $800.

The revised network, adjusted for the time and cost assigned to Activity 1-2, is shown in Figure 10.17. The critical path is not changed but remains ① - ② - ④ - ⑤. The project completion time has been reduced by 8 days to 50 days, which is still greater than the crashed completion time of 40 days. Thus, we must continue the procedure.

Continue crashing?

The Second Crashing

Since Activity 1-2 has been crashed, either Activity 2-4 or Activity 4-5 should be chosen for crashing based on its crash cost per day. Since both activities have the same crash costs of $100, we may choose Activity 2-4 arbitrarily. Notice, however, that we cannot reduce Activity 2-4 for more than 2 days since doing so will generate a new critical path (i.e., ① - ③ - ④ - ⑤). Therefore, we can crash only up to 2 days. This crash will reduce Activity 2-4 to 18 days, resulting in a project completion time of 48 days. The additional cost for this crash is $200. The revised network is shown in Figure 10.18.

The Third Crashing

The project completion time of 48 days is still greater than the completely crashed completion time of 40 days. Thus, we can continue our crashing procedure. As shown in Figure 10.18, now there are two critical paths: ① - ② - ④ - ⑤ and ①

Figure 10.18   Cost Network with Activities 1-2 and 2-4 Crashed

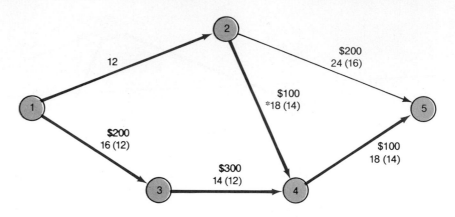

Project completion time = 48 days
*Activity 2–4 partially crashed by 2 days

- ③ - ④ - ⑤. By crashing Activity 4-5, the only joint activity (i.e., the common activity for both critical paths), we can reduce the project completion time without crashing more than one activity. We may, in fact, crash more than one activity if we can reduce the project completion time and reduce the cost by doing so; for example, we may crash an activity on each of the two critical paths. Here, we can reduce by 4 days the duration for Activity 4-5. Thus, as shown in Figure 10.19, the project completion time has been reduced to 44 days, and the resultant additional crashing cost is $400.

The Fourth Crashing

Which uncrashed activity to select?

We still have two critical paths, as shown in Figure 10.19. This time, however, we cannot reduce only one activity since there is no single uncrashed activity through which both critical paths pass. If we crash only one activity, one of the two critical paths will be still critical (unreduced) and the project completion time will remain unchanged at 44 days. Thus, in this case, both Activities 1-3 and 2-4 should be crashed simultaneously. This selection is based on the fact that Activity 2-4 is the only activity left to be crashed and Activity 1-3 has less crash cost than Activity 3-4. In general, if there are several uncrashed activities to choose from several critical paths, we should select the activity from each critical path that has the minimum crashing cost.

One more thing to note is that we can crash each activity down to the lower limit established by one of them (whichever has the minimum crash time). In this example, both Activities 1-3 and 2-4 can be reduced by 4 days. Thus, Activity 1-3 has been reduced to 12 days (16 − 4 = 12), whereas Activity 2-4 has been reduced further to 14 days (18 − 4 = 14), as illustrated in Figure 10.20. Consequently, the total project completion time is 40 days and the additional crashing cost is $1,200 ($200 × 4 + $100 × 4 = $1,200).

Figure 10.19   Cost Network with Activities 1-2, 2-4, and 4-5 Crashed

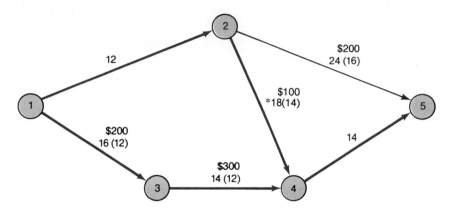

Project completion time = 44 days

Figure 10.20   Cost Network with Activities 1-2, 4-5, 2-4, and 1-3 Crashed

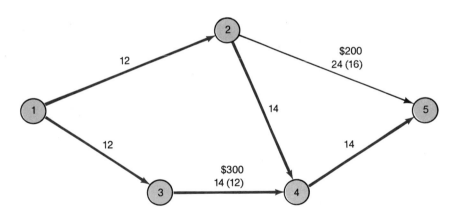

Project completion time = 40 days

When to stop the procedure?

Figure 10.20 shows that the activity times of Activities 1-2, 2-4, and 4-5 have been reduced to their limits. In other words, there cannot be any more crashing because the project completion time of 40 days will remain unchanged even if we crash either Activity 2-5 or 3-4 or both. Thus, the minimum completion time for this project is 40 days, and the total additional cost for crashing the 4 activities is $2,600 ($800 + $200 + $400 + $1,200 = $2,600). The total cost of this project is then $13,200: $10,600 (normal cost) + $2,600 (additional crashing cost) = $13,200.

Table 10.9   Summary of the Crashing Procedure

Crashing Step Number	Activities Crashed	Time Reduced	Revised Project Completion Time	Additional Cost	Revised Project Cost
0	—	—	58 days	—	$10,600
1	1-2	8 days	50	$ 800	11,400
2	2-4	2	48	200	11,600
3	4-5	4	44	400	12,000
4	1-3 & 2-4	4	40	1,200	13,200
		18 days		$2,600	

Figure 10.21   Time-Cost Trade-off Relationship

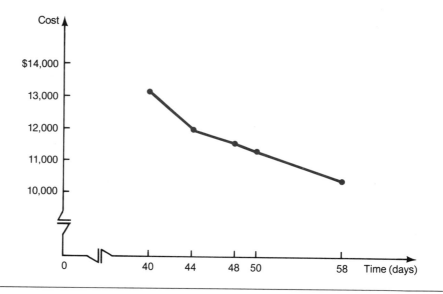

Table 10.9 summarizes the result of this cost analysis. Figure 10.21 presents the time-cost trade-off relationship through the crashing process.

The Final Analysis

Based on our analysis, it is obvious that if the incentive of crashing the project is worth more than the crashing cost of $2,600, it is desirable to crash it. Otherwise, it is, of course, not worth crashing the project. In addition to this standard time-cost trade-off analysis, we can perform several sensitivity-type analyses. For example, we may want to find answers to questions such as: What is the minimum cost required to complete the project in 45 days? Given that we can afford only $12,000, what would be the best way to schedule the project? This type of question can be answered by using the same time-cost trade-off analysis procedure.

ESTIMATING ACTIVITY TIMES IN PERT

Thus far, our discussion has been focused on the CPM technique in which we assume that a single estimate of each activity duration can be obtained with certainty. Such an assumption is not warranted in many situations. PERT is more effective in handling cases in which activity duration times are not known with certainty.

Basic assumptions of PERT

The PERT technique makes the following basic assumptions: (1) activity times are statistically independent and could be associated with a known distribution (usually a beta distribution); (2) there are a sufficient number of activities involved in the network and thus the summed totals of activity times based on their means and variances will be normally distributed; and (3) three estimates of the activity duration can be obtained for each activity—optimistic, most likely, and pessimistic times.

Three time estimates

We can define the three time estimates for each project activity as follows:

Optimistic (shortest) time represents the duration required to complete an activity under the most ideal conditions. It is denoted by *a*.

Most likely (model) time is the expected duration of an activity under normal conditions. It is denoted by *m*.

Pessimistic (longest) time represents the duration of an activity under unusual conditions, such as machine breakdowns, material shortages, bad weather, and the like. It is denoted by *b*.

Activity time distribution

As noted previously, it is assumed that the distribution of the three time estimates is best approximated by a *beta* distribution. In a beta distribution, it is simple to determine such parameters as mean and standard deviation by using the following formula:

$$\text{Mean:} \quad t_e = \frac{a + 4m + b}{6}$$

$$\text{Standard deviation:} \quad \sigma_e = \frac{b - a}{6}$$

where t_e = mean duration for an activity in the PERT network.

By using t_e values, it is possible to make probability statements about the expected completion time for the project. Suppose that we have obtained the following three time estimates: $a = 8$, $m = 17$, and $b = 20$. Then, we can compute

$$t_e = \frac{8 + 4(17) + 20}{6} = \frac{96}{6} = 16$$

$$\sigma_e = \frac{20 - 8}{6} = 2$$

The expected duration of activity is 16 days with the standard deviation of 2 days. In this example, the most likely time ($m = 17$) is closer to the pessimistic time ($b = 20$) than to the optimistic time ($a = 8$). Thus, the activity time distribution is skewed to the right, as shown in Figure 10.22. Based on the information we obtain from the three time estimates, we can further analyze the network problem. For

---

Figure 10.22   Beta Distribution of a PERT Activity Time

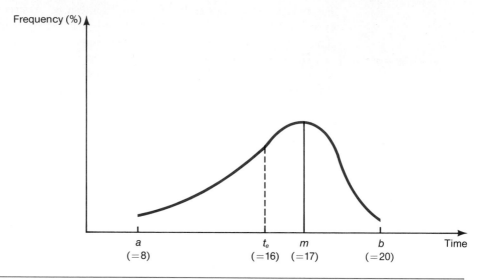

example, we can determine the expected project completion time, the variance of the critical path, and the probability associated with completing the project before a specified period of time.

CASETTE 10.2   *DINO'S INC. OF CALIFORNIA*

Dino's Inc. of California is a California-based firm that operates a chain of fast food restaurants, Dino's, throughout the United States. The company has been extremely successful owing to its innovative menu and promotional activities. One of Dino's recent successful menu innovations was Beefalo Burger de Dino.

Dino's product development process is centered in two groups: the Product Development Committee, which reviews and makes final decisions on new products, and the Research and Development Department, which provides technical support. The product development process involves eight distinct activities: (1) idea generation, (2) business analysis, (3) screening, (4) development, (5) quality assurance, (6) testing, (7) approval of the committee, and (8) commercialization.

The management of Dino's has been very concerned about the duration of the product development process, and it is keenly interested in obtaining information concerning the possibility of reducing the completion time of the whole process. The Product Development Committee decided to ask Cindy Hall, a senior systems analyst, to analyze the problem and make recommendations.

Cindy is an experienced systems analyst with extensive working knowledge of PERT and CPM. Because of Dino's excellent information systems, Cindy was able

Table 10.10 Activity Time Estimates for Dino's Inc.

Activity	Description	Predecessor	a (Optimistic)	m (Most Likely)	b (Pessimistic)
A	Idea generation	none	8	12	16
B	Business analysis	A	12	15	24
C	Screening	A	5	7	15
D	Development	B	4	6	14
E	Quality assurance	B	2	4	6
F	Testing	C	6	10	14
G	Approval of committee	E,F	2	4	12
H	Commercialization	D,G	13	15	23

Table 10.11 The t_e, σ_e, and σ_e^2 for Each Activity

Activity	Expected (Mean) Time $\left(\dfrac{a + 4m + b}{6}\right)$	Standard Deviation $\left(\dfrac{b - a}{6}\right)$	Variance $\left(\dfrac{b - a}{6}\right)^2$
A*	12	4/3	16/9
B*	8	5/3	25/9
C	16	2	4
D	7	5/3	25/9
E*	4	4/3	16/9
F	10	4/3	16/9
G*	5	5/3	25/9
H*	16	5/3	25/9

*Critical activity.

to obtain time estimates for each activity without much difficulty. Cindy compiled the relevant data, as shown in Table 10.10.

In order to obtain the expected project completion time, the critical path of the network must be determined. In a PERT network, we can compute t_e (mean completion time) and σ_e (standard deviation) for each activity. The variance of the activity time distribution, $\sigma_e^2 = [(b - a)/6]^2$, is also useful for further analysis. Cindy computed t_e, σ_e, and σ_e^2 for each activity, as presented in Table 10.11. Based on the activity precedence relationship information compiled in Table 10.10 and the activity time data presented in Table 10.11, Cindy developed a PERT network and its critical path, as shown in Figure 10.23.

Cindy examined the past project records and found that the distribution of each activity completion time is about *normal*. Thus, the expected activity times for critical activities (i.e., activities on the critical path) are also normally distributed. Accordingly, Cindy makes the assumption that the summation of all of the time estimates

Figure 10.23   Critical path

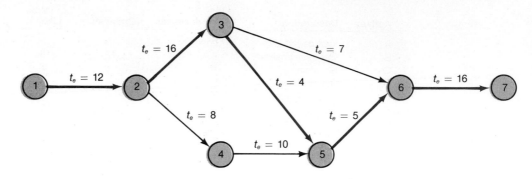

Expected completion time, $E(t) = 53$ days

of critical activities, which is the expected project completion time, would be normally distributed according to the central limit theorem of probability theory. The expected project completion time of Dino's new product development is 53 days, as shown in Figure 10.23.

Given the normal distribution assumption, the probability of completing the project in 53 days or less is 0.5. We can develop a more precise normal curve of the project completion time if we determine the standard deviation of the time estimates for critical activities. The standard deviation is computed as follows:

Computing standard deviations

$$\sigma_{cp} = \sqrt{\sum \sigma_e^2}$$

where

σ_{cp} = standard deviation of the expected project completion time
$\sum \sigma_e^2$ = sum of variance of all activities on the critical path

Since Cindy has already computed the variance of each critical activity, σ_{cp} is easily computed as shown in Table 10.12. The standard deviation of the expected project completion time is 3.45 days. Now Cindy can easily find the probability of completing the project on or before a specified time (or on or after a specified time).

For some time Dino's management has been trying to complete the product development within 50 days, but without success. In order to find the probability of this completion time, Cindy decided to use the formula that computes the *standardized random variate* (Z). The formula is as follows:

Standardized random variate

$$Z = \frac{X - E(t)}{\sigma_{cp}}$$

where

X = desired project completion time
$E(t)$ = expected project completion time

Table 10.12 *Computation of Project Standard Deviation*

Activities on Critical Path	σ_e	σ_e^2
A	4/3	16/9
B	5/3	25/9
E	4/3	16/9
G	5/3	25/9
H	5/3	25/9
		$\Sigma\sigma_e^2 = 107/9$

$$\sigma_{cp} = \sqrt{\Sigma_e^2} = \sqrt{107/9} = 3.45$$

σ_{cp} = standard deviation of activities on the critical path

Z = number of standard deviation of a normal distribution (standardized random variate)

Using the above formula, Cindy determined the standardized random variate, Z, as follows

$$Z = \frac{50 - 53}{3.45} = -0.87$$

We can find the probability corresponding to any Z value in the standard normal distribution table in Appendix 5. The probability for the Z value of 0.87 is 0.8078. Since $Z = -0.87$, in this case we must subtract 0.8078 from the standard deviate of 1.0. Thus, we obtain $1.0 - 0.8078 = 0.1922$. In other words, the probability of completing Dino's new product development within 50 days is 0.1922, or 19.22 percent. This reasoning is illustrated in Figure 10.24.

Suppose that Dino's is also interested in finding the probability of completing the project in 60 days. The computation for this probability (p) is

$$p \text{ (60 or fewer days)} = p\left(Z \le \frac{60 - 53}{3.45}\right)$$

$$= p\left(Z \le \frac{7}{3.45}\right)$$

$$= p\,(Z \le 2.0290)$$

$$= 0.97927$$

Thus, the probability of completing the project in 60 days or less is 0.9793, or 97.93 percent.

In addition to determining the probability $(p = 0.1922)$ of completing the new product development project within 50 days, Cindy made several other suggestions. These suggestions were based on probability analysis of the earliest completion times at each node, determined by summing the activity times and variances along the critical path. Also, she analyzed the possible impact of the variances of noncritical

Figure 10.24   *Normal Distribution of Expected Project Time*

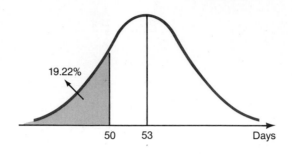

activities on the probability of the project completion. Soon after this study, Cindy was promoted to the position of Manager of Systems Analysis.

APPLYING COMPUTERS TO PROJECT PLANNING

Computer packages

As we have seen in previous sections of this chapter, it is a time-consuming job to analyze PERT/CPM networks by hand. It might be impossible to perform certain network analyses without the help of computers, especially when the networks are large and complex. There are available today a number of computer packages that are capable of analyzing sophisticated network problems such as scheduling multiple projects simultaneously, providing cost and resource information, choosing the best procedure, and analyzing probabilistic network problems. In summary, the real-world scheduling network analysis can be performed effectively by using computers for the specific objectives of each analysis.

REAL-WORLD APPLICATIONS

GERT and VERT

Surveys of managers and practicing management scientists, similar to those cited in Chapter 1, indicate that network techniques are applied to a variety of managerial problems. Of course, it is not clear whether these surveys were referring to the actual use of PERT/CPM or to many different types of networking techniques. We believe that PERT/CPM, or stochastic network techniques such as graphical evaluation and review technique (GERT) and venture evaluation and review technique (VERT), are often used by large technology-oriented organizations and federal agencies. However, these techniques are not widely applied by medium-sized or small organizations, primarily because of a lack of technical staff.

Nevertheless, we believe the Gantt chart and PERT/CPM have many sound concepts to offer, such as the precedence relationship, events, activities, the critical path, slack analysis, probabilistic analysis of the network, time-cost trade-off analysis, and the like. Thus, we believe project planning will remain an important part of management science. It is especially so with the advent of today's inexpensive but powerful micro- or personal computers.

Application of PERT/CPM in Government

A study was published in 1979 concerning the extent of real-world applications of PERT/CPM and the factors related to its successful applications in a federal government agency.[1] Specifically, this study focuses on the use of PERT/CPM by 19 national forest offices in the states of Oregon and Washington. These offices, which are organizations within the U.S. Department of Agriculture, administer 23 million acres of land and account for over 25 percent of the raw timber sold from national forest land in the continental United States.

Among the many tasks performed by the forest office administrators, one of the most complex is the project scheduling required for a timber sale. Thus, in the early 1960s, national forest administrations were eager to apply PERT/CPM techniques. By 1970, there was a computer package developed for this purpose called "Critical Path Man Scheduling." The program is capable of handling 99 timber sales containing as many as 4,500 activities and 99 different resource craft skills. During the past 17 years, 18 of the 19 forests in the region have applied the program to some aspect of the timber sales activities.

Factors for successful applications

Although the application rate was extremely high, only 4 out of 18 PERT/CPM introductions were evaluated as successful. A further investigation revealed two important factors for the successful introduction of PERT/CPM: (1) the organizational level of the person making the original introduction, and (2) the stated purpose of the original introduction. If the person introducing PERT/CPM is at a higher organizational level, it is more likely that PERT/CPM application would continue in the organization. Also, if the stated purpose is broad and general, the chance of successful PERT/CPM application would be enhanced.

This study supports the notion that PERT and CPM are valuable techniques. However, in order for the success of their real-world applications to be increased, they must be carefully tailored to fit the manager and his or her decision problems at hand. In other words, it is imperative to determine beforehand what type of information can be generated by these techniques. The failure to do so may have been the primary reason behind the fewer than expected successful applications of PERT and CPM in the national forest offices.

SUMMARY

In this chapter we have discussed several valuable tools for project planning. They are the Gantt chart, the general project network, CPM, and PERT. Although the Gantt chart is the simplest and perhaps the most widely used tool among practicing managers, it can show only the duration of various project activities on a time scale.

---

[1] C. W. Dane, C. F. Gray, and B. M. Woodworth, "Factors Affecting the Successful Application of PERT/CPM Systems in a Government Organization," *Interfaces,* 9:5 (Nov. 1979), 94–98.

If we want to analyze interrelationships among project activities, we need to develop a network. A network can provide such useful information as activities, events, precedence relationships, earliest expected time, latest allowable time, total slack, free slack, and, perhaps most importantly, the critical path.

PERT and CPM techniques are built on the general concept of project networks. CPM utilizes time-cost trade-off analysis based on two time and cost estimates: normal time and crash time, and normal cost and crash cost. On the basis of this data, CPM can manipulate the critical path while establishing desired trade-offs between the project time and cost.

PERT introduces probabilistic aspects to the project network. It uses three project activity time estimates: optimistic, most likely, and pessimistic. On the basis of these time estimates, we can develop a probability distribution for project completion time. Thus, we can easily determine the probability of project completion within a certain specified time period. This information is invaluable to management in project planning.

References

Cleland, D. I., and King, W. R. *Systems Analysis and Project Management,* 2nd ed. New York: McGraw-Hill, 1975.

Dane, C. W., Gray, C. F., and Woodworth, B. M. "Factors Affecting the Successful Application of PERT/CPM Systems in a Government Organization." *Interfaces,* 9:5 (Nov., 1979), 94–98.

Davis, E. W. *Project Management: Techniques, Applications, and Managerial Issues.* Norcross, Ga.: American Institute of Industrial Engineers, #AIIE-PP & C-76-1, 1976.

Elmaghraby, S. B. *Activity Networks: Project Planning and Control by Network Models.* New York: Wiley, 1977.

Ford, L. R., and Fulkerson, D. R. *Flows in Networks.* Princeton, N.J.: Princeton University Press, 1962.

Gallagher, C. A., and Watson, H. J. *Quantitative Methods for Business Decisions.* New York: McGraw-Hill, 1980.

Lee, S. M., Moeller, G. L., and Digman, L. A. *Network Analysis for Management Decisions: A Stochastic Approach.* Boston: Kluwer-Nijhoff, 1982.

Lee, S. M., Moore, L. J., and Taylor, B. W. *Management Science.* Dubuque, Iowa: W. C. Brown, 1981.

Wiest, J., and Levy, F. *Management Guide to PERT-CPM,* 2nd ed. Englewood Cliffs, N.J.: Prentice-Hall, 1977.

Assignments

10.1 What is a project?

10.2 Describe a project familiar to you by listing the various activities and events of that project.

10.3 Construct a Gantt chart for the project described in Problem 10.2.

10.4 Your term project in the management science class is to analyze the inventory control system of a local manufacturing firm. Describe the necessary activities and their precedence relationships.

10.5 Your term project must be organized in the following sequences: introduction, review of the related literature, research methods, results, discussion of the results, conclusions, and bibliography. You have ten weeks to complete the term project. Construct a Gantt chart for this project.

10.6 Develop a network for the term project based on your Gantt chart.

10.7 What is a dummy activity? Why do we need it?

10.8 Define the following terms: *critical path, noncritical activities, earliest expected time, latest allowable time, total slack, floating slack, free slack, project crashing.*

10.9 What are the two basic steps we must follow in crashing a project?

10.10 What are the important characteristics of a beta distribution?

10.11 Define the three time estimates we use in a PERT network.

10.12 Given that PERT network activities have the following time estimates, determine their mean activity times and standard deviations:

	Activity Time		
Activities	**Optimistic**	**Most Likely**	**Pessimistic**
A	5	10	15
B	3	9	18
C	10	14	22
D	6	10	13
E	12	20	32

10.13 A network activity has the following duration time and cost estimates. Determine the activity time-cost relationship graphically.

Activity Time	Activity Cost
Normal 12 days	Normal $1,200
Crash 8 days	Crash 2,000

10.14 Construct a Gantt chart in order to schedule the following activities:

Activity	Predecessor	Duration (Days)
A	—	10
B	A	7
C	A	4
D	B	9
E	C,D	6

10.15 Construct a project network for the following activities:

Activity (Nodes)	Duration (Days)
1-2	8
2-3	12
2-4	10
3-4	13
3-5	9
4-6	20
5-6	15

10.16 The open-heart surgery team at Methodist General Hospital has developed the following general sequence of activities for a typical patient:

Activity	Predecessor	Duration (Days)
A. Patient check-in	—	1
B. Patient information file	—	1
C. General physical exam	A	2
D. Specialized lab tests	A,B	4
E. Patient rest and preparation	C,D	3
F. Surgery	E	1
G. Intensive care	F	2
H. Recovery care and discharge	G	5

a. Construct a network for the above activities.
b. Determine the earliest expected time for each event.
c. Determine the latest allowable time for each event.
d. Identify the critical path.
e. Determine the expected project completion time.

10.17 A project being planned involves the following activities:

Activity (Nodes)	Duration (Weeks)
1-2	4
1-3	2
2-4	4
2-6	5
3-4	5
3-5	6
4-6	3
5-6	4

a. Construct a network and determine the following information: *ET, LT, TS,* and *FS*.
b. Determine the critical path and the expected project completion time.

10.18 Consider the following project network:

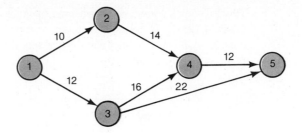

a. Compute *ET* and *LT* at each of the events.
b. Determine *TS* and *FS* for each activity.
c. Identify the critical path and determine the expected project completion time.

10.19 Identify the critical path and determine the expected project completion time for the following network:

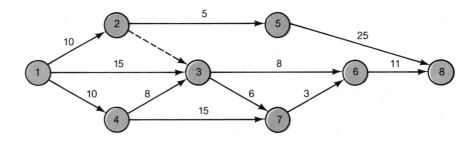

10.20 Jackie Costello has just finished her undergraduate degree in linguistics. After exploring the job market for over a year, she finally decided to go back to school and study for an MBA degree. She has not applied to any school as yet. However, she would like to find out how long it would take to get admitted to a land-grant university. Jackie has identified the following necessary activities for getting an admission:

Activity	Predecessor	Duration (Days)
A. Select universities	—	14
B. Obtain application forms	A	21
C. Take GMAT and send the score	A	50
D. Complete and send applications	B	14
E. Wait for answers	C,D	30
F. Make the final decision	E	10

a. Construct a network for Jackie.
b. Identify the critical path.
c. Determine the expected time (the number of days) in which Jackie may be able to decide which university to attend.

10.21 Thomas Jones, who owns and operates a chain of grocery stores called "Groceries 4 Less," is considering a new computer system for accounting and inventory control. A local computer sales office sent the following information about the computer system installation:

Activity	Precedence	Duration (Weeks)
A. Select the computer model	—	6
B. Design input/output system	A	8
C. Design monitoring system	A	8
D. Assemble computer hardware	B	20
E. Develop the main programs	B	18
F. Develop input/output routines	C	10
G. Create data base	E	8
H. Install the system	D,F	2
I. Test and implement	G,H	7

a. Construct a network for this problem.
b. Identify the critical path by computing the *ET, LT, TS,* and *FS* values.
c. Determine the project completion time.

10.22 A construction company has a shopping center development project. The project involves the following activities and relevant information:

Activity	Activity Time (Weeks) Normal	Activity Time (Weeks) Crash	Activity Cost Normal	Activity Cost Crash
1-2	14	10	$700	$1,100
1-3	12	6	600	900
2-4	16	12	1,600	2,400
3-4	13	10	650	950
2-6	13	10	2,600	3,500
4-6	16	12	1,600	2,600
4-5	15	11	750	950
6-7	12	8	2,400	3,600
5-7	12	6	1,800	2,400

a. Construct a network for the project.
b. Determine the project completion time and total cost based on normal activity times and costs.
c. Determine the project completion time and total cost based on crash activity times and costs.
d. Compute the minimum cost required to crash the project.
e. Compute the cost savings as compared to the total cost involved when all activities of the network are crashed.
f. If the company has only a total of $2,000 available for project crashing, which activities should be crashed?

10.23 Consider a PERT network having activity time estimates as follows:

	Time (Days)		
Activity	*a*	*m*	*b*
1-2	12	24	46
2-3	12	15	30
3-4	9	21	45
4-5	7	9	14

a. Compute the mean time (t_e) of each activity.
b. Determine the expected project completion time.
c. Compute the standard deviation of the project completion time.

10.24 Consider a PERT network having the following activity time estimates:

	Time (Weeks)		
Activity	*a*	*m*	*b*
1-2	2	6	10
2-3	6	14	22
3-4	4	6	20
4-5	10	10	10
5-6	2	20	26
6-7	6	12	18

a. Determine the expected project completion, $E(t)$.
b. Compute the standard deviation for the project.

10.25 Consider a project having the following activities and their time estimates:

Activity	**Most Optimistic**	**Most Likely**	**Most Pessimistic**
1-2	10	22	22
1-3	20	20	20
1-4	4	10	16
2-6	2	14	26
3-6	8	8	20
3-7	8	14	20
3-5	4	4	4
4-5	0	12	12
5-7	4	16	28
6-7	2	8	14

a. Construct a PERT network for the project.
b. Compute the t_e value for each activity.

   c. Compute the σ_e value for each activity.

   d. Identify the critical path and determine the expected project completion time.

10.26 Consider a PERT network that has the expected project completion time of 120 days and a standard deviation of 20 days.

   a. Determine the probability of completing the project within 90 days.

   b. Determine the probability of completing the project between 85 days and 135 days.

10.27 Consider the following network having three activity time estimates:

		Time (Days)		
Activity	Predecessor	Most Optimistic	Most Likely	Most Pessimistic
A	—	2	4	6
B	A	8	12	16
C	A	14	16	30
D	B	4	10	16
E	C,B	6	12	18
F	E	6	8	22
G	D	18	18	30
H	F,G	8	14	32

   a. Construct a PERT network for the project.

   b. Determine the critical path and compute the expected project completion time.

   c. Determine the probability of completing the project within 80 days.

   d. What is the probability the project will require at least 75 days?

10.28 Consider the following project network:

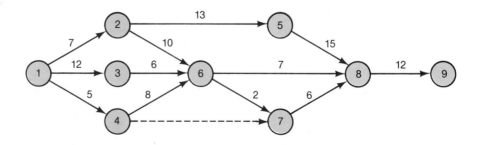

   a. Compute the *ET, LT, TS,* and *FS* values.

   b. Determine the critical path.

   c. Determine the expected project time.

11 INVENTORY MODELS

Every company, regardless of type or size, maintains inventories of some kind. Thus, it is not surprising that maintaining and financing inventories represent a major cost of doing business. The level of inventory to carry is an important decision variable at all stages of manufacturing, marketing, financing, and distributing. Proper inventory control plays an important role in successful operations management. There are two questions that are critical to successful inventory management: (1) When should we replenish the inventory (place an order for a given item)? (2) How many units should we order at a time?

To obtain answers to these questions, quantitative models can be applied. As a matter of fact, inventory control models represent perhaps the oldest management science techniques. As such, there are almost unlimited variations of inventory models developed for unique management situations. In this chapter we will focus on the most fundamental inventory models.

Learning Objectives *From the study of this chapter, you will learn the following:*

1. The importance of inventory control systems for organizational success.
2. Different types of inventories.
3. The purposes of holding inventories.
4. Basic inventory decision problems.
5. Components of total annual inventory costs.
6. Understanding the EOQ model and its variations or extensions.
7. Inventory models under probabilistic conditions.
8. The meaning of the following terms:

Holding cost	*Setup cost*
Ordering cost	*Safety stocks*
Shortage cost	*Lead time*
The EOQ model	*Demand during lead time*
Order quantity	*Material requirements planning (MRP)*
Reorder point	*Kanban*
Inventory cycle	*Lotless repetitive manufacturing system*
Economic lot size	*Inventory system under uncertainty*

CHARACTERISTICS OF INVENTORY SYSTEMS

All types and sizes of organizations, be they manufacturers, agricultural firms, wholesalers, retailers, hospitals, or government agencies, maintain inventories. The total dollar investment in inventories for any particular sector of the economy is substantial. For example, factory inventories in May, 1981, were valued by the U.S. Department of Commerce at $256 billion.

Need for inventory

Inventory is any resource that is set aside for future use. We need inventories because the demand and supply of goods are usually not matched perfectly at any given time or place. As customers, we would like to see stores always carry all of the items we may want on the spur of the moment. For example, we expect a grocery store to carry enough inventories of Coke, light bulbs, or detergent. However, we would not expect a car dealer to have the exact car we may want—a powder-blue station wagon with white interior, cassette player and AM-FM radio, 30-miles-per-gallon diesel engine, and genuine leather upholstery.

Different types of inventories

In many organizations, inventories represent costly unearning or idle resources. As a matter of fact, inventories have been referred to as the graveyard of American business, because excess inventories cause many business failures. There are many different types of inventories. Some examples are:

Raw materials—coal, iron ore, cotton, crude oil, etc.

Semifinished products—copper wire, plastic sheets, threads, lumber, etc.

Finished products—television sets, shoes, designer jeans, frozen pizzas, etc.

Human resources—standby utility personnel such as the utility crew on an assembly line, standby cabin attendants of an airline, reserve personnel of the army, etc.

Financial or other fixed resources—cash on hand, accounts receivable, warehouse space, etc.

Some reasons for keeping inventories

We tend to think that the best decision about inventories is to limit them just enough to meet future demand. However, the real-world situation is far more complex than that. Inventories are maintained for many different reasons. Some of the important reasons are:

1. Satisfaction of fluctuating demand. Sufficiently high levels of inventories are maintained to meet future peak demand. For example, many public utilities store excess gas or electric-generating capacity to meet peak demand during a cold winter (gas) or during a hot summer (electricity for air conditioning).

2. Protection against a short supply of materials. Inventories may be kept at relatively high levels to avoid a period of short supply. Some possible causes of such situations are strikes at the supplying company or in the transportation industry, international tension such as the oil embargo of 1974 or the Iranian situation in 1980, or declining natural resources.

3. Hedge against price inflation. Inventories may be kept at high levels as a hedge against expected price inflation. For certain goods (coal, silver, gold, copper, etc.) storage costs are negligible when compared to price increases due to inflation and materials shortage.

4. Benefits of quantity discounts. Another possible reason to carry high inventories may be the availability of quantity discounts for large purchases.

5. Savings on negotiation costs. In international trade, purchasing often requires costly and painstaking negotiations. Also, there is a general trend toward enormous increases in efforts and negotiation costs whenever a change takes place in the management of a foreign corporation. Thus, ordering large quantities of goods at one time is widely practiced.

6. There are many other reasons that prompt firms to carry high levels of inventories. A manufacturing firm, to become a dominant customer, may order large quantities for a period of time in order to establish bargaining power or control over supply sources. Or a company may carry certain levels of inventories to maintain an even production level and thus avoid the layoff of employees.

A buffer between supply and demand

Since organizations do not have crystal balls to precisely forecast future demands, they need to carry inventory as a buffer between supply and demand. However, this approach can create chaos for management when there are many stock items (or SKU's—stock-keeping units). For example, if a company has 30,000 stock items, inventory decisions can be a real mess. Since prices change frequently and in an unorderly fashion, the items and supply sources may also change frequently. Therefore, individual items may require unique management considerations.

Another factor that further complicates the inventory situation is the literally unlimited number of ways to solve inventory problems. For example, a firm can order 10 units of an item once a week or it can order 2,600 units every five years. Or, to approximate the fluctuating demand, the company can order fluctuating quantities on an irregular basis.

Because of all of these characteristics of inventory systems, a seat-of-the-pants or a purely judgmental approach to the inventory problem is not a reasonable way to manage operations in today's complex environment. Mathematical models can be effectively utilized to search for good solutions to inventory problems. This is why inventory analysis was one of the first areas of application of management science principles.

History of inventory models

One of the earliest models of inventory management was the Harris Economic Lot Size equation, developed around 1915. The Harris model was expanded by F. W. Raymond in the early 1930s. There was very little additional work published on inventory management until Moses Abramovitz published the result of his research on inventories and business cycles for the National Bureau of Economic Research in 1950. Since that time, an avalanche of research work has been reported concerning scientific inventory control.

BASIC INVENTORY DECISIONS

How much and when to replenish

The two basic inventory decisions are *how much* and *when* items are to be replenished so as to minimize the total inventory costs. Although it is possible to consider these two decisions separately, in some cases they can be made simultaneously. In other words, the valves of the two variables must be found at the same time. We can choose either of these approaches according to the assumptions of our model.

Three components of inventory cost

In developing inventory models, the objective is to minimize the total inventory costs. The total inventory costs have three components: holding costs, ordering costs, and shortage costs.

Holding Costs

Holding costs

Holding costs or *carrying costs* represent costs that are associated with storing a certain level of inventory. These costs include the following components:

Interest incurred or opportunity cost in having capital tied up in inventories.

Storage costs such as insurance, taxes, rental fees, utilities, and other maintenance costs of the storage space.

Warehousing or storage operation costs, including handling, record keeping, information processing, and the actual taking of a physical inventory.

Costs associated with deterioration, shrinkage, obsolescence, and damage.

The total holding costs are dependent on how many items are stored and for how long. Therefore, holding costs are expressed in terms of *dollar cost for carrying one unit of inventory per unit of time*. Holding costs can also be expressed in terms of *a percentage of the average inventory value*. Common ranges for holding costs are 15 to 20 percent of average inventory value for consumer goods, and 20 to 30 percent for industrial goods.

Ordering Costs

Ordering costs

Ordering costs represent costs that are associated with replenishing inventories. These costs are not dependent on how many items are ordered at a time. Instead, they are based on the number of times orders are prepared. In other words, it is assumed that the cost of preparing an order is constant. Ordering costs include overhead, clerical work, data processing, and other expenses that are incurred in searching the supply sources: purchasing, expediting, transporting, receiving, inspecting, and the like. Ordering costs can be determined by dividing the total annual costs incurred in preparing orders by the number of orders processed during the year. Thus, ordering costs are usually expressed in terms of *dollar cost per order*.

Shortage Costs

Shortage costs

Shortage costs or *stock-out costs* are those costs that occur when demand exceeds the available inventory in stock. These costs are dependent on how much shortage has occurred and for how long. Thus, shortage costs are expressed in terms of *dollar cost per unit of short item per unit time*. In some cases, when only the magnitude of the shortage is considered, these costs can be expressed in terms of *dollar cost per short unit*.

Shortages and stock-outs may occur when there is unexpected high demand before inventories are replenished. Or shortages may be due to the established inventory policy of the company. If shortages can be filled by back ordering, without permanently losing the customers, the shortage costs would be only temporary and minor. Usually, however, shortages result in long-term lost customers (lost profit) or a permanent goodwill cost owing to unsatisfied customers.

ECONOMIC ORDER QUANTITY (EOQ) MODEL

EOQ model

The economic order quantity (EOQ) model, which is often referred to as the classic or basic inventory model, is the simplest and most elementary of the inventory models. Since it is so basic and simple, it may not be appropriate for many real-world inventory situations. Nevertheless, it is a good starting point for developing more realistic inventory models.

EOQ Model Assumptions

The optimum order quantity

The objective of the EOQ model is to determine the *optimum order quantity* that will minimize the total inventory cost. The EOQ model is simple because it is based upon some rigid assumptions. As we develop more realistic models, we will need to modify or eliminate some of these assumptions. The EOQ model assumes the following:

The demand for inventory is known with certainty, such as one unit per day.

The demand for inventory is known with certainty, such as one unit per day.

Inventory replenishment is instantaneous (once the order is placed, it is received simultaneously).

No excess inventories or shortages are necessary or needed (inventory is replenished only when inventory is exactly zero).

The holding cost per unit and ordering cost are constant regardless of the order quantity.

Figure 11.1   The Classic Inventory Model

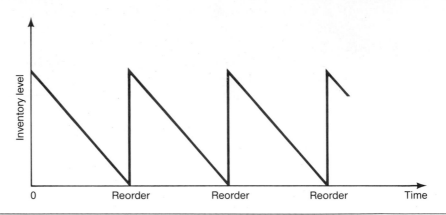

The assumptions of the EOQ model are reflected in Figure 11.1, which represents the inventory level over a period of time. Based on the known demand rate, the inventory level decreases until it reaches zero. Then, an order is placed on the assumption of an instantaneous replenishment. When the order quantity is received, the inventory level jumps up to the previous high level. The decreasing process of the inventory level then repeats itself.

EOQ Model Symbols

To formulate the EOQ model, we must define the following symbols as model variables and parameters:

$$TC = \text{total annual inventory cost}$$
$$HC = \text{holding cost per unit per year}$$
$$THC = \text{total annual holding cost}$$
$$OC = \text{ordering cost per order}$$
$$TOC = \text{total annual ordering cost}$$
$$Q = \text{quantity per order}$$
$$D = \text{annual demand for items in inventory}$$

Before formulating the model, we should reiterate here that the objective of the EOQ model is to determine the optimum order quantity so that the sum of all of the costs related to managing the inventory system can be minimized. Shortage costs are not considered in the EOQ model because, given the model's assumptions, it is impossible for shortages to occur. Thus, inventory costs consist entirely of holding and ordering costs, and the objective is to minimize the sum of these two components.

Figure 11.2 graphically illustrates the relationships of *TC, THC,* and *TOC.* We will discuss the mathematical functions for each of the costs in the next section. In Figure 11.2, it is evident that the total holding cost *(THC)* is a linear function. When the quantity per order is increased, *THC* increases at a constant rate. On the other

Figure 11.2   The Classic EOQ Inventory Decision Model

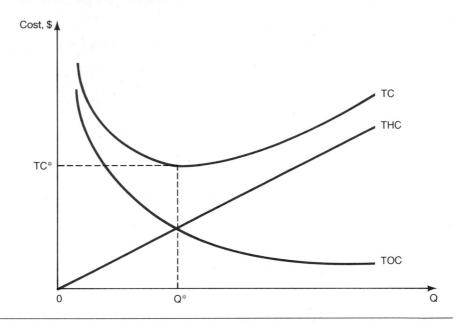

hand, total ordering cost *(TOC)* is a nonlinear function. When the quantity per order is increased, *TOC* decreases at a gradual rate.

Total inventory cost *(TC)*, which is the sum of *THC* and *TOC*, first decreases as the order quantity size increases but begins to rise from the point where the *THC* and *TOC* functions intersect. The optimum order quantity *(Q*)*, which corresponds to the minimum total inventory cost *(TC*)*, can be determined graphically at the point where *THC* equals *TOC*.

EOQ Model Formulation

Total Inventory Cost The total annual inventory cost is the sum of two components: (1) total annual holding cost and (2) total annual ordering cost.

$$
\begin{array}{ccc}
\textbf{Total annual} & & \textbf{Total annual} & & \textbf{Total annual} \\
\textbf{inventory cost} & = & \textbf{holding cost} & + & \textbf{ordering cost} \\
TC & = & THC & + & TOC
\end{array}
$$

Total Annual Holding Cost The total annual holding cost is determined by multiplying the holding cost per unit per year *(HC)* by the inventory level measured in

The total holding cost

units. Although we can easily determine *HC*, it is not so simple to measure the inventory level, unless we do so for each day, because the inventory level fluctuates from day to day based on the demand rate.

Since the demand rate is assumed to be constant over time and to be known with certainty, we can compute the average inventory on hand and use it as the inventory level. When the demand is known and constant, the average inventory level is simply

The average inventory level

the midpoint of the highest and lowest inventory levels on hand. The highest inventory level equals Q, the order quantity, and the lowest inventory level is zero. Thus, we can compute the average inventory level as $(Q + 0)/2 = Q/2$:

$$\textbf{Average inventory level} = \frac{Q}{2}$$

Now we can compute the total holding cost as

$$THC = HC \cdot \frac{Q}{2}$$

The total ordering cost

Total Annual Ordering Cost The total annual ordering cost *(TOC)* is the product of the ordering cost per order *(OC)* times the number of orders processed per year. The number of orders we need to process per year is easily computed by dividing the known annual demand *(D)* by the quantity ordered per order (Q). Thus, the number of orders per year will be

$$\textbf{Number of orders per year} = \frac{D}{Q}$$

Now we are ready to compute the total annual ordering cost as follows:

$$TOC = OC \cdot \frac{D}{Q}$$

Optimum Order Quantity As we already know, the total inventory cost is the sum of the total holding cost and the total ordering cost. Thus, we can write

$$THC = THC + TOC$$
$$= HC \cdot \frac{Q}{2} + OC \cdot \frac{D}{Q}$$

In the above equation, we have left out the total merchandise purchase cost because it is not usually considered to be a part of the total inventory cost. However, if we are interested in computing the total merchandising cost, we can add $(P \cdot D)$, where P is the per-unit purchase price.

The optimum order quantity

Now it is possible for us to determine the optimum order quantity, Q^*. As we demonstrated in Figure 11.2, the optimum order quantity is found at the point where the total holding cost line intersects the total ordering cost curve. Thus, if we equate the total holding cost with the total ordering cost and solve for Q, we can obtain the value of Q^*:

$$THC = TOC$$

$$HC \cdot \frac{Q}{2} = OC \cdot \frac{D}{Q}$$

$$\frac{HC \cdot Q}{2} = \frac{OC \cdot D}{Q}$$

$$HC \cdot Q^2 = 2 \cdot OC \cdot D$$

$$Q^2 = \frac{2 \cdot OC \cdot D}{HC}$$

$$Q^* = \sqrt{\frac{2OC \cdot D}{HC}}$$

The optimum value of Q can also be determined at the lowest point on the total cost curve in Figure 11.2. To use this approach, the derivation of the total cost equation with respect to Q must be computed by using calculus:

Using calculus to find the optimum order quantity

$$TC = \frac{HC \cdot Q}{2} + \frac{OC \cdot D}{Q}$$

$$\frac{dTC}{dQ} = \frac{-OC \cdot D}{Q^2} + \frac{HC}{2}$$

Since this derivative represents the slope of the total cost curve, the optimum quantity of Q is the point where the slope is zero. Thus,

$$\frac{-OC \cdot D}{Q^2} + \frac{HC}{2} = 0$$

Consequently, we can obtain

$$Q^* = \sqrt{\frac{2OC \cdot D}{HC}}$$

To determine the optimum order quantity for any specific inventory model, we simply plug the values of *HC, OC,* and *D* into the EOQ model. We will now examine the application of the EOQ model and its component cost functions through a casette problem.

CASETTE 11.1   *TELEVISION TECHNOLOGY, INC.*

Television Technology, Inc. is a local retail store that specializes in the sale and service of televisions, video cassette players, and television parts. The company is an exclusive dealer for Star-Colorvision TV sets. Arjay Swing, the owner of the company, wants to determine the optimum number of TV sets to order each time so that the total inventory cost is minimized.

Working with the sales and accounting records, Arjay has been able to uncover the following information:

Annual demand *(D)* = 360 sets
Holding cost *(HC)* = $50 per set
Ordering cost *(OC)* = $20 per order

Arjay contacted the Small Business Center at the local university and requested some help in analyzing this inventory problem. Professor Robert Judd assigned Susan Wiseman to the project as part of her class work.

Based on available data, Susan decided that the demand for television sets is constant at one set per day. Furthermore, since the distribution center is only 20 miles away, inventory replenishment can be assumed to be instantaneous (orders can be delivered in the same day). As a matter of fact, Susan accepted all of the assumptions of the EOQ model.

Total Holding Cost

The total holding cost *(THC)* can be determined by

$$THC = HC \cdot \frac{Q}{2}$$

Since $HC = \$50$, Susan could easily determine that

$$THC = \$50 \cdot \frac{Q}{2} = \$25Q$$

The above *THC* function is obviously a linear function. Thus, the total holding cost will increase at a constant rate of $25 for each unit increase in the order quantity. Susan decided to examine three possible ordering policies: (1) a yearly order, (2) quarterly orders, and (3) monthly orders.

The total annual holding cost for the three ordering policies can be determined easily as follows:

Yearly Order. A yearly order policy requires that the order quantity be equal to the total annual demand ($D = 360$):

$$Q = 360: \quad \begin{aligned} THC &= \$25Q \\ &= \$25 \times 360 \\ &= \$9,000 \end{aligned}$$

Quarterly Order. Based on a quarterly ordering policy, $Q = D/4 = 360/4 = 90$. Thus,

$$Q = 90: \quad \begin{aligned} THC &= \$25Q \\ &= \$25 \times 90 \\ &= \$2,250 \end{aligned}$$

Monthly Order. When orders are processed each month, $Q = D/12 = 360/12 = 30$. Thus,

$$Q = 30: \quad \begin{aligned} THC &= \$25Q \\ &= \$25 \times 30 \\ &= \$750 \end{aligned}$$

Susan plotted on a graph the total annual holding costs for the three ordering policies, as shown in Figure 11.3.

Total Ordering Cost

The annual total ordering cost can be computed by

$$TOC = OC \cdot \frac{D}{Q}$$

Since $D = 360$ and $OC = \$20$, Susan proceeded as follows:

$$TOC = \frac{\$20 \times 360}{Q} = \frac{\$7,200}{Q}$$

The above *TOC* function is a nonlinear function. The total ordering cost will decrease as the order quantity, Q, is increased gradually. Susan examined the behavior of the *TOC* function for the three ordering policies we examined earlier.

Yearly Order. Since only one order is processed annually, *TOC* would be

$$Q = 360: \quad TOC = \frac{\$7,200}{360} = \$20$$

Quarterly Order

$$Q = \frac{D}{4} = \frac{360}{4} = 90: \quad TOC = \frac{\$7,200}{90} = \$80$$

Figure 11.3   Total Annual Holding Cost (THC) Function

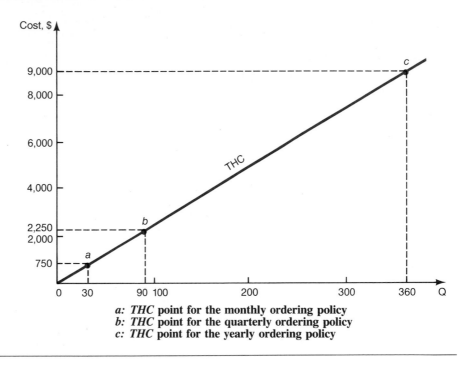

a: **THC point for the monthly ordering policy**
b: **THC point for the quarterly ordering policy**
c: **THC point for the yearly ordering policy**

Monthly Order

$$Q = \frac{D}{12} = \frac{360}{12} = 30: \qquad TOC = \frac{\$7,200}{30} = \$240$$

Susan plotted the above *TOC* values for the three ordering policies on a graph, as shown in Figure 11.4. The *TOC* function shows that the total ordering cost decreases as the ordering quantity increases. This should make good sense, because as the order quantity is increased, the number of orders per year will decrease, and thus TOC will also decrease.

Total Inventory Cost

The total inventory cost is the sum of *THC* and *TOC*. Thus, Susan computes *THC* for the three ordering policies as follows:

Ordering Policy	THC	TOC	TC
Yearly	$9,000	$20	$9,020
Quarterly	2,250	80	2,330
Monthly	750	240	990

On the basis of the above analysis, it is clear that the monthly ordering policy is the best among the three ordering policies we have evaluated. However, the monthly ordering policy ($Q = 30$) may not be the optimum order quantity.

Figure 11.4   Total Annual Ordering Cost (TOC) *Function*

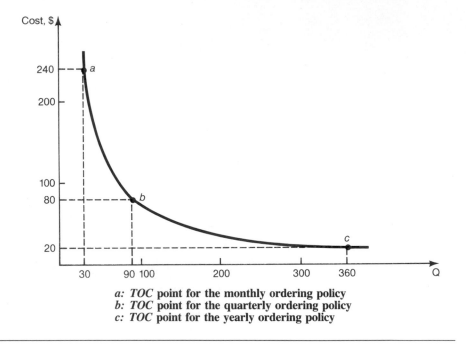

a: TOC **point for the monthly ordering policy**
b: TOC **point for the quarterly ordering policy**
c: TOC **point for the yearly ordering policy**

Determination of EOQ

To determine the optimum order quantity, Susan must determine the economic order quantity, Q^*. Since Q^* can be found when the *THC* and *TOC* functions intersect, the relationship can be written as

$$THC = TOC$$

$$\frac{HC \cdot Q}{2} = \frac{OC \cdot D}{Q}$$

Determining EOQ   Solving for Q^*, we can find

$$Q^* = \sqrt{\frac{2OC \cdot D}{HC}}$$

where
Q^* = optimum order quantity
D = annual demand
HC = holding cost per unit per year
OC = ordering cost per order

For the Television Technology problem, the optimum order quantity Q^* can be determined as follows:

$$Q^* = \sqrt{\frac{2 \times 20 \times 360}{50}} = \sqrt{\frac{1440}{5}} = \sqrt{288} = 16.97 \cong 17$$

Figure 11.5 TC, THC, TOC, *and the Determination of* **Q***

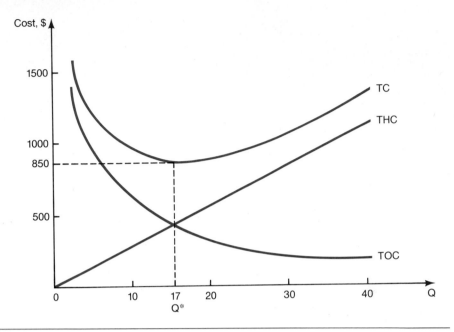

This optimum solution indicates that the economic order quantity is 17 television sets at a time. Since the annual demand is 360 sets, we can determine the number of orders as follows:

$$\text{Number of orders} = \frac{D}{Q^*} = \frac{360}{17} = 21.18 \cong 21$$

Figure 11.5 presents the graphical solution of the Television Technology inventory problem. The minimum total inventory cost *(TC)* is found at the intersection point of the total holding cost *(THC)* and the total ordering cost *(TOC)* functions. It is obvious that Q^* is approximately 17.

Managerial Information

Obtaining managerial information

The EOQ model is used not only to determine the economic order quantity, Q^*. We can also generate much managerial information about the inventory system under consideration. Examples of the type of valuable information we can obtain from the EOQ model are as follows:

The inventory cycle

Inventory Cycle The inventory cycle represents the number of days the inventory would last from the day of order (receipt) to the day when it reaches zero. The length of each inventory cycle can be determined by dividing the number of business days per year by the number of orders processed per year. Thus, for the Television Technology problem we can determine the inventory cycle as follows:

Business days per year $= 360$

Demand rate $= 1$ set per day

Figure 11.6   *Inventory Cycle and the Maximum and Average Inventory Levels*

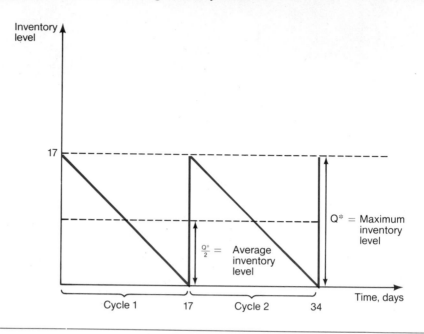

$$\text{Number of orders per year } = \frac{D}{Q^*} = \frac{360}{17} \cong 21$$

$$\text{Inventory cycle } = \text{ Business days } \div \text{ Number of orders}$$

$$= 360 \div 21 \cong 17 \text{ days}$$

The inventory cycle is presented in Figure 11.6. From this figure we can also determine the maximum inventory level and the average inventory level. The maximum inventory level is exactly the value of Q^*, and the average inventory level is, of course, $\dfrac{Q^*}{2}$:

$$\text{Maximum inventory level } = Q^* = 17$$
$$\text{Average inventory level } = \frac{Q^*}{2} = 8.5$$

It should be pointed out here that the inventory cycle equals the maximum inventory level in this particular problem. This is a coincidence because of the total demand ($D = 360$), demand rate ($DR = 1$), and business days per year (360). In most real-world problems, the inventory cycle does not equal the maximum inventory level.

Cost information

Cost Information. Once the EOQ model determines Q^*, we can determine *THC*, *TOC*, and subsequently *TC*. Furthermore, we can also determine the dollar value of each order quantity. Since we have already determined that $Q^* = 17$, we can compute *THC*, *TOC*, and *TC* as follows:

$$\text{THC} = \frac{HC \cdot Q^*}{2} = \frac{\$50 \times 17}{2} = \$425$$

$$TOC = \frac{OC \cdot D}{Q^*} = \frac{\$20 \times 360}{17} = \$424$$

$$TC = \$425 + \$424 = \$849$$

It should be noted in the above computations that *THC* and *TOC* should be equal. The difference of one dollar between them results because of the rounding of Q^* to 17. If we use the precise value of $Q^* = 16.97$, we would derive more accurate values for *THC* and *TOC*.

The optimum total inventory cost, *TC**, can also be derived through a general formula. For example, we can write *TC** as follows:

$$TC^* = THC + TOC$$

$$= \frac{HC \cdot Q^*}{2} + \frac{OC \cdot D}{Q^*} \left(\text{since } Q^* = \sqrt{\frac{2 \cdot OC \cdot D}{HC}} \right)$$

$$= \frac{HC \cdot \sqrt{\dfrac{2 \cdot OC \cdot D}{HC}}}{2} + \frac{OC \cdot D}{\sqrt{\dfrac{2 \cdot OC \cdot D}{HC}}} \text{ (deriving a common denominator)}$$

$$= \frac{2 \cdot OC \cdot D + HC \left(\dfrac{2 \cdot OC \cdot D}{HC} \right)}{2 \cdot \sqrt{\dfrac{2 \cdot OC \cdot D}{HC}}}$$

$$= \frac{4 \cdot OC \cdot D}{2 \cdot \sqrt{\dfrac{2 \cdot OC \cdot D}{HC}}} = \frac{OC \cdot D}{\sqrt{\dfrac{2 \cdot OC \cdot D}{HC}}} \text{ (combining all terms in the radical)}$$

$$= \sqrt{\frac{(2 \cdot OC \cdot D)^2 \cdot HC}{2 \cdot OC \cdot D}} = \sqrt{2 \cdot OC \cdot HC \cdot D}$$

Now we can find *TC** by substituting parameter values in the above formula as follows:

$$TC^* = \sqrt{2 \cdot OC \cdot HC \cdot D} = \sqrt{2 \cdot 20 \cdot 50 \cdot 360} = 848.53$$

The dollar value of each order quantity, based on Q^*, can be easily determined if the cost of each television set is known. For example, if the cost of each television set is $500, we can determine the dollar value of an optimum order quantity as follows:

$$Q^* = 17: \quad \text{cost of a television set} = \$500$$
$$\text{Dollar value of } Q^* = 17 \times \$500 = \$8,500$$

MODIFICATIONS IN THE EOQ MODEL

Modifications in the EOQ model

In applying the EOQ model, a number of modifications are possible. Some of these may result from the relaxation or removal of certain model assumptions, or from changed definitions of model parameters. In this section we will examine three modifications in the EOQ model. These modifications enable us to expand the model for a more realistic application or to analyze an inventory model in a different way depending on the requirements of the situation.

Holding Cost as a Proportion of Value

The first modification

As we discussed earlier in this chapter, holding cost (*HC*) can be expressed as a proportion or percentage of average dollar value of inventory. In other words, total annual holding cost (*THC*) is determined by multiplying the average dollar value of inventory by the percentage holding cost per year. This approach may be appropriate when the unit holding costs of individual items are difficult to measure.

Let us define the following new parameters:

HCP = holding cost as a percentage of the annual inventory dollar value

P = price or value per unit of inventory item

Now we can reformulate the total annual holding cost as follows:

$$THC = HCP \cdot P \cdot \frac{Q}{2}$$

In the above formula, $HCP \cdot P$ replaced the previous unit holding cost, *HC*. Thus, the optimum order quantity can be determined by

$$Q^* = \sqrt{\frac{2 \cdot OC \cdot D}{HCP \cdot P}}$$

In the Television Technology inventory problem presented as Casette 11.1, let us assume that the percentage holding cost *(HCP)* is 20 percent of the average annual inventory, and that the price of the television set is $500. Then, the optimum order quantity becomes

$$Q^* = \sqrt{\frac{2 \cdot OC \cdot D}{HCP \cdot P}} = \sqrt{\frac{2 \times 20 \times 360}{.2 \times 500}} = \sqrt{\frac{14,400}{100}}$$

$$= \sqrt{144} = 12$$

In the above computation, the unit holding cost is in fact doubled (*HC* = *HCP* $\cdot$ *P* = .2 × $500 = $100), as compared to the previous holding cost of $50. Therefore, it makes sense to decrease the order quantity from 17 to 12. In this way we can reduce the average inventory level (from 8.5 to 6 units) to reduce *THC*. However, the number of orders, and consequently *TOC,* will increase.

Time Horizon as a Model Variable

The second modification

If we specify the time horizon over which the inventory analysis is to apply, the demand for items in inventory must be specified during that time horizon. The holding cost is also specified as the cost of holding one unit in inventory per unit of time (e.g., per day). This approach is especially appropriate when holding costs change frequently over time. The following model variables need to be redefined:

$$T = \text{time horizon for the inventory analysis}$$
$$D = \text{total demand during time horizon } T$$
$$HC = \text{holding cost per unit } \textit{per unit of time} \text{ (e.g., per day)}$$

A major change in the above definition of *HC* is that it is measured for a unit of time (e.g., per day) rather than for the entire time horizon (e.g., per year). Now we can determine *THC, TOC,* and *Q** as follows:

$$THC = HC \cdot \frac{Q}{2} \cdot T$$

$$TOC = OC \cdot \frac{D}{Q}$$

$$Q^* = \sqrt{\frac{2 \cdot OC \cdot D}{HC \cdot T}}$$

Returning to our Television Technology example, suppose that the time horizon is 6 months (180 business days). Thus, the demand during the time horizon would be 180 television sets. If we assume that the holding cost *per day* is 14 cents, we can determine the optimum order quantity as

$$Q^* = \sqrt{\frac{2 \times 20 \times 180}{.14 \times 180}} = 16.9 \cong 17$$

Reorder Point

The third modification

Lead time

The reorder point

Thus far in our discussion of the EOQ model, we have assumed that an order is received at the same instant it is placed. In reality, however, such a case would be a rarity. It is more realistic to assume that there exists some time lag between the time an order is placed and the time that order is received. This time lag is often referred to as *lead time*. Figure 11.7 illustrates the lead time for each of the orders (inventory cycles). Since there is a lead time, items are ordered before the inventory level reaches zero. Thus, the *reorder point* is the point at which an order is placed.

The assumptions for obtaining the reorder point are: (1) constant and known demand rate per time period (e.g., per day), and (2) constant and known lead time. We can now find the reorder point by simply finding the demand during the lead time. The demand rate per unit of time is simply the quotient of the total demand for the time horizon *(D)* divided by the number of days. Let us define the following parameters before we derive the reorder point:

$$R = \text{reorder point, expressed in terms of inventory level in units}$$
$$DR = \text{demand rate per unit of time (e.g., per day)}$$
$$LT = \text{lead time, expressed in unit of time (e.g., days)}$$

Now we can express the demand rate and reorder point as follows:

$$DR = \frac{D}{360}, \text{ assuming 360 business days per year}$$

$$R = LT \cdot \frac{D}{360}$$

Going back to the Television Technology inventory problem of Casette 11.1, let

Figure 11.7   Reorder Point in the Inventory Cycle

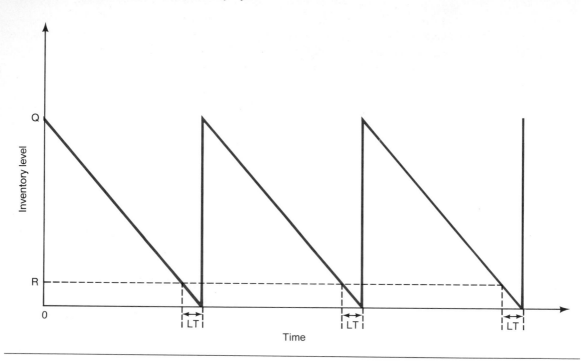

us suppose that the company has a constant lead time of 5 days. Then, the reorder point would be

$$R = LT \cdot \frac{D}{360} = 5 \times \frac{360}{360} = 5$$

Thus, the company should reorder when the inventory level of television sets falls to 5 sets.

It should be noted here that the optimum order quantity, Q^*, is not affected by the existence of a lead time. However, it is important to determine the reorder point and to process orders accordingly. Otherwise, determination of Q^* and TC^* becomes impossible because all of the necessary assumptions will not be satisfied.

EXTENSIONS OF THE EOQ MODEL

Several extensions of the EOQ model

There are many different extensions of the basic EOQ model that are developed either for special purposes or under specific conditions. In this section we will examine several such models.

Noninstantaneous Receipt Model

In previous models, we have assumed that once an order is placed, the entire order is received instantaneously. In other words, it has been assumed that there is no delivery lead time for replenishments. However, this assumption is not always realistic. In reality, the delivery process for most products may be gradual rather than instantaneous. In this section, we will eliminate the assumption of instantaneous receipt, but the other assumptions of the initial model will remain unchanged. In the noninstantaneous receipt model, it is necessary to assume that goods are received at

A gradual receipt model   a constant rate over time. Let us define the following parameters:

V = inventory receipt rate (rate at which items are received over time), assumed to start at the time the order is placed and assumed to be a constant rate

DR = demand rate per unit of time (e.g., per day), assumed to be a constant rate

All other parameters or variables are unchanged from the initial model.

Average Inventory In the initial EOQ model, the average inventory is half of the maximum inventory level (Q). In the noninstantaneous receipt model, however, the maximum inventory level must be adjusted since the items are received over time. The average inventory can be obtained as follows:

$$\frac{Q}{V} = \text{number of days required to receive one entire order (order receipt period)}$$

$$\frac{Q}{V} \cdot DR = \text{number of units demanded (usage rate) during the order receipt period}$$

$$Q - \left(\frac{Q}{V} \cdot DR\right) = \text{maximum inventory level for a given order cycle}$$

With constant rates of receipt and use, the average inventory level is half of the maximum level. Thus,

$$\text{Average inventory level} = \frac{1}{2}\left[Q - \left(\frac{Q}{V} \cdot DR\right)\right]$$

The average inventory level can be modified to obtain

$$\text{Average inventory level} = \frac{Q}{2}\left(1 - \frac{DR}{V}\right)$$

In the above expression, $\dfrac{DR}{V}$ represents the proportion of an order receipt that will be required to meet demand. Therefore, $\left(1 - \dfrac{DR}{V}\right)$ will be the proportion of an order receipt that will become an increment to the inventory level during the delivery cycle.

The Inventory Model The inventory level for a noninstantaneous receipt case is shown in Figure 11.8. As we can observe in the graph, the total inventory level rises gradually as the order receipt rate is assumed to be greater than the usage rate (i.e., $V > DR$). Thus, the inventory level rises at a constant rate of $V - DR$. The inventory level will reach the maximum level $Q - [(Q/V) \cdot DR]$. When the order receipt is completed for a given order, the inventory level begins to fall at the constant demand rate, DR.

Figure 11.8   Inventory Model with Noninstantaneous Receipt

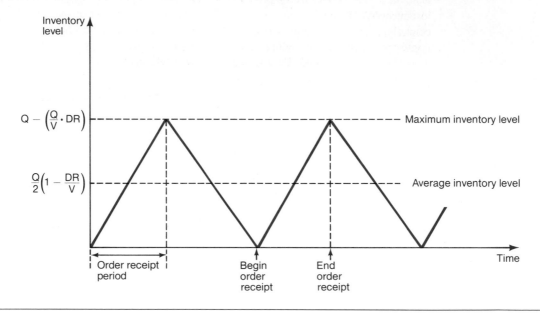

Now we can develop the inventory model:

$$THC = HC \cdot \frac{Q}{2} \left(1 - \frac{DR}{V} \right)$$

$$TOC = OC \cdot \frac{D}{Q}$$

$$TC = HC \cdot \frac{Q}{2} \left(1 - \frac{DR}{V} \right) + OC \cdot \frac{D}{Q}$$

The total inventory cost is still minimum at the point where the total holding cost equals the total ordering cost. Thus, we can write

$$THC = TOC$$

$$HC \cdot \frac{Q}{2} \left(1 - \frac{DR}{V} \right) = OC \cdot \frac{D}{Q}$$

$$Q^2 = \frac{2 \cdot OC \cdot D}{HC \left[1 - (DR/V) \right]}$$

Therefore, the optimum order quantity is

$$Q^* = \sqrt{\frac{2 \cdot OC \cdot D}{HC \left[1 - (DR/V) \right]}}$$

The optimum order quantity

The basic formula for Q^* is the same as in the initial EOQ model except that the holding cost (HC) is multiplied by the proportion of the order receipt that is allocated to inventory, $1 - (DR/V)$. This multiplier takes care of the fact that items ordered are received over time rather than instantaneously.

As an example of the application of this model, let us go back to the original Television Technology problem of Casette 11.1. Let us assume the following values for the model parameters:

$$HC \text{ (holding cost per unit per year)} = \$50$$
$$OC \text{ (ordering cost per order)} = \$20$$
$$D \text{ (total annual demand)} = 360 \text{ sets}$$
$$DR \text{ (demand rate per day)} = 1 \text{ set}$$
$$V \text{ (receipt rate per day)} = 2 \text{ sets}$$

Then, the optimum order quantity would be

$$Q^* = \sqrt{\frac{2 \cdot 20 \cdot 360}{50 \, (1 - 1/2)}} = \sqrt{\frac{14{,}400}{25}} = \sqrt{576} = 24$$

In the above computation, the unit holding cost is discounted by 50 percent. This is because that 50 percent, or the proportion DR/V of the goods received, will be sold immediately; thus, no holding cost will be charged. Since the total holding cost will be reduced by 50 percent, the total inventory cost can be reduced by ordering in large quantities. The optimum order quantity is thus increased from the previous Q^* of 17 to 24.

Economic Lot-Size (ELS) Model

The ELS model

The setup cost

The economic lot-size model is an interesting extension of the noninstantaneous receipt model we considered in the previous section. The ELS model is an application of the EOQ concept to the production management area. In most production problems, an important cost consideration is the *setup cost*. Setup cost represents the expenses incurred in preparing the production facilities for an upcoming run. For example, let us suppose that a furniture manufacturer is preparing to produce 2,000 colonial-style dining tables. The company must dismantle the previous production setup for Mediterranean-style sofas, prepare the machines and assemblies for the new run, and take care of any training or clerical work. Thus, the setup cost includes all expenses, both materials and personnel, that are related to dismantling the old setup and preparing for the new production run.

If the setup cost is a major component of the production cost, as it usually is in many manufacturing situations, it may be more economical to produce items in large lots rather than in small but frequent lots to meet the demand. When large lots of goods that exceed the demand rate are produced, the inventory level will gradually increase. When the inventory level reaches a certain high point, production will be stopped. Then, the inventory level decreases gradually as demand is satisfied from the existing inventory. When the inventory level is decreased to a sufficiently low level, another production lot is processed to begin the second cycle.

The ELS process is illustrated graphically in Figure 11.9. Each cycle consists of two basic phases: Phase 1 represents the production period and thus an increase of the inventory level, and Phase 2 represents the inventory depletion period.

To analyze the ELS model, let us define the following parameters:

$$HC = \text{holding cost per unit per year}$$
$$SU = \text{setup cost per production lot}$$
$$THC = \text{total annual holding cost}$$
$$TSU = \text{total annual setup cost}$$
$$D = \text{demand rate over time on an annual basis}$$

Figure 11.9   *Inventory Level for Economic Lot-Size Model*

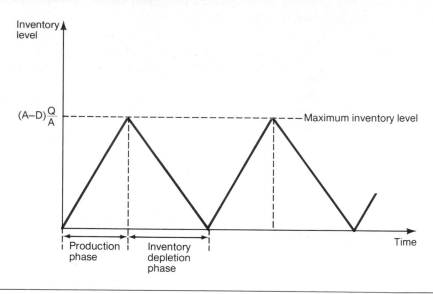

$$A = \text{production rate over time on an annual basis}$$
$$Q = \text{production lot size}$$
$$TC = \text{total annual production cost}$$

Now we are ready to develop the relationships that are necessary to determine the optimum lot size, Q^*.

Determining the optimum lot size

Length of the Production Phase During the production phase, the total production quantity would be lot Q. Since the production rate is A and the demand rate is D, the inventory level will increase at the rate of $A - D$, assuming that $A > D$. The length of the production phase in terms of days will be the lot size divided by the production rate:

$$\text{Length of production phase} = \frac{Q}{A}$$

The Maximum Inventory Level During the production phase, the inventory level increases at the rate of $A - D$ until it reaches the maximum level at the end of this phase. Since the increase in the production level is gradual throughout the production phase, we can state

$$\text{Maximum inventory level} = (A - D)\frac{Q}{A}$$

The Average Inventory Level Since we have determined the maximum inventory level above, the average inventory level is simply half of the maximum inventory level:

$$\text{Average inventory level} = \frac{(A - D)\, Q}{2A}$$

Total Annual Holding Cost The total annual holding cost is determined by multiplying the average inventory level by the unit holding cost per unit per year. Thus, we can write

$$THC = \frac{HC \cdot (A - D) \cdot Q}{2A}$$

Length of Inventory Depletion Phase At the end of the production phase, production stops completely. Since the demand rate continues, the inventory will be depleted gradually. The length of the inventory depletion period, then, would be simply the maximum inventory level divided by the demand rate:

$$\text{Length of inventory depletion phase} = \frac{(A - D)Q}{D \cdot A}$$

Number of Annual Inventory Cycles The number of inventory cycles represents the number of times the inventory level goes through the production (inventory increase) and inventory depletion phases. The number of inventory cycles will be simply the same as the number of times the production lot is processed. Thus, the number of inventory cycles is determined by the total annual demand divided by the production lot size:

$$\text{Number of inventory cycles} = \frac{D}{Q}$$

Total Annual Setup Cost The total annual setup cost corresponds to the total annual ordering cost in the EOQ model. Since a setup cost occurs every time we have a production phase, the total annual setup cost is the product of the setup cost per production lot multiplied by the number of annual inventory cycles:

$$TSU = \frac{SU \cdot D}{Q}$$

Optimum Production Lot Size The optimum lot size, Q^*, is found in the usual manner, equating the total annual holding costs to the total annual setup cost:

$$\frac{HC \cdot (A - D) \cdot Q}{2A} = \frac{SU \cdot D}{Q}$$

$$HC \cdot (A - D) \cdot Q^2 = 2A \cdot SU \cdot D$$

$$Q^* = \sqrt{\frac{2A \cdot SU \cdot D}{HC\,(A - D)}}$$

CASETTE 11.2   *SUNERGY PRODUCTS, INC.*

Sunergy Products, Inc. is a relatively new firm that specializes in producing various solar energy products. The company is best known for its solar panels. It produces panels of different types, sizes, and purposes. However, it also produces various other solar energy products such as plastic pipes and valves, heat storage units, and water circulation devices.

The company is primarily concerned about determining the production lot size of its primary product, solar panels for residential use. The demand for the panels is 5,000 per year, or 25 panels per day for 200 plant operation days. The setup cost for each production run is estimated to be $1,000. The inventory holding cost per panel per year is $50. The production rate during the production phase is 30 panels per day.

Bob Reznicek, a new inventory analyst, has been assigned the task of determining the optimum production lot size and other relevant information such as total inventory cost, number of cycles, maximum inventory level, and lengths of the production and inventory depletion phases.

Bob first defined and determined the values of certain model parameters:

D (total annual demand) $= 5,000$ panels
A (total annual production capacity) $= 6,000$ panels
HC (holding cost per unit per year) $= \$50$
SU (setup cost per production run) $= \$1,000$

Optimum Production Lot Size

$$Q^* = \sqrt{\frac{2A \cdot SU \cdot D}{HC\ (A - D)}} = \sqrt{\frac{2(6,000)\ (1,000)\ (5,000)}{50\ (6,000 - 5,000)}}$$

$$= \sqrt{1,200,000} = 1,095.45 \cong 1,095 \text{ units per lot}$$

Length of Production Phase

$$\text{Length of production phase} = \frac{Q^*}{A} = \frac{1,095}{6,000} = 0.1825 \text{ years}$$

Since the company has 200 working days, the length of the production phase will be 37 operation days.

Maximum Inventory Level

$$\text{Maximum inventory level} = (A - D)\frac{Q^*}{A} = (6,000 - 5,000)\frac{1,095}{6,000}$$

$$= 182.5 \cong 182 \text{ or } 183 \text{ units}$$

Average Inventory Level

$$\text{Average inventory level} = \frac{\text{maximum inventory level}}{2}$$

or

$$\text{Average inventory level} = \frac{(A - D)\ Q^*}{2A} = \frac{(6,000 - 5,000)(1,095)}{2\ (6,000)}$$

$$= 91.25 \cong 91 \text{ units}$$

Length of Inventory Depletion Phase

$$\text{Length of inventory depletion phase} = \frac{\text{maximum inventory level}}{\text{demand rate}}$$

or

$$\text{Inventory depletion phase} = \frac{(A - D)\ Q^*}{D \cdot A} - \frac{(6,000 - 5,000)\ (1,095)}{(5,000)\ (6,000)}$$

$$= 0.0365 \text{ years, or 7 operation days}$$

Length of Inventory Cycles and Number of Inventory Cycles

Length of inventory cycles = production phase + inventory depletion phase
$$= 37 + 7 = 44 \text{ days}$$

$$\text{Number of inventory cycles} = \frac{D}{Q^*} = \frac{5,000}{1,095}$$
$$= 4.57 \text{ cycles per year}$$

Total annual holding cost

$$THC = \frac{HC \cdot (A - D) \cdot Q^*}{2A} = \frac{\$50 \times (6,000 - 5,000)(1,095)}{(2)(6,000)}$$
$$= \$4,562.50$$

Total Annual Setup Cost

$$TSU = \frac{SU \cdot D}{Q^*} = \frac{(\$1,000)(5,000)}{(1,095)} = \$4,566.21$$

Total Annual Inventory Cost

$$TC = THC + TSU = \$4,562.50 + \$4,566.21 = \$9,128.71$$

In the above computation of the total annual inventory cost, the total annual holding cost does not exactly equal the total annual setup cost. These two cost components must be equal, given the optimum lot size, Q^*. If we use the exact value of $Q^* = 1,095.4451$, the two costs will be exactly equal.

On the basis of this solution procedure, Bob was able to develop the production process of solar panels at Sunergy Products, Inc. as shown in Figure 11.10.

Figure 11.10   Solar Panel Production Process of Sunergy Products, Inc.

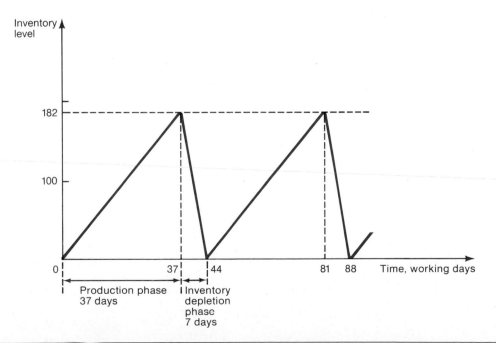

Quantity Discount Model

The quantity discount model

Quite frequently, manufacturers and vendors offer price discounts on orders of large quantities. To take advantage of such discounts, a firm will need to evaluate whether or not the size of a particular order should be greater than the present EOQ. If a large quantity is ordered each time in order to receive a quantity discount, the average inventory will increase. Consequently, the total annual holding cost will be increased. On the other hand, when the order quantity is increased, the number of orders per year will decrease. Thus, the total ordering cost will be decreased. Therefore, we can conclude that it is desirable to order a larger quantity than the EOQ if the increase in the total holding cost is less than the sum of the savings in the total ordering cost and the purchase cost of the item.

The total inventory cost for a quantity discount model would be

$$TC = \text{total holding cost} + \text{total ordering cost} + \text{total purchasing cost}$$

$$TC = HCP \cdot P\frac{Q}{2} + OC\frac{D}{Q} + P \cdot D$$

where

HCP = holding cost as a percentage of the annual inventory dollar value
P = purchase price

In the above model, it should be noted that the total holding cost is expressed as a percentage of the average dollar value of the inventory held instead of a dollar

Figure 11.11   Inventory Analysis Model for Quantity Discount

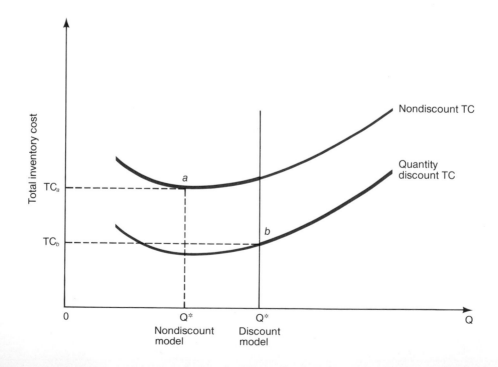

holding cost per unit held. We discussed this model previously as a variation of the EOQ model. Also, we added the total annual purchasing cost component to the model.

The solution procedure for this model is as follows: (1) Compute *TC with* a quantity discount; (2) compute *TC without* a quantity discount; and (3) compare the two *TC's* and determine the optimum order quantity, Q^*, which results in the minimum total cost.

The quantity discount modeling approach is graphically illustrated in Figure 11.11. The nondiscount *TC* curve is higher than the discount *TC* curve since a higher total purchasing cost is included. Point *b* indicates the minimum order quantity that is required for receiving a price break. We are interested only in the *TC* curves that are indicated by bold lines in the two *TC* curves. If our order quantity is less than the quantity required for discount, the higher price is charged and the nondiscount *TC* curve takes effect. On the other hand, if our order quantity is greater than or equal to the quantity required for a price break, the lower price is charged and the discount *TC* curve becomes relevant. In Figure 11.11, we will take the quantity discount because the total inventory cost is lower at point *b* than at point *a*.

CASETTE 11.3	*SMITH AUTOPARTS COMPANY*

James Robert Smith has been operating Smith Autoparts Company for the past 20 years. Jim Bob's main problem has always been inventory control. He has only 2,000 square feet of storage space. Also, he does not wish to tie up too much money in inventory.

A new vendor of a certain type of muffler that fits most foreign-made compact cars has approached Jim Bob with a quantity dsicount scheme. World Muffler Products, Inc. is offering a 10 percent price break for orders of 50 or more mufflers. Jim Bob struggled with this proposal by putting some figures down on paper. When the figures became too complicated, he just gave up. He approached Mark Simpson, an industrial engineer at a large local manufacturing firm that produces outboard motors for boats.

Mark asked Jim Bob several questions about the operations and cost data of Smith Autoparts, and he quickly recognized the problem as a quantity discount inventory analysis case. He obtained the following information:

D (total annual demand) = 300 mufflers
HCP (holding cost as a percentage of the annual inventory dollar value) = .2
OC (ordering cost per order) = \$20
P_1 (purchase price of muffler without discount) = \$50
P_2 (unit purchase price for 50 or more mufflers) = \$45

Total Inventory Cost without the Discount To find the nondiscount *TC*, Mark computes the optimum order quantity as follows:

$$Q^* = \sqrt{\frac{2 \cdot OC \cdot D}{HCP \cdot P_1}} = \sqrt{\frac{2(20)(300)}{(.2)(50)}} = 35$$

Now, Mark computes *TC* as follows:

$$TC = HCP \cdot P_1 \frac{Q}{2} + OC \cdot \frac{P}{Q} + P_1 \cdot D$$

$$= (.2)(50)\frac{35}{2} + (20)\frac{300}{35} + (50)(300) = \$15,346.43$$

Total Inventory Cost with the Discount

$$Q^* = \sqrt{\frac{2 \cdot OC \cdot D}{HCP \cdot P_2}} = \sqrt{\frac{2(20)(300)}{(.2)(45)}} \cong 37$$

Since Q^* is less than 50, the minimum quantity required to receive the discount price, Q must be set to the required order size. Thus, Q is set to 50:

$$TC = HCP \cdot P_2 \frac{Q}{2} + OC \cdot \frac{D}{Q} + P_2 \cdot D$$

$$= (.2)(45)\frac{50}{2} + (20)\frac{300}{50} + (45)(300) = \$13,845.00$$

Comparison of the Two Total Inventory Costs In comparing the two total inventory costs, it is clear that Smith Autoparts should order 50 mufflers at a time rather than 35 because the company can save \$1,501.43 annually. Mark summarized the analysis and presented it to Jim Bob as follows:

Q and Cost Information	Without Discount	With Discount
Quantity per order (Q)	35	50
Total holding cost (THC)	\$175.00	\$120.00
Total ordering cost (TOC)	171.43	225.00
Total purchase cost	15,000.00	13,500.00
Total inventory cost	\$15,346.43	\$13,845.00

On the basis of this information, Jim Bob started a long business relationship with World Muffler Products. Mark received much satisfaction from solving an interesting problem, and, in addition, he received a \$300 certificate toward automobile maintenance work at any of the shops that purchase parts from Smith Autoparts.

Inventory Model with Planned Shortages

Models with inventory shortages

In previous models, it has been assumed that there is no inventory shortage. In other words, an order is received at the moment the inventory level reaches zero. We will now consider an instantaneous order receipt model in which inventory shortages are allowed to occur because they can be back ordered. Therefore, all demands will be met eventually since all back orders will be satisfied before meeting new demands at the moment of replenishment. This approach is appropriate when the products we are dealing with are expensive or custom-made, or when the specifications are very complicated. This approach is also useful when there is very little penalty cost involved with shortages. Mail order companies frequently use this inventory system.

Figure 11.12   Inventory Model with Planned Shortages

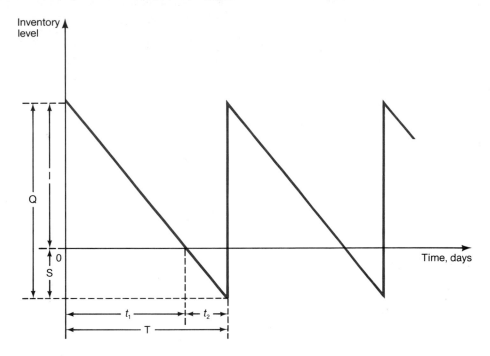

An analysis of the inventory model with planned shortages is presented graphically in Figure 11.12. The level of on-hand inventory (I) does not equal the maximum order quantity level (Q) because back orders are filled first when an order is received. Thus, the number of items that are back ordered is represented by the difference between Q and I (or $Q - I$). Because of the lowered inventory level, we can anticipate that the total inventory holding cost will be reduced. However, we must consider the shortage costs. Shortage costs are dependent on the number of back ordered items and the duration of shortages. Shortage costs include the labor and handling costs of back ordered items as well as the cost due to a loss of goodwill.

The definitions and descriptions of the model variables used here will be the same as in the previous models, along with several new ones:

Q = order quantity per order
HC = holding cost per unit per year
OC = ordering cost per order
SC = shortage cost per unit per year
S = shortage quantity back ordered per order
I = maximum inventory level ($Q - S$)
D = annual demand quantity
THC = total annual holding cost
TOC = total annual ordering cost
TSC = total annual shortage cost
TC = total annual inventory cost

T = inventory cycle time period, on an annual basis

t_1 = time period when inventory is available in a cycle, on an annual basis

t_2 = time period when there are shortages in a cycle, on an annual basis

The total annual inventory cost function for the model is expressed as:

Total inventory cost = total holding cost

+ total ordering cost + total shortage cost

$$TC = THC + TOC + TSC$$

Now we are ready to determine each of the cost components and model variables for the inventory model with planned shortages.

Total Holding Cost Since the inventory level ranges from zero to I, where $I = Q - S$, the average inventory level over the time period t_1 is

$$\frac{I + 0}{2} = \frac{I}{2}$$

Thus, the total holding cost during one inventory cycle T is

$$HC \text{ per cycle } T = HC \cdot t_1 \cdot \frac{I}{2}$$

To convert this holding cost per inventory cycle into an annual cost, we must understand the geometrical relationship of t_1 to I shown by the triangular arc in Figure 11.12 during period t_1. If we extend the triangular area, we obtain a similar relationship of T to Q. Thus, we can write

$$\frac{t_1}{I} = \frac{T}{Q}$$

From the above relationship we can solve for t_1 as follows:

$$t_1 = \frac{T \cdot I}{Q}$$

By substituting the above value of t_1 into the total holding cost per inventory cycle model, we obtain

$$\text{Holding cost per cycle } T = HC \cdot t_1 \cdot \frac{I}{2}$$

$$= HC \cdot \left(\frac{T \cdot I}{Q} \right) \cdot \frac{I}{2}$$

$$= \frac{HC \cdot T \cdot I^2}{2Q}$$

If there are N number of inventory cycles per year, we can write $T \cdot N = 1$ year. Thus, the number of inventory cycles per year is $N = 1/T$. The total annual holding cost is the product of the total holding cost per inventory cycle multiplied by the number of cycles per year. Thus, we can obtain

$$THC = \frac{HC \cdot T \cdot I^2}{2Q} \cdot N = \frac{HC \cdot T \cdot I^2}{2Q} \cdot \left(\frac{1}{T} \right)$$

$$THC = \frac{HC \cdot I^2}{2Q}$$

Total Ordering Cost The total annual ordering cost is the product of the unit ordering cost multiplied by the number of orders processed per year. Thus, *TOC* is not affected by the allowance of shortages:

$$TOC = OC \cdot \frac{D}{Q}$$

Total Shortage Cost In Figure 11.12, we can clearly see that the shortage level ranges from zero to S, where $S = Q - I$. Thus, the average shortage level during the shortage time period t_2 is $S/2$. We can develop the shortage cost per inventory cycle as follows:

$$\text{Shortage cost per cycle } T = SC \cdot t_2 \cdot \left(\frac{S}{2}\right)$$

Since the geometric relationship of t_2 to S is precisely the same as the relationship of T to Q, we can write $t_2/S = T/Q$. Again, we can solve for t_2 and obtain

$$t_2 = \frac{T \cdot S}{Q}$$

By substituting the value of t_2 into the shortage cost function, we obtain the following shortage cost per inventory cycle:

$$\text{Shortage cost per cycle } T = SC \cdot t_2 \cdot \frac{S}{2} = SC \cdot \left(\frac{T \cdot S}{Q}\right) \cdot \frac{S}{2}$$

$$= \frac{SC \cdot T \cdot S^2}{2Q}$$

Since there are N number of inventory cycles per year ($N = 1/T$) and the shortage is simply the order quantity minus the maximum inventory level ($S = Q - I$), we can derive the total annual shortage cost as

$$TSC = \frac{SC \cdot T \cdot S^2}{2Q} \cdot N = \frac{SC \cdot T \cdot (Q - I)^2}{2Q} \cdot \left(\frac{1}{T}\right)$$

$$TSC = \frac{SC \cdot (Q - I)^2}{2Q}$$

Total Annual Inventory Cost The total annual inventory cost model with planned shortages is determined by summing the three cost components:

$$TC = \frac{HC \cdot I^2}{2Q} + \frac{OC \cdot D}{Q} + \frac{SC \cdot (Q - I)^2}{2Q}$$

Determination of Optimum Values of Q, I, S, T, and TC Next, we should find the optimum values of Q, I, and S as well as T and TC. The method for obtaining these solutions involves partial differentiation of the total cost function with respect to Q and I, setting each partial derivative to zero and solving the resulting equations simultaneously. This method is beyond the scope of this book, but it may be found in other books such as *Management Science*, by Lee, Moore, and Taylor, and *Introduction to Operations Research* by Hillier and Liberman.

The optimum solutions for the model variables, however, are given below:

$$Q^* = \sqrt{\frac{2 \cdot OC \cdot D}{HC}} \cdot \sqrt{\frac{HC + SC}{SC}}$$

$$I^* = \sqrt{\frac{2 \cdot OC \cdot D}{HC}} \cdot \sqrt{\frac{SC}{HC + SC}}$$

$$S^* = Q^* - I^*$$

$$T^* = \sqrt{\frac{2 \cdot OC}{HC \cdot D}} \cdot \sqrt{\frac{HC + SC}{SC}}$$

$$TC^* = \sqrt{2 \cdot HC - OC \cdot D} \cdot \sqrt{\frac{SC}{HC + SC}}$$

CASETTE 11.4   *AMERICAN RUBBER PRODUCTS, INC.*

American Rubber Products, Inc. is a family-owned wholesaler of rubber products for households. One of its typical carrying items is the rubber belt for vacuum cleaners, which it sells to retailers in boxes. The company has had a long-standing corporate policy of no inventory shortage. However, this policy has resulted in a high level of annual holding cost of inventories. The manager of the Materials Management Division, James Hines, has been assigned the task of evaluating the implications of an inventory policy for planned shortages.

On the basis of company records, Jim has estimated the following demand and cost information:

D (total annual demand) $= 100$ boxes
HC (holding cost per box per year) $= \$4$
OC (ordering cost per order) $= \$2$
SC (storage cost per box per year) $= \$8$

Jim proceeded to determine the optimum values for the following decision variables:

Optimum Order Quantity

$$Q^* = \sqrt{\frac{2 \cdot OC \cdot D}{HC}} \cdot \sqrt{\frac{HC + SC}{SC}}$$

$$= \sqrt{\frac{2(2)(100)}{4}} \cdot \sqrt{\frac{4 + 8}{8}}$$

$$= 10 \cdot \sqrt{\frac{12}{8}} \approx 12 \text{ boxes}$$

Maximum Inventory Level

$$I^* = \sqrt{\frac{2 \cdot OC \cdot D}{HC}} \cdot \sqrt{\frac{SC}{HC + SC}}$$

$$= \sqrt{\frac{2(2)(100)}{4}} \cdot \sqrt{\frac{8}{4 + 8}}$$

$$= 10 \cdot \frac{2}{3} \simeq 8 \text{ boxes}$$

Inventory Cycle

$$T^* = \sqrt{\frac{2 \cdot OC}{HC \cdot D}} \cdot \sqrt{\frac{HC + SC}{SC}}$$

$$= \sqrt{\frac{2(2)}{4(100)}} \cdot \sqrt{\frac{4 + 8}{8}}$$

$$= \frac{1}{10} \cdot \sqrt{\frac{3}{2}} \simeq 0.122 \text{ year}$$

Assuming 365 working days per year, $0.122 \times 365 \cong 45$ days.

Total Annual Inventory Cost

$$TC^* = \sqrt{2 \cdot OC \cdot HC \cdot D} \cdot \sqrt{\frac{SC}{HC + SC}}$$

$$= \sqrt{2(2)(4)(100)} \cdot \sqrt{\frac{8}{4 + 8}}$$

$$= 40 \cdot \sqrt{\frac{2}{3}} \simeq \$32.65$$

On the basis of the above computations, Jim made the following conclusions:

1. The company should order 12 boxes of belts at a time.

2. The company may allow a shortage of 4 boxes before placing another order for 12 boxes.

3. The inventory reaches the maximum level of 8 boxes.

4. The optimum time between orders is approximately 45 days.

Jim Hines proceeded to compare the above results with the current no-shortage policy of the company, as shown below:

Important Variables	EOQ Model, No-Shortage Policy	Planned Shortage Model
Order quantity (*Q*)	10 boxes	12 boxes
Maximum inventory level (*I*)	10 boxes	8 boxes
Back order (*S*)	0 box	4 boxes
Inventory cycle (*T*)	37 days	45 days
Total inventory cost (*TC*)	$40.00	$32.65

Based on this result, American Rubber Products adopted a planned shortage inventory policy. This new policy is appropriate in view of the number of the company's diverse products (50 different rubber belts for various brands and types of vacuum cleaners).

THE INVENTORY MODEL UNDER UNCERTAINTY

Inventory model under uncertainty

The inventory models we have discussed thus far in this chapter require two basic assumptions: (1) demand is constant and known with certainty, and (2) lead time is constant and known with certainty. These two assumptions make the model somewhat unrealistic. In this section, we will discuss inventory models in which one or both of the above assumptions are untenable. In other words, we will discuss inventory models with an uncertain demand but with a certain lead time, as well as models with probabilistic demand and lead time.

Inventory Model with Safety Stocks

The safety stock model

In many real-world situations, organizations maintain certain safety stocks. These safety stocks serve as a buffer or security for emergencies or unexpected excess demands. For example, public utility firms maintain high levels of safety stocks in anticipation of severe weather conditions (tornadoes, floods, snowstorms, etc.).

In the inventory model with safety stocks, demand is considered to be probabilistic while the lead time is assumed to be constant and known with certainty. Since the lead time is constant, the order quantity from the classic EOQ model can be utilized as an approximated order quantity. However, demand is uncertain. Thus, we should compute the expected (average) demand during lead time so that the reorder point can be determined. In other words, we are assuming that demand is constant and known over lead time. Actual demand varies continuously, of course, and consequently shortages or stock-outs may occur during any lead time period. Thus, it is desirable to hold safety stocks or buffer stocks of inventory to avoid such possible shortages.

The inventory level with safety stocks is illustrated graphically in Figure 11.13. In the second inventory cycle we would have faced inventory shortages if we did not hold safety stock. On the other hand, in the third cycle we would have had a surplus of inventory even without the safety stock. The implication of this model is that surpluses and shortages will be balanced out over time (a year), and they will approximate the expected demand pattern. The average excess inventory held over time is shown by the shaded area in the figure.

The demand during lead time

In this model, we are primarily interested in finding the optimum quantity of safety stock to hold. As the actual demand over any period of time is uncertain, it must be considered as a probability distribution. Many firms have records of demand during lead time (*DDLT*). This information can be used to generate a probability distribution of *DDLT*. For example, let us suppose that a firm has experienced the demand during the lead time as shown in Table 11.1. On the basis of the data provided, we can easily compute the probability distribution for *DDLT*.

Figure 11.13   Inventory Model with Safety Stock

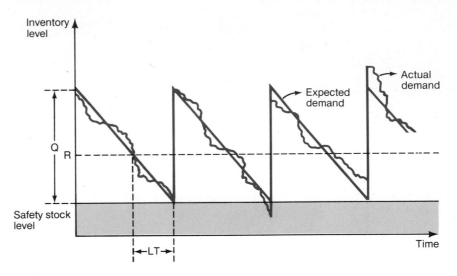

Table 11.1   Development of a Probability Distribution for DDLT

Demand during Lead Time (*DDLT*)	Frequency	Probability of *DDLT* (Relative Frequency)
10 units	10 times	.10
20	20	.20
30	40	.40
40	20	.20
50	10	.10
		1.00

Annual Safety Stock Cost   In the inventory model with safety stocks, we must develop a probabilistic model that involves safety stocks, expected demand, and expected shortages. As previously mentioned, the approximated optimum order quantity is determined by using the classic EOQ model. However, the reorder point, which may include safety stock, will be determined separately as a probabilistic model.

If the level of safety stock is high, the total holding cost will be high, but the shortage (stock-out) cost will be low. On the other hand, if we lower the safety stock level sufficiently, the holding cost will be low but the shortage cost will increase. Thus, we need to achieve a balance by analyzing the trade-off between the two costs.

Let us define the following new variables:

$$SI = \text{safety stock inventory level}$$
$$SHC = \text{annual safety stock holding cost}$$

The unused safety stocks will incur holding costs that are the product of the unit

Table 11.2   The Expected Shortage for Selected Reorder Points

Reorder Point	Safety Stock	DDLT	Shortage	P(DDLT)	Expected Shortage [E(S)]	
30	0	30	0	.4	0	
		40	10	.2	2	4
		50	20	.1	2	
40	10	40	0	.2	0	1
		50	10	.1	1	
50	20	50	0	.1	0	

Safety stock holding cost

holding cost (*HC*) and the safety stock level. Then, we can compute the annual safety stock holding cost as follows:

$$SHC = HC \cdot SI$$

Annual Expected Shortage Cost Let us examine the *DDLT* distribution presented in Table 11.1. If we set the reorder point at 50 units, we would not face a shortage since 50 units represent the maximum demand during a lead time. If the reorder point is set at 40 units, we would experience an inventory shortage for an average of 10 percent of the time because a demand of 50 units will occur for 10 percent of the lead time. Similarly, if we set the reorder point at 20 units, we would expect shortages of 10 units for 40 percent, 20 units for 20 percent, and 30 units for 10 percent of the time.

The expected (average) demand during lead time for the above example is found as follows:

$$E(DDLT) = .1(10) + .2(20) + .4(30) + .2(40) + .1(50) = 30 \text{ units}$$

The expected DDLT

On the basis of the expected demand during lead time of 30 units, we can select a reorder point (*R*). If we select 40 units as a reorder point, the average excess of 10 units [*R* − *E(DDLT)*] is regarded as the safety stock. If a reorder point of 20 units is selected, the expected shortage would be 10 units. The expected shortages for reorder points of 30, 40, and 50 can be computed as shown in Table 11.2.

Table 11.2 clearly shows that if we do not allow any safety stock, the expected shortage will be 4 units. If we allow a safety stock of 10 units (i.e., a reorder point of 40 units), the expected shortage is only one unit. If we keep a large safety stock (e.g., 20 units), then there will be no stock-outs.

The total shortage cost

The expected shortage we computed is for only one inventory order (inventory cycle). Thus, the total expected shortage per year would be found by multiplying the expected shortage cost per inventory order by the number of orders per year.

Total shortage cost = shortage cost · number of orders · expected shortage per inventory order cycle

$$TSC = SC \cdot N \cdot E(S)$$

where   *SC* = shortage cost per unit
   N = number of annual orders, *D/Q*
   E(S) = expected shortage units per order cycle

CASETTE 11.5	**BOLD BODYBUILDERS, INC.**

Bold Bodybuilders, Inc. is a specialty sporting goods store that carries equipment and accessories for body builders. Since the store caters to a special group of clients, it is essential for the company to keep up with new trends in the body building area.

Joe Staub (Super Staub), the owner and manager of the store, attends all national, regional, and local body building contests. A popular new product made a debut at a recent Chicago contest—Geni, a piece of body building equipment for women. Bold Bodybuilders has become the exclusive distributor of the Geni line in the three-state region.

After carrying the line for a year, Joe decided to analyze the company's inventory policy for Genies. On the basis of the past year's record, Joe has accumulated the following data:

HC (annual holding cost per Geni) = $20
SC (shortage cost per Geni per year) = $10
D (annual demand) = 1,200 Genies
N (number of orders per year) = 10

Probabilistic Demand Data	
DDLT	*P(DDLT)*
100 units	.1
110	.2
120	.4
130	.2
140	$\underline{.1}$
	1.0

Safety Stock Holding Cost

Joe Staub easily computed the safety stock holding cost with the following equation:

$$SHC = HC \cdot SI$$

where

SHC = safety stock holding cost
SI = safety stock inventory level

Safety Stock Level (SI) · Holding Cost (HC) =		Annual Safety Stock Holding Cost (SHC)
0	$20	$ 0
10	20	200
20	20	400

In the above computation, it should be noted that $Q^* = 120$. This is simple to compute as follows:

$$N = \frac{D}{Q^*}$$

$$10 = \frac{1200}{Q^*}$$

$$Q^* = 120$$

Since the company orders 120 Genies at a time, the safety stock level will be zero if *DDLT* is 120 or greater. If *DDLT* = 100, the safety stock level will be 20 units. On the other hand, if *DDLT* = 110, then *SI* = 10.

Expected Shortage Cost

Joe realized that the expected shortage cost could be determined by computing the combined product of the shortage cost per unit, the number of orders per unit, and the expected number of shortages per order cycle (lead time or inventory cycle):

$$TSC = SC \cdot N \cdot E(S)$$

where   *TSC* = total annual shortage cost
              E(S) = expected number of shortages per order cycle

The expected number of shortages per order cycle can be computed as follows:

Reorder Point	DDLT	Shortage	P(DDLT)	E(S)
120	120	0	.4	0
	130	10	.2	2 } 4
	140	20	.1	2
130	130	0	.2	0
	140	10	.1	1 } 1
140	140	0	.1	0

Now, based on the above information and computed data, the total annual shortage cost can be determined as follows:

Safety Stock Level (SI)	Shortage Cost (SC)	Number of Orders (N)	Expected Shortage per Order Cycle [E(S)]	Total Annual Shortage Cost (TSC)
0	$10	10	4	$400
10	10	10	1	100
20	10	10	0	0

Total Expected Cost

The total annual cost involved in the safety stock decision is the sum of the safety stock holding cost and the expected shortage cost. Joe summarized his analysis as follows:

Safety Stock Level (SI)	Safety Stock Holding Cost (SHC)	Expected Shortage Cost (TSC)	Total Expected Cost
0	$ 0	$400	$400
10	200	100	300
20	400	0	400

It is clear from the above calculation that the total expected cost can be minimized when the company keeps a safety stock level of 10 Genies (i.e., a reorder point of 130 Genies). This solution is based on an *expected* cost value derived from the probability distribution of *DDLT* during one year. For the company to implement this safety stock level policy, it needs an accurate data base for a lengthy period of time. Such a data base is imperative in order to balance out variations in actual costs and to examine trade-offs between a policy of no safety stocks and one of holding an adequate level of safety stocks.

Inventory Model with Uncertain Demand and Lead Time

Uncertain demand and lead time

In this section we will consider an inventory model in which both the demand rate and the lead time are assumed to be probabilistic. Since both demand and lead time are uncertain, we cannot determine the optimum order quantity, Q^*, independently without considering the lead time. By the same token, the optimum reorder point, R^*, cannot be determined without examining the demand rate. In other words, we must determine an optimum combination of Q^* and R^*.

In this model, the total annual inventory cost will be the sum of the total holding cost, total ordering cost, and total shortage cost:

$$TC = THC + TOC + TSC$$

We shall examine each cost component in detail.

Total Holding Cost Since both demand and lead time are uncertain, the average inventory level is dependent on the reorder point (R) as well as on the order quantity (Q). If we assume that no shortage will occur during an order cycle, the average inventory pattern will be as shown in Figure 11.14.

We can easily determine the average inventory level as

$$\text{Average inventory level} = \frac{Q}{2} + \Delta Q$$

The holding cost

In Figure 11.14, ΔQ is considered a safety stock level. Since $R = \Delta \hat{Q} + \Delta Q$, we can determine ΔQ as follows:

$$\Delta Q = R - \Delta \hat{Q}$$

As we explained earlier, $\Delta \hat{Q}$ is the expected demand during a lead time. Thus, we obtain

$$\Delta Q = R - E(DDLT)$$

Now we can determine the total annual holding cost as follows:

$$THC = HC \cdot \left[\frac{Q}{2} + R - E(DDLT) \right]$$

where
HC = annual holding cost per unit
Q = order quantity
$E(DDLT)$ = expected demand during a lead time

Total Ordering Cost The total annual ordering cost is simply the product of the

Figure 11.14   Average Inventory Pattern with Uncertain Demand Rate and Lead Time (No Shortage Assumption)

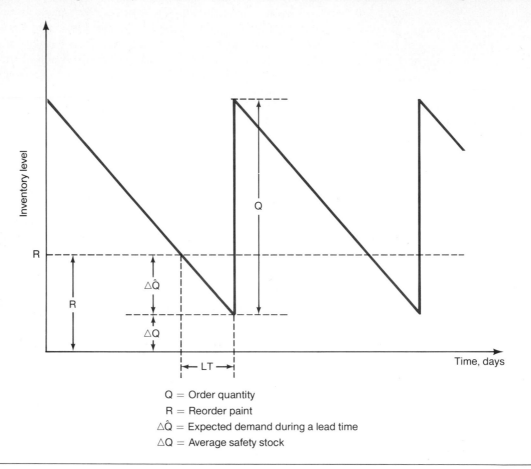

Q = Order quantity
R = Reorder paint
△Q̂ = Expected demand during a lead time
△Q = Average safety stock

The ordering cost   ordering cost per order multiplied by the number of orders processed per year. Thus, there will be no change in the computation of *TOC*:

$$TOC = OC \cdot \frac{D}{Q}$$

where OC = ordering cost per order
                     D = total annual demand

Total Shortage Cost   Shortages occur only when demand during a lead time is greater than the sum of the expected demand and the safety stock level. For example, suppose that the expected demand during a lead time is 2 units and the firm has a safety stock of 3 units. Then, a shortage will occur only if demand during a lead time is greater than 5 units.

Since the reorder point (*R*) should be equal to the expected demand during a lead time ($\Delta\hat{Q}$) plus the safety stock (ΔQ), as seen in Figure 11.14, we can write

$$R = \Delta\hat{Q} + \Delta Q$$

Table 11.3 *Relationships of* Q *and* R *to Inventory Cost Components*

Order Quantity (Q)	THC	TOC	TSC
High	↑	↓	↓
Low	↓	↑	↑

Reorder Point (R)	THC	TOC	TSC
High	↑	—	↓
Low	↓	—	↑

Then, a shortage occurs only when $DDLT > R$. The expected shortage per lead time $[E(S)]$ can be computed as follows:

$$\text{Expected shortage per lead time} = E(DDLT > R)$$

The total shortage cost   The total annual shortage cost is simply the product of the expected shortage per lead time multiplied by the annual per-unit shortage cost multiplied by the number of lead times. Since a lead time occurs whenever we process an order, the number of annual lead times would be D/Q. Now we can determine the total annual shortage cost as follows:

$$TSC = E(DDLT > R) \cdot SC \cdot \frac{D}{Q}$$

where
$$E(DDLT > R) = \text{expected shortage per lead time}$$
$$SC = \text{annual per-unit shortage cost}$$

Now we can obtain the total annual inventory cost:

$$TC = THC + TOC + TSC$$
$$= HC \cdot \left[\frac{Q}{2} + R - E(DDLT) \right] + OC \cdot \frac{D}{Q} + E(DDLT > R) \cdot SC \cdot \frac{D}{Q}$$

In the EOQ model section, we discussed the relationship of the order quantity (Q) to the total annual holding cost (THC) and to the total annual ordering cost (TOC). If we set Q very high, THC will be high because the average inventory level is high. However, a high-level Q will result in a low TOC because the number of orders (D/Q) will decrease. In the above TC function, we can also see that a high-level Q tends to decrease the total shortage cost (TSC) because the number of lead times (D/Q) would decrease. If we decrease the level of Q, the reverse will be true.

If we set the reorder point (R) very high, THC will increase as the average inventory level becomes high. On the other hand, a high-level Q will decrease TSC as the safety stock level increases. However, R has no direct influence on TOC. The relationships of Q and R values to THC, TOC, and TSC are summarized in Table 11.3. Because of the intertwined relationships of Q and R to the various components of the total inventory cost, the optimum order quantity Q^* and optimum reorder point R^* cannot be determined independently of each other.

CASETTE 11.6	*MODERN OFFICE EQUIPMENT, INC.*

Modern Office Equipment, Inc. specializes in designing and providing modern equipment for efficient executive offices. The company's newest line is Exec-Desk, a genuine wood desk with a built-in computer terminal, dictating machine, a small duplicating machine, and a telephone drawer. It also offers a priority filing system for confidential materials.

Exec-Desk has become an important product for the sales of other equipment and services of Modern Office Equipment. Thus, the company has decided to undergo a complete analysis of the inventory patterns of the Exec-Desk. Laura Compton, a rising systems analyst, was assigned to evaluate the system and make appropriate recommendations to the Vice-President for Materials Management.

After an intensive review and analysis of the existing data, Laura was able to determine the following:

> Current cost of Exec-Desk: $3,000
> Annual holding cost per desk (*HC*): 5% of cost or $150
> Ordering cost per order (*OC*): $30
> Annual demand (*D*): 220 desks (for 220 working days)
> Annual per-unit shortage cost (*SC*): $80
> Shortage units are back ordered

Daily demand rate (*DR*): uncertain

Demand Rate	Probability
0	.3
1	.4
2	.3
	1.0

Lead time (*LT*): uncertain

Lead Time	Probability
1	.25
2	.50
3	.25
	1.00

A search procedure for Q* and R*

To systematize the analysis process, Laura decided to evaluate the inventory system step by step.

The Basic Problem

The basic inventory problem is to determine the optimum order quantity (Q^*) and optimum reorder point (R^*) that will minimize the total inventory cost (TC^*).

Expected Demand during Lead Time

Laura realizes that Q^* and R^* cannot be determined independently of each other. She has jotted down the following key points:

1. Shortage occurs only during a lead time if the demand during a lead time is greater than the reorder point ($DDLT>R$).

2. The magnitude of inventory shortage is a function of the reorder point, daily demand rate, and lead time.

3. To determine Q^* and R^*, the expected shortage during lead time $[E(DDLT>R)]$ must be determined.

4. The expected shortage during a lead time can be determined only if the expected demand during lead time $[E(DDLT)]$ is known.

5. To determine the expected demand during lead time, $E(DDLT)$, all of the possible demand quantities during a lead time must be known.

Demand during Lead Time (**DDLT***) and Probabilities*

To analyze the demand during a lead time, Laura checked the inventory pattern during the last three lead time periods. Figure 11.15 presents the inventory pattern of the Exec-Desk. The actual inventory level and possible shortages are determined by *R, DR,* and *LT.*

Laura proceeded to determine the possible demand quantities during a lead time. We shall see only her calculation for *DDLT* of 6, 5, and 4 units, shown below:

Demand during Lead Time (*DDLT*)	Required Lead Time (*LT*)	Probability of Lead Time [*P(LT)*]	Demand Rate (*DR*)			Probability of Demand Rate [*P(DR)*]		
			Day 1	Day 2	Day 3	Day 1	Day 2	Day 3
6	3 days	.25	2	2	2	.3	.3	.3
5	3	.25	2	2	1	.3	.3	.4
			2	1	2	.3	.4	.3
			1	2	2	.4	.3	.3
4	3	.25	2	2	0	.3	.3	.3
			2	0	2	.3	.3	.3
			0	2	2	.3	.3	.3
			2	1	1	.3	.4	.4
			1	2	1	.4	.3	.4
			1	1	2	.4	.4	.3
4	2	.50	2	2	—	.3	.3	—

Since the maximum *LT* is 3 days and the maximum *DR* is 2 units, the maximum *DDLT* would be 6. The probability of *DDLT* = 6 can be computed by $P(LT) \times P(DR)$. Thus, we can obtain

$$P(DDLT = 6) = (.25) \times (.3) \times (.3) \times (.3) = .00675$$

Figure 11.15   Inventory Pattern of Exec-Desk

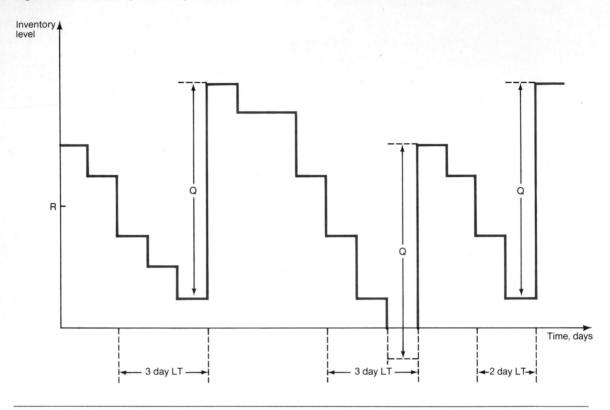

Proceeding in this fashion, Laura was able to determine $P(DDLT = 5)$ as follows:

$$P(DDLT = 5) = P(LT = 3) \cdot P(DR = 2, 2, 1 \text{ combination})$$
$$= (.25)(.3)(.3)(.4) = .009$$

or

$$= (.25)(.3)(.4)(.3) = .009$$

or

$$= (.25)(.4)(.3)(.3) = \underline{.009}$$

Thus, $P(DDLT = 5) = .027$

On the basis of this computation procedure, Laura computed the $DDLT$, the $P(DDLT)$, and the cumulative probability that demand during a lead time will be greater than the given quantity $[P(DDLT > Z)]$, as shown in Table 11.4. The last column $[P(DDLT > Z)]$ is simply a cumulative probability that demand during a lead time will be greater than Z, which is the $DDLT$ quantity we see in the first column. For example, the maximum $DDLT$ is 6. The probability of $DDLT = 6$ is .00675. Then, the probability that demand during a lead time will be greater than 6 is zero. This is shown by $P(DDLT > 6)$.

Table 11.4 Demand during Lead Time Probability Distribution

Possible Demand during Lead Time (DDLT)	P(DDLT)	Cumulative Probability [P(DDLT > Z)]
0	.12675	.87325
1	.24700	.62625
2	.30125	.32500
3	.19000	.13500
4	.10125	.03375
5	.02700	.00675
6	.00675	.00000

Expected Shortage per Lead Time

Expected shortage per lead time

Laura proceeded to determine the expected shortage per lead time for various reorder points (R). If R is set at 6 units (i.e., when the stock level reaches 6 units, an order is placed immediately), there will never be a shortage because $P(DDLT > 6)$ is zero. If R is set at 5, there will be a shortage of 1 unit if $DDLT$ is 6. The probability of $DDLT > 5$ is .00675. Then, the expected shortage per lead time for $R = 5$ units will be $(6 - 5) \times .00675 = .00675$ units.

If R is set at 4 units, Modern Office Equipment can expect shortages 3.375 percent of the lead times. Now the expected shortage per lead time can be determined as follows:

1. If $DDLT = 6$, the shortage will be 2 units $(6 - 4)$. Since $P(DDLT = 6) = .00675$, the expected shortage is $2 \times .00675 = .0135$.

2. If $DDLT = 5$, the shortage will be 1 unit $(5 - 4)$. Since $P(DDLT = 5) = .027$, the expected shortage is $1 \times .027 = .027$.

Therefore, the company would experience an expected shortage per lead time of .0405 units. In other words, if we examine 10,000 lead times, we would expect a total shortage of 405 units. In a similar manner, Laura determined the expected shortage per lead time for various reorder points. The expected shortage per lead time is simply a cumulative of the cumulative probabilities [$P(DDLT > Z)$]. The expected shortage is computed in Table 11.5.

Computation of Total Inventory Costs for Various **Q** and **R**

Laura has no formal training in simulation. Thus, she decided to solve for the optimum Q^* and R^* by means of a step-by-step search method. If she sets R at a certain low quantity and determines the optimum Q for that R, she could determine the total inventory cost (TC) with the given combination of R and Q. She can increase R by one unit and once again determine the optimum Q and TC. If TC increases gradually

Computing TC

and then decreases, she would be able to find the optimum R^* and Q^* that produce the minimum TC.

Table 11.5   Computation of Expected Shortage per Lead Time

Reorder Point (R)	P(DDLT > R)	E(DDLT > R)
0	.87325	2.00000
1	.62625	1.12675
2	.32500	0.50050
3	.13500	0.17550
4	.03375	0.04050
5	.00675	0.00675
6	.00000	0.00000

Laura's search procedure started with the following computations:

Expected Demand during Lead Time. The expected demand during lead time, $E(DDLT)$, is a component required for computing the total holding cost. $E(DDLT)$ can be easily determined if the expected lead time, $E(LT)$, and the expected demand rate per day, $E(DR)$, can be computed.

The probability distribution for lead time is as follows:

LT	P(LT)
1	.25
2	.50
3	.25
	1.00

Then, the expected lead time-is

$$E(LT) = (1 \times .25) + (2 \times .50) + (3 \times .25)$$
$$= .25 + 1.00 + .75 = 2 \text{ days}$$

The probability distribution for the demand rate per day is as follows:

DR	P(DR)
0	.3
1	.4
2	.3
	1.0

Thus, the expected demand rate is computed as

$$E(DR) = (0 \times .3) + (1 \times .4) + (2 \times .3) = .4 + .6 = 1 \text{ unit per day}$$

Now Laura is able to determine the expected demand during lead time as follows:

$$E(DDLT) = E(LT) \times E(DR) = 2 \times 1 = 2 \text{ units}$$

Optimum Order Quantity. The optimum order quantity, Q^*, can be determined from the total inventory cost function:

$$TC = THC + TOC + TSC$$

$$= HC \cdot \left[\frac{Q}{2} + R - E(DDLT) \right] + OC \cdot \frac{D}{Q} + SC \cdot \left(\frac{D}{Q} \right) \cdot E(DDLT > R)$$

By using the partial derivation procedure, Laura proceeded as follows:

$$\frac{d(TC)}{dQ} = HC \cdot \left[\frac{Q}{2} + R - E(DDLT) \right] + OC \cdot \frac{D}{Q}$$

$$+ SC \cdot \left(\frac{D}{Q} \right) \cdot E(DDLT > R)$$

$$= \frac{HC}{2} - \frac{OC \cdot D}{Q^2} - \frac{SC \cdot D \cdot E(DDLT > R)}{Q^2}$$

At the minimum total inventory cost point, the partial derivative (slope) must be zero. Thus, we can proceed as follows:

$$0 = \frac{HC}{2} - \frac{OC \cdot D}{Q^2} - \frac{SC \cdot D \cdot E(DDLT > R)}{Q^2}$$

$$\frac{D[OC + SC \cdot E(DDLT > R)]}{Q^2} = \frac{HC}{2}$$

$$Q^2 \cdot HC = 2 \cdot D[OC + SC \cdot E(DDLT > R)]$$

$$Q^* = \sqrt{\frac{2 \cdot D[OC + SC \cdot E(DDLT > R)]}{HC}}$$

If we select a given reorder point (e.g., $R = 3$), then we can easily determine the optimum order quantity, Q^*, by the above formula.

Total Inventory Cost for Selected Reorder Points To determine the optimum Q^* and R^* that would yield the minimum TC^*, Laura decided to compute TC for selected reorder points.

$R = 2$: From Table 11.5 we can find $E(DDLT > R)$. If $R = 2$, $E(DDLT > 2)$ will be .5005. Now, Q^* can be determined for $R = 2$ as follows:

$$Q^* = \sqrt{\frac{2 \cdot D[OC + SC \cdot E(DDLT > 2)]}{HC}}$$

$$= \sqrt{\frac{2 \cdot 220(30 + 80 \times .5005)}{150}}$$

$$= \sqrt{205.45} = 14.33$$

$$\simeq 14$$

Given that $Q = 14$ and $R = 2$, TC becomes

$$TC = HC \cdot \left[\frac{Q}{2} + R - E(DDLT) \right] + OC \cdot \frac{D}{Q} + SC \cdot \left(\frac{D}{Q} \right) \cdot E(DDLT > R)$$

$$= \$150 \left(\frac{14}{2} + 2 - 2\right) + \$30 \cdot \frac{220}{14} + \$80 \times \left(\frac{220}{14}\right) \times .5005$$

$$= \$1,050.00 + \$471.43 + \$629.20 = \$2,150.63$$

R = *3:* Following the same computation procedure, we can compute *Q** for *R* = 3:

$$Q^* = \sqrt{\frac{2 \cdot 220(30 + .1755 \cdot 80)}{150}} = \sqrt{129.184} = 11.3659$$

$$\simeq 11$$

$$TC = \$975.00 + \$600.00 + \$280.80 = \$1,855.80$$

R = *4:*

$$Q^* = \sqrt{\frac{2 \cdot 220(30 + .0404 \cdot 80)}{150}} = \sqrt{97.504} = 9.87$$

$$\simeq 10$$

$$TC = \$1,050.00 + \$660.00 + \$71.28 = \$1,781.28$$

R = *5:*

$$Q^* = \sqrt{\frac{2 \cdot 220(30 + .00675 \cdot 80)}{150}} = \sqrt{89.584} = 9.465$$

$$\simeq 9$$

$$TC = \$1,125.00 + \$733.33 + \$13.20 = \$1,871.53$$

Determination of Optimum *Q** and *R**

The procedure that Laura utilized in searching for the optimum order quantity (*Q**) and reorder point (*R**) was as follows:

Step 1: Set *R* at a low quantity.
Step 2: Determine *Q** for the given *R*.
Step 3: Compute *TC* with the given *R* and *Q**.
Step 4: Record *TC*. If this *TC* is greater than the previous *TC,* go to Step 5. Otherwise, go to Step 6.
Step 5: Increase *R* by one and return to Step 2.
Step 6: Stop.

This procedure is presented as a flowchart in Figure 11.16. Laura's computational search procedure is summarized in Table 11.6. The optimum order quantity and the reorder point are 10 and 4 respectively. With *Q** = 10 and *R** = 4, the total inventory cost is \$1,781.28. It is interesting to note that as *R* increases, the total shortage cost decreases. When *R* is increased, the total holding cost also increases but *Q* gradually decreases. Thus, the combined effect of these simultaneous changes of *R* and *Q* would first decrease *THC* and then increase it. As *Q* is decreased, *TOC* gradually increases, of course, as the number of orders per year increases.

Figure 11.16 Flowchart of the Search Procedure for Q* and R*

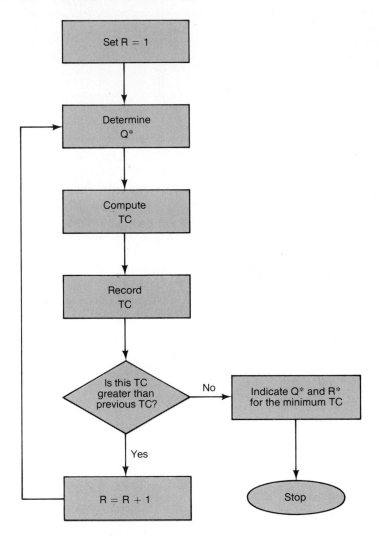

Table 11.6 Summary of the Search Procedure for Q* and R*

R	Q	TC	THC	TOC	TSC
2	14	$2,150.63	$1,050.00	$471.43	$629.20
3	11	1,855.80	975.00	600.00	280.80
4*	10*	1,781.28	1,050.00	660.00	71.28
5	9	1,871.53	1,125.00	733.33	13.20

Laura presented the result of her analysis to the Vice President for Materials Management. On the basis of this analysis, Modern Office Equipment was able to develop an efficient inventory policy for Exec-Desks.

ANALYTICAL VS. SIMULATION APPROACH

In developing and solving inventory models, we would like to employ analytical approaches whenever possible. Analytical approaches use a direct, or "pure," form of computation in determining the optimum order quantity by calculus. For example, the EOQ model is a good representation of the analytical approach.

Analytical vs. simulation approach

In the previous section, we discussed probabilistic inventory models in which the lead time and demand rates are stochastic. In analyzing these models, we employed a search procedure that is a combination of an analytical and a simulation approach. In real-world inventory problems, many model parameters and variables are interrelated and stochastic. Frequently, therefore, the last resort in analyzing the inventory problem under uncertainty is simulation. We will discuss simulation in Chapter 14. If you are interested in pursuing more advanced inventory models, you should consult the References at the end of this chapter.

MATERIAL REQUIREMENTS PLANNING (MRP) AND KANBAN

The inventory models we have discussed thus far are based on the general assumption that the demand pattern is essentially constant over time. Such an assumption is often valid for many finished goods. The same assumption, however, is quite unrealistic for subassembly items. The primary reason for this is that the demand for subassembly items is usually "lumpy" rather than "steady" because it is dependent on the demand for finished goods. For example, in producing a three-wheel all-terrain motorcycle, the demand for subassemblies of the three-wheels occurs at a very high level for a short duration of the production time.

The MRP system

For such lumpy demand, it is very costly to hold required items in inventory for an entire production time. The usual EOQ model has very little value for such a case. If we can devise an inventory system that will deliver the required items *just in time* for them to be used, the total inventory cost will be reduced greatly. Material requirements planning is such a system.

Elements of an MRP system

The MRP system consists of three elements: (1) a master production schedule, (2) a bill of materials file, and (3) an inventory master file. Based on the production schedule, the MRP system determines what subcomponents will be required when and in what quantities by searching through the bill of materials file and the inventory master file. The MRP system can be used advantageously in the lot-sizing problem we discussed previously. This system plans the timing of the lot so that the required subcomponents would be available in the week of production. However, MRP has no effect on economic lot-size determination of the optimum lot size.

MRP has been heralded as the best inventory control system for the job-lot production that requires various subcomponents. It is an efficient system in that it minimizes the inventory level because inventory is dependent on the production schedule.

The Kanban system

The *Kanban* system, a Japanese term for a repetitive manufacturing control system, attempts to carry the MRP philosophy of correct order timing much further. Kanban refers to a set of subcomponents-delivery and reorder cards. The system is also referred to as a *just-in-time* system. The Kanban system at Toyota, for example,

The Toyota Kanban system

is designed to allow major components to arrive just in time to go into final end products, subcomponents just in time to go into major components, parts just in time to go into subcomponents, and so forth.

Contrasts between MRP and Kanban

The major difference between MRP and Kanban is in the time frame. In MRP, "just in time" usually implies the right week of production or assembly work. In Kanban, on the other hand, "just in time" means the right day or even hour of production. Although MRP can also utilize a finer time frame, it is often more economical, because of the setup costs involved, to develop lots that are sufficient in size to allow production for a period of several weeks. In Kanban, an important key input, the setup cost, is altered in the EOQ model. If the setup cost is reduced, economic lot sizes can be adjusted downward. This process allows the Japanese factory to deliver parts "just in time."

Several organizations, including Toyota and Kawasaki Motors Corporation, USA, have reported successful implementation of the Kanban system. It appears that several Japanese manufacturing systems have great potential in terms of their impact in developing more efficient inventory control systems. If you are interested in Kanban, you should consult the References at the end of this chapter.

REAL-WORLD APPLICATIONS

Inventories represent a major business investment. Proper management and control of inventory systems are important not only for individual organizations but also for the national economy. Inventory management does not mean a physical count of every item in stock. Nor does it mean a mathematical analysis of every stock keeping

The critical few principle

unit (SKU). There is the principle of *critical few* in the inventory situation. That is, a small proportion of SKU's contributes a very large proportion of the total sales. Also, 2 percent of inventory items cause 50 percent of inventory control problems. Thus, management must exercise good judgment in selecting certain critical items for analysis.

The availability of various computer software and consulting services has made

Computerized inventory system

inventory management more systematic. There are a number of computer-based materials management systems offered by such organizations as IBM, Arthur Andersen and Co., and TRES. These systems are capable of keeping perpetual inventory records, analyzing trends, computing EOQ's, printing purchase orders, and controlling warehousing operations and inventories.

There are numerous published studies that deal with inventory models. Many practitioners argue that the EOQ model is abused and overused. They contend that the EOQ model is used even in situations in which the required assumptions are not satisfied. To design a proper inventory management system, the manager must understand the properties as well as the limitations of certain modeling approaches. The EOQ model remains the basic starting point for developing other advanced or modified inventory models.

SUMMARY

Inventories represent a considerable investment for many organizations. This is especially true for manufacturing, wholesaling, and retailing companies, and for public utilities, hospitals, and government agencies such as the Department of Defense. Thus, it is extremely important to minimize total inventory costs as much as possible while achieving the organization's production and/or service objectives. In this chapter, we have studied the basic EOQ model, a number of variations of the EOQ model, and inventory problems under uncertainty.

In the deterministic EOQ type models, the optimum order quantity is determined by balancing the total holding cost and the total ordering cost. In probabilistic inventory models, the optimum order quantity and optimum reorder point must be determined in order to minimize the total inventory cost, which includes shortage costs in addition to the holding and ordering costs.

The inventory situation is usually unique for any given organization. Thus, it is difficult to develop a general inventory model that can be applied widely. In this chapter, we have studied many special models for various inventory situations. These models can be adapted to different situations. We can also use simulation to analyze inventory systems under stochastic conditions of demand and lead time. Regardless of which approach or model we develop, the basic purpose of the inventory model remains the same: to determine when and how much to order at one time so that the organization's production and/or service objectives can be achieved while minimizing the total inventory cost.

References

Buffa, E. S., and Taubert, W. H. *Production-Inventory Systems: Planning and Control,* rev. ed. Homewood, Ill: Irwin, 1972.

Hillier, F. S., and Lieberman, G. J. *Introduction to Operation Research,* 3rd ed. San Francisco: Holden-Day, 1980.

Lee, S. M.; Moore, L. J.; and Taylor, B. W. *Management Science.* Dubuque, Iowa: W. C. Brown, 1981.

McMillan, C., and Gonzales, R. *Systems Analysis,* 3rd ed. Homewood, Ill.: Irwin, 1973.

Schonberger, R. J. *Operations Management.* Dallas: Business Publications, 1981.

Starr, M. K., and Miller, D. W. *Inventory Control: Theory and Practice.* Englewood Cliffs, N.J.: Prentice-Hall, 1962.

Sugimori, Y., *et al.* "Toyota Production System and Kanban System: Materialization of Just-in-Time and Respect-for-Humans System." *International Journal of Production Research,* 15:6 (1977), 553–564.

Turban, E., and Meredith, J. R. *Fundamentals of Management Science,* 2nd ed. Dallas: Business Publications, 1981.

Assignments

11.1 Why is inventory management important for the national economy, a firm, and the customer?

11.2 What are some examples of inventories that are familiar to you?

11.3 What are some of the reasons that we keep inventories?

11.4 What are the two basic inventory decisions? Why are they important?

11.5 Holding costs represent an important component of the total annual inventory cost. Discuss some examples of costs that may be included in holding costs.

11.6 What are the three major components of the total annual inventory cost? Explain each component briefly.

11.7 The EOQ model is said to be so basic and elementary that it does not really represent complex real-world situations. Why, then, should we study the EOQ model?

11.8 Discuss several assumptions that are required in the EOQ model.

11.9 In the EOQ formulation, the optimum order quantity is found when $THC = TOC$. Why is this true?

11.10 In the economic lot-size model (*ELS*), which cost replaces the total ordering cost component?

11.11 In the inventory model under uncertainty, what conditions are assumed to be uncertain?

11.12 In an inventory model under uncertainty, which costs are affected by Q and R?

11.13 What are the major differences between MRP and Kanban?

11.14 Why is it sometimes necessary to employ simulation to analyze inventory systems?

11.15 Do you think it is possible for American corporations to adapt Japanese manufacturing systems? Why or why not?

11.16 You are given the following parameters:

$$D = 100 \text{ units per year}$$
$$HC = \$18 \text{ per unit per year}$$
$$OC = \$20 \text{ per order}$$

a. Plot the *THC* on a graph for $Q = 5$, $Q = 10$, and $Q = 20$.
b. Plot the *TOC* on the graph for $Q = 5$, $Q = 10$, and $Q = 20$.
c. Plot the *TIC* for $Q = 5$, $Q = 10$, and $Q = 20$.
d. Determine the optimum order quantity.
e. What is the optimum number of orders per year?

11.17 The First Gateway Bank just introduced the "Money Now" checking system. The bank requires a minimum balance of $500 in order for the customer to be able to write as many checks as desired without paying any service charge. As a promotional scheme, Gateway will give away to new checking account customers the popular brass belt buckles that have been used as free gifts to savings accounts depositors.

The additional brass buckles required have created a new inventory problem. Mary Kaye Snyder, Assistant Manager of Customer Services, has revised the inventory data as follows:

$$D = 800 \text{ buckles per year}$$
$$HC = \$3 \text{ per buckle}$$
$$OC = \$20 \text{ per order}$$

a. How many buckles should Mary Kaye order at each time?

b. Determine the total annual inventory cost with the optimum order quantity.

11.18 Christenson's Television Service is a local dealer of SONY television sets. Mike Olson, the manager of the store, has been trying hard to find ways to lower the inventory level because of the increasing holding cost and the limited storage space. Mike has estimated the store sells about 800 SONY sets annually. The estimated holding cost is $30 per set and the ordering cost is $20 per order.

a. Determine the optimum order quantity.

b. Determine the number of orders.

c. Describe the inventory pattern graphically.

d. What is the total inventory cost per year?

11.19 Weber Babyfood Company produces sugarless applesauce for infants. The company's factory produces 200,000 jars of applesauce every year. The demand for the applesauce is estimated to be 180,000 jars per year. To produce applesause, a setup cost of $1,000 is required for the production line. The annual inventory holding cost is estimated to be $.25 per jar of applesauce per year.

a. Determine the economic lot size.

b. Determine the optimum number of production runs.

c. Determine the length of time between the start of each production run, assuming 300 working days in a year.

11.20 Ace Chemicals, Inc. has just introduced a new detergent, Snow-White. Ace's monthly production capacity is 20,000 boxes of Snow-White. The annual demand for the detergent has been predicted to be 200,000 boxes at a constant rate. The setup cost for the production of Snow-White is $500 per production run, and the *monthly* holding cost is estimated to be $.25 per box.

a. Determine the optimum lot size.

b. Determine the optimum number of production runs.

c. Determine the length of time between the start of each production run, assuming 20 working days per month.

11.21 Ryan's Liquor Shoppe orders Scotch whiskey 4 times a year. The lead time for reordering is estimated to be 5 days. The average demand for Scotch whiskey is 2 cases per day (300 business days). Ryan's has estimated the stock-out cost to be $50 per case and the inventory holding cost to be approximately $30 per case per year. Based on the past reorder periods, the actual demand distribution is shown below:

Demand during Lead Time (*DDLT*)	Frequency
40 cases	32 times
45	64
50	128
55	64
60	32

Ryan's is considering carrying 0, 5, or 10 boxes of safety stock.

a. Determine the total annual shortage cost (*TSC*) and the safety stock holding cost (*SHC*).

b. Determine the optimum level of safety stock.

11.22 Mr. Dan Brown, owner of the New England Seafood Store, has the only seafood store in town that carries Maine lobsters. The demand for lobsters has been sufficiently high to warrant the continued air transportation of lobsters from Boston. However, Mr. Brown cannot order too many lobsters because of the ever-increasing holding costs and the limited salt water tank space.

Mr. Brown asked his son-in-law, Jimmy Stuart, a recent graduate of a business college, to give him some help in determining the best inventory policy for lobsters. After looking over the company's past records, Jimmy came up with the following data:

$$D = 4,000 \text{ lobsters per year}$$
$$HC = \$.50 \text{ per lobster per year}$$
$$OC = \$40 \text{ per order (including air freight)}$$
$$LT = 3 \text{ days}$$
$$\text{Store business days} = 300 \text{ per year}$$

a. Determine the optimum order quantity (Q^*) for lobsters.

b. Determine the demand rate (*DR*) per day.

c. Determine the optimum order point (R^*).

d. Compute the total inventory cost with the optimum Q^* and R^*.

11.23 The Purchasing Manager of St. Mary's Municipal Hospital was contacted by a new vendor who offered a quantity discount for disposable syringes. The ordering cost for the item is $80 per order and the holding cost is 25 percent of the average inventory value on an annual basis. The annual demand for the syringes is 40,000 boxes at a constant rate. The hospital currently pays $80 per box for the syringes. However, the new vendor offered a $4-per-box discount if the hospital would order a minimum of 2,000 boxes at a time.

Should the hospital take advantage of this offer? Show a comparative analysis of all of the costs involved for the two alternatives.

11.24 Goldstar Electronics Company manufactures a transistor circuit that is used to produce solid-state television sets. Goldstar has agreed to supply the circuit to Panavision TV, Inc. for the next 3 years. Panavision has ordered 4,000 circuits per year during the contract period. Goldstar's annual production capacity is 8,000 circuits. The holding cost is $10 per unit per year, and the setup cost per production run is estimated to be $2,000. Given this information, determine:

    a. The optimum production lot size,

    b. The length of the production phase,

    c. The average inventory level, and

    d. The optimum total annual inventory cost.

    e. Illustrate the inventory level graphically.

11.25 Rocky Snowmobile Rental Company operates a snowmobile rental business near Vail, Colorado. The company uses an average of 2,000 gallons of gasoline each month. The ordering cost of gasoline is $50, and the holding cost is 10 percent of the unit cost. The cost of the gasoline is currently $1.40 per gallon if the company orders less than 2,000 gallons. However, the cost would be $1.30 per gallon if it orders more than 2,000 gallons.

    a. How much gasoline should the company order at a time? Show a comparative analysis of the two alternatives.

    b. Suppose the cost of gasoline would be $1.20 per gallon if the company orders more than 5,000 gallons. Then, how much gasoline should the company order at a time?

11.26 Mr. Howard Davis, the owner of a hardware store, is faced with an inventory problem for a particular item. Because of a high inventory holding cost, Mr. Davis is considering allowing shortages but he does not want to create any damaging goodwill problems with his customers. His estimated annual demand for the item is 4,000 units. The ordering cost is estimated to be $100 per order, and the holding cost is $5 per unit per year. The shortage cost per unit is approximately $10.

    a. Determine the optimum order quantity.

    b. Determine the maximum inventory level.

    c. Illustrate the inventory level for the first three inventory cycles.

    d. Compute the optimum total inventory cost.

11.27 Western Regional Center is a state-supported mental health institution. It has 300 patients in the minimum security ward. The patients have been engaged in various arts and crafts that are money-making activities. The center's most popular products have been hand-painted egg decorations for such special occasions as Christmas, Easter, and Mother's Day.

    Arts and crafts activities are not only money-making activities for patients and the institution, but they also have tremendous therapeutic value. Thus, the patient's activities are relatively stable over time, although the actual demand for decorated eggs is definitely seasonal. Dixie Johnson, the Coordinator of Arts and Crafts, has been purchasing goose and duck eggs from several sources. In order to systematize the purchasing procedure, Dixie has been analyzing the egg decoration activities. She came up with the following information:

$$HC = \$2 \text{ per egg per year}$$
$$SC \rightarrow \$20 \text{ per egg per year}$$
$$D = 7,200 \text{ eggs per year}$$
$$N \text{ (number of orders)} = 12 \text{ per year}$$

Demand during Lead Time (DDLT)	Probability (DDLT)
100	.10
110	.20
120	.20
130	.30
140	.10
150	.05
160	.05

a. Determine the total annual shortage cost (*TSC*).
b. Compute the optimum level of safety stock.

11.28 Sprint Print Company has been an exclusive printer of all state court proceedings and legislative sessions. The company has been purchasing its paper from Continental Paper and Pulp, Inc. Inventory information currently available at Sprint Print is as follows:

$$\text{Demand} = 120,000 \text{ pounds of paper type A1}$$
$$HC = \$10 \text{ per pound per year}$$
$$OC = \$30 \text{ per order}$$
$$SC = \$5 \text{ per pound}$$

LT	P(LT)	DR	P(DR)
5	.30	400	.50
6	.40	410	.50
7	.30	—	—
	1.00		1.00

a. Compute the expected lead time and expected demand rate.
b. Compute the expected demand during a lead time.
c. What is the expected shortage if *R* is set at 800 pounds?
d. If we assume that the optimum *R* is 1,200 pounds, what would be the optimum order quantity?

11.29 The Boshgarian Oriental Rug Company sells fine imported rugs. The company has a long-term contract with a large department store. The contract calls for a total of 5,000 oriental rugs in the 6' × 9' size. The company has been negotiating with an Indian rug dealer, and the dealer has offered the following quantity discount schedule:

Quantity	Price per Rug
0–999	$500
1,000–2,999	450
3,000–4,999	400
5,000 or more	350

The company estimates the following:

$$HC = 20 \text{ percent of price of rug per year}$$
$$OC = \$150 \text{ per order}$$

a. Determine the EOQ for each price level and ascertain its feasibility.
b. Compare the total inventory costs at various quantity levels and recommend the best inventory policy for the company.

11.30 You are given the following information:

$$HC = 10 \text{ percent of cost per unit per year}$$
$$\text{Purchase cost} = \$200 \text{ per unit}$$
$$OC = \$40 \text{ per order}$$
$$D = 500 \text{ units per year}$$
$$SC = 20 \text{ percent of cost per unit per year}$$

LT	P(LT)	DR	P(DR)
1	.25	1	.25
2	.50	2	.50
3	.25	3	.25
	1.00		1.00

DDLT	P(DDLT)	P(DDLT > Z)
0	.0000	1.0000
1	.0613	0.9387
2	.1520	0.7867
3	.2011	0.5856
4	.2188	0.3668
5	.1718	0.1950
6	.1101	0.0849
7	.0578	0.0271
8	.0232	0.0039
9	.0039	0.0000

a. Assuming that there is complete certainty concerning the lead time and the demand rate, compute the EOQ.

b. Under the condition of certainty, if the ordering cost is not known (while other cost information is known) but the EOQ is known to be 35, what will be the ordering cost?

c. Under the condition of uncertainty, if the optimum R is assumed to be 5, what should be the optimum Q?

Waiting lines are a fact of life. From traffic lights to hamburger stands, our society forces us to wait. Although a catsup commercial glamorizes waiting with the catchword "anticipation", we usually consider any waiting experience very unpleasant. As a matter of fact, whenever we face a waiting situation, we attempt to avoid it or to shorten the waiting time.

Waiting lines occur when the time of arrival of someone needing a service and/or the time required to provide that service vary from a fixed schedule. Waiting lines not only affect our personal lives but they can critically influence business operations. Operating systems from computer networks to production operations, from shipping docks to airports, can become inefficient because of waiting lines.

Since there is virtually an unlimited number of variations of waiting line systems, it is impossible to discuss all of them in this chapter. As a matter of fact, there are perhaps more unique and exotic models in waiting line theory than in any other management science approaches. Therefore, in this chapter we will have a quick walk through only the most commonly used queuing models.

Learning Objectives   From the study of this chapter, you will learn the following:

1. The basic components of a waiting line system.
2. The basic structure of a waiting line system.
3. Waiting line decision problems.
4. Arrival and service time distributions.
5. Queue discipline.
6. Kendall's notation.
7. Different types of queuing models.
8. The relationship between queuing problems and simulation.
9. The implication of applying queuing models to real-world problems.
10. The meaning of the following terms:

Waiting line (queue) system	Exponential distribution
Calling population	Erlang distribution
Service facility	Constant distribution
Queue length	First-come first-served queue discipline
Channel	Priority queue discipline
Phase	Balking
Poisson distribution	

11. *The primary parameters of a queuing system:*

L *Mean length of the system, including waiting and service, in terms of numbers of arrivals*

L_q *Mean length of the waiting line only, in number of arrivals*

W *Mean time spent by an arrival in the system, including waiting and service*

W_q *Mean time spent waiting by an arrival*

P_0 *Probability of no unit in the system*

P_n *Probability of n units in the system*

ρ *Utilization rate of service facility*

λ *Arrival rate in number of arrivals per unit of time*

μ *Mean service rate in number of departures per unit of time*

THE WAITING LINE PROCESS

Waiting is part of life

Having to wait is a real pain. As a student you should be an expert in waiting. Wherever you go, there seems to be a line waiting for you. You face a string of waiting lines when you seek to register for required courses, obtain a parking permit, make necessary class changes, purchase football tickets, buy books, get a haircut, and get an interview with a company recruiter. Almost everyone has experienced some waiting time at a bank, a grocery store, a highway tollbooth, a hamburger shop, or a busy discount store. At a grocery store we carefully check which line is the shortest and has customers with only a few items in their carts. But we often discover that the cashier at the short line happens to be a slow trainee and that the customer in front of us has several items without price tags. Someone has even developed a law of waiting lines to describe such a situation—"The other line moves faster."

Law of waiting lines

Waiting lines are often referred to as *queues*. Queues can consist of automobiles, assembly parts, people, animals, or other objects waiting for service. People's attitudes toward waiting are quite diverse. The British are well known for their patience and jolliness in "queuing up" at a waiting line. On the other hand, we have seen pictures of grim-faced Poles and Russians waiting in long lines leading to state-run food distribution centers.

Queues

Waiting lines are important for any organized society. Thus, the study of waiting lines, which is often referred to as *queuing theory*, is one of the oldest and most fruitful topics of management science. The pioneering work of queuing theory was done by the Danish mathematician A. K. Erlang. His study, published in 1913, involved an analysis of telephone service delays due to varying demands. Since then, queuing theory has been applied to many real-world problems.

A. K. Erlang

Waiting lines may be clearly observable in many situations such as lines at theaters, grocery stores, or hotel telephone switchboards. However, the more subtle or abstract forms of waiting lines may have profound managerial implications. For example, a breakdown of equipment results in a queue for repair. Customers at a gift-wrapping service counter take a number and browse around the store while waiting. Customers at a restaurant are often seated in the bar while they wait for a table. Table 12.1 presents a variety of familiar waiting line situations we see in our daily lives.

Table 12.1   *Examples of Waiting Line Systems*

Situation	Arrivals	Queue	Service Facility
Airport	Airplanes	Stacked planes or planes on holding patterns	Runway
Air terminal	Passengers	Gate waiting room	Airplane
Assembly line	Components	Assembly line	Workers or machines
Bakery	Customers	Customers with numbers	Sales counter
Bank	Customers	Customers in line	Teller
Car wash	Automobiles	Dirty cars in line	Washing facility
Computer center	Programs or jobs	Stacked programs	Computer
Course registration	Students	Students in line	Registration desk
Doctor's office	Patients	Waiting room	Medical staff
Fire station	Fire alarms or calls	Fires	Firemen and trucks
Grocery store	Customers	Customers in line	Checkout counter
Machine repair shop	Machine breakdowns	Repair requests	Repair shop
Police department	Service calls	Crimes in progress or service needs	Policemen
Shipping dock	Ships	Waiting ships	Loading and unloading facility
Stadium	Ticket holders	Waiting line	Entrance
Street intersection	Automobiles	Cars in line	Traffic light
Telephone company	Calls	Callers on line	Operator
Tollbooth	Automobiles	Cars in line	Toll payment

Although no one likes waiting in a line, it may be extremely costly to completely eliminate waiting by increasing the service capacity. For example, a branch bank that serves about 150 people per day could completely eliminate waiting if it had 20 tellers at work at all times. Common sense tells us that we need a balance between the costs involved in waiting and the desired service level.

The source of queuing problems

The manager's decision problem is to decide on the most appropriate service capacity or service rate. There will be absolutely no queuing problem if customers arrive according to a set schedule for fixed service times. The only thing the manager has to decide in such a case is the service capacity that will exactly correspond with customer arrivals. Many production assemblies are set up according to such an exact scheduling scheme.

Uncertain arrival and service times

In most real-world situations, however, customer arrivals and the service times are unpredictable. The manager at the student union can tell us when the cafeteria is busiest during the day, but he probably would not even be able to guess when each customer will arrive. Also, the time required to serve each customer (some people cannot quickly make up their minds about what to eat) will vary considerably. In other words, most waiting line situations may involve many unpredictable elements.

A manager with extensive experience and good judgment may intuitively come up with a pretty good balance between waiting and service cost. For example, a small family-owned grocery store owner may stop stocking shelves and run the second cash register when the customer line becomes too long. A toy store manager hires part-time help during the holiday season on the basis of the previous year's experience. In many complex waiting line situations, however, intuition is not sufficient to determine the proper balance between waiting and service capacity. Or the problem may involve such substantial cost or risk, as in capital investment problems or airport control tower operations, that queuing analysis may be very beneficial.

The need for queuing analysis

As we mentioned earlier, there are almost an infinite number of variations of queuing models describing particular characteristics of waiting line systems. Queuing theory encompasses all of such mathematical models. The general purpose of these models is to determine the characteristics of the steady state of the system, such as the average length of the waiting line, the average waiting time, and the average service time. The steady-state behavior can provide us with a sound basis for determining optimum service capacity.

Studying the steady state of the system

Components of a Waiting Line System

A waiting line system is described by the following components: *arrivals, waiting lines* or *queues, queue discipline, service facility,* and *departures,* as shown in Figure 12.1. Let us examine these components in greater detail.

Components of a queuing system

Arrivals The arrival of an entity (customer, automobile, airplane, etc.) in need of some service is the first component. Arrivals can occur in a number of different ways. Arrivals can be constant, as in an assembly line. Often, however, arrivals occur in random fashion. We may be able to describe the rate of arrivals according to some probability distribution. Then, we could infer some rational cost analysis despite the fact that arrivals do not conform to fixed schedules. The source of arrivals is often referred to as the *calling population.* We need to develop a clear description of the calling population in order to understand and analyze a waiting line problem.

Arrivals

The calling population

Waiting Lines When arrivals occur in such a way that they have to wait for service, waiting lines or queues develop. Waiting lines may be desirable if we want efficient utilization of service facilities. A waiting line ensures that the service facility will be kept busy. But if you happen to be in a waiting line, you may take a dim view of a long waiting period and may well decide to take your business to another place where the waiting time is shorter. The fast-food industry (McDonald's, Burger King, Wendy's, etc.) has prospered by catering to the desire of customers to cut down on waiting time.

Queue Discipline From the waiting line, arrivals move to the service facility according to a decision rule that prescribes how they are to be served. This rule is referred to as queue discipline. It is most frequently assumed that customers are served on a first-come first-served basis. Other decision rules are possible, of course. Last-come first-served, random service, or some sort of priority decision rule is often found in

Queue discipline

Figure 12.1   A General Waiting Line System

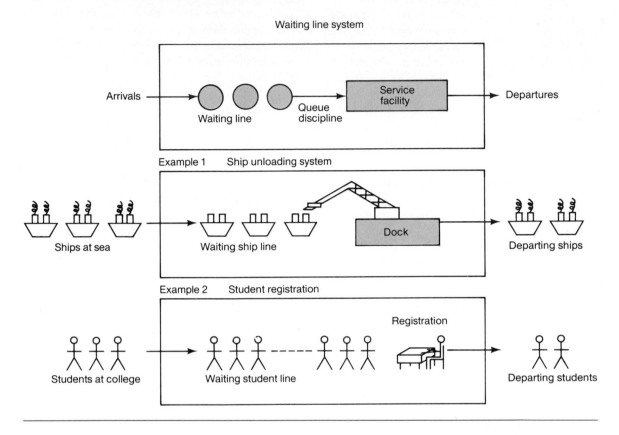

real-world applications. In this chapter, we will consider only the first-come first-served discipline.

Service Facility The service facility or server is the next component of the waiting line system. There are many possible configurations of service facility, such as a single server (e.g., a ticket counter), multiple servers (e.g., several bank tellers), or sequential servers (e.g., a package deal of gasoline pumping, car wash, and vacuum job). In addition, the rate of service at the facility may be constant, as in a washing machine's cycle or a blast furnace process. But service rates can vary just as arrival rates can. A visit to a dentist may be less than ten minutes for a quick checkup, or it may drag on for hours. A letter written by a manager may take only a few minutes, or may take weeks, months, or forever. The rate of service, just as the rate of arrivals, can be described according to a number of distributions.

Service facility

Departures Once arrivals are served, they become departures. Departing customers are not usually allowed to reenter the system immediately. Of course, this happens in real-world situations—forgetting something at the grocery store and going back to the checkout counter is one example. However, frequent reentries by departing enti-

Departures

ties may affect the arrival rates. Thus, it is generally assumed that departing customers do not reenter the system immediately.

Variations of queuing problems

There are a number of specific factors in the above described components that have an impact on the analysis of the general waiting line system. The population of arrivals may consist of any positive finite number or an infinite calling population. The queue may be limited to some maximum number. There may be multiple servers. The order of service may be first-come first-served, last-come first-served, or some other priority system. Service itself may consist of more than one station, such as the system found in driver's license facilities. Waiting may be required to register for the license, to take a written test, to take an eye test, to take a road test, to have a photograph taken, and finally, to pay for the license.

Structures of queuing systems

Basic Structures of Waiting Line Systems

Waiting line systems can be classified into four basic structures, based on the nature of the service facilities involved. The four classifications are illustrated in Figure 12.2. If a service facility involves parallel service stations, they are known as *channels*. On the other hand, if numbers of sequential steps are involved in the service, they are referred to as *phases*.

Channels and phases

The simplest waiting line structure is a single-channel, single-phase system, such as a single barber in a barbershop. Many hairstyling shops have more than one hairstylist, an example of a multiple-channel, single-phase system. If a customer wants a hairstyling and a manicure, it may require waiting for the stylist and then waiting for the manicurist, an example of a two-phase system. The same type of waiting systems is seen at places like Disney World and Universal Studios, where visitors queue to buy tickets and then wait for a tram or monorail ride.

This classification is by no means exhaustive. Multiple queues often have different characteristics at service counters, such as in department stores. In some multiple-channel waiting lines, switching between servers may be possible. Although reality is often very complex, the fundamentals of queuing theory for the basic structures we have discussed can be effectively used for the analysis of waiting line problems.

CASETTE 12.1   *STUDENT UNION HAIRSTYLING SALON*

Norman Dwork has been operating the Hairstyling Salon at the university student union for the past 30 years. He often talks to his customers about the good old days when the crew cut was the "in" thing. He had four barbers working for him then, and all five chairs were busy most of the time. He still has three barber chairs in his shop. But he is now the only stylist working in the shop.

A simple example

The salon's service hours are 8:00 AM–1:30 PM and 2:30 PM–5:00 PM Monday through Friday. Although there is a definite pattern of volume during the day, customers come to the salon at random intervals during any given hour. The time required to provide a good style cut for a customer is also a random variable. Since Norman does not have an appointment system, his customers are served strictly on a first-come, first-served basis.

The busiest time during a given day is from 11:30 AM to 1:00 PM, the lunch period for most of the faculty, staff, and students. Norman asked his wife, the cashier

Figure 12.2   Four Basic Waiting Line Structures

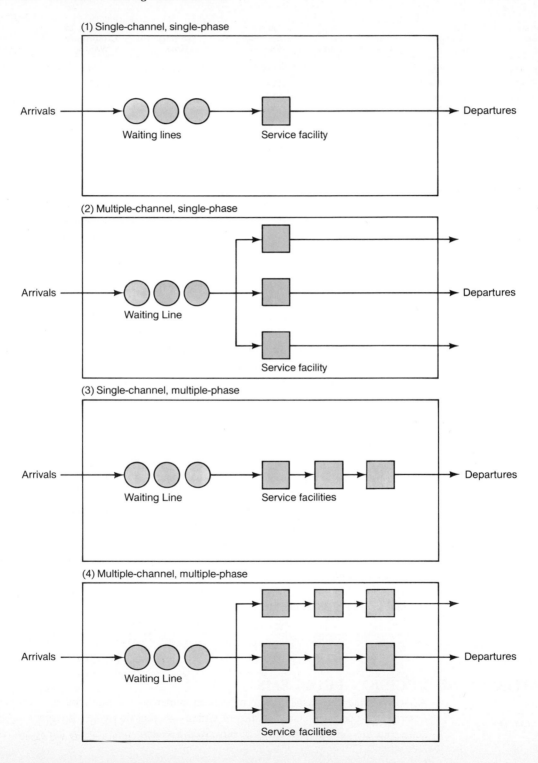

Table 12.2   *Student Union Hairstyling Salon Customer Service Data*

Customer Arrival Time	Time Styling Begins	Styling Time Required (Min.)	Time Service Ends	Customer Waiting Time	Number of Customers Waiting	Norman's Idle Time (Min.)
11:32 AM	11:32 AM	8	11:40 AM	0	0	2
11:35 AM	11:40 AM	7	11:47 AM	5	1	0
11:38 AM	11:47 AM	5	11:52 AM	9	2	0
11:45 AM	11:52 AM	12	12:04 PM	7	1	0
11:46 AM	12:04 PM	9	12:13 PM	18	2	0
12:00 PM	12:13 PM	6	12:19 PM	13	2	0
12:02 PM	12:19 PM	5	12:24 PM	17	1	0
12:07 PM	12:24 PM	9	12:33 PM	17	0	0
12:25 PM	12:33 PM	8	12:41 PM	8	0	4
12:45 PM	12:45 PM	9	12:54 PM	0	0	0
12:48 PM	12:54 PM	7	1:01 PM	6	0	0

and occasional shampooer, to keep a log to check the waiting pattern of his customers during the busiest period. Table 12.2 presents a summary of the customer service data during the 11:30 AM to 1:00 PM period on Monday.

The table is a good summary of customer flows, customer waiting times, lengths of waiting times, styling time variances, and Norman's working time. The table clearly indicates that Norman's hairstyling work begins when a customer arrives at the salon and Norman is not already engaged in the styling work for a previously arrived customer. A waiting line is created on the basis of two elements: the customer arrival time and the styling time required for customers.

The arrival time and service time

The table also provides important information about the salon operation. Since the salon has eight chairs available for customer waiting, the number of customers indicated in the table provides no special problems to Norman. However, the length of customer waiting time worries Norman. Will a customer wait 18 minutes for a haircut? Customers may perceive the waiting time as too long and not come back in the future. Such customer perceptions may cause a permanent business loss.

Norman is also concerned about a large number of customers waiting more than seven or eight minutes. Should he consider hiring a part-time stylist during the busy hours? Or should he subscribe to additional popular reading materials such as *National Geographic*, *Reader's Digest*, *Sports Illustrated*, *Time*, and *Ladies' Home Journal*? Determining accurate answers to these questions simply cannot be based on intuitive judgment. Waiting line models are helpful in answering such questions.

WAITING LINE DECISION PROBLEMS

As we indicated previously, there have been numerous queuing models developed to describe the operating characteristics of various waiting line systems. Operating characteristics are described in terms of how well a system functions in the *steady state*.

The steady and transient states

The *transient states,* the starting up and shutting down of the system, are not usually analyzed. The steady state system characteristics, such as expected length of a waiting line, customer waiting time, and percent of idle time of service facility, are described by the expected value concept. These operating characteristics are only the necessary inputs to a broader framework of analysis required for waiting line decision making.

The basic cost question

Waiting line problem analysis must answer various service-related questions. Eventually, however, it should answer the basic question, "How can we minimize the total expected cost involved in the system's operation?" within certain managerial policies concerning service in the problem. To answer this primary question, we must determine the optimum level of service. For example, let us consider the problem of a hamburger shop owner. He or she certainly would like to see the employees working steadily throughout their working hours, generating revenue. This would require a constant waiting line in front of each and every cash register. The customers, however, may base their decision of where to take their business on the minimum waiting time required. The owner can minimize the customer waiting time by hiring more servers. Since customers do not arrive according to a desired schedule, the owner will face conflicting trade-offs between the number of servers hired, which results in increased payroll cost, and the quality or level of service provided, which results in increased waiting costs.

Most business problems that can benefit from waiting line models often involve cost analysis. Businesses typically provide service facilities, and customers are usually found in the waiting lines. Employees can also be found in waiting lines, eating up payroll time while waiting to use a copy machine, a telephone line, or a tool crib.

The service and waiting costs

Service facilities, such as drive-in teller stations, often require substantial investment. The level of service must eventually be related to the other parameters and variables of the waiting line system.

Total expected system cost is the sum of two separate cost components: *service costs* and *waiting costs.* Our objective is to minimize the total expected cost of the waiting line system. Figure 12.3 presents the relationship of our decision variable, level of service, to expected service cost, waiting cost, and total cost.

As the level of service increases (e.g., as the number of checkout counters increases in a grocery store), the cost of serving increases. On the other hand, as the level of service increases, the customer waiting time will decrease and consequently

The service cost vs. waiting costs

the expected waiting cost (e.g., lost customers due to long waiting lines) will decrease. We cannot eliminate customer waiting completely. But we can minimize the expected total system cost by analyzing the relationship between the service and waiting costs. As shown in Figure 12.3, if the service cost increases monotonically and the waiting cost decreases monotonically, the total system cost is minimized when the increase of service cost equals the decrease of waiting cost.

Service Costs

The service costs include payroll, equipment, facilities, and other related costs in providing the service. Thus, as the level of service increases, the service costs will naturally increase. In our hamburger shop example, if the owner hires a second

Service costs

checkout worker, service costs increase by the wage of the second worker, the cost of the second cash register, and the uniform and other related costs for the second

Figure 12.3   Relationship of Level of Service to Typical Waiting and Service Costs

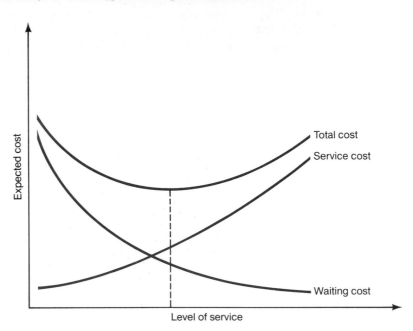

worker. The exact cost of employing the second server may be straightforward. However, it may also require a careful analysis of the complexities that are unique in the given situation.

   We can also analyze service costs through evaluating the costs associated with server or service facility idle time. When we increase the level of service, the idle time for servers will obviously increase. For example, when the hamburger shop installs a second checkout counter, the server idle time experienced with only one checkout counter will naturally increase. Whether we analyze service costs through calculating the additional cost of servers or measuring the idle service time cost, we would usually derive the same result.

Waiting Costs

Waiting costs

When the level of service is increased, we expect waiting time, and consequently waiting costs, to decrease. But since waiting costs usually depend on the arrival of customers and customers' reactions to the waiting line, it is often difficult to measure waiting costs directly. In the hamburger shop example, it is difficult to determine how much revenue is lost because the lines are too long. Managerial judgment, perhaps tempered by experience, may provide an estimate of waiting costs. If the waiting situation occurs in the work situation, such as workers waiting in line at a copy machine, the cost of waiting should reflect the cost of productive resources lost during the waiting time.

The Total System Cost

The total system service cost

Now we can clearly see that the decision problem is one of balancing waiting time costs and service costs. Thus, a general decision model statement for a waiting line problem can be described as follows:

$$\text{Minimize } TC(S) = IC_1 + WC_2$$

where

$TC(S)$ = total expected cost for the service level S
I = total expected server idle time for a specified period (each hour, each day, etc.)
C_1 = cost associated with a unit of server idle time
W = total expected waiting time for all arrivals for a specified period
C_2 = cost associated with customer waiting per unit of time

In our decision model, the level of service, S, is the decision variable. Our model should be evaluated for each level of service under consideration. We will consider the following simple example as an illustration of how a total system formula can be applied.

EXAMPLE 12.1   A PORT UNLOADING PROBLEM

A company has two unloading facilities at a port. The management is attempting to determine whether or not to man both facilities for a particular day. Since the arrival rates of customers (ships) fluctuate randomly, estimates of the expected arrivals for a given day would be required for the analysis.

Balancing the service and waiting costs

The company has obtained the following information:

Model Parameter	One Dock	Two Docks
Total expected dock idle time for the day (I)	1 hr.	12 hr.
Total expected ship waiting time for the day (W)	4 hr.	1 hr.
Estimated cost per unit of dock time (C_1)	$2,000/hr.	
Estimated cost per unit of ship waiting time (C_2)	$60,000/hr.	

On the basis of the above data, we can calculate the total expected system cost for operating one or two docks as follows:

$$TC(S = 1) = (1)(\$2,000) + (4)(\$60,000)$$
$$= \$2,000 + \$240,000$$
$$= \$242,000$$

$$TC(S = 2) = (12)(\$2,000) + (1)(\$60,000)$$
$$= \$24,000 + \$60,000$$
$$= \$84,000$$

It is apparent from the above analysis that the cost of ship waiting time far outweighs the cost of dock idle time. Thus, even though manning the second dock facility results in a large amount of idle time for the dock workers and the port facility (if the company owns the port as well as the ships) the company should provide the additional dock workers to operate the second dock.

From the above example, it should be obvious that solving waiting line problems requires the assumption that model parameters are known. Management must be able to determine sufficiently accurate estimates of C_1 (cost associated with a unit of server idle time) and C_2 (cost associated with customer waiting per unit of time).

No general optimization theory

As we noted earlier, unlike linear programming or the other optimization techniques we have studied, there exists no general optimization theory for waiting line problems. The total system cost approach we discussed above is a means of analyzing waiting line problems as a decision making model. Thus far we have identified the general components of the decision making model for waiting line problems. The mathematical formulation required to solve queuing problems can vary widely according to the characteristics of the problem under study. Some of these formulations will be presented in this chapter. Many queuing problems, however, do not fit developed waiting line formulations. For this reason, waiting line theory has been developed primarily to provide a wide variety of descriptive measures of the system's operating performance.

ASSUMPTIONS FOR WAITING LINE MODELS

To analyze the waiting line situation, we need estimates of such operating characteristics as expected server idle time and expected customer waiting time. Waiting line theory provides formulas that allow calculation of operating characteristics based on specific assumptions.

Key operating characteristics

The operating characteristics most frequently obtained in the analysis of waiting lines are:

Probability of any specified number of customers being in the system.

Mean (expected) waiting time for each customer.

Mean (expected) length of the waiting line.

Mean time in the system (waiting plus being served) for each customer.

Mean number of customers in the system.

Probability that the service facility will be idle.

To determine the operating characteristics outlined above, we must make certain assumptions about waiting line parameters. We will discuss several of the most important assumptions that affect the operating characteristics of the waiting line system.

The characteristics of a waiting line system can be classified by six parameters. They are:

1. Arrival distribution.

2. Service time distribution.

Six parameters **3.** Number of servers.

4. Queue discipline.

5. Maximum number of customers allowed in the system.

6. Number of potential customers in the calling population.

Kendall's notation In 1953, D. G. Kendall introduced a compact notational scheme to describe the characteristics of waiting line systems. The *Kendall notation* has since been widely accepted as a systematic means of describing queuing models. Kendall's notation can be used as a shorthand means of portraying a waiting line system. For example, abbreviations for the six parameters listed above can be placed in the appropriate position of the following format:

(Arrival distribution/Service distribution/Number of servers):
(Queue discipline/Maximum customers/Calling population)

Arrival Distribution

The pattern of arrivals is described by the arrival distribution. The number of arrivals per unit of time is not usually based on a precise schedule but occurs in a random fashion according to one of many probability distributions. The most frequently used assumption about customer arrivals is the *Poisson distribution*.

The Poisson distribution In the Poisson distribution, named after the French mathematician Siméon D. Poisson (1781–1840), the number of arrivals during a certain time interval is independent of the number of arrivals in previous time intervals. The Poisson distribution has proven useful for the simple reason that many statistical studies of queuing processes have resulted in Poisson-distributed arrivals.

The general formula for the Poisson probability distribution is

$$P(r) = \frac{e^{-\lambda}(\lambda)^r}{r!}$$

where

r = number of arrivals per unit of time
$P(r)$ = probability of r arrivals

$$\lambda = \text{mean arrival rate}$$
$$e = \text{the base of natural logarithms, } 2.71828$$
$$r! = r(r - 1)(r - 2) \cdots (3)(2)(1)$$

Unique features of the Poisson distribution

Assuming random independent arrivals, we can describe the arrivals as a Poisson distribution.[1] Each arrival is also independent of the state of the system. The Poisson distribution has the unique feature that the mean is equal to the variance. Therefore, if we know the mean, we can describe the entire Poisson distribution. The Poisson distribution is a *discrete* probability distribution, since it provides the probability of the number of arrivals per unit of time. This means that we need to deal only with whole numbers. Figure 12.4 portrays the shape of the general Poisson distribution. As the mean (λ) becomes larger, the distribution becomes flatter and more bell-shaped.

Let us consider an example. If the mean arrival rate of ships at a port is one every 12 hours, the probabilities associated with a different number of arrivals per hour would be

$$P(r) = \frac{e^{-\lambda}(\lambda)^r}{r!}$$

For $r = 1$, $P(1) = \dfrac{2.71828^{(-1/12)}(1/12)^1}{1!} = .9200(1/12) = .0767$

r	P(r)
0	.9200
1	.0767
2	.0032
3	.0001
4	.0000

A negative exponential distribution

If the number of arrivals per unit of time can be described by a Poisson distribution, with a mean rate of λ, then the time between arrivals is distributed as a *negative exponential* probability distribution, with a mean of $1/\lambda$. The negative exponential distribution is continuous, allowing any fraction. For example, if the mean arrival rate per 1-hour period is 6, then the mean time between arrivals is 10 minutes (1 hour/6). The relationship between the arrival rate and the time between arrivals is as follows:

Arrival Rate	Time between Arrivals
Poisson	Negative exponential
Mean = λ	Mean = $1/\lambda$
λ = 6 arrivals per hour	$1/\lambda$ = (1/6)(1 hour) = 10 minutes

Arrival rates can be described by other distributions as well. If arrivals follow a schedule, without variance, they are deterministic. Assembly line processes may be set at this arrival distribution.

---

[1] A table of Poisson probability values for various values of r and λ is presented in Appendix 3.

Figure 12.4   The General Shape of the Poisson Distribution

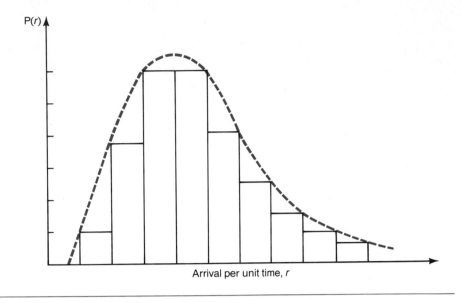

The assumption of the *Erlang distribution* is very important in waiting line theory. As we noted earlier, queuing theory was pioneered by A. K. Erlang to analyze waiting effects on a telephone system. Most of the empirically determined distributions can be described as Erlang distributions. This is a very important value of the Erlang distribution. The Erlang distribution density function is:

The Erlang distribution

$$f(t) = \frac{(\mu k)^k}{(k - 1)!} \, t^{k-1} e^{-k\mu t}$$

where

$$t = \text{service time}$$
$$f(t) = \text{probability density associated with } t$$
$$k = \text{number of service phases}$$
$$\mu = \text{mean service rate}$$
$$e = \text{natural number (2.71828)}$$

In the above formula, μ is the mean and k is the parameter that determines the dispersion of the distribution. This distribution is shown, with several values of k, in Figure 12.5. If $k = 1$, we obtain the negative exponential distribution; if $k = \infty$, we obtain a constant distribution. It should be noted that k must be a positive integer.

A general explanation of k can be obtained by considering a multiple-phase queuing operation. In a multiple-phase queuing situation, a server can perform several functions. For example, a druggist can take the prescription, fill it, make the proper records and ring up the cash register. If a single server performs several functions for a customer during one service operation, and all of the k service functions have identical exponential distributions with mean $1/k\mu$, then the aggregate service distri-

Figure 12.5   Erlang Distribution for Selected Values of k

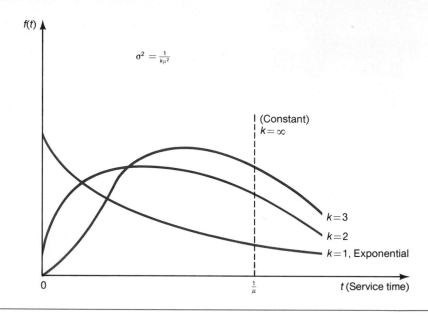

bution will be $1/\mu$ and the variance σ^2 will be $1/k^2$. Even if the physical process does not fit this description, the Erlang distribution may fit the arrival distribution.

The arrival distribution symbols in Kendall's notation are given below:

Symbol	Description
M	Poisson
D	Deterministic
E_k	Erlang, with parameter k
GI	General independent

Any arrival distribution not described by the first three symbols can be noted by the symbol GI.

Service Time Distribution

Service time distribution

Service times in a waiting line process may also be described by any one of a large number of different probability distributions. The most commonly assumed distribution for service times is the negative exponential distribution.

The assumption of negative exponential service times is not valid nearly as often as is the assumption of the Poisson arrival distribution. Therefore, we must check this assumption very carefully before selecting the service time distribution.

Figure 12.6   Negative Exponential Probability Density Distribution

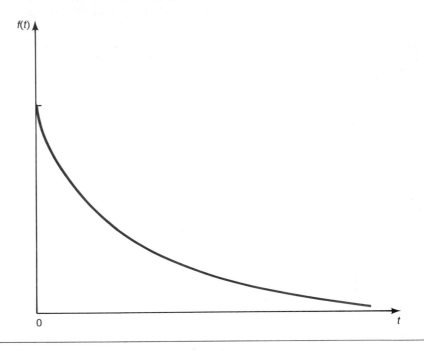

The general formula for the negative exponential probability density function is

$$f(t) = \mu e^{-\mu t}$$

where

$$t = \text{service time}$$
$$f(t) = \text{probability density associated with } t$$
$$\mu = \text{mean service rate}$$
$$1/\mu = \text{mean service time}$$
$$e = 2.71828 \dots$$

The negative exponential service time assumes random time for service. The probability of serving a customer is independent of how much time has already elapsed on the service for that customer or for any prior customers. It is also independent of the number of customers waiting for service. (This last assumption limits us a great deal, as service in reality may speed up when people are waiting.)

As was pointed out before, the negative exponential distribution is continuous. Figure 12.6 illustrates the negative exponential distribution. In this figure we can easily see that short service times have the highest probability of occurrence. As service time increases, the probability function diminishes gradually toward zero.

A cumulative probability distribution

The area under the curve for the negative exponential distribution is obtained from its cumulative distribution function. The area under the curve to the left of T (T being any time selected) is described as

$$F(T) = f(t \le T) = 1 - e^{-\mu T}$$

As an example, if the mean service time $(1/\mu)$ of a dock unloading facility is 1 ship unloaded every 8 hours, the probability that service would take T or fewer hours would be calculated from the formula given above as follows:[2]

Service Times of at Most T (Hr.)	$F(T)$ Probability
0	.0000
1	.1175
2	.2212
3	.3127
4	.3935
5	.4647
8	.6321
12	.7769
18	.8946
24	.9507
40	.9933

T	$F(T)$
1	$1 - e^{-\mu T} = 1 - 2.71828^{-(1/8)(1)} = 1 - .8825 = .1175$
2	$1 - e^{-\mu T} = 1 - 2.71828^{-(1/8)(2)} = 1 - .7788 = .2212$
3	$1 - e^{-\mu T} = 1 - 2.71828^{-(1/8)(3)} = 1 - .6873 = .3127$

Service time distributions can take the same distribution forms as arrival distributions. Service distribution symbols in Kendall's notation are:

Symbol	Description
M	Negative exponential
D	Constant
E_k	Erlang, with parameter k
GS	General distribution

Number of Servers

The number of servers

The next waiting line system characteristic we will consider is the number of parallel servers. Servers can be equipment (washing machines, cranes, etc.), people (barbers, bank tellers), or systems combining both. If there is more than one server in a system, these servers can be arranged in a parallel system in which each server provides the same type of service to different customers. Alternatively, when servers are in series, services are performed in sequence. In Kendall's notation, the number of parallel servers is indicated by the appropriate integer.

It is important to remember that in a waiting line system the service rate (from all servers combined) must exceed the arrival rate; otherwise the waiting line will

---

[2]A table of values of e^x and e^{-x} is presented in Appendix 4.

Figure 12.7 Relationship of Waiting Line Length to Arrival/Service Rate Ratio

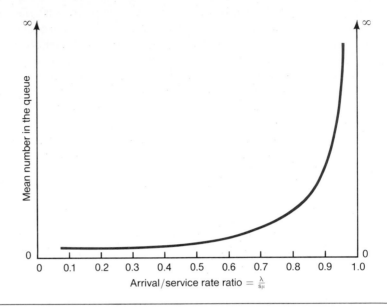

grow infinitely long. If the arrival rate exceeds the service rate, it will be necessary to add parallel servers to ensure that arrivals will receive service. It should be apparent that if an average of four customers an hour arrives at a barbershop with only one barber, and the barber services three customers per hour, every hour will find an additional customer in the waiting line. To restore reasonable schedules to the lives of all concerned, an additional server (barber) will be required. For the queuing system to attain equilibrium, the rate of service multiplied by the number of parallel servers must exceed the rate of arrival. This is demonstrated in Figure 12.7.

Queue Discipline

Service discipline symbols

Queue discipline, as we discussed earlier, is the decision rule that determines the order in which waiting customers will be selected for service. It is normally assumed that customers are serviced on a first-come first-served basis. Other decision rules are possible, however. Last-come first-served, random service, or some other sort of priority decision rule is often found in real-world applications. The symbols and descriptions of queue discipline are shown below:

Symbol	Description
FCFS	First-come first-served
LCFS	Last-come first-served
SIRO	Service in random order (random service order)
GD	General distribution (other decision rules)

Infinite vs. Finite Waiting Line Length

Length of the waiting line

The maximum number of customers awaiting service can affect the waiting line model. Many models may be appropriately described by an unlimited queue length. But there may be limited space available for customers awaiting service. For example, the driveway and parking lot at a hamburger establishment may have a limited capacity. Although cars attempting to enter a car wash often back up into the street, there may be traffic ordinances against such a situation.

Balking

The behavior of customers may also be such that a limited queue length may be appropriate for a model. Customers may refuse to enter a long line even if space is available. For example, your hunger pains may cause you to seek another source of food if your favorite hamburger shop has 64 customers awaiting service. This decision to not enter a waiting line is referred to as *balking*. Balking can result in an effective limited queue despite ample space available for waiting. Although infinite queues are easier to work with from a mathematical standpoint, finite queues are often more realistic. In Kendall's notation, the maximum queue length is indicated by the appropriate integer or by the symbol ∞.

Maximum Population in the System

Calling population

The calling population in waiting line theory is the source of arrivals to be served. If you are considering a waiting line problem in which there is a large number of potential customers, it would be reasonable to assume that the calling population is infinite. However, if the source of arrivals for service is such that removal of one member of that population would affect the probability of arrival, it would be appropriate to use a model having a finite calling population. In Kendall's notation, the calling population is indicated by the appropriate integer or by the symbol ∞.

WAITING LINE MODELS

Variety of waiting line models

Now we are ready to study the most widely used waiting line models and their required assumptions. Before looking at some of these models, it is important for us to note that waiting line systems are in a transient state when they begin operations, during which state they approach equilibrium, or steady-state conditions. This simply means that service facilities may begin their operations without a queue of waiting customers. At the beginning of the day, unless customers arrive before opening time, there are no customers forced to wait for service. It might take a period of system operating time before the steady-state conditions described by queuing formulas could accurately predict system parameters.

Complex queuing models have been developed that allow an estimation of service time as a function of the time elapsed since operations began. Waiting lines begin operations empty, meaning a higher probability of shorter lines. This chapter, however, will present only steady-state models.

The waiting line models we are about to study are categorized on the basis of their required assumptions. In order to refresh our memory, it would be a good idea to repeat Kendall's notation format:

(Arrival distribution/Service distribution/Number of servers):
(Queue discipline/Maximum customers/Calling population)

(D/D/1):(FCFS/∞/∞)

Initially, we will look at the deterministic waiting line system. This model assumes the following:

1. Deterministic (constant) arrival.

2. Deterministic (constant) service time.

3. Number of servers = 1, or a single-channel system.

4. Queue discipline is first-come, first-served.

5. Maximum number of customers is assumed to be infinite, ∞.

6. Calling population is also assumed to be infinite, ∞.

This model is actually a special case of the stochastic waiting line model, with zero variance in arrival and service time rates. Each of the models will be discussed through variations of a casette problem.

CASETTE 12.2   **THE TITANTIC QUEUE**

Barney Harrelson reported to work in June, fresh from a business college and armed with the latest in quantitative tools. He had obtained a position with Titantic Oil Port Systems, Inc. (TOPSI), a new petroleum refinery company, and had been assigned to the North Atlantic Division.

The North Atlantic Division of TOPSI came into being to meet the critical demand for petroleum products in the northeastern United States. TOPSI's president, Eric Reed, had long held an interest in a small but unproductive farm just south of Thule, Greenland. TOPSI built a refinery on the farm site, obtained agreements with various crude oil producers, and was set for operations. Mr. Reed decided to go to Boston himself to set up marketing operations, entrusting the details of the refinery operation to his executive vice-president (and favorite nephew), Lafe Erickson.

Lafe was interested in efficiency and had drawn up a plan of operations for the terminal where crude oil is to be delivered at the average rate of two 480,000 barrel tankers per day during the open shipping season (when ice conditions allowed). Lafe designed the unloading facilities to handle that delivery rate. The tankers charge demurrage of $600 per hour for idle waiting time. Lafe calculated the port facility cost $800 per hour to build and operate. Lafe's proposed schedule for the first week of operation is shown in Table 12.3.

Table 12.3   The Titanic Oil Port Systems: Constant Arrival/Constant Service Time

Ship	Arrival Hour	Service Begins	Service Time (Hr.)	Service Ends	Ship Waiting Time (Hr.)	Dock Idle Time (Hr.)	Ships Waiting
Ill Wind	0	0	12	12	0	0	0
Typhoon	12	12	12	24	0	0	0
Zephyr	24	24	12	36	0	0	0
Sirocco	36	36	12	48	0	0	0
Monsoon	48	48	12	60	0	0	0
Whirlwind	60	60	12	72	0	0	0
Gale	72	72	12	84	0	0	0
Tokyo Maru	84	84	12	96	0	0	0
Squall	96	96	12	108	0	0	0
Mistral	108	108	12	120	0	0	0
Simoom	120	120	12	132	0	0	0
Trade Wind	132	132	12	144	0	0	0
Samiel	144	144	12	156	0	0	0
Levanter	156	156	12	168	0	0	0
14 ships unloaded			168		0	0	

Based on the constant arrival and constant service time, the following analysis can be made.

$$\text{Mean arrival rate, } \lambda = \frac{14 \text{ ships}}{168 \text{ hours}} = \frac{1 \text{ ship}}{12 \text{ hours}}$$

$$\text{Mean service rate, } \mu = \frac{14 \text{ ships}}{168 \text{ hours}} = \frac{1 \text{ ship}}{12 \text{ hours}}$$

Mean length of the system, $L = 1$ ship in system

Mean time in the system, $W = 12$ hours in system

Mean length of the waiting line, $L_q = 0$ ships waiting

Mean waiting time, $W_q = 0$ hours waiting

Now the total cost per week can be calculated as follows:

Demurrage (W_q):   0 hours × \$600/hr. =   \$0
Operation: 168 hours × \$800/hr. = \$134,000
Total cost = \$134,000

(M/M/1):(FCFS/∞/∞)

This model assumes the same conditions as the first model except that it assumes a Poisson distribution for arrival rates, and service time is described by the negative exponential distribution. It is the classical model of waiting line theory.

The operating characteristics of this model are:

λ = mean arrival rate ($1/\lambda$ = mean time between arrivals)

μ = mean service rate ($1/\mu$ = mean service time)

$$n = \text{number of customers (units) in the system (includes those waiting and in service)}$$

L = mean number in the system

L_q = mean number in the waiting line (queue length)

W = mean time in the system

W_q = mean waiting time (in the queue)

ρ = service facility utilization factor

I = percentage of server idle time

By assuming Poisson distribution arrival rates and exponential service times, we can determine the parameters of the model as follows:

The percentage of time the service facility is operating,

$$\rho = \frac{\lambda}{\mu}$$

The probability of no units in the system,

$$P_0 = 1 - \frac{\lambda}{\mu}$$

The probability of n units in the system,

$$P_n = \left(\frac{\lambda}{\mu}\right)^n \left(1 - \frac{\lambda}{\mu}\right)$$

The probability of k or more units in the system,

$$P_{n \geq k} = \left(\frac{\lambda}{\mu}\right)^k$$

Mean (expected) number of units in the system,

$$L = \frac{\lambda}{\mu - \lambda}$$

Mean number of units in the queue,

$$L_q = \frac{\lambda^2}{\mu(\mu - \lambda)}$$

Mean time in the system,

$$W = \frac{1}{\mu - \lambda}$$

Mean waiting time,

$$W_q = \frac{\lambda}{\mu(\mu - \lambda)}$$

Percentage of server idle time,

$$P_0 = 1 - \frac{\lambda}{\mu}$$

Sometimes we may be able to obtain only part of the above information. To determine information on other parameters, the following relationships can aid us in completing our information:

$$P_n = P_0 \left(\frac{\lambda}{\mu}\right)^n$$

$$P_0 = 1 - \rho$$

$$L_q = L - \frac{\lambda}{\mu} = \lambda \cdot W_q$$

$$L = L_q + \frac{\lambda}{\mu} = \lambda \cdot W$$

$$W_q = W - \frac{1}{\mu} = \frac{L_q}{\lambda}$$

$$W = W_q + \frac{1}{\mu} = \frac{L}{\lambda}$$

Given knowledge of λ and μ, when we know any of the parameters L_q, L, W_q, or W, we can determine the other three parameters. The probability of zero customers in the system will, of course, equal the percentage of time the service facility is idle.

CASETTE 12.3   ***OPERATION THULE***

Barney Harrelson had been hired to help in planning operations at Thule. Lafe Erikson, who believed in motivation, informed Barney that his bonus would be based on the efficiency of the crude oil receiving operation. Barney examined the schedule. It did not appear promising, and his career at Thule seemed doomed. All would be well if the ships arrived on schedule and the unloading operation progressed smoothly. But Barney had always been the worrying sort. There were many sources of delay for shipping en route to Thule, including storms and icebergs. The unloading operation was also fraught with potential delays. The tankers required secure anchoring for unloading, and it took time to hook up the piping system in rough weather (which occurred at Thule 364 days a year, and 179 of the 180 annual operating days). And even though Lafe had obtained a very favorable price on some pumps from the Arctic Pump Wholesaling Company, Barney was somewhat concerned with pump reliability.

Barney recalculated the schedule of operations based upon a Poisson distribution rate of arrival and an exponentially distributed rate of service time. Using the system set up by Lafe, Barney found little probability of unloading all of the tankers arriving during the open-sea season before the ice closed in, and calculated an infinite demur-

Table 12.4   Operation Thule-Poisson Arrival/Exponential Service

Ship	Arrival Hour	Service Begins	Service Time (Hr.)	Service Ends	Ship Waiting Time (Hr.)	Dock Idle Time (Hr.)	Ships Waiting
Ill Wind	0	0	1	1	0	0	0
Typhoon	9	9	7	16	0	8	0
Zephr	53	53	28	81	0	37	5
Sirocco	61	81	5	86	20	0	4
Monsoon	64	86	4	90	18	0	3
Whirlwind	66	90	2	92	24	0	3
Gale	76	92	4	96	16	0	3
Tokyo Maru	79	96	17	113	17	0	3
Squall	90	113	3	116	23	0	3
Mistral	93	116	2	118	23	0	2
Simoom	99	118	12	130	19	0	2
Trade Wind	114	130	20	150	16	0	2
Samiel	119	150	1	151	31	0	1
Levanter	138	151	6	157	13	0	0
End of week	168					11	
			112		224	56	

rage expense. Although Lafe felt the young man tended to worry too much, Lafe also was concerned a bit when faced with the contingencies that he had overlooked. To be on the safe side, Lafe agreed to increase the pumping system from a capacity of 40,000 barrels per hour to 60,000 barrels per hour, yielding a cost to TOPSI of $1,200 per hour for operation and depreciation. Lafe had Barney recalculate the schedule of operations, based upon a Poisson rate of tanker arrival and an exponential rate of service. The first week's operation proceeded as shown in Table 12.4.

$$\lambda = \frac{14 \text{ ships arrive}}{168 \text{ hours}} = \frac{1 \text{ ship}}{12 \text{ hours}}; \quad \mu = \frac{14 \text{ ships unloaded}}{112 \text{ hours}} = \frac{1 \text{ ship}}{8 \text{ hours}};$$

$$\rho = \frac{\lambda}{\mu} = \frac{1/12}{1/8} = \frac{2}{3} \text{ or } \frac{112}{168} = \frac{2}{3}$$

$$L = \frac{\lambda}{\mu - \lambda} = \frac{1/12}{1/8 - 1/12} = 2 \text{ ships in harbor}$$

$$W = \frac{L}{\lambda} = \frac{2}{1/12} = 24 \text{ hours in harbor per ship}$$

$$L_q = \frac{\lambda^2}{\mu (\mu - \lambda)} = \frac{\lambda}{\mu} L = \frac{1/12}{1/8} \times 2 = \frac{4}{3} \text{ ships waiting for service}$$

$$W_q = \frac{L_q}{\lambda} = \frac{4/3}{1/12} = 16 \text{ hours waiting} \times 14 \text{ ships} = 224 \text{ hours}$$

The total cost per week is calculated as follows:

$$\text{Demurrage:} \quad 224 \text{ hours} \times \$600/\text{hr.} \quad = \$134,000$$
$$\text{Operation:} \quad 112 \text{ hours} \times \$1,200/\text{hr.} = \underline{\$134,400}$$
$$\text{Total cost} = \$268,800$$

Mr. Reed found the first week's account of unloading operations somewhat unsettling in that there was as much cost for demurrage as for operation. Also, the shipping companies had complained because their crews were getting unruly while waiting in Thule. There is a saying, "If you find out that you have only a month to live, spend it in Thule. It will seem like a lifetime."

Mr. Reed gently reminded Lafe that his future would be much more pleasant if he found a way to reduce costs in the unloading operation. Lafe took his favorite uncle's advice to heart, and told Barney to come up with better alternatives by morning.

Since days in Thule are quite long in the open season, Barney had time to gather information on three alternative systems. The primary cause of unloading delay appeared to be the pumping system. It was true that the tankers arrived in a most haphazard manner, but TOPSI had no control over arrivals.

The existing dock facility allowed only one ship to berth at a time. Barney gathered information on three proposals, each involving a different pump arrangement. Pump reliability was related to cost, and since Barney was attempting to develop a cost effective operation, he conducted the following analysis with the objective of minimizing total cost:

Pump System	Capacity (Bbl./Hr.)	Cost/Operating Hr.	Distribution of Service Time
Brand X	1 × 60,000	$2,100	Normal: $\sigma_\mu = 3.5$
Brand Y	1 × 60,000	$2,400	Constant: $\sigma_\mu = 0$
Brand Z	2 × 30,000	$1,800	Erlang ($k = 2$): $\sigma_\mu = 5.63$
Existing	1 × 60,000	$1,200	Exponential: $\sigma_\mu = 8$

Barney brushed the snow off his quantitative methods book, and analytically examined the expected outcome of the three alternatives. As a check, he developed distributions of service times conforming to the three alternatives, and examined the expected outcome of each alternative against the first week's distribution of arrival times. We will now look at three queuing models, each using a different distribution of service time.

(M/GI/1):(FCFS/∞/∞)

This model assumes arrival rates distributed as Poisson, as before. But the service rates are allowed to take on any distribution. It is possible to accurately describe the rate of service according to the normal distribution, the beta distribution, or any other kind of distribution.

If we assume that the service times are independent, with some common probability distribution (*any* distribution, as long as it is the same for all services), and that their mean $(1/\mu)$ and standard deviation (σ) are known, then we can use the following equations to analyze the system performance:

$$\rho = \frac{\lambda}{\mu}$$

$$P_0 = 1 - \frac{\lambda}{\mu}$$

$$L_q = \frac{\lambda^2\sigma_\mu^2 + (\lambda/\mu)^2}{2(1 - \lambda/\mu)}$$

$$L = L_q + \frac{\lambda}{\mu}$$

$$W_q = \frac{L_q}{\lambda}$$

$$W = W_q + \frac{1}{\mu}$$

CASETTE 12.4   *Operation Thule—Pump X*

Barney's analysis of the Brand X pump, with normally distributed service time, is presented in Table 12.5.

Table 12.5   Operation Thule—Pump X: Poisson Arrival/Normal Service ($\sigma_\mu = 3.5$)

Ship	Arrival Hour	Service Begins	Service Time (Hrs.)	Service Ends	Ship Waiting Time (Hrs.)	Dock Idle Time (Hrs.)	Ships Waiting
Ill Wind	0	0	4	4	0	0	0
Typhoon	9	9	8	17	0	5	0
Zephyr	53	53	5	58	0	36	0
Sirocco	61	61	8	69	0	3	2
Monsoon	64	69	6	75	5	0	1
Whirlwind	66	75	8	83	9	0	2
Gale	76	83	7	90	7	0	1
Tokyo Maru	79	90	12	102	11	0	3
Squall	90	102	10	112	12	0	2
Mistral	93	112	5	117	19	0	2
Simoom	99	117	13	130	18	0	2
Trade Wind	114	130	15	145	16	0	2
Samiel	119	145	3	148	26	0	1
Levanter	138	148	8	156	10	0	0
End of week	168					12	
			112		133	56	

On the basis of the information in Table 12.5, Barney computed the weekly operation cost as follows:

$$\lambda = \frac{14 \text{ ships}}{168 \text{ hours}} = \frac{1 \text{ ship}}{12 \text{ hours}}; \quad \mu = \frac{14 \text{ ships}}{112 \text{ hours}} = \frac{1 \text{ ship}}{8 \text{ hours}};$$

$$\rho = \frac{112}{168} = \frac{2}{3}; \quad \sigma_\mu = 3.5$$

$$L_q = \frac{\lambda^2 \sigma_\mu^2 + \rho^2}{2(1 - \rho)} = \frac{(1/144)(3.5)^2 + 4/9}{2(1 - 2/3)} = .7943 \text{ ship}$$

$$L = \rho + L_q = \frac{2}{3} + .7943 = 1.461 \text{ ships}$$

$$W_q = \frac{L_q}{\lambda} = \frac{.7943}{1/12} = 9.531 \text{ hours} \times 14 \text{ ships} = 133.4 \text{ hours}$$

$$W = W_q + \frac{1}{\mu} = 9.531 \text{ hours} + \frac{1}{1/8 \text{ hour}} = 17.531 \text{ hours}$$

$$P_0 = 1 - \rho = 1 - \frac{2}{3} = .333$$

The total cost per week is calculated as follows:

Demurrage:	133 hours × $600/hr.	= $ 79,800
Operation:	112 hours × $2,100/hr.	= $235,200
	Total cost	= $315,000

(M/D/1):(FCFS/∞/∞)

This model assumes Poisson arrival rates, with constant service time rates. This model is very useful for those applications in which there is no variance in service rate. One example among many might be an analysis of the waiting line system at an automatic car wash. Many services relying on a high degree of automation have deterministic service times.

The formulas for the parameters of this model are a special case of the (M/GI/1): (FCFS/∞/∞) model, with $\sigma^2 = 0$.

$$\rho = \frac{\lambda}{\mu}$$

$$P_0 = 1 - \frac{\lambda}{\mu}$$

$$L_q = \frac{(\lambda/\mu)^2}{2(1 - \lambda/\mu)}$$

$$L = L_q + \frac{\lambda}{\mu}$$

$$W_q = \frac{L_q}{\lambda}$$

$$W = W_q + \frac{1}{\mu}$$

CASETTE 12.5   OPERATION THULE—PUMP Y

The analysis of the Brand Y pump, with constant service time, is shown in Table 12.6.

Table 12.6   Operation Thule—Pump Y: Poisson Arrival/Constant Service

Ship	Arrival Hour	Service Begins	Service Time (Hr.)	Service Ends	Ship Waiting Time (Hr.)	Dock Idle Time (Hr.)	Ships Waiting
Ill Wind	0	0	8	8	0	0	0
Typhoon	9	9	8	17	0	1	0
Zephyr	53	53	8	61	0	36	0
Sirocco	61	61	8	69	0	0	2
Monsoon	64	69	8	77	5	0	1
Whirlwind	66	77	8	85	11	0	2
Gale	76	85	8	93	9	0	2
Tokyo Maru	79	93	8	101	14	0	3
Squall	90	101	8	109	11	0	2
Mistral	93	109	8	117	16	0	2
Simoom	99	117	8	125	18	0	2
Trade Wind	114	125	8	133	11	0	1
Samiel	119	133	8	141	14	0	1
Levanter	138	141	8	149	11	0	0
End of week	168						
			112		112	56	

Barney's analysis of Operation Thule with Pump Y is as follows:

$$\lambda = \frac{14 \text{ ships}}{168 \text{ hours}} = \frac{1 \text{ ship}}{12 \text{ hours}}; \quad \mu = \frac{14 \text{ ships}}{112 \text{ hours}} = \frac{1 \text{ ship}}{8 \text{ hours}}; \quad \rho = \frac{1/12}{1/8} = 2/3$$

$$\sigma_\mu = 0; \quad L_q = \frac{\lambda^2 \sigma_\mu^2 + \rho^2}{2(1 - \rho^2)} = \frac{(1/12)^2(0)^2 + (2/3)^2}{2(1 - 2/3)} = 2/3 \text{ ship}$$

$$L = \rho + L_q = 2/3 + 2/3 = 1.333 \text{ ships}$$

$$W_q = \frac{L_q}{\lambda} = \frac{2/3}{1/12} = 8 \text{ hours} \times 14 \text{ ships} = 112 \text{ hours}$$

$$W = W_q + \frac{1}{\mu} = 8 \text{ hours} + 8 \text{ hours} = 16 \text{ hours}$$

The total cost per week is calculated as follows:

Demurrage:	112 hours × $600	=	$ 67,200
Operation:	112 hours × $2,400	=	$268,800
		Total cost =	$336,000

$(\text{M/E}_k/1):(\text{FCFS}/\infty/\infty)$

This model includes service times following the Erlang distribution, and it has proved to be highly useful in practice because of the flexibility of the service distribution. We should remember that the negative exponential and constant service distributions are special cases of the Erlang distribution, with k parameters of 1 and 0 respectively.

To analyze the operating characteristics for the Erlang service time model, we can set $\sigma^2 = 1/k\mu^2$ and use the model for arbitrary service times:

$$\rho = \frac{\lambda}{\mu}$$

$$P_0 = 1 - \rho$$

$$L_q = \frac{\lambda^2\sigma^2 + (\lambda/\mu)^2}{2(1 - \lambda/\mu)} = \frac{(k + 1)\,\rho^2}{2k(1 - \rho)}$$

$$\sigma^2 = \frac{1}{k\mu^2}$$

$$L = L_q + \frac{\lambda}{\mu}$$

$$W_q = \frac{(k + 1)_\rho}{2k(\mu - \lambda)} = \frac{L_q}{\lambda}$$

$$W = W_q + \frac{1}{\mu}$$

CASETTE 12.6   *OPERATION THULE—PUMP Z*

Barney worked up an analysis for the Brand Z pump as shown in Table 12.7. On the basis of this analysis, he calculated the weekly operation cost as follows:

Table 12.7   Operation Thule—Pump Z: Poisson Arrival/Erlang Service ($\text{k} = 2$)

Ship	Arrival Hour	Service Begins	Service Time (Hr.)	Service Ends	Ship Waiting Time (Hr.)	Dock Idle Time (Hr.)	Ships Waiting
Ill Wind	0	0	6	6	0	0	0
Typhoon	9	9	7	16	0	3	0
Zephyr	53	53	11	64	0	37	1
Sirocco	61	64	5	69	3	0	2
Monsoon	64	69	4	73	5	0	1
Whirlwind	66	73	21	94	7	0	4
Gale	76	94	6	100	18	0	4
Tokyo Maru	79	100	3	103	21	0	3
Squall	90	103	10	113	13	0	2
Mistral	93	113	8	121	20	0	3
Simoom	99	121	19	140	22	0	3
Trade Wind	114	140	3	143	26	0	2
Samiel	119	143	4	147	24	0	1
Levanter	135	147	5	152	9	0	0
End of week	168					16	
			112			168	56

$$\lambda = \frac{14 \text{ ships}}{168 \text{ hours}} = \frac{1 \text{ ship}}{12 \text{ hours}}; \quad \mu = \frac{14 \text{ ships}}{112 \text{ hours}} = \frac{1 \text{ ship}}{8 \text{ hours}}; \quad \rho = \frac{2}{3};$$

$$\sigma_\mu = 5.63 \text{ (actual data)}; \quad \sigma^2 = \frac{1}{k\mu^2} = \frac{1}{2(1/8)^2} = 32; \quad \sigma = 5.66$$

$$L_q = \frac{\lambda^2 \sigma_\mu^2 + (\lambda/\mu)^2}{2(1 - \lambda/\mu)} = \frac{(1/12)^2(5.63)^2 + (2/3)^2}{2(1 - 2/3)} = 1.0 \text{ ship}$$

$$L_q = \frac{k + 1}{2k} \frac{\rho^2}{(1 - \rho)} = \frac{3}{4} \frac{(2/3)^2}{1/3} = 1.0 \text{ ship}$$

$$L = L_q + \frac{\lambda}{\mu} = 1 + \frac{2}{3} = 1.67 \text{ ships}$$

$$W_q = \frac{k + 1}{2k} \frac{\rho}{\mu - \lambda} = \frac{3}{4} \frac{(2/3)}{(1/24)} = 12 \text{ hours} \times 14 \text{ ships} = 168 \text{ hours}$$

$$W = W_q + \frac{1}{\mu} = 12 + 8 = 20 \text{ hours}$$

The total cost per week is calculated as follows:

$$
\begin{aligned}
\text{Demurrage:} \quad & 168 \text{ hours} \times \$\ \ 600 = \$100{,}800 \\
\text{Operation:} \quad & 112 \text{ hours} \times \$1{,}800 = \underline{\$201{,}600} \\
& \text{Total cost} = \ \ \ 302{,}400
\end{aligned}
$$

Barney prepared a recap of his analysis of available pump alternatives for Lafe, summarized as follows:

Pump System	Service Time Distribution (σ_μ)	Ship Waiting Time per Week	Demurrage ($600/Hr.)	Operating Cost/Hr.	Operating Cost (112 Hr.)	Total Expected Cost
Brand X	Normal (3.5)	133	$ 79,800	$2,100	$235,200	$315,000
Brand Y	Constant (0)	112	67,200	2,400	268,800	336,000
Brand Z	Erlang (5.6)	168	100,800	1,800	201,600	302,400
Existing	Exponential (8)	224	134,400	1,200	134,400	268,800

This analysis indicated that the excessive cost of operating more reliable pumping systems outweighed the expected gains in reducing demurrage. Lafe relayed the analysis to Mr. Reed, who, when presented with the costs of reducing the tanker waiting time, responded by sending Thule four Ping-Pong tables to keep unruly mariners occupied.

(M/M/1):(FCFS/m/∞)

This model is the same as the classical model we investigated earlier, with the added restriction of a limited queue. The model is very useful in practice, both for those cases where waiting is actually limited and for those cases that experience a high degree of balking activity by potential customers when there are waiting lines of some length.

We must modify our model to consider the limited length of waiting lines. For this model, the service rate does *not* have to exceed the arrival rate ($\mu > \lambda$) for us to obtain steady-state conditions. The operating characteristics of this system are:

$$m = \text{maximum number of customers in the system}$$

$$P_0 = \frac{1 - \lambda/\mu}{1 - (\lambda/\mu)^{m+1}}$$

$$P_n = (P_0)\left(\frac{\lambda}{\mu}\right)^n \quad (\text{for } n \leq m)$$

$$L = \frac{\lambda/\mu}{1 - \lambda/\mu} - \frac{(m+1)(\lambda/\mu)^{m+1}}{1 - (\lambda/\mu)^{m+1}}$$

$$L_q = L - \frac{\lambda(1 - P_m)}{\mu}$$

$$W = \frac{L}{\lambda(1 - P_m)}$$

$$W_q = W - \frac{1}{\mu}$$

P_m (the value of P_n for $n = m$) is the probability that customers are lost from the system.

CASETTE 12.7   *THE ICELAND CONNECTION*

With the passage of summer, tanker captains averted mutinous action from overexposure to Thule by exchanging radio messages. If there were two tankers waiting to be unloaded, other inbound tankers would divert to the more comfortable climes of Iceland.

This reaction resulted in the following operating changes for the unloading facility:

$$P_0 = \frac{1 - 2/3}{1 - (2/3)^3} = \frac{9}{19} = .4737$$

$$P_n = \frac{9}{19}(2/3)^2 = .2105 \text{ probability tanker will divert}$$

$$L = \frac{(2/3)}{(1/3)} - \frac{(3)(2/3)^3}{1 - (2/3)^3} = .74 \text{ ship}$$

$$L_q = \frac{14}{19} - \frac{(1/12)(1 - 4/19)}{1/8} = .21 \text{ ship}$$

$$W = \frac{14/19}{(1/12)(1 - 4/19)} = 11.2 \text{ hours}$$

$$W_q = 11.2 - 8 = 3.2 \text{ hours}$$

Of 14 ships bound for Thule, 78.95 percent continue, or an average of 11.05 ships per week.

The total cost per week is calculated as follows:

$$\begin{aligned}
\text{Demurrage:} \quad & 11.05 \text{ ships} \times 3.2 \text{ hours} \times \$600 = \$\ 21,216 \\
\text{Operation:} \quad & \text{(since crew costs are unchanged)} = \underline{\$134,400} \\
& \text{Total cost} \qquad\qquad\qquad\quad = \$155,616
\end{aligned}$$

With the 78.95 percent productivity level (21.05 percent of the tankers will divert), the total cost of $155,616 is the equivalent of $197,107 cost at the full operation level. This result actually provided a benefit to TOPSI, because demurrage was reduced more than productivity fell. Because the reduction in production bolstered the market, Mr. Reed sent his nephew Lafe a hearty thank you note.

M/M/1):(FCFS/∞/m)

This model allows consideration of limited calling populations. The probabilities of arrival in this model are a function of the number of customers in the system. If both the service times and the time spent outside the system between services are in the form of exponential distributions with means of $1/\lambda$ and $1/\mu$ respectively, then the operating characteristics can be described as follows:

$$P_0 = \frac{1}{\displaystyle\sum_{n=0}^{N} \frac{N!}{(N-n)!}\left(\frac{\lambda}{\mu}\right)^n} \quad \text{(where } N = \text{population size)}$$

$$P_n = \frac{N!}{(N-n)!}\left(\frac{\lambda}{\mu}\right)^n P_0 \quad \text{(where } n = 1, 2, \cdots, N)$$

$$L_q = N - \frac{\lambda + \mu}{\lambda}(1 - P_0)$$

$$L = L_q + (1 - P_0) \quad \text{or} \quad L = N - \frac{\mu}{\lambda}(1 - P_0)$$

$$W_q = \frac{L_q}{(N - L)\lambda}$$

$$W = W_q + \frac{1}{\mu}$$

CASETTE 12.8   *END OF OPEN-SEA SEASON AT THULE*

Deep into the open-sea season, there was a cutback in the number of companies renewing contracts to deliver crude oil to Thule. Only the braver (or more desperate) risked the oncoming ice. Barney found that there were only six tankers in the Atlantic that would schedule delivery. This obviated the limited queue length, and any queue length up to the maximum of five was possible. Of course, there usually was no waiting line. The rate of arrivals declined, on average, to one every 48 hours. This meant the pump system was operating only one-sixth of the time. Thus, the operating characteristics will be as follows:

$$P_0 = \frac{1}{\sum\limits_{n=0}^{6} \left[\frac{720}{(6-n)!} \left(\frac{1}{6}\right)^n \right]}$$

$$P_0 = .26492$$
$$P_1 = .26492$$
$$P_2 = .22077$$
$$P_3 = .14718$$
$$P_4 = .07359$$
$$P_5 = .02453$$
$$P_6 = .00409$$
$$L = 6 - 6(.73508) = 1.59 \text{ ships}$$

$$L_q = 6 - \left[\frac{(1/48 + 1/8)(.73508)}{1/48} \right] = .85 \text{ ship}$$

$$W_q = \frac{.85}{(6 - 1.59)(1/48)} = 9.25 \text{ hours}$$
$$W = 9.25 + 8 = 17.25 \text{ hours}$$

$$\frac{168 \text{ hours}}{48 \text{ hours}} = 3.5 \text{ ships per week}$$

The total cost per week is calculated as follows:

Demurrage: 9.25 hours $\times$ 3.5 ships $\times$ \$600 = \$ 19,425
Operations: \$134,400
                                      Total cost = \$153,825

At the 25 percent productivity level, the total cost of \$153,825 is the equivalent of \$615,300 cost at the full operation level. When Mr. Reed saw the equivalent cost of operating, he became extremely concerned with tanker safety and closed down operations at Thule for the winter.

(M/M/s):(FCFS/∞/∞)

This model allows consideration of multiple-channel servers. It is extremely useful in cost analysis that compares alternative service systems, for it allows us to predict the impact of adding servers.

In this model, we will assume Poisson arrivals and exponential service times. Arrivals are assumed to come from an infinite pool of customers. There is no limit to the length of the queue. Service is first-come, first-served. Other conditions would require model modifications.

The mean effective service rate for the system is $s(\mu)$, where s is equal to the number of servers. Here, again, we have to have $s\mu$ exceed the customer arrival rate, λ. We assume that the service time distribution for each server is the same.

Steady-state parameters[3] of this model are:

---

[3]A table of values of P_0 for various combinations of $\lambda/s\mu$ is presented in Appendix 5.

$$P_0 = \cfrac{1}{\left[\displaystyle\sum_{n=0}^{s-1} \frac{(\lambda/\mu)^n}{n!}\right] + \left[\dfrac{(\lambda/\mu)^s}{s!(1 - \lambda/s\mu)}\right]}$$

$$P_n = \frac{(\lambda/\mu)^n}{n!} P_0 \quad \text{(if } n \le s)$$

$$P_n = \frac{(\lambda/\mu)^n}{s!s^{(n-s)}} P_0 \quad \text{(if } n > s)$$

$$\rho = \frac{\lambda}{s\mu}$$

$$L_q = \frac{P_0(\lambda/\mu)^s\rho}{s!(1 - \rho)^2}$$

$$L = L_q + \frac{\lambda}{\mu}$$

$$W_q = \frac{L_q}{\lambda}$$

$$W = W_q + \frac{\lambda}{\mu}$$

CASETTE 12.9 **PLANNING FOR THE NEW SEASON AT THULE**

Since operations were shut down for the winter, Lafe kept Barney occupied with analysis of the coming summer's operations. TOPSI had found the rewards for providing fuel to New England to be great. Mr. Reed obtained a larger share of the market, and operations for the coming year were to be doubled.

The arrival rate of tankers at Thule was to be one every six hours. Clearly, the existing unloading system, with capacity of unloading a tanker every eight hours on average, was inadequate. Lafe had developed the dock system so that up to four berths were possible. This allowed Mr. Reed to assure shippers that diversion of tankers was no longer necessary. Barney was assigned the task of determining how many pumping systems TOPSI should install at Thule. Each system would be similar to the existing one, costing \$134,400 per week to operate. The operating characteristics of the three possible pumping systems are examined below:

(1) $\qquad s = 2; \quad \lambda = \dfrac{1}{6}; \quad \mu = \dfrac{1}{8}; \quad \rho = \dfrac{1/6}{1/8(2)} = \dfrac{2}{3}$

$$P_0 = \cfrac{1}{\left[\displaystyle\sum_{n=0}^{2} \frac{(4/3)^n}{n!}\right] + \dfrac{(4/3)^2}{2(1/3)}} = \frac{1}{1 + 4/3 + 8/3} = .2$$

$$L_q = \frac{.2(4/3)^2(2/3)}{2(1/3)^2} = 1.067 \text{ ships}$$

$$L = 1.067 + \frac{4}{3} = 2.4 \text{ ships}$$

$$W_q = \frac{1.067}{1/6} = 6.4 \text{ hours}$$

$$W = 6.4 + 1.33 = 7.33 \text{ hours}$$

28 ships per week $\times$ 6.4 hours = 179.2 hours idle

(2) $s = 3$; $\rho = \dfrac{1/6}{1/8(3)} = \dfrac{4}{9}$

$$P_0 = \frac{1}{\displaystyle\sum_{n=0}^{1} \frac{(4/3)^n}{n!} + \frac{(4/3)^3}{3!(1 - 4/9)}} = \frac{1}{1 + 4/3 + 8/9 + 32/45} = .2542$$

$$L_q = \frac{.2542(4/3)^3(4/9)}{6(5/9)^2} = .145 \text{ ship}$$

$$L = .145 + 1.333 = 1.478 \text{ ships}$$

$$W_q = \frac{.145}{1/6} = .87 \text{ hour}$$

$$W = .87 + \frac{4}{3} = 2.20 \text{ hours}$$

28 ships per week $\times$ .87 hour = 24.36 hours idle

(3) $s = 4$; $\rho = \dfrac{1/6}{1/8(4)} = 1/3$

$$P_0 = \frac{1}{\displaystyle\sum_{n=0}^{3} \frac{(4/3)^n}{n!} + \frac{(4/3)^4}{4!(2/3)}} = \frac{1}{1 + 4/3 + 8/9 + 32/81 + 16/81} = .2621$$

$$L_q = \frac{.2621(4/3)^4(1/3)}{24(2/3)^2} = .0259 \text{ ship}$$

$$L = .0259 + 1.3333 = 1.359 \text{ ships}$$

$$W_q = 6 \times .0259 = .155 \text{ hour}$$

$$W = .155 + 1.3333 = 1.489 \text{ hours}$$

28 ships per week $\times$ .155 hour = 4.34 hours idle

The total weekly cost is as follows:

	$s = 2$	$s = 3$	$s = 4$
Demurrage ($600 $\times$ W_q)	$107,520	$14,616	$2,604
Operations ($134,400 $\times$ s)	268,800	403,200	537,600
	$376,320	$417,816	$540,204

Therefore, TOPSI prepared for the oncoming season, looking forward to a prosperous year with two unloading systems. Table 12.8 presents a summary of the operating characteristics and formulas for the various waiting line models we have discussed.

SIMULATION OF WAITING LINE SYSTEMS

Simulation of queuing systems

In this chapter we have looked at several analytic models of queuing systems, presenting equations that allow prediction of system parameters. However, the discussion of these numerous models, restricted by so many assumptions and by no means exhaustive, leads one to appreciate the many real applications that defy the categorization required by the available models.

You have been given a taste of the analysis of waiting line systems in this chapter, and have obtained at least rough approximations of system operating characteristics. The techniques of simulation, which will be discussed in Chapter 14, can be employed in the analysis of queuing systems. The interested reader should therefore explore simulation with queuing applications in mind.

REAL-WORLD APPLICATIONS

Applications to real-world problems

A large number of studies dealing with real-world applications of waiting line models have been reported in the management science literature. Most of these studies deal with unique characteristics of waiting line systems and related managerial decision problems. In this section we will examine two of the recently published real-world applications of waiting line models.

Machine Manning Schedule

The Becton Dickinson Division of Becton Dickinson Company is a supplier of hypodermic needles and syringes for health care.[4] This study was undertaken because escalating costs and a limited labor pool were drastically curtailing the company's ability to increase its production capacity. The critical problem faced by the company was to expand its manufacturing capacity while keeping costs at the current level and also maintaining a high level of product quality. The predominant factor that affected costs was direct labor. Machine attendants comprised over 50 percent of the labor force. The major function of a machine attendant's job was to clear jams in the production flow. Thus, the major question to be answered by this queuing study was whether or not the direct labor manning structure could be improved so that frequent jams and downtime of the production line could be minimized.

On the basis of previous data and observations, the company made the following assumptions: each service facility had a Poisson input and a queue discipline of FCFS. It was also assumed that, in the steady state of the system, the mean arrival rate and mean service rate per operator were both constants independent of the state

[4]M. A. Vogel, ''Queuing Theory Applied to Machine Manning,'' *Interfaces*, 9:4 (Aug., 1979), 1–6.

Table 12.8 Operating Characteristics and Formulas for Various Queuing Models

	$(M/M/1){:}(FCFS/\infty/\infty)$	$(M/GI/1){:}(FCFS/\infty/\infty)$	$(M/D/1){:}(FCFS/\infty/\infty)$	$(M/E_k/1){:}(FCFS/\infty/\infty)$	$(M/M/1){:}(FCFS/m/\infty)$	$(M/M/1){:}(FCFS/\infty/m)$	$(M/M/s){:}(FCFS/\infty/\infty)$
Arrival distribution	Poisson	Poisson	Poisson	Poisson	Poisson	Poisson	Poisson
Service distribution	Exponential	Arbitrary	Constant	Erlang	Exponential	Exponential	Exponential
σ^2_μ	$1/\mu^2$	σ^2	0	$1/k\mu^2$	$1/\mu^2$	$1/\mu^2$	$1/\mu^2$
Servers	1	1	1	1	1	1	s
Queue limit	∞	∞	∞	∞	m	∞	∞
Population	∞	∞	∞	∞	∞	m	∞
Service stages	1	1	1	k	1	1	1
P_0	$1-\rho$	$1-\rho$	$1-\rho$	$1-\rho$	$\dfrac{1-\rho}{1-\rho^{m+1}}$	$\dfrac{1}{\displaystyle\sum_{n=0}^{N}\dfrac{N!}{(N-n)!}\rho^n}$	$\dfrac{1}{\displaystyle\sum_{n=0}^{s-1}\dfrac{(\lambda/\mu)^n}{n!}+\dfrac{(\lambda/\mu)^s}{s!(1-\lambda/s\mu)}P_0}$
P_n	$(1-\rho)\rho^n$	$(1-\rho)\rho^n$	$(1-\rho)\rho^n$	$(1-\rho)\rho^n$	$P_0(\rho)^n$	$\dfrac{N!}{(N-n)!}\rho^n P_0$	If $n\le s$, $\dfrac{(\lambda/\mu)^n}{n!}P_0$; If $n>s$, $\dfrac{(\lambda/\mu)^n}{s!s^{(n-s)}}P_0$
L	$\dfrac{\lambda}{\mu-\lambda}$	$L_q+\rho$	$L_q+\rho$	$L_q+\rho$	$\dfrac{\rho}{1-\rho}-\dfrac{(m+1)\rho^{(m+1)}}{1-\rho^{(m+1)}}$	$L_q+(1-P_0)$	$L_q+\dfrac{\lambda}{\mu}$
L_q	$\dfrac{\lambda^2}{\mu(\mu-\lambda)}$	$\dfrac{\lambda^2\sigma^2_\mu+\rho^2}{2(1-\rho)}$	$\dfrac{\rho^2}{2(1-\rho)}$	$\dfrac{(k+1)\rho^2}{2k(1-\rho)}$	$L-\dfrac{\lambda(1-P_m)}{\mu}$	$N-\dfrac{\lambda+\mu}{\lambda}(1-P_0)$	$\dfrac{P_0(\lambda/\mu)^s\rho}{s!(1-\rho)^2}$
ρ	λ/μ	λ/μ	λ/μ	λ/μ	λ/μ	λ/μ	$\lambda/\mu s$
W	$\dfrac{1}{\mu-\lambda}$	$W_q+\dfrac{1}{\mu}$	$W_q+\dfrac{1}{\mu}$	$W_q+\dfrac{1}{\mu}$	$\dfrac{L}{\lambda(1-P_m)}$	$W_q+\dfrac{1}{\mu}$	$W_q+\dfrac{1}{\mu}$
W_q	$\dfrac{\rho}{\mu-\lambda}$	$\dfrac{L_q}{\lambda}$	$\dfrac{L_q}{\lambda}$	$\dfrac{(k+1)\rho}{2k(\mu-\lambda)}$	$W-\dfrac{1}{\mu}$	$\dfrac{L_q}{(N-L)\lambda}$	$\dfrac{L_q}{\lambda}$

of the waiting line. These characteristics were used, in conjunction with management input concerning cost estimates, to arrive at a waiting line model.

The study resulted in a revised manning schedule that was implemented throughout the plant. The company reduced the number of machine operators, through reassignment and normal attrition, by 115 in the entire plant. The cost saving in direct labor that resulted from this study was $575,000 during the first year. The company also reported that production levels increased by 80 percent during the two-year period of model implementation.

Bank Teller Staff Level Determination

The Bankers Trust Company of New York was increasingly concerned about rising labor costs.[5] The bank's Management Service Group was assigned a project to determine the appropriate teller staff level necessary to provide a consistently high level of customer service. The study was to be based on an analysis of variable service demand at each of the bank's branches.

Management had reliable data that identified a relatively constant customer arrival pattern for any given branch, as well as an average service time for each customer at each branch. However, this average customer service time varied considerably from branch to branch. Each branch had unique operational characteristics. Thus, service times and customer arrival patterns were determined through studies conducted over a period of time.

Bankers Trust's teller staffing system had a series of subsystems: a staff planning system, an administrative system, and an implementation plan. The staff planning system consisted of three main functions—data collection, data analysis, and determination of required staff. Once the customer arrival rates and the average customer service time were estimated and the appropriate level of desired service was determined, the teller staffing model was utilized to arrive at the required number of open teller locations per hour for each hour of the day and week. The user selected appropriate staffing requirements based on the performance criteria of expected rate, service time, and service level desired. Once the hourly teller requirements were determined, a branch staffing plan was formalized. This plan reflected the number of full- and part-time tellers needed, the number of customer representatives present, and management's service objective.

The administrative system attempted to achieve the following: use of part-time personnel to meet fluctuating traffic patterns; utilization of backup personnel to cover for absenteeism, turnover, and vacations so that customer service levels could be maintained; and development of a management reporting system to focus on the staffing goals and objectives. To achieve staff savings as quickly as possible, management proceeded along several concurrent paths to recruit and use part-time tellers.

The implementation plan consisted of four elements: specification of service levels, line-staff interaction, control-performance evaluation, and follow-up action. The proximity to competing banks and the profitability of each branch were two of the many factors considered when determining the service level goal for the branch.

The result of this study was reported to be very impressive after its implemen-

[5]H. Deutsch and V. A. Mabert, "Queuing Theory and Teller Staffing: A Successful Application," *Interfaces,* 10:5 (Oct., 1980), 63–66.

tation at 104 branches. About $1,000,000 was saved from the annual payroll for branch operations. The cost to study and implement the staffing plan was $110,000. In addition to the significant cost savings, the study reported that bank branches provided better and more consistent services than before.

SUMMARY

In this chapter we have examined waiting line models and their applications to management decision making problems. In a waiting line system, the basic situation is: arrivals enter the system when they enter a line to wait their turn to be served, then they progress to the service facility where they are served, and they immediately depart the system once they are served. The basic purpose of waiting line theory is to minimize the total expected operating cost for the system. This can be achieved through a proper management of the system so that the cost of waiting and the cost of service can be balanced.

Waiting line models are not the end in decision making; they are just the beginning of the structuring of a decision making framework. Thus, waiting line models are often developed for the purpose of understanding the operating characteristics of the system rather than of finding exact solutions to a queuing problem. Waiting line systems are evaluated in two phases. The first phase involves the analysis of the steady-state operating characteristics of the system by using waiting line theory or simulation. The second phase attempts to minimize the total expected operating cost of the system by using the estimated waiting and service costs.

You have been introduced to a number of different waiting line models that are useful in determining steady-state operating characteristics under different assumptions. When an appropriate model does not exist for a particular problem, a simulation approach may be used. Management scientists frequently debate the capability of waiting line models to reflect complex real-world situations. However, an increasing number of real-world applications of waiting line models appears in management science literature. This is a clear indication that queuing models are important tools for management decision making.

References

Buffa, E. S. *Operations Management: Problems and Models,* 3rd ed. New York: Wiley, 1972.

Feller, W. *An Introduction to Probability Theory and Its Applications,* Vol. I, 3rd ed. New York: Wiley, 1968.

Hillier, F., and Lieberman, G. J. *Operations Research,* 3rd ed. San Francisco: Holden-Day, 1979.

Kendall, D. G. "Stochastic Processes Occurring in the Theory of Queues and Their Analysis by Means of the Imbedded Markov Chain." *The Annals of Mathematical Statistics,* 24 (1953), 338–354.

Kleinrock, L. *Queueing Systems* (2 vols.). New York: Wiley, 1975.

Morse, P. M. *Queues, Inventories, and Maintenance.* New York: Wiley, 1958.

Panico, J. A. *Queuing Theory: A Study of Waiting Lines for Business, Economics and Science.* Englewood Cliffs, N.J.: Prentice-Hall, 1969.

Saaty, T. L. *Elements of Queueing Theory.* New York: McGraw-Hill, 1961.

Assignments

12.1 In an operation involving waiting lines, what happens when the arrival rate exceeds the service rate?

12.2 What can be done to reestablish a stable operation if the arrival rate exceeds the service rate?

12.3 Does the existence of a very long waiting line for professional service (such as in a doctor's office) provide any indication of the economic appropriateness of the fees being charged?

12.4 How does customer impatience affect waiting lines?

12.5 Under what conditions might faster service be detrimental?

12.6 What sources exist for gathering data for queuing analysis?

12.7 Give an example of a last-in, first-out queue discipline.

12.8 Give an example of a random order queue discipline.

12.9 Give an example of a preemptive priority queue discipline.

12.10 Many business operations face uneven waiting lines. How do grocery stores, as an example, deal with fluctuating waiting lines?

12.11 In waiting line situations involving multiple servers, why is it more efficient to have a single-pooled waiting line than individual waiting lines in front of each server?

12.12 Why will limited queue lines reach a steady state even when the arrival rate exceeds the service rate?

12.13 Why will models with limited calling populations reach a steady state even though the arrival rate may exceed the service rate?

12.14 What is the effect of scheduling arrivals (such as barber appointments) on a waiting line?

12.15 The transient state of a queuing system is expected to have smaller than average waiting lines. Under what conditions might initial waiting lines be longer than average?

12.16 If customers arrive at a checkout counter in a totally random manner (Poisson distribution) at the mean rate of 5 customers per hour, what is the probability of exactly 0, 1, 2, 3, and 4 arrivals per hour? What is the probability of at least 4 arrivals per hour?

12.17 It takes an average of 2 hours for a mechanic to service a disabled truck. What is the probability a repair will be completed in:
   a. 30 minutes or less?
   b. 1 hour or less?
   c. 90 minutes or less?
   d. 2 hours or less?

12.18 The Ace Wrecking Company operates a large fleet of trucks. These trucks have averaged one call for mechanical service every 4 hours. Trucks generate revenue for Ace of $20 per hour. Ace's ace mechanic, Thumbs Swenson, costs the company $12 per hour in wages, fringes, and equipment. Thumbs was found to average 20 minutes on a truck without help from the truck driver (2 hours per truck with the truck driver's help). (Assume an M/M/1:FCFS/∞/∞ model.)
   a. What is the probability of 0, 1, or 2 trucks in need of repair at any one time?
   b. What is the average number of trucks requiring repair at any one time?
   c. What is the average time a truck is out of service after breaking down?
   d. What is the average amount of time a truck waits for Thumbs?
   e. On the average, how many trucks are idle while waiting for Thumbs?

12.19 As the trucks got older, Ace Wrecking Company (presented in Problem 12.18) found the rate of mechanical failures increased. In the second year of operation, Ace suffered a truck breakdown once every hour. The increased severity of the mechanical failures also required additional mechanic time. The average repair time per truck increased to 30 minutes.
   a. What is the probability of 0, 1, or 2 trucks in need of repair?
   b. What is the average number of trucks that are inoperative?
   c. What is the average time a truck is inoperative?
   d. What is the average number of trucks waiting for the mechanic?
   e. What is the average idle time for a truck that is waiting for a mechanic?
   f. What is the cost to Ace in lost revenue by not having enough mechanics?
   g. Would it pay to add a mechanic?

12.20 Sal Maglie has operated a small tonsorial parlor in Poughkeepsie for a number of years. Sal has experienced a wide variety of business conditions over that time. With the development of his business, conditions have changed a great deal. Sal has kept meticulous records of operations over the years. There have been distinct changes in the distribution of customer arrivals as well as Sal's haircut time.

   When Sal was learning to cut hair, the rate of service varied a lot. He averaged 30 minutes per haircut, distributed exponentially. About one customer per hour, arriving randomly, risked his head in Sal's shop.

   Calculate the basic parameters of this system (P_0, P_1, P_2, L, L_q, W, W_q, ρ).

12.21 Sal Maglie became a better barber with time, and was able to cut hair in a more normal time distribution. This had a positive effect upon business. Sal took only 15 minutes, on average, to cut hair, with random variance ($\mu = 4$/hour, $\sigma^2 = .05$). Customers randomly arrived at the rate of 3 per hour.

    a. What was the effect on the number of customers waiting, and the amount of time they waited, due to a variance of .05 versus $1/\mu^2$, or .0625, for the exponential distribution?

    b. Between the two service distributions, is there any difference in the probability of n customers in the system?

    c. Do the formulas for the arbitrary distribution work for the exponential distribution?

12.22 The 1950s saw an increase in demand for haircuts. Sal Maglie became an excellent barber, capable of giving a crew cut or a trim in 10 minutes flat. The arrival rate of customers still varied but averaged 5 per hour. Sal was interested in the implications of giving a haircut at a constant rate of every 10 minutes, or varying the time according to the desire of the customer to talk.

    a. If the customers talked, what would be the implications of varying haircut time with a standard deviation of 6 minutes ($\sigma_\mu^2 = .01$ hour) or the exponential distribution standard deviation of 10 minutes ($\sigma_\mu^2 = 1/\mu = .0278$)?

    b. Calculate the average number of customers in the system, the average waiting line, the average time a customer would spend in the barbershop, and the average waiting time.

12.23 Sal Maglie, being older and overworked, joined the barber's union in the 1960s. The cultural shock of the 1960s also caused a change in demand by customers. Sal now had a clientele desiring both shampoos and styling, two distinct operations. Since he could now charge exorbitant prices, he took as much time as the customer desired. The mean time for a shampoo was the same as that for a styling, each taking an average of 10 minutes. The service was distributed according to the Erlang distribution, with parameter $k = 2$. The arrival rate of customers declined to 2 per hour. The total service rate, of course, was 3 per hour.

    Compare the number of customers in the shop and the waiting times of those customers for the Erlang and exponential distributions.

12.24 (M/M/1):(FCFS/∞/∞). Frank's Slow Cook Diner features special-order hamburgers. Customers wander in at the rate of 5 per hour. Determine the number of people who will be waiting in line, the average time they will have to wait, and the probabilities of 0, 1, 2, and more than 2 waiting customers, given the following different service rates:

    a. A service rate of five ($\lambda = 5$).

    b. A service rate of seven ($\lambda = 5$).

    c. A service rate of nine ($\lambda = 5$).

12.25 (M/M/1):(FCFS/∞/∞). Larsen E. Whipsnade is a rising young attorney. He wants to determine the optimum time to spend consulting with each client. Larsen E. feels the more time spent with a client, the more satisfied the client will be and the more willing he will be to pay a not-so-nominal consulting fee. On the other hand, longer consulting time results in other clients having to wait longer. If clients wait too long, they are likely to consult other solicitors. Given the arrival rate of 4 clients per hour, randomly distributed, determine total clients in the office, average client time in the office, and the probabilities of 0, 1, 2, and more than 2 clients in Larsen E.'s office. Use the service rates given below.

a. Average consulting time of 15 minutes ($\lambda = 4$).

b. Average consulting time of 10 minutes ($\lambda = 4$).

c. Average consulting time of 7.5 minutes ($\lambda = 4$).

12.26 (M/GI/1):(FCFS/∞/∞). Larsen E. Whipsnade (see problem 12.25) decided on an average service rate of 6 clients per hour, and later determined that the distribution of service times was described by a variance of 1/144 hours (a 5-minute standard deviation). What effect does this added information have on the expected number of clients in the office, the average time a client spends in the office, and the probability of no customers in the office ($\lambda = 4$, $\mu = 6$)?

12.27 (M/D/1):(FCFS/∞/∞). Dirty Dan's Car Wash uses a fixed-time assembly line requiring 3 minutes to wash a car, including drying time. If customers arrive in a random manner at the average rate of 8 per hour, calculate the expected number of cars in the system and the average time each customer can expect to spend at Dirty Dan's.

12.28 (M/E_k/1):(FCFS/∞/∞). The Bureau for the Elimination of Bureaucracy requires all individuals filing a complaint to be processed at 2 stations. The first station prepares a file for the complaint. The second station prepares a file for the complainer. Both stations require an average service time of 5 minutes, randomly varying. Given the arrival of a complainer every 15 minutes on the average, calculate the average time someone filing a complaint would spend in the Bureau filling out forms, the number of people filing complaints expected to be in the system at any one time, and the probability that no one is in the office for the purpose of filing a complaint.

12.29 (M/E_k/1):(FCFS/∞/∞). The Bureau for the Elimination of Bureaucracy (cited in Problem 12.28) plans to add a third station to perform some of the work required at Stations 1 and 2. This will result in all 3 stations requiring an average of 3 1/3 minutes per complaint. The arrival rate would still be 4 per hour. What would be the average number of people filing complaints at any one time? How long could they expect to spend in the Bureau filling out forms?

12.30 (M/M/1):(FCFS/m/∞). Fred's Quick Lube provides speedy oil changes and chassis lubrication for automobiles. Fred conducted a study of past arrival and service rates, finding an average of 4 customers per hour and an average service time of 10 minutes (6 per hour). Both rates were randomly distributed. Fred fears that if 3 customers are in the system, potential customers will leave. Fred wants to know the impact of this event on the probabilities of being idle, having only 1 customer in the system, 2 customers in the system, or 3 customers in the system. Use the formulas for an unlimited queue length to identify probabilities, and compare the results with the formulas for a limited queue length of 3.

12.31 (M/M/1):(FCFS/m/∞). Ace Bullwinkle operates a flying school. He owns a small landing strip outside of Walla Walla, Washington. On the average, one of Ace's students needs to land every hour. It takes an average of 6 minutes for one of Ace's students to accomplish a landing. The variance from this time is distributed according to the Poisson distribution. The students will wait to land if only one other student is attempting a landing. Otherwise, from impatience as well as from fear of running out of fuel, students will go to Walla Walla International Airport to land, and thereby incur a $20 fee for Ace. Ace is considering new alternatives, and needs to know the probabilities of 0, 1, 2, and more than 2 students in need of landing. He also needs to know the average number of students in the process of landing and the average time they spend doing so, including waiting time. Calculate these parameters for an unlimited queue model and for a model using a limited queue of 2.

12.32 (M/M/1):(FCFS/m/∞). Acme Widget is manufacturing widget assemblies. Forklift trucks are crucial to this operation. Acme's Maintenance Department provides service to forklift trucks. Forklifts are supposed to check in for service every 1,000 operating hours. Service time averages 6 minutes, with Poisson distributed variance. Forklift arrivals occur 9 times an hour on the average.

Because forklift operators are paid incentive wages, they tend to skip service when 2 other forklifts are at the service station. This has led to an increase in the rate of mechanical failures of forklifts. The Maintenance Department manager would like to know the probability of 0, 1, 2, and more than 2 forklifts being at a maintenance station, as well as the average number of forklifts and the average time spent by a forklift at the maintenance station.

  a. Identify these parameters for a model with an unlimited queue and for a model with a maximum queue length of 2.
  b. What are the same parameters for a system with no more than 2 customers?

12.33 (M/M/1):(FCFS/m/m). Speed Rench has been the mechanic for Shoddy Construction, Inc. for many years. He used to take care of a small fleet of 1940 Reo trucks that suffered a truck breakdown every half hour. Speed required 12 minutes on the average to fix these trucks. There were only 5 trucks in this fleet.

Shoddy finally wised up and liquidated the 1940 Reo trucks, replacing them with brand-new models. The manager determined that these turcks, even though there were 50 of them, broke down at the same rate as the old fleet (one every half hour). Speed still required an average of 12 minutes to fix whatever was wrong, but he voiced a severe complaint that he had nothing to do.

  a. Analyze these two systems using an arrival rate of 2 per hour and a service rate of 5 per hour, the Poisson distribution for arrivals, and the negative exponential distribution for service time.
  b. Calculate L, W, P_0, P_1, P_2, P_3, P_4, and P_5 for both systems.
  c. Make the first system a limited population model with 5 customers. Assume an unlimited calling population for the second system. Find out why Speed is underworked in the second system.

13 DYNAMIC PROGRAMMING

Dynamic programming is a mathematical modeling technique that is useful in solving a select set of problems involving a sequence of interrelated decisions. Dynamic programming provides a systematic means of solving multistage problems over a planning horizon or a sequence of events. As an example, a stock investment problem can be analyzed by dynamic programming to determine the allocation of funds that will maximize the total profit over a number of years. Decision making in this case, as in many similar cases, requires a set of decisions separated by time. Each year can be a stage in which a decision must be made.

Dynamic programming is a powerful tool that allows segmentation or decomposition of complex multistage problems into a number of simpler subproblems. These subproblems are often much easier for us to handle. In this chapter, we will discuss the basic nature, problem formulation, and solution procedures of dynamic programming.

Learning Objectives *From the study of this chapter, you will learn the following:*

1. The basic nature of dynamic programming.
2. Segmentation of a problem into subproblems.
3. The backward solution approach for a dynamic programming problem.
4. The basic features of a dynamic programming problem.
5. The complete enumeration approach for a dynamic programming problem.
6. The solution approach of dynamic programming.
7. The basics of probabilistic dynamic programming.
8. The meaning of the following terms:

Decomposition or segmentation	*Sequential decision making*
Backward approach	*Stage*
State	*Policy decision*
Return	*Recursive relation*
Probabilistic dynamic programming	*Deterministic dynamic programming*

THE BASIC NATURE OF DYNAMIC PROGRAMMING

Most management science techniques are designed to analyze a decision problem by finding the optimum solution under a given set of conditions. The usual approach is to solve the model and derive a solution in one operation. Of course, we have seen some exceptions. In decision tree analysis, which we studied in Chapter 9, an example of sequential decision making was analyzed through various states of nature and their associated probabilities. In many ways, dynamic programming is similar to decision tree analysis in that both techniques are useful for analyzing complex problems by breaking them down into interrelated subproblems in which decisions can be made sequentially. Therefore, dynamic programming is a convenient way to analyze a complex problem by breaking it down into smaller subproblems.

This *decomposition* or *segmentation* approach is a unique characteristic of dynamic programming. For this reason, dynamic programming is also referred to as a *multistage* or *sequential* decision process. Since the problem is segmented into smaller interrelated subproblems, the decision outcome of a subproblem at one stage (or time period) will be affected by the decision outcome of the previous-stage subproblem.

Sequential decision making

The pioneering work in dynamic programming was done by Richard Bellman. His important work *Dynamic Programming* was published in 1957. Further development and applications have flourished since then. In dynamic programming, we do not have a universal solution method such as the simplex method for linear programming problems. Instead, dynamic programming utilizes a variety of methods to solve the multistage problem. Because of its flexibility, this technique has been applied to a variety of decision problems, including those in the areas of resource allocation, inventory control, production planning, equipment maintenance and replacement, investment planning, product assortment, process design and control, and manpower planning.

History of dynamic programming

Segmentation and Sequential Decisions

Segmenting the problem

The first important concept of dynamic programming is the segmentation of the problem into a set of smaller subproblems. Each of the subproblems is called a *stage*. The entire problem now becomes a sequence of stages. Thus, dynamic programming becomes a sequential decision process.

For example, let us suppose that we are interested in making an investment decision during a period of four years. We can segment the problem into four yearly subproblems. Our investment problem is to determine where to invest and how much to invest in each year in order to maximize the total return at the end of the four-year period. Therefore, we can segment the problem, shown in Figure 13.1, as a sequence of decisions.

The Backward Approach

In Figure 13.1, the arrows, representing the linkage between stages and the stage numbers, are arranged in a left to right order. The linkage direction is also from left to right, and it indicates the direction of the information flow required for sequential decision making. For example, the investment decision in the second quarter must be based on funds available at the end of the first quarter. In other words, we must first make the decision about what should be invested in the fourth year based on the capital available at the end of the third year. Such an approach is often referred to as the *backward* or *rollback* approach in which we first attempt to make the decision that is closest to the final target.

The backward approach

In dynamic programming, most problems are solved with this backward approach. However, this is by no means the universal solution approach of dynamic program-

Figure 13.1 Segmentation of the Investment Problem into Four Yearly Stage Problems

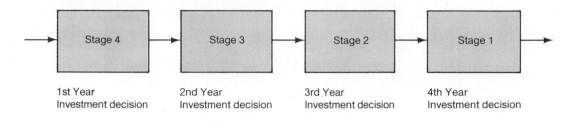

| Stage 4 | Stage 3 | Stage 2 | Stage 1 |

1st Year
Investment decision

2nd Year
Investment decision

3rd Year
Investment decision

4th Year
Investment decision

ming. In certain problems, dynamic programming may utilize the *forward* approach, which starts the solution process from the point that is farthest from the target. The appropriateness of the approach we take will depend on the unique characteristics of the problem under consideration.

Although many dynamic programming problems are segmented on the basis of time, that is not a requirement. If a problem can be segmented into a sequence of interrelated subproblems, or if it is initially composed of a set of smaller problems, dynamic programming can be applied as a solution technique. To understand the general characteristics and terminology of dynamic programming, let us examine a "shortest-route" problem.

CASETTE 13.1   THE WASHINGTON, D.C. CONFERENCE

Roger Miller is a systems analyst at Pacific Instruments, Inc., a Los Angeles-based producer of medical instruments. Roger coauthored an article with Susan Allen, a

A shortest-route problem

senior production engineer, entitled "A Multistage Production Planning Model via Dynamic Programming." The paper has been accepted for presentation at a national conference scheduled for May in Washington, D.C.

When Roger and Susan submitted the required travel authorizations to their respective supervisors, they were told that the trip to Washington, D.C. must be by the company's plane. The company has a small Cessna plane that is available to executives for business trips. The plane requires frequent stops to refuel and it must avoid severe weather conditions.

The pilot, after studying the typical weather conditions for May, determined a network of possible routes to Washington, D.C. The network, along with the required flying time for each leg, is presented in Figure 13.2. Roger and Susan quickly recognized that this traveling problem can be analyzed as a shortest-route problem, a typical dynamic programming application.

The Basic Features of Dynamic Programming

Determining nodes and arcs

The shortest-route problem is made up of nodes (stations) and arcs (routes). In Figure 13.2, the nodes indicate cities on the possible travel routes. The arcs indicate the flight routes from city to city. The numbers over each arc indicate the flying time

Figure 13.2   A Shortest-Route Travel Network

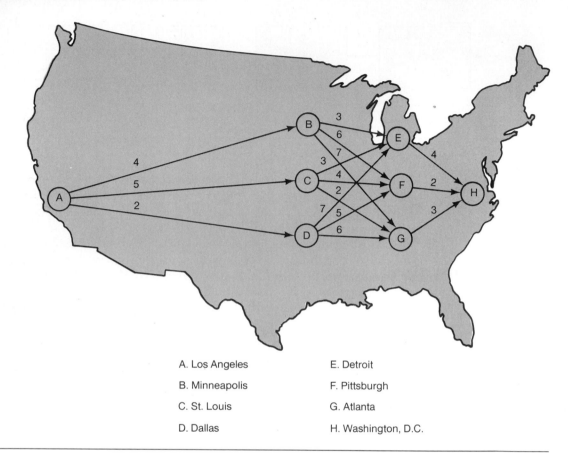

A. Los Angeles	E. Detroit
B. Minneapolis	F. Pittsburgh
C. St. Louis	G. Atlanta
D. Dallas	H. Washington, D.C.

required between two adjacent cities. Roger and Susan are attempting to determine the fastest route from Los Angeles to Washington, D.C. Thus, they revised the travel network as a dynamic programming problem, as shown in Figure 13.3.

Let us examine the basic features of dynamic programming in the shortest-route problem.

A state

State A state is the condition that a problem under analysis has in a particular stage. It is represented as a node of a system configuration and is identified by a label, such as A, B, etc. One or a number of states may be associated with a stage. In our shortest-route problem, a city corresponds to a state. For example, in Stage 2 we have three states: B (Minneapolis), C (St. Louis), and D (Dallas).

A stage

Stage A dynamic programming problem can be segmented in a number of stages. A stage is a decision point represented by an arc. In our example, Roger and Susan must decide which flying route to take for a particular leg of the journey. The stages are determined as follows: In Los Angeles they must decide which route to take—to B (Minneapolis), C (St. Louis), or D (Dallas). Once they arrive at B, C, or D, their

Figure 13.3   A Network of Cities in a Shortest-Route Problem

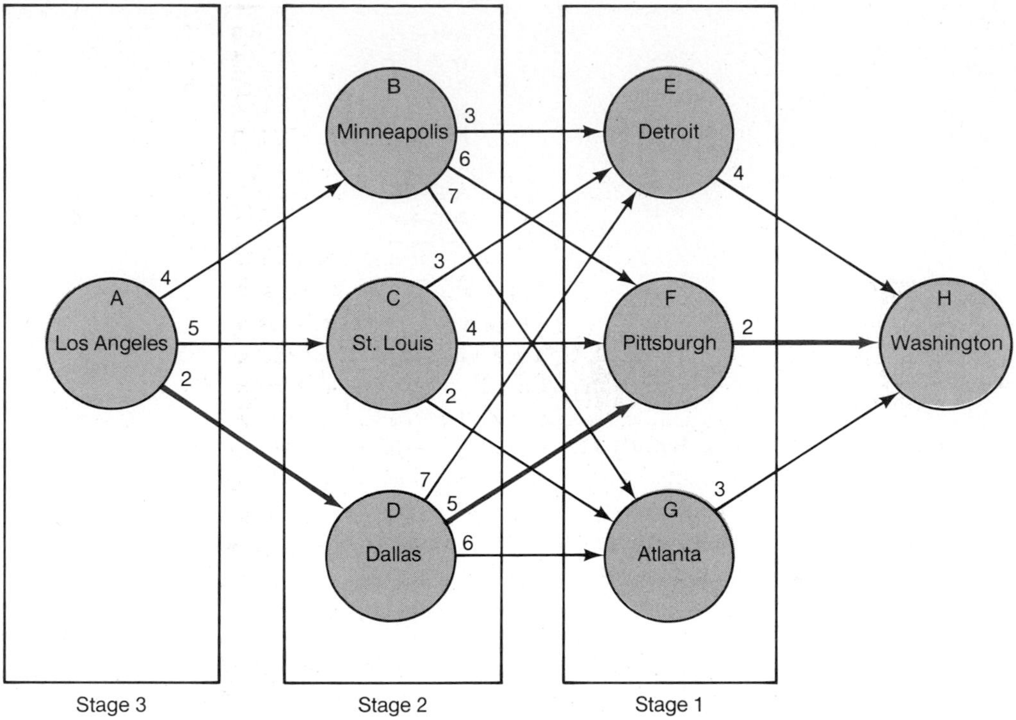

next decision would be to travel to E (Detroit), F (Pittsburgh), or G (Atlanta). Regardless of the location in the third leg (Cities E, F, or G), they must travel to Washington, D.C. Thus, this shortest-route problem can be segmented into three stages.

In each stage, Roger and Susan can be at one and only one state. Thus, a stage is a single step in a sequential decision making process. A decision made at each step results in the transition from one state to an adjacent state. In Figure 13.2, one stage corresponds to the transition from one column of cities to the next column of cities.

Policy decision

Policy Decision A policy decision refers to a plan to make a decision based on a predetermined policy under each possible condition. A policy decision must be made from the set of available alternatives at each stage. For example, in Figure 13.3, if Roger and Susan are at St. Louis, three different travel alternatives exist: to Detroit, Pittsburgh, or Atlanta. Obviously, the best decision is to travel from St. Louis to Atlanta because this travel plan has the least flying time (two hours vs. three or four).

Return

Return A return or reward is the value of the state that is generated over one stage. It is also referred to as *immediate return*. In the shortest-route problem, the immediate return is the time (or distance, cost, etc.) required in moving from one state to the next state.

Table 13.1   Complete Enumeration of the Shortest-Route Problem

Possible Routes	Travel Time
A–B–E–H	4 + 3 + 4 = 11
A–B–F–H	4 + 6 + 2 = 12
A–B–G–H	4 + 7 + 3 = 14
A–C–E–H	5 + 3 + 4 = 12
A–C–F–H	5 + 4 + 2 = 11
A–C–G–H	5 + 2 + 3 = 10
A–D–E–H	2 + 7 + 4 = 13
A–D–F–H	**2 + 5 + 2 = 9** ← Minimum
A–D–G–H	2 + 6 + 3 = 11

Total return

Total Return Total return is a function of returns generated from the initial state to the current state. The function can be simply a sum, a multiplication, or a more complex operation. In the shortest-route problem, total return corresponds to the accumulated travel time from the initial state to the current state. The shortest total return will be the optimum value in our example.

The principle of optimality

The most important concept of dynamic programming is the *principle of optimality*. Given the current state, an optimum policy decision for the remaining stages is independent of the policy decisions adopted in the previous stages. In other words, each subproblem is determined only by the solution (or the parameters from the solution) of its immediate predecessor. For example, in Figure 13.3, determining which route we should take from Dallas is based on the travel time of the immediate predecessor (Los Angeles to Dallas) and the travel time from the current state (Dallas to Atlanta, Dallas to Pittsburgh, and Dallas to Detroit). This principle must be satisfied before we try to solve a problem by dynamic programming. The principle may seem somewhat ambiguous at first glance, but it means only that *at any stage of the problem, future decisions are independent of prior decisions.*

The Complete Enumeration Approach

For a simple problem, we can easily analyze all possible alternatives. The shortest-route problem has only nine possible routes from Los Angeles to Washington, D.C., as shown in Table 13.1. It is obvious that route A–D–F–H is the best route because it provides the shortest travel time. This best route is also indicated in Figure 13.3 by bold lines. The minimum travel time required by the company plane is nine hours by taking route A–D–F–H.

The problem with the enumeration approach

The complete enumeration approach is an easy way to identify the optimum solution if the problem under consideration is a very simple one. For a large and complex travel network problem, however, it is unrealistic to use the complete enumeration approach. The time and effort required to evaluate every possible route may indeed be prohibitive. Thus, dynamic programming is needed for such problems.

Solution by Dynamic Programming

Solution steps of dynamic programming

Step 1: Segmentation As we discussed previously, the first step of dynamic programming is the segmentation or decomposition of the problem into smaller subproblems or stages. The shortest-route problem has been broken down into three stages, as shown in Figure 13.3. Stages are numbered from right to left so that the backward approach may be used.

Step 2: The Backward Approach In dynamic programming, we often use the backward approach, in which the last part of the problem is analyzed first. For example, let us assume that Roger and Susan are in Washington, D.C. Now we need to examine from which state (city) they should travel in order to minimize the flying time to Washington, D.C.

Solution of Stage 1

Stage 1 When Roger and Susan reach Washington, D.C., they will be at the final destination. Before reaching Washington, D.C., they must be at State E (Detroit), F (Pittsburgh), or G (Atlanta) regardless of how they got there. These three states are in Stage 1. Since this is the last leg of the trip, the travel route from each state to Washington, D.C. is given and there is no other choice. For example, if Roger and Susan are in Detroit, the only route to Washington, D.C. open to them is Detroit → Washington, D.C. A similar reasoning applies to each state in Stage 1. Table 13.2 presents the analysis for Stage 1.

Stage 2 For Roger and Susan to reach any state in Stage 1, they must have been at States B (Minneapolis), C (St. Louis), or D (Dallas) in Stage 2. It is important to examine the best route from each of these states to the final destination, Washington, D.C. Since we have already examined the states of Stage 1 in Table 13.2, we need

Solution of Stage 2

only to evaluate the routes in Stage 2. For example, from State B there are three alternative routes to States E, F, or G in Stage 1. The first route (B–E) requires three hours and the time required for the last leg, E–H, was computed as four hours in Stage 1. Of the three alternatives open for State B, the best route is B–E with the total required time of seven hours to Washington, D.C., as shown in Table 13.3. The best route is selected for each state in the table. It should be noted that the "best time from Stage 1 to Washington" is obtained from the previous table, Table 13.2.

Solution of Stage 3

Stage 3 For Roger and Susan to reach Stages B, C, or D in Stage 2, they must start from the initial point, State A (Los Angeles). They have three alternative routes to States B, C, or D. Table 13.4 presents the computation summary.

The best route is now identified. It is A–D–F–H for a total of nine hours of

Table 13.2 The First-Stage Analysis

State	Alternative Routes	Time Required to Washington	Best Route
E	E–H	4 hr.	4 hr.
F	F–H	2	2
G	G–H	3	3

Table 13.3   The Second-Stage Analysis

State	Alternative Routes	Time Required to Stage 1	Best Time from Stage 1 to Washington	Total Travel Time	Best Route
	B–E	3 hr.	4 hr.	7 hr.	←
B	B–F	6	2	8	
	B–G	7	3	10	
	C–E	3	4	7	
C	C–F	4	2	6	
	C–G	2	3	5	←
	D–E	7	4	11	
D	D–F	5	2	7	←
	D–G	6	3	9	

Table 13.4   The Third-Stage Analysis

State	Alternative Routes	Time Required to Stage 2	Best Time from Stage 2 to Washington	Total Travel Time	Best Route
	A–B	4 hr.	7 hr.	11 hr.	
A	A–C	5	5	10	
	A–D	2	7	9	←

flying time. This solution corresponds to the one we obtained by the complete enumeration method. The sequence of decisions we have made at each stage is based on the backward approach, as shown in Figure 13.4.

THE STRUCTURE OF DYNAMIC PROGRAMMING

Dynamic programming approach

We have discussed the basic structure of the dynamic programming problem through the shortest-route problem presented as Casette 13.1. The fundamental idea of dynamic programming involves *segmentation, sequential decision making,* and the *recursive relation.* Segmentation is accomplished through decomposing the problem into subproblems, each of which is often referred to as a stage. Sequential decision making is required to move from a decision point in a given stage to the next decision point.

The recursive relation

The recursive relation function ties together the sequential decisions at each stage. This function represents the relationships among the immediate return, the total return, and the optimum total return.

Before we present the general structure of dynamic programming, let us first define the following terminology and symbols:

Figure 13.4 Sequential Optimization of the Shortest-Route Problem

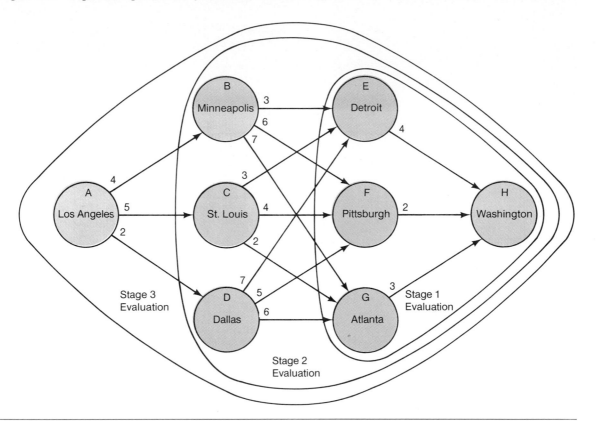

Terminology	Symbol	Definition
Stage	n	A transition from a node (e.g., a city) to an adjacent node (city) for the current stage
State	s_n	A node (e.g., a city) in the current stage
Policy decision	x_n	A decision made among alternatives at Stage n in a state (e.g., distance from a city to an adjacent city)
Return	c_{x_n}	Cost or payoff (e.g., travel time) incurred by x_n
Total return	$f_n(s_n)$	Total cost or payoff (e.g., travel time) from the current state (city) to the terminal stage (final destination city)
	$x_n^\star$	The optimum value (e.g., the distance of the best route) for each x_n
	$f_n^\star(s_n)$	The optimum value (e.g., the minimum total distance) for each $f_n(s_n)$

The recursive relation in a typical shortest-route problem can be developed as follows:

Figure 13.5   *One-Stage Shortest-Route Problem of Casette 13.1*

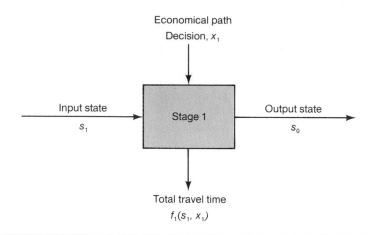

$$f_n^* (s_n) = \min [c_{x_n} + f_{n-1}^* (s_{n-1})]$$

For example, with two stages remaining, the recursive function $f_2^*(s_2)$ is to minimize $c_{x2} + f_1^*(s_1)$, and the optimum decision at this stage is to find the value of x_2 associated with $f_2^*(s_2)$. The subscript $n - 1$ represents the previous stage, regardless of whether we use a backward or a forward approach. Thus, the best route to take at Stage 2 in the shortest-route problem, as shown in Table 13.3, is determined by finding the minimum total travel time to Stage 2 $[f_2^*(s_2)]$. This minimum total travel time to Stage 2 can be determined by finding the sum of the travel time from Stage 2 to Stage 1 (c_{x2}) and the minimum travel time from Stage 1 to the final destination $[f_1^*(s_1)]$.

The exact form of the recursive function (or relationship) may differ from problem to problem. For the shortest-route problem, the functional operation required to link the immediate return with the total return was the addition ($+$) operation. However, this may be a multiplication operation or another type of operation. Also, the objective of the problem may be to maximize the total payoff rather than to minimize the total cost. Thus, the general form of the recursive relationship can be described as

$$f_n^*(s_n) = \text{max or min } [f_n^*(s_n, x_n)]$$

Since dynamic programming may utilize diverse forms of recursive relationships, subject only to the basic characteristics of the problem and the principle of optimality, the best way to examine the benefits of dynamic programming is to see how it is applied. For this purpose, we will look at several additional examples.

Before proceeding, however, we need to introduce the term *deterministic* dynamic programming. In deterministic dynamic programming, the state at the next stage is determined completely by the state and the policy decision at the current stage. In other words, we are certain of the costs of the alternatives. When the determination of the next state requires a probability distribution, such a case is referred to as

Figure 13.6   Three-Stage Shortest-Route Problem of Casette 13.1

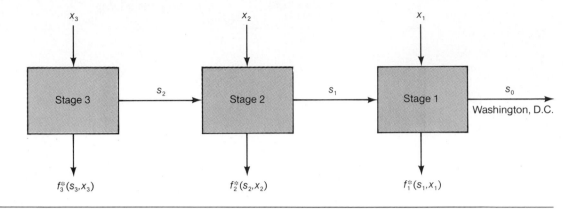

Probabilistic dynamic programming

probabilistic dynamic programming. We will discuss probabilistic problems later in this chapter.

Figure 13.5 presents a typical one-stage diagram of deterministic dynamic programming, in conjunction with the shortest-route problem. The input state, s_1, represents different routes from Stage 2 to Stage 1. Economical path decision, x_1, indicates the shortest travel time from Stage 1 to the final destination. The total travel time, f_1 (s_1, x_1), represents the minimum cumulative travel time to the final destination. Finally, the output state, s_0, indicates the travel route from Stage 1 to the final destination.

Figure 13.6 shows the entire three-stage diagram of the shortest-route problem presented in Casette 13.1. It is clear in Figure 13.6 that there is only one path from a state s_n to a next state s_{n+1} in deterministic dynamic programming.

The shortest-route travel problem we discussed in Casette 13.1 is clearly deterministic since every path from a city in one stage to a city in the next stage is determined by the state (i.e., city) and policy decision (i.e., minimum travel time), but not by any probability distribution. We assumed that the travel time was known with certainty.

CASETTE 13.2   DOWNJOHN PHARMACEUTICAL CORPORATION

Downjohn is the producer of the widely used cold medicine "Context." The company has been successful in increasing its market share in many areas. However, the company has experienced difficult distribution problems. The product is perishable and must be refrigerated. Tardy distribution will cause the medicine to spoil. The company has recently created the Product Distribution Department because of the importance of distribution to the company's success.

Marcia Antonelli is the newly apointed manager of the Product Distribution Department. She has been contemplating the establishment of a systematic method of distributing the product to three primary market areas—the Northeast, Midwest, and

Table 13.5 Forecasted Sales and Profits in the Three Market Areas

Product Sales (1,000 lb.)	Expected Profit ($1,000)		
	Northeast	Midwest	South
0	$ 0	$ 0	$ 0
1	8	6	6
2	15	12	12
3	23	20	19
4	30	28	28
5	36	36	36
6	40	40	43

South districts. The product is distributed by company airplanes because of the product's perishability. Marcia has been informed by the Sales Manager that the maximum quantity of the product available for distribution in the three market areas is 6,000 pounds per month.

Marcia asked her assistant, Sam Jones, how much profit the company could expect in the three market areas. Sam, who has a Master's degree in management science, analyzed the past sales data based on several forecasting models. The forecasted sales and profits in each of the market areas are presented in Table 13.5. Because of shipping costs, the company has a policy that calls for transporting the product in units of 1,000 pounds.

The basic decision problem facing Marcia is how the company should distribute its product to the three market areas to maximize profits. Initially, Marcia thought the problem was rather simple. However, as she began to analyze it, the problem soon became quite complex. Reluctantly, Marcia asked Sam for help. After a few days of study, Sam came up with a systematic method for solving this problem.

Defining the basic terms Sam's solution procedure, based on dynamic programming, begins with definitions of basic terms:

1. *State:* The quantity of product to be distributed to each market area.

2. *Stage:* Each market for the product.

3. *Decision:* To determine how much of the product is to be assigned to each market.

4. *Return:* Profit from each market.

5. *Total return:* Accumulated profit at each stage.

On the basis of the above definitions, Sam developed the market stage relationships shown in Figure 13.7. Unlike the shortest-route problem, there is no concern

Figure 13.7 *The Downjohn Product Distribution Problem*

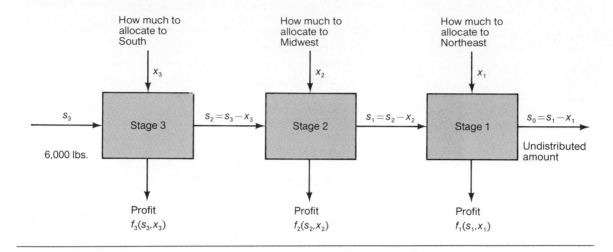

about which market is treated as the first stage and which as the last. Thus, Sam begins the solution from the Northeast market district, treating it as the first stage.

Stage 1

Solution of Stage 1

For the Northeast market area, the company can distribute quantities (in 1,000-pound lots) of 0, 1, 2, 3, 4, 5, or 6 pounds of the product. The quantity of the product available for distribution in the Northeast market area is denoted by s_1. Since our problem is to maximize profits, the recursive relationship for this problem can be expressed as follows:

$$f_n^*(s_n,x_n) = \max [c_{x_n} + f_{n-1}^*(s_{n-1})]$$

The total return, $f_1 (s_1, x_1)$, in the first stage is exactly the same as the return c_{x1}, assuming that all of the product would be sold. The computed returns from the quantities distributed and sold in the Northeast market district are presented in Table 13.6.

Table 13.6 *The Downjohn First-Stage Analysis*

Quantity, s_1, to Be Distributed (1,000 Lb.)	Decision x_1, Quantity to Be Allocated to Northeast (1,000 Lb.), and Associated Profit, $f_1(s_1)$ ($1000)							Optimum Return, $f_1^*(s_1,x_1)$ ($1,000)
	0	1	2	3	4	5	6	
0	$0							$0
1	0	$8						8
2	0	8	$15					15
3	0	8	15	$23				23
4	0	8	15	23	$30			30
5	0	8	15	23	30	$36		36
6	0	8	15	23	30	36	$40	40

Stage 2

Solution of Stage 2

In Stage 2, we must decide how the available products need to be allocated to the Northeast and the Midwest market areas. In this stage, we can define the following:

s_2 = quantity of the product distributed to both the Northeast and the Midwest market areas

x_2 = quantity of the product allocated to the Midwest market area

$s_2 - x_2$ = quantity of the product allocated to the Northeast market area

State variable s_2 can take a value of 0, 1, 2, 3, 4, 5, or 6, as shown earlier in Tables 13.5 and 13.6. For each possible value of s_2, we can consider several alternatives in allocating the product to the Midwest and the Northeast market areas. The recursive equation for this stage is

$$f_2^* (s_2, x_2) = \max [c_{x_2} + f_1^*(s_1)]$$

We can consider all seven possible values of s_2. For example, if $s_2 = 0$, then no allocation is possible. Thus, the expected profit (return) will be, of course, zero. If $s_2 = 1$, the value of total returns for $f_2(s_2 = 1)$ would be

$$f_2(s_2 = 1, x_2) = \max \begin{cases} c_{x_2} + f_1(s_1 = 1) = 0 + 8 = 8 & \text{(for } x_2 = 0) \\ c_{x_2} + f_1(s_1 = 0) = 6 + 0 = 6 & \text{(for } x_2 = 1) \end{cases}$$

In other words, the two alternatives open to Downjohn would be as follows:

Alternative 1	Midwest	Northeast
Allocation	0	1
Return	$0	$8

Alternative 2	Midwest	Northeast
Allocation	1	0
Return	$6	$0

From the above calculation, it is clear that when $s_2 = 1$ the first allocation scheme is a better alternative because its total return ($8 + $0 = $8) is greater than that of the second alternative ($0 + $6 = $6). In other words, if there is only one 1,000-pound lot of the product available for allocation, the entire amount should be distributed to the Northeast market.

We can use the same approach for the remaining values of s_2. For example, if $s_2 = 2$, we can evaluate three available allocation alternatives as follows:

Allocation to Midwest, x_2 (1,000 Lb.)	Allocation to Northeast, $s_2 - x_2$ (1,000 Lb.)	Immediate Return from Midwest, c_{x_2} ($1,000)	Optimum Return from Northeast, $f_1^*(s_1)$ ($1,000)	Total Return, $f_2(s_2, x_2)$ ($1,000)
0	2	$0	$15	$15
1	1	6	8	14
2	0	12	0	12

Table 13.7   Analysis of Allocation Alternatives for s₂ = 4

Allocation to Midwest, x_2 (1,000 Lb.)	Allocation to Northeast, $s_2 - x_2$ (1,000 Lb.)	Immediate Return ($1,000)	Optimum Return in Stage 1 ($1,000)	Total Return, $f^2(s_2,x_2)$ ($1,000)	Optimum Alternative, $f_2^*(s_2,x_2)$
0	4	$0	$30	$30	←
1	3	6	23	29	
2	2	12	15	27	
3	1	20	8	28	
4	0	28	0	28	

Table 13.8   The Downjohn Second-Stage Analysis

Quantity, s_3, to Be Distributed (1,000 Lb.)	Decision x_2, Quantity to Be Allocated to Midwest (1,000 Lb.) and Associated Profit, $f_2(s_2,x_2)$($1,000)							Optimum Return, $f_2^*(s_2,x_2)$ ($1,000)
	0	1	2	3	4	5	6	
0	ⓢ0							0
1	⑧	$6						8
2	⑮	14	$12					15
3	㉓	21	20	$20				23
4	㉚	29	27	28	$28			30
5	㊱	㊱	35	35	㊱	ⓢ36		36
6	㊹	42	42	43	43	㊹	$40	44

The computation becomes more tedious as the value of s_2 increases. However, the procedure is exactly the same. For example, if $s_2 = 4$, we can evaluate five possible allocation alternatives, as shown in Table 13.7. Now we are ready to develop a complete table of computations for all of the possible values of s_2, as presented in Table 13.8. In this table, the optimum decision value of x_2 (quantity to be allocated to the Midwest market) for various values of s_2 are circled.

Stage 3

Now the computation for the third stage can be performed in a similar manner. The recursive relationship for the third stage is

Solution of Stage 3

$$f_3^*(s_3, x_3) = \max [c_{x_3} + f_2^*(s_2)]$$

For example, if $s_3 = 2$, we can evaluate the available allocation alternatives as follows:

Table 13.9   The Downjohn Third-Stage Analysis

Quantity, s_3, to Be Distributed (1,000 Lb.)	Decision x_3, Quantity to Be Allocated to South (1,000 Lbs.) and Associated Profit, $f_3(s_3,x_3)$($1,000)							Optimum Return $f_3^*(s_3,x_3)$ ($1,000)	Optimum Alternative
	0	**1**	**2**	**3**	**4**	**5**	**6**		
0	($0							0	
1	8	$6						8	
2	15	14	$12					15	
3	23	21	20	$19				23	
4	30	29	27	27	$28			30	
5	36	36	35	34	36	$36		36	
6	44	42	42	42	43	44	$43	44	←

Allocation to South, x_3 (1,000 Lb.)	Allocation to Northeast and/or Midwest $(s_3 - x_3)$ (1,000 Lb.)	Immediate Return from South, c_{x3} ($1,000)	Optimum Return in Stage 2, $f_2^*(s_2)$ ($1,000)	Total Return, $f_3(s_3,x_3)$ ($1,000)
0	2	$0	$15	$15
1	1	6	8	$14
2	0	12	0	$12

Based on the return value c_{x3} and f_2^* (s_2), the total return, f_3 (s_3,x_3), is computed in Table 13.9.

Identifying the optimum decision

Now we are ready to identify the maximum return and the optimum decision alternative. From Table 13.9 we can easily ascertain that $f_3^*(s_3) = 44 (i.e., $44,000) and $x_3^* = 0$ or 5. If we choose $x_3^* = 0$ (no allocation to the South), we would have 6,000 pounds of the product for the Northeast and Midwest market areas. On the other hand, if we choose $x_3^* = 5$, we will have only 1,000 pounds left for sale in either the Northeast or the Midwest market. Thus, we have alternative optimum solutions. The value of state variable s_2 would be as follows:

$$\text{If } x_3 = 0, \text{ then } s_2 = 0, 1, 2, 3, 4, 5, 6$$
$$\text{If } x_3 = 5, \text{ then } s_2 = 0, 1$$

The two solution pairs (x_2, x_3) are either (5, 0) or (0, 5). Now we can proceed to the first-stage problem to find the value of x_1. Since Downjohn would sell all of the product except 1,000 pounds in either case, the only possible value for s_1 is 1. Therefore, we can obtain $x_1 = 1$ from Table 13.6.

Summarizing the result, we can derive the following two solutions:

	Allocation (1,000 Lb.)	
Market	Solution 1	Solution 2
Northeast	1	1
Midwest	5	0
South	0	5
Total Profit ($1,000)	$44	$44

In the previous two casettes, we dealt with typical problems that could be solved by dynamic programming. In Casette 13.3, we will study another example of a typical application of dynamic programming—production scheduling and inventory control.

CASETTE 13.3 ACE MANUFACTURING COMPANY

A production-inventory problem

Hagar Prudence, a systems engineer in the Ace Manufacturing Company, developed a new component to be used in mining equipment. Hagar was promoted to Production Manager of Ace's newly established mining tool plant. As a new production manager, Hagar felt he should develop a systematic way of minimizing production cost while satisfying customer demand. Hagar sought to make his department the most productive in the company.

The first thing Hagar analyzed was future demand. He knew future demand for the new component would be very unstable and subject to great fluctuation. He decided the only reliable forecast would be relatively short term. The estimated demands for four future planning periods are shown in Table 13.10.

Table 13.10 Demand Forecast for Ace Manufacturing

Planning Period	Estimated Batches (Units)
1	$S_4 = 2$ (60 units)
2	$S_3 = 3$ (90 units)
3	$S_2 = 2$ (60 units)
4	$S_1 = 4$ (120 units)

The production cost of this new component is $1 per unit. Setup cost is $90. Ace produces the product in batches of 30 units owing to the very expensive setup cost and marketing problems. Because of packing and delivery operations, the product has been sold wholesale also in batches of 30 units. The maximum production capacity is 180 units per period. Other fixed costs associated with production are not included here because those costs are not affected by the decision at each period. The total production cost is expressed as follows:

$$\text{Total production cost} = \$90 + \$30x_i \quad (\text{for } 0 < x_i \le 6)$$

or
$$\$0 \quad (\text{for } x_i = 0)$$

where x_i = the multiple of 30 units of products for Period i.

Hagar estimates that the inventory holding cost is \$15 for a batch of 30 units per period. Since this is a new product, he can safely assume the final period to be zero to avoid the unnecessary cost of storage. After determining the important cost factors and demand, the objective is clear: minimize total production cost while satisfying customer demand. Since the problem is one of multiperiod optimization, he decides to use dynamic programming.

Hagar defined the basic terms as follows:

1. *Stage:* The number of periods remaining, n.

2. *State:* The amount of inventory at the beginning of the stage, I_n.

3. *Decision:* The production level at each stage. The decision variable is expressed by x_n.

4. *Return:* Total production cost for the current stage, $f_n (I_n)$.

5. *Total return:* The accumulated sum of total production costs up to the current stage.

Figures 13.8 and 13.9 show one-stage and four-stage diagrams of the problem.

To find the current inventory level, Hagar made the transition equation for inventory level a function of three variables: the previous inventory level, I_n; the production level of the previous period, x_n; and the product sold in the previous period, S_n. It is assumed that the product sold in any period is equal to the demand forecast given in Table 13.10.

The transition equation for inventory level is

$$I_{n-1} = I_n + x_n - S_n$$

The total production cost (i.e., return) for each stage is

$$c_n (x_n, I_n) = 90 + 30x_n + 15I_n \quad (\text{for } 0 < x_n \le 6)$$

or
$$0 \quad (\text{for } x_n = 0)$$

The recursive function Finally, the general recursive relationship was easily obtained using the functions described above. The recursive function for total production cost is

$$f_n(I_n) = \min [c_n(x_n, I_n) + f^*_{n-1}(I_n + x_n - S_n)]$$

subject to
$$x_n + I_n \ge S_n$$
$$0 \le x_n \le 6$$

Once all of the necessary relationships were established, Hagar started with the last period (i.e., Period 4) and proceeded backward. Since at every stage the optimum decision (the production level that yields the minimum production cost) is determined by the previous optimum value, he was confident that the principle of optimality was satisfied.

Figure 13.8   One-Stage Diagram of Minimum Production Cost for Ace Manufacturing

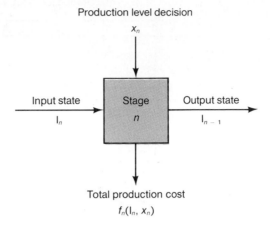

Production level decision

x_n

Input state — Stage n — Output state

I_n .... I_{n-1}

Total production cost

$f_n(I_n, x_n)$

Figure 13.9   Four-Stage Diagram for Ace Manufacturing

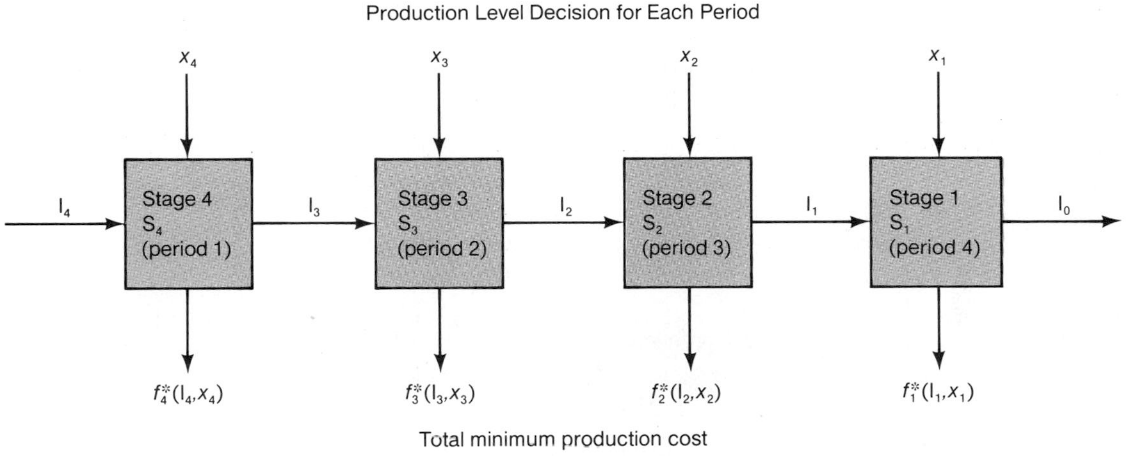

Production Level Decision for Each Period

x_4 x_3 x_2 x_1

I_4 → | Stage 4 S_4 (period 1) | → I_3 → | Stage 3 S_3 (period 2) | → I_2 → | Stage 2 S_2 (period 3) | → I_1 → | Stage 1 S_1 (period 4) | → I_0

$f_4^*(I_4, x_4)$ $f_3^*(I_3, x_3)$ $f_2^*(I_2, x_2)$ $f_1^*(I_1, x_1)$

Total minimum production cost

Stage 1

First, we will examine the single-stage problem. The total production cost associated with the state variable I_n would be

$$f_1(I_1) = \min [c_1 (x_1, I_1) + f_0 (I_1 + x_1 - S_1)]$$

However, $f_0 (I_1 + x_1 - S_1) = 0$, since it is assumed that there will be no inventory at the end of Period 4. Therefore

$$f_1 (I_1) = \min c_1 (x_1, I_1)$$

Using the above equation, we find that the total production cost $f_1(I_1)$, the minimum production cost $f_1^*(I_1)$, and the optimum decision variable x_1^* are determined as shown in Table 13.11.

Table 13.11   Single-Stage Problem

State Variable I_1	Total Production Cost, $f_1(I_1)$ x_1					Minimum Return, $f_1^*(I_1)$	Optimum Decision, x_1^*
	0	1	2	3	4		
0					$210	$210	4
1				$180 +15		195	3
2			$150 +30			180	2
3		$120 +45				165	1
4	$60					60	0*

Note that the possible values of inventory levels are the integer values from 0 to 4. Since there is a demand for 120 units (i.e., 4 batches of 30 units) for Period 4, depending on the different values of inventory level I_1, we can make different decisions. Since $S_1 = 4$ (120 units), $I_1 + x_1 = 4$. For example, if $I_1 = 4$, then $x_1 = 0$. In this case, the only cost involved will be the inventory cost of $15 per batch, or $60. On the other hand, if $I_1 = 3$, then $x_1 = 1$. In this case, the total cost will be $90 (setup cost) + $30 ($1 $\times$ 30 units) + $45 (inventory cost, $15 $\times$ 3 batches) = $120 + $45 = $165.

Stage 2

Now let us look at the two-stage problem, which includes Periods 3 and 4. The sum of production and inventory must be greater than or equal to the forecasted demand of 6 batches (180 units) for Periods 3 and 4. Thus, the possible values of I_2 would range from 0 to 6. We can calculate the sum of production and inventory costs in a similar manner.

The total production cost is calculated by summing the production cost in the current stage [i.e., $c_2(x_1, I_2)$] and the total production cost in the previous stage [i.e., $f_1^*(I_2 + x_2 - S_2)$]. Mathematically, the function is

$$f_2(I_2) = \min [c_2(x_2, I_2) + f_1^*(I_2 + x_2 - S_2)]$$

The results of the two-stage problem are presented in Table 13.12. Each cost entry consists of two costs—production cost (including setup cost) and inventory cost. For example, if $I_2 = 0$ and $x_2 = 2$, then the production cost for Period 3 will be $90 + $60 = $150 and the inventory cost will be zero. However, since the total demand is 6 batches (180 units), production for Period 4 will be $x_1 = 4$. The minimum return for this decision is $210, as shown in Table 13.11. Thus, the return $f_2(I_2 = 0, x_2 = 2)$ is $360. This calculation procedure identifies the optimum value of x_2.

Stage 3

We now face the three-stage problem, which includes Periods 2, 3, and 4. At the beginning of Period 1, there was no inventory. Thus, we know that inventory in Period 2 is determined by subtracting the sales in Period 1 from the production in Period 1. In other words, $I_3 = x_4 - S_4$. The forecasted sales in Period 1 are determined as 2 ($S_4 = 2$). Thus, we can easily determine that I_3 can range from 0 to 4.

Table 13.12 Two-Stage Problem

State Variable I_2	Total Production Cost, $f_2(I_2)$ x_2 0	1	2	3	4	5	6	Minimum Return, $f_2^*(I_2)$	Optimum Decision, x_2^*
0			$150 +210	$180 +195	$210 +180	$240 +165	($270 +60)	$330	6*
1		$135 +210	165 +195	195 +180	225 +165	(255 +60)		315	5
2	($30 +210)	150 +195	180 +180	210 +165	240 +60			240	0
3	(45 +195)	165 +180	195 +165	225 +60				240	0
4	(60 +180)	180 +165	210 +60					240	0
5	(75 +165)	195 +60						240	0
6	(90 +60)							150	0

Table 13.13 Three-Stage Problem

State Variable, I_3	Total Production Cost, $f_3(I_3)$ x_3 0	1	2	3	4	5	6	Minimum Return, $f_3^*(I_3)$	Optimum Decision, x_3^*
0				$180 +330	$210 +315	($240 +240)	$270 +240	$480	5
1			$165 +330	195 +315	(225 +240)	255 +240	285 +240	465	4
2		$150 +330	180 +315	(210 +240)	240 +240	270 +240	300 +240	450	3
3	($45 +330)	165 +315	195 +240	225 +240	255 +240	285 +240	315 +150	375	0*
4	(60 +315)	180 +240	210 +240	240 +240	270 +240	300 +150		375	0

The total production and inventory cost $f_3(I_3)$ is determined by

$$f_3(I_3) = \min [c_3(x_3, I_3) + f_2^*(I_3 + x_3 - S_3)]$$

The computation is exactly the same as the previous stage. The minimum total production cost, $f_3^*(I_3)$, is obtained with optimum decision x_3^*. The results are shown in Table 13.13. For example, if $x_3 = 3$ and $I_3 = 2$, then the total production cost

Table 13.14 Four-Stage Problem

State Variable I_4	Total Production Cost, $f_4(I_4)$ x_4						Minimum Return, $f_4^*(I_4)$	Optimum Decision, x_4^*
	0	1	2	3	4	5	6		
0			$150 +480	$180 +465	$210 +450	$240 +375	$270 +375	$615	5*

would be $90 (setup cost) + $90 (production cost of 3 batches) = $180, and the inventory cost will be $30. Since the forecasted demand for Period 2 is 3 batches (90 units), then, if $I_3 = 2$, we must produce at least 1 batch. If we produce 3 batches in Period 2, then $x_3 = 3$ and we will have 2 surplus batches. Since the total demand for Periods 3 and 4 is 6 batches, we must still produce 4 more batches during Periods 3 and 4. Thus, $I_2 = 2$. We find $f_2^*(I_2 = 2) = 240 in Table 13.12. Thus, the total cost for $x_3 = 3$ and $I_3 = 2$ will be $210 + $240 = $450, as shown in Table 13.13.

Stage 4

The last stage is easy to calculate because the only value of I_4 is zero. The total production cost $f_4(I_4)$ is

$$f_4(I_4) = \min [c_4(x_4, I_4) + f_3^*(I_4 + x_4 - S_4)]$$

Using the same computation procedure, we obtain the optimum solution of the four-stage problem as shown in Table 13.14. This is the optimum solution for the entire problem. The total production cost for the four periods is $615.

Optimum Solution

Now we have to determine the optimum decision variable at each stage:

Stage 4 Clearly, $x_4^* = 5$.

Stage 3 Since $I_3 = I_4 + x_4 - S_4$, while $I_4 = 0$, $x_4 = 5$, and $S_4 = 2$, we obtain $I_3 = 3$. From Table 13.13, we obtain $x_3^* = 0$.

Stage 2 Since $I_2 = I_3 + x_3 - S_3$, while $I_3 = 3$, $x_3 = 0$, and $S_3 = 3$, we obtain $I_2 = 0$. From Table 13.13, we obtain $x_2^* = 6$.

Stage 1 Since $I_1 = I_2 + x_2 - S_2$, while $I_2 = 0$, $x_2 = 6$, and $S_2 = 2$, we obtain $I_2 = 4$. From Table 13.13, we obtain $x_1^* = 0$.

The optimum solution is shown below:

Period	Production Quantity Cost (Batch)		Demand (Batch)	Inventory Quantity Cost (Batch)		Production & Inventory Cost
1	5	$240	2	3	$45	$285
2	0	0	3	0	0	0
3	6	270	2	4	60	330
4	0	0	4	0	0	0
					total cost	$615

PROBABILISTIC DYNAMIC PROGRAMMING

Probabilistic dynamic programming

In the previous section, we discussed deterministic dynamic programming. We know that deterministic dynamic programming deals with problems in which a transition from one state to another is known with certainty, yielding a series of returns that result in a total return. However, in many cases we face situations in which a transition from one state to another is associated with a probability distribution. In other words, a state of the next stage is determined by the probability distribution, which in turn is determined by the previous state. This probability, referred to as *transition probability,* is an important concept in decision making under risk. This advanced topic of dynamic programming is beyond the scope of this book. If you are interested in this topic, consult the books listed in the References.

REAL-WORLD APPLICATIONS

Real-world applications

There have been a number of interesting real-world applications of dynamic programming. Some of these studies deal with such diverse problems as inventory control, investment analysis, manpower scheduling, resource allocation, police force development, network optimization, and the like. Most of these studies report design and implementation of dynamic programming models for sequential decision making problems. In this section, we will consider two application examples of dynamic programming.

Dynamic Programming for Ship Fleet Management

This study deals with a decision problem to determine the optimum policy for scaling down a fleet of general cargo ships.[1] The shipping company operates 34 cargo ships in a particular trade area. With the advent of container ships and many new technological changes, over the next 10 years the company will be forced to scale down its fleet to 12 ships.

In the face of falling demand, the company must decide which particular ships to sell as the demand decreases. Several important decision criteria for choosing ships to sell are: current operating costs, earnings, and current and future resale prices of the various ships. Another important factor to consider is the possibility of utilizing the charter or hire market. This option allows the company to sell a ship prematurely and replace it with a chartered ship to meet market commitments.

The decision problem is to determine the optimum sequence through which the company's ships are sold and chartered ships are taken on. The modeling approach consists of two stages. The first stage determines a priority order for selling the existing ships. The second stage applies dynamic programming to determine the optimum number of chartered ships based on the priority replacement order developed in the first stage.

The study reports the determination of the optimum level of chartering through the use of dynamic programming. In addition, the authors contend that the computer program could be utilized to evaluate various other proposed schemes to replace the

[1]T. A. J. Nicholson and R. D. Pullen, "Dynamic Programming Applied to Ship Fleet Management," *Operational Research Quarterly,* 22:3 (1971), 211–220.

cargo ships. Based on this study, the company was said to reduce its capital invest-ment in cargo ships from £31.83 million to £28.90 million. A very successful appli-cation it was indeed.

Mine-Mill Production Scheduling

This study explores the application of dynamic programming to the operation of a mine-mill complex.[2] More specifically, the study focuses on one primary aspect of a mine operation—determination of an optimum production schedule.

The data utilized to develop the dynamic programming model for production scheduling were: "deposit size, feed grade, maximum tonnage throughput, minimum controllable variation in throughput, fixed mining cost, fixed concentrating cost, var-iable mining cost, variable concentrating costs, a quadratic equation relating through-put to grade, market price for the concentrate, smelter charges, transport cost to the smelter and the acceptable return on investment."

Based on the application of a dynamic programming model, the author was able to make the following general conclusions:

1. The stability of the production schedule is dependent on the size of deposits.

2. The operating range of the mine-mill is determined by the proportion of fixed costs to total costs. If fixed costs are very high, the possible operating range becomes very small.

3. The production schedule can incorporate the rates of increase in the product price and production costs.

4. The dynamic programming model of the production schedule yielded a 4–5 per-cent higher present worth of operation than a constant-level production schedule, and it was 15–20 percent higher than a constant production level that gave the highest net cash flow per ton of ore.

This study clearly demonstrated the effectiveness of dynamic programming ap-plication to the production schedule of a mine mill.

SUMMARY

Dynamic programming is a powerful technique for solving multistage problems. Dy-namic programming deals with state variables, stages, decisions (variables), returns, and a recursive relationship for subproblems (e.g., single-stage, two-stage). Dynamic programming uses decomposition of complex programs into smaller and simpler sub-problems. The computation procedure is almost identical for each subproblem, and for each subproblem a suboptimum solution is obtained. Dynamic programming elim-

[2]R. J. Roman, "Mine-Mill Production Scheduling by Dynamic Programming," *Operational Research Quarterly,* 22:4 (1971), 319–328.

inates much of the computational effort required in complete enumeration. Depending on the characteristics of the operators in recursive relationships, the computational procedure may be rather cumbersome. Nevertheless, it is much better than enumeration of all of the possible solution vectors.

In this chapter we have dealt only with finite-stage dynamic programming (deterministic and probabilistic). If you are interested in more advanced techniques and applications of dynamic programming, consult the following References.

References

Bellman, Riehard. *Dynamic Programming*. Princeton, N.J.: Princeton University Press, 1957.

Bellman, Richard, and Dreyfus, Stuart. *Applied Dynamic Programming*. Princeton, N.J.: Princeton University Press, 1962.

Howard, Ronald A. "Dynamic Programming." *Management Science,* 12:5 (Jan., 1966), 317–345.

Kaufman, Arnold, and Cruon, R. *Dynamic Programming: Sequential Scientific Management*. New York: Academic Press, 1967.

Nemhauser, George L. *Introduction to Dynamic Programming*. New York: Wiley, 1966.

Wagner, Harvey M. *Principles of Operations Research*. Englewood Cliffs, N.J.: Prentice-Hall, 1969.

White, D. J. *Dynamic Programming*. San Francisco: Holden-Day, 1969.

Assignments

13.1 What is the difference between dynamic programming and linear programming?

13.2 Explain the following terms: *decomposition* (or *segmentation*), *multistage* (or *sequential*) decisions.

13.3 Discuss the principle of optimality.

13.4 Discuss the differences and similarities between the *backward* approach and the *forward* approach.

13.5 Why is dynamic programming a better method than complete enumeration?

13.6 Define the following terms: *stage, state, policy decision, return, total return*.

13.7 List the typical application areas of dynamic programming.

13.8 Describe the additive recursive relationship and explain it by using the terms in Problem 13.6.

13.9 How does probabilistic dynamic programming differ from deterministic dynamic programming?

13.10 John Lynch inherited $3,000 from his grandmother and decided to invest it in stocks. A local brokerage firm suggested three stocks: X, Y, and Z. The following table indicates the probable return for each stock:

Investment	Return on Investment		
($1,000)	Stock X	Stock Y	Stock Z
$0	0%	0%	0%
1	5	5	4
2	15	15	26
3	40	40	40

Obviously, John wants to maximize the total return, which is the sum of the individual returns. It is assumed that the return from each stock is independent of investments in other stocks.

    a. Illustrate the problem graphically with states, stages, decisions, and returns.

    b. Determine the transition function.

    c. Determine the optimum mix of stocks by using dynamic programming.

13.11 The Harwell Software Company plans to develop an efficient procurement plan over the next two years. The estimated demand for the critical items the company intends to purchase is given as follows:

Year:	1	2
Demand:	100	200

The procurement cost is estimated to be 20¢ per unit with the condition that the quantities be purchased in multiples of 100 at the beginning of each period; a maximum of 400 units can be purchased. Holding cost is $.10 per unit per year. The current maximum storage capacity is 200 units. Total cost is expressed as the sum of procurement cost and holding cost for two years. Assume that there is no stock on hand at the beginning of the first year and at the end of the second year.

    a. Develop the dynamic programming formulation with the illustration of states, stages, decisions, returns, and transition function.

    b. Determine the optimum quantity of procurement.

13.12 The Harwell Software Company has developed a new mathematical programming software for mini- and microcomputers and has contracted to develop the package over the next four production periods. The lack of skilled programmers and other engineering capabilities limits the production of the package to 10 units per period. The storage cost per unit of software is $20. The table below shows the production costs and sales contracted:

Period	Production Cost	Sales Contracted
1	$350	6
2	$360	7
3	$400	12
4	$380	6

Jim Harwell, President and Chief System Analyst, wants to satisfy the contracts within the current capacity of the firm; he also wants to minimize cost. Note that the ending state is expressed as the beginning inventory plus the production quantity minus sales.

    a. Formulate the dynamic programming problem.
    b. Show the solution procedure stage by stage. (*Hint:* Four stages are needed.)
    c. Determine the optimum quantity of product and total cost.

13.13 The Water Resource Management Council of the county is responsible for providing water to the towns in the county. This council decided to provide water to the newly developing town of Plainview. A systems analyst group has estimated the costs to be incurred for adding new capacity such as pipes and other necessary equipment. The estimated costs are given in the illustration below:

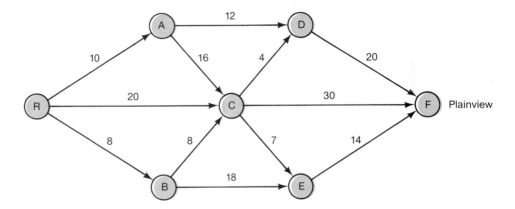

    a. Formulate the dynamic programming problem.
    b. Solve the problem by the complete enumeration method.
    c. Show the solution procedure step by step.
    d. Determine the most economic path to use for providing water to Plainview.

13.14 The Jensen Laboratories has three popular products for general health care: Comtol I, Comtol II, and Comtol X. The company currently has three machines that can produce any of the three products. The production scheduling is prepared in such a manner that once a machine is set up for one product that machine must run for a week without being changed. The production scheduler is responsible for determining how many machines are to be used to produce each product. The following table presents the estimated profit for the three products in terms of machines scheduled:

Number of Machine	Forecasted Profit per Week ($100)		
	Comtol I	Comtol II	Comtol X
1	$50	$45	$15
2	57	75	48
3	82	96	84

a. Formulate the problem by using dynamic programming.

b. Determine the optimum number of machines for the coming week.

13.15 Refer to Problem 13.14. Suppose that the company decided that each machine would be used to produce each product. To maximize the profit, the production manager decides that two more machines will be installed to produce any one of the three products. The new machines are assumed to have the same capability as the machines currently in use. The estimated profits for the fourth and fifth machines to be added are as follows:

Number of Machine	Forecasted Profit per Week ($100)		
	Comtol I	Comtol II	Comtol X
4	$ 95	$105	$ 92
5	108	112	110

a. Formulate the problem by using dynamic programming.

b. Determine the optimum number of machines for the coming week.

13.16 Richard Armando, a Maine fisherman, owns his own fishing boat. His boat is usually inspected every two years. At a time of inspection, he decides whether the boat is to be overhauled or replaced. If the boat does not pass the inspection, he sells it for scrap material. The cost figures for overhaul and the scrap values of boats with different ages are given in the table below:

Boat's Age	Overhaul Cost	Scrap Value
2	$ 3,000	$20,000
4	7,000	10,000
6	10,000	4,000

The current market price for a new fishing boat is about $50,000. The boat that Mr. Armando owns is about four years old. When the boat is six years old, Mr. Armando plans to sell it for scrap material.

    a. Formulate the problem by using dynamic programming. (*Hint:* There are only two decision variables—replace and overhaul.)

    b. Determine the optimum replacement plan.

13.17 Refer to Problem 13.16. Mr. Armando decided to continue using the fishing boat because of a lack of cash on hand. He figured out that he could use the fishing boat up to eight years and that the overhaul cost and the scrap value of the boat at the eighth year would be $15,000 and $2,000 respectively.

    a. Formulate the problem by using dynamic programming.

    b. Determine the optimum replacement plan.

    c. Is his new replacement plan the same as the one in Problem 13.16?

13.18 General Aviation International has developed a medium-range plan for developing a new type of computerized aviation system called Project OWL. Since the top management insists upon efficiency and effectiveness in planning any project, the manager of the Planning Department is very concerned about the risk of failure. The Operations Research Group estimated the probability of success for three different projects as follows:

Amount Invested ($ Million)	Probability of Success		
	Project OWL I	Project OWL II	Project OWL III
1	.7	.6	.8
2	.8	.7	.9
3	.95	.95	.9

Note that the manager decided to allocate the budget in block amounts of $1 million. The maximum amount for each project is $3 million, and the total available budget is $5 million.

    a. Determine the optimum allocation of the budget for each project that will maximize the probability of success.

    b. Show the dynamic programming formulation by using a state, stage, return, and transition function.

13.19 Refer to Problem 13.18. The Operations Research Group also estimated the probability of failure for the three projects as follows:

Amount Invested ($Million)	Probability of Failure		
	Project OWL I	OWL II	OWL III
$1	.3	.4	.2
2	.2	.3	.1
3	.05	.05	.1

What would be the optimum budget allocation in order to minimize the probability of failure? Is the answer to this problem the same as the answer to Problem 13.18?

13.20 Karen Oliver, the Marketing Manager of Ragoo Toy Company, faces a pricing decision for a new toy, Walking Bear. She is considering three different prices: $10, $12, and $14. Since the toy market is very competitive and demand fluctuates, she has to decide on a price for each of the next three years. After studying the market, she calculated the potential profit over three years as shown below:

Price	Potential Profit ($ Million)		
	1st year	2nd year	3rd year
$10	$7	$3	$5
12	5	4	7
14	3	7	8

Ms. Oliver wants to maximize the potential profit during the next three years.
  a. Formulate the problem by using dynamic programming.
  b. Determine the optimum pricing plan over three years.
  c. What is the maximum profit?

13.21 Refer to Problem 13.20. After conferring with her boss, the Vice-president of Marketing, Ms. Oliver is told that the price of Walking Bear should not fluctuate very much, up or down. After considering the possible solutions to this restriction, she decides that any price change, up or down, should be made within a range of $2.
  a. Formulate the problem by using dynamic programming.
  b. Determine the maximum profit and the optimum prices.

13.22 The Alaskan Tourist Company owns four small but luxurious sailboats for traveling the Alaskan coastal sea via three different routes. The management of the company wants to optimize the allocation of these four boats on the three routes in terms of profit. The expected profits per month are as follows:

Number of Boats Allocated	Expected Profit ($1,000)		
	Route 1	Route 2	Route 3
1	$2.8	$0.8	$1.8
2	3.6	2.0	2.4
3	4.0	3.6	3.8
4	4.2	5.2	4.8

  a. Formulate the problem by using dynamic programming.
  b. Determine the optimum allocation of the sailboats.

13.23 Refer to Problem 13.22. Assume that the Alaskan Tourist Company wants to purchase two more sailboats because of expanding tourism. The expected profits for the additional two boats are as follows:

Number of Boats Allocated	Expected Profit ($1,000)		
	Route 1	Route 2	Route 3
5	$4.7	$5.6	$5.5
6	5.0	6.0	6.2

What would be the new optimum allocation plan?

13.24 The Miller and Associates Construction Company obtained a new contract for constructing a football stadium for Lakeview High. The construction schedule is determined as follows:

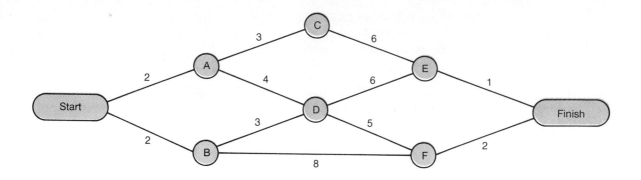

a. Use dynamic programming to isolate the longest-time path.
b. Use dynamic programming to isolate the shortest-time path.

13.25 Refer to Problem 13.24. The company is reconsidering the problem in terms of costs. The cost data are shown in the following table:

Node:	A	B	C	D	E	F
Cost ($1000):	$20	$40	$60	$100	$36	$200

a. Determine the minimum cost path by using dynamic programming.
b. Determine the maximum cost path by using dynamic programming.

13.26 The Red Valley Mine Company wants to purchase a new custom truck for delivering coal and other materials. The current price of this truck is $15,000. Recently the operating cost for this truck became a concern because of skyrocketing gasoline prices. The local chamber of commerce provided the following data for the operating costs and resale prices of the truck:

Year	Operating Cost ($1,000)	Resale Price ($1,000)
1	$ 5	$12
2	7	10
3	10	7

Since this type of truck is heavily used in the mine, no single truck can be used for more than three years. Every year the company decides whether or not it should buy a new truck. Assume that all of the values are adjusted as present values.
    a. Show the solution procedure of dynamic programming by using a state, stage, return, and transition function.
    b. Determine the optimum replacement plan of the company.

13.27 Refer to Problem 13.26. The Rock Valley Mine Company wants to extend the current replacement plan through a fifth year period. The operating costs and resale prices for the additional two years are given below:

Year	Operating Cost ($1,000)	Resale Price ($1,000)
4	$12	$6
5	15	5

Determine the new optimum replacement plan of the company.

13.28 The Portland Shipbuilding Company produces three types of racing sailboat: Snipe, Hampton, and Lightning. Each type of boat needs a certain amount of fiberglass for its hull construction. Currently, the company has 20 tons of fiberglass in stock and cannot receive more fiberglass in the near future because of a labor strike. Thus, the allocation of fiberglass to each type of sailboat is critical at present. The probable returns for these three different types of sailboats, shown below, depend on the quantity of fiberglass allocated. Note that the allocation of fiberglass is made in units of 5 tons.

Fiberglass (5-ton Unit)	Expected Profit		
	Snipe	Hampton	Lightning
5	$200,000	$120,000	$160,000
10	$350,000	$350,000	$220,000
15	N/A	N/A	$380,000

a. Develop the dynamic programming formulation by using a state, stage, return, and transition equation.
b. Determine the optimum allocation plan of the company to maximize the return.

13.29 Refer to Problem 13.28. The Portland Shipbuilding Company wants to diversify its products to meet the demand. After conferring with the Chief Engineer, the management of the company decided to add another type of sailboat, to be called the Rebel. The probable returns for this type of boat are $170,000, $320,000, and $390,000 for each successive level of allocation, respectively.
a. Determine the optimum allocation plan and probable total return.
b. Did the company make the right decision in terms of probable return?

14 SIMULATION

For all the prowess of management science, many real-world problems cannot be easily analyzed by the modeling techniques we have discussed thus far in this text. Many standard analytical techniques based on algorithms, such as linear programming and transportation methods, are often too restrictive for dynamic decision problems. Some decision problems are characterized by complex interrelationships among the decision variables, random events, and simultaneous changes of the model parameters. When all available analytical models fail, one possible avenue open to us is to conduct an experiment. Simulation is one such experimentation technique. It is based on mathematical models or logical trial-and-error approaches. Simulation is widely applied to evaluate the behavior of many real-world systems, such as inventory, production, sales, manpower, and the like. In this chapter, we will study the basic nature, characteristics, and important approaches of simulation.

Learning Objectives *From the study of this chapter, you will learn the following:*

1. Many different types of simulation in real-world situations.
2. The advantages and disadvantages of simulation.
3. The various characteristics of simulation models.
4. The general process of simulation.
5. Application of the Monte Carlo process.
6. Generation of random numbers and their transformation for determining random variables.
7. Incorporation of optimization in simulation.
8. The application areas of simulation.
9. The meaning of the following terms:

Simulation	*Transformation*
Random number	*GPSS*
Descriptor	*SIMSCRIPT*
Flowchart	*SIMULA*
Monte Carlo	*GASP IV*
Uniform probability distribution	*DYNAMO*
Artificial intelligence	*Heuristics*
Business games	*Industrial dynamics*

THE NATURE OF SIMULATION

We are most familiar with physical simulations. "It's great . . . things are just spectacular. Voyager 2 is racing by Saturn at 54,000 mph, skimming just 63,000 miles over the ringlets within the C-ring, surrounded by B-ring," an excited scientist at the Jet Propulsion Laboratory comments on the television set. He continues, "After examining Enceladus, one of Saturn's collection of at least 17 moons, Voyager 2 will continue its long journey to distant Uranus. Please watch the simulator." Now we see an artist's simulated journey of Voyager 2 far into the dark universe.

Examples of simulation

We are exposed to many such physical simulations. The ground flight simulator duplicates flying conditions for training pilots. Most experiments conducted by the manned space flight programs of NASA are based on simulated space conditions. Many of the board games children play are also simulations—"Monopoly," "Acquire," "Life," and the like. Other simulations we often see are:

Management games used for training and development.

Simulation models of the world, urban systems, and corporations.

Corporate planning simulation models.

Water resource simulation models.

Inventory-production simulators.

Probabilistic network models.

Queuing models for airport traffic control.

Air quality simulation models.

Econometric models to predict economic conditions.

World energy models.

Simulation—a popular technique

As we saw in Chapter 1, simulation is one of the most widely used techniques of management science. The primary reason for this popularity is its applicability to a wide range of management problems. Simulation is effective in generating a large amount of information concerning the performance or behavior of a system under various conditions and/or assumptions.

What Is Simulation?

What is a simulation?

Simulation is much like a model. A model is a representation of reality. Instead of representing reality, however, simulation simply imitates it. But the two are alike in that both a model and simulation mean many different things to different people.

Figure 14.1   Management Science Modeling Solution Process

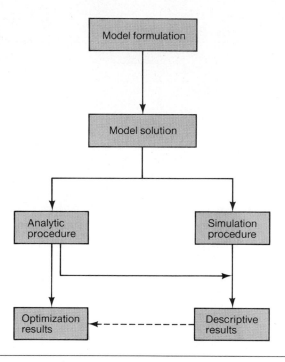

When a beautiful lady tells us that she aspires to become a model, we surely would not think of a well-formulated linear programming model.

The process of simulation involves "operating" or "running" the model to obtain operational information of the system. Operational information should be so designed to help the manager in making the decision. Today, simulation generally refers to computer-based simulation. Thus, we can define simulation in the management science context as: *A numerical technique of experimentation to determine the dynamic behavior of a management system on the digital computer*. Although powerful computers allow us to simulate complex systems, simulation can also be carried out manually for simple problems.

In simulation, instead of seeking an optimum solution through algorithms as in analytical modeling approaches, we attempt to obtain descriptive information through experimentation. The descriptive results of simulation are often referred to as *descriptors*. The system descriptors can be valuable for predicting behavior or performance of a system under various conditions. For example, change in the inventory level under various combinations of daily demand and lead time, as we studied in Chapter 11, gives us a pretty good idea of what to expect when the demand rate changes.

Although simulation output is always in the form of descriptive results, it is certainly possible to include a search rule in the simulator so that the results can be evaluated in such a way that the optimum solution to the decision problem can be identified. Thus, we can visualize the model solution phase of the management science process as shown in Figure 14.1. The dashed arrow in the figure, leading from

Descriptive results from simulation

Figure 14.2   The Simulation Process

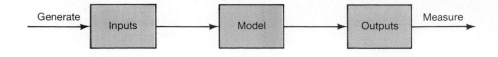

the block containing descriptive results to the block containing optimization results, represents the optimum solution possibility of simulation.

The simulation process

A simplified version of the simulation process is illustrated in Figure 14.2, where the model is shown as a box. The simulation process requires the generation of input data to be fed into the model, and the model should be designed in such a way as to provide the output that can be used to measure or evaluate the performance (objective criteria) variables. In order to design an effective simulation model, we must identify the system under study by carefully considering its important variables and performance criteria.

Characteristics of simulation

On the basis of our discussion thus far, we can summarize the characteristics of simulation as follows:

Simulation is a technique of experimentation to determine the behavior of a system under various conditions.

A computer-based model is used to generate descriptive results.

An optimum solution routine can be included in the simulation process.

Simulation requires necessary data, and its results must be evaluated based on objective criteria.

Simulation does not necessarily represent reality but merely imitates it.

Simulation is usually applied when a decision problem under analysis is too complex to be solved by analytical models (e.g., linear programming and EOQ models).

Why Simulate?

In recent years, computers have become more powerful in terms of speed and computational power. Speed of computation is getting faster, even for large-scale models, while the cost is decreasing dramatically. A small personal computer costing less than $2,000 can be as powerful as a gigantic computer that used to fill up a room in the 1960s. Another significant development is in the area of dedicated (specially designed) simulation languages for various managerial problems.

Table 14.1 Advantages and Disadvantages of Simulation

Advantages	Disadvantages
Allows controlled experimentation	Model development can be costly and/or time consuming
Reveals new facts about the problem	
Allows a patchwork approach to model formulation	Requires powerful computers
Is an effective training tool	Is very sensitive to model formulation
Has a broad range of applications	Gives no guaranteed optimum solution
Allows "what if" questions	Encourages tendency to overlook other techniques

Simulation as a decision making tool

Although the attempts to simulate a situation under investigation have not always been successful, simulation has grown rapidly as a decision making tool in many organizations. The increasing application of simulation is a good indication that simulation has many advantages. Table 14.1 presents the major advantages and disadvantages of simulation. Let us discuss the advantage and disadvantages of simulation in greater detail.

Advantages Computer-based simulation has the following advantages:

Advantages of simulation

1. The first, and perhaps the most important, advantage of simulation is that it provides a means to study the real-world system or situation without actually changing it. In many social systems, it is often impossible to experiment, or an experiment may involve a high level of risk. For example, a change of price for a product can be a risky business. Even when such a change is made on the basis of a rigorous analysis, it can still lead to disaster. There are many such cases in real-world situations: change of tax systems, tactical changes in warfare, psychological experiments, policy changes in détente with the Soviet Union, change of government regulations, a gasoline coupon system, and the like.

If such real-world systems can be simulated on a computer, the decision maker can observe the potential outcome of various changes without altering the real system. Thus, many alternatives can be explored and their results can be studied in a formal way. Simulation is especially valuable for analyzing complex systems that defy other analytical techniques.

2. Simulation requires a thorough analysis of the problem in order to generate the required data. This process can reveal some hidden interrelationships or previously unrecognized defects in the system.

3. The simulation model, regardless of the complexity of the problem, does not need to be an overwhelming large-scale model at the beginning. Usually, a simulation model is the aggregate of many simple models representing interrelationships among system variables and components. Thus, the simulation model can be built slowly, step by step.

4. The simulation model is usually designed on the basis of the manager's perspective of the system rather than on that of the management scientist. This is an important factor in the eventual implementation of the model results. We will discuss implementation thoroughly in Chapter 15.

5. Simulation can be an effective training tool for managers and employees alike. Management games based on simulation are widely used by business schools and the in-house training programs of many organizations.

6. Simulation has a broad range of applications, from such operations problems as inventory control to such strategic planning problems as mergers and capital budgeting. Computer-based simulation is particularly effective for analyzing complex organizational problems.

7. Simulation provides descriptive results rather than prescriptive (optimum) results. Thus, the manager has ample opportunity to ask "what if" type sensitivity analysis questions. Such information provides much confidence concerning the range of possible outcomes to a certain decision alternative.

Disadvantages Although computer simulation is a very effective technique for many decision problems, it has some disadvantages:

Disadvantages of simulation

1. Development of a simulation model, especially a complex computer-based model, can be a very costly and slow proposition. Since an effective simulation model requires accurate data and precise interrelationships among the variables, it may become a formidable task in terms of cost, manpower, time, and expertise.

2. Most simulation models require powerful digital computers for computation. Therefore, simulation is not a quick and inexpensive approach to complex decision problems.

3. Simulation model results are usually very sensitive to model formulation. Thus, if the model contains some inaccurate relationships or interdependencies, the results may be quite misleading.

4. Simulation provides descriptive model results. Thus, either an optimum solution (or a very good solution) cannot be guaranteed or identification of an optimum (or a good) solution becomes an additional task after the simulation work is completed.

5. Simulation may become the jack-of-all-trades to some managers. Thus, some analytical techniques, which are simpler and more effective for finding even better solutions, may be overlooked.

Besides the advantages and disadvantages of simulation, we had better remember the adage, "When all else fails, simulate." This implies that simulation should be the last resort only if other available techniques cannot solve the problem. As we pointed out earlier, the purpose of simulation is to conduct systematic experiments for a real system. Therefore, the results obtained from simulation must be complementary to analytical solutions, regardless of whether or not analytical solutions exist.

Characteristics of Simulation Models

There are many different types of simulation models, depending on the nature of the problem under investigation. Let us discuss the following characteristics:

Static vs. Dynamic We can use simulation to analyze both static and dynamic situations. In most cases, the simulation models we construct are dynamic in nature. For example, economic forecasting models and national energy models are dynamic simulation models that analyze real-world systems. Examples of static simulation models might be plant layout design, space allocation, warehouse location, and the like.

Deterministic vs. Stochastic Virtually all of the real-world situations we face are stochastic (probabilistic) rather than deterministic. Whenever a system involves randomness in its variables or parameters, the model we construct should be stochastic. For example, if a hamburger shop has a waiting line, the customer waiting time in the line is a random variable. If we design a simulation model to observe the customer waiting patterns, it will be a stochastic model. However, if the expected value of the waiting time is available, we can use this information to construct a deterministic simulation model.

Continuous vs. Discrete A variable is said to be continuous if its value changes continuously over time. On the other hand, a variable is said to be discrete if its value changes discretely over time. We must choose appropriate variables for the problem under study because the variable selection greatly affects the nature of a simulation model. Continuous simulation models are often used for large-scale problems such as econometric (economic forecasting) models and energy planning models. Discrete simulation is used for detailed operational problems such as production scheduling, inventory control, and manpower planning.

Aggregated vs. Detailed The level of detail and the degree of aggregation are perhaps the most important characteristics of simulation. These two characteristics are determined according to the purpose of the particular simulation modeling. For example, if the top decision maker is interested in gross quantities such as total sales, total inventories, total production, manpower capacity, and the like, a simulation model should be an aggregated model. On the other hand, if a middle manager of a manufacturing firm is concerned with detailed operational information, the simulation model should be a detailed one.

Time Slice In most problem situations, the variables involved in a simulation model change over time. Therefore, the simulation process should be capable of revealing the current status of the important variables at each time period. Thus, determining the appropriate size of the time slice between time periods is a critical concern. In a simulation model designed for weekly analysis, such as material requirements planning (MRP) models, the time slice can be a day or even an hour. However, in an econometric simulation model designed for forecasting economic conditions, the time slice can be a month, a quarter, or a year.

THE PROCESS OF SIMULATION

The step-by-step process of simulation

Simulation is usually carried out in a sequence of several steps. These steps are important elements of the successful system experimentation process. The simulation process is presented in Figure 14.3.

Step 1: Problem Formulation A simulation model may be designed to generate information about the behavior of an existing system or to help develop a new system. Because a hospital may be experiencing rising operation costs, it may design a simulation model to uncover the contributing causes of the increasing costs. Similarly, an investment firm may experiment with alternative financing schemes for a new shopping center development project.

Formulating the problem

The initial step of the simulation process is to identify and formulate the problem or the purpose of the study. Objective or performance criteria, variables, decision rules, and parameters must be clearly defined. If the experimental objectives are not clearly specified by management, the simulation process has no definite guidelines. Thus, it is necessary to modify abstract objectives to more definite operational goals whenever possible.

Step 2: Analysis of Model Requirements In this step, all of the required data concerning variables and parameters must be identified. It is important to determine which variables and parameters are needed to measure the system performance. It is important in this step to classify the variables into two basic types: controllable and uncontrollable (see Chapter 2). Controllable variables are those within the influence of the decision maker. Uncontrollable variables are those influenced by exogenous factors. The simulation model should include controllable variables while holding other variables constant. The division of variables into two classifications is not always clear, and some experience is needed for proper definition.

Identifying the variables and parameters

Generally, data for parameters can be obtained from historical data. If such historical data are not available, they can be estimated from other information sources or judgments. It is also possible at this step to identify which variables are deterministic or stochastic.

Step 3: Model Development In most situations, it is effective to formulate a number of submodels according to their functions before aggregating them into a whole model. Obviously it is much easier to analyze smaller subsystems separately than to analyze a large and complex system in one operation. Once a number of submodels is formulated, the whole model can be developed by linking the submodels according to their logical relationship. The linkage must have a flexibility that allows easy revisions for possible changes.

Formulating submodels

In developing a simulation model, flowcharts are often very useful. A flowchart is simply a graphic aid that simplifies the logical process being used in simulation— it provides a visual aid to the mental process of simulation. We have already used flowcharts throughout this text. The most widely used flowchart outlines are shown in Figure 14.4.

Step 4: Programming the Model by Computer Language In this step, a model written by a natural language is transformed into a model written by a computer language. This transformation, often the most time-consuming and painful step, is necessary in order to run the model on the computer. However, a proper formulation of submodels makes this step much simpler. Also, a proper selection of a simulation language can be an important factor in the success of the model.

Using the computer

Figure 14.3   The Process of Simulation

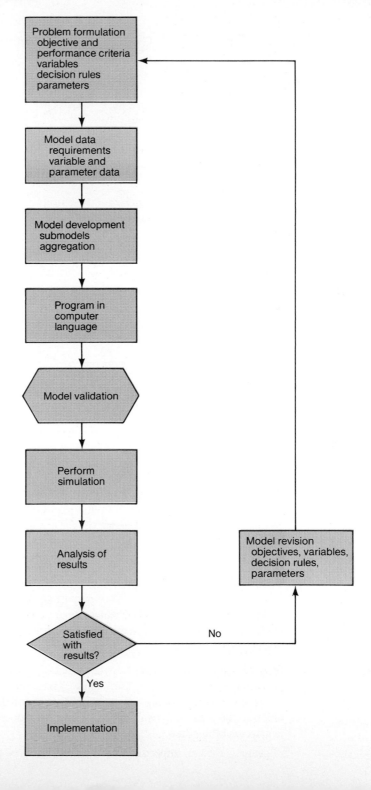

Figure 14.4   Basic Flowchart Outlines

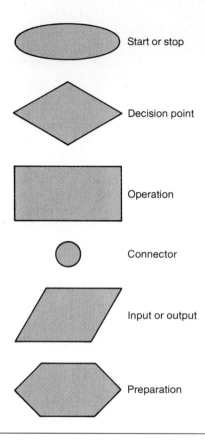

Start or stop

Decision point

Operation

Connector

Input or output

Preparation

Step 5: Validation of the Simulation Model In order to validate the simulation model, a number of test runs are often required. The results of these runs should be compared with the real data under similar conditions. If the test outputs deviate significantly from the real data, the whole process of modeling should be reexamined carefully.

Testing the model

Step 6: Perform Simulation Once the simulation model is designed and validated, it is run according to the scheme or purpose of the experiment. The simulation results under various experimental schemes are observed, and, if necessary, revisions are made in the model. In this step, user participation is extremely important in order to obtain practical results.

Running the model

Step 7: Analysis of Results Simulation usually yields operating statistics in the form of averages and probability distributions. Thus, analysis of results can be either simple or complex depending on the characteristics of the simulation objectives. In addition to the many technical aspects of analysis, successful interpretation is an important factor in this step.

Analyzing the results

In practice, the seven steps described above are not necessarily distinct steps nor are they in a rigid sequence. Some of these steps overlap, some can be simplified, and others may need to be expanded. The basic determining factors are: the objective of the study, the type of model, the capability of the simulation, the language used, and the availability of data. What is important is the completeness of the required analysis rather than strict adherence to the sequence of steps.

SIMULATION OF STOCHASTIC MODELS

Many decision problems that involve probabilistic (stochastic) events are difficult to solve by applying analytical techniques. This is especially true if a problem involves several random variables. We remember studying inventory problems with random lead times and random demand rates. Also, many waiting line problems involve random arrival rates and random service times. Such problems are good candidates for a simulation study. The majority of real-world applications of simulation is based on stochastic models.

The Monte Carlo Process

The Monte Carlo process

The *Monte Carlo* process is a procedure that generates values of a random variable based on one or more specific probability distributions. Thus, the Monte Carlo process is not a simulation method or a simulation model per se, although it has become almost synonymous with stochastic simulation. In actuality, the Monte Carlo process is simply an important technique that is extensively used for stochastic simulation.

History of the Monte Carlo idea

The Monte Carlo process was originated from the statistical sampling process. The basic idea of Monte Carlo is that the probabilities of certain events can be approximated by a sampling process based on a certain probability distribution. In general, the use of the Monte Carlo technique is attributed to John von Neumann and associates, who used the technique in various research efforts, including the development of the atomic bomb during World War II.

Random number generation

The Monte Carlo process is basically a two-stage procedure, as presented in Figure 14.5. In the first stage, when a command is given, a random number generator produces a number. By definition, the random numbers generated have a uniform probability distribution. In other words, each number should have an equal probability of being selected. The random number generator can be a simple device such as a deck of cards, a die, or colored balls in a hat, or it can be a complex computer-based device.

An example of a Monte Carlo process

The second stage of the Monte Carlo process is the transformation procedure. This manipulates the random number into the value that is useful, according to a specified distribution. For example, in an inventory problem the Monte Carlo process involves the following:

1. Generate a random number in order to determine a lead time.

2. Fit the random number generated into the probability distribution of the lead time.

3. Transform the random number into an appropriate lead time.

Figure 14.5   The Monte Carlo Process

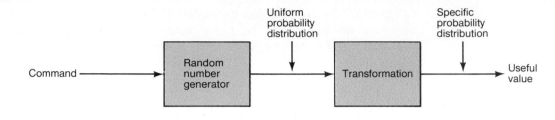

Examples of random variables

The basis of the Monte Carlo process is the generation of the values of random variables included in the simulation model. The following examples of random variables can provide us with useful insights:

Waiting line model
   Time between customer arrivals at a service location.
   Time between machine breakdowns.
   Service time (to serve a customer or repair a machine).

Project management model
   Time to complete an activity in a project.

Inventory model
   Lead time for a specific order.
   Demand per day.
   Time to process an order after it is received.
   Order quantity, when it is received.

Since random variables are included in almost all simulation models, we need to know how to obtain the random values for random variables. First we will look at the simple manual method of generating random values. Then, we will proceed to computer-based methods of generating uniform random numbers and their transformation into appropriate probability distributions.

Simple Random Number Generation and Transformation For simple problems, we can easily generate uniformly distributed random numbers without using a computer-based system. For example, we can use such methods as reading down the table of random numbers (see Appendix 7), rolling dice, flipping coins, spinning a number wheel, or the numbers-in-a-hat method.

A manual random number generator

Let us assume that the probability distribution given in Table 14.2 represents the demand per day for a particular product. Here, the random variable is the quantity demanded on a particular day. We are going to use an unbiased spinning wheel, as shown in Figure 14.6. Each segmented sector represents a demand according to its

Table 14.2   Probability Distribution of Demand per Day

Demand (D)	P(D)
0	0.1
1	0.2
2	0.3
3	0.3
4	0.1

Figure 14.6   Simulated Sampling by Spinning a Roulette Wheel

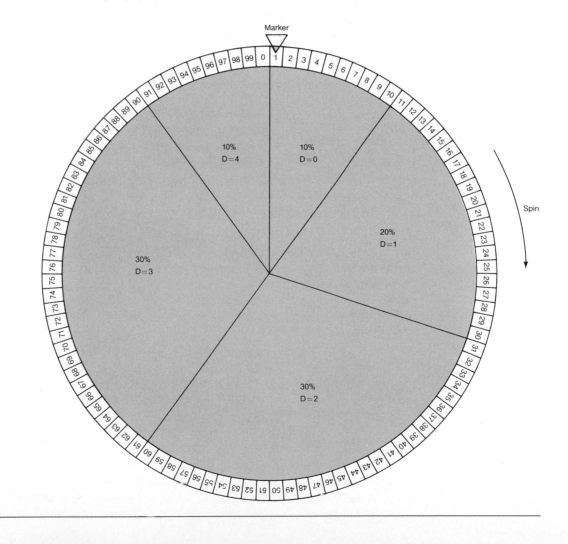

Table 14.3   Cumulative Probability Distribution of Daily Demand

Demand (D)	P(D)	Cumulative Probability, F(D) = P(Demand ≤ D)	Random Number Interval
0	0.1	0.1	0.01–0.10
1	0.2	0.3	0.11–0.30
2 ←————	0.3 ←	0.6 ←	0.31–0.60 ←
3	0.3	0.9	0.61–0.90
4	0.1	1.0	0.91–1.00

$r = 0.50$

corresponding probability. For example, 10 percent of the spinning wheel area is occupied by $D = 0$. By *unbiased* we mean that the result of a spin will be the same regardless of the starting position of the roulette wheel or the spinning power.

Spinning a roulette wheel can generate a random number for a random variable, in this case the demand on a particular day. If we continue using this method, over many spins of the wheel the relative frequency of demand generated will approximate the probability distribution given in Table 14.2. This procedure is, in fact, a Monte Carlo process.

Although the spinning wheel method provides us with the randomly selected daily demand in one operation, most Monte Carlo processes require the transformation stage. The transformation stage may be based on a tabular form, a graphical method, or a mathematical transformation technique. Here we will examine the tabular and graphical methods. The mathematical transformation will be discussed later in this chapter.

Transforming random values

Tabular Method The tabular method is perhaps the simplest and easiest way to transform a random number. This method is based on the cumulative probability function. Table 14.3 presents the same basic data presented in Table 14.2 but with two additional columns. The third column presents the cumulative probability distribution of daily demand, $F(D)$. The fourth column is for the intervals of random numbers that match the cumulative probability distribution. For example, the probability of 2 units demanded is 0.3. In the cumulative probability column, we can see that the range of this demand ($D = 2$) is between 0.3 and 0.6. Thus, if we generate a 2-digit random number between 0 and 1, then the random number interval should be exactly as shown in the fourth column.

Utilizing a cumulative probability distribution

Now we are ready to make any transformation. For example, suppose we generated a random number r. The number we found is 0.50. Since 0.50 falls in the 0.31–0.60 range of intervals, the daily demand represented by this random number can be easily determined by simply following the arrows in Table 14.3. In this case, the daily demand will be 2 units.

A graphical method

Graphical Method The graphical method is also a simple way to transform a uniformly distributed random number into a meaningful number in a specific distribution. In order to use the graphical method, we must prepare a graph of the cumulative probability distribution. For our daily demand determination example, the cumulative

Figure 14.7 *Cumulative Probability Distribution of Daily Demand*

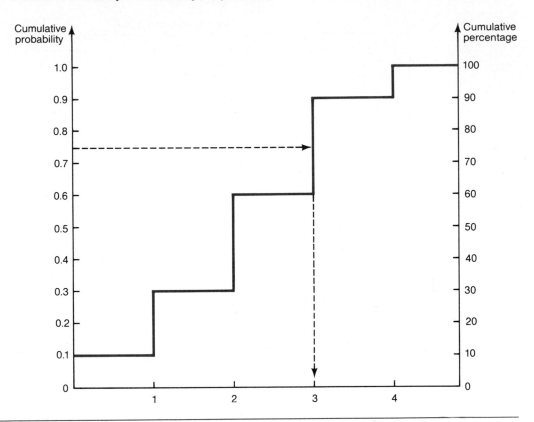

probability distribution of daily demand is expressed by $F(D)$, as shown in Table 14.3. Figure 14.7 provides the graphical presentation of $F(D)$.

Suppose that a random number is generated and it is found to be 0.75. By tracing the graph we can easily determine that the corresponding daily demand for this particular random number is 3 units, as shown in Figure 14.7. Notice that the length of the vertical lines at each demand, D, corresponds exactly to the probability of each demand, $P(D)$. For example, let us consider $D = 1$. The probability of a daily demand for 1 unit, $P(1)$, is shown by the vertical line from 0.1 to 0.3, yielding a probability of 0.2, or 20 percent.

CASETTE 14.1 MACHINE REPAIR PROBLEM
OF THE MILWAUKEE CONSTRUCTION COMPANY

The Milwaukee Construction Company is a medium-sized construction firm specializing in erecting professional office buildings. Currently, the company has three identical cranes. These cranes represent the most valuable equipment the company has in

Figure 14.8   Functional Block Diagram for the Machine Shop Operation

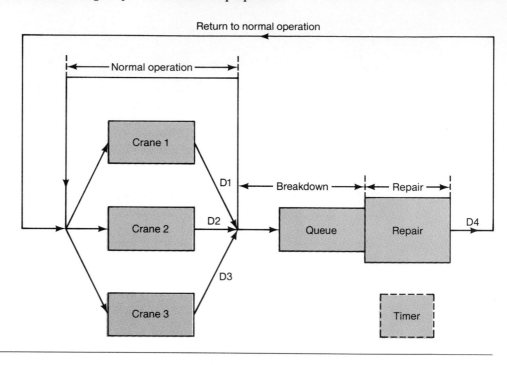

terms of cost and use. The company has only one repairman for the cranes. Thus, in case of a crane breakdown, construction work may be delayed. Mr. William Cane, President of the company, is naturally very interested in finding ways to reduce the breakdown rate of the three cranes.

Another of Mr. Cane's concerns is reducing repair time. No accurate statistics are currently available for both the frequency of crane breakdown and repair time. After conferring with his staff, Mr. Cane decided to ask a local consulting firm, Infotech, for help. Bert Erlanger, a management scientist at Infotech, paid a visit to Milwaukee Construction and examined the problem.

Bert concluded that there was little chance of utilizing any analytical technique to study the crane breakdown problem. Thus, he decided to use a simulation approach to collect the data about crane utilization. Bert is a firm believer in user participation. Hence, he explained to Mr. Cane how the simulation process works and showed that the study results come from a valid representation of the real system.

Modeling the Machine Shop Operation

A machine shop model

Bert decided that the best way to demonstrate the simulation process is to first work the problem out manually. Thus, he developed a simple model to represent the machine shop operation, as shown in Figure 14.8.

Every block in Figure 14.8 indicates the location where a miniature crane (or a simpler indicator, such as a card) is to be put. We can easily note that the condition

Table 14.4 **Crane-Status Table**

Time Period (Half-Hour)	Crane 1			Crane 2			Crane 3		
	Oper.	Queue	Repair	Oper.	Queue	Repair	Oper.	Queue	Repair
1	✓					✓	✓		
2	✓					✓	✓		
3	✓					✓	✓		
4		✓				✓	✓		
5			✓	✓			✓		
.									
.									
.									
23			✓	✓					✓
24	✓			✓					✓

of the machine shop can be broken down into three stages: normal operation, breakdown, and repair. When all three crane blocks are filled up, it is obvious that all cranes are in normal operation. When a crane is moved into the QUEUE or REPAIR block, it is waiting for repair or is being repaired. Since there are three cranes, three of the five blocks must be filled at all times.

The next thing Bert introduced in the model is TIMER. This is not necessarily a real timer. Nevertheless, it indicates the amount of time elapsed during operation. For example, let us get a deck of 24 cards, with a numerical label, ranging from 1 to 24, printed on each card. In order to represent a 12-hour operation period, each card will represent one half-hour time block. Thus, by putting these 24 cards in sequence on the TIMER block and checking the number of the card on the top, we can ascertain the duration of crane operation time. In simulation, it is important to store the timed operational statistics.

Developing the crane status table

Table 14.4 presents the crane-status tabulation. The first column indicates the passage of time (i.e., time period). The time period number must be identical to the card number on the TIMER block. For each crane, there are three condition columns: operating, queuing, and repairing. One of these columns must be checked at a given time period for each crane, depending in which block in Figure 14.8 each crane is located. Then, at the end of simulation, crane downtime can be easily computed by counting the number of checkmarks in the queue and repair columns and multiplying them by one half-hour.

Stochastic Variables

Defining the stochastic variables

As we discussed earlier, it is important to classify variables as either deterministic or stochastic. For a deterministic variable, there is no need to generate random numbers. However, for a stochastic variable, we need some sort of mechanism that generates random numbers according to an appropriate statistical distribution.

In the machine breakdown problem of the Milwaukee Construction Company, there are basically two stochastic variables: (1) a variable that indicates whether a crane is in normal operation or in need of repair, and (2) a variable that indicates whether or not a crane under repair can be returned to normal operating condition.

Table 14.5   *Repair Time and Probability of Occurence*

	Repair Time Period (Half Hour)	Probability of Occurrence
	1	0.3
	2	0.2
	3	0.3
	4	0.2

Stochastic Variable—Crane Breakdowns Since there exist no reliable data on crane breakdowns, Bert Erlanger decided to assume that a crane breakdown occurs in a random fashion. On the basis of his observations and interviews with the crane operators, however, he roughly estimated that a crane breakdown occurs once in every 12 half-hours (i.e., every 6 hours). In other words, the probability that a crane breakdown occurs in a given time period (half hour) is approximately 0.083.

Generating random numbers for crane breakdowns

Now we are ready to generate random numbers. Let us prepare 3 decks of cards, each deck contains 10 cards from 0 to 9. The reason for preparing 3 card decks is that we need to generate a number that has 3 digits below the decimal point (e.g., 0.125 is derived when we draw a 1 from Deck 1, 2 from Deck 2, and 5 from Deck 3). Since we draw each of 3 cards from a different card deck, the randomness of the value generated is guaranteed.

The random number (r) that we generate by this mechanism is always between zero and 1 (i.e., $0 \leq r < 1.000$). It should be obvious by now that we are generating a number that represents a probability. Since the probability of machine breakdown is estimated to be 0.083, we can establish the following decision rule:

> If $r > 0.083$, crane is in normal operation.
> If $r \leq 0.083$, crane is in need of repair.

For example, let us suppose that the cards we drew from the 3 decks at Time Period 10 are 1, 3, and 5. Then, we have a probability value of 0.135. This number is clearly greater than the probability of crane breakdown of 0.083. Thus, the crane under analysis is considered to be in normal operating condition. Conversely, if we draw a random number that is less than or equal to 0.083, the crane will be considered broken down and in need of repair.

Stochastic Variable—Repair Time A similar mechanism can be developed to generate

Generating random numbers for repair time

random numbers for repair time. On the basis of historical data, Bert could estimate the repair time. The repair time duration ranges from one time period (a half hour) to 4 time periods (2 hours). Table 14.5 presents the repair time duration and corresponding probabilities.

Since the probability is represented by one number below the decimal point, we can use a single deck of cards containing cards from 0 to 9. We shuffle the deck and draw a card. If the number is drawn is 5, then the probability is 0.5. Now we must check the area in which this probability falls. Figure 14.9 presents 4 probability areas for the 4 possible repair time periods. Since probability 0.5 falls in Area P_2, we can interpret that the required repair is 2 half-hour periods, or one hour.

Figure 14.9   Crane Repair Time under Uniform Distribution

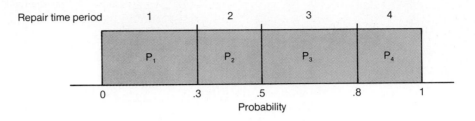

We developed two random-number-generating mechanisms in order to determine values of the two stochastic variables: breakdown and repair time. These values determined by random numbers must be checked at points D1, D2, D3, and D4 in Figure 14.8. These points represent *decision points*.

The Simulation Procedure

The simulation procedure

In the previous section, Bert Erlanger introduced two important concepts: simulation modeling and random number generation. Now we are ready to perform simulation for the machine repair problem. The simulation procedure can be either very simple or very complex, depending on the level of detail needed. The simulation procedure of the machine repair problem, presented in Figure 4.10 as a flowchart diagram, attempts to obtain information about crane utilization.

The entire procedure consists of five subprocedures: (1) initialization, (2) time-advance, (3) check-crane-breakdown, (4) check-repair, and (5) computer-output. Notice that each subprocedure is named according to its basic task. Now, let us examine each subprocedure in detail.

Initializing the simulation process

Initialization This subprocedure prepares for the simulation run. Block 0 sets all three cranes in operating positions (i.e., the three blocks of cranes in Figure 14.8) and also sets the TIMER at zero by putting time card 0 on the TIMER block in Figure 14.8. Preparation of a set of card decks for random number generation and the Crane-Status Table are not included in the flowchart. However, they are assumed to be included in this subprocedure. Admittedly, this step is simple, but without a proper utilization step no valid simulation is possible.

The time-advance mechanism

Time-Advance Blocks 1 and 2 accomplish the task of advancing time. These blocks check the available time cards on the TIMER, and if a card is available, then time is advanced by putting a new time card on top of the previous time cards on the TIMER. The time-advance is an important function of the simulation procedure.

Determining the crane breakdown

Check-Crane-Breakdown Blocks 3 and 10 perform the task of determining whether or not each crane is broken down. First, Crane 1 is examined for its operational condition. If it is operational, a random number is generated by drawing three numbers from three different card decks, as we explained earlier. By comparing this random number with the probability of machine breakdown ($P = 0.083$), we can determine whether or not the crane is broken down. If the crane is broken down ($r \leq 0.083$), we record this change of status for Crane 1 in the Crane-Status Table and move the

Figure 14.10   Simulation Procedure for the Machine Repair Problem

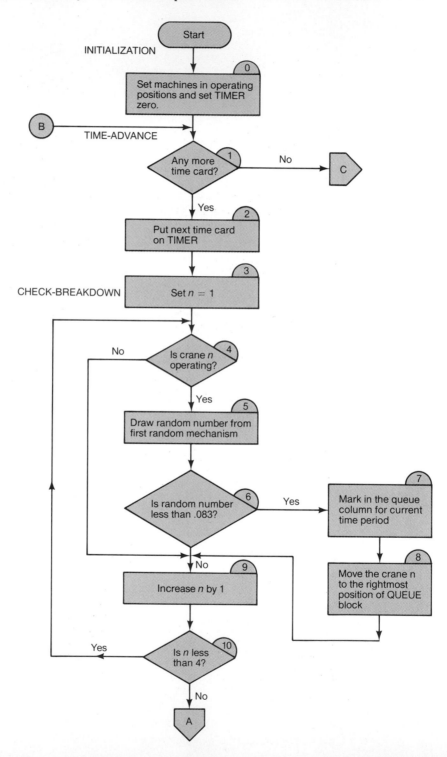

Figure 14.10 *(continued)*

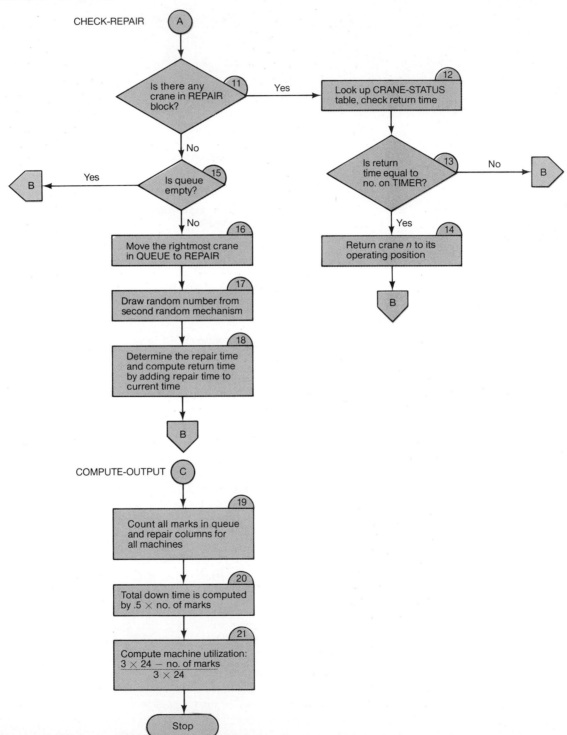

Table 14.6   *Event List of a Single Simulation Run*

Time	Events (or Transactions)
1	Crane 2 is in repair, repair time = 4 units
2	—
3	—
4	Crane 1 is broken down and in queue
5	Crane 1 is in repair, repair time = 3 units
	Crane 2 returns to operation
6	—
7	—
8	—
9	Crane 1 returns to operation
10	—
11	Crane 3 is broken down , repair time = 3 units
12	—
13	Crane 2 is broken down and in queue, repair time = 2 units
14	Crane 3 returns to operation
	Crane 2 is in repair
15	—
16	Crane 2 returns to operation
17	—
18	Crane 3 is broken down, repair time = 4 units
19	Crane 1 is broken down and in queue, repair time = 2 units
20	—
21	—
22	Crane 3 returns to operation
	Crane 1 is in repair, repair time = 2 units
23	—
24	Crane 1 returns to operation

crane to the QUEUE block (see Blocks 7 and 8). If the crane is not broken down, we proceed to the next crane until the operational conditions of all of the cranes are checked (Blocks 3, 9, and 10).

Check-Repair In this subprocedure, we determine whether or not the repair of a crane is completed. We determine the repair time through the second random number generator, as explained earlier. Thus, if a crane is already in the repair shop, we can simply compare the TIMER time and return time. If these two times are identical, the crane has been repaired and it returns to normal operating condition (Blocks 11 to 14).

Determining the repair time

After a crane completes its repair service, we must examine the QUEUE block to see whether or not there is any other crane waiting for repair work (Block 15). If there is no crane waiting for repair, then, because no additional checking is necessary, we go back to Block 1 and advance to the next time period. If there is one or more cranes in QUEUE, we move the rightmost crane to the REPAIR block and indicate this change in the appropriate column of the Crane-Status Table.

There is one more task remaining. That is to determine the repair time of the crane that just moved into REPAIR by using the second random number generator.

Table 14.7 Crane-Status Table for a Single Run

Time Period (Half Hour)	Crane 1			Crane 2			Crane 3		
	Oper.	Queue	Repair	Oper.	Queue	Repair	Oper.	Queue	Repair
1	√					√	√		
2	√					√	√		
3	√					√	√		
4	√					√	√		
5	√			√			√		
6			√	√			√		
7			√	√			√		
8			√	√			√		
9	√			√			√		
10	√			√			√		
11	√			√					√
12	√			√					√
13	√					√			√
14	√					√	√		
15	√					√	√		
16	√			√			√		
17	√			√			√		
18	√			√					√
19		√		√					√
20		√		√					√
21		√		√					√
22			√	√			√		
23			√	√			√		
24	√			√			√		

By simply adding the repair time to the current time, we can obtain the return time of the crane. Blocks 16 to 18 accomplish this task.

Compute-Output This subprocedure concludes the simulation procedure. We attempt to obtain information about crane utilization. Thus, we first compute the downtime and then compute the crane utilization time by the simple formula presented in Block 21.

Derive the result

Result of a Single Simulation Run

A single simulation run

Let us examine the *event list* of one actual simulation run for the span of 24 time periods (12 hours), as shown in Table 14.6. This event list is actually based on the information in the Crane-Status Table shown in Table 14.7. Table 14.8 summarizes the downtime and waiting time for each crane during the 24 time periods; the table also presents the total crane downtime and crane utilization in terms of percentage (69.4 percent).

After completing the simulation work for the Milwaukee Construction Company, Bert Erlanger made the following observation: "In order to obtain reliable output, Milwaukee Construction should run a lot more simulations than 24 time periods, perhaps about 10,000 time periods." This statement clearly makes sense. Since there are two stochastic variables, a great number of runs would make the results more

Table 14.8   Machine Utilization for a Single Run

Machine	Downtime (Hr.)	Waiting Time (Hr.)
Crane 1	4.0	1.5
Crane 2	3.5	0.5
Crane 3	3.5	0

Machine utilization = 0.694
Total waiting time = 2 hr.
Waiting time in worst case = 1.5 hr.

reliable. Nevertheless, it must be added here that it is not a simple matter to determine exactly how many simulation runs would guarantee valid results. In order to answer this question, we need much experience in applying various simulation approaches to real-world problems and perhaps a great deal of rigorous analytical work.

GENERATING RANDOM NUMBERS

Systematic ways to generate random numbers

An essential element of stochastic simulation is the generation of random numbers. In a simple simulation model, we can use a manual procedure to generate random numbers (dice, a roulette wheel, a deck of cards, numbers in a hat, etc.). However, in most simulation models we need a more systematic way to generate random numbers as they play such a significant role in the validity of the simulation results.

Table of Random Numbers

The random number table

Appendix 7 presents an excerpt from a random number table. The random numbers in the table were generated by a numerical technique. A long sequence of numbers generated by a numerical technique usually repeats itself after a certain number of iterations. Thus, these numbers are not true random numbers. Consequently, they are often referred to as *pseudorandom numbers*. True random numbers are usually generated by some physical process such as electrical noise, which is naturally random.

Pseudorandom numbers

In using the random number table, we can use one of two approaches: (1) select a number in a random fashion (e.g., close your eyes and place your pencil on the random number table); or (2) select a number according to a fixed pattern (e.g., pick every third number from the top). You can use your creativity in using the table.

Mid-Square Method

The mid-square method

The mid-square method was first studied by John von Neumann. This method employs a starting number, referred to as a *seed* value, and generates a series of random numbers. For example, if we use 4,745 as the initial value, then it is squared and selected middle-digit numbers are used as a random number. Then, this random number is squared to find the next random number, and so on, as in the following example:

$$\text{Seed value} = 4{,}745$$
$$(4{,}745)^2 = 22\boxed{5150}25;\ r_1 = 5{,}150$$
$$(5{,}150)^2 = 26\boxed{5225}00;\ r_2 = 5{,}225$$
$$(5{,}225)^2 = 27\boxed{3006}25;\ r_3 = 3{,}006$$
$$(3{,}006)^2 = \cdots,\ \text{etc.}$$

Of course, these random numbers must be divided by 10,000 in order to generate a decimal number between 0 and 1. This method yields a set of pseudorandom numbers that can be used in a simulation model. However, this is not an efficient way to generate random numbers because of its computational complexities and time requirement.

Mid-Product Method

The mid-product method

The mid-product method is similar to the mid-square method in that both use a seed value and select middle-digit numbers. The only difference is that in the mid-product method, instead of squaring the value, we multiply a constant. For example, let us use the same seed value as before (4,745) and a constant of 123. Then the random number generation process will be:

$$\text{Seed value} = 4{,}745;\ \text{constant} = 123$$
$$123(4{,}745) = 5\boxed{8363}5;\ r_1 = 8{,}363$$
$$123(8{,}363) = 10\boxed{2864}9;\ r_2 = 2{,}864$$
$$123(2{,}864) = 3\boxed{5227}2;\ r_3 = 5{,}227$$
$$123(5{,}227) = \cdots,\ \text{etc.}$$

This method generates a set of pseudorandom numbers as does the mid-square method. However, it also shares the same basic inefficiency as the mid-square method.

Random Number Transformation

There are a number of different methods to generate random numbers by the computer. Some of these methods use complex procedures, such as the multiplicative congruential method. Discussions of these procedures are beyond the scope of this text. Instead, we will discuss how uniform random numbers are transformed into random numbers for a given distribution. There are a number of methods of transformation, such as the inverse transformation, the tabular method, the method of convolution, and so on. We will study the *inverse transformation* method because it is the simplest and the most fundamental technique of generating random numbers from a probability distribution.

The inverse transformation method

The basic approach of inverse transformation is to get random numbers from the cumulative probability distribution that may be based on historical data. Suppose that we wish to generate random numbers from a probability distribution $F(x)$. If we have a uniform random number, r, and if we know how to determine x from $F(x)$, then we can generate numbers with distribution $F(x)$ by first generating r and then taking $x = F^{-1}(x)$. This inverse transformation method is illustrated in Figure 14.11.

The inverse transformation method is the same basic approach we used in the tabular method (Table 14.3) and the graphical method (Figure 14.7), where we used

Figure 14.11   Inverse Transformation Procedure

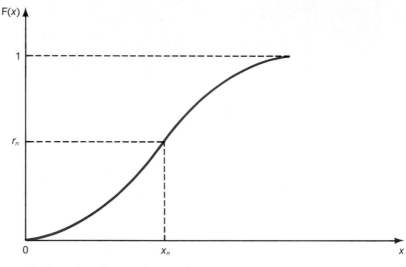

(1) Generate uniform random number r_n

(2) Find x_n by using $F^{-1}(x)$.

a discrete distribution. If we had a continuous distribution, the cumulative distribution would be represented by a continuous function, as shown in Figure 14.11.

A computer-based simulation model

In a computer-based simulation model, we can use one of a number of different random number generators as a subroutine in the system. Even though random number generators have a wide variety of computational schemes and their purposes differ sometimes (e.g., a normal random number generator or an exponential random number generator), the basic approach used is almost the same. Appendix 8 presents a computer program to generate values of random variables. Figure 14.12 presents a flowchart for the random generation of daily demand that we discussed in Table 14.3.

CASETTE 14.2   AN INVENTORY PROBLEM AT PEACH COMPUTERS, INC.

An inventory problem

Peach Computers, Inc. specializes in selling various personal computers. Recently, the company has been experiencing widely fluctuating inventories for its Saturn X computers. William Sharpe, the Office Manager, is interested in experimenting with various inventory policy options before selecting an acceptable one. The primary policy decisions are concerned with the order quantity and the reorder point.

The office has good historical data concerning past lead time, weekly demand, and associated inventory costs. Although Bill has not been able to pinpoint the unit shortage cost, there are some lost sales when computers are not available for sale. Thus, Bill would like to obtain information about the total inventory cost and the

Figure 14.12   Flowchart of Random Generation of Daily Demand

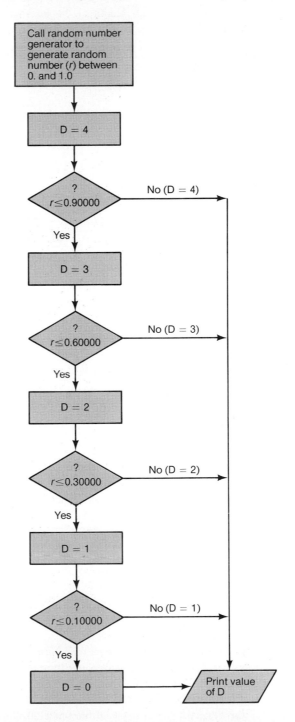

Note: Program generates the value of *D* as the "last" value set equal to *D*.

probability of computer shortage associated with a given order quantity and reorder point.

After a thorough search of the historical data, Bill was able to determine the following:

Annual holding cost per computer (*HC*): $104 ($2/week)
Ordering cost per order (*OC*): $30

Weekly Demand Distribution	
Computers	Probability
0	0.3
1	0.4
2	0.3
	1.0

Lead Time Distribution	
Weeks	Probability
1	0.25
2	0.50
3	0.25
	1.00

Simulation Procedure

Bill would like to experiment with order quantities ranging from 5 to 10 and reorder points from 2 to 5. In order to establish a valid pattern for inventory levels throughout a year (52 weeks) for each of the 24 combinations of order quantities and reorder points (6 different order quantities × 4 different reorder points = 24), Bill would like to run a sufficient number of simulation runs to draw valid conclusions.

An important subprocedure of this simulation study is the determination of total demand during a lead time. Since lead time varies from 1 to 3 weeks, weekly demand must be calculated for as many weeks as the selected lead time. Table 14.9 presents the cumulative probabilities and random number intervals for the weekly demand and lead time. Figure 14.13 presents the flowchart of the procedure for determining the demand during lead time (*DDLT*).

In order to determine the total annual inventory cost for various combinations of order quantity (*Q*) and reorder point (*R*), the simulation model is designed as shown in Figure 14.14. This process adjusts the inventory level, initiates the necessary orders, and computes the total inventory cost for various combinations of Q and R.

Simulation Results

The beginning inventory level of Saturn X computers in the first week is assumed to be 5 units. Table 14.10 presents the results of the first 5 runs based on an order quantity of 5 units and a reorder point of 2.

Bill first conducted a complete simulation of the problem for 24,000 runs, 1,000 runs for each combination of the order quantity (*Q*) and reorder point (*R*). The result

Table 14.9 Monte Carlo Process for the Inventory Problem

	Weekly Demand		
Units	Probability	Cumulative Probability	Random Number Intervals
0	0.3	0.3	1–30
1	0.4	0.7	31–70
2	0.3	1.0	71–100

	Lead Time		
Weeks	Probability	Cumulative Probability	Random Number Intervals
1	0.25	0.25	1–25
2	0.50	0.75	26–75
3	0.25	1.00	76–100

Table 14.10 Five Inventory Simulation Runs ($Q = 5$, $R = 2$)

Week	Lead Time		Weekly Demand		Ending Inventory	Holding Cost/ Week	Ordering Cost	Total Cost
	Random Number	Weeks	Random Number	Units				
0					7			
1	—	—	56	1	6	$12	—	$12
2	—	—	91	2	4	8	—	8
3	62	2	88	2	2	4	$30	34
4	—	—	16	0	2	4	—	4
5	—	—	59	1	6	12	—	12

of the computer run is presented in Figure 14.15. Although the difference in the average total annual inventory cost is relatively small among the 24 combinations, there are significant differences in the average annual stock-out.

Bill believes that Peach Computers cannot afford to lose customers because of a continuous shortage of Saturn X computers. Thus, the absolute ceiling of average stock-outs is set at 5 computers per year. On the basis of this policy decision, Peach Computers decided to adopt an inventory policy of EOQ $= 9$, $R = 3$. With this policy, the company can expect the minimum total inventory cost of $1,586.15 per year.

Figure 14.13   Determining the Demand during Lead Time

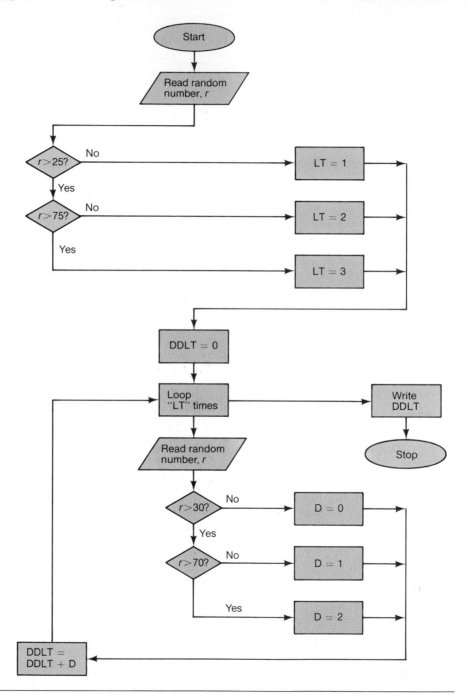

Figure 14.14   Peach Computer Inventory Simulation Model

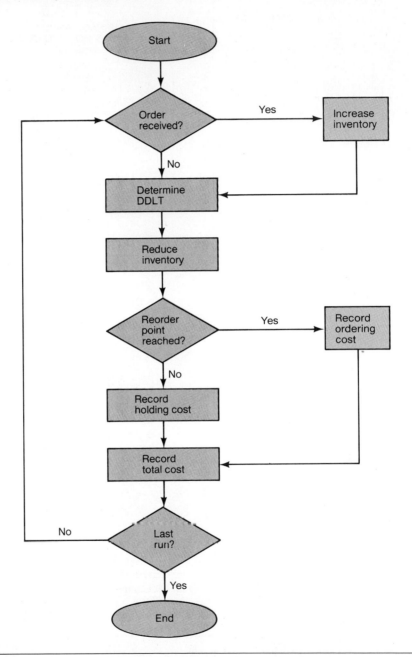

Figure 14.15   Inventory Simulation Results, 24,000 runs

```
.invensim output
```

Q = 5	R	AVERAGE ANNUAL ORDER & HOLDING COST	AVERAGE ANNUAL STOCK-OUT
	2	1596.02	13.93
	3	1598.43	4.88
	4	1597.22	1.17
	5	1594.08	0.19

Q = 6	R	AVERAGE ANNUAL ORDER & HOLDING COST	AVERAGE ANNUAL STOCK-OUT
	2	1601.60	14.02
	3	1601.47	4.96
	4	1596.31	1.14
	5	1596.89	0.19

Q = 7	R	AVERAGE ANNUAL ORDER & HOLDING COST	AVERAGE ANNUAL STOCK-OUT
	2	1598.00	14.16
	3	1594.87	4.85
	4	1594.09	1.12
	5	1598.15	0.19

Q = 8	R	AVERAGE ANNUAL ORDER & HOLDING COST	AVERAGE ANNUAL STOCK-OUT
	2	1592.07	13.79
	3	1592.80	4.91
	4	1591.65	1.15
	5	1603.15	0.17

Q = 9	R	AVERAGE ANNUAL ORDER & HOLDING COST	AVERAGE ANNUAL STOCK-OUT
	2	1595.23	13.94
	3	1586.15	4.79
	4	1594.31	1.05
	5	1599.98	0.16

Q = 10	R	AVERAGE ANNUAL ORDER & HOLDING COST	AVERAGE ANNUAL STOCK-OUT
	2	1595.62	14.01
	3	1594.00	4.90
	4	1593.09	1.16
	5	1595.02	0.18

Table 14.11   Total Inventory Cost for Various Q and R Combinations

Quantity Ordered (Q)	Reorder Point (R)			
	3	4	5	6
10	$1,215	$1,110	$980	$1,025
11	1,079	1,002	874	926
12	945	836	746	795
13	926	812	728	774
14	981	864	769	821

OPTIMIZATION IN SIMULATION

Deriving an optimum solution through simulation

As we discussed earlier, the simulation model usually provides descriptive results about the behavior of a system under study. However, for certain problems, we may be able to use a subroutine in the model in such a way that simulation, through its search process, will provide us with the best solution. The best solution selected by this procedure is *optimum* in the sense that it is the best among the solutions generated by simulation. However, it is not the same as the optimum solution that we obtain from a linear program.

An example

The optimum solution derived by an analytical technique such as linear programming is truly optimum. The best solution derived by a simulation model is only approximate or quasi-optimum. Nevertheless, if the simulation process is carefully designed and includes a large enough number of runs to derive valid conclusions, simulation can produce a "good" approximate optimum solution.

As we demonstrated in Casette 14.2, we can easily determine the best combination of order quantity (Q) and reorder point (R) that yields the minimum total inventory cost. For example, suppose that the total inventory cost (TC) function is given as follows:

$$TC = THC + TOC + TSC$$

where

THC = total annual holding cost
TOC = total annual ordering cost
TSC = total annual stock-out cost

Now, we can set Q to a certain number and vary the value of R and determine the total inventory cost for that combination by selecting the lead time and demand rate through a Monte Carlo process. If we simulate 100 runs for each combination, the average TC of the combination can be taken as a good approximation. On the basis of this process, the simulation model can compare the average TC for each Q and R combination and select the best inventory policy. In order to assist the decision maker, we can construct a summary table as shown in Table 14.11. In this summary, the minimum total inventory cost ($728) is obtained when $Q = 13$ and $R = 5$.

SIMULATION LANGUAGES

Construction of a simulation model usualy requires the development of a computer program. This phase of simulation modeling is often a very time-consuming step. Fortunately, there are several widely used general simulation languages available. A selection of the most appropriate simulation language for the given problem can save us much time and cost.

Generalized simulation languages

Most simulation programs have many similar functions, such as generating random numbers, advancing time, recording intermediate results for analysis, and the like. In recognition of such similarities, a generalized simulation was developed in the 1950s. Since then, several other simulation languages have been developed.

Best-known languages

The best-known and most widely available simulation languages are GPSS (General Purpose Simulation System), SIMSCRIPT, SIMULA, GASP IV, and DYNAMO. We will discuss each of these simulation languages briefly.

GPSS

This is one of the most widely used simulation languages available today. It was developed by IBM in the early 1960s. Its latest version is GPSS/360. Although GPSS is often classified as a flowchart-oriented language, it is also effective for systems with complex processes. Thus, it is quite compatible with problems that involve queues or networks. Knowledge of computer programming is not a prerequisite for using GPSS.

SIMSCRIPT

SIMSCRIPT, developed by the RAND Corporation in the early 1960s, is a generalized simulation and programming language. Its latest version is SIMSCRIPT II. The use of SIMSCRIPT requires a knowledge of computer programming.

SIMULA

SIMULA was developed by O. J. Dahl and K. Nygaard and released by the Norwegian Computing Center in 1965. The latest version is SIMULA 67. This language is quite similar to SIMSCRIPT.

GASP IV

GASP is not a complete, generalized simulation language. Rather, it is a set of subroutines in FORTRAN. GASP II was developed by A. Pritsker and P. Kiviat in 1967, and its current version, GASP IV, was developed by Pritsker and N. R. Hurst in 1973. Since GASP IV is written entirely in FORTRAN IV, it has an important advantage over other simulation languages in terms of its flexible subroutine modification capabilities for different purposes.

DYNAMO

DYNAMO was developed by P. Fox and A. Pugh at M.I.T. in 1959. This language was an outgrowth of J. Forrester's *Industrial Dynamics* modeling approach. It is particularly efficient in analyzing the dynamic behaviors of large-scale industrial systems. DYNAMO requires very little computer programming knowledge for its use.

APPLICATIONS OF SIMULATION

Some application examples

Simulation has been applied to many decision problems that are too complex to be analyzed by analytical techniques. What is impressive about simulation is that a great number of the studies dealing with this topic are about applications to real-world problems. Let us briefly discuss some of the best-known application areas of simulation.

Queuing Problems

Perhaps the most prevalent application area of simulation is queuing problems. As we discussed in Chapter 12, in many real-world queuing problems, the only avenue open to systematic analysis is simulation.

Inventory Problems

Many inventory problems involve several random variables such as lead time, demand rate, time required to process an order, and quantity received. As we saw in Casette 14.2, simulation is an effective tool for analyzing complex inventory problems.

Network Problems

In many network problems, all parameters are not as neatly provided as we need for using PERT or CPM. There are many random events we must deal with in network systems, such as probabilistic activity times, branching, and performance. Many stochastic network simulation programs have been developed recently. Three of these are GERT IIIZ, Q-GERT, and VERT III.

Operations Planning

Many operations management problems, including production, inventory control, warehousing, plant layout, assembly line balancing, location-allocation, and maintenance, involve complex stochastic processes. Simulation has been applied extensively to these problems.

Financial Planning

Many financial problems are influenced by external factors (e.g., state of the economy, interest rates, monetary policy, and foreign trade). Thus, it is difficult to use analytical techniques for such problems. Simulation has been applied to such financial problems as overall corporate financial planning, capital budgeting, working capital management, and cash flow analysis.

Policy Analysis

Recently there have been reported many interesting applications of simulation that deal with public policies. Among these are operational policy decisions for schools, police departments, fire departments, sewage treatment plants, judiciary systems, land development, water resources, environmental protection, and tax systems.

Artificial Intelligence and Heuristic Programming

Artificial intelligence

Artificial intelligence deals with simulating human thought through computers. Although the attempt to make the computer think intelligently is still far from complete, much progress has been made in using the computer to search, recognize patterns, prove mathematical relationships, and learn from experience.

Heuristic programming

An area related to artificial intelligence is heuristic programming. Heuristics are basically step-by-step procedures that are used to obtain satisficing solutions to complex problems. Heuristic programming is the general approach that uses heuristics to derive "good enough" solutions to poorly structured problems. Simulation has a great potential in these new areas of human decision making.

Business Games

Business games

Many business games (management games, decision games, simulation games, marketing games, investment games, operational games, and the like) are useful educational or training tools that simulate realistic settings for decision making. The basic purpose of simulation games is to provide the participants with an intuitive feel for the effect of interrelated variables on a decision outcome.

System Simulation

Industrial dynamics

System simulation usually involves an analysis of the dynamic behavior of a very large-scale system, such as the national economic system, the world population problem, or an urban system. System simulation is based on the *Industrial Dynamics* modeling approach developed by J. Forrester. The simulation model includes many mathematical equations for the flow of resources or their interactions in a computer program. Then, through time lags and feedback systems built into the model, the simulation model provides information concerning the effects of various policies or inputs.

REAL-WORLD APPLICATIONS

Application to real-world problems

In view of the general applicability of simulation and today's easy access to inexpensive computing facilities, it is natural to expect wide applications of simulation. The literature of management science certainly supports this trend. Furthermore, we expect that this trend will continue at an accelerating rate. We believe that simulation will play an even greater role in the application of management science to real-world decision problems in the years to come. In this section we will briefly review two interesting real-world applications of simulation.

A Simulation Model for a Mining Operation

This award-winning study is concerned with a successful application of dynamic simulation to the process of selecting, examining, and modifying the design of mining equipment.[1] This study was conducted by Canadian Bechtel Limited for Syncrude Canada Limited. Syncrude is a consortium of several government and oil companies authorized by the Alberta government of Canada to implement petroleum recovery from the vast quantities of crude oil locked in the Athabasca tar sands. It has been estimated that the Athabasca tar sands contain up to 600 billion barrels of oil, with the recoverable volume estimated at 300 billion barrels.

Syncrude had been applying a simulation program to model its dragline/train operations. Bechtel came on the job in 1972 and began evaluating the base case mining concept. This approach led to a consideration of a bucketwheel scheme. Thus, Bechtel utilized dynamic simulation to investigate the total system availability and production level for several versions of the bucketwheel scheme. Syncrude concurred that simulation was an expedient way to analyze blockages and bottlenecks and to size the bucketwheel equipment appropriately. Thus, Bechtel was given the project to develop, within a 7-week period, a new simulation model for the 105,000-barrel-per-day bucketwheel excavator scheme.

The simulation model designed was organized in five modules: mining, transportation, storage, extraction, and weather. The impact of this study was said to be

---

[1] F. Paul Wyman, "Simulation of Tar Sands Mining Operations," *Interfaces,* 8:1 (1977), 6–20.

considerable. Its impact on the state of the art of actual mining practice was a new scheme designed for mining tar sand. The impact upon Syncrude was said to be most significant because the selection of mining equipment of this order of magnitude is an irreversible decision once it is made. The simulation study was useful to Syncrude in estimating production capability under various engineering considerations. Furthermore, this study provided information on the most economical balance of equipment sizes to achieve the desired production level.

A Simulation Model for a Disease Control

Bovine brucellosis is a highly contagious disease among cattle. It causes fertility problems, thereby reducing productivity in beef and dairy products. Furthermore, this disease can be transmitted to humans. Thus, many countries, including the United States, are engaged in various eradication campaigns. This study[2] focuses on a nationwide eradication campaign in Australia.

Vaccination of female breeding stock has been used extensively to control brucellosis. However, the ultimate eradication can be achieved only by the slaughter of all infected animals. The general campaign procedure in Australia is as follows:

All breeding animals in all herds are blood tested.

All infected animals found must be slaughtered within 21 days of testing.

Blood testing must continue at 30- to 60-day intervals until the herd is found free of brucellosis in 2 consecutive tests.

A routine check test is carried out on the herd after the second clear test. If the herd remains clear, then it is declared "provisionally free" of brucellosis.

An area becomes "provisionally free" of brucellosis when all of the herds have been tested at least once and the prevalence of the disease is less than 0.2 percent.

This simulation study was designed to project testing workloads and culling numbers for the campaign. The model simulates the following operations: (1) actual testing and slaughtering procedure, and (2) scheduling new herds for periodic testing. The model includes such inputs as estimates of retests, slaughter rates, and initial disease status. In the simulation model, a herd moves from one state to another until it achieves the state of provisional disease freedom through the process of each retesting and subsequent slaughtering. On the basis of Monte Carlo procedures, a herd's path to the state of provisional disease freedom can be simulated.

This simulation study provided valuable information concerning the magnitude of the campaigns needed to control the disease. The estimated time required to achieve

---

[2]A. C. Beck and L. W. Valentine, "A Simulation Model to Aid Decision Making in a Campaign to Eradicate Brucellosis from Cattle," *Interfaces*, 10:1 (1980), 28–37.

provisional freedom varies from 7.3 years for 2 disease control teams to 10.5 months for 15 teams. The time required to complete all testing varies from 8.4 years for 2 teams to 2.2 years for 15 teams. The simulation model also predicted that about 7,600 herd tests would be required to complete the campaign in the Richmond-Tweed area.

The study proved very informative in that it provided information concerning the time, manpower, and resource requirements to complete the campaign. In addition, the study revealed the estimated number of head of cattle that needed to be slaughtered to complete the campaign. An estimated 9,500 head of cattle had to be slaughtered, representing about 4.8 percent of all of the breeding stock in the area.

SUMMARY

Most of the management science techniques we have studied prior to this chapter are designed for specific types of problems. For example, linear programming is an optimization technique for constrained decision problems. These techniques are based on restrictive and sometimes unrealistic assumptions. Many of the real-world problems we face are often too complex to impose such restrictive assumptions.

Simulation is a method for conducting experiments based on logical procedures or mathematical models. As such, simulation does not require any inherent assumptions. Simulation is a highly flexible and powerful management science tool for many real-world problems. This flexibility results in some undesirable side effects, such as the diverse model structures, the problem of model validity, and the complexity of output analysis. However, individual creativity and a strict set of technical procedures can help us to alleviate most of these problems.

Perhaps the most significant element of simulation is the Monte Carlo process. It is an extremely useful process to generate values of random variables. The Monte Carlo process involves basically two phases: (1) generation of a uniformly distributed random number, and (2) transformation of the selected random number into a corresponding value for the random variable.

Simulation has been widely applied to a variety of real-world problems. In addition to typical operational problems, such as queuing, inventory control, financial planning, and production operations, it is becoming increasingly important in the area of artificial intelligence and heuristic programming. The computer-based simulation approach is a valuable management science tool today and will be more so in the future.

References

Beck, A. C., and Valentine, L. W. "A Simulation Model to Aid Decision Making in a Campaign to Eradicate Brucellosis from Cattle." *Interfaces,* 10:1 (1980), 28–37.

Forrester, J. *Industrial Dynamics.* Cambridge, Mass.: M.I.T. Press, 1961.

Kiviat, P. J., Villaneuva, R., and Markowitz, H. M. *The Simscript II Programming Language.* Englewood Cliffs, N.J.: Prentice-Hall, 1969.

Lee, S. M., Moore, L. J., and Taylor, B. W. *Management Science.* Dubuque, Iowa: W. C. Brown, 1981.

Meier, R. C., Newell, W. T., and Pazer, H. L. *Simulation in Business and Economics.* Englewood Cliffs, N.J.: Prentice-Hall, 1969.

Pritsker, A. A. B. *The GASP IV Simulation Language.* New York: Wiley, 1974.

Pritsker, A. A. B. *Modeling and Analysis Using Q-GERT Networks,* 2nd ed. New York: Wiley, 1977.

Pugh, A. L. *DYNAMO II User's Manual.* Cambridge, Mass.: M.I.T. Press, 1970.

Schriber, T. S. *Simulation Using GPSS*. New York: Wiley, 1974.

Wheelwright, S. C., and Makridakis, S. G. *Computer-Aided Modeling for Managers*. Reading, Mass.: Addison-Wesley, 1972.

Wyman, F. P. *Simulation Modeling: A Guide to Using SIMSCRIPT*. New York: Wiley, 1970.

Wyman, F. P. "Simulation of Tar Sands Mining Operations." *Interfaces*, 8:1 (1977), 6–20.

Assignments

14.1 What is simulation? Define it by using your own words.

14.2 What are the major differences between an analytical solution procedure and simulation?

14.3 Describe any decision problem familiar to you that could be analyzed by simulation more appropriately than by analytical techniques.

14.4 What are the types of results we can obtain from simulation of a model?

14.5 Describe a decision problem that is not suited for simulation. (*Hint:* Consider several of the disadvantages of simulation discussed in this chapter.)

14.6 Define the following terms briefly: *random variable, pseudorandom number, cumulative distribution, random number generation, transformation, Monte Carlo method.*

14.7 Among all of the advantages of simulation we discussed in this chapter, what is the most important advantage in your opinion? Why?

14.8 Briefly describe the basic steps of the simulation process and indicate how various types of information are processed through each step.

14.9 Explain briefly how the tabular method and the graphical method work in the random-number-generation process.

14.10 Categorize simulation languages in terms of their orientation toward flowchart or process.

14.11 Briefly define the following terms: *artificial intelligence, business games, heuristics, industrial dynamics.*

14.12 It is possible to incorporate an optimization process in simulation. Does that mean that the optimum solution we derive through simulation would be exactly the same as the true optimum solution?

14.13 What are the major characteristics of simulation models?

14.14 Why is the transformation procedure necessary in the Monte Carlo process?

14.15 What is the primary reason that many random number generators produce pseudorandom numbers rather than true random numbers?

14.16 By using a random selection procedure, generate 10 random numbers from the table of random numbers (Appendix 7).

14.17 Generate 10 random numbers by the mid-square method. Use 1,779 as the initial seed value and select 4 middle-digit numbers.

14.18 Generate 10 random numbers by the mid-product method. Use 1,779 as the seed value and 253 as the constant. Select the middle 4 digits as numbers.

14.19 The time between arrivals of customers at the information desk of a local IRS office is given by the following probability distribution:

Time between Arrivals (Min.)	Probability
1	0.10
2	0.25
3	0.35
4	0.20
5	0.10

   a. Construct a cumulative probability distribution.
   b. Simulate the arrival of 10 customers by the tabular method.
   c. Compute the expected time between arrivals and compare it with the mean time between arrivals derived by simulation.

14.20 Cusomter service time of the teller machine at the Midland Commercial Bank is considered as a random variable and is defined by the following probability distribution:

Service Time (Minutes)	Probability
3	0.10
4	0.20
5	0.30
6	0.25
7	0.10
8	0.05

a. Construct a cumulative probability distribution.

b. Suppose there are 10 customers to be served. Simulate their service time by using the graphical method.

14.21 Aqua-Science Laboratories produces a number of different types of marine science equipment. This company has two different assembly lines to produce its most popular sonar equipment, Aqua-Sonics. The process time for each assembly line is regarded as a random variable and is described by the following probability distribution:

Process Time (Minutes)	Assembly 1	Assembly 2
3	0.10	0.15
4	0.40	0.35
5	0.30	0.25
6	0.20	0.25

a. Construct a cumulative probability distribution of the process time for each assembly line.

b. Develop a random number mechanism to generate the process time for 20 units of the product and compute the average process time for the product.

14.22 The time between two consecutive customers arriving at an auto repair shop is considered a random variable and has the following probability distribution:

Time between Arrivals (10 min.)	Probability
1	0.10
2	0.20
3	0.30
4	0.15
5	0.13
6	0.12

a. Construct a cumulative probability distribution of the interarrival time.

b. Simulate the customer arrival for 10 customers and compute the mean time between arrivals.

14.23 Abdul Mohammed has been the Port Manager in the state of Oman. After several hectic years of his tenure, he has learned to manage the port efficiently. Realizing the importance of the port as the major window of export for his country, Mohammed would like to establish an effective port management policy. Since simulation appears to be the best method for analyzing this type of problem, he organized a management science group to conduct a feasibility study of this project.

Assume that you are a member of the management science group. Given the probability distribution for interarrival time between ships as shown below, construct a cumulative probability distribution and illustrate it graphically. Indicate on the graph how the time between ship arrivals can be obtained as a random variable based on the generation of random numbers between zero and 1.

Time between Ship Arrivals (Days)	Probability
1	0.05
2	0.10
3	0.20
4	0.30
5	0.20
6	0.10
7	0.05

14.24 By using the probability data in Problem 14.23 and the random number table in Appendix 7, generate uniform random numbers first and then determine the corresponding interarrival times for the first 20 ships. In selecting random numbers from Appendix 7, select any two-digit number (e.g., 35, 74) at a time. Complete the following table of 20 observations:

	Random Number	Interarrival Times
No ship—1st ship		
1st ship—2nd ship		
2nd ship—3rd ship		
.		
.		
.		
19th ship—20th ship		

14.25 Assume that most ships entering this port, described in Problem 14.23, need about 5 days to unload, clean, and prepare for departure. Determine by simulation the values for the random variables specified in the following table. (Use the Monte Carlo process and let the days start with day zero.)

Ship Number	Arrival Day	Time to Arrival of Next Ship	Day Unloading Begins	Departure Day	Waiting Time	No. of Ships Waiting
1						
2						
3						
.						
.						
.						
10						

14.26 Compute the following summary statistics for the ship docking simulation of Problem 14.25:

a. Mean time between ship arrivals.
b. Mean time that ships wait to unload.
c. Mean number of ships waiting to unload.
d. Mean time that ships spend waiting to unload and being unloaded.
e. Proportion of arrivals that enter an empty port.
f. Frequency distribution of ship waiting time.
g. Frequency distribution of number of ships waiting.

14.27 Refer to Problem 14.25. Assume that the time required to unload, clean, and prepare for departure is a random variable that ranges from 3 days to 6 days with the following probability distribution:

Time to Unload, Clean, and Prepare for Departure (Days)	Probability
3	0.1
4	0.2
5	0.4
6	0.3

a. For the first 20 ships, construct a cumulative probability distribution and determine the time to unload, clean, and prepare for departure by using the random number table in Appendix 7.
b. Assuming a random unloading time for this case, construct a new table similar to the table shown in Problem 14.25. (Note that the simulation results now include the joint interaction of two random variables, interarrival time and unloading time.)

14.28 On the basis of the processes used to obtain simulation results from Problems 14.23–14.27 (regarding unloading time as a random variable), develop a flowchart of ship docking simulation and identify 5 basic components of the Monte Carlo process.

14.29 John Demsky is the Inventory Manager for the Weight Watchers' Clinic. Recently, the demand for Diet 15 has shown wide fluctuations. John wants to determine the expected demand for Diet 15 in stock during a reorder period, i.e., the time lapse from the stock reorder until the ordered goods are received. The most important information John is seeking to find is how far in advance he should reorder before the stock level is reduced to zero. On the basis of the historical data concerning lead time and demand, John realizes that these two variables are random variables, described by the probability distributions shown below:

Lead Time (Days)	Probability	Demand per Day	Probability
1	0.5	1	0.1
2	0.3	2	0.3
3	0.2	3	0.4
		4	0.2

a. Simulate this problem by using the Monte Carlo process. Show the demand during lead time (*DDLT*) for 30 reorders and determine the expected demand during lead time. (*Hint:* The lead time must first be randomly generated, followed by separate random generations of daily demand rates for each day of lead time.)

b. From the simulation results, construct a frequency distribution of the demand during lead time.

14.30 Refer to Problem 14.29. After determining the frequency distribution of the demand during lead time, John wishes to set his reorder point so that the probability of stock-out during a lead time is no greater than 0.1 (the percentage of reorder periods during which shortages occur should be no more than 10 percent). This policy represents a 90 percent service level for customers.

a. At what level should John set his reorder point in order to provide 90 percent service level to his customers?

b. Where should the reorder point be set to maintain a service level of 80 percent? Of 60 percent?

15 IMPLEMENTATION OF MANAGEMENT SCIENCE

Most of the readers of this book are likely to become decision makers who will be involved in implementing management science studies. Thus, it is perfectly fitting to close this book with a discussion of a broad management perspective concerning the actual application of management science. We have seen enough evidence that the successful application of management science requires more than just a good knowledge of management science techniques.

There is no question whatever that management science has a great potential for improving management decision making. Nevertheless, we are far from reaching this potential. As a matter of fact, there is increasing concern among practicing managers about the role and direction of management science. In this chapter, we will first attempt to construct a proper perspective about management science by studying its development. Then, we will explore ways to improve organizational effectiveness and performance through successful implementation of management science.

Learning Objectives   *From the study of this chapter, you will learn the following:*

1. *The developmental history of management science.*
2. *The meaning of management science implementation.*
3. *Several typical problems involved in implementation.*
4. *Differences between managers and management scientists in the perceived barriers to the application of management science.*
5. *The basic role of the management scientist.*
6. *Differences between the concepts of management by information and management by ideology.*
7. *Factors that are important for successful management science implementation.*
8. *Strategies for managing resistance to organizational change.*
9. *Several ways to improve each phase of the management science process.*
10. *The future of management science.*
11. *The meaning of the following terms:*

Decision support systems   *Management by ideology*
Implementation   *Situational normativism*
Management by information   *Cost/benefit analysis*

DEVELOPMENT OF MANAGEMENT SCIENCE

As we have discussed throughout the previous chapters, a phenomenal advance has been made in the field of management science since the end of World War II. Many new techniques have been developed through technical breakthroughs, new applications of existing techniques have been explored, and complex decision problems have been solved through the use of computers. In this book we have purposely selected the most widely used basic management science techniques for study.

The process of management science application

We need a good working knowledge of modeling techniques in order to analyze decision problems. Nevertheless, modeling is only a part of the entire process of management science application. Today, more than ever, management scientists and practicing managers are concerned about the actual implementation of management science. For example, a recent study reports over 300 studies that deal with the implementation issue of management science.[1] This concern clearly indicates the growing maturity of the management science field as a profession.

Gaither's survey

According to Gaither's study, approximately 50 percent of the manufacturing firms surveyed use management science.[2] Over 90 percent of these firms rate the results of the management science applications as very good to excellent. However, the actual picture of management science implementation in organizations is not always that rosy. We are beginning to find reports of failures in applying management science to decision problems. One study even had this catchy title: "How to Fail with OR in Government without Really Trying."

We have seen many claims of successful management science implementation of one sort or another. Yet management science is increasingly concerned about its future, especially its role in the most important part of the management science process—implementation. Before we discuss this critical issue, let us briefly discuss the developmental phases of management science so that we can develop a proper perspective about management science implementation.

Development phases of management science

The Embryonic Stage (Prior to the 1960s)

After World War II, a small number of professionals began to analyze well-defined operational problems by using quantitative tools. Most of these scientists were transferred from other disciplines such as mathematics, statistics, engineering, the natural sciences, and the like. They were primarily interested in learning and developing new techniques in order to find optimum solutions to clearly defined problems in such areas as production scheduling, inventory control, and blending procedures.

Developing new techniques

During this time, two well-known professional associations were organized: the Operations Research Society of America (ORSA) and The Institute of Management Science (TIMS). These organizations also began to publish their journals, reporting new advances in management science techniques and applications. Academic interest was very limited. In fact, there were only a handful of universities offering formal programs in management science or operations research.

ORSA and TIMS

---

[1] R. Wysocki, "OR/MS Implementation Research: A Bibliography," *Interfaces,* 9:2 (1979), 37–41.

[2] N. Gaither, "The Adoption of Operations Research Techniques by Manufacturing Organizations," *Decision Sciences,* 6 (1975), 797–813.

The Rapid Growth Stage (1960–Late 1970s)

Formal educational programs

The period from 1960 to the late 1970s saw a dramatic growth of management science in academic institutions. A great number of institutions began to offer formal degree programs in management science and related fields. The profession has put its emphasis on the education of future decision makers.

The rapid growth of management science has brought the follwoing positive results:

Some positive results

1. It provided a special impetus to utilize the enormous computational power of computers. Many ''canned'' programs became available for easy applications of various techniques.

2. It stimulated the development of the computer-based management information systems (MIS). The computer-based MIS required quantitative data inputs, systematic data analysis, and timely use of the data base. This approach gave birth to the decision support system (DSS) concept.

3. Many college graduates with management science education moved into management positions in various organizations. Their understanding and appreciation of the potential contributions of management science provided an environment conducive to the further growth of management science.

Some negative results

The enormous educational growth of management science has also resulted in some negative consequences:

1. Many management scientists conducted only academic, theoretical, or pure research for the refinement of minute details of various techniques that had little or no relevance to real-world problems.

2. Many practitioners began to be disillusioned, partially because of their inability to comprehend the esoteric research reports and partially because of the irrelevance of the studies.

''Have gun will travel''

3. A tendency to emphasize the techniques over the actual problems to be solved began to develop. This ''intellectual masturbation'' or ''have gun will travel'' approach was denounced by practitioners and managers alike.

4. There was a general neglect or lack of understanding of the decision environment, organizational values, conflicting nature of multiple organizational objectives, data requirements, organizational politics, and behavioral implications of the solution implementation.

The Maturing Stage (Late 1970s——)

A self-evaluation period

Although the maturing stage began earlier than the late 1970s, it has become more evident during the years since then. The profession of management science began a self-evaluation. Management scientists began to ask the question, ''Are we doing the job we are supposed to be doing?'' Many leading management scientists began to speak out on the failures of management science as well as its successes. Several important characteristics of this stage are:

New developments in the profession

1. A more pragmatic approach is being taken by both managers and management scientists concerning the true value, role, and limitations of management science.

2. A greater emphasis is being placed on the analysis of the decision environment and the nature of the problem, as compared to the previous emphasis on developing abstract models.

3. Management scientists now recognize the importance of obtaining *satisficing* solutions to certain problems rather than finding the *optimum* solutions.

4. A greater effort is being placed on the better integration of environmental, behavioral, and quantitative analyses in problem solving. Managers and management scientists are striving to gain a clearer understanding of the quantitative aspects of the problem and the impact of various model assumptions.

5. The computer technology is utilized more vigorously in pursuing heuristic solutions to ill-structured managerial problems. Decision scientists are attempting to develop computer-based interactive processes for evolving successively better answers to the problems.

Tool using rather than tool tuning

The greater emphasis on the actual implementation of management science indicates that the profession is moving in the right direction. During this period, a new professional organization, the American Institute for Decision Sciences (AIDS), has joined APICS (the American Production and Inventory Control Society), TIMS, ORSA, and others as an active advocate of actual implementation of management science. Also, a joint publication of ORSA-TIMS, *Interfaces,* has emerged as an important indication that management scientists are determined to do their work through ''tool using'' rather than ''tool tuning.''

PROBLEMS OF IMPLEMENTATION

What Is Implementation?

Implementation of management science basically means the actual use of the output of a management science project by managers to improve organizational performance. It is not easy to define what degree of use would be required to label a management

Figure 15.1 The Process of Management Science

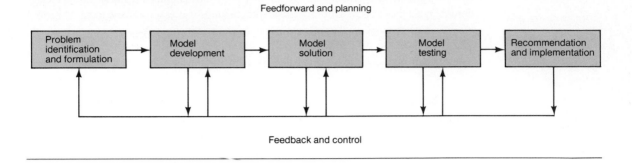

Feedforward and planning

| Problem identification and formulation | Model development | Model solution | Model testing | Recommendation and implementation |

Feedback and control

Different views of implementation

science project as implemented. There are differing views about successful implementation. The practicing manager tends to declare implementation a success when management science output helps the manager to achieve his or her intended objectives. On the other hand, the management scientist tends to think that a successful implementation has occurred if the project provided valuable new information, experience, or insights about the problem.

A broader and more realistic index of implementation is to view implementation as a continuous cycle or process of management science. In this framework, implementation does not start after the solution to a model is obtained or the recommendation is accepted by the manager. Instead, implementation encompasses the entire process of management science, involving all of the following phases:

The implementation process

Identification and formulation of a problem.

Development of a model.

Solution of the model.

Testing of the solution.

Recommendation and implementation.

Integrated steps

Figure 15.1 presents the process of management science. This process is not a series of isolated operating steps. Typically there are feedback and feedforward activities at each phase. For example, the model formulation effort may indicate that the needed data are not available. Then, we may need to go back to the first step to examine the problem once again. This process will be more fully discussed when we examine implementation strategies in a later section of this chapter.

Implementation a continuous process

The concept of a continuous life cycle of implementation has been supported by a number of researchers. Gupta reported an interesting study about implementation difficulties of management science in the U.S. Postal Service.[3] His study clearly demonstrates that a successful implementation requires successful achievement of various criteria at each phase of the entire process of management science.

Obviously we do not have a unified definition of implementation. Nevertheless, a successful implementation is often associated with the following characteristics:

1. An improved organizational performance through the use of the model results or information generated by the process.

Successful implementation

2. An improved communication or work relationship among the interdisciplinary parties involved (the manager, management scientist, operations personnel, staff specialists, and others).

3. Carefully planned and monitored activities in each phase of the entire process.

4. A continuous and dynamic process of updating, feedforward, feedback, review, control, and communication.

Typical Problems Involved in Implementation

The kind of picture we have drawn in this book may look rosy for management science. In some organizations, such an optimistic picture may be justified. However, numerous organizations are experiencing many difficulties in their attempts to apply

Conflict between managers and management scientists

management science to decision analysis. In reality, we often see practicing managers and management scientists operate as two separate groups, each with its own language, methods, and goals. Each has much to contribute to and learn from the other. Yet, managers often accuse management scientists of dealing with "technological nonsense," whereas management scientists scorn managers as "ignorant pragmatists." The British philosopher, C. P. Snow, once observed that science and the humanities operate as two distinct cultures. His advice was: "What we need to do is humanize the scientist and simonize the humanist."

When organizations face certain problems in implementation, the typical causes listed are often opinionated finger pointing such as: lack of interpersonal and communication skills on the part of management scientists, cultural and educational differences between managers and management scientists, improper identification of the problem by managers, unworkable model formulation by management scientists, lack of understanding of the decision environment by management scientists, lack of understanding of management science by managers, and formulating too complex models for simple problems (the scalpel for a hamburger syndrome).

Grayson's reasons for not using management science

C. Jackson Grayson, a student of management science and former chairman of

---

[3]J. N. D. Gupta, "Management Science Implementation: Experiences of a Practicing O.R. Manager," *Interfaces*, 7:3 (1977), 84–90.

the Price Commission in the federal government, lists the following reasons for not applying management science:

1. Shortage of time—most important decisions require immediate solutions; no time to fool around with problem formulation, data collection, model design, testing the model solution, etc.

2. Lack of data—often the required data for the model are inaccessible, nonexistent, or not in the form usable to the model.

3. Resistance to change—implementation requires organizational change, which is often resisted by managers and operational personnel.

4. Long response time—the management scientist tends to take a systematic but time-consuming way to analyze a problem, and managers would rather use a quick judgmental decision than wait for a good solution after six months.

5. Simplifications and assumptions—important environmental or behavioral constraints are often swept under the rug by the management scientist in designing the model. For example, time constraints, data inaccessibility, bureaucratic power structures, organizational values, and the manager's priority structure of objectives are often simplified out of the model.[4]

Although the above five reasons may sound reasonable, they are more eloquent excuses than legitimate causes for not applying management science. These five reasons exist for any major project that organizations undertake. For example, a change of organizational structure, which is usually not a management science project, may encounter the same five problems.

Causes of implementation difficulties

We may be able to shed some light on more meaningful causes of implementation difficulties by citing two survey studies. The first survey, published in 1977 by Green, Newsom, and Jones, provides managers' (vice-presidents') perceptions on barriers to the use of management science. Table 15.1 presents the survey results. The second survey, conducted by Watson and Marett in 1979, presents practicing management scientists' perceptions about the barriers to management science implementation. Table 15.2 presents the second survey.

There is a general trend of agreement between managers and management scientists concerning the major barriers to application. The most important barriers appear to be educational or technical knowledge, perceptional differences about the value of management science, and lack of appropriate data. However, there also are some differences on several important issues. Managers generally tend to be more cost or time conscious. Thus, they often pursue "quick and dirty" solutions. On the other

[4]C. Jackson Grayson, Jr., "Management Science and Business Practice," *Harvard Business Review,* 51:4 (1973), 41–48.

Table 15.1   Managers' Perceived Barriers to Management Science Application

Rank	Barrier
1	Benefits of using techniques are not clearly understood by managers.
2	Managers lack knowledge of quantitative techniques.
3	Managers are not exposed to quantitative techniques early in their training.
4	Required data is difficult to quantify.
5	Only a small portion of management is trained in the use of quantitative techniques.
6	Management is successful without using techniques.
7	Managers in key positions lack knowledge of quantitative techniques.
8	The cost of developing models and using techniques is too high.
9	The data required in using the techniques are not available.
10	Managers are not quantitatively oriented.
11	Recent college graduates with quantitative training have not yet attained positions of influence.
12	Managers are unwilling or unable to use the computer for decision making and/or computers are not available.
13	The expense of employing quantitative specialists is too great.
14	Senior management personnel do not encourage the use of techniques by younger management personnel.
15	Management distrusts or fears the use of techniques.

Source: T. B. Green, W. B. Newsom, and S. R. Jones, "A Survey of the Application of Quantitative Techniques to Production/Operations Management in Large Organizations," *Academy of Management Journal,* 4 (Dec. 1977), 669–676.

Table 15.2   Management Scientists' Perception of Barriers to Management Science Application

Rank	Barrier
1	Selling management science techniques to management meets with resistance.
2	Neither top nor middle management has the educational background to appreciate management science techniques.
3	Lack of good clean data.
4	There is never time to analyze a real problem using a sophisticated approach.
5	Lack of understanding by those who need to use the results.
6	Hard to define problems for applications.
7	The payoff from using unsophisticated methods is sufficient.
8	Shortage of personnel.
9	Poor reputation of management scientists as problem solvers.
10	Individuals feel threatened by management scientists and their techniques.

Source: H. J. Watson and P. G. Marett, "A Survey of Management Science Implementation Problems," *Interfaces,* 9:4 (1979), 124–128.

Different concerns

hand, management scientists tend to be more concerned with developing mathematically elegant models than with attempting to just extract information that is needed by managers.

*Important factors for
successful implementation*

Many other recent studies have identified a number of factors that are important for successful implementation of management science. Some of these factors are:

The degree of management participation and support.

Technical competence and organizational influence of the management scientist.

Relevance of management science to organizational problems.

Effectiveness of the model—simplicity, robustness, adaptability, and ease of communication.

Resources allocated to management science projects.

Organizational climate for innovation and change.

Organizational commitment to long-range strategic planning.

Commitment of all personnel to organizational values and purpose.

Communication among all levels of the organization.

Unique aspects of the organization, problem, decision environment, or personnel.

MANAGEMENT PERSPECTIVE OF IMPLEMENTATION

Role of the Management Scientist

Management science implementation is much like the successful introduction of a new product. In order to introduce a new product, an organization must go through a market research, feasibility study, product design, production, distribution, sales, and maintenance or service. Each phase of the process must be successfully completed in order to have a successful result. For example, a sloppy sales effort will certainly ruin a fine product.

*The role of management
scientist*

Many empirical studies suggest that for successful implementation the management scientist must work harmoniously with the manager. We believe management scientists should take the initiative in changing their work behavior. It is extremely difficult for managers to change their work patterns. Furthermore, the end product is supposed to be management, not management science.

Traditional educational programs train a student of management science to formulate and solve models. Rarely is a student exposed to the relationship between the abstract organizational purpose and the model. Worse yet, most management science courses are technique-oriented rather than implementation-oriented. Thus, most management scientists do not have the broad management perspective required for successful implementation.

H. Z. Halbrecht, the president of a management consulting firm, told the following story in a professional meeting:

An interesting story

A recent Ph.D. in operations research was hired by a metropolitan city government. His job was to find a good location for a sewage disposal plant somewhere in one of the boroughs. A few weeks later he came to his supervisor. He had the model; he had spent an awful lot of money on computer time; and he announced, "I've got the optimum location for it." When his supervisor heard "optimum" he started to duck, but thought he would listen to him anyway. Then the fellow showed how he came up with the location. Now, everybody who is high-up in any city administration (who has also got a little bit of brains and who has lasted more than six months) has an address book in his pocket, because it's great to know all the theories about public administration and city management, but before you do anything drastic, it's nice to know who lives in the area that you are going to pick for the sewage disposal plant. And, by an odd coincidence, the optimum location picked was two blocks from the Chairman of the City Finance Committee's home. The supervisor suggested that that was not the "optimum" location, and this fellow got furious. He said, "I will tell you that this is the optimum location. Are you looking for a political solution or for a truthful solution?" The man who replaced the first fellow was put on that assignment and was told to find the best "workable" solution.[5]

The above story tells us that the management scientist should know more than the analytical techniques to design models and that he should help implement the results of the design model. There have been several recent attempts to narrow the gap between management and management science. First, there has been a rapid decentralization of management science activities in organizations. Instead of maintaining a separate management science group, many firms have sprinkled management scientists throughout the organization in areas where they can be really valuable. Many management scientists are assigned to significant functional management positions, or as aides to the top managers. They are given line responsibilities for results.

Narrowing the gap between management and management science

Another trend is the managers' demand for implementation of the model by management scientists. This approach helps alleviate the problem of unworkable, theoretical model design on the part of management scientists. A third trend has been thorough on-the-job training of management scientists in the broad organizational purpose and values, unique organizational characteristics, and behavioral aspects of management science implementation. *It is the responsibility of management to integrate management scientists into the mainstream of the organization's operations.*

Responsibility of management

The basic problem of implementation is not the weaknesses inherent in manage-

---

[5]Quoted with the permission of *Decision Sciences* from H. Z. Halbrecht, "If Your Students Aren't Marketable, What's Your Future?" *Decision Sciences*, 4:3 (1973), xx.

Two important factors

ment science itself. Rather, the root of the problem lies in two factors: (1) management's failure to integrate all functions of organization members into its basic purpose, and (2) management scientists' failure to broaden their views and insights about their roles in the organization. Thus, the basic problem of implementation rests on the misconception, by both managers and management scientists, of the role and purpose of management science in organizations.

The Concept of Management by Ideology

Management by information

The process of management science is based on the approach of *management by information*. Management by information certainly makes sense, for we live in a dynamic environment, and the high cost associated with error is forcing organizations to seek more concrete information. However, management by information has the following characteristics: a high degree of organizational instrumentation, emphasis on measurable short-term objectives, a top-down communication of objectives, a technology-based functional structure, a general lack of organizational commitment on the part of its members, and a problem-solving approach of management.

Management by ideology

An emerging concept of management is a broad approach of *management by ideology*. Management by ideology emphasizes superordinate organizational values and philosophies, long-term strategic objectives, a two-way (top-down and bottom-up) communication system, cooperation and harmony-oriented functional structures, a strong commitment to the organizational values on the part of the members, and consultative decision making.

The Japanese management philosophy

The Japanese management system is closely related to management by ideology. Under this system, the superordinate organizational values, philosophies, and purposes are clearly communicated throughout the organization. The basic approach of management is to pursue long-range achievement of the organizational purpose. Based on this stable management approach, middle and lower management personnel are encouraged to use management by information to develop intermediate objectives for top management review, such as profit, market share, research and development, human resource development, operational efficiency, and the like. These intermediate objectives are simply means of achieving the superordinate organizational purpose.

American managers often scorn Japanese managers for their slowness in making decisions. One Japanese executive's answer to this accusation was, "Yes, we are very slow in making our decisions, so sorry. But you American managers take forever to implement the decisions you make so promptly." How true it is! The entire process of management science can be more quickly completed if a longer time period is used for proper preparations and persuasion of all of the personnel involved. As a well-known top American executive once said, "Most managers would rather live with a problem they can't solve than use a solution they don't understand."

Short-term objectives vs. long-term goals

We believe the fundamental problem of implementation lies in the basic approach of management practiced by organizations. If firms pursue only short-term monetary objectives as the ultimate organization goals, they will attract only mercenaries—those who will try to get the result at all costs. Once his or her résumé becomes impressive, he or she will be knocking on the office door of a headhunter. In such an environment, a successful management science implementation is not likely. It takes too much time and effort to carry out a well-prepared management science project.

Figure 15.2   Management Science in the Management by Ideology Framework

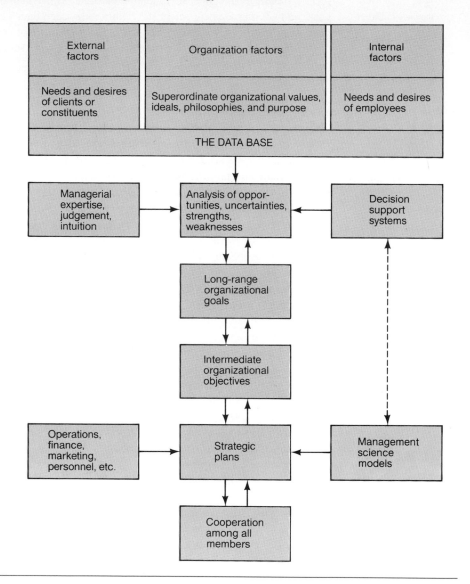

Hayes and Abernathy have echoed the same basic idea.[6] They contend that one of the problems behind the financial and productivity woes of many large American firms is their emphasis on short-term monetary objectives, often at the expense of long-term organizational goals. The same reasoning applies to the many implementation problems experienced by organizations. Thus, we propose that management by ideology,

[6]R. H. Hayes and W. J. Abernathy, "Managing Our Way to Economic Decline," *Harvard Business Review,* 58 (1980), 67–77.

supported by management science, should replace the management by information approach blindly pursued by so many organizations. We will make some more definitive suggestions in the next section. Figure 15.2 presents a broad overview of the role and position of management science in the management by ideology framework.

IMPLEMENTATION STRATEGIES

The success of management science application is determined by the organization's efforts in implementing the model results. If implementation is properly planned with appropriate effort, time, resources, and determination, the organization will most likely enjoy maximum benefits from the management science process.

Implementation strategies

Numerous implementation strategies of management science have been suggested by many researchers and practitioners. In order to attain successful implementation, there are several key issues that need to be addressed. Some of these issues are:

Who should be responsible for the implementation?

Who should be involved in the process?

What problems are most likely to be encountered?

What strategies should be used to resolve these problems?

What are the required resources for implementation?

How can we plan ahead for implementation?

We will briefly discuss these questions from both empirical and theoretical viewpoints and provide important guidelines and strategies for implementation.

Organizational Factors Important for Successful Implementation

Organizational factors

The organizational factors discussed below have been pointed out by many empirical studies as important for successful implementation.

Top Management Involvement and Support Many studies have pointed out that visible involvement and support of top management are crucial for the management science process to succeed. The very purpose of management science is to improve the organizational performance and effectiveness outlined by top management. Also, implementation usually requires large-scale changes in organizational structure, policy and work procedures, and job responsibilities. Thus, top management involvement is imperative.

Consistent Management Philosophy Management science projects are based on the belief that greater efficiency can be achieved in the organization when systematic analysis is applied to decision making for long-term organizational objectives. If management's philosophy is contrary to the underlying principles of management science, implementation cannot be successful. The organization must have a management philosophy that encourages creativity, innovation, and change.

Effective Communication The management science process, contrary to what many people think, is a human process. In order to bring out the best imagination, creativity, and efforts from various members of the organization, clear communication is essential. Effective communication results in *commitment* to the common purpose rather than reluctant *compliance* on the part of organization members.

Effective Management Information System A management information system is concerned with collecting, storing, processing, and transmitting information that is essential for effective decision making. The management science process is an important element of the broad concept of decision support systems (DSS). An effective information system is required to carry out such important steps as quantification of organizational objectives, formulation of the model, model testing, and feedback analysis.

Managerial and Technical Skills Management science implementation requires various managerial and technical skills. Managers must possess conceptual skills in formulating and communicating organizational objectives. On the other hand, management scientists must have technical competence in order to collect required data, quantify many abstract objective criteria, construct models, and analyze the implications of the model solutions. Perhaps the most crucial skills required of everybody are human skills—abilities to listen and communicate, develop human relationships, coach and counsel, and motivate others to work toward a common goal.

Proper Integration of Management Science with Other Functions Management science cannot exist in a vacuum. It must be properly integrated with the other functions of management. Many successful organizations integrate management science within each of their line functions. Thus, management scientists work as line personnel while practicing their professional skills.

Commitment to Reduce Bureaucracy Implementation of management science model results usually requires a great deal of interaction, coordination, communication, and cooperation among personnel and departments. Thus, management science projects frequently require additional paperwork and bureaucracy for implementation. In order to avoid the ''bogged down'' situation, it is important that top management make a commitment to reduce bureaucracy and paperwork as much as possible.

Preparing for Organizational Change

Organizational change

Implementation frequently results in significant changes in the organization, not only in management practice and organizational structure but also in work policies and procedures. Thus, organization members may need to work, behave, and think differently. For an effective implementation, we must minimize the negative consequences of such change. Organizational change is a complex field in itself, and our discussion here can only be brief. Let us simply discuss some of the important issues involved in preparing for organizational change.

Management Assessment The first major step required for organizational change is managerial assessment of the problem at hand, the situation, the cost/benefit considerations, and whether or not the organization is ready to use management science. The assessment should involve more than an appraisal of expected benefits vs. associated costs (including organizational disturbance and unrest). It is not advisable to embark on a management science project because of the "other firms do it" syndrome without fully recognizing the required organizational change.

Planning for a change

Planning for Organizational Change Planning is essential for any significant organizational change. The planning process for implementation should produce and communicate the following information:

What needs to be changed.

Why change is necessary.

How change will be carried out.

Who will be involved in the change process.

When change will take place.

Expected organizational benefits from change.

The planning period for implementation is perhaps the most sensitive phase for organization members. The way implementation planning is carried out has enormous impact upon the eventual effectiveness of implementation. Once a go-ahead decision has been made to implement the model results, the operational manager must take charge and outline the following important aspects:

Immediate changes that are necessary.

Appointment of a task force or planning group for implementation.

Needs assessment for change in policies, work procedures, information requirements and flows, training and development programs, job descriptions, functional relationships among various work units, and communication systems.

A group approach

Perhaps the best way to initiate implementation planning is through a task force group composed of all key operational personnel (linking pin concept), management scientists, and some external experts (if appropriate). In order to provide prestige and credibility as well as appropriate responsibility to the task force group, top managers must be actively involved in the implementation planning process.

Lewin's idea

Managing Resistance to Change According to a theory of social change proposed by Kurt Lewin,[7] any situation in which change is proposed has dynamic forces working in opposing directions. The *driving forces* attempt to move the situation toward the direction of a desired change. The opposing forces, referred to as *restraining forces,* attempt to resist the driving force and keep the situation from moving toward the desired change. A dynamic equilibrium is achieved between the two sets of opposing forces. Lewin contends that any increase in the driving force will most likely be accompanied by an increase in the restraining forces. Thus, the achievement of a desired change in a smooth and permanent way would be through three basic steps: (1) identifying and blunting the courses of the restraining forces, (2) increasing the driving forces toward the desired change, and (3) achieving a new level of equilibrium between the opposing forces closer to the desired change by reinforcing positive behaviors.

How to manage resistance to change

Some of the most widely accepted strategies of managing resistance to change are:

Involve key personnel throughout the process.

Open channels of communication—no secrets.

Create and maintain top management's interest in and commitment to the desired changes.

Recognize and honor established work procedures or group norms as much as possible.

Provide reinforcement for positive behaviors toward the desired change.

Improving the Process of Management Science

We have already stressed the importance of successful completion of each phase of the management science process for a successful final implementation. Let us briefly discuss several essential factors that must be considered in each phase.

Problem Identification and Formulation The identification and formulation of a decision problem is the responsibility of the manager. The manager must determine the existence of a gap between where the organization "is or will be at" and where it "ought to be at" at the end of a planning horizon in a given area of operation. This identification process requires a clear understanding of the organizational purpose, long-range goals, intermediate objectives, and activities that would contribute to the improvement of organizational effectiveness. Therefore, it is imperative for the man-

Understanding the organization's value and purpose

[7]K. Lewin, "Group Decision and Social Change," in *Readings in Social Psychology,* edited by T. N. Newcomb and E. P. Hartley (New York: Holt, Rinehart & Winston, 1947), 340–344.

agement scientist to have a clear understanding of the managerial decision process. We must avoid and reject the general tendency to believe that the identification and formulation of a problem phase is conditioned by the management scientist's knowledge of management science techniques. In other words, management should not allow the management scientist to construct a model for the problem simply because he or she can solve it. Instead, the manager must work with the management scientist in identifying, formulating, and solving the actual problem that needs to be analyzed.

Situational normativism

Several practitioners have reported that one approach that is useful for avoiding such problems is *situational normativism,* proposed by M. L. Shakun.[8] This behavioral approach advocates the construction of a descriptive model of a real-world situation involving participants, their values and aspirations, and the decision rules of the existing system. This model can be used as a gaming device to test the applicability of various management science models. Furthermore, it encourages and necessitates an interaction between the manager and the management scientist. Consequently, this approach can lead to a successful implementation.

Model Development There is no doubt that this phase is the most exciting and interesting part for the management scientist. Thus, some inexperienced management scientists may want to jump right into this phase and have fun rather than labor over problem identification and formulation. A model hastily developed without proper effort to identify and formulate the problem may be based on many unverified as-

Testing assumptions

sumptions. Models with untested assumptions are not only unrealistic but they can also lead to unsuccessful implementation.

Another critical problem involved in model development is inaccessibility or nonavailability of required data. Management scientists frequently design models first and hope that the manager will somehow come up with the required data. Obviously a model can dictate its data requirement. However, a model does not and cannot generate data for itself. Therefore, the actual model development phase must be preceded by a data securing system.

Model Solution Once the model is properly developed, usually very few problems are faced in the model solution phase. Of course, large-scale models based on sophisticated techniques (e.g., nonlinear integer programming) may not be easy to solve, even with the help of the most advanced computer. This phase is an appropriate time to test the various model assumptions. Also, the problem should be attacked by using

Using the simplest tools

the simplest possible tool rather than the most sophisticated technique available.

Solution Testing Before the final recommendations are prepared for the manager, the model solution should be thoroughly tested. Some researchers have suggested the gaming approach, based on a simulation of the decision environment, as a testing device. In testing the solution, actual data should be used whenever possible. Furthermore, it is very important to test the sensitivity of the model to the various model

Answering ''what if'' questions

assumptions and to changes in model parameters. Sensitivity analysis based on an analytical or simulation-based approach can provide valuable information for ''what if'' questions.

---

[8]M. L. Shakun, ''Management Science and Management: Implementing Management Science via Situational Normativism,'' *Management Science,* 18 (1972), 367–377.

Recommendation and Implementation Management scientists are trained to obtain the optimum solution. If the management scientist simply presents the optimum solution to the decision maker, the manager has only two options: accept the recommended solution or reject it. We are already familiar with the story of the sewage disposal plant fiasco for a large city. A much better and more pragmatic approach is to provide the manager with a number of different options with associated resource requirements and benefits. Such a recommendation enables the manager to select a workable decision based on rich information concerning the various decision options.

Providing different alternatives

Also, the management scientist can be directly involved with the manager in exploring different options before arriving at a good solution. The shared purpose and commitment are important factors for successful implementation.

Gupta's idea

Gupta, on the basis of his real-world experience in the U.S. Postal Service, suggests the following strategies for successful implementation:

Analyze the decision situation and construct its descriptive model.

Establish the cause and effect relationship of decision factors influencing the manager's thinking.

Explore or develop appropriate information systems to secure the needed data.

Construct a mathematical model with explicit recognition of data requirements and availability.

Identify the managerial and organizational changes required by the model.

Obtain multiple and competitive solutions to the model.

Analyze each solution in terms of the consequences on decision factors.

Prepare a realistic cost/benefit analysis of each competitive solution.

Provide the manager with multiple solutions with consequences and cost/benefit analysis.

Aid the manager and his/her staff in implementing the manager's decision, if he/she requests it.[9]

Cost/Benefit Analysis for Implementation

When people are involved in an exciting management science project, cost considerations are often completely overlooked or put aside. However, it is important to derive a good estimate of the total cost of the project. The easiest cost components to estimate

The cost/benefit issue

---

[9]Gupta, *op.cit.*

are direct personnel costs, indirect personnel costs (external consultants), computer time costs, and other required resources for developing the model. However, the often neglected but significant costs are those stemming from work disruptions, decreased employee productivity and morale, and possible failure of the final implementation process.

Management scientists and managers who are directly involved often exaggerate the benefits of management science projects. The possible benefits are often expressed in terms of estimated increases in profit, sales, or employee productivity, and decreases in costs, waste, or resource requirements. However, what is often ignored or neglected are the lasting implicit costs associated with employee dissatisfaction, obsolescence of skills, decrease in employee commitment to organizational goals, and the like. Similarly, the lasting benefits such as new skills acquired by employees and increased worker involvement are often ignored.

THE FUTURE OF MANAGEMENT SCIENCE

Management science has advanced dramatically during the past 30 years, especially in the technical and technological areas. On the other hand, many new or continuing problems have been encountered in the area of organizational impact of management science. Let us discuss these trends in greater detail.

Technical Progress

New and more powerful tools

The decision environment and the types of problems that organizations face are becoming increasingly more complicated. We need more powerful and sophisticated techniques to analyze complex problems. Indeed, several important advances have been made. First, a number of new techniques have been developed to analyze complex decision problems. As we learned in Chapter 6, during the past 10 years goal programming and other approaches have been developed for multiple objective decision making. Also, several algorithms for large-scale nonlinear, integer, and network programming problems have been proposed.

The second advance we have seen is in the expanded use of existing techniques. For example, there has been such an improvement in the efficiency of linear programming, network models, and simulation techniques that they are routinely applied to many complex problems. We believe that a continuous refinement and expansion of existing techniques will take place in the future.

Expanded applications

A third area of advancement in management science is the development of more realistic descriptive models for managerial problems. Until recently, management scientists have primarily been engaged in developing normative-type models for clearly defined operational problems. Many management scientists are now attempting to design models to obtain satisficing solutions to ill-structured problems. Such a modeling approach will undoubtedly find greater acceptance in the organization.

Technological Progress

Technical progress provides the necessary means to perform systematic decision analysis. However, actual applications of management science to real-world problems require the use of computers. The remarkable progress in computer technology, both in the hardware and software areas, has allowed a greater sophistication of decision models.

It is now possible to construct and solve very elaborate production, inventory, financial planning, and market analysis models that require a great deal of computational capacity on the part of the computer.

Computer-related advances in information processing

With the continuing inventions and innovations in computer science, the application of management science is expected to become an even more important managerial function in the future. With the advent of computer-based management information systems (MIS) and decision support systems (DSS), management science modeling may become a relatively routine activity.

We have seen some remarkable changes in decision making based on the time-sharing mode of computing. With the convenience of a time-sharing facility, a continuous monitoring of the decision system is possible. For example, the production-inventory system can be updated on a continuous basis without going through a periodic overhaul of the model. Today, we are witnessing the age of powerful yet inexpensive micro- and personal computers. Easy access to micro- or time-sharing computers has already stimulated the use of management science techniques by small organizations. For example, many farming co-op organizations and individual farmers now utilize linear programming to plan their crops through the AGNET (Agricultural Computer Network) system.

Time-sharing

Software packages

Another important advance in computer technology that has had a significant impact on the application of management science is the standardization of various techniques in the form of software packages. With further advances in this area, perhaps we will see more widespread use of management science in the future.

Interactive decision systems

One promising development that has already had enormous organizational impact is the interactive decision system. This system allows the decision maker to be involved directly in the entire management science process. In the interactive system, the decision maker interfaces with the model and data base via an on-line computer terminal. The communication language is often very similar to everyday English. For example, currently there are interactive linear and goal programming systems available for actual application. An important advantage of the interactive system is, in addition to its attractiveness for implementation, that it allows sensitivity analysis through ''what if'' dialogues with a minimum amount of effort.

Organizational Impact

When management science application was first introduced in various organizations, the management scientist was an isolated person in the organization. He or she designed a mathematical model whenever the need arose but remained isolated from the actual implementation of the study. Today, however, managers recognize the potential impact of management science projects on the organization as well as on the work behavior of those directly affected by them.

The management science group (sometimes identified as the OR, MS, administrative analysis, managerial analysis, methods and analysis, or corporate planning group) has a continuous workload and ongoing interrelationships with various operational departments and service units (computer center, statistical records, etc.). Also, the recent trend toward decentralized management science activities may result in a greater effectiveness of management science in the future.

In spite of its technical prowess, management science has a somewhat cloudy future. The primary problem is that so many management scientists are interested

Figure 15.3   Three Stages of the Management Science Process

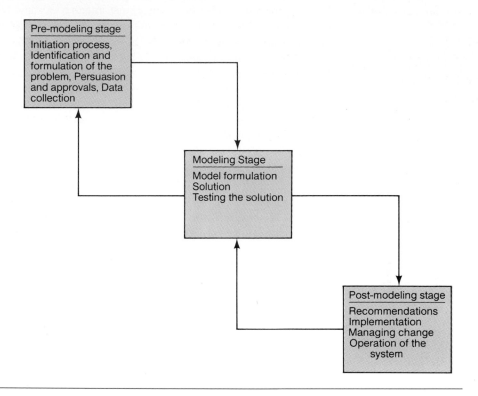

only in the technical aspects of management science implementation. The management science process consists of three basic stages: the premodeling stage; the modeling stage; and the postmodeling stage. The premodeling stage involves much of the behavioral and political pains of conceiving the idea, identifying the problem, collecting the necessary data, and getting the required approvals of key individuals. The modeling stage includes the formulation, testing, and solution of the model. The postmodeling stage is concerned with the pains of persuasion, confrontation, and finally living with the system throughout the implementation phase. Figure 15.3 presents the three stages of the management science process.

Stages of the management science process

If management scientists insist on simply doing the modeling work, they have very little to offer. In order to realize the true potential of management science, management scientists must change their perceptions concerning their roles and functions in the organization. As a matter of fact, it is the responsibility of management to see that management scientists are individuals capable not only of performing the modeling task but of completing the entire management science project.

True potential of management science

We must emphasize once again that a person who simply has tools is not necessarily valuable. A truly valuable person is the one who has both tools and the mental ability to use those tools for different purposes in varying situations. Also, management must have stable values, philosophies, and purposes for the organization. These superordinate

*Top-down and bottom-up
interface*

organizational goals must be communicated throughout the organization in a cascade fashion. In order to achieve these goals, middle managers and employees must use their imagination to innovate, change, and improve existing systems. This top-down and bottom-up interface is the key to management by ideology.

Management science should be no exception to this basic pattern. The group-oriented work patterns such as quality circles and small groups, as evident in Japanese management practices, would greatly enhance the work of management science. Management scientists are well-educated professionals with advanced degrees. They are usually specialists with narrow backgrounds. In order to play their roles effectively, they must learn the structure, functions, work methods, and behavioral aspects of the organization. Furthermore, they must be patient persuaders and advisers. In other words, the effective management scientist must be what Kenneth Boulding calls "a

*A specialist with a
universal mind*

specialist with a universal mind." We believe it is highly plausible that many business schools will continue to modify their curricula so that students will be more broadly educated, especially in the humanities and liberal arts. What we need is not more management scientists who can use tools. Instead, we need management scientists with creativity linked to conceptual and human skills who will carry through the entire management science project.

SUMMARY

This chapter has attempted to provide an overview of what management science implementation involves. Implementation is generally regarded as a continuous process encompassing the entire cycle of the management science project. There are many possible problems that can arise during the implementation process. We have studied some innovative strategies that can be used to alleviate some of the problems of implementation. However, the most important factor for successful implementation appears to be a proper management perspective about the role of management science.

We have seen many successful applications of management science. In order to ensure continued success, the management scientist must broaden his or her vision beyond the model building stage. There are many people who are competent model builders. But there are few who have the broad management perspective, creativity, and conceptual and human skills to make a real impact on the organization. The future decision environment cries out for sophisticated analysis in the hands of creative professionals who can work with managers. We believe the age of management by information has given way to the concept of management by ideology. Management science has much to contribute in this new era of management.

References

Boulding, K. "The Specialist with a Universal Mind." *Management Science,* 14:12 (1969), 647–653.

Churchman, C. W.; Ackoff, R. L.; and Arnoff, E. L. *Introduction to Operations Research.* New York: Wiley, 1958.

Gaither, N. "The Adoption of Operations Research Techniques by Manufacturing Organizations." *Decision Sciences,* 6 (1975), 797–813.

Grayson, C. J., Jr. "Management Science and Business Practice." *Harvard Business Review,* 51:4 (1973), 41–48.

Green, T. B.; Newsom, W. B.; and Jones, S. R. "A Survey of the Application of Quantitative Techniques to Production/ Operations Management in Large Organizations." *Academy of Management Journal,* 4 (Dec. 1977), 669–676.

Griener, L. "Patterns of Organizational Change." *Harvard Business Review,* 45 (1967), 119–130.

Gupta, J. N. D. "Management Science Implementation: Experiences of a Practicing O.R. Manager." *Interfaces,* 7:3 (1977), 84–90.

Halbrecht, H. Z. "If Your Students Aren't Marketable, What's Your Future?" *Decision Sciences,* 4:3 (1973), xiii–xix.

Harvey, A. "Factors Making for Implementation Success and Failure." *Management Science,* 16 (1970), 312–321.

Hayes, R. H., and Abernathy, W. J. "Managing Our Way to Economic Decline." *Harvard Business Review,* 58 (1980), 67–77.

Lee, S. M., Moore, L. J., and Taylor, B. W. *Management Science.* Dubuque, Iowa: W. C. Brown, 1981.

Lee, S. M.; and Schwendiman, G., eds. *Japanese Management.* New York: Praeger, 1983.

Lee, S. M.; and Schwendiman, G., eds. *Management by Japanese Systems.* New York: Praeger, 1983.

Lewin, K. "Group Decision and Social Change." In *Readings in Social Psychology,* edited by T. N. Newcomb and E. L. Hartley. New York: Holt, Rinehart & Winston, 1947, 340–344.

Ouchi, W. *Theory Z.* Reading, Mass.: Addison-Wesley, 1981.

Schultz, R. L., and Slevin, D. P., eds. *Implementing Operations Research/Management Science.* New York: Elsevier, 1975.

Shakun, M. L. "Management Science and Management: Implementing Management Science via Situational Normativism." *Management Science,* 18 (1972), 367–377.

Watson, H. J., and Marett, P. G. "A Survey of Management Science Implementation Problems." *Interfaces,* 9:4 (1979), 124–128.

Wysocki, R. K. "OR/MS Implementation Research: A Bibliography." *Interfaces,* 9:2 (1979), 37–41.

Assignments

15.1 What are the three broad phases of management science development?

15.2 What are some important characteristics of the maturing stage of management science?

15.3 Is management science implementation different from other projects in organizations? Why or why not?

15.4 What are the basic steps of the management science process?

15.5 Do you agree with C. Jackson Grayson's reasons for not applying management science? Provide your argument on each reason listed by Grayson.

15.6 Why do you think there are significant differences between the manager and management scientist in the perceived barriers to the management science application?

15.7 Is management science always applicable to management problems? Why or why not?

15.8 Why is there a definite gap between management practice and the management science approach?

15.9 In solving a difficult problem, should a management scientist take the initiative and lead the manager toward implementation? Why or why not?

15.10 Some organizations have separate management science departments. Such departments usually operate as service departments. Their services to other departments are usually charged based on a profit generating scheme (each department is operated as a profit center). At the end of the fiscal year, the management science department is responsible for its profit or loss positions. What are some advantages and disadvantages to the profit center concept of management science service?

15.11 Contrast the concepts of management by information and management by ideology.

15.12 What are some workable strategies that could be used to manage the following organizational change?

Notice to Students:

Effective immediately, any student who did not get the desired courses through the general registration must go to each individual department and go through the priority system. The priority system allows into the class only a handful of students who desperately need the course. Items required on the priority slip are:

1. *Undergraduate advisor's verification.*
2. *Instructor's approval.*
3. *Department chairperson's approval.*
4. *Dean's signature.*
5. *Stamp of the Registrar.*

15.13 Management scientists are said to be very competent for certain tasks but ineffective in others. Discuss the overall process of management science and point out the steps or phases in which management scientists are usually either competent or ineffective.

15.14 Do you think the advances in computer technology will enhance or decrease the use of management science in the future?

15.15 Management science projects are usually undertaken by a team (group). The composition of team members is crucial for successful implementation. Suppose an automobile company is considering production of a new model. The company president wants to organize a management science team to analyze the feasibility of this new model. What kind of people should be involved in this team?

$$\text{Maximize } Z = 150x_1 + 250x_2$$
$$\text{subject to} \quad 4x_1 + 2x_2 \leq 80$$
$$x_1 + 3x_2 \leq 60$$
$$x_1, x_2 \geq 0$$

```
CMS

.LINGO
**LINGO START . . .
⟨TYPE YOUR INPUT FILE NAME AND TYPE; IF YOU DO NOT HAVE ,
...JUST RETURN.⟩
.
EXECUTION BEGINS...

ENTER NUMBER OF ROWS, NUMBER OF VARIABLES, AND AN INTEGER 1.
LEAVE SPACES BETWEEN VALUES
?
.2 4 1
ENTER NUMBER OF DECISION VARIABLES
?
.2

ENTER 1 FOR MAXIMIZATION OR –1 FOR MINIMIZATION
?
.1

ENTER 1 IF YOU WISH SENSITIVITY ANALYSIS OTHERWISE ENTER –1
?
.1

ENTER NUMBER OF LESS THAN OR EQUAL CONSTRAINTS
?
.2

ENTER IN ROW ORDER THE SUBSCRIPT VALUES OF VARIABLES IN THE INITIAL
SOLUTION. SEPARATE BY SPACES
?
.3 4

ENTER RIGHT-HAND-SIDE VALUES
?
.80 60
```

ENTER CONTRIBUTION COEFFICIENTS OF OBJ. FUNCTION
?
.0 0 −150 −250

ENTER COLUMN SUBSCRIPTS OF SIMPLEX TABLE
?
.3 4 1 2

ENTER TECHNOLOGICAL COEFFICIENTS FOR ROW # 1
? 00007
.1 0 4 2

ENTER TECHNOLOGICAL COEFFICIENTS FOR ROW # 2
? 00007
.0 1 1 3

PROBLEM kS   ITERATION   0

		C(J) =	0.0	0.0	−150.000	−250.000
C(I)	BASIS	B(I)	X(3)	X(4)	X(1)	X(2)
0.0	X(3)	80.000	1.000	0.0	4.000	2.000
0.0	X(4)	60.000	0.0	1.000	1.000	3.000
	Z(J)	0.0	0.0	0.0	0.0	0.0
	Z(J)−C(J)		0.0	0.0	150.000	250.000

PROBLEM kS   ITERATION   1

		C(J) =	0.0	0.0	−150.000	−250.000
C(I)	BASIS	B(I)	X(3)	X(4)	X(1)	X(2)
0.0	X(3)	40.000	1.000	−0.667	3.333	0.0
−250.00	X(2)	20.000	0.0	0.333	0.333	1.000
	Z(J)	−5000.000	0.0	−83.333	−83.333	−250.000
	Z(J)−C(J)		0.0	−83.333	66.667	0.0

PROBLEM kS   ITERATION   2

		C(J) =	0.0	0.0	−150.000	−250.000
C(I)	BASIS	B(I)	X(3)	X(4)	X(1)	X(2)
−150.00	X(1)	12.000	0.300	−0.200	1.000	0.0
−250.00	X(2)	16.000	−0.100	0.400	0.0	1.000

Z(J)	−5800.000	−20.000	−70.000	−150.000	−250.000
Z(J)−C(J)		−20.000	−70.000	0.0	0.0

OPTIMUM SOLUTION FOUND

***** FINAL SOLUTION *****

VARIABLE NO.	VALUE
X(1)	12.000
X(2)	16.000
Z −	5800.000

***** LP SENSITIVITY ANALYSIS *****

RIGHT-HAND-SIDE RANGING

CONSTRAINT NO.	LL	B(I)	UL
1	40.00	80.00	240.00
2	20.00	60.00	120.00

BASIS VARIABLE COEFFICIENT RANGING

VARIABLE NO.	LL	C(J)	UL
X(1)	83.33	150.00	500.00
X(2)	75.00	250.00	450.00

NONBASIS VARIABLE COEFFICIENT RANGING

VARIABLE NO.	LL	C(J)	UL

ENTER 1 IF YOU WISH TO RUN ANOTHER LINEAR PROGRAMMING PROBLEM,
OTHERWISE ENTER 0
?
.0
R;

Appendix 2 INTERACTIVE GOAL PROGRAMMING EXAMPLE PROBLEM (EXAMPLE 6.2)

$$\text{Minimize } Z = P_1 d_1^- + P_2 d_4^+ + 5P_3 d_2^- + 3P_3 d_3^- + P_4 d_1^+$$

$$\text{subject to} \quad x_1 + x_2 + d_1^- - d_1^+ = 80$$

$$x_1 \qquad + d_2^- \qquad = 70$$

$$x_2 + d_3^- \qquad = 45$$

$$x_1 + x_2 + d_4^- - d_4^+ = 90$$

$$x_1, x_2, d_i^-, d_i^+ \geq 0$$

CMS

```
.GPGO
⟨⟨⟨ REGULAR GOAL PROGRAMMING ⟩⟩⟩
⟨RUN , HELP OR STOP? ENTER ONE OF THEM ⟩
⟨USERS UNFAMILIAR WITH GP ARE STRONGLY RECOMMENDED TO TYPE 'HELP' ⟩
⟨IF YOU WANT TO STOP RUNNING, ENTER 'STOP' WHENEVER THERE IS A
QUERY.⟩
.RUN

⟨BATCH OR INTERACTIVE? IF BATCH, SPECIFY FILE NAME & TYPE⟩
⟨OTHERWISE JUST HIT RETURN.⟩

⟨DO YOU WANT TO STORE OUTPUT IN DISK?  ANSWER 'YES' OR 'NO'.⟩
.NO
EXECUTION BEGINS...
 ENTER # OF ROWS
?
.4
 ENTER # OF VARIABLES
?
.2
 ENTER # OF PRIORITY LEVELS
?
.4
 ENTER THE 4 SIGN SYMBOLS
?
.'B' 'L' 'L' 'B'
 NOW ENTER INFORMATION FOR THE PRIORITY STRUCTURE
 ENTER 'NEG' OR 'POS', ROW #, PRIORITY, WEIGHT
?
.'NEG' 1 1 1
 MAKE ANOTHER ENTRY...OR ENTER " 'END',0,0,0"
?
.'POS' 4 2 1
```

```
 MAKE ANOTHER ENTRY...OR ENTER " 'END',0,0,0"
?
.'NEG' 2 3 5
 MAKE ANOTHER ENTRY...OR ENTER " 'END',0,0,0"
?
.'NEG' 3 3 3
 MAKE ANOTHER ENTRY...OR ENTER " 'END',0,0,0"
?
.'POS' 1 4 1
 MAKE ANOTHER ENTRY...OR ENTER " 'END',0,0,0"
?
.'END' 0 0 0
 NOW ENTER INFORMATION ON TECHNOLOGY COEFFICIENTS
 ENTER ROW #, COLUMN #, VALUE
?
.1 1 1
 MAKE ANOTHER ENTRY...OR ENTER "0,0,0"
?
.1 2 1
 MAKE ANOTHER ENTRY...OR ENTER "0,0,0"
?
.2 1 1
 MAKE ANOTHER ENTRY...OR ENTER "0,0,0"
?
.3 2 1
 MAKE ANOTHER ENTRY...OR ENTER "0,0,0"
?
.4 1 1
 MAKE ANOTHER ENTRY...OR ENTER "0,0,0"
?
.4 2 1
 MAKE ANOTHER ENTRY...OR ENTER "0,0,0"
?
.0 0 0
 NOW ENTER THE 4 RIGHT-HAND-SIDE VALUES AS MANY AS POSSIBLE PER LINE.
?
.80 70 45 90
 THE RIGHT-HAND-SIDE INPUT    PAGE 01
1    80.00000
2    70.00000
3    45.00000
4    90.00000
 THE SUBSTITUTION RATES INPUT PAGE 02
```

ROW 1									
1.000	0.0	0.0	0.0	−1.000	0.0	1.000	1.000	0.0	0.0
0.0	0.0	0.0	0.0						

ROW 2									
0.0	1.000	0.0	0.0	0.0	0.0	1.000	0.0	0.0	0.0
0.0	0.0	0.0	0.0						

ROW 3									
0.0	0.0	1.000	0.0	0.0	0.0	0.0	1.000	0.0	0.0
0.0	0.0	0.0	0.0						

ROW 4									
0.0	0.0	0.0	1.000	0.0	−1.000	1.000	1.000	0.0	0.0
0.0	0.0	0.0	0.0						

THE OBJECTIVE FUNCTION-INPUT PAGE 03

PRIORITY   4
    0.0   0.0   0.0   0.0   1.000   0.0   0.0   0.0   0.0   0.0
    0.0   0.0   0.0   0.0

PRIORITY   3
    0.0   5.000   3.000   0.0   0.0   0.0   0.0   0.0   0.0   0.0
    0.0   0.0   0.0   0.0

PRIORITY   2
    0.0   0.0   0.0   0.0   0.0   1.000   0.0   0.0   0.0   0.0
    0.0   0.0   0.0   0.0

PRIORITY   1
  1.000   0.0   0.0   0.0   0.0   0.0   0.0   0.0   0.0   0.0
    0.0   0.0   0.0   0.0

SUMMARY OF INPUT INFORMATION PAGE 04
NUMBER OF ROWS...................... 4
NUMBER OF VARIABLES 14
NUMBER OF PRIORITIES................ 4
ADDED PRIORITIES 0
THE INITIAL ZJ-CJ MATRIX

PRIORITY   4
    0.0   0.0   0.0   0.0   −1.000   0.0   0.0   0.0   0.0   0.0
    0.0   0.0   0.0   0.0

PRIORITY   3
    0.0   0.0   0.0   0.0   0.0   0.0   5.000   3.000   0.0   0.0
    0.0   0.0   0.0   0.0

PRIORITY   2
    0.0   0.0   0.0   0.0   0.0   −1.000   0.0   0.0   0.0   0.0
    0.0   0.0   0.0   0.0

PRIORITY   1
    0.0   0.0   0.0   0.0   −1.000   0.0   1.000   1.000   0.0   0.0
    0.0   0.0   0.0   0.0

ITERATIONS 3
THE SIMPLEX SOLUTION PAGE 05

THE BASIC VARS.   THE RIGHT-HAND SIDE
    8(X 2)   20.00000
    7(X 1)   70.00000
    3(−D 3)   25.00000
    5(+D 1)   10.00000

THE SUBSTITUTION RATES

ROW   1
    0.0   −1.000   0.0   1.000   0.0   −1.000   0.0   1.000   0.0   0.0
    0.0   0.0   0.0   0.0

ROW   2
    0.0   1.000   0.0   0.0   0.0   0.0   1.000   0.0   0.0   0.0
    0.0   0.0   0.0   0.0

ROW   3
    0.0   1.000   1.000   −1.000   0.0   1.000   0.0   0.0   0.0   0.0
    0.0   0.0   0.0   0.0

ROW   4
 −1.000   0.0   0.0   1.000   1.000   −1.000   0.0   0.0   0.0   0.0
    0.0   0.0   0.0   0.0

THE ZJ-CJ MATRIX

PRIORITY   4
 −1.000   0.0   0.0   1.000   0.0   −1.000   0.0   0.0   0.0   0.0
    0.0   0.0   0.0   0.0

PRIORITY   3
    0.0   −2.000   0.0   −3.000   0.0   3.000   0.0   0.0   0.0   0.0
    0.0   0.0   0.0   0.0

PRIORITY   2
      0.0   0.0   0.0   0.0   0.0   − 1.000   0.0   0.0   0.0   0.0
      0.0   0.0   0.0   0.0
PRIORITY   1
    −1.000   0.0   0.0   0.0   0.0   0.0   0.0   0.0   0.0   0.0
      0.0   0.0   0.0   0.0
AN EVALUATION OF THE OBJECTIVE FUNCTION
4   10.00
3   75.00
2   0.0
1   0.0
ANALYSIS OF DEVIATIONS FROM RHS-STATED GOALS   PAGE 06

ROW	RHS-VALUE	D+	D−
1	80.00000	10.00000	0.0
2	70.00000	0.0	0.0
3	45.00000	0.0	25.00000
4	90.00000	0.0	0.0

ANALYSIS OF DECISION VARIABLES

VARIABLE	AMOUNT
2	20.00000
1	70.00000

ANALYSIS OF THE OBJECTIVE FUNCTION   PAGE 08

PRIORITY	NONACHIEVEMENT
4	10.00000
3	75.00000
2	0.0
1	0.0

DO YOU WISH TO ADD ANY NEW CONSTRAINTS OR DELETE
ANY TO YOUR PRESENT SERIES OF CONSTRAINTS? IF SO ENTER A "1"
OTHERWISE ENTER A "0"
?
.0
DO YOU DESIRE TO MAKE MODIFICATIONS? IF SO ENTER A "1"
OTHERWISE ENTER A "0"
?
.0
R;

Appendix 3 POISSON PROBABILITY VALUES

r	0.10	0.20	0.30	0.40	0.50	λ 0.60	0.70	0.80	0.90	1.00
0	.9048	.8187	.7408	.6703	.6066	.5488	.4966	.4493	.4066	.3679
1	.0905	.1637	.2222	.2681	.3033	.3293	.3476	.3595	.3659	.3679
2	.0045	.0164	.0333	.0536	.0758	.0988	.1217	.1438	.1647	.1839
3	.0002	.0011	.0033	.0072	.0126	.0198	.0284	.0383	.0494	.0613
4	.0000	.0001	.0003	.0007	.0016	.0030	.0050	.0077	.0111	.0153
5	.0000	.0000	.0000	.0001	.0002	.0004	.0007	.0012	.0020	.0031
6	.0000	.0000	.0000	.0000	.0000	.0000	.0001	.0002	.0003	.0005
7	.0000	.0000	.0000	.0000	.0000	.0000	.0000	.0000	.0000	.0001

r	1.10	1.20	1.30	1.40	1.50	λ 1.60	1.70	1.80	1.90	2.00
0	.3329	.3012	.2725	.2466	.2231	.2019	.1827	.1653	.1496	.1353
1	.3662	.3614	.3543	.3452	.3347	.3230	.3106	.2975	.2842	.2707
2	.2014	.2169	.2303	.2417	.2510	.2584	.2640	.2678	.2700	.2707
3	.0738	.0867	.0998	.1128	.1255	.1378	.1496	.1607	.1710	.1804
4	.0203	.0260	.0324	.0395	.0471	.0551	.0636	.0723	.0812	.0902
5	.0045	.0062	.0084	.0111	.0141	.0176	.0216	.0260	.0309	.0361
6	.0008	.0012	.0018	.0026	.0035	.0047	.0061	.0078	.0098	.0120
7	.0001	.0002	.0003	.0005	.0008	.0011	.0015	.0020	.0027	.0034
8	.0000	.0000	.0001	.0001	.0001	.0002	.0003	.0005	.0006	.0009
9	.0000	.0000	.0000	.0000	.0000	.0000	.0001	.0001	.0001	.0002

r	2.10	2.20	2.30	2.40	2.50	λ 2.60	2.70	2.80	2.90	3.00
0	.1225	.1108	.1003	.0907	.0821	.0743	.0672	.0608	.0550	.0498
1	.2572	.2438	.2306	.2177	.2052	.1931	.1815	.1703	.1596	.1494
2	.2700	.2681	.2652	.2613	.2565	.2510	.2450	.2384	.2314	.2240
3	.1890	.1966	.2033	.2090	.2138	.2176	.2205	.2225	.2237	.2240
4	.0992	.1082	.1169	.1254	.1336	.1414	.1488	.1557	.1622	.1680
5	.0417	.0476	.0538	.0602	.0668	.0735	.0804	.0872	.0940	.1008
6	.0146	.0174	.0206	.0241	.0278	.0319	.0362	.0407	.0455	.0504
7	.0044	.0055	.0068	.0083	.0099	.0118	.0139	.0163	.0188	.0216
8	.0011	.0015	.0019	.0025	.0031	.0038	.0047	.0057	.0068	.0081
9	.0003	.0004	.0005	.0007	.0009	.0011	.0014	.0018	.0022	.0027
10	.0001	.0001	.0001	.0002	.0002	.0003	.0004	.0005	.0006	.0008
11	.0000	.0000	.0000	.0000	.0000	.0001	.0001	.0001	.0002	.0002
12	.0000	.0000	.0000	.0000	.0000	.0000	.0000	.0000	.0000	.0001

					λ					
r	3.10	3.20	3.30	3.40	3.50	3.60	3.70	3.80	3.90	4.00
0	.0450	.0408	.0369	.0334	.0302	.0273	.0247	.0224	.0202	.0183
1	.1397	.1304	.1217	.1135	.1057	.0984	.0915	.0850	.0789	.0733
2	.2165	.2087	.2008	.1929	.1850	.1771	.1692	.1615	.1539	.1465
3	.2237	.2226	.2209	.2186	.2158	.2125	.2087	.2046	.2001	.1954
4	.1733	.1781	.1823	.1858	.1888	.1912	.1931	.1944	.1951	.1954
5	.1075	.1140	.1203	.1264	.1322	.1377	.1429	.1477	.1522	.1563
6	.0555	.0608	.0662	.0716	.0771	.0826	.0881	.0936	.0989	.1042
7	.0246	.0278	.0312	.0348	.0385	.0425	.0466	.0508	.0551	.0595
8	.0095	.0111	.0129	.0148	.0169	.0191	.0215	.0241	.0269	.0298
9	.0033	.0040	.0047	.0056	.0066	.0076	.0089	.0102	.0116	.0132
10	.0010	.0013	.0016	.0019	.0023	.0028	.0033	.0039	.0045	.0053
11	.0003	.0004	.0005	.0006	.0007	.0009	.0011	.0013	.0016	.0019
12	.0001	.0001	.0001	.0002	.0002	.0003	.0003	.0004	.0005	.0006
13	.0000	.0000	.0000	.0000	.0001	.0001	.0001	.0001	.0002	.0002
14	.0000	.0000	.0000	.0000	.0000	.0000	.0000	.0000	.0000	.0001

					λ					
r	4.10	4.20	4.30	4.40	4.50	4.60	4.70	4.80	4.90	5.00
0	.0166	.0150	.0136	.0123	.0111	.0101	.0091	.0082	.0074	.0067
1	.0679	.0630	.0583	.0540	.0500	.0462	.0427	.0395	.0365	.0337
2	.1393	.1323	.1254	.1188	.1125	.1063	.1005	.0948	.0894	.0842
3	.1904	.1852	.1798	.1743	.1687	.1631	.1574	.1517	.1460	.1404
4	.1951	.1944	.1933	.1917	.1898	.1875	.1849	.1820	.1789	.1755
5	.1600	.1633	.1662	.1687	.1708	.1725	.1738	.1747	.1753	.1755
6	.1093	.1143	.1191	.1237	.1281	.1323	.1362	.1398	.1432	.1462
7	.0640	.0686	.0732	.0778	.0824	.0869	.0914	.0959	.1002	.1044
8	.0328	.0360	.0393	.0428	.0463	.0500	.0537	.0575	.0614	.0653
9	.0150	.0168	.0188	.0209	.0232	.0255	.0281	.0307	.0334	.0363
10	.0061	.0071	.0081	.0092	.0104	.0118	.0132	.0147	.0164	.0181
11	.0023	.0027	.0032	.0037	.0043	.0049	.0056	.0064	.0073	.0082
12	.0008	.0009	.0011	.0013	.0016	.0019	.0022	.0026	.0030	.0034
13	.0002	.0003	.0004	.0005	.0006	.0007	.0008	.0009	.0011	.0013
14	.0001	.0001	.0001	.0001	.0002	.0002	.0003	.0003	.0004	.0005
15	.0000	.0000	.0000	.0000	.0001	.0001	.0001	.0001	.0001	.0002

					λ					
r	5.10	5.20	5.30	5.40	5.50	5.60	5.70	5.80	5.90	6.00
0	.0061	.0055	.0050	.0045	.0041	.0037	.0033	.0030	.0027	.0025
1	.0311	.0287	.0265	.0244	.0225	.0207	.0191	.0176	.0162	.0149
2	.0793	.0746	.0701	.0659	.0618	.0580	.0544	.0509	.0477	.0446
3	.1348	.1293	.1239	.1185	.1133	.1082	.1033	.0985	.0938	.0892
4	.1719	.1681	.1641	.1600	.1558	.1515	.1472	.1428	.1383	.1339
5	.1753	.1748	.1740	.1728	.1714	.1697	.1678	.1656	.1632	.1606
6	.1490	.1515	.1537	.1555	.1571	.1584	.1594	.1601	.1605	.1606
7	.1086	.1125	.1163	.1200	.1234	.1267	.1298	.1326	.1353	.1377
8	.0692	.0731	.0771	.0810	.0849	.0887	.0925	.0962	.0998	.1033
9	.0392	.0423	.0454	.0486	.0519	.0552	.0586	.0620	.0654	.0688
10	.0200	.0220	.0241	.0262	.0285	.0309	.0334	.0359	.0386	.0413
11	.0093	.0104	.0116	.0129	.1043	.0157	.0173	.0190	.0207	.0225
12	.0039	.0045	.0051	.0058	.0065	.0073	.0082	.0092	.0102	.0113

r	5.10	5.20	5.30	5.40	5.50	λ 5.60	5.70	5.80	5.90	6.00
13	.0015	.0018	.0021	.0024	.0028	.0032	.0036	.0041	.0046	.0052
14	.0006	.0007	.0008	.0009	.0011	.0013	.0015	.0017	.0019	.0022
15	.0002	.0002	.0003	.0003	.0004	.0005	.0006	.0007	.0008	.0009
16	.0001	.0001	.0001	.0001	.0001	.0002	.0002	.0002	.0003	.0003
17	.0000	.0000	.0000	.0000	.0000	.0001	.0001	.0001	.0001	.0001

r	6.10	6.20	6.30	6.40	6.50	λ 6.60	6.70	6.80	6.90	7.00
0	.0022	.0020	.0018	.0017	.0015	.0014	.0012	.0011	.0010	.0009
1	.0137	.0126	.0116	.0106	.0098	.0090	.0082	.0076	.0070	.0064
2	.0417	.0390	.0364	.0340	.0318	.0296	.0276	.0258	.0240	.0223
3	.0848	.0806	.0765	.0726	.0688	.0652	.0617	.0584	.0552	.0521
4	.1294	.1249	.1205	.1161	.1118	.1076	.1034	.0992	.0952	.0912
5	.1579	.1549	.1519	.1487	.1454	.1420	.1385	.1349	.1314	.1277
6	.1605	.1601	.1595	.1586	.1575	.1562	.1546	.1529	.1511	.1490
7	.1399	.1418	.1435	.1450	.1462	.1472	.1480	.1486	.1489	.1400
8	.1066	.1099	.1130	.1160	.1188	.1215	.1240	.1263	.1284	.1304
9	.0723	.0757	.0791	.0825	.0858	.0891	.0923	.0954	.0985	.1014
10	.0441	.0469	.0498	.0528	.0558	.0588	.0618	.0649	.0679	.0710
11	.0244	.0265	.0285	.0307	.0330	.0353	.0377	.0401	.0426	.0452
12	.0124	.0137	.0150	.0164	.0179	.0194	.0210	.0227	.0245	.0269
13	.0058	.0065	.0073	.0081	.0089	.0099	.0108	.0119	.0130	.0142
14	.0025	.0029	.0033	.0037	.0041	.0046	.0052	.0058	.0064	.0071
15	.0010	.0012	.0014	.0016	.0018	.0020	.0023	.0026	.0029	.0033
16	.0004	.0005	.0005	.0006	.0007	.0008	.0010	.0011	.0013	.0014
17	.0001	.0002	.0002	.0002	.0003	.0003	.0004	.0004	.0005	.0006
18	.0000	.0001	.0001	.0001	.0001	.0001	.0001	.0002	.0002	.0002
19	.0000	.0000	.0000	.0000	.0000	.0000	.0001	.0001	.0001	.0001

r	7.10	7.20	7.30	7.40	7.50	λ 7.60	7.70	7.80	7.90	8.00
0	.0008	.0007	.0007	.0006	.0006	.0005	.0005	.0004	.0004	.0003
1	.0059	.0054	.0049	.0045	.0041	.0038	.0035	.0032	.0029	.0027
2	.0208	.0194	.0180	.0167	.0156	.0145	.0134	.0125	.0116	.0107
3	.0492	.0464	.0438	.0413	.0389	.0366	.0345	.0324	.0305	.0286
4	.0874	.0836	.0799	.0764	.0729	.0696	.0663	.0632	.0602	.0573
5	.1241	.1204	.1167	.1130	.1094	.1057	.1021	.0986	.0951	.0916
6	.1468	.1445	.1420	.1394	.1367	.1339	.1311	.1282	.1252	.1221
7	.1489	.1486	.1481	.1474	.1465	.1454	.1442	.1428	.1413	.1396
8	.1321	.1337	.1351	.1363	.1373	.1381	.1388	.1392	.1395	.1396
9	.1042	.1070	.1096	.1121	.1144	.1167	.1187	.1207	.1224	.1241
10	.0740	.0770	.0800	.0829	.0858	.0887	.0914	.0941	.0967	.0993
11	.0478	.0504	.0531	.0558	.0585	.0613	.0640	.0667	.0695	.0722
12	.0283	.0303	.0323	.0344	.0366	.0388	.0411	.0434	.0457	.0481
13	.0154	.0168	.0181	.0196	.0211	.0227	.0243	.0260	.0278	.0296
14	.0078	.0086	.0095	.0104	.0113	.0123	.0134	.0145	.0157	.0169
15	.0037	.0041	.0046	.0051	.0057	.0062	.0069	.0075	.0083	.0090
16	.0016	.0019	.0021	.0024	.0026	.0030	.0033	.0037	.0041	.0045
17	.0007	.0008	.0009	.0010	.0012	.0013	.0015	.0017	.0019	.0021
18	.0003	.0003	.0004	.0004	.0005	.0006	.0006	.0007	.0008	.0009
19	.0001	.0001	.0001	.0002	.0002	.0002	.0003	.0003	.0003	.0004

					λ				
r	7.10	7.20	7.30	7.40	7.50	7.60	7.70	7.80	7.90	8.00

r	7.10	7.20	7.30	7.40	7.50	7.60	7.70	7.80	7.90	8.00
20	.0000	.0000	.0001	.0001	.0001	.0001	.0001	.0001	.0001	.0002
21	.0000	.0000	.0000	.0000	.0000	.0000	.0000	.0000	.0001	.0001

					λ				
r	8.10	8.20	8.30	8.40	8.50	.8.60	8.70	8.80	8.90	9.00
0	.0003	.0003	.0002	.0002	.0002	.0002	.0002	.0002	.0001	.0001
1	.0025	.0023	.0021	.0019	.0017	.0016	.0014	.0013	.0012	.0011
2	.0100	.0092	.0086	.0079	.0074	.0068	.0063	.0058	.0054	.0050
3	.0269	.0252	.0237	.0222	.0208	.0195	.0183	.0171	.0160	.0150
4	.0544	.0517	.0491	.0466	.0443	.0420	.0398	.0377	.0357	.0337
5	.0882	.0849	.0816	.0784	.0752	.0722	.0692	.0663	.0635	.0607
6	.1191	.1160	.1128	.1097	.1066	.1034	.1003	.0972	.0941	.0911
7	.1378	.1358	.1338	.1317	.1294	.1271	.1247	.1222	.1197	.1171
8	.1395	.1392	.1388	.1382	.1375	.1366	.1356	.1344	.1332	.1318
9	.1256	.1269	.1280	.1290	.1299	.1306	.1311	.1315	.1317	.1318
10	.1017	.1040	.1063	.1084	.1104	.1123	.1140	.1157	.1172	.1186
11	.0749	.0776	.0802	.0828	.0853	.0878	.0902	.0925	.0948	.0970
12	.0505	.0530	.0555	.0579	.0604	.0629	.0654	.0679	.0703	.0728
13	.0315	.0334	.0354	.0374	.0395	.0416	.0438	.0459	.0481	.0504
14	.0182	.0196	.0210	.0225	.0240	.0256	.0272	.0289	.0306	.0324
15	.0098	.0107	.0116	.0126	.0136	.0147	.0158	.0169	.0182	.0194
16	.0050	.0055	.0060	.0066	.0072	.0079	.0086	.0093	.0101	.0109
17	.0024	.0026	.0029	.0033	.0036	.0040	.0044	.0048	.0053	.0058
18	.0011	.0012	.0014	.0015	.0017	.0019	.0021	.0024	.0026	.0029
19	.0005	.0005	.0006	.0007	.0008	.0009	.0010	.0011	.0012	.0014
20	.0002	.0002	.0002	.0003	.0003	.0004	.0004	.0005	.0005	.0006
21	.0001	.0001	.0001	.0001	.0001	.0002	.0002	.0002	.0002	.0003
22	.0000	.0000	.0000	.0000	.0001	.0001	.0001	.0001	.0001	.0001

					λ				
r	9.10	9.20	9.30	9.40	9.50	9.60	9.70	9.80	9.90	10.00
0	.0001	.0001	.0001	.0001	.0001	.0001	.0001	.0001	.0001	.0000
1	.0010	.0009	.0009	.0008	.0007	.0007	.0006	.0005	.0005	.0005
2	.0046	.0043	.0040	.0037	.0034	.0031	.0029	.0027	.0025	.0023
3	.0140	.0131	.0123	.0115	.0107	.0100	.0093	.0087	.0081	.0076
4	.0319	.0302	.0285	.0269	.0254	.0240	.0226	.0213	.0201	.0189
5	.0581	.0555	.0530	.0506	.0483	.0460	.0439	.0418	.0398	.0378
6	.0881	.0851	.0822	.0793	.0764	.0736	.0709	.0682	.0656	.0631
7	.1145	.1118	.1091	.1064	.1037	.1010	.0982	.0955	.0928	.0901
8	.1302	.1286	.1269	.1251	.1232	.1212	.1191	.1170	.1148	.1126
9	.1317	.1315	.1311	.1306	.1300	.1293	.1284	.1274	.1263	.1251
10	.1198	.1210	.1219	.1228	.1235	.1241	.1245	.1249	.1250	.1251
11	.0991	.1012	.1031	.1049	.1067	.1083	.1098	.1112	.1125	.1137
12	.0752	.0776	.0799	.0822	.0844	.0866	.0888	.0908	.0928	.0948
13	.0526	.0549	.0572	.0594	.0617	.0640	.0662	.0685	.0707	.0729
14	.0342	.0361	.0380	.0399	.0419	.0439	.0459	.0479	.0500	.0521
15	.0208	.0221	.0235	.0250	.0265	.0281	.0297	.0313	.0330	.0347
16	.0118	.0127	.0137	.0147	.0157	.0168	.0180	.0192	.0204	.0217
17	.0063	.0069	.0075	.0081	.0088	.0095	.0103	.0111	.0119	.0128
18	.0032	.0035	.0039	.0042	.0046	.0051	.0055	.0060	.0065	.0071
19	.0015	.0017	.0019	.0021	.0023	.0026	.0028	.0031	.0034	.0037

r	9.10	9.20	9.30	9.40	9.50	λ 9.60	9.70	9.80	9.90	10.00
20	.0007	.0008	.0009	.0010	.0011	.0012	.0014	.0015	.0017	.0019
21	.0003	.0003	.0004	.0004	.0005	.0006	.0006	.0007	.0008	.0009
22	.0001	.0001	.0002	.0002	.0002	.0002	.0003	.0003	.0004	.0004
23	.0000	.0001	.0001	.0001	.0001	.0001	.0001	.0001	.0002	.0002
24	.0000	.0000	.0000	.0000	.0000	.0000	.0000	.0001	.0001	.0001

r	11.	12.	13.	14.	15.	λ 16.	17.	18.	19.	20.
0	.0000	.0000	.0000	.0000	.0000	.0000	.0000	.0000	.0000	.0000
1	.0002	.0001	.0000	.0000	.0000	.0000	.0000	.0000	.0000	.0000
2	.0010	.0004	.0002	.0001	.0000	.0000	.0000	.0000	.0000	.0000
3	.0037	.0018	.0008	.0004	.0002	.0001	.0000	.0000	.0000	.0000
4	.0102	.0053	.0027	.0013	.0006	.0003	.0001	.0001	.0000	.0000
5	.0224	.0127	.0070	.0037	.0019	.0010	.0005	.0002	.0001	.0001
6	.0411	.0255	.0152	.0087	.0048	.0026	.0014	.0007	.0004	.0002
7	.0646	.0437	.0281	.0174	.0104	.0060	.0034	.0019	.0010	.0005
8	.0888	.0655	.0457	.0304	.0194	.0120	.0072	.0042	.0024	.0013
9	.1085	.0874	.0661	.0473	.0324	.0213	.0135	.0083	.0050	.0029
10	.1194	.1048	.0859	.0663	.0486	.0341	.0230	.0150	.0095	.0058
11	.1194	.1144	.1015	.0844	.0663	.0496	.0355	.0245	.0164	.0106
12	.1094	.1144	.1099	.0984	.0829	.0661	.0504	.0368	.0259	.0176
13	.0926	.1056	.1099	.1060	.0956	.0814	.0658	.0509	.0378	.0271
14	.0728	.0905	.1021	.1060	.1024	.0930	.0800	.0655	.0514	.0387
15	.0534	.0724	.0885	.0989	.1024	.0992	.0906	.0786	.0650	.0516
16	.0367	.0543	.0719	.0866	.0960	.0992	.0963	.0884	.0772	.0646
17	.0237	.0383	.0550	.0713	.0847	.0934	.0963	.0936	.0863	.0760
18	.0145	.0256	.0397	.0554	.0706	.0830	.0909	.0936	.0911	.0844
19	.0084	.0161	.0272	.0409	.0557	.0699	.0814	.0887	.0911	.0888
20	.0046	.0097	.0177	.0286	.0418	.0559	.0692	.0798	.0866	.0888
21	.0024	.0055	.0109	.0191	.0299	.0426	.0560	.0684	.0783	.0846
22	.0012	.0030	.0065	.0121	.0204	.0310	.0433	.0560	.0676	.0709
23	.0006	.0016	.0037	.0074	.0133	.0216	.0320	.0438	.0559	.0669
24	.0003	.0008	.0020	.0043	.0083	.0144	.0226	.0329	.0442	.0557
25	.0001	.0004	.0010	.0024	.0050	.0092	.0154	.0237	.0336	.0446
26	.0000	.0002	.0005	.0013	.0029	.0057	.0101	.0164	.0246	.0343
27	.0000	.0001	.0002	.0007	.0016	.0034	.0063	.0109	.0173	.0254
28	.0000	.0000	.0001	.0003	.0009	.0019	.0038	.0070	.0117	.0181
29	.0000	.0000	.0001	.0002	.0004	.0011	.0023	.0044	.0077	.0125
30	.0000	.0000	.0000	.0001	.0002	.0006	.0013	.0026	.0049	.0063
31	.0000	.0000	.0000	.0000	.0001	.0003	.0007	.0015	.0030	.0054
32	.0000	.0000	.0000	.0000	.0001	.0001	.0004	.0009	.0018	.0034
33	.0000	.0000	.0000	.0000	.0000	.0001	.0002	.0005	.0010	.0020
34	.0000	.0000	.0000	.0000	.0000	.0000	.0001	.0002	.0006	.0012
35	.0000	.0000	.0000	.0000	.0000	.0000	.0000	.0001	.0003	.0007
36	.0000	.0000	.0000	.0000	.0000	.0000	.0000	.0001	.0002	.0004
37	.0000	.0000	.0000	.0000	.0000	.0000	.0000	.0000	.0001	.0002
38	.0000	.0000	.0000	.0000	.0000	.0000	.0000	.0000	.0000	.0001
39	.0000	.0000	.0000	.0000	.0000	.0000	.0000	.0000	.0000	.0001

r	25.0	30.0	40.0	50.0	75.0	100.0
0	.0000	.0000	0	0	0	0
1	.0000	.0000	0	0	0	0
2	.0000	.0000	0	0	0	0
3	.0000	.0000	0	0	0	0
4	.0000	.0000	0	0	0	0
5	.0000	.0000	0	0	0	0
6	.0000	.0000	.0000	0	0	0
7	.0000	.0000	.0000	0	0	0
8	.0001	.0000	.0000	0	0	0
9	.0001	.0000	.0000	0	0	0
10	.0004	.0000	.0000	0	0	0
11	.0008	.0000	.0000	.0000	0	0
12	.0017	.0001	.0000	.0000	0	0
13	.0033	.0002	.0000	.0000	0	0
14	.0059	.0005	.0000	.0000	0	0
15	.0099	.0010	.0000	.0000	0	0
16	.0155	.0019	.0000	.0000	0	0
17	.0227	.0034	.0000	.0000	0	0
18	.0316	.0057	.0000	.0000	0	0
19	.0415	.0089	.0001	.0000	0	0
20	.0519	.0134	.0002	.0000	0	0
21	.0618	.0192	.0004	.0000	0	0
22	.0702	.0261	.0007	.0000	0	0
23	.0763	.0341	.0012	.0000	0	0
24	.0795	.0426	.0019	.0000	0	0
25	.0795	.0511	.0031	.0000	0	0
26	.0765	.0590	.0047	.0001	.0000	0
27	.0708	.0655	.0070	.0001	.0000	0
28	.0632	.0702	.0100	.0002	.0000	0
29	.0545	.0726	.0138	.0004	.0000	0
30	.0454	.0726	.0185	.0007	.0000	0
31	.0366	.0703	.0238	.0011	.0000	0
32	.0286	.0659	.0298	.0017	.0000	0
33	.0217	.0599	.0361	.0026	.0000	0
34	.0159	.0529	.0425	.0038	.0000	0
35	.0114	.0453	.0485	.0054	.0000	0
36	.0079	.0378	.0539	.0075	.0000	0
37	.0053	.0306	.0583	.0102	.0000	0
38	.0035	.0242	.0614	.0134	.0000	0
39	.0023	.0186	.0629	.0172	.0000	0
40	.0014	.0139	.0629	.0215	.0000	0
41	.0009	.0102	.0614	.0262	.0000	0
42	.0005	.0073	.0585	.0312	.0000	.0000
43	.0003	.0051	.0544	.0363	.0000	.0000
44	.0002	.0035	.0495	.0412	.0000	.0000
45	.0001	.0023	.0440	.0458	.0001	.0000
46	.0001	.0015	.0382	.0498	.0001	.0000
47	.0000	.0010	.0325	.0530	.0001	.0000
48	.0000	.0006	.0271	.0552	.0002	.0000
49	.0000	.0004	.0221	.0563	.0003	.0000

r	25.0	30.0	40.0	λ 50.0	75.0	100.0
50	.0000	.0002	.0177	.0563	.0005	.0000
51	.0000	.0001	.0139	.0552	.0007	.0000
52	.0000	.0001	.0107	.0531	.0011	.0000
53	.0000	.0000	.0081	.0501	.0015	.0000
54	.0000	.0000	.0060	.0464	.0021	.0000
55	.0000	.0000	.0043	.0422	.0028	.0000
56	.0000	.0000	.0031	.0376	.0038	.0000
57	.0000	.0000	.0022	.0330	.0050	.0000
58	.0000	.0000	.0015	.0285	.0065	.0000
59	.0000	.0000	.0010	.0241	.0082	.0000
60	.0000	.0000	.0007	.0201	.0103	.0000
61	.0000	.0000	.0004	.0165	.0126	.0000
62	.0000	.0000	.0003	.0133	.0153	.0000
63	.0000	.0000	.0002	.0105	.0182	.0000
64	.0000	.0000	.0001	.0082	.0213	.0000
65	0	.0000	.0001	.0063	.0246	.0000
66	0	.0000	.0000	.0048	.0279	.0001
67	0	.0000	.0000	.0036	.0313	.0001
68	0	.0000	.0000	.0026	.0345	.0002
69	0	.0000	.0000	.0019	.0375	.0002
70	.000	.0000	.0000	.0014	.0402	.0003
71	0	.0000	.0000	.0010	.0424	.0004
72	0	.0000	.0000	.0007	.0442	.0006
73	0	0	.0000	.0005	.0454	.0008
74	0	0	.0000	.0003	.0460	.0011
75	0	0	.0000	.0002	.0460	.0015
76	0	0	.0000	.0001	.0454	.0020
77	0	0	.0000	.0001	.0442	.0026
78	0	0	.0000	.0001	.0425	.0033
79	0	0	.0000	.0000	.0404	.0042
80	0	0	.0000	.0000	.0379	.0052
81	0	0	.0000	.0000	.0350	.0064
82	0	0	.0000	.0000	.0321	.0078
83	0	0	.0000	.0000	.0290	.0094
84	0	0	.0000	.0000	.0259	.0112
85	0	0	.0000	.0000	.0228	.0132
86	0	0	.0000	.0000	.0199	.0154
87	0	0	.0000	.0000	.0172	.0176
88	0	0	.0000	.0000	.0146	.0201
89	0	0	0	.0000	.0123	.0225
90	0	0	0	.0000	.0103	.0250
91	0	0	0	.0000	.0085	.0275
92	0	0	0	.0000	.0069	.0299
93	0	0	0	.0000	.0056	.0322
94	0	0	0	.0000	.0044	.0342
95	0	0	0	.0000	.0035	.0360
96	0	0	0	.0000	.0027	.0375
97	0	0	0	.0000	.0021	.0387
98	0	0	0	.0000	.0016	.0395
99	0	0	0	.0000	.0012	.0399

r	25.0	30.0	λ 40.0	50.0	75.0	100.0
100	0	0	0	.0000	.0009	.0399
101	0	0	0	.0000	.0007	.0395
102	0	0	0	.0000	.0005	.0387
103	0	0	0	.0000	.0004	.0376
104	0	0	0	0	.0003	.0361
105	0	0	0	0	.0002	.0344
106	0	0	0	0	.0001	.0325
107	0	0	0	0	.0001	.0303
108	0	0	0	0	.0001	.0281
109	0	0	0	0	.0000	.0258
110	0	0	0	0	.0000	.0234
111	0	0	0	0	.0000	.0211
112	0	0	0	0	.0000	.0188
113	0	0	0	0	.0000	.0167
114	0	0	0	0	.0000	.0146
115	0	0	0	0	.0000	.0127
116	0	0	0	0	.0000	.0110
117	0	0	0	0	.0000	.0094
118	0	0	0	0	.0000	.0079
119	0	0	0	0	.0000	.0067
120	0	0	0	0	.0000	.0056
121	0	0	0	0	.0000	.0046
122	0	0	0	0	.0000	.0038
123	0	0	0	0	.0000	.0031
124	0	0	0	0	.0000	.0025
125	0	0	0	0	.0000	.0020
126	0	0	0	0	.0000	.0018
127	0	0	0	0	.0000	.0012
128	0	0	0	0	.0000	.0010
129	0	0	0	0	.0000	.0007
130	0	0	0	0	.0000	.0006
131	0	0	0	0	.0000	.0004
132	0	0	0	0	.0000	.0003
133	0	0	0	0	.0000	.0003
134	0	0	0	0	.0000	.0002
135	0	0	0	0	.0000	.0001
136	0	0	0	0	.0000	.0001
137	0	0	0	0	.0000	.0001
138	0	0	0	0	.0000	.0001

Appendix 4 VALUES OF e^x AND e^{-x}

x	e^x	e^{-x}	x	e^x	e^{-x}
0.00	1.000	1.000	3.00	20.086	0.050
0.10	1.105	0.905	3.10	22.198	0.045
0.20	1.221	0.819	3.20	24.533	0.041
0.30	1.350	0.741	3.30	27.113	0.037
0.40	1.492	0.670	3.40	29.964	0.033
0.50	1.649	0.607	3.50	33.115	0.030
0.60	1.822	0.549	3.60	36.598	0.027
0.70	2.014	0.497	3.70	40.447	0.025
0.80	2.226	0.449	3.80	44.701	0.022
0.90	2.460	0.407	3.90	49.402	0.020
1.00	2.718	0.368	4.00	54.598	0.018
1.10	3.004	0.333	4.10	60.340	0.017
1.20	3.320	0.301	4.20	66.686	0.015
1.30	3.669	0.273	4.30	73.700	0.014
1.40	4.055	0.247	4.40	81.451	0.012
1.50	4.482	0.223	4.50	90.017	0.011
1.60	4.953	0.202	4.60	99.484	0.010
1.70	5.474	0.183	4.70	109.95	0.009
1.80	6.050	0.165	4.80	121.51	0.008
1.90	6.686	0.150	4.90	134.29	0.007
2.00	7.389	0.135	5.00	148.41	0.007
2.10	8.166	0.122	5.10	164.02	0.006
2.20	9.025	0.111	5.20	181.27	0.006
2.30	9.974	0.100	5.30	200.34	0.005
2.40	11.023	0.091	5.40	221.41	0.005
2.50	12.182	0.082	5.50	244.69	0.004
2.60	13.464	0.074	5.60	270.43	0.004
2.70	14.880	0.067	5.70	298.87	0.003
2.80	16.445	0.061	5.80	330.30	0.003
2.90	18.174	0.055	5.90	365.04	0.003
3.00	20.086	0.050	6.00	403.43	0.002

Appendix 5 VALUES OF P_0 FOR VARIOUS COMBINATIONS OF $\dfrac{\lambda}{s\mu}$

$R = \lambda/s\mu$

FOR MULTICHANNEL POISSON/EXPONENTIAL QUEUING PROCESS: PROBABILITY OF ZERO IN SYSTEM

NUMBER OF CHANNELS: s

R	2	3	4	5	6	7	8	9	10	15
0.02	0.96079	0.94177	0.92312	0.90484	0.88692	0.86936	0.85215	0.83527	0.81873	0.74082
0.04	0.92308	0.88692	0.85215	0.81873	0.78663	0.75578	0.72615	0.69768	0.67032	0.54881
0.06	0.88679	0.83526	0.78663	0.74082	0.69769	0.65705	0.61878	0.58275	0.54881	0.40657
0.08	0.85185	0.78659	0.72615	0.67032	0.61878	0.57121	0.52729	0.48675	0.44933	0.30119
0.10	0.81818	0.74074	0.67031	0.60653	0.54881	0.49659	0.44933	0.40657	0.36788	0.22313
0.12	0.78571	0.69753	0.61876	0.54881	0.48675	0.43171	0.38289	0.33960	0.30119	0.16530
0.14	0.75439	0.65679	0.57116	0.49657	0.43171	0.37531	0.32628	0.28365	0.24660	0.12246
0.16	0.72414	0.61838	0.52720	0.44931	0.38289	0.32628	0.27804	0.23693	0.20190	0.09072
0.18	0.69492	0.58214	0.48660	0.40653	0.33959	0.28365	0.23693	0.19790	0.16530	0.06721
0.20	0.66667	0.54795	0.44910	0.36782	0.30118	0.24659	0.20189	0.16530	0.13534	0.04979
0.22	0.63934	0.51567	0.41445	0.33277	0.26711	0.21437	0.17204	0.13807	0.11060	0.03688
0.24	0.61290	0.48519	0.38244	0.30105	0.23688	0.18636	0.14660	0.11532	0.09072	0.02732
0.26	0.58730	0.45640	0.35284	0.27233	0.21007	0.16200	0.12492	0.09632	0.07427	0.02024
0.28	0.56250	0.42918	0.32548	0.24633	0.18628	0.14082	0.10645	0.08045	0.06081	0.01500
0.30	0.53846	0.40346	0.30017	0.22277	0.16517	0.12241	0.09070	0.06720	0.04978	0.01111

x										
0.32	0.00823	0.04076	0.05612	0.07728	0.10639	0.14644	0.20144	0.27676	0.37913	0.51515
0.34	0.00610	0.03337	0.04687	0.06584	0.09247	0.12981	0.18211	0.25510	0.35610	0.49254
0.36	0.00452	0.02732	0.03915	0.05609	0.08035	0.11505	0.16460	0.23505	0.33431	0.47059
0.38	0.00335	0.02236	0.03263	0.04778	0.06981	0.10195	0.14872	0.21649	0.31367	0.44928
0.40	0.00248	0.01836	0.02729	0.04069	0.06065	0.09032	0.13433	0.19929	0.29412	0.42857
0.42	0.00184	0.01494	0.02279	0.03465	0.05267	0.07998	0.12128	0.18336	0.27559	0.40845
0.44	0.00136	0.01225	0.01902	0.02950	0.04573	0.07080	0.10944	0.16860	0.25802	0.38889
0.46	0.00101	0.01003	0.01587	0.02511	0.03968	0.06265	0.09870	0.15491	0.24135	0.36986
0.48	0.00075	0.00822	0.01324	0.02136	0.03442	0.05540	0.08895	0.14221	0.22554	0.35135
0.50	0.00055	0.00671	0.01104	0.01816	0.02984	0.04896	0.08010	0.13043	0.21053	0.33333
0.52	0.00041	0.00544	0.00920	0.01544	0.02586	0.04323	0.07207	0.11951	0.19627	0.31579
0.54	0.00030	0.00444	0.00767	0.01311	0.02239	0.03814	0.06477	0.10936	0.18273	0.29870
0.56	0.00022	0.00366	0.00638	0.01113	0.01936	0.03362	0.05814	0.09994	0.16986	0.28205
0.58	0.00017	0.00298	0.00531	0.00943	0.01673	0.02959	0.05212	0.09119	0.15762	0.26582
0.60	0.00012	0.00243	0.00441	0.00799	0.01443	0.02601	0.04665	0.08306	0.14599	0.25000
0.62	0.00009	0.00198	0.00366	0.00675	0.01243	0.02282	0.04167	0.07550	0.13491	0.23457
0.64	0.00007	0.00161	0.00303	0.00570	0.01069	0.01999	0.03715	0.06847	0.12438	0.21951
0.66	0.00005	0.00131	0.00251	0.00480	0.00918	0.01746	0.03304	0.06194	0.11435	0.20482
0.68	0.00004	0.00106	0.00207	0.00404	0.00786	0.01522	0.02930	0.05587	0.10479	0.19048
0.70	0.00003	0.00085	0.00170	0.00338	0.00670	0.01322	0.02590	0.05021	0.09569	0.17647
0.72	0.00002	0.00069	0.00140	0.00283	0.00570	0.01144	0.02280	0.04495	0.08702	0.16279
0.74	0.00001	0.00055	0.00114	0.00235	0.00483	0.00986	0.01999	0.04006	0.07875	0.14943
0.76	0.00001	0.00044	0.00093	0.00195	0.00407	0.00846	0.01743	0.03550	0.07087	0.13636
0.78	0.00001	0.00035	0.00075	0.00160	0.00341	0.00721	0.01510	0.03125	0.06335	0.12360
0.80	0.00001	0.00028	0.00060	0.00131	0.00284	0.00610	0.01299	0.02730	0.05618	0.11111
0.82	0.00000	0.00022	0.00048	0.00106	0.00234	0.00511	0.01106	0.02362	0.04933	0.09890
0.84	0.00000	0.00017	0.00038	0.00085	0.00190	0.00423	0.00931	0.02019	0.04280	0.08696
0.86	0.00000	0.00013	0.00029	0.00067	0.00153	0.00345	0.00772	0.01700	0.03656	0.07527
0.88	0.00000	0.00010	0.00022	0.00052	0.00120	0.00276	0.00627	0.01403	0.03060	0.06383
0.90	0.00000	0.00007	0.00017	0.00039	0.00092	0.00215	0.00496	0.01126	0.02491	0.05263
0.92	0.00000	0.00005	0.00012	0.00028	0.00068	0.00161	0.00377	0.00867	0.01947	0.04167
0.94	0.00000	0.00003	0.00008	0.00019	0.00047	0.00113	0.00268	0.00627	0.01427	0.03093
0.96	0.00000	0.00002	0.00005	0.00012	0.00029	0.00070	0.00170	0.00403	0.00930	0.02041
0.98	0.00000	0.00001	0.00002	0.00005	0.00013	0.00033	0.00081	0.00194	0.00454	0.01010

Appendix 6 AREA UNDER THE STANDARD NORMAL CURVE

Z	.00	.01	.02	.03	.04	.05	.06	.07	.08	.09
0.0	.50000	.50399	.50798	.51197	.51595	.51994	.52392	.52790	.53188	.53586
0.1	.53983	.54380	.54776	.55172	.55567	.55962	.56356	.56749	.57142	.57535
0.2	.57926	.58317	.58706	.59095	.59483	.59871	.60257	.60642	.61026	.61409
0.3	.61791	.62172	.62552	.62930	.63307	.63683	.64058	.64431	.64803	.65173
0.4	.65542	.65910	.66276	.66640	.67003	.67364	.67724	.68082	.68439	.68793
0.5	.69146	.69497	.69847	.70194	.70540	.70884	.71226	.71566	.71904	.72240
0.6	.72575	.72907	.73237	.73536	.73891	.74215	.74537	.74857	.75175	.75490
0.7	.75804	.76115	.76424	.76730	.77035	.77337	.77637	.77935	.78230	.78524
0.8	.78814	.79103	.79389	.79673	.79955	.80234	.80511	.80785	.81057	.81327
0.9	.81594	.81859	.82121	.82381	.82639	.82894	.83147	.83398	.83646	.83891
1.0	.84134	.84375	.84614	.84849	.85083	.85314	.85543	.85769	.85993	.86214
1.1	.86433	.86650	.86864	.87076	.87286	.87493	.87698	.87900	.88100	.88298
1.2	.88493	.88686	.88877	.89065	.89251	.89435	.89617	.89796	.89973	.90147
1.3	.90320	.90490	.90658	.90824	.90988	.91149	.91309	.91466	.91621	.91774
1.4	.91924	.92073	.92220	.92364	.92507	.92647	.92785	.92922	.93056	.93189
1.5	.93319	.93448	.93574	.93699	.93822	.93943	.94062	.94179	.94295	.94408
1.6	.94520	.94630	.94738	.94845	.94950	.95053	.95154	.95254	.95352	.95449
1.7	.95543	.95637	.95728	.95818	.95907	.95994	.96080	.96164	.96246	.96327
1.8	.96407	.96485	.96562	.96638	.96712	.96784	.96856	.96926	.96995	.97062
1.9	.97128	.97193	.97257	.97320	.97381	.97441	.97500	.97558	.97615	.97670
2.0	.97725	.97784	.97831	.97882	.97932	.97982	.98030	.98077	.98124	.98169
2.1	.98214	.98257	.98300	.98341	.98382	.98422	.98461	.98500	.98537	.98574
2.2	.98610	.98645	.98679	.98713	.98745	.98778	.98809	.98840	.98870	.98899
2.3	.98928	.98956	.98983	.99010	.99036	.99061	.99086	.99111	.99134	.99158
2.4	.99180	.99202	.99224	.99245	.99266	.99286	.99305	.99324	.99343	.99361
2.5	.99379	.99396	.99413	.99430	.99446	.99461	.99477	.99492	.99506	.99520
2.6	.99534	.99547	.99560	.99573	.99585	.99598	.99609	.99621	.99632	.99643
2.7	.99653	.99664	.99674	.99683	.99693	.99702	.99711	.99720	.99728	.99736
2.8	.99744	.99752	.99760	.99767	.99774	.99781	.99788	.99795	.99801	.99807
2.9	.99813	.99819	.99825	.99831	.99836	.99841	.99846	.99851	.99856	.99861
3.0	.99865	.99869	.99874	.99878	.99882	.99886	.99899	.99893	.99896	.99900
3.1	.99903	.99906	.99910	.99913	.99916	.99918	.99921	.99924	.99926	.99929
3.2	.99931	.99934	.99936	.99938	.99940	.99942	.99944	.99946	.99948	.99950
3.3	.99952	.99953	.99955	.99957	.99958	.99960	.99961	.99962	.99964	.99965
3.4	.99966	.99968	.99969	.99970	.99971	.99972	.99973	.99974	.99975	.99976
3.5	.99977	.99978	.99978	.99979	.99980	.99981	.99981	.99982	.99983	.99983
3.6	.99984	.99985	.99985	.99986	.99986	.99987	.99987	.99988	.99988	.99989
3.7	.99989	.99990	.99990	.99990	.99991	.99991	.99992	.99992	.99992	.99992
3.8	.99993	.99993	.99993	.99994	.99994	.99994	.99994	.99995	.99995	.99995
3.9	.99995	.99995	.99996	.99996	.99996	.99996	.99996	.99996	.99997	.99997

Appendix 7 TABLE OF RANDOM NUMBERS

```
39 65 76 45 45    19 90 69 64 61    20 26 36 31 62    58 24 97 14 97    95 06 70 99 00
73 71 23 70 90    65 97 60 12 11    31 56 34 19 19    47 83 75 51 33    30 62 38 20 46
72 20 47 33 84    51 67 47 97 19    98 40 07 17 66    23 05 09 51 80    59 78 11 52 49
75 17 25 69 17    17 95 21 78 58    24 33 45 77 48    69 81 84 09 29    93 22 70 45 80
37 48 79 88 74    63 52 06 34 30    01 31 60 10 27    35 07 79 71 53    28 99 52 01 41

02 89 08 16 94    85 53 83 29 95    56 27 09 24 43    21 78 55 09 82    72 61 88 73 61
87 18 15 70 07    37 79 49 12 38    48 13 93 55 96    41 92 45 71 51    09 18 25 58 94
98 83 71 70 15    89 09 39 59 24    00 06 41 41 20    14 36 59 25 47    54 45 17 24 89
10 08 58 07 04    76 62 16 48 68    58 76 17 14 86    59 53 11 52 21    66 04 18 72 87
47 90 56 37 31    71 82 13 50 41    27 55 10 24 92    28 04 67 53 44    95 23 00 84 47

93 05 31 03 07    34 18 04 52 35    74 13 39 35 22    68 95 23 92 35    36 63 70 35 33
21 89 11 47 99    11 20 99 45 18    76 51 94 84 86    13 79 93 37 55    98 16 04 41 67
95 18 94 06 97    27 37 83 28 71    79 57 95 13 91    09 61 87 25 21    56 20 11 32 44
97 08 31 55 73    10 65 81 92 59    77 31 61 95 46    20 44 90 32 64    26 99 76 75 63
69 26 88 86 13    59 71 74 17 32    48 38 75 93 29    73 37 32 04 05    60 82 29 20 25

41 47 10 25 03    87 63 93 95 17    81 83 83 04 49    77 45 85 50 51    79 88 01 97 30
91 94 14 63 62    08 61 74 51 69    92 79 43 89 79    29 18 94 51 23    14 85 11 47 23
80 06 54 18 47    08 52 85 08 40    48 40 35 94 22    72 65 71 08 86    50 03 42 99 36
67 72 77 63 99    89 85 84 46 06    64 71 06 21 66    89 37 20 70 01    61 65 70 22 12
59 40 24 13 75    42 29 72 23 19    06 94 76 10 08    81 30 15 39 14    81 83 17 16 33

63 62 06 34 41    79 53 36 02 95    94 61 09 43 62    20 21 14 68 86    84 95 48 46 45
78 47 23 53 90    79 93 96 38 63    34 85 52 05 09    85 43 01 72 73    14 93 87 81 40
87 68 62 15 43    97 48 72 66 48    53 16 71 13 81    59 97 50 99 52    24 62 20 42 31
47 60 92 10 77    26 97 05 73 51    88 46 38 03 58    72 68 49 29 31    75 70 16 08 24
56 88 87 59 41    06 87 37 78 48    65 88 69 58 39    88 02 84 27 83    85 81 56 39 38

22 17 68 65 84    87 02 22 57 51    68 69 80 95 44    11 29 01 95 80    49 34 35 86 47
19 36 27 59 46    39 77 32 77 09    79 57 92 36 59    89 74 39 82 15    08 58 94 34 74
16 77 23 02 77    28 06 24 25 93    22 45 44 84 11    87 80 61 65 31    09 71 91 74 25
78 43 76 71 61    97 67 63 99 61    80 45 67 93 82    59 73 19 85 23    53 33 65 97 21
03 28 28 26 08    69 30 16 09 05    53 58 47 70 93    66 56 45 65 79    45 56 20 19 47

04 31 17 21 56    33 73 99 19 87    26 72 39 27 67    53 77 57 68 93    60 61 97 22 61
61 06 98 03 91    87 14 77 43 96    43 00 65 98 50    45 60 33 01 07    98 99 46 50 47
23 68 35 26 00    99 53 93 61 28    52 70 05 48 34    56 65 05 61 86    90 92 10 70 80
15 39 25 70 99    93 86 52 77 65    15 33 59 05 28    22 87 26 07 47    86 96 98 29 06
58 71 96 30 24    18 46 23 34 27    85 13 99 24 44    49 18 09 79 49    74 16 32 23 02

93 22 53 64 39    07 10 63 76.35    87 03 04 79 88    08 13 13 85 51    55 34 57 72 69
78 76 58 54 74    92 38 70 96 92    52 06 79 79 45    82 63 18 27 44    69 66 92 19 09
61 81 31 96 82    00 57 25 60 59    46 72 60 18 77    55 66 12 62 11    08 99 55 64 57
42 88 07 10 05    24 98 65 63 21    47 21 61 88 32    27 80 30 21 60    10 92 35 36 12
77 94 30 05 39    28 10 99 00 27    12 73 73 99 12    49 99 57 94 82    96 88 57 17 91
```

Appendix 8 A COMPUTER PROGRAM TO GENERATE VALUES OF RANDOM VARIABLES

```
PROGRAM TO RANDOMLY GENERATE
VALUES OF D (DEMAND) ACCORDING
TO PROBABILITY DISTRIBUTION
GIVEN IN TABLE 14.3
      N = 1000
      ISEED = 2671
      WRITE (6,10)
10 FORMAT (///18X, 'RN', 10X, 'D'//)
      DO 20 I = 1,N
      RN = DRAND (ISEED)
      D = 4.
      IF (RN.LE..9) D = 3.
      IF (RN.LE..6) D = 2.
      IF (RN.LE..3) D = 1.
      IF (RN.LE..1) D = 0.
20 WRITE (6,30) I, RN, D
30 FORMAT (6X, I5, 3X, F10.8, F9.1)
      STOP
      END
      FUNCTION DRAND (ID)
C  SUBPROGRAM TO RANDOMLY
C  GENERATE RANDOM NUMBERS
C  (RN) BETWEEN 0 AND 1.0
C
      ID = ID*65539
      IF (ID) 1,1,2
1     ID = ID + 2147483647+1
2     DRAND = ID* .4656613E-9
      RETURN
      END
```

INDEX